FIRST APPEARANCES

FIRST APPEARANCES

David Hofstede

Zanne-3 Publishing
Las Vegas, Nevada

First Appearances

Published by:

Zanne-3 Publishing
P.O. Box 70596
Las Vegas, NV 89170-0596 U.S.A.

Photo credits and acknowledgments: Universal Pictures, Walt Disney Productions, Paramount Pictures. Warner Bros., MGM, 20th Century-Fox, Allied Artists, Cannon Films, United Artists

Any omission or incorrect information should be transmitted to the author or publisher, so it can be rectified in any future edition of this book.

ISBN: 0-9629176-6-4

Library of Congress Catalog Card Number: 96-90003

Copyright © 1996 by David Hofstede

Printed in the United States of America

TABLE OF CONTENTS

PREFACE--HOW FIRST IS "FIRST"?

The "First Appearance" designation refers to the performer's *feature* film debut, which in several cases is not the first film footage that exists of that performer. Back in Hollywood's Golden Age, one- and two-reel short subjects were often presented along with a newsreel, serial and cartoon before the main feature began. Among the many stars who first appeared in these short subjects were June Allyson, Humphrey Bogart and Judy Garland. It was a difficult decision whether to single out these shorts or not, because technically they do represent the first time these actors appeared before a movie camera. The problem, then, is where to draw the line. Should student films made in college also be considered? Or armed forces training films? For the purposes of consistency, it seemed to make sense to designate the feature film appearance. However, in those cases when other footage exists before that debut, titles and years have been listed in the appropriate chapter, so those who wish to track down these rare items can do so. Also, for the sake of consistency, television appearances have also been listed, but do not count as a first appearance.

For every rule there are exceptions, and that is also the case here. Charlie Chaplin made dozens of one and two-reelers, in which he created and developed his trademark Little Tramp character, and he was firmly established as a star by the time he made his first feature film appearance. In this case, the feature debut occurs in the midst of an already thriving career, and loses much of its importance. For Chaplin, Laurel & Hardy and Mary Pickford, short films are listed. Shirley Temple is another exception; the "Baby Burlesks" in which she first appeared and was discovered are widely available on video, and clearly showcase the talent and charisma that would make Shirley the most beloved child star of all time. Since Temple herself has referred to these films as "the best things I ever did," it seemed the right choice. Of course, her feature film debut in *Red-Haired Alibi* is pointed out in the bio.

The next question was whether to include only first <u>billed</u> appearances, or instead opt for the first movie in which the performer, or some part of the performer, can be glimpsed, if only for a scant few seconds. Many stars got their start as extras, and can be seen in crowd scenes of several films before they earned their first billing and first line of dialogue. Another difficult decision, but in light of the previous choice to eliminate short films, etc. from consideration, it didn't made sense to pass over what in some cases were a half-dozen more appearances to get to one in which the performer receives screen credit. The core definition of "first appearance" has already been stretched, and to do so further would devoid it of any meaning. So, although Lana Turner is seen only from the back for less than five seconds in *A Star is Born* (1954), and Sigourney Weaver can barely be viewed in an extreme long shot near the end of *Annie Hall*, these are their respective first feature appearances and have been designated thus.

WHEN ARE STARS BORN?

In some cases, the answer is indisputable--Julie Andrews in *Mary Poppins*, Kathleen Turner in *Body Heat*. But for a great many others, the choice of which performance in which film, if any, was responsible for the conferring of stardom on a comparatively unknown performer is a subjective one. Would you select *Zulu* or *The Ipcress File* for Michael Caine? *San Francisco* or *Captains Courageous* for Spencer Tracy? *High Sierra* or *The Maltese Falcon* for Humphrey Bogart? I tried to base my decision on as much impartial information--film reviews, box-office success, movie magazine buzz--as possible, plus the definition of movie star supplied by Veronica Lake; "The proven ability to draw people into movie theaters." But undoubtedly there are instances when the author's personal preference won the day.

DEDICATION/ ACKNOWLEDGMENTS

First Appearances would not have appeared at all without the help of many people, to whom the book is gratefully dedicated. To the helpful staff at the libraries of UCLA and the Academy of Motion Picture Arts & Sciences, to Leo G. Willette, Eddie Brandt and many others who provided video copies of obscure films, to Wendy Bousman and the folks at Video Park in Las Vegas, to the University of Nevada, Las Vegas (they're not just for basketball anymore), to Ron Zayas for his cover design, to my parents for their constant support, to Tom Bergeron, Laurie Hibberd, Jim and Bob, for helping me to start every day with a smile and a positive attitude, and to the teachers who told me I could succeed if only I'd apply myself--thank you.

BUD ABBOTT (1895-1974) AND LOU COSTELLO (1906-1959)

FIRST APPEARANCE: *One Night in the Tropics* (Universal, 1940)

A STAR IS BORN: *Buck Privates* (Universal, 1941)

Biographical sketches of Abbott and Costello seem to dwell as much on backstage discord as they do on the performance chemistry that made the comedy team one of the best-loved in motion pictures. The situation was exacerbated by the hatchet job made-for-TV movie *Bud and Lou* (1978), which portrayed the pair as at each other's throats for thirty years. According to the children of both men, who gathered to write the foreword to the excellent career review *Abbott and Costello in Hollywood*, Bud and Lou would be saddened to learn that the friction between them had become a prominent part of their history; "They were literally with each other more than they were with our mothers," write the second-generation Abbotts and Costellos; "You can't be together for that amount of time and not fight, yet you can't be together that long and not be friends."

Bud Abbott's father was an advance man for the Barnum and Bailey Circus; his mother performed in the show as a bareback rider. Bud, born in New Jersey, was one of four Abbott offspring who all landed in showbiz, though only Bud broke through the burlesque ranks to stardom. At the age of sixteen he worked in the box office of the Brooklyn Theater, where he met such legends as W.C. Fields and Fannie Brice, and spent more time watching the acts and analyzing their timing and routines than he did watching the till. He held other jobs at various theaters over the next decade, and first appeared on a stage as the straight man for vaudeville comic Billy Gilbert. In 1918 he married chorus girl Betty Smith and moved to Cleveland, where with borrowed money he started his own show, entitled *Broadway Flashes*. The show was a hit, and Abbott went on to produce other comedy revues and develop a reputation, opposite a variety of comedians including his wife, as the best straight man in the business.

Lou Cristillo was also New Jersey-born, but there were no show business roots in his family. While Abbott studied the great burlesque comics, Cristillo was at the movies, where he watched Charlie Chaplin shorts over a dozen times and used the routines in his role as high school class clown. After the graduation ceremony, in which he performed a pratfall before collecting his diploma, Lou went to Hollywood and changed his last name to Costello, after actress Helene Costello. In 1927 he began landing parts in crowd scenes, including one in the Laurel and Hardy short *Battle of the Century*. He worked as a stuntman in over sixty films, then returned to the less-dangerous field of comedy, traveling the country in various skits and revues.

Abbott and Costello first met in 1933, when Lou and Bud's wife Betty teamed to do a routine. They had known of each other before and would cross paths several more times before they finally attempted a bit together. The result was an immediate hit. They officially became a team in 1936, and gradually worked their way up from $20-a-week spots on the burlesque circuit to featured billing in the Broadway show *Streets of Paris* (1939). They gained national fame on Kate Smith's radio program, and when Hollywood beckoned they were ready.

One Night in the Tropics was the first of ten films made by Abbott and Costello between 1940 and 1941. The forgettable plot revolved around the romantic struggles of Steve (Robert Cummings), Cynthia (Nancy Kelly), Steve's old girlfriend Mickey (Peggy Moran) and his best friend Jim (Allan Jones). After several misunderstandings all problems are solved during a vacation to tropical San Marcos. Bud and Lou play flunkies who work at a nightclub, and they are the sole reason to see the film. The story is flat and the Jerome Kern score was the composer's only effort that did not produce a hit, but when Abbott and Costello launch into their routines the movie picks up instantly. "Only the comedy of A & C saves the picture from general tediousness," wrote *Variety*. No wonder that when the film was rereleased their billing was boosted from third to first, and fifteen minutes of the dull goings-on between their appearances were excised.

Unlike Laurel and Hardy, who were still developing as a team in their early pictures, Abbott and Costello were polished veterans of radio and the stage, and the split-second timing of their patter was perfect from their first moment on screen, in which they perform a money-changing sketch known to all A & C fans. Next up is the classic "Who's on First?" routine, which is now in the Baseball Hall of Fame and would certainly be in the Comedy Hall of Fame if such a place existed. Later, Costello's simple refusal to put mustard on a hot dog develops into a hilarious sketch in which Abbott blames his partner for the collapse of the mustard industry. "Go ahead, pick your friends," Costello yells, "me or mustard."

It was only natural after the attention Bud and Lou received that Universal would now build projects around them, rather than inserting the team into standard programmers. Abbott and Costello were clearly the stars of their next film, *Buck Privates*, though the studio threw in the Andrews Sisters for extra box-office insurance. The set-up is simple; con men Slicker Smith and Herbie Brown (A & C) inadvertantly join the army while running from an angry cop. As in *One Night in the Tropics*, A & C recycled many of their best stage routines, and ad-libbed extra material which equaled anything in the script. The dice game scene, in which Lou insists that he's never played craps but lets slip phrases like "Let it ride!" and "A little Joe!" is a gem, and the "Drill" routine is as side-splitting as anything in their filmography. "Their antics have as much innuendo as a thousand-pound bomb, but nearly as much explosive force," wrote the *New York Times*.

The film was made in twenty days for less than $250,000, and outgrossed *How Green Was My Valley*, *Citizen Kane* and *Sergeant York* on its way to a $4 million take. Most of the credit belongs to Bud and Lou, but the Andrews Sisters' renditions of "Apple Blossom Time" and the Oscar-nominated "Boogie Woogie Bugle Boy" are also memorable, and there was much flag-waving throughout that was very welcome at the time. Historians will also appreciate the scene between Costello and Shemp Howard, the member of another legendary comedy team.

Universal loved the profits generated by the Abbott and Costello pictures, but never enough to increase their budget, add any major costars, or even put color film in the camera. Had they started at another studio the duo might have reached even greater heights, but what they accomplished with 'B' movie money and shooting schedules is still delighting audiences fifty years later.

ONE NIGHT IN THE TROPICS
Directed by A. Edward Sutherland; Written by Gertrude Purcell and Charles Grayson, from the novel *Love Insurance* by Earl Derr Biggers; Produced by Leonard Spigelgass; Music by Jerome Kern, Dorothy Fields and Oscar Hammerstein II

Cast
Allan Jones (Jim Moore), Nancy Kelly (Cynthia Merrick), BUD ABBOTT (ABBOTT), LOU COSTELLO (COSTELLO), Robert Cummings (Steve Harper), Peggy Moran (Mickey Fitzgerald)

BUCK PRIVATES
Directed by Arthur Lubin; Written by Arthur T. Horman (special material for Abbott and Costello by John Grant); Produced by Alex Gottlieb; Music by Don Raye, Hughie Prince, Sonny Burke, Vic Schoen, Albert Von Tilzer and Neville Fleeson

Cast
BUD ABBOTT (SLICKER SMITH), LOU COSTELLO (HERBIE BROWN), The Andrews Sisters (Themselves), Lee Bowman (Randolph Parker III), Jane Frazee (Judy Gray), Nat Pendleton (Sergeant Michael Collins)

WOODY ALLEN (1935-   )

<u>FIRST APPEARANCE</u>: *What's New, Pussycat* (United Artists, 1965)

<u>A STAR IS BORN</u>: *Take the Money and Run* (Cinerama, 1969)

It's impossible to separate Woody Allen the actor from Woody Allen the filmmaker. Only four times in his career has Allen stepped before the cameras without also serving as writer and director. But whether he's performing his own script or somebody else's, every character Allen plays is only a slight variation on the insecure, book-smart but bumbling nebbish he first created as a stand-up comedian. Like Charlie Chaplin and Jacques Tati, Allen has built a career out of inventing new situations--mostly comic, sometimes tragic--for his cinematic alter-ego.

Allen Stewart Konigsberg was born in Brooklyn, New York (not exactly a news flash if you've seen any of his movies), and raised in comfortable, middle-class surroundings. He was a shy, melancholy child whose search for interpersonal and spiritual comfort started early and later found its way into several Woody Allen films. "I had this intense sense of failure," he once told the *New York Times*. "But although I never laughed out loud I was a funny kid. My viewpoint was funny and I said funny things."

Allen's sense of humor frequently landed him in the high school principal's office, but at the age of fifteen he was already earning money as a joke writer for a public relations firm, where his material was supplied to such clients as Arthur Murray and Sammy Kaye. Two years later, Allen was a staff writer at NBC, earning $75 a week. After being expelled from both New York University and City College of New York, he returned to the career in which he had already been successful. He was a writer for *The Tonight Show* in 1957, and joined the legendary creative team behind Sid Caesar's *Your Show of Shows* in 1961.

After much persuasion from friends and business associates, Allen became a stand-up comic. He debuted his surrealistic, self-deprecating routines in the nightclubs and coffee houses of Greenwich Village, and by 1964 he was one of the nation's most popular comedians, and one of the first to parlay his success into a career in motion pictures.

Allen wrote the script for *What's New Pussycat?*, a frenetic sex comedy starring Peter O'Toole (a last-minute replacement for Warren Beatty) and Peter Sellers. O'Toole plays Michael James, the editor of a Paris fashion magazine who seeks help from psychiatrist Fritz Fassbender (Sellers). When Michael becomes engaged, he asks Fritz how he can resist the temptation of other women, who seem to offer themselves on a daily basis. The shrink would kill to have that problem, and so would Michael's friend Victor (Allen), a wardrobe man at a strip club who also loves Michael's fiance`, but who would settle for anything in a dress. After numerous trials and temptations, Michael makes it to the altar.

Playboy magazine called *What's New Pussycat?* "inspired lunacy," and they were half right. Lunacy it is, but there's not much inspiration in Allen's first screenplay, which was more accurately described by the *New York World-Telegram* as "a shrieking, reeking, conglomeration of dirty jokes, dreary camp and blatant ambi-sexuality wrapped around a tediously plodding plot and stale comedy routines." *Playboy* only liked it because of the procession of girlwatching opportunities provided by Ursula Andress, Paula Prentiss, Capucine and Romy Schneider.

Overall the reviews were mixed, but the film has not aged well and, if it weren't for *Casino Royale* (1967), *What's New Pussycat?* would be Allen's worst film as both writer and actor. The few jokes that work are the ones that go by the fastest, such as an unbilled cameo by O'Toole's drinking buddy Richard Burton, and Allen walking past Vincent Van Gogh, Henri de Toulouse-Lautrec and Edouard Manet at a Paris cafe`. Allen's trademark perplexity in romance, wry observations and nervous mannerisms are already in evidence, but his character, like the movie, goes nowhere.

Allen wrote new and frequently hilarious dialogue to a cheesy old Japanese spy movie and released it as *What's Up, Tiger Lily?* (1966). The following year he was an actor only in *Casino Royale*. His next original feature as both writer and actor was also his first as director; *Take the Money and Run* is a satiric documentary about the life and loves of a career criminal named Virgil Starkwell (Allen). It's more a series of individual skits than a standard storyline, but the episodic structure is hard to criticize when almost every episode is terrific. Any conversation about the film begins with "Remember the scene when..."--my favorites include Virgil's attempt to play a cello in a marching band, and his prison break with a gun carved out of soap, which dissolves into suds in a thunderstorm.

 Take the Money and Run is the most consistently appealing film of Allen's pre-*Annie Hall* period, when his only goal was to make an audience laugh. In his first lead role as an actor, he builds on the built-in humor of a nervous nebbish becoming a bank robber, and ventures beyond what he could accomplish as a stand-up comic, proving himself an adept physical comedian as well.

WHAT'S NEW PUSSYCAT?
Directed by Clive Donner; Written by Woody Allen; Produced by Charles K. Feldman; Music by Burt Bacharach

Cast
Peter Sellers (Dr. Fritz Fassbender), Peter O'Toole (Michael James), Romy Schneider (Carole Werner), Capucine (Renee Lefebrvre), Paula Prentiss (Liz), WOODY ALLEN (VICTOR SHAKAPOPULIS)

TAKE THE MONEY AND RUN
Directed by Woody Allen; Written by Woody Allen and Mickey Rose; Produced by Charles H. Joffe; Music by Marvin Hamlisch

Cast
WOODY ALLEN (VIRGIL STARKWELL), Janet Margolin (Louise), Marcel Hillaire (Fritz)

JUNE ALLYSON (1923-   )

FIRST APPEARANCE: *Best Foot Forward* (MGM, 1943)

A STAR IS BORN: *Two Girls and a Sailor* (MGM, 1944)

"The girl next door" is an overused expression, so if the cliche` police mandated that only one actress could retain girl-next-door status, the choice would have to be June Allyson. Petite in stature, kind in heart, attractive but accessible, boundless energy, and talent that relies as much on enthusiasm as virtuosity, Allyson was the kind of girl that, after you've finished fantasizing about Lana Turner, you would be proud to marry and bring home to mom.

History does not record the names of Miss Allyson's neighbors in New York City, to whom she really *was* the girl next door. Jan Allyson's parents divorced before her first birthday, and she lived with her grandmother for much of her early childhood. An injury at the age of eight forced Jan to wear a back brace for several years. She started swimming to strengthen her muscles, and also taught herself to dance by watching Fred Astaire and Ginger Rogers movies. When she announced in high school that after eighteen viewings of *The Gay Divorcee`* (1934) she had learned Ginger's steps cold, her friends dared her to audition for a Broadway show. Jan took the dare and won a spot in the chorus of *Sing Out the News* (1938). But after two months she was ordered by her mother to quit the show and finish high school.

In 1939, she returned to Broadway as June Allyson and earned chorus roles in *Very Warm for May* (1939), *Higher and Higher* (1939), and *Panama Hattie* (1940). For *Panama Hattie* she understudied the lead role played by Betty Hutton, and played the part five times when Miss Hutton had the measles. Broadway producer George Abbott and MGM producer Arthur Freed were both in attendance at one of her performances, and both offered contracts. Allyson put Hollywood on hold and took a supporting role in Abbott's musical *Best Foot Forward* (1941). When MGM bought the film rights, Allyson and several other cast members reprised their stage roles in their motion picture debuts.

It's senior prom time at the Winsocki Military Institute as the movie opens, and starlet Lucille Ball (playing herself) is on her way to accept an invitation she received in the mail from one of the cadets. Her agent thinks the date will make great publicity, but the press gets a bigger story than anticipated when Lucy is mobbed at the prom and attacked by her escort's girlfriend.

During her first day on the set, Allyson was told to go home and cure her cold. "I haven't got a cold," she responded, "I talk like this all the time." Her role as Ethel, one of the girls at the prom, is a small one that only hints at her full potential, but her husky voice separated her from the crowd of chorines. She performs "The Three 'B's" with Gloria DeHaven and Nancy Walker, but the song is not as memorable as the trio who sing it. The film's big number is the closer, "Buckle Down, Winsocki," a catchy, familiar tune that is zestfully rendered by the entire cast. Nancy Walker and Lucille Ball supply enough comedy to make up for the mediocre score.

Following *Best Foot Forward*, which did respectable business, Allyson appeared with Mickey Rooney in *Girl Crazy* (1943), with most of the MGM lot in *Thousands Cheer* (1943) and again with Lucille Ball in *Meet the People* (1944). Her growing popularity with audiences encouraged the studio to try Allyson in a lead role; in *Two Girls and a Sailor* she was once again joined at the hip with Gloria DeHaven, but this time it was at the top of the bill and in some sprightly duets that outshone the best efforts of a slew of guest stars. The musical became one of the year's most popular offerings.

Allyson and DeHaven play the singing Deyo sisters, Patsy and Jean. Every night after their last show they invite a dozen soldiers and sailors back to their apartment, which has been converted into an intimate canteen (were the 1940s really this innocent?). Jean wishes they could do more for our men in uniform, and her wish is granted when Johnny, a millionaire sailor

(Van Johnson) buys them a warehouse and converts it into a canteen/nightclub. So much for plot. The movie is almost all music, and almost all wonderful.

In addition to Allyson and DeHaven, entertainment at the canteen is provided by Lena Horne, Gracie Allen, Jimmy Durante (performing "Inka Dinka Doo"), and the orchestras of Harry James and Xavier Cugat. Allyson solos admirably on "Young Man With a Horn," but she is just as appealing serving donuts to the G.I.s as she is singing on stage, and that's the best explanation I can give for the longevity of her career. *Two Girls and a Sailor* launched June Allyson but it's anyone's guess why it didn't do the same for the lovely Gloria DeHaven, who never got much further up the MGM depth chart than this.

BEST FOOT FORWARD
Directed by Edward Buzzell; Written by Irving Brecher; Produced by Arthur Freed; Music by Martin Blane

<u>Cast</u>
Lucille Ball (Herself), William Gaxton (Jack O'Riley), Virginia Weidler (Helen Schlessinger), Tommy Dix (Elwood), Nancy Walker (Nancy), Gloria DeHaven (Minerva), JUNE ALLYSON (ETHEL)

TWO GIRLS AND A SAILOR
Directed by Richard Thorpe; Written by Richard Connell and Gladys Lehman; Produced by Joe Pasternak; Music and songs by Arthur Freed, Roger Edens, Nacio Herb Brown, Harry James, Sammy Fain

<u>Cast</u>
Van Johnson (John Dyckman Brown III), JUNE ALLYSON (PATSY DEYO), Gloria DeHaven (Jean Deyo), Jimmy Durante (Billy Kipp), Tom Drake (Frank Miller)

JULIE ANDREWS (1935-   )

FIRST APPEARANCE: *Mary Poppins* (Disney, 1964)

A STAR IS BORN: *Mary Poppins*

Julie Andrews' Oscar-winning performance as Mary Poppins was one of the most self-assured and successful motion picture debuts of all time. First appearances this profound can often lead to typecasting, but rather than seek out a good axe-murderer role Andrews instead made *The Sound of Music* one year later. The result--another lovable governess, another musical, another of the decade's most popular films; now, it was too late. That second spoonful of silver screen sugar forever transformed Andrews into the personification of wholesome sweetness and light.

She was born Julia Elizabeth Wells in Walton-on-Thames, England, but became Julie Andrews when her mother, Barbara, divorced her father and married music hall singer Edward Andrews. Julie's musical talent was first noticed during a World War II air raid, when the family took refuge in a London underground shelter. Her stepfather hoped to raise the spirits of those gathered by leading a singalong, and eight-year-old Julie's voice was heard soaring over the impromptu chorus. A throat specialist later confirmed what seemed obvious--her singing voice was already as fully developed as an adult's. She began taking singing lessons at age twelve, and in less than a year she made her professional debut at the London Hippodrome.

After an adolesence spent on the stage in her parents' traveling variety show, Julie won the title role in *Cinderella* at the London Palladium in December of 1953. She was "discovered" during this performance by director Vida Hope, whose Broadway-bound musical *The Boy Friend* was packing houses down the street. In September of 1954, Julie played Polly Brown in the New York production and was hailed as the find of the season. In 1956, after starring in the made-for-TV movie *High Tor* with Bing Crosby, she returned to Broadway as Eliza Doolittle opposite Rex Harrison as Professor Henry Higgins in Lerner and Loewe's *My Fair Lady*, a Tony award-winning triumph that ran for six years.

A film adaptation was inevitable, and everyone assumed that Rex Harrison and Julie Andrews would reprise their roles. Everyone except for Warner Bros. boss Jack Warner, who paid $5 million for the rights and planned to sink $20 million more into the film. At those prices he wanted established box-office draws Cary Grant and Audrey Hepburn to play the leads. Grant, however, told Warner that not only wouldn't he play Higgins, he wouldn't even see the movie if Harrison wasn't in it. Warner relented, but he refused to let Eliza be played by an unknown stage actress. So Julie was out, and Audrey--even though her vocals in the musical numbers would have to be dubbed by Marni Nixon--was in.

Meanwhile, Andrews had opened to more glowing notices in *Camelot*, her third straight Broadway smash. Walt Disney paid her a backstage visit, and offered her the title role in *Mary Poppins*. At first Disney had planned to remain faithful to the P.L. Travers books and cast a middle-aged woman in the role--Bette Davis and Mary Martin were among the candidates. But the demands of flying via umbrella and dancing with Dick Van Dyke seemed a bit much for the over-40 stars, and after Disney heard Julie's glorious voice in `Camelot` he had no Warner-like qualms about her unknown status.

The film is set in London circa 1910; Jane and Michael Banks (Karen Dotrice and Matthew Garber), have driven a succession of nannies out the door, much to the exasperation of their parents (David Tomlinson and the superb Glynis Johns). Mary Poppins takes the position, and the children find themselves transported into a series of magical, musical adventures. The children learn much from her influence but their father learns a great deal more. He abandons his obsession for punctuality and decorum and rediscovers the joy of his family's love. Her true mission now accomplished, Mary Poppins flies off into the sunset.

Mary Poppins earned thirteen Academy Award nominations and became the "other" big musical of 1964. *My Fair Lady* received twelve nominations, but Audrey Hepburn was blatantly and unfairly chastised for "stealing" Julie's role and was passed over. Had she been nominated, however, Andrews still would have and should have won. Although Andrews' musical performances stand out, particularly on the tender ballads "Stay Awake" and "Feed the Birds," she also captured all the complexities of the "practically perfect" nanny with a completely perfect performance. The character's wilder eccentricities were trimmed from Travers to Disney, but Mary Poppins must still be cocksure, bossy and sometimes sarcastic while always remaining the cheerful epitome of British stiff-upper-lip refinement.

It's hard to find fault anywhere with *Mary Poppins*; the casting is flawless, from costars Dick Van Dyke and Glynis Johns to one-scene appearances by Ed Wynn and Jane Darwell, the mix of live action and animation in the "Jolly Holiday" sequence is amazing, and the score represented a career pinnacle for longtime Disney composers Richard and Robert B. Sherman. However, despite Julie Andrews' instant stardom when the film premiered, and her subsequent Oscar victory, she would be aced out of the film adaptation of her other Broadway triumph three years later, when Vanessa Redgrave was cast as Queen Guinevere in *Camelot*.

MARY POPPINS
Directed by Robert Stevenson; Written by Bill Walsh and Don DaGradi, based on the books by P.L. Travers; Produced by Walt Disney and Bill Walsh; Music by Richard M. and Robert B. Sherman

Cast
JULIE ANDREWS (MARY POPPINS), Dick Van Dyke (Bert), David Tomlinson (Mr. Banks), Glynis Johns (Mrs. Banks), Hermione Baddeley (Ellen), Reta Shaw (Mrs. Brill), Karen Dotrice (Jane Banks), Matthew Garber (Michael Banks), Arthur Treacher (Constable Jones), Reginald Owen (Admiral Boom), Ed Wynn (Uncle Albert), Jane Darwell (The Bird Woman)

ANN-MARGRET (1941-   )

FIRST APPEARANCE: *A Pocketful of Miracles* (United Artists, 1961)

A STAR IS BORN: *Bye Bye Birdie* (Columbia, 1963)

Just as Ann-Margret burst onto the Hollywood scene, the movie musical fizzled out. She made a few of them anyway, and proved as good a dancer as Cyd Charisse and a better singer, but the material was by and large substandard; to see Ann-Margret at her best meant going to Caesars Palace, not the movie theatre. Although she is also a talented dramatic actress, as evidenced by her Oscar nomination for *Carnal Knowledge* (1971), Pauline Kael correctly noted that her curvaceous figure was all that seemed to matter in her movies, and that she was most often cast as "a lewd mechanical doll."

The small village of Valsjoybyn, Sweden, was Ann-Margret Olsson's home for the first seven years of her life. In 1946 she moved with her mother to the United States to join her father, who had left Sweden shortly after Ann-Margret was born. The family settled in Fox Lake, Illinois, and later moved to the Chicago suburb of Wilmette.

"My mother was determined that I would have the singing, dancing, and piano lessons she had always wanted but was too poor to have in Sweden," said Ann-Margret, but this was not a case of a stage mother pushing her daughter into show business. Ann-Margret dreamed of a career on the stage from the age of four, and went willingly to her lessons. Before she enrolled in Northwestern University in 1959, she had already made her professional debut as a bandsinger in Kansas City. In the summer of 1960, she made her Las Vegas debut at the Nevada Club. When more bookings followed, she decided to put college on hold. George Burns discovered her in the lounge of the Dunes Hotel, and hired her as his opening act at the Sahara. That led to a recording contract with RCA, television appearances with Jack Benny and a screen test with Twentieth Century-Fox.

The test was successful, and Ann-Margret made her film debut in *A Pocketful of Miracles*, Frank Capra's remake of his 1933 film *Lady For A Day*. Bette Davis starred as Apple Annie, a street peddler who sells apples to finance her taste for gin. Glenn Ford plays Dave the Dude, a gangster who always buys an apple from Annie for luck. For years Annie corresponds with her daughter Louise, who lives in Europe and believes that her mother is a socialite named Mrs. E. Worthington Manville. But when Louise writes that she is returning to America with her fiance`, a Spanish nobleman, Annie believes her charade is about to end. But with Dave the Dude's help, Annie is transformed into the woman she had created in her letters.

The 1933 version rates the edge, though *Pocketful of Miracles* gains some historical importance by being Frank Capra's last film as producer and director. The tried-and-true *Pygmalion* gimmick works well enough again, but it happens a full hour into the film, which plays more like a sentimental made-for-TV movie made to run two weeks before Christmas. The pace is a problem, but Capra was still a master at tugging heartstrings. The scene in which Annie's cover story is saved at the very last minute is a classic bit of Capra-corn.

Bette Davis seems oddly miscast as Apple Annie, though she improves considerably after she plays the role within a role of Mrs. E. Worthington Manville. Glenn Ford and costars Hope Lange and Peter Falk (who earned an Oscar nomination as Dave's right-hand man) seem right at home in the colorful Damon Runyon universe from which this tale emerged.

Ann-Margret first appears at about the eighty minute mark. Wearing clothes from the Neiman-Marcus junior miss department, with her hair darkened to a demure auburn shade and set in a pony tail, she looks more like Shelley Fabares on *The Donna Reed Show* than the future kitten with a whip. It's a standard ingenue role, but there is one lovely moment when she sings "I Gave My Love a Cherry" in her delicate, breathy soprano.

She followed *A Pocketful of Miracles* with *State Fair* (1962) and *Bye Bye Birdie* (1963), but Ann-Margret actually became a star between movies, during an appearance on the 1962

Academy Awards telecast. Her performance of the nominated song "Bachelor in Paradise" stole the show. "What she appeared to be was a girl in her first formal who'd set out for the Junior Prom," wrote one reviewer, " and then she began to sing. . . and a transformation took place. From Little Miss Lollipop to Sexpot-Banshee. Her rendition was definitive. She squeezed it out, ground it out, belted it out, wrung it out, and flung it out. In the space of three minutes, Ann-Margret became the hottest name in town."

Bye Bye Birdie was her first project after this legendary performance, and it is the best musical in her filmography (though Elvis fans will surely opt for Viva Las Vegas--1964). Set in the 1950s, the featherweight plot is launched when rock singer and teen idol Conrad Birdie is drafted, and publicity whiz Rosie DeLeon (Janet Leigh) arranges for Birdie to kiss one female fan goodbye on The Ed Sullivan Show. Chosen at random for this honor is small-town girl Kim McAfee (Ann-Margret). DeLeon's actual objective in setting up the stunt is to get Birdie to perform a song written by her boyfriend (Dick Van Dyke), thus assuring him financial security so he will finally propose marriage.

The film is a clever send-up of the hysteria generated in America by the first blast of rock and roll, with Birdie obviously an ersatz Elvis Presley. Director George Sidney does a marvelous job in opening up the musical sequences from their original Broadway form. Every song is imaginatively staged--most better than they deserved-- only "Put on a Happy Face" emerged from the score and entered the national consciousness. Enthusiastic performances emerge from Leigh, Van Dyke and Paul Lynde, but Jesse Pearson, who plays the supposedly irresistable Conrad Birdie, can't even match Fabian in charisma. In a cameo as himself, Ed Sullivan acts with all the raw emotional fervor he projected as host of his long-running variety show.

"Modern musician worship is given the perfect embodiment in the innocent, yet strongly sexual power of Ann-Margret" wrote the Motion Picture Guide. She was playing a sweet sixteen-year-old, but her pouts and winks and gyrations send out a different message. Her hair is back to fiery red, her dresses are cut lower and her skirts are cut higher. Her vivacity as a dancer is captured in the stand-out production number "Got a Lot of Livin' to Do," but in the opening and closing renditions of the title song, which she performs with a coy Betty Boop inflection against a bare blue screen backdrop, Ann-Margret proved she needs no embellishment to attract undivided attention.

A POCKETFUL OF MIRACLES
Directed and produced by Frank Capra; Written by Hal Kanter, Harry Tugend and Jimmy Cannon, based on the story Madame La Gimp by Damon Runyon and the screenplay Lady For A Day by Robert Riskin; Music by Walter Scharf, James Van Heusen and Sammy Cahn

Cast
Glenn Ford (Dave "The Dude" Conway), Bette Davis (Apple Annie), Hope Lange (Queenie Martin), Arthur O'Connell (Count Alfonso Romero), Peter Falk (Joy Boy), Thomas Mitchell (Judge Henry G. Blake), ANN-MARGRET (LOUISE)

BYE BYE BIRDIE
Directed by George Sidney; Written by Irving Brecher, based on the musical by Michael Stewart; Produced by Fred Kohlmar; Music by Charles Strouse and Lee Adams

Cast
Janet Leigh (Rosie DeLeon), Dick Van Dyke (Albert Peterson), ANN-MARGRET (KIM MCAFEE), Maureen Stapleton (Mama), Bobby Rydell (Hugo), Jesse Pearson (Conrad Birdie), Ed Sullivan (Himself), Paul Lynde (Mr. McAfee)

FRED ASTAIRE (1899-1987)

FIRST APPEARANCE: *Dancing Lady* (MGM, 1933)

A STAR IS BORN: *Flying Down to Rio* (RKO, 1933)

Fred Astaire's name is synonymous with dance on film, and with a level of excellence that had previously been reserved only for classically-trained artists from the world of ballet. In fact, it was George Balanchine, the legendary ballet choreographer, who singled out Astaire as "the most interesting, the most inventive, the most elegant dancer of our time." Astaire was also a revolutionary force in the development of the musical; "Not only did he create his own choreography in most films, he also participated in the decision-making process of how his dances would be photographed, scored, and edited," wrote essayist Jeanine Basinger. Astaire pioneered the serious presentation of dance in motion pictures, both by his on-screen influence and his behind-the-scenes collaboration.

His most familiar screen persona was that of an assertive but happy-go-lucky bachelor who breaks down the resistance of the woman he loves through a courtship of dance. Although Astaire was a capable dramatic actor, a talented light comedian, and an engaging vocalist who has probably introduced more Irving Berlin and George Gershwin standards than any singer, the characters he played were only memorable when they gracefully moved in sync with a melody. Whether he was gliding across the floor with Ginger Rogers in an elegant adagio or banging out a tap duel with Eleanor Powell, Astaire attained a virtuosity that approached perfection, and made it seem effortless.

Fred Austerlitz was born in Omaha, Nebraska, and at the age of four he was enrolled by his mother in the ballet school where his sister Adele was already taking lessons. When both children displayed exceptional natural ability, the Austerlitzes moved to New York so that Fred and Adele could enroll in a school operated by Ned Wayburn, the originator of modern tap dancing. They made their vaudeville debut as a dance team in 1906, billed as "Juvenile Artists Presenting an Electric Musical Toe-Dancing Novelty." By 1917, the Austerlitz children had changed their name to Astaire, and were appearing on Broadway. Among the shows in which Fred and Adele danced were *Lady be Good* (1925), *Funny Face* (1927) and *The Band Wagon* (1931), which marked the final appearance of the team. Adele retired after her marriage to Lord Charles Cavendish, and Fred, already a stage veteran with over twenty years in show business, continued his career in Hollywood.

Some reference sources list the Mary Pickford silent film *Fanchon the Cricket* (1915) as Astaire's film debut. Supposedly, Fred and Adele perform an adagio number that is the only footage of their partnership. Astaire writes in his biography *Steps in Time* that he and Adele were visitors on the set, but says nothing about appearing in the film. Adele Astaire also emphatically denied that she and Fred shared the screen with Mary Pickford, according to Pickford biographer Scott Eyman. The film is believed lost, so absolute proof may be impossible, but perhaps the best evidence of the Astaires' non-participation is the *Variety* review of *Fanchon the Cricket*, which was published on May 14, 1915, and makes no mention of a talented young dance team. Anyone who ever saw the Astaires has claimed that Adele was Fred's most simpatico partner, so it seems highly unlikely that a performance by them would be overlooked in a review.

Astaire did appear in one short film entitled *Municipal Bandwagon* (1931) before making his feature debut in *Dancing Lady* (1933), a creaky musical with an offbeat but wonderful grab-bag cast of future legends. Stars Joan Crawford and Clark Gable are joined by Astaire, Nelson Eddy, Eve Arden and--no kidding--the Three Stooges. And the film still isn't all that great. The dancing lady in the title is Janie Barlow (Crawford), an out-of-work hoofer who is plucked from a burlesque house and placed in a Broadway show by a lovestruck Park Avenue playboy. There, she becomes torn romantically between her benefactor and the show's whip-cracking director (Gable).

Although she appeared in several musicials in the early days of her career, Joan Crawford dances a lot like Broderick Crawford. But when she becomes Fred Astaire's first partner on screen, he makes her look fine, as he would do with all his future costars who needed the support. Unfortunately, he can't do much about her singing. He first appears, playing himself, one hour into the film in a brief rehersal scene, and when he returns for opening night he is garbed in the top hat and tails that would become his uniform for the next fifty years. Although the routines he performs, such as the ludicrous "Let's Go Bavarian," are nowhere near his highlight reel, every step is already impeccable.

Next, Astaire took a featured role in *Flying Down to Rio*, in which he was paired with an up-and-coming comedienne and chorine named Ginger Rogers. Dolores Del Rio stars as a South American beauty with two suitors--her long-time fiance` (Raoul Roulien) and a handsome American bandleader (Gene Raymond). After Raymond and his band (which includes Astaire as accordion player Fred Ayres and Rogers as singer Honey Hale) fly down to Rio, they visit a nightclub where some dancers are performing the carioca. "I'd like to try this thing just once," says Fred to Ginger. "We'll show them a thing or three," she replies. From the first moment they begin to move in unison, it is obvious that, unlike Joan Crawford, Ginger didn't need Astaire to look proficient. Together they spin and glide through Hermes Pan's intricately choreographed routine, which borrows elements from ballroom, tap and tango.

"The Carioca" is the only number they perform, but the public reaction was instantaneous and overwhelming; the dance launched a national craze, and the film made enough money to rescue RKO from bankruptcy. Astaire and Rogers became forever united as the movies' greatest dance team and, as successful as each would become in solo projects, it was their ten collaborations that still stand as the pinnacle achievement of the movie musical.

DANCING LADY
Directed by Robert Z. Leonard; Written by Allen Rivkin and P.J. Wolfson, based on the novel by James Warner Bellah; Produced by David O. Selznick; Music and songs by Lou Silvers, Dorothy Fields, Jimmy McHugh

Cast
Joan Crawford (Janie Barlow), Clark Gable (Patch Gallagher), Franchot Tone (Tod Newton), FRED ASTAIRE (HIMSELF), Nelson Eddy (Himself), Moe Howard, Jerry Howard, Larry Fine (Three Stooges)

FLYING DOWN TO RIO
Directed by Thornton Freeland; Written by Cyril Hume, H.W. Hanemann and Edward Gelsey, based on a play by Anne Caldwell; Produced by Lou Brock; Music by Vincent Youmans, Edward Eliscu and Gus Kahn

Cast
Dolores Del Rio (Belinha de Rezende) Gene Raymond (Roger Bond), Raoul Roulien (Julio Rubeiro), Ginger Rogers (Honey Hale) FRED ASTAIRE (FRED AYRES)

LAUREN BACALL (1924-   )

FIRST APPEARANCE: *To Have and Have Not* (Warner Bros., 1944)

A STAR IS BORN: *To Have and Have Not*

      Lauren Bacall's silver screen debut was the kind of showcase that few actresses receive in a career; a lead role opposite Humphrey Bogart, in a film directed by Howard Hawks and written by William Faulkner, based on a book by Ernest Hemingway. No one could ask for a better opportunity for overnight stardom. The downside, of course, is that if it didn't work she couldn't blame the material. But Lauren Bacall seemed the only choice for the film from the moment she walked into frame; her feline delivery enhanced Faulkner's words, and at the tender age of nineteen she matched Bogart's world-weary cynicism stride for stride. Bogie was so impressed with his leading lady that he married her one year later.

      According to Hollywood legend, the film was first conceived from an argument between Hemingway and Hawks during a Florida fishing trip. Angry over Hemingway's refusal to work on a screenplay, the director vowed to make a movie out of the author's worst book. "What is my worst book?" Hemingway asked. "That piece of junk called *To Have and Have Not*." Hawks responded. When Hemingway maintained that the novel was unfilmable, Hawks said he'd get William Faulkner to pen the script, because "he can write better than you can anyway."

      To Have and Have Not became Howard Hawks' *Casablanca*. Comparisons were made in every review, and were accentuated by Humphrey Bogart again being cast as a reluctant hero who helps the French cause against Germany in World War II. Set on the island of Martinique in 1940, the story has Captain Harry Morgan (Bogart) refusing to allow French loyalists to use his fishing boat on a covert mission. He relents after having his own problems with the Germans, and inevitably is drawn deeper into the underground movement. The casting of Bogart was a natural, but the role of Marie (Slim) Browning, a sardonic chanteuse who finds a kindred spirit in Captain Harry, would be more difficult to fill.

      Betty Bacall was born just five years after Bogart made his film debut. She attended the American Academy of Dramatic Arts in New York City, where she would form a lifelong friendship with fellow student Kirk Douglas. The Academy prepared its pupils for a career on the stage, but Bacall's longest-running job in the theater was as an usher. She managed a couple of minor credits in plays that closed in less than a month, but at the age of eighteen she turned to modeling to pay the bills. Her first assignment, just like her later introduction to the movies, was a plum--a *Harper's Bazaar* layout that landed Bacall on the cover of the magazine's January, 1943 issue. The alluring photos brought phone calls from the offices of Columbia Pictures, David O. Selznick and Howard Hawks. Bacall forgot about the stage, signed with Hawks and left the east coast for the west.

      Bacall screen-tested for *To Have and Have Not* with the scene that became the film's most famous--Marie seductively exits Harry's hotel room, but reminds him that to see her again, all he has to do is whistle. "You know how to whistle, don't you? You just put you lips together...and...blow." Watching her purr that line in the finished .product, it's not hard to see how she won the role. It was Hawks who changed Betty Bacall's name to Lauren, and suggested that she lower the timbre of her voice as much as possible for line-readings and for the three songs she performs in the film. Throughout production the producers were uncertain about using Bacall's singing, and since no female singer could adequately match her contralto speaking voice, the task of dubbing her musical numbers was given to Andy Williams! Finally they decided against dubbing, and Bacall's Marlene Dietrich-like performances do manage to get the message across. Her eyes make the difference.

      The film is less remembered for its music than for the many classic give-and-take dialogue exchanges between Bogie and Bacall, a tough-talk competition with few equals in the movies. Bacall seems to exude self-assurance, but she was so nervous when filming began that her visible trembling was blowing takes. To solve the problem, she kept her head tilted down, with her chin almost touching her chest, while focusing her eyes in the opposite direction. Thus was born "The Look" which captivated audiences and launched her career.

Time magazine described Bacall as a combination of divas Bette Davis, Greta Garbo, Mae West, Marlene Dietrich, Jean Harlow and Glenda Farrell, but noted that much of her personality is "completely new to the screen;" "She has a javelinlike vitality, a born dancer's eloquence in movement, fierce female shrewdness and a special sweet-sourness. With these faculties, plus a stone-crushing self-confidence and a tombstone voice, she manages to get across the toughest girl a piously regenerate Hollywood has dreamed of in a long, long while." *Variety* put it more succinctly--"She can slink, brother, and no fooling!"

TO HAVE AND HAVE NOT
Directed and produced by Howard Hawks; Written by Jules Furthman and William Faulkner, from the novel by Ernest Hemingway; Music by Franz Waxman, songs by Hoagy Carmichael, Johnny Mercer, Stanley Adams, Harry Akst and Grant Clarke

Cast
Humphrey Bogart (Harry Morgan), Walter Brennan (Eddie), LAUREN BACALL (MARIE BROWNING), Dolores Moran (Helene De Bursac), Hoagy Carmichael (Cricket), Walter Molnar (Paul De Bursac), Sheldon Leonard (Lt. Coyo)

ANNE BANCROFT (1931-   )

FIRST APPEARANCE: *Don't Bother to Knock* (20th Century-Fox, 1952)

A STAR IS BORN: *The Miracle Worker* (United Artists, 1962)

Ronald Reagan was dubbed "The Teflon President," because negative news stories about his policies did not affect his popularity. Using the same metaphor, Anne Bancroft could be considered "The Teflon Actress." She still brings an aura of quality and class to a movie, despite the fact that for every *Miracle Worker* in her filmography, there are two *Treasure of the Golden Condor*s.

Twentieth Century-Fox obviously didn't know what to do with Bancroft after they put her under contract, so she is not entirely to blame for her stalled early career. Her first fifteen films include such bargain-bin releases as *Demetrius and the Gladiators* (1954), *Walk the Proud Land* (1956), and *The Girl in Black Stockings* (1957), in which she was billed ahead of Mamie Van Doren but behind Lex Barker. Her best roles, beginning with *The Miracle Worker*, established her as a first-rate portrayer of characters with a formidable physical presence and an iron will, but even after *The Pumpkin Eater* (1964) and *The Graduate* (1967), one Academy Award and four nominations, she still turns up in junk like *Bert Rigby, You're a Fool* (1989) and *Love Potion #9* (1992). And as quickly as these mistakes are made they are forgotten, and Bancroft emerges, as always, untarnished.

A native of the Bronx, New York, Anne-Marie Italiano was a born show-off who from the age of three would sing for for WPA workers in her neighborhood. She was active in the Drama Club at Christopher Columbus High School and, in 1947, after briefly contemplating a career as a lab technician, she entered the American Academy of Dramatic Arts. Under the name Anne Marno, she won a recurring role on the early television sitcom *The Goldbergs*, and appeared in *Studio One* and other dramatic anthology programs. After a screen test, Twentieth Century-Fox signed her up, and Anne Marno became Anne Bancroft.

Don't Bother to Knock gave Marilyn Monroe her first leading role, and was intended to be the film that proved she could act. This it could not accomplish, but the film and Monroe's character are so poorly written that they could hardly be considered a fair judge of talent. Nell (Monroe), an unbalanced young woman still mourning the death of her boyfriend in a plane crash, is released from a mental institution and gets a job babysitting in a hotel. Jed Towers (Richard Widmark), after being dumped by girlfriend Lyn Lesley (Bancroft), spots Nell though his hotel window and talks his way into an invitation to her room. He quickly realizes that Nell is cracking up, and grows concerned for the little girl in her charge.

Bancroft's character is the singer in the hotel's lounge, and her small part contains more lyrics than lines. Lyn Lesley is a tough cookie, Gloria Grahame-type role, that Bancroft plays with the appropriate laconic tone. The big surprise is how well she handles the vocals; her husky voice slides smoothly and gracefully through "I'll Take Manhattan" and other standards. Unfortunately, she wouldn't get another chance to sing in movies until *To Be Or Not to Be* (1983), in which she and husband Mel Brooks perform "Sweet Georgia Brown" in Polish.

Bancroft spent the next five years toiling in the trenches, before giving up on movies and heading back to New York. "I learned a great deal in Hollywood, even though I'm not particularly proud of the fifteen or so films I made." she told *Theatre* Magazine. In 1958, the actress that Hollywood judged fit for Audie Murphy westerns won a Tony Award for her performance in *Two for the Seesaw*, and then starred as Annie Sullivan in *The Miracle Worker*, opposite Patty Duke as Helen Keller. The result was a masterpiece of theater that provided Bancroft with the role of a lifetime and a second career in motion pictures. This time, she brought her own material.

Annie Sullivan probably would have been played by Deborah Kerr if Hollywood had anything to say about it, but play producer Fred Coe, director Arthur Penn and writer William

Gibson all went west to oversee the film adaptation, and it was their mandate that Bancroft and Duke reprise their roles. Their insistence was justified when both actresses earned Academy Awards. Duke, as a defiant, blind and deaf wild child, delivers what is arguably the best performance by a teenager in the history of motion pictures. Bancroft is every bit as superb as Helen's tenacious teacher, who engages her reluctant student in a fierce battle of wits and of wills, that frequently explodes into violent physical confrontation.

The classic scene, of course, is at the water pump when Helen learns to communicate with sign language, but the scene that brought the house down on stage began with Annie watching with revulsion as Helen walks around the breakfast table, grabbing food from everyone's plate. Annie will not allow her food to be taken, and thus begins a ten-minute brawl that transforms the Keller kitchen into a war zone. The intensity of their struggle is astonishing, so much so that it is hard to imagine how Duke and Bancroft summoned the strength to play the scene hundreds of times during the theatrical run.

She is compelling in the clinches, but Bancroft also conveys Annie's quick wit, gentle humor, and above all her determination to ignite the intelligence that she knows exists within the quiet, dark world of Helen Keller. "Giving up," she says in a lilting Irish accent, "is my idea of original sin."

DON'T BOTHER TO KNOCK
Directed by Roy Baker; Written by Daniel Taradash, based on the novel by Charlotte Armstrong; Produced by Julian Blaustein; Music by Lionel Newman

Cast
Richard Widmark (Jed Towers), Marilyn Monroe (Nell), ANNE BANCROFT (LYN LESLIE), Donna Corcoran (Bunny), Elisha Cook, Jr. (Eddie)

THE MIRACLE WORKER
Directed by Arthur Penn; Written by William Gibson, based on his play and the book by Helen Keller; Produced by Fred Coe; Music by Laurence Rosenthal

Cast
ANNE BANCROFT (ANNIE SULLIVAN), Patty Duke (Helen Keller), Victor Jory (Capt. Keller), Inga Swenson (Kate Keller), Andrew Prine (James Keller)

BRIGITTE BARDOT (1934-)

FIRST APPEARANCE: *Le Trou Normand [Crazy for Love]* (Cite-Films, 1952)

A STAR IS BORN: *Et...Dieu Crea La Femme [And...God Created Woman]* (Iena-UCIL-Condor/Kingsley International, 1956)

Fun, guilt-free sex was the promise made by Brigitte Bardot in a string of delightfully decadant films, that landed like atomic bombs in repressed 1950s America. You didn't see as much as you might remember in those teasing glimpses of BB behind shower curtains and wet t-shirts, but it was demonstrably more than could be seen in American movies of the time, which is why her imported charms played in the peek-a-boo grindhouses as well as the legitimate art theaters. Today, her exploits would barely rate a PG-13, but four decades ago Bardot was scandalous.

What endeared her to some and further outraged others was how she relished her reputation. She loved making the movies, shocking audiences with nude scenes, and living her on-screen persona by having affairs with several leading men. Bardot's unapologetic participation in what was then considered pornography made her the most famous French woman since Joan of Arc, and, unexpectedly, earned her praise for creating a modern revolutionary character for women.

Born in Paris, France, Brigitte Bardot was a shy, sheltered child who grew up in comfort and privilege. A British nurse, a chalet near Versailles, winters skiing at Meribel, private schools and ballet lessons formed the memories of her early years. At a 1948 ballet recital, an editor for *Jardin des Modes* magazine watched fourteen-year-old Brigitte perform, and offered her the chance to model for a teenage fashion spread. Less than one year later, she was on the cover of *Elle* magazine, but since her mother insisted that Brigitte's name not appear, as modeling was not considered appropriate for someone in the Bardot social circle, the girl was identified only by her initials--BB.

Film director Marc Allegret saw the pictures, and asked his friend Roger Vadim for his opinion. "Interesting," replied Vadim, who then contacted Brigitte's parents to ask their permission to put their daughter in the movies. Acting was thought to be even more lowbrow than modeling, but Vadim could be very persuasive, and Brigitte was allowed to film a screen test. It would take several more tests, plus acting lessons taught by Vadim, before Brigitte was judged ready for her first film. By then she was eighteen--and married to her acting coach.

Le Trou Normand is a charming comedy set in the small French village of Courteville. The owner of an inn dies, and wills the business to his slow-witted nephew Hypolite (Bourvil), but only if the 32-year-old man will return to elementary school and earn a diploma. Hypolite's Aunt Augustine (Jeanne Marten) has designs on the property, and uses her pretty but conceited daughter Javotte (Bardot) in a scheme to take advantage of Hypolite's crush on his cousin.

Bardot avails herself well as bad girl Javotte Lemoine, who isn't nearly as bad as she pretends. During a wonderful scene late in the film, Javotte learns that Hypolite has tried to fail his test on purpose, after Augustine promises him Javotte in exchange for the inn. At first she laughs at the simple-minded man's affection, but then she takes pity on him, and shows some unexpectedly genuine kindness before leaving town for good. When Javotte hears that Hypolite passed the test anyway, her smile has a natural warmth and sweetness that is harder to find in later Bardot vehicles.

Fifteen films came between *Le Trou Normand* and Bardot's breakthrough in *And...God Created Woman*. America was first exposed to "BeBe" in the latter film, and the resulting sensation led to the importing of her earlier features, many of which were re-cut to emphasize Bardot's contribution. Because of this, Bardot gets top billing in the prints of *Le Trou Normand* that were shipped over here. Those expecting to see BeBe in scantily-clad temptress mode must have been disappointed; clothed in the modest dress of a rural schoolgirl, with her mousy brown hair tucked into a bun, she looks much younger than her eighteen years.

Four years later, in the opening moments of *And...God Created Woman*, a sex goddess was born; Bardot sunbathes nude behind a white sheet hanging over a clothesline, in an opening sequence that has become legendary. Never has plot mattered less in a blockbuster film; Juliette Hardy (Bardot), a sexually-uninhibited beauty, marries the kind-hearted Michel (Jean-Louis Trintignant) just to stay out of an orphanage. In time Juliette comes to care for her devoted husband, but she still seduces Michel's older brother Antoine (Christian Marquand). That's it. The film was tailor-made by director Vadim as an exercise in Bardot-worship, and nobody remembers any scene that she was not in.

The role of "shameless creature" Juliette Hardy is one she had played before, in films like *Manina, La Fille Sans Voiles* (1952) and *La Lumiere d'en Face* (1955), but *And...God Created Woman* displayed her for the first time in color and CinemaScope, which made the film more acceptable to foreign audiences. It also had Vadim behind the camera, and whatever his other shortcomings at storytelling, he knew how to present his wife to best advantage. In the love scene between Juliette and Antoine, and in Juliette's brazen, defiant skirt-twirling dance in the last scene, Vadim proves he knows the tricks of sensuality on film that they don't teach at UCLA.

"In a lifetime of seeing movies, I have never seen an actress convey sex so simply and so devastatingly," wrote Matt White in his review. "She had me blushing in the nervous darkness of the cinema." The film received an "X" rating in England, and even after extensive censoring was banned in Dallas, Texas. Two theater owners in Philadelphia were arrested after one showing.

Bardot always suggested more than she showed, but those suggestions were awfully powerful. Taking stock of her full blond mane of curly hair, large, wide-open eyes, lips pursed in a seductive pout, her bust so full and her waist so tiny, the swivel of her hips and her flat, barefoot walk, her smoldering expressions and willingness to share her charms, it is clear that the movies have never created a more unabashed, living, walking sexual fantasy. Only her badly-dubbed voice did not seem computer-designed for enticement. "You've never seen anything like it," raved the *New York Daily News*; "If Loren, Monroe (and) Mansfield see Brigitte in this film, they will more than likely feel so inadequate they will leave the screen."

LE TROU NORMAND
AKA Crazy for Love
Directed by Jean Boyer; Written by Arlette de Pitray; Produced by Jacques Bar; Music by Paul Misraki and Jean Boyer

Cast
Bourvil (Hypolite), Jeanne Marken (Augustine), BRIGITTE BARDOT (JAVOTTE LEMOINE), Nadine Basile (Madeleine)

ET...DIEU CREA LA FEMME
AKA And...God Created Woman
Directed by Roger Vadim; Written by Roger Vadim and Raoul J. Levy; Produced by Raoul J. Levy; Music by Paul Misraki

Cast
BRIGITTE BARDOT (JULIETTE HARDY), Curt Jurgens (Eric Carradine), Jean-Louis Trintignant (Michel Tardieu), Christian Marquand (Antoine Tardieu), Georges Poujouly (Christian Tardieu)

WARREN BEATTY (1937-   )

FIRST APPEARANCE: *Splendor in the Grass* (Warner Bros., 1961)

A STAR IS BORN: *Splendor in the Grass*

He was one of the last leading men to fit the "clean-cut and handsome" mold when such attributes were still a prerequisite for stardom. He broke into movies with a lead role, and had the young stud territory pretty much to himself throughout the 1960s. Warren Beatty's dashing looks and well-publicized escapades with thirty years of leading ladies (from Natalie Wood in his movie debut to Annette Bening in 1991's *Bugsy*) have reduced most coverage of his career to fifty percent critical assessment and fifty percent snickering tabloid gossip. He has proven himself a filmmaker of unique vision and insight, with a keen ability to find a novel take on a familiar subject, as well as an actor with a knack for antiheros in perpetual adolesence. But it's reasonable to conclude that his accomplishments have been obscured by his libertine reputation. To chastise Beatty for this would be presumptuous and arrogant, and blaming the press is like spitting into the wind. It will be interesting to study, however, the extent to which marriage and fatherhood will impact evaluation of his career.

Warren's older sister Shirley was the first to embrace show business, but he would often join with her and their mother in reading scenes for practice. After her graduation from high school in Arlington, Virginia, Shirley adapted her mother's maiden name (McLean) and took off for Broadway. Warren became president of his high school class and, after receiving his diploma in 1955, he turned down ten football scholarships and enrolled in the School of Speech and Drama of Illinois's Northwestern University. One year later he left for New York and the Stella Adler Theatre School. While studying with Ms. Adler he played cocktail-hour piano in a bar on 58th Street, and worked construction on the third tube of the Lincoln Tunnel.

His first professional experience, as it was for so many other New York actors in the late fifties, was in the plethora of live television drama series, including *Studio One* and *Playhouse 90*. In between, Beatty took stage work wherever it was offered, and it was during his time with the New Jersey Playhouse that he was discovered by playwright William Inge and director Joshua Logan. He screen-tested with another up-and-comer named Jane Fonda for a proposed new film by Elia Kazan, but when that fell through Beatty was cast in Inge's play *A Loss of Roses*. The play earned mixed reviews when it opened in New York in November of 1959, but Warren Beatty's portrayal of a fatherless teenager who falls in love with a carnival actress was described as "mercurial, sensitive, excellent" by the *Herald-Tribune*, and other critics also offered praise. *A Loss of Roses* closed after 25 performances, but Beatty was in demand as soon as the last curtain fell. He signed a non-exclusive movie contract with MGM, and made his film debut with Warner Bros. in *Splendor in the Grass*.

It was familiar territory for Beatty--another William Inge script inspired by the author's own youth in Kansas, circa 1925, and once again he was cast as a tortured adolescent torn between family and love. He was 24 years old but could still pass--barely--as a high school senior.

Bud Stamper (Beatty) and Deanie Loomis (Natalie Wood) are sweethearts whose relationship is derailed by the warped good intentions of their parents. Bud's oil-rich father Ace (Pat Hingle) has his son's entire future mapped out--four years at Yale and a white collar career. Deanie, whose family lives on the proverbial wrong side of the tracks, is encouraged to marry Bud, but her screwed-up mother (Audrey Christie) attempts to squelch her daughter's sexual feelings with dire warnings of the shattered lives led by those who gave in ("Boys don't respect a girl they can go all the way with"). Deanie stays pure but Bud loses the battle with his hormones and starts dating the town slut. When she learns the truth, Deanie attempts suicide and is taken to a mental institution. Bud, after dealing with the financial collapse of his father and the death of his sister, leaves Yale and marries an Italian waitress (Zohra Lampert). He meets up with Deanie again years later, but the passion they once shared has been destroyed from within and without.

Splendor in the Grass hasn't aged well--the characters played to scenery-chewing excess by Hingle and Christie are so warped that they are hard to take seriously. Some of the lines in Inge's script, which unbelievably won an Oscar, could have emerged from drive-in exploitation flicks like *Delinquent Daughters* (1944) and *Bad Girls Do Cry* (1954). The names of Inge and Elia Kazan suggest a pedigree, but at heart it's the same formula spiel.

But if the film seems dated, the performances of Warren Beatty and Natalie Wood do not. There was more than a little James Dean in Beatty's reading of the brooding, confused, misunderstood Bud Stamper, but he is deftly able to suggest Dean without imitating him. "Ten years of intensive work put in by a notable talent could not improve upon this particular characterization." wrote the *New York Post*, "The way in which he projects his personality and emotions in front of the camera is an amazing achievement for a young man so lacking in experience." Natalie Wood is equally superb as the devoted, fragile Deanie. Together they create some genuinely moving moments.

SPLENDOR IN THE GRASS
Directed and produced by Elia Kazan; Written by William Inge; Music by David Amram

<u>Cast</u>
Natalie Wood (Deanie Loomis), WARREN BEATTY (BUD STAMPER), Pat Hingle (Ace Stamper), Audrey Christie (Mrs. Loomis), Barbara Loden (Ginny Stamper), Zohra Lampert (Angelina), Sandy Dennis (Kay)

INGRID BERGMAN (1915-1982)

FIRST APPEARANCE: *The Count of the Monk's Bridge* (Svenskifilmindustri, 1934)

A STAR IS BORN: *Intermezzo* (Selznick/United Artists, 1939)

If the word "luminous" did not already exist in the English language, its creation would be necessary to describe Ingrid Bergman. There were other actresses with flawless skin, honey blond hair and a shining smile, but no female movie star before or since Bergman could magnify her physical features with a radiant inner light. Her exotic, lightly-accented voice was similar in pitch to that of the previous big Swedish import, Greta Garbo, but Bergman's wholesome, approachable farm girl freshness was the antithesis of Garbo's aloof persona.

Both of Ingrid's parents died before her twelfth birthday, and she was raised by a stern, elderly uncle. She created an imaginary world to escape the sadness of her situation and the taunts of five cousins who ridiculed her shyness and awkward demeanor. Her choice of a career in performing was a natural extension of a childhood spent in a Swedish suburb of the Neighborhood of Make Believe.

The skills she developed in her sanctuary of fantasy led to a try-out with Sweden's Royal Dramatic Theater School, where in 1933 she was selected from 75 applicants for one of eight places. Two years later, while her fellow students were still studying, Ingrid Bergman had become a star. She was offered a studio contract after her first film appearance, in the undistinguished comedy *Munkbrogreven*, or *The Count of the Monk's Bridge*. The film could be mistaken for a Stockholm travelogue, and the numerous sequences of Sweden's picturesque capital is the only footage of interest today besides that of Bergman's debut. She plays a maid in a cheap hotel, who encounters a band of drinking buddies during their uproarious travels from tavern to tavern. One doesn't immediately associate the Swedish film industry with madcap frivolity, but the genre was a popular one in the thirties and *The Count of the Monk's Bridge* was typical of its kind.

Though seventh-billed in a brief role, Bergman was noticed by critics who described her as "sunny of spirit," but a tad overweight. Her reputation as a talented ingenue increased gradually over the course of ten films, and achieved a pinnacle with *Intermezzo* (1936), a sweet and simple love story; Holger Brandt, a concert violinist (Gosta Ekman) finds himself drawn to Anita, his children's beautiful young piano teacher. Though he is happily married, Holger falls in love with Anita and leaves his family. They tour the concert stages of Europe together, but their happiness is impaired when Holger begins to miss his wife and children. Anita bows out and Holger returns home, where he is forgiven by his family.

The film was popular enough to reach the art houses in America, where it was greeted with fervent praise from critics. The reviews were read by Elsa Neuberger, an employee in producer David O. Selznick's story office in New York. Neuberger saw a matinee of *Intermezzo* at the Cinema de Paris Theatre, and agreed with the critics that Ingrid Bergman stole the movie. She cabled her boss, who secured the American rights to remake the film and dispatched a representative to Sweden to lure the 23-year-old Bergman to Hollywood. When Selznick's aide arrived in Stockholm, she was somewhat surprised to discover that the maiden whose performance resonated with an almost childlike naivete` was already a wife and a mother to an infant daughter. When Ingrid hesitated about leaving home, Selznick began shopping for another leading lady. Loretta Young had the inside track before Bergman finally accepted and boarded a ship for New York.

Filming began with Gregory Ratoff at the helm, but it was Selznick who continued to call the shots. "There is no single thing about the physical production of this picture that compares in importance with the photography of Miss Bergman," he wrote in a memo, which explained his decision to bring in Gregg Toland, the most inventive cinematographer of his era, to replace Harry Stradling. Toland's job, according to Ronald Haver`s book *David O. Selznick's*

Hollywood, was to capture the "curious charm" and "combination of exciting beauty and fresh purity" Bergman had in the Swedish version. It was cinematographer Ake Dahlqvist, who worked on seven of Bergman's Swedish films including *Intermezzo*, that created the look that caught the Selznick studio's attention. Ten years earlier, Dahlqvist had photographed the screen test that brought Greta Garbo to Hollywood.

Selznick insisted on endless retakes of key moments in the film, and even called Bergman back to the studio on the day she was to return to Sweden for one more take of Anita's momentous first meeting with Holger. The remake of *Intermezzo* was released in 1939, and Ingrid Bergman was once again lauded for her touching performance and her exquisite natural beauty. Leslie Howard replaced Gosta Ekman as the smitten violinist, and the haunting "Intermezzo Theme," written by Heinz Provost, was wisely retained from the original film and became a huge hit. Bergman had successfully resisted the producer's insistence that she change her name (too German, thought Selznick) and was back with her family when she was told by telephone of the film's success. The option on her one-picture contract was exercised, and Bergman returned to Hollywood to stay. Three years later, she walked into Rick's cafe` in *Casablanca*, and into movie history. *Intermezzo* was remade once more in 1980 as *Honeysuckle Rose*, with Amy Irving in the role that Ingrid Bergman rode to stardom.

THE COUNT OF THE MONK'S BRIDGE
Directed by Edvin Adolphson and Sigurd Wallen; Written by Gosta Stevens, based on the play *Greven Fran Gamla Sta'n* by Arthur and Sigfried Fischer; Produced by AB Fribergs Filmbyra; Music by Jules Sylvain

Cast
Valdemar Dahlqvist, Sigurd Wallen, Eric Abrahamson, Weyler Hildebrand, Artur Cederborg, Edvin Adolphson, INGRID BERGMAN

INTERMEZZO
Directed by Gregory Ratoff; Written by George O'Neil, based on a story by Gosta Stevens and Gustav Molander; Produced by David O. Selznick; Music by Heinz Provost

Cast
Leslie Howard (Holger Brandt), INGRID BERGMAN (ANITA HOFFMAN), Edna Best (Margit Brand), John Halliday (Thomas Stenborg)

JACQUELINE BISSET (1941-   )

FIRST APPEARANCE: *The Knack...and How to Get It* (United Artists, 1965)

A STAR IS BORN: *The Deep* (Columbia, 1977)

"One of these days," wrote *New York Times* film critic Vincent Canby, "the splendid-looking Jacqueline Bisset is going to get a role that matches her talent as well as her beauty." Over a decade has passed since Canby's optimistic prediction, but it still hasn't happened. Francois Truffaut's *Day for Night* (1973) should have made further proof of Bisset's talent unnecessary, but continental films do not make many stars in America. Such dilemmas have been the story of her career; Bisset's bad movies, *The Greek Tycoon* (1978) and *Class* (1983) among others, are well-publicized, mainstream releases, while her best work--*Day For Night*, *The Sunday Woman* (1976)--goes virtually unnoticed.

Jacqueline Fraser Bisset grew up in a centuries-old thatch-roofed cottage in Reading, England, 35 miles west of London. Her father was a doctor and her mother was a lawyer, so it is not surprising that Jacqueline's education was a priority. But after completing her secondary grades, she bypassed college for a career in modeling. "I didn't like it, I just wanted to make money," she told the *New York Post*, and after appearing in *Vogue* and other top fashion magazines, and a few television commercials, Bisset was almost, but not quite, able to quit her day job as a waitress.

She achieved enough recognition selling milk and butter on TV to land bit parts in several European films, the first being Richard Lester's very British comedy *The Knack...and How to Get It*. This was Lester's first film after the smash *A Hard Day's Night* (1964), and it has the same playful, irreverent tone that worked so well with The Beatles. But this time, despite an excellent cast and some lovely vignettes, the result is a smug, pretentious comedy in which the director's surreal style seems more self-indulgent than creative.

Michael Crawford, long before his run in Broadway's *Phantom of the Opera*, is Colin, school teacher and exasperated landlord to Tolen (Ray Brooks), a super-cool ladykiller who offers to teach Colin "the knack" for attracting women. As Colin debates the offer, young Nancy (Rita Tushingham) arrives in London looking for the YWCA, and sees Colin pushing a brass bed through the city streets. A relationship seems imminent, until Tolen starts putting his patented moves on the impressionable country girl.

It's not so much a plot as a string of offbeat episodes, with hit-and-miss results. In England, *The Knack* was a huge success that made a star out of tiny, crosseyed Rita Tushingham, whose deadpan, small-town reactions to London's eccentricities provide the film's best moments. But if you're looking for Bisset, she's in the very first scene, a dream sequence of Colin's in which he imagines dozens of beautiful, identically-clad girls lined up outside Tolen's apartment. Because the actresses were supposed to resemble a succession of interchangable mannequins, and because the camera movement is swirling and near-constant, it's tough to find Bisset in the crowd. Repeat viewings reveal that she's the first girl picked from the line by Tolen, at which time she passes through the frame in under five seconds.

Thus began what Bisset's *Current Biography* listing described as the "decorative prop" stage of her career, which was typified by her portrayal of Giovanna Goodthighs in *Casino Royale* (1967) and a seductive schoolgirl in *Two for the Road* (1967). In 1968 she played her first featured role in *The Sweet Ride*, and received her first popular notice as a last-minute replacement for Mia Farrow in *The Detective*, opposite Frank Sinatra. In 1970 she appeared in the megahit *Airport*, but better roles did not follow. After her career-best work in *Day for Night*, she was again relegated to supporting roles in less-than-inspired projects.

The Deep made Jacqueline Bisset a household name, but for reasons that had nothing to do with the quality of the film or of Bisset's performance. She plays Gail Berke, girlfriend and scuba diving companion to David Sanders (Nick Nolte). Together they discover artifacts off the coast of Bermuda that might be worth a fortune, as well as a large cache of morphine. On the surface, David and Gail are pursued by gangsters who want the drugs, and beneath the waves they become a would-be meal for sharks and a giant moray eel.

Dismissed as a rip-off of *Jaws* (1975) upon its release, *The Deep* is kept afloat by several exciting underwater sequences and a clever resolution to its buried treasure mystery. The underwater photography is outstanding and the cast, for the most part, is able to sell the sometimes uneven script. But the film's strongest selling point was Bisset's scuba scenes, which she played in the kind of white see-through T-shirt worn by drunken co-eds on spring break. This sequence, which opens the film, rivaled the spaceships in *Star Wars* and John Travolta's strut in *Saturday Night Fever* as the most talked-about movie image in 1977. This was certainly not the way Bisset would have chosen to crack the 'A'-list of actresses, but what was even more lamentable is that she was unable to capitalize on her sudden notoriety. *The Deep* recouped its $8 million cost in its first three days of release, but it could not jump-start Bisset's career. Her next film, *The Greek Tycoon*, was a flop, and in 1982 she hit rock bottom with *Inchon* (1982).

Although she turned fifty in 1994, Bisset's stunning beauty remains undiminished, but there is always hope that she will one day emerge from the decorative prop dungeon, where she has already been stranded for far too long.

THE KNACK...AND HOW TO GET IT
Directed by Richard Lester; Written by Charles Wood, from the play by Ann Jellicoe; Produced by Oscar Lewenstein; Music by John Barry

Cast
Rita Tushingham (Nancy Jones), Ray Brooks (Tolen), Michael Crawford (Colin) ...JACQUELINE BISSET (GIRL)

THE DEEP
Directed by Peter Yates; Written by Peter Benchley and Tracy Keenan Wynn, based on the novel by Benchley; Produced by Peter Guber; Music by John Barry

Cast
Robert Shaw (Romer Treece), JACQUELINE BISSET (GAIL BERKE), Nick Nolte (David Sanders), Louis Gossett (Henri Cloche), Eli Wallach (Adam Coffin)

HUMPHREY BOGART (1899-1957)

FIRST APPEARANCE: *A Devil With Women* (Fox, 1930)

A STAR IS BORN: *The Maltese Falcon* (Warner Bros., 1941)

"Bogart is a man with a past," wrote French critic André Bazin. "When he comes into a film it is already 'the morning after'; his face scarred by what he has seen, and his step heavy from all that he has learned, having ten times triumphed over death, he will surely survive for us one more time." Bazin's summation, eloquent and incontestable, is applicable only to the mature phase of Bogart's career, which began with his 42nd release, *The Maltese Falcon*. Typecast early on as a gangster, he rarely triumphed over death in most of the films he made during his first decade in the business.

A Christmas baby born in New York City, Humphrey Bogart was educated at the prestigious Andover Academy in Massachusetts, but left school during the First World War to enlist in the Navy. After the war, he returned to New York but did not return to school. Instead, he accepted a job offer from producer William A. Brady, who lived next door to the Bogarts. Starting as a clerical worker in Brady's office, he was later promoted to assistant stage manager, and in 1920 he appeared on stage for the first time, in a road company production of *The Ruined Lady*. He played a houseboy, and was given one line of dialog. On opening night, he dropped the tray of dishes he was supposed to carry out, and the audience howled.

Two years later he made his Broadway debut, and for the next thirteen years Bogart was steadily employed in a long succession of plays, often cast as a "Tennis, anyone?" type of upper-crust collegiate. He tried repeatedly to land motion picture jobs, but failed in screen test after screen test because of a protruding upper lip. His father, a surgeon, fixed the slight deformity, and Bogart landed a contract at Fox with his very next attempt.

The first appearance of Humphrey Bogart on film was in a ten-minute short entitled *Broadway's Like That* (1930). His first feature was *A Devil With Women*, filmed later that same year. His character survives to the closing credits and even walks away with the girl, atypical achievements for Bogie in the 1930s. Victor McLaglen stars as Jerry Maxton, a soldier of fortune hired to bring down a notorious bandit in an unnamed Central American country. Bogart plays Tom Standish, carefree nephew to a millionaire, who joins Maxton's mission for kicks. After several adventures, Maxton apprehends the bandit with the help of femme fatale Rosita Fernandez (Mona Maris), who lures the villain into Maxton's clutches. The hero now looks forward to celebrating his victory with Rosita, but she rides off with Tom instead.

Fox had hoped that *A Devil With Women* would be the first in a series of films starring McLaglen as Jerry Maxton, but the public's lukewarm reception forced a change of plans. Bogart, in his Banana Republic cotton twill ensemble, plays the kind of spoiled gentry role he played so often on stage. He brings a certain brash charm to Tom Standish, but the performance is interesting primarily in the way it contrasts with the world-weary persona that would define Bogart later on. Critics, who had no way of knowing that at the time, gave him mild praise; "An ingratiating performance. . . Mr. Bogart is both good-looking and intelligent." was the *New York Times*' assessment.

Bogart's first impact in motion pictures came with a series of gangster roles at Warner Bros., beginning with *Three on a Match* (1932). One could argue for Bogart's performance as killer Duke Mantee in *The Petrified Forest* as his breakthrough, but rave reviews did not lead to better roles. "I'm sick to death of being a one-dimensional character," he complained in an early interview. "I'm just a guy in a tight suit and a snap-brim hat. I have no function except to carry the plot and get killed in the end to prove that virtue is triumphant."

The turnabout came with *High Sierra* (1941) in which Bogie gave a mesmerizing portrayal of Mad Dog Roy Earle, an aging life-termer with the chance to pull one last job. The character is homicidal and fanatical, but not entirely unsympathetic. Bogart creates a purpose in Earle's race against his own mortality, in a world he no longer understands, that is almost noble. John Huston, who cowrote the screenplay for *High Sierra*, made his directorial debut that year in *The Maltese Falcon*. George Raft was offered the role of detective Sam Spade, but turned it down because he didn't want to work with a rookie director. Bogart had no such qualms, and the two men forged a friendship on the set that lasted until Bogart's death.

Still the ultimate detective film, *The Maltese Falcon* weaves a labyrinthine plot of intrigue and deception, revolving around the title bird, a priceless medieval artifact. Sam Spade is brought into the fray by Brigid O'Shaughnessy (Mary Astor), under the guise of searching for her missing sister. Gradually, Spade begins to unravel Brigid's true motives; he falls in love, but won't "take the fall" for her, after discovering that she murdered his partner.

Every aspect of the production contributes to the film's status as a classic. Huston's script contains more quotable dialog than any film ever made, right down to the perfect final line. Threatened with dismissal if he went over budget or the tight shooting schedule, Huston plotted every step of the filmmaking process in meticulous detail, and made every shot count.

As Sam Spade, Humphrey Bogart was anything but one-dimensional. At the age of 42, he reinvented himself for the screen, capturing perfectly all of Spade's complexities, his eccentric sense of honor, his tough talk and his cynical nature. What also emerged, somewhat surprisingly, is a new kind of romantic antihero, a loner who pretends to be immune to love, though he is no less vulnerable than the rest of us. In 1943, Bogart brought the same spirit to *Casablanca*, and the world's list of all-time favorite films would never be the same.

A DEVIL WITH WOMEN
Directed by Irving Cummings; Written by Dudley Nichols and Henry M. Johnson, based on the novel *Dust and Sun* by Clements Ripley; Music by Peter Brunelli, songs by James Monaco and Cliff Friend

Cast
Victor McLaglen (Jerry Maxton), Mona Maris (Rosita Fernandez), HUMPHREY BOGART (TOM STANDISH), Luana Alcaniz (Dolores), Michael Vavitch (Morloff)

THE MALTESE FALCON
Directed and written by John Huston, based on the novel by Dashiell Hammett; Produced by Hal Wallis and Henry Blanke; Music by Adolph Deutsch

Cast
HUMPHREY BOGART (SAM SPADE), Mary Astor (Brigid O'Shaughnessy), Gladys Geroge (Iva Archer), Peter Lorre (Joel Cairo), Lee Patrick (Effie Perine), Sydney Greenstreet (Casper Gutman), Barton MacLane (Lt. Dundy)

MARLON BRANDO (1924-   )

FIRST APPEARANCE: *The Men* (Kramer/United Artists, 1950)

A STAR IS BORN: *A Streetcar Named Desire* (Warner Bros./20th Century-Fox, 1951)

I have never completely bought into the contention that Marlon Brando revolutionized acting, or revolutionized Hollywood. It is an east-coast conceit, created to take credit for a movement that was already underway out west. Those in the film business will tell you they were doing just fine with acting before Brando, thank you very much, and if there was any revolution going on it was in the new acceptance of socially relevant storylines and more graphic depictions of sex and violence. Whether this was a step back or a step forward is still open for debate. Either way, Brando arrived at the right time with the right piece of material to test the newly liberal waters--Tennessee Williams' *A Streetcar Named Desire*. His performance, already honed to prefection after a year of practice on the New York stage, became the defining moment in the breakdown of Hollywood's restrictive self-censorship.

Make no mistake--Marlon Brando is an actor of enormous ability and amazing instincts, but if he truly "extended the boundaries of the acceptable a perceptible degree," as the otherwise level-headed critic Richard Schickel writes in a fawning biography, it is only because the motion picture medium was already inclined in that direction.

He was born in Omaha, Nebraska, the oldest of three siblings. His mother Dorothy was an amateur actress who suffered from alcoholism, his father Marlon Sr. was a salesman. The marriage was cordial but remote. Before Marlon Jr., who preferred the nickname "Bud," became a teenager, the family moved to Evanston, Illinois and then to a farm in upstate Libertyville. One of his closest boyhood friends was Mr. Peepers himself, Wally Cox. After an unhappy stint in military school, Brando moved to New York to live with his sister and pursue his interest in acting. One of his first jobs was as an elevator operator at Best's Department Store.

Brando joined Stella Adler's acting class at the New School in Greenwich Village in 1942. Adler saw in Brando an intuitive gift, which she refined and directed right on up to his debut on Broadway two years later in *I Remember Mama*. The play was a hit, but Brando's notices in the supporting role of youngest son Nils were mixed. More stage work followed, culminating in Elia Kazan's production of *A Streetcar Named Desire*. Jessica Tandy played Blanche DuBoise, Kim Hunter played Stella, and Karl Malden played Mitch. *Streetcar* was a major triumph, and allowed Brando to write his own ticket in motion pictures. He was determined not to become one of those Hollywood people, whatever that means, but when a $40,000 salary offer was presented, Brando admitted "I don't have the character to turn down such big money."

His first film was *The Men* , Stanley Kramer's drama about a hospital ward that is home to parapalegic World War II veterans. They each accept their cruel condition to various degrees except for Ken (Brando), who remains embittered and remote. Eventually he begins to make progress with the help of other patients and his fiancee`, Ellen (Teresa Wright).

The most interesting aspect of the film is its frank look at rehabilitation from paralyzing injury, and the day-to-day struggles, both physical and mental, that each of "the men" must face. The drama is inherent in the situation, and was ill-served by the heavy-handed dialogue and musical cues--even the title seems a bit pretentious. Brando's brooding performance should have cut through some of that, but it is nowhere near his best work. His flat, somewhat mumbled line-readings were intriguing but incongruous with the rest of the cast. Only Everett Sloan, as the tough-love doctor in charge of the ward, avoids soap opera cliche`. During production, Brando went out to a bar in his wheelchair with some fellow cast members, and was approached by a religious woman who suggested he pray for recovery. Brando did so on the spot, and then began to slowly rise from the chair. He stood up, and then broke into a tapdance as the woman fainted dead away. Had more of this black humor found its way into the film, *The Men* might have better achieved its noble objective of presenting parapalegics as human beings, not objects of pity.

Brando's next project was the film adaptation of *Streetcar*, which reunited director Elia Kazan, Kim Hunter and Karl Malden, and replaced Jessica Tandy with Vivien Leigh. A few cuts were necessary to satisfy the Catholic Legion of Decency, but on the whole the story survived intact; Blanche DuBois arrives in New Orleans to visit her sister, Stella. Stella's brutish husband Stanley Kowalski takes an instant dislike to the flighty Blanche, and repeatedly grills her about the DuBois family home, which he believes is part his under the Napoleanic Code of Louisiana. Blanche, who is already on the verge of a mental breakdown, is hesitant to provide any details. Eventually her entire sordid history is laid bare. While Stella gives birth to Stanley's child, Stanley rapes Blanche and shatters what's left of her sanity. When Stella returns she moves out with the baby.

The theater snobs insisted that the film and Brando's performance were a mere shadow of what happened on stage, forgetting or ignoring the fact that a close-up and a creative camera angle can heighten drama in a way that would be impossible in a theater. The experience and confidence of all the principals (including Leigh, who had played Blanche on the London stage) was apparent and certainly contributed to the film's success. Unlike *The Men*, in which Brando's rhythm did not connect with that of other actors, the chemistry in *Streetcar* is perfect. Brando and Leigh scorch the screen with their verbal skirmishes, which build to a climax that can still leave an audience drained. Oscars were doled out to Leigh, Hunter and Malden, but the Brando performance now considered seminal was beaten by Humphrey Bogart in *The African Queen*.

THE MEN
Directed by Fred Zinnemann; Written by Carl Forman; Produced by Stanley Kramer; Music by Dimitri Tiomkin

Cast
MARLON BRANDO (KEN), Teresa Wright (Ellen), Everett Sloane (Dr. Brock), Jack Webb (Norm), Richard Erdman (Leo), Arthur Jurado (Angel)

A STREETCAR NAMED DESIRE
Directed by Elia Kazan; Written by Tennessee Williams, adapted by Owen Saul; Produced by Charles K. Feldman; Music by Alex North

Cast
Vivien Leigh (Blanche DuBois), MARLON BRANDO (STANLEY KOWALSKI), Kim Hunter (Stella Kowalski), Karl Malden (Mitch)

RICHARD BURTON (1925-1984)

FIRST APPEARANCE: *The Last Days of Dolwyn* (London Films, 1948)

A STAR IS BORN: *The Robe* (20th Century-Fox, 1953)

An accomplished Shakespearian actor, Richard Burton was not as proficient at adapting his classical training to popular material as Laurence Olivier or John Gielgud. As Hamlet and Othello, his performances at the Old Vic Theatre are still used as a measuring stick; at the movies, he has been repeatedly victimized by poor choices and poor material. There isn't another actor of his caliber with as many turkeys in his filmography. Thankfully, there are also a few examples of Burton in top form on screen, such as *Becket* (1964), *Who's Afraid of Virginia Woolf?* (1966) and *Equus* (1977) that display the talent that is so familiar to his theater audiences.

Richard Burton was born Richard Jenkins in Pontrhydfen, South Wales, the youngest of thirteen children. As a boy soprano, he won a prize at an annual Welsh singing festival, and avoided any teasing from classmates by also winning a prize fight at the age of fifteen. He developed an interest in acting while still in high school, and took the last name of his drama teacher, Philip Burton, as a stage name. When he was seventeen, Burton answered a newspaper ad placed by producer Emlyn Williams, and won a supporting role in Williams' production of *The Druid's Rest*, which ran in Liverpool and London throughout 1943.

Burton earned a full scholarship to Oxford University, but left after one year to enlist in the Royal Air Force. He was demobilized with the rank of sergeant in 1947. The following year, he began his distinguished stage career at London's Globe Theatre. Burton made his Broadway debut in 1950 in *The Lady's Not for Burning*, and first played Hamlet at the 1953 Edinburgh Festival. Two years later he was in *Henry V* and *Othello*, alternating as Othello and Iago.

It was Emlyn Williams, who gave Burton his first job on the stage, who also launched the actor's film career. Williams served as writer, director and star of *The Last Days of Dolwyn*, and created a part especially for Burton. The story is set in the tiny Welsh village of Dolwyn, where the quiet, content lives of the populace are threatened by an outsider with plans to buy up the entire district for a water development project. When his scheme is thwarted by the citizens of Dolwyn, he tries to exact his revenge by setting fire to the village. Gareth (Burton), the son of one of Dolwyn's matriarchs, kills the man in a fight. Gareth's mother (Edith Evans) then carries out a shocking act to cover up the murder.

Much of the film is in Welsh, and when the cast speaks in English, their pronounced Welsh accents make some of the dialogue difficult to understand. This is probably the reason that the *The Last Days of Dolwyn* achieved only a very limited release in the United States. However, the film is almost worth seeing for its scenery alone, and Williams' tender, forthright storyline unfolds leisurely and is easy to follow even when the dialogue is not.

Edith Evans is exquisite as the kindly peasant woman whose radiant smile masks a will of iron. Burton, as Evans' headstrong son, figures prominently only in the last reel, when the story takes a surprising and not altogether satisfying turn. By this time he had already worked hard to lose his Welsh accent, but he reclaims it here and is able to recall the almost poetry-like delivery shared by the rest of the cast. *The New York Times* described his performance as "superior," which is a tad extravagant, but if he doesn't stand out as much as might be expected, it is only because of the talent that surrounds him.

With the help of a friend, producer Alexander Korda, Richard Burton arrived in Hollywood in 1952 and was not without work for long. His first American film, *My Cousin Rachel* (1952), brought him space in several "faces to watch" columns and an Academy Award nomination for Best Supporting Actor. He was promoted to leading man in his next film, *The Robe*, though like the rest of the cast he took second billing to CinemaScope. The film, a lavishly-mounted Biblical epic, was one of Hollywood's first unabashed attempts to lure audiences away from their new television sets with a show too big from the small screen. The experiment worked--*The Robe* set box-office records and ushered in a slew of larger-than-life epics.

Burton plays Marcellus Gallio, Roman Tribune, who incurs the wrath of Emperor Caligula, and is punished with an extended field trip to Jerusalem. He oversees the crucifixion of Jesus, and thinks little of it at the time, but later becomes profoundly affected by the experience, even after returning to Rome. Believing himself cursed after touching the robe worn by Jesus on his way to the cross, Marcus tries to locate its whereabouts, and is gradually converted to Christianity by his former slave, Demetrius (Victor Mature) and the apostle Peter (Michael Rennie). When Caligula learns that Marcus has been converted, he sentences the Tribune to death.

The best performances are found in the supporting roles; Michael Rennie as Peter, Betta St. John as Miriam, a girl whose life is changed by Jesus and who plays a key role in the conversion of Marcellus, and Jean Simmons, at her most Audrey Hepburn-like, standing by her beloved under threat of a death sentence. Richard Burton manages one genuinely stirring moment at Marcellus' climactic trial, though the scene is marred somewhat by Jay Robinson's over-the-top performance as Caligula. Burton's voice is the first to be heard when the movie opens, and sets the appropriate tone of majestic significance that the rest of the film only halfway achieves.

The Robe's attempt to emulate the Cecil B. DeMille school of Biblical epics is successful in its sincerity, but less so in actual craftsmanship. The 135-minute film is often stodgy and slow, and sometimes, as when crashes of lightning and cymbals punctuate every pivotal moment, borderline laughable. But the movie was exceptionally reviewed at the time and, opening so soon on the heels of *My Cousin Rachel*, secured Richard Burton's status in Hollywood.

THE LAST DAYS OF DOLWYN

Directed and written by Emlyn Williams; Produced by Anatole de Grunwald; Music by John Greenwood

Cast

Edith Evans (Merri), Emlyn Williams (Rob), RICHARD BURTON (GARETH), Anthony James (Dafydd), Barbara Couper (Lady Dolwyn)

THE ROBE

Directed by Henry Koster; Written by Philip Dunne, based on the novel by Lloyd C. Douglas, adapted by Gina Kaus; Produced by Frank Ross; Music by Alfred Newman

Cast

RICHARD BURTON (MARCELLUS GALLIO), Jean Simmons (Diana), Victor Mature (Demetrius), Michael Rennie (Peter), Jay Robinson (Caligula), Dean Jagger (Justus), Torin Thatcher (Sen. Gallio), Richard Boone (Pilate), Betta St. John (Miriam)

JAMES CAGNEY (1899-1986)

FIRST APPEARANCE: *Sinner's Holiday* (Warner Bros., 1930)

A STAR IS BORN: *The Public Enemy* (Warner Bros., 1931)

In 1932, when the greater part of James Cagney's brilliant film career still lay ahead of him, critic Lincoln Kirstein defined the essence of Cagney's appeal; "an inspired sense of timing, an arrogant style, a pride in the control of his body and a conviction and lack of self-consciousness that is unique in the deserts of the American screen."

Cagney was a dancer first, a fact that should be apparent even to those who haven't seen *Yankee Doodle Dandy* (1942). In his portrayals of gangsters, heroes and cowboys, his sharp staccato movements blended the grace of a ballet dancer with the cocky swagger of a streetcorner huckster. The voice that snarled in rat-a-tat cadence was an ideal complement to his physical inquietude.

James Cagney was born in 1899 above his father's saloon on New York's lower east side. The neighborhood produced all the data Cagney needed to later play bullies and crooks, but he never conducted first-hand research in the field. Boxing might have been a career before his mother forbade it--Cagney was the New York state lightweight title runner-up, but instead he listened to mom and entered Columbia University to study fine arts. Six months later he was forced to drop out after his father died at the age of 42.

Cagney's first theater experience was with the Lenox Hill Settlement House. He joined as a scenery painter, but when his brother Henry took sick Jimmy stepped in to perform his part. He appeared in two more Lenox Hill productions, then moved up to the vaudeville show *Every Sailor*. Cagney had second thoughts after being asked to perform in drag, but $25 a week in 1919 was enough to put him in a dress for two months. A self-taught dancer, he attended an open audition for the Broadway show *Pitter Patter*, and landed a spot in the chorus. Thus began ten years of steady work in the theater, during which time he opened his own dancing school, the Cagne' School of Dance, and tried unsuccessfully to break into movies.

In March of 1930 he appeared opposite newcomer Joan Blondell in the melodrama *Penny Arcade*. The play opened to mixed reviews and lasted just 24 performances, but Al Jolson liked it enough to buy the screen rights. Jolson, as big a star as existed in the world at that time, sold the property to Warner Bros. with the stipulation that Cagney and Blondell reprise their roles. In the film, retitled *Sinner's Holiday*, the Delano family hire an ex-con named Angel after he saves young Jennie Delano from the unwanted advances of a ruffian named Mitch McKane. Jennie's brother Harry (played by Cagney) kills Mitch after an argument, and confesses the crime to his mother. Ma Delano tries to frame Angel for the crime, but Jennie overhears the scheme and informs on her brother.

Cagney, 31 years old in his film debut, received favorable notices; "His fretful tenseness during the closing scenes is conveyed with sincerity" wrote the *New York Times*. The raw emotion he imparts in Harry Delano's confession, when he sobs and buries his head in his mother's breast, earned Cagney a five-year contract with Warner Bros. and set a precedent of strong mother-son relationships in his movies. Warner Bros. producer Darryl F. Zanuck took credit for initiating the pattern, which continued with *The Public Enemy* (1930), *The Irish in Us* (1935), *Each Dawn I Die* (1939) and most notably *White Heat* (1949); "I gave Cagney one redeeming trait. He was a no-good bastard but he loved his mother, and somehow or other you felt a certain affection and rooting interest for him, even though he is despicable."

Cagney, who would never get the chance to thank Jolson for his launch, became one of the busiest members of the Warner Bros. stock company. He appeared in four films over the next six months, all of them programmers like *Sinner's Holiday* that are now interesting only as early entries in his filmography. *The Public Enemy* (1931) was his first lead role, and so mesmerizing was Cagney as gangster Tom Powers that he was forever defined as the movies' most charismatic bad guy. Powers, a cop's son, grows up in the slums with a taste for the good life, and little regard for how he achieves it. With his buddy Matt Doyle he starts committing small robberies and works his way up to rum-running. When Matt is gunned down, Tom takes on the rival gang that was responsible single-handed. During his hospital stay Tom is reconciled with his family, but he cannot escape the retribution of the gang he attacked. Powers's brutalized corpse is delivered on his mother's doorstep.

Esquire's film critic called Cagney's performance "as great as anything I've seen in movies," and praised his "balletlike control of his body," and his "extraordinary command of expression." The excellent cast also included Cagney's old pal Joan Blondell, Jean Harlow and, for the first week, Louise Brooks. Mae Clarke replaced Brooks just in time to get a grapefruit smacked in her face, and instant eternal life as a trivia question. It is certainly the film's most famous scene, but there are others that remain vivid in the memory; Cagney, again using his dancer's instincts, staggering bullet-ridden through a rainstorm, is an unforgettable image captured by cinematographer Devereaux Jennings, and the final scene has lost none of its chilling effect.

Director William Wellman vowed to make "the toughest gangster picture ever filmed," and his quest for authenticity actually induced him to use real bullets in some of the action scenes. Wellman also deserves credit for making the grapefruit scene so powerful, after he learned that Cagney and Clarke had agreed to fake the actual blow. The director secretly convinced Cagney to really hit her, and when they filmed the scene Clarke's shock and anger were real, because she didn't know the grapefruit, and the sadistic extra little twist Cagney gives it, was coming. Clarke was outraged, but Wellman accurately predicted that the scene "will be talked about for a century" and would make Cagney "the biggest star in the business."

There were protests from what passed for feminists in the thirties, but one guy who loved the scene was Clarke's ex-husband Monte Brice, who attended dozens of *Public Enemy* screenings to watch his wife get plastered. One time he laughed so hard he was asked to leave the theater.

SINNER'S HOLIDAY
Directed by John G. Adolfi; Written by Harvey Thew and George Rosener, based on the play *Penny Arcade* by Marie Baumer

Cast
Grant Withers (Angel Harrigan), Evelyn Knapp (Jennie Delano), JAMES CAGNEY (HARRY DELANO), Joan Blondell (Myrtle), Lucille LaVerne (Ma Delano)

THE PUBLIC ENEMY
Directed by William Wellman; Written by Kubec Glasmon and John Bright; Produced by Darryl F. Zanuck; Music by Jean Kenbrovin, John W. Kellette, Harry Barris and Gordon Clifford

Cast
JAMES CAGNEY (TOM POWERS), Jean Harlow (Gwen Allen), Edward Woods (Matt Doyle), Joan Blondell (Mamie), Beryl Mercer (Ma Powers), Donald Cook (Mike Powers), Mae Clarke (Kitty)

MICHAEL CAINE (1933-   )

FIRST APPEARANCE: *A Hill in Korea* (British Lion, 1956)

A STAR IS BORN: *The Ipcress File* (Universal, 1965)

Michael Caine's name appears in the credits of more films in the 1970s and 1980s than any other leading man. Accepting work with little regard for the quality of the project, a custom begat from a childhood of short-lived jobs and long-lived poverty, Caine has appeared in an average of two films a year throughout his three-decade career. He finds the challenge of giving a good performance in a bad film strangely appealing; "Anybody," he has said, "can look good with a good script and a good director." To be fair, Caine also has several outstanding efforts to his credit, including *Alfie* (1966), *The Man Who Would Be King* (1975), *Educating Rita* (1983), and his Academy Award- winning performance in *Hannah and Her Sisters* (1986). Unfortunately, Caine was unable to accept his Oscar in person, as he was busy filming *Jaws: The Revenge.*

Born in a charity hospital in one of London's poorest neighborhoods, Maurice Joseph Micklewhite was a bright child who showed little interest in school, until he enrolled in a drama class to be near a girl he liked. During World War II, while his father served in the British army, Maurice, his mother and his brother lived with twelve other evacuated families in a large farmhouse in rural Norfolk. Returning to London after the war, he became a frequent visitor to the gallery of the Old Vic Theatre, where he was discouraged to find that none of the actors on stage spoke with his Cockney accent.

He quit school at sixteen and was drafted two years later, serving in Berlin and Korea between 1951 and 1953. Discharged after a severe bout with malaria, Maurice answered a newspaper ad for an assistant stage manager position with a Sussex repertory company. He played occasional bit parts, then joined another company as a supporting actor. He moved back to London, changed his name to Michael Caine after *The Caine Mutiny*, and tried to join the first-string of his profession in the West End, with only moderate success.

Caine's military experience, not his acting experience, brought about his first movie offer. The producers of *A Hill in Korea* needed someone who had fought in the Korean conflict to serve as a technical advisor. Caine, who had spent time on several hills in Korea, got the job and a small role in the film. Though the story is based on actual events, it is obvious that much of Caine's advice on procedural accuracy was ignored. Still, *A Hill in Korea* gets the "was is hell" message across with unpretentious clarity.

The film focuses on the efforts of one army patrol, under the command of Lieutenant Butler (George Baker), to clear out a village of enemy soldiers. Days of shared jokes and stories among the men give way to tense nights of reconnaissance. After apparently completing their mission, the patrol discovers that getting out of the village is more dangerous than getting in.

"Only the closeups of their sweaty faces, and calling each other's names brings individuality to the actors," wrote *Variety* in an otherwise positive review. Baker, Harry Andrews and Ronald Lewis are featured, but movie buffs checking out the back corners of the frame will see Steven Boyd and Robert Shaw as well as Michael Caine, who delivers the occasional line with his Cockney accent uninhibited.

Caine, a workaholic long before he was famous, appeared in more than 100 television dramas in a five-year period, but did not make a name for himself until he understudied Peter O'Toole in the 1959 play *The Long, the Short and the Tall.* When O'Toole left the show, Caine toured in the lead role, and better offers began to materialize. After a scene-stealing supporting role in *Zulu* (1964), he was sought out by producer Harry Saltzman, who was enjoying international success with the James Bond series. Saltzman offered Caine the role of Harry Palmer, a secret agent who would never be confused with 007, in a film adaptation of

Len Deighton's *The Ipcress File*.

Sgt. Harry Palmer, an undisciplined, nine-to-five surveillance agent, is assigned to investigate the abduction of a scientist. Following a hunch, Palmer orchestrates a raid on a warehouse and finds a piece of audiotape labeled "Ipcress," that is connected to the scientist's disappearance. Palmer, who seems to be barely paying attention half the time, solves the case, survives a harrowing brainwash attempt, and exposes his boss as a double agent.

The bespectacled, overweight Harry Palmer did not look or act like a secret agent--even his name sounded more suited to an accountant--which was Saltzman's reason for casting Caine in the first place. He is not a tactical genius or fearless superhero--where James Bond goes to Monte Carlo on a case, Palmer goes to the supermarket--but when tested under fire, he rises to the occasion.

The Ipcress File makes the whole business of espionage rather dull, and that's the point. That the film itself is not dull is largely due to Michael Caine, the outstanding John Barry score, and the shamelessly indulgent direction of Sidney J. Furie, who never found an odd camera angle he didn't like. Drawing openly upon the working-class background that he concealed so deftly in *Zulu*, Caine perfectly registers Palmer's bemused attitude at his own line of work, where the agents spend as much time spying on each other as they do on the enemy. The film exceeded all box-office expectations, and was followed by two sequels.

A HILL IN KOREA
Directed by Julian Amyes; Written by Ian Dalrymple and Anthony Squire, based on a novel by Max Catto; Music by Malcolm Arnold

Cast
George Baker (Lt. Butler), Harry Andrews (Sgt. Payne), Stanley Baker (Cpl. Ryker), Michael Medwin (Pvt. Docker), Ronald Lewis (Pvt. Wyatt), Steven Boyd (Pvt. Sims). . . MICHAEL CAINE (PVT. LOCKYER)

THE IPCRESS FILE
Directed by Sidney J. Furie; Written by Bill Canaway and James Doran, based on the novel by Len Deighton; Produced by Harry Saltzman; Music by John Barry

Cast
MICHAEL CAINE (HARRY PALMER), Nigel Green (Dalby), Guy Doleman (Major Ross), Sue Lloyd (Jean), Gordon Jackson (Jock Carswell), Aubrey Richards (Radcliffe)

CHARLIE CHAPLIN (1889-1977)

FIRST APPEARANCE: *Making a Living* (Keystone, 1914)

A STAR IS BORN: *Tillie's Punctured Romance* (Keystone, 1914)

After Thomas Edison, who gave the movies a form, and D.W. Griffith, who gave them a language, there is no more important figure in the history of cinema than Charlie Chaplin. He elevated the motion picture comedy from a novelty to an art form within two years of his first film, and created an alter-ego, the Little Tramp, that is beloved in every civilized country in the world. His films *The Gold Rush* (1925), *City Lights* (1931) and *Modern Times* (1936) are still ranked with the medium's greatest achievements.

Charlie Chaplin was born in abject poverty, in one of London's most downtrodden boroughs. His parents, both singers on the variety stage, divorced when Charlie was still young, and Charlie lived with his mother until her death. At the age of fourteen, he was forced to leave school to earn a living. A job with a printing press establishment brought in enough money for food, but Chaplin felt the same passion for show business that stirred his parents. Using their connections, he had already gained some music hall experience as part of a dancing team billed as the Lancashire Lads. In 1905, he played a pageboy in a Sherlock Holmes play starring William Gillette.

Chaplin honed his skills at comedy, music and mime with a troupe of performers headed by Fred Karno. Gradually, he progressed from bit player to solo performer, and by the time he left Karno he was the star of the act. In 1913, Chaplin signed his first movie contract with the Keystone Company, owned by Mack Sennett. He stayed with Sennett for less than a year, but in that time Chaplin made fifty short films and one feature, and though his best work still lay ahead, he had already established himself as one of the new industry's most talented and innovative filmmakers.

Making A Living (1914) is interesting not only as the film debut of Charlie Chaplin, it is also the only film that predates the first appearance of his most famous character, the Little Tramp. Wearing a gray top hat, a checkered waistcoat, a cravat, a monocle and a long, Snidely Whiplash-like mustache, Charlie played a sharp-dressed but penniless dude who hits his best friend up for a loan, and then returns the favor by trying to steal his friend's girl and his job as a reporter. The movie ends with the obligatory chase scene, which commences in a lady's bedroom and ends on the cow-catcher of a moving train.

Chaplin was outraged when he saw the finished film, believing that all of his best moments, most of which he suggested during production, were shortened or cut out completely. He received good notices--"The clever player who takes the part of a sharper. . .is a comedian of the first water," said one trade paper--but Chaplin was already lobbying for more creative control over his films. "All I need to make a comedy is a park, a policeman and a pretty girl," said Chaplin to Mack Sennett, and as the weeks passed he set out to prove it.

As with all of Sennett's players, Chaplin churned out movies at an astonishing pace. *Making a Living* was released on February 2, 1914; *Kid Auto Races* was released on February 7, and *Mabel's Strange Predicament* on February 9, followed by four more films in March and another four in April. In *Kid Auto Races*, Chaplin is first seen in the familiar bowler hat, ill-fitting clothes and clipped mustache of the Little Tramp. "By the time I walked on to the stage he was fully born," said Chaplin of the character. From August, 1914 on, he directed all the films in which he appeared except for *Tillie's Punctured Romance*.

The selection of *Tillie's Punctured Romance* as Chaplin's breakthrough is, at best, arbitrary. *The Knockout*, released just three months after his debut, was billed as a Chaplin film, even though he appeared for only about two minutes, as the referee of a boxing match between Roscoe "Fatty" Arbuckle and Edgar Kennedy. Such was the rapid rise in the comedian's popularity. *Tillie's Punctured Romance* is significant, however, as the first feature-length film comedy, and for its casting of nearly every performer under contract to Sennett, and still represents something of a landmark in Chaplin's career.

Marie Dressler stars as Tillie Banks, a naive country girl who is wooed by a con man (Chaplin), who is only interested in her father's money. After he abandons her, Tillie gets a job at a restaurant, but is soon rich once again after the death of a millionaire uncle. Charlie learns of her inheritance and returns once again, this time with a marriage proposal. Their uproarious wedding is followed by a frenetic slapstick chase, prompted by Charlie getting caught with another girl.

Dressler reprised the role she had played on Broadway; Chaplin and Mabel Normand, who played the other woman, were Sennett's two biggest film stars, and the success of *Tillie's Punctured Romance* brought similar fame to Dressler. Though the story figures more prominently than it does in most films from the period, there are times when *Tillie* plays like an awkwardly-protracted two-reeler. Chaplin, once more removed from his Little Tramp persona, is an effective comic villain, who gets his just desserts after being chased off a pier and into the ocean by the Keystone Kops.

MAKING A LIVING
Directed by Henry Lehrman; Written by Reed Heustis

Cast
CHARLIE CHAPLIN (SLICKER), Virginia Kirtley (Girl), Alice Davenport (Mother), Henry Lehrman (Reporter), Minta Durfee (Woman), Chester Conklin (Policeman)

TILLIE'S PUNCTURED ROMANCE
Directed by Mack Sennett; Written by Hampton Del Ruth, based on the play *Tillie's Nightmare* by Edgar Smith

Cast
Marie Dressler (Tillie Banks), CHARLES CHAPLIN (CHARLIE), Mabel Normand (Mabel), Mack Swain (John Banks), the Keystone Kops

GLENN CLOSE (1947-   )

FIRST APPEARANCE: *The World According to Garp* (Warner Bros., 1982)

A STAR IS BORN: *The Big Chill* (Columbia, 1983)

Glenn Close is an emphatic presence on screen. Her cool good looks and no-nonsense demeanor made for ideal casting as Michael Douglas's psychotic one-night-stand in *Fatal Attraction* (1987), which has become one of the benchmark films of the 1980s. But whether Close is playing the scorned woman of every philanderer's nightmare, or virtue personified in *The Natural* (1984), she demonstrates a strength of conviction that is always formidable.

The first Closes arrived in America in the late seventeenth century, and helped found the town of Greenwich, Connecticut. Glenn and her three siblings grew up on a five-hundred acre estate in Greenwich owned by her grandfather. She was named after her godmother, Glenn Andrews, a longtime family friend. Although she was privy to all the perks of American aristocracy, Close had already settled on the lowbrow career of an actress by the age of seven. In 1960, her childhood detoured into Africa after her father, a Harvard-educated surgeon, established a clinic in the Belgian Congo. Glenn continued her education in Swiss boarding schools, and then returned to New England to attend Rosemary Hall, an exclusive girls' school in Connecticut.

Close's first taste of acting came in her performance as Romeo in the school's annual Shakespeare play. After graduating in 1965, she traveled with the vocal group Up With People, got married in 1969, got divorced two years later, and in 1975 graduated from William and Mary College with a B.A. in drama. After a stint with the New Phoenix Repertory Company, Close made her Broadway debut in *Love for Love* (1975). She worked on and off-Broadway for the next five years, earning a Tony nomination as P.T. Barnum's wife in the musical *Barnum*.

Director George Roy Hill was casting a film adaptation of John Irving's beloved novel *The World According to Garp* at the time and, in a 1984 interview, he recalled seeing Close in *Barnum* and being struck by her "combination of dignity, warmth and extremely rare serenity." Hill offered her the role of Jenny Fields, Garp's imperturable mother. Close left the *Barnum* cast in 1981, after over three hundred performances, to make her film debut.

Summarizing *The World According to Garp* is more difficult than summarizing *War and Peace*. Ostensibly it's the life story of one T.S. Garp, conceived under bizarre circumstances, raised at a preppie boy's school where his mother works as a nurse, and maturing into adolesence and adulthood in a universe where the bizarre and mundane coexist and everyone is slightly off-center. Maybe that sounds like real life, and maybe the bleak message that pervades *The World According to Garp* has some credibility. Or maybe the movie, like the book, deserves Roger Ebert's criticism as "cruel, annoying and smug." There are no halfway reactions to this material--you will either find it deep, or just quirky.

Casting could not be better. Robin Williams as Garp was more subdued and sympathetic than anyone expected, and Glenn Close deserved the Supporting Actress Oscar nomination she received for her portrayal of the unflappable Jenny Fields. Although her warm smile and demeanor rarely changes, Jenny is the most vivid and fully-realized character in the film. Close plays her with a trace of Katharine Hepburn in her voice, which is most prominent when Jenny explains to the dumbstruck dean of his school how Garp was conceived. Her description of outlandish events with a detatched, matter-of-fact delivery is very much in sync with the tone of the book.

Glenn Close is on screen for most of the film's first hour, but whatever edge she may have received in the Oscar derby for the prominence of the role was offset by the movie's non-stop weirdness. The Academy doesn't like weird, and in this case neither did the paying public. *Garp* barely broke even, thanks mostly to the drawing power of Robin Williams.

However, the film did bring Glenn Close to the attention of writer-director Lawrence Kasdan, who cast her in *The Big Chill*, a seriocomic look at how the children of the 1960s are coping twenty years later.

The plot is deceptively simple; seven old friends who attended Michigan University are brought back together for the funeral of another friend named Alex (who was played by Kevin Costner before the role was cut). After the funeral, and accompanied by Alex's girlfriend (Meg Tilly), they spend a weekend together remembering dreams of the past, and facing the realities of the present. Their discussions and revelations are the cornerstone of *The Big Chill*, and there hasn't been such quotable conversation in a film since *My Dinner With Andre* (1981). Its themes are accessible to all ages, but for Baby Boomers the film takes on a poignant resonance that can induce shivers.

The Big Chill assembled the kind of stars-everywhere cast that is usually only found in MGM films of the 1940s; Close is joined by Kevin Kline, Jeff Goldblum, JoBeth Williams, Tom Berenger, William Hurt and Mary Kay Place. Kasdan, except for a lovely, sweeping crane shot at Alex's burial, wisely keeps out of the way and lets the actors act. Superb ensemble performances and an irresistable soundtrack of 1960s hits turned *The Big Chill* into one of 1983's most popular films.

It's possible to receive one Academy Award nomination and remain a relative unknown, but you can't do it two years in a row. Although her performance was not markedly better or more prominent than that of her costars, Close was again singled out by the Academy for exemplary work. Sarah, Close's character, had an affair with Alex five years earlier, and is thus affected by his death in a different way than the rest of the group. She's a bit more reflective than the others, but on the whole Sarah has the same number of playful and serious moments, and the same ambiguous feelings about how her life has changed. "Sometimes," she says after a typical parenting speech to her daughter, "I don't believe what I hear myself say."

THE WORLD ACCORDING TO GARP
Directed by George Roy Hill; Written by Steve Tesich, based on the novel by John Irving; Produced by George Roy Hill and Robert L. Crawford

Cast
Robin Williams (T.S. Garp), Mary Beth Hurt (Helen Holm), GLENN CLOSE (JENNY FIELDS), John Lithgow (Roberta Muldoon)

THE BIG CHILL
Directed by Lawrence Kasdan; Written by Lawrence Kasdan and Barbara Benedek; Produced by Michael Shamberg

Cast
GLENN CLOSE (Sarah), Tom Berenger (Sam), William Hurt (Nick), Jeff Goldblum (Michael), Mary Kay Place (Meg), Kevin Kline (Harold), Meg Tilly (Chloe), JoBeth Williams (Karen)

CLAUDETTE COLBERT (1905-   )

FIRST APPEARANCE: *For the Love Of Mike* (First National, 1927)

A STAR IS BORN: *The Sign of the Cross* (Paramount, 1932)

Claudette Colbert is nearly impossible to categorize, because she seemed so at ease in every type of character and every type of film. Comedies, slapstick and sophisticated, comprise the greater part of her career's work, but she was also effective as a lascivious siren in *The Sign of the Cross* and *Cleopatra* (1934) and as a modern woman in mature dramas such as *Since You Went Away* (1944). The only discernible common denominator in her film persona is a projection of canny intelligence, that always seemed to emerge as much from Colbert as from the character she played.

Born in Paris, Claudette Chauchion moved to New York with her parents when she was five years old. At Washington Irving High School she studied art, and after graduation she worked in a dress shop, hoping to one day become a fashion designer, supplementing her income by giving French lessons in the evenings. An acting career was first suggested to Claudette by playwright Anne Morrison, who went so far as to arrange for her friend to play a small role in the play *The Wild Westcotts* (1923). After reading her three lines on stage, Claudette gave herself a new last name and never went back to the dress shop.

Colbert learned her craft on stage in a succession of roles that gradually increased in prominence. In 1929, her performance as a sexy snake charmer in *The Barker* became an unintentional audition for her first movie role, in Frank Capra's *For the Love of Mike*. The film, a United Nations *Three Men and a Baby*, was a comedy about a Jewish man (George Sidney), an Irish man (Hugh Cameron) and a Dutch man (Ford Sterling), who find a baby boy on their doorstep. They raise the boy to adulthood, and put him through Yale University, where he wins the big boat race against Harvard and the heart of his Italian girlfriend, Mary (Colbert).

The film was shot in New York, and has been lost virtually since its original release. Critics of the day were not surprised that no writer was credited, and saved their highest praise for the Yale sequences, shot on location by Ernest Haller (who would later work on *Gone With the Wind*). Of Colbert, the *New York Times* observed "she seems quite at home before the camera." Both Colbert and producer-director Capra harshly criticized the film later. Photos from the film show Colbert in full flapper regalia, looking adoringly on her boyfriend, and all available evidence suggests she was asked to do little else. "I'll never make another motion picture," she declared.

She kept her word for two years, but was then drawn back by a tempting offer from Paramount Pictures. Colbert appeared in a series of uninspired films, first in New York and later in Hollywood. How she landed her breakthough role--Empress Poppaea in Cecil B. DeMille's *The Sign of the Cross*, is uncertain; DeMille said he chose Colbert after seeing her walk by his window on the soundstage. Other sources claim that Colbert obtained a copy of the script and demanded to play the role. Either way, the casting worked.

Frederic March starred as Marcus Superbus, Prefect of the Roman Empire, who is loved by Poppaea, the wife of Emperor Nero (Charles Laughton), but who would rather spend time with Mercia (Elissa Landi), a simple Christian lass. After Nero burns Rome, he blames the Christians for his crime and orders Marcus to round them up. Marcus tries to hide Mercia, but after she is caught he begs Nero to spare her life. The spurned Poppaea makes certain that the girl is sent to the arena. Marcus joins her in facing the lions. The lions win.

The Sign of the Cross was recut in 1944, to allow for the inclusion of a nine minute, World War II prologue, featuring a beautiful love letter to Rome written by Dudley Nichols, and a comparison between Nero and Adolf Hitler. It's an interesting bit of wartime propaganda, but when it was added several scenes from the original film were excised. The burning of Rome, and the scenes of carnage in the arena before an audience of thousands are DeMille at his most flamboyant, but most of the violence was cut, as were scenes depicting cannibalism and thinly-veiled lesbianism.

Claudette Colbert's scenes, fortunately, survived intact. She is first seen in the very famous milk bath sequence, which would still get the film a 'PG-13' rating today. Colbert, clearly revealed to be topless, splashes and cavorts in asses milk, which developed such a foul smell under the hot studio lights that Colbert fainted more than once. Her provocative costumes--or lack thereof--certainly helped her to get noticed, but it was her performance that gave her movie career a long overdue surge.

While most of the actors automatically read their lines with the formal, flawless enunciation that seems appropriate to grand Biblical epics, Colbert opts for a more contemporary manner. "I shall beg your pardon tomorrow," Marcus tells Poppaea after running down her carriage. "How about tonight?" she purrs, with a seductive lilt in her voice that is more Mae West than Roman empress. Later, after Poppaea seals Mercia's fate, Marcus explodes with fury. "You harlot!" he screams. Poppaea responds with a sly smile and a shrug of her shoulders, and then walks off without a word; a very cool response in any historical era.

FOR THE LOVE OF MIKE
Directed an produced by Frank Capra; based on a story by John Moroso

Cast
Ben Lyon (Mike), George Sidney (Abraham Katz), Ford Sterling (Herman Schultz), Hugh Cameron (Patrick O'Malley), CLAUDETTE COLBERT (MARY)

THE SIGN OF THE CROSS
Directed and produced by Cecil B. DeMille; Written by Waldemar Young and Sidney Buchman, based on the play by Wilson Barrett; Music by Rudolph Kopp

Cast
Frederic March (Marcus Superbus), Elissa Landi (Mercia), CLAUDETTE COLBERT (EMPRESS POPPAEA), Charles Laughton (Nero), Ian Keith (Tigellinus), Joyzelle Joyner (Ancaria)

RONALD COLMAN (1891-1958)

FIRST APPEARANCE: *The Toilers* (Diamond Super Ltd., 1919)

A STAR IS BORN: *Beau Geste* (Famous Players/Paramount, 1926)

He was an English gentleman, slight of build and gentle in manner, who projected a quiet, distinctive confidence and courage. "Ronald Colman is, on the whole, good for humanity," wrote Colman biographer Roland Wild. "Doctors might prescribe a dose of him for depressed patients or for those with acute melancholia." A touching tribute yet perhaps somewhat odd, considering how often Colman played tragic figures who expired in an act of noble self-sacrifice. Nobody did it better, though, especially when it came time for last words; Ronald Colman's voice, as melodious an instrument as has ever been heard in motion pictures, made us wonder if anyone has ever made a more graceful departure from this mortal coil. Maybe the depressed patients should stick to Colman's equally memorable comedic roles in *The Talk of the Town* (1942) and *Champagne for Caesar* (1950).

Born in Richmond, Surrey, England, Ronald Charles Colman grew up with every intention of granting his father's wish to have a son at Cambridge. But when Charles Colman died when Ronald was sixteen, the dream was abandoned, and Ronald went to work as a shipping clerk to support his mother and four siblings. Amateur theatricals were a pleasant diversion for the talented Colman, who would act, sing, and play the banjo in touring dramatic societies, whenever his regular job would allow.

In 1914, Ronald Colman volunteered for military service, and was among the first 100,000 English soldiers to fight on French soil in World War I. Just two months later, the decorated, twenty-three year old Private was wounded in combat, and discharged in May of 1915. He turned once again to acting, this time as a career instead of a pastime. He made his London stage debut as a walk-on player in *The Maharanee of Arakan*, where his dashing looks and rich, clear voice were quickly noticed. Before the year was over, he was playing juvenile leads.

An appearance in the play *Damaged Goods* (1916) prompted an offer from British film pioneer George Dewhurst, who offered Colman a lead role in the comedy short subject *The Live Wire*. The movie was made, but never released. All copies, along with those of *The Toilers* (Colman's actual film debut) and six other early releases, were presumed destroyed in the London Blitz of 1941.

What we know of *The Toilers* is that Colman played Bob, the selfish adopted son of a fisherman's widow. He deserts his stepmother (Gwynne Herbert) for a rich socialite (Mollie Terraine), but when the romance sours he returns to the simple life to seek the forgiveness of his family. A *Bioscope* review called the film "poor and unconvincing material," and did not single out Colman as a talent worth watching. The actor's own recollections, recorded in Roland Wild's biography, are also disparaging; "My hands and arms went round and round like windmills," Colman said, "and I was all over the place like a jumping jack."

Colman's breakthrough came when he played opposite Lillian Gish in *The White Sister* (1923), the first American film to be shot on location in Italy. He signed a contract with the Metro-Goldwyn studio in 1924, but became a star when he was loaned out to Paramount for Herbert Brenon's epic, *Beau Geste*. Percival Christopher Wren's tale of a brave, last stand by the French Foreign Legion at the mysterious Fort Zinderneuf has been told four times on the silver screen, but never as well as when Ronald Colman played the title role.

Wren's description of Michael "Beau" Geste seems to have been written with Colman in mind; "remarkable physical beauty, mental brilliance, irresistable charm, stubborn determination, and the reckless courage of a youthful d'Artagnan." Michael and his brothers Digby (Neil Hamilton) and John (Ralph Forbes) leave England to join the Foreign Legion after they are each suspected of stealing a priceless jewel. It was a theft born of noble intent, though the truth is not revealed until two brothers have perished. In the Legion, Beau and Digby serve under the tyrranical Sergeant-Major Lejaune (Noah Beery) at Fort Zinderneuf, a remote outpost in the Sahara Desert. When the fort is attacked by thousands of Arab invaders, Beau and Digby forget their discord with Lejaune and stand against the marauders.

Mystery, action and romance are served up generously in this landmark film; the nearly one million dollar budget all shows up on the screen in several amazing sequences, especially the final assault on Fort Zinderneuf. Thousands of extras, many of them actual ex-legionnaires, were hired to ride toward a fort built in a desolate part of the Arizona desert near the Mexican border. Marvelous cinematography and production design stand out above the uniformly excellent technical credits, not the least of which is Herbert Brenon's flawless direction.

Two schools of acting are visible in *Beau Geste*, one pointing to the motion picture medium's past, one to its future; Noah Beery as Lejaune and William Powell as the lowlife thief Boldini illustrate the broad, sweeping, pop-eyed performance style expected of silent film villains, while Ronald Colman's more controlled performance, relying on subtle gesture and facial expression, foreshadowed the paradigm in talking pictures. Michael Geste's heroic spirit, modest dignity and strong sense of duty and honor are effortlessly conveyed by Colman with little more than the arching of an eyebrow and a wistful smile.

Had *Beau Geste* not been released one year before the first Academy Awards presentation, Ronald Colman would not have waited another twenty-two years to receive an Oscar (for 1947's *A Double Life*). The resonance of the "beautiful gesture" performed by Beau sets the pattern for Colman's later portrayals of Sidney Carton in *A Tale of Two Cities* (1935), and Richard Heldar in *The Light That Failed* (1939).

THE TOILERS
Directed by Tom W. Watts; Written by Eliot Stannard and R.C. Sheriff, based on the novel *The Toilers of the Sea* by Victor Hugo; Produced by George Dewhurst

Cast
Manora Thaw (Rose), George Dewhurst (Jack), Gwynne Herbert (Mother), RONALD COLMAN (BOB)

BEAU GESTE
Directed by Herbert Brenon; Written by Paul Schofield and John Russell, based on the novel by Percival Christopher Wren; Produced by Adolph Zukor and Jesse L. Lasky; Music by Hugo Riesenfeld

Cast
RONALD COLMAN (MICHAEL "BEAU" GESTE), Neil Hamilton (Digby Geste), Ralph Forbes (John Geste), Alice Joyce (Lady Brandon), Mary Brian (Isobel), Noah Beery (Sgt. Lejaune), William Powell (Boldini), Victor McLaglen (Hank), Norman Trevor (Major de Beaujolais), Donald Stuart (Buddy)

SEAN CONNERY (1930-   )

FIRST APPEARANCE: *No Road Back* (RKO, 1957)

A STAR IS BORN: *Dr. No* (United Artists, 1962)

Although he had already appeared in ten films, audiences around the world first met Sean Connery at the same time they met Secret Agent James Bond, thus forging a connection between actor and role that has yet to subside. The casting was so perfect that for many fans of the 007 series, Connery is still the only James Bond that counts. Although he worked steadily after leaving the series in 1971, it was not until 1986's *The Name of the Rose* that he was able to emerge from Bond's tuxedoed shadow.

Born in Fountainbridge, Scotland, Thomas Connery (Sean was a nickname) grew up in modest circumstances, showing little interest in school or anything else. At ten years old his life almost changed dramatically, when his parents arranged for Sean to sail to Australia as a war evacuee. The boat sank before he could leave. Sean left school at the age of thirteen, and began drifting from job to job. He spent time in the Royal Navy, and later worked as a coffin polisher and a figure model for art students. His interest in physical fitness culminated with his being elected as Scotland's representative in the 1953 Mr. Universe contest.

Connery placed third in the competition, but more important was his meeting with some of the other entrants, who were working in the London production of *South Pacific*. Some cast members were about to depart before the show embarked on a national tour, and Connery was encouraged to audition for one of their parts. He was accepted, and for the next year he performed backing vocals on "There Is Nothing Like a Dame," as an American sailor. Finding the work enjoyable, Connery later landed minor roles in other stage productions, and made his television debut in 1956 opposite Robert Shaw in *The Escaper's Club*. In 1957, he made his feature film debut as a penny-ante gangster in *No Road Back*.

Skip Homeier starred as John Railton, a young medical student who returns to England after completing his education in the United States. His blind and deaf mother (Margaret Rawlings) has financed John's education by fencing stolen property, as John discovers after he is nearly framed for a robbery, during which a night watchman is murdered. At the last moment, mom confesses to her involvement in the crime network, and saves her son from the gallows.

The story sounds perfect for a seedy film noir, and director Montgomery Tully admirably creates suspense with a low budget and a less-than-polished cast. Skip Homeier looks confused most of the time, which fortunately is appropriate for the character, and Patricia Dainton is impressive as John's fiancee`, who is also a part of the fencing racket. Sean Connery plays Spike, one of the hoods who participates in Ma Railton's last heist. He is on screen for about fifteen minutes altogether, but has very little to do outside of look threatening. His imposing physique and permanent scowl lend an appropriate air of menace to his strong but silent character. Connery's hair is a little higher and his wardrobe a bit less tailored than it would be when he played Bond, but he already projects an effortless, cocksure confidence that was a principal trait of his most famous role.

Connery next costarred in a BBC production of Rod ·Serling's *Requiem for a Heavyweight*, and he was impressive enough to earn rave reviews and several movie offers. It was his performance as an Irish country bumpkin in Walt Disney's *Darby O'Gill and the Little People* (1959) that convinced producer Albert Broccoli to test Connery for *Dr. No*, the first James Bond film. Other candidates for the role included Patrick McGoohan and Roger Moore.

Author Ian Fleming was not always happy with the way his creation was played in the movies, but he was smart enough to demand a percentage of all box-office revenues. Producers Broccoli and Harry Saltzman agreed to Fleming's terms, and signed a multipicture deal with United Artists. *Dr. No*, despite a lukewarm critical reception, became a huge hit, and introduced most of the trademark scenes that fans now expect in every series entry.

At this point, the filmmakers still showed some concern about paying attention to the books, and the script of *Dr. No* is somewhat consistent with its source material; A British Secret Service agent is murdered in Jamaica, and 007 (the number is a rank that signifies the license to kill) is assigned to the case. James Bond teams up with FBI agent Felix Leiter (Jack Lord), and together they uncover a plot by the insidious Dr. No (Joseph Wiseman) to divert missiles launched at Cape Canaveral from his island fortress. Bond foils the doctor's plans to blackmail the U.S. government.

Dr. No was one of the more realistic (as opposed to cartoon) violent Bond films, and Bond himself is still more of a human being here than a superhero; he actually registers fear in the scene where he wakes up with a tarantula, and becomes physically ill afterward. Joseph Wiseman, by contrast, borders on inhuman as megalomaniac Dr. No, the prototypical Bond opponent. Bernard Lee and Lois Maxwell begin their stints as M and Miss Moneypenny, reliable presences for much of the series, and Ursula Andress sets the standard for "Bond girls," in measurements if not in acting ability, as Honey Rider.

We first meet James Bond, appropriately, at the Baccarat table of a London casino. From the moment Connery looks lazily up from the table to light a cigarette, and utters the classic self-introduction "Bond. James Bond," the role is his. He is handsome, but not in a male model way, and older than the average movie sex symbol, with a receding hairline and ears that are a bit too prominent. But Connery's poise and debonair charm made it easy to believe in 007's ladykilling power.

NO ROAD BACK
Directed by Montgomery Tully; Written by Charles Leeds and Montgomery Tully, basd on the play *Madame Tictac* by Falkland D. Cary and Philip Weathers; Produced by Steven Pallos and Charles Leeds; Music by John Veale

Cast
Skip Homeier (John Railton), Paul Carpenter (Clem Hayes), Patricia Dainton (Beth), Norman Wooland (Inspector Harris), Margaret Rawlings (Mrs. Railton), Eleanor Summerfield (Marguerite), Alfie Bass (Rudge), SEAN CONNERY (SPIKE)

DR. NO
Directed by Terence Young; Written by Richard Maibaum, Johanna Harwood and Berkley Mather, based on the book by Ian Fleming; Produced by Albert R. Broccoli and Harry Saltzman; Music by Monty Norman

Cast
SEAN CONNERY (JAMES BOND), Ursula Andress (Honey Rider), Joseph Wiseman (Dr. No), Jack Lord (Felix Leiter), Lois Maxwell (Miss Moneypenny), Bernard Lee (M)

GARY COOPER (1901-1961)

FIRST APPEARANCE (Billed): *The Winning of Barbara Worth* (Goldwyn/United Artists, 1926)

A STAR IS BORN: *The Virginian* (Paramount, 1929)

Early in his film career, Gary Cooper would occasionally be cast as a villain, but after *The Virginian* he put away his black hat for good. Like John Wayne, golden age Hollywood's other good guy, Cooper was tall and handsome and specialized in cleaning up the wild west. But unlike the Duke, Cooper would play brave men who were also shy and insecure. His best films utilized this contrast, which made his formidable presence less threatening to male moviegoers, and all the more desirable to their dates. His finest characters--"John Doe", Longfellow Deeds, Sergeant York, Will Kane--were simple men of inherent nobility, and when they stood up for what's right, not for glory or money or any personal gain, but just because it *was* right, he had the whole theater on his side.

Frank James Cooper spent his childhood winters in Helena, Montana, and his summers on a large cattle ranch fifty miles north of town. His parents tried to instill some of their native British gentility into Frank and his brother Arthur, but Frank preferred the rough and tumble life of the cowboys who worked on the ranch. His best friend was a ranch hand named Zeb who taught him how to hunt, shoot a six-gun and ride a horse. Mrs. Cooper was not amused, and suggested a pallette-cleansing visit to England. Frank and Arthur's frontier upbringing left them ill-prepared for the strict headmasters at the Dunstable School in Bedfordshire, where they spent three years before returning to Montana at the outbreak of World War I.

At the age of sixteen, Frank Cooper grew fourteen inches, got expelled from high school, and attended every western at Helena's only theater. He still spent summers working on the ranch, but quickly realized that the life of a cowboy was more romantic on a movie screen than it was in reality. His father, now a county judge, pulled enough strings to get Frank back in school and, after graduating, he became a tour guide at Yellowstone National Park. In 1921 he enrolled in Iowa's Grinnell College, where he was rejected by the dramatic society three times. One of Cooper's many college girlfriends had suggested he could make a fortune in movies, and that vote of confidence was reason enough to board a train for Hollywood.

He arrived in Los Angeles on Thanksgiving Day of 1924. After stints as a milkman and a door-to-door salesman, Cooper tracked down an old friend from the ranch named Jim Galen, who was working in westerns as an extra. Galen, who told Cooper that Hollywood "can never find enough people to ride horses," introduced his friend to director Al Neitz, one of the busiest men in the area of Tinseltown known as Poverty Row. Here, westerns and other 'B' movies were churned out by the dozen by such generic companies as Majestic, Mascot, and Beacon Pictures. Cooper would become the only performer to emerge from the ranks of Poverty Row into stardom.

For ten dollars a day, Cooper appeared as an extra in anywhere from twelve to fifty films. "Some days," he once told a reporter, "I was a cowboy before lunch and an Injun in the afternoon." The exact number is impossible to determine because the same footage was used in more than one film, and almost all these movies are now lost. The actual first appearance of Gary (then still Frank) Cooper is open for debate, but it might be as a background cowboy in Al Neitz's *Warrior Gap* or *A Six-Shootin' Romance*, both released in 1925. That same year, another man named Frank Cooper was convicted of murder in Los Angeles. An agent, Nan Collins, advised that Cooper make a change before his name became famous for the wrong reason. She suggested Gary, after her hometown of Gary, Indiana. Said Cooper later, "Good thing she didn't come from Poughkeepsie."

Collins also prepared test footage of Cooper demonstrating his skills as a horseman, which she showed to director Henry King. After watching the test, King gave Gary Cooper his first billed role in *The Winning of Barbara Worth* (1926), and a raise to fifty dollars a week. The story revolves around a scheme to reclaim desert lands owned by Jefferson Worth (Charles Lane) by using the Colorado River for irrigation purposes. Engineers Willard Holmes (Ronald Colman) and Abe Lee (Gary Cooper) work together on the project, but after hours they compete for the affections of Barbara Worth (Vilma Bankey), Jefferson's daughter. The project is sabotaged by faulty materials and a double-crossing financial backer, resulting in a thrilling climax in which a spectacular flood pours through a busted dam and floods the town. Abe does not survive, but Willard and Barbara pledge their love among the ruins.

"Gary Cooper is a youth who will be heard of on the screen, and possibly blossom out as an 'ace' lead," wrote *Variety*. Though he appears in only a few scenes, Cooper received enough attention to earn a contract with Paramount. There he made more forgotten films, romanced Clara Bow and built a reputation as a reliable western lead. His rising star received its biggest boost with the demise of silent film, and the title role in one of the most popular western stories of all time. Owen Wister's novel *The Virginian* had already been filmed in 1921 and 1923, before Cooper saddled up in 1929. Another version debuted in 1946, and a *Virginian* television series ran from 1962 to 1971. The '29 vintage seems a rather creaky old oater today, but Cooper's performance makes it definitive.

The film was prepared as a vehicle for Richard Dix, but when he held out for more money director Victor Fleming suggested Gary Cooper as a replacement. As the Virginian, he makes his first appearance singing, and illustrates why there are no musicals in his filmography. He plays the foreman of a Wyoming ranch who watches as friends and workers sell out their loyalty to a rustler named Trampas (Walter Huston). He makes the painful decision to turn in his buddies, but Trampas escapes and puts a bullet in the Virginian. He is nursed back to health by Miss Molly, the pretty new schoolmarm. On their wedding day, Trampas returns for a showdown.

Walter Huston creates the most fully-realized character in the piece. Cooper is less consistent; when he tries to stare down Trampas during the party for Miss Molly, he looks more constipated than angry. But later, he approaches Molly to apologize for an earlier joke, and Cooper's hesitant speech and awkward movement of his gangly arms seem just right. It's a sweet moment. The rest is cliche` now though at the time it wasn't, and even so the climactic showdown is still exciting. Compare The Virginian's victory with the last act of *High Noon* (1952), a worthy opposing bookend for the first notch in Gary Cooper's six-gun.

THE WINNING OF BARBARA WORTH
Directed by Henry King; Written by Frances Marion, based on the novel by Harold Bell Wright; Produced by Samuel Goldwyn; Music by Ted Henkel

Cast
Ronald Colman (Willard Holmes), Vilma Bankey (Barbara Worth), Charles Lane (Jefferson Worth), Paul McAllister (The Seer), E.J. Ratcliffe (James Greenfield), GARY COOPER (ABE LEE)

THE VIRGINIAN
Directed by Victor Fleming; Written by Howard Estabrook, Edward E. Paramore, Jr., Grover Jones and Keene Thompson, based on the novel by Owen Wister; Produced by Louis D. Lighton

Cast
GARY COOPER (THE VIRGINIAN), Walter Huston (Trampas), Mary Brian (Molly Wood), Richard Arlen (Steve), Helen Ware ("Ma" Taylor), Chester Conklin (Uncle Hughey), Eugene Pallette (Honey Wiggin)

KEVIN COSTNER (1955-   )

FIRST APPEARANCE: *Sizzle Beach, U.S.A.* (Troma, 1986)

A STAR IS BORN: *No Way Out* (Orion, 1987)

It's wise to be wary of comparisons between stars of yesterday and stars of today, since most of them are hatched by agents and publicists. But sometimes the link between generations is more substantial; try describing Kevin Costner, then transfer every word into an essay on Gary Cooper, and very little will have to be deleted. Costner's physical appearance, his voice, flat with a trace of western drawl, his affinity for characters with rural backgrounds and simple, straightforward values, all identify him as the spiritual heir to Coop. If only he'd say "Yup" more.

Kevin Costner was born in Los Angeles, California, the city where his parents relocated after losing their Oklahoma farm in the Great Depression. Bill Costner got a job at Southern California Edison, which forced his family to move repeatedly throughout Kevin's childhood. Kevin attended four different high schools, excelling in sports but always feeling like an outsider. After graduation he attended California State University at Fullerton, where he majored in marketing and finance.

Costner began to consider acting as a profession after auditioning for a college production of *Rumplestiltskin*. He wasn't cast, but the experience so intrigued him that he joined a community theater group. Costner earned his marketing degree and took a job in the field, but thirty days later he quit to become an actor. "I guess I took a risk, but I felt it was a bigger risk not to do what my mind and heart were telling me," he said in a *Good Housekeeping* interview. "I didn't have a plan for success, but I never felt like turning back. Ever."

He moved to Hollywood and was hired as a stage manager at Raleigh Studios, where he made the contacts that led to his film debut. The finished product was so dreadful that it never achieved a sizable release. *Sizzle Beach, U.S.A.* is a jiggle movie about three buxom women who move into a Malibu beach house and spend most of their days changing clothes and taking showers. The film makes no attempt to tell a story or create interesting characters, and is shameless in its non-stop display of female flesh. I haven't seen so many breasts on parade since the Folies Bergere.

Technical credits are beyond negligent--scenes in which articles of clothing appear and disappear are edited together, and every shot seems to be held either too long or not long enough. There's also not an actor in sight, and that includes Costner as wealthy stable owner John Logan. He plays a couple of flirty scenes with one of the Malibu tarts, who succumbs to his charms without much opposition. Costner is no matinee idol yet (and if Logan is so rich, couldn't he afford a better haircut?), and even though his line readings are the most natural of anyone in the film, there are times when he underplays so much that you want to poke him to make sure he's still awake. The opening credits of the *Sizzle Beach, U.S.A.* video release were changed to promote Costner to "special guest star" status. "I was totally naive, and we shot it on weekends over the course of a year, so I had no idea what the finished picture even looked like," he said years later. If he's lucky, he'll never find out.

The 1980s were kinder. After bit parts in several movies including *Night Shift* (1982) and *Testament* (1983), Costner played a supporting role in *The Big Chill* (1983). Although his entire contribution was cut before the film was released, writer/director Lawrence Kasdan remembered Costner and cast him in *Silverado* (1985). He received his first significant role and his first critical notice, most of which was positive. This was followed by *American Flyers* (1985) and then *The Untouchables* (1987), in which he starred as Eliot Ness. The film was the fifth most popular release that year, and enhanced the careers of everyone involved except for Costner, who seemed to blend into the wallpaper.

The problem, besides the fact that David Mamet's script portrayed Ness as a dullard, was that there were hardly any women in the movie. Costner's biggest strength is as a romantic lead, as he proved in *No Way Out* (1987), the film that finally established him as a charismatic leading man.

Costner plays Lieutenant Commander Tom Farrell, a naval hero who is hired by Secretary of Defense David Brice (Gene Hackman) to serve as a liason to the CIA. Farrell falls in love with Susan Atwell (Sean Young), who is also Brice's mistress. When the jealous Brice kills her in a fit of rage, he tries to cover up the murder by blaming it on "Yuri," a Russian spy who is rumored to have infiltrated the Pentagon. Farrell is assigned to the case, which takes several surprising turns before he is able to expose Brice as the killer.

Although Costner is still underplaying, he does it this time with better material and the confidence of an "uncomplicated, retrograde American archetype," as one writer described him. The twist at the end of *No Way Out* was one too many, and ruined the film for a lot of ticket buyers. But it was Costner's believalbility as an all-American hero that made the twist so hard to swallow, which is something of a compliment, and despite the flaw the film is exciting and fast-paced.

Tom's tryst in the back of a limosuine with Susan was brought up in every review, but their relationship is more meaningful than a one-ride stand, and for all its sexual heat there was also a refreshing sweetness to the scenes between Costner and Sean Young. Costner's first memorable moment on screen occurs when Tom learns of Susan's death from a file folder in Brice's office. Forced to keep his heartbreak a secret, his face registers a medley of tortured expressions.

SIZZLE BEACH, U.S.A.
Directed by Richard Brander; Written by Craig Kusaba; Produced by Eric Louzil; Music by The Beach Towels

Cast
Terry Congie (Janice), Leslie Brander (Sheryl), Roselyn Royce (Dit), KEVIN COSTNER (JOHN LOGAN)

NO WAY OUT
Directed by Roger Donaldson; Written by Robert Garland, based on the book *The Big Clock* by Kenneth Fearing; Produced by Laura Ziskin and Robert Garland; Music by Maurice Jarre, Paul Anka, Michael McDonald and Richard Marx

Cast
KEVIN COSTNER (LT. CMDR. TOM FARRELL), Gene Hackman (David Brice), Sean Young (Susan Atwill), Will Patton (Scott Pritchard), Howard Duff (Willy Duvall)

JOAN CRAWFORD (1906-1977)

FIRST APPEARANCE: *Lady of the Night* (MGM, 1925)

A STAR IS BORN: *Our Dancing Daughters* (MGM, 1928)

Much has been made of the "gender transgression" in Joan Crawford's persona. Other actresses combined masculine and feminine qualities in their characters (Katharine Hepburn being an obvious example), but these qualities have never been so exaggerated as they have been in Crawford. Her portrayals of tough, ambitious, working women were so forceful that they overpowered the best efforts of her male costars. Her face could be beautiful on screen, but it could also be downright scary.

No actor ever worked harder at building and maintaining a "movie star" image than Joan Crawford. She was tremendously loyal and devoted to her fans, and wore the outer trappings of her opulent lifestyle in part because she knew it was how they expected to see her. But Crawford's private life was as much a performance as the eighty roles she played in her six-decade career, and when the image that was so meticulously crafted was destroyed by Christina Crawford's book *Mommie Dearest*, and the film adaptation (in which Faye Dunaway portrayed Joan as, in the words of one reviewer, a combination of Medea and Medusa), it may have been justified, but it was also inescapably tragic.

When asked about her childhood, Crawford would often reply, "I never had one." She was born Lucille LeSueur in San Antonio, Texas, and moved with her mother six weeks later to Lawton, Oklahoma. Her father had abandoned her mother before Lucille was born. A scandal involving her stepfather, Henry Cassin, forced the family to move once more, this time to Kansas City. At the age of eleven, Lucille started working as a cleaning woman and cook in a private school, where she was beaten with a broom handle by the principal for any indiscretion. She stayed three years despite the abuse, and then left to pursue her dream of becoming a dancer.

She won chorus jobs in Chicago and Oklahoma City and, after attracting the attention of J.J. Shubert, a similar job in the Broadway shows *Innocent Eyes* (1923) and *The Passing Show* (1924). A talent scout for MGM spotted Lucille and offered her a contract. At first she turned it down, but the offer of $75 a week for five years proved irresistible. She was billed as Lucille LaSueur for her first four films, but then the studio demanded a name change and sponsored a contest in *Movie Weekly* magazine. Lucille's fate was decided by a woman in New York named Marie Tisdale, whose suggestion of Joan Crawford won second prize (the first prize winner, "Joan Arden" was already taken). Lucille hated the name, because it sounded like "crawfish."

In her very first film appearance, Lucille/Joan wasn't billed at all. In *Lady of the Night*, Norma Shearer played a dual role as Florence, a judge's daughter and society debutante, and Molly, a petty thief from the slums. Molly falls for David, a wealthy gentleman (Malcolm McGregor), but their relationship lasts only until David sees Florence. In one scene, the two lookalike women confront each other, and it was Crawford's assignment to represent whichever character Shearer was not playing. The camera was always over her shoulder, and the back of her head was all that was visible. *Lady of the Night* was a showcase for Shearer, but for the future Joan Crawford it was a rather degrading debut. She complained to the studio, and after that she worked steadily, appearing in four other films in 1925, three more in 1926 and six more in 1927. The best of these early outings was probably Tod Browning's *The Unknown* (1927), in which she played opposite Lon Chaney.

Our Dancing Daughters was no different or better than other romantic melodramas of the day, but it gave Crawford her first lead role. She played Diana, a vivacious party girl who ignores warnings that she is "too free" with her affections in public, and that "men are still old-fashioned when it comes to marriage." As a result, she loses her boyfriend Ben (Johnny Mack

Brown) to another woman. But after Ben's wife dies he returns to Diana, his one true love, in a weird but happy ending.

As a dancer Crawford is energetic but not particularly graceful, though she moves with a feverish conviction that betrayed a fear of what will happen when the music stops. In close-ups she proves Norma Desmond's point about how "They had faces then." Crawford has the entrancing eyes and hypnotic gaze of the great silent rnovie sirens, and she shows a flair for comedy that was not utilized often in her subsequent career (1939's *The Women* is a notable exception). Crawford's scenes are certainly the most watchable in *Our Dancing Daughters*, which gets sidetracked too often into a drippy subplot involving Diana's drippy friend Beatrice and her even drippier boyfriend. However, the chic art deco settings created by Cedric Gibbons are more interesting now than anything that happened in front of them.

Crawford sneaked the script for *Our Dancing Daughters* out of MGM, knew it was right for her, and campaigned forcefully to play Diana Medford. The film spawned two sequels, was one of MGM's biggest moneymakers of 1928, and made Joan Crawford a star overnight, but sixty years later it's hard to see why. The reason, I guess, is that her portrayal of the vivacious flapper personified the carefree jazz age, when life was non-stop playtime for the well-to-do. "I'm known as Diana the dangerous," she tells Ben, and it is her live-for-today attitude and shameless enthusiasm for men and gin that must have captivated audiences of the day.

LADY OF THE NIGHT
Directed by Monta Bell; Written by Alice D.G. Miller, based on a story by Adela Rogers St. John;

Cast
Norma Shearer (Molly/Florence), Malcolm McGregor (David), George K. Arthur (Chunky), Fred Esmelton (Judge Banning)...JOAN CRAWFORD (DOUBLE FOR NORMA SHEARER)

OUR DANCING DAUGHTERS
Directed by Harry Beaumont; Written by Josephine Lovett; Produced by Hunt Stromberg; Music by Ballard MacDonald, William Axt and David Mendoza

Cast
JOAN CRAWFORD (DIANA MEDFORD), Johnny Mack Brown (Ben Blaine), Nils Asther (Norman), Dorothy Sebastian (Beatrice), Anita Page (Ann)

TOM CRUISE (1962-   )

FIRST APPEARANCE: *Endless Love* (PolyGram Pictures, 1981)

A STAR IS BORN: *Risky Business* (Warner Bros., 1983)

He has been described as the closest thing going to a young Jimmy Stewart--clean-cut good looks, instinctive comic timing, and a gift for projecting innate decency. Thomas Cruise Mapother IV's genial personality was beneficial in his pre-teen years, when he was the new student in over a dozen different schools while his father traveled the country looking for work. After his parents divorced, Cruise settled with his mother and sisters in Louisville, Kentucky, where he could at last look forward to seeing the same faces for more than one semester. However, his long undiagnosed dyslexia meant that school would still hold its share of trials.

In 1980, Cruise auditioned on a whim for a high school production of *Guys and Dolls*. He earned a lead role, and fell in love with performing. When the feeling didn't wear off after the last curtain dropped in the school auditorium, he left for New York to pursue an acting career. Cruise paid a few dues, but not that many, before his matinee idol looks began to land him roles.

The first of these was *Endless Love*, the ill-fated film adaptation of Scott Spencer's acclaimed novel. It told the touching story of David Axelrod and Jade Butterfield, two lovestruck and starcrossed teenage lovers played by Martin Hewitt and Brooke Shields. When Jade's father forbids the relationship, a distraught David sets fire to the Butterfield porch, hoping to look the hero by alerting the family. Instead, he overdoes the lighter fluid and burns down their house. Cruise plays Billy, who suggests the idea of romance through arson to his friend David. Sounds like a pivotal part, but in fact Cruise worked only one day on the film, and appears in only one scene.

Director Franco Zeffirelli had attempted to recapture the passion of adolescent love he had depicted so superbly in his 1968 production of *Romeo and Juliet*. But *Endless Love* was a failure in every respect; the source material certainly wasn't Shakespeare, and the passion of the protagonists was not adequately conveyed by the sullen Martin Hewitt and the vapid Brooke Shields. For his part, Cruise dutifully took of his shirt and uttered his handful of lines in a voice an octave higher than what is familiar to audiences now.

The role didn't ask for more than a smile and well-developed pectorals, and the producers probably didn't care that Cruise was capable of so much more. But Cruise had enough confidence in his talent to never again compromise his integrity. He turned down a slasher film at a career juncture when most actors would kill for any role, but got roped into *Losin' It* (1983) by promises that the final script would be more polished than the version he read. As it turned out, the teen sex comedy costarring Shelley Long was a forgettable flop.

After distinguishing himself in supporting roles alongside half of young Hollywood in *Taps* (1981) and *The Outsiders* (1983), Cruise was offered the lead role in a film called *Risky Business*. At first, it appeared to be another movie about teenage hormones run amok. But writer/director Paul Brickman had devised a well-crafted, character-driven comedy that brought class and respectability to a genre unaccustomed to such treatment. Critics who walked in expecting another pathetic *Porky's* clone walked out comparing the film to *The Graduate*.

Set in an upscale suburb of Chicago, *Risky Business* is the story of 18-year-old Joel Goodsen, who is left alone by his parents for a weekend. Joel is a good boy, but is in desperate need to lose his virginity. He calls an escort service, and a beautiful working girl named Lana gives him a night he will never forget. But when the sun comes up she's still there, waiting for her $300 fee. Joel is late for school, and offers to let Lana stay in the house until he can raise some cash. When he returns, Lana has disappeared along with a valuable crystal sculpture that used to be on the living room mantel. Joel tries to track Lana down, which leads to a variety of complications including the driving of his father's Porsche into Lake Michigan, and the conversion of the Goodsen home into a brothel. Somehow the house is put back in order and the Porsche is repaired before mom and dad return.

Prior to *Risky Business* Cruise had played rebels of varying intensity, from the psychotic military student in *Taps* to the troubled leather-jacketed hood in *The Outsiders*. *Risky Business* became the first film to present what has become the predominant Cruise persona on screen -- a stalwart good guy, virtuous and resourceful, but with a mischievous streak that always leads to trouble (*Top Gun*--1986, *Days of Thunder*--1990, *A Few Good Men* --1992).

Paul Brickman's perceptive script and sure-handed direction, plus the most engaging of foils in Rebecca De Mornay (Lana) gave Tom Cruise everything he needed to prove his ability, but *Risky Business* contained an added bonus--a star-making moment so instantly engaging that 40 years from now it will be the first film clip played at his life-achievement award ceremony; dressed in a pink shirt and white underpants, Joel dances joyfully through his living room, lip-synching to Bob Seger's "Old Time Rock and Roll." We know as we watch him play air guitar and jump around on the couch that it's probably the most reckless thing that Joel Goodsen ("good son") has ever done. It's one of the most charmingly innocent attempts at decadance ever conceived.

ENDLESS LOVE
Directed by Franco Zeffirelli; Written by Judith Rascoe, based on the novel by Scott Spencer; Produced by Dyson Lovell; Music by Jonathan Tunick

Cast
Brooke Shields (Jade), Martin Hewitt (David), Shirley Knight (Anne), Don Murray (Hugh), Richard Kiley (Arthur), Beatrice Straight (Rose)...TOM CRUISE (BILLY)

RISKY BUSINESS
Directed and written by Paul Brickman; Produced by Jon Avnet; Music by Tangerine Dream

Cast
TOM CRUISE (JOEL), Rebecca De Mornay (Lana), Joe Pantollano (Guido), Richard Masur (Rutherford), Bronson Pinchot (Barry), Curtis Armstrong (Miles)

LINDA DARNELL (1923-1965)

FIRST APPEARANCE: *Hotel For Women* (20th Century-Fox, 1939)

A STAR IS BORN: *The Mark of Zorro* (20th Century-Fox, 1940)

Of all the screen goddesses who adorned costume dramas in the 1940s, Linda Darnell generally gets the least amount of credit for her acting ability. Her performances in *A Letter to Three Wives* (1949) and *No Way Out* (1950) provide evidence to the contrary, but for most of her career 20th Century-Fox was content to limit her roles to set decoration, and Darnell sufficiently met the minimal requirements of her casting.

"I had no great talent, and I never wanted to be a movie star," Darnell confessed, "but my mother had always wanted it for herself, and I guess she projected through me. I was going to become a star or mom was going to bust in the attempt." Linda, born Monetta Eloyse Darnell in Dallas, Texas, was taking tap dance lessons and entering talent contests before she started kindergarten. At the age of eleven she was able to pass for sixteen, and was hired to model clothes at a local department store. When she was fourteen, her mother sent photographs of Linda to a 20th Century-Fox talent scout, claiming that her daughter was eighteen. Two years later, Fox sent her an invitation to Hollywood.

Darnell arrived at the studio in the spring of 1939, where she received a seven-year, $75-a-week contract and a new first name. After three weeks of formal acting lessons, she was cast in *Hotel For Women*, a project especially designed to showcase the studio's up-and-coming players. Ann Sothern, the only "name" in the cast, is top-billed, but Darnell has the lead role of Marcia Bromley, a naive Syracuse lass who moves to New York City to marry her childhood sweetheart. She checks into the Hotel Sherrington, the headquarters for attractive girls on the prowl for rich husbands.

Of course, it is Marcia who is discovered and skyrocketed into sudden fame as the "Cambridge cigarette girl." She is wined and dined by a succession of millionaires on the make, including her boyfriend's father, but Marcia, like all movie Cinderellas, knows when it's time to leave the ball and settle down with the right Prince Charming.

Hotel For Women was based on the real-life recollections of socialite Elsa Maxwell, who cowrote the story. Reviewers scoffed at the "expose'" aspirations of the script, concluding that nothing had been added to the pitfalls awaiting sweet young things on reaching the big town that has not been told over and over again on the screen. Sixteen-year-old Linda Darnell was lauded as a beautiful newcomer, though the *New York Times* could not resist observing that "she will probably not be challenging Miss Bette Davis's academy title for quite a few years."

The studio didn't much care that Darnell won praise only for her beauty and voluptuous figure; any publicity was considered an endorsement, so she remained at the top of Fox's starlet depth chart, and was cast opposite Tyrone Power in *Daytime Wife* (1939). Her next film, *Star Dust* (1940), was cowritten by the talent scout who discovered her, and was based on Linda's own emergence into the Hollywood galaxy.

She was arguably already a star, but any lingering doubt was removed after her next film, *The Mark of Zorro.* Although Darnell was not markedly better, and her role as Lolita Quintero was actually smaller than those she had already played, the film was by far her most prestigious, and one of Fox's biggest box-office hits of 1940.

The Mark of Zorro is that rarest of remakes that actually equals the quality of its classic predecessor. Tyrone Power played the role immortalized by Douglas Fairbanks in the 1920 version, and with this one performance he pulled into contention with Errol Flynn for the title of Hollywood's premier swashbuckler. The story was transferred from the Fairbanks version intact-- the foppish Don Diego (Power) returns to California, then ruled by the corrupt Don Luis Quintero. He becomes a symbol of the resistance as Zorro, while playing the fool by day. Darnell plays Quintero's niece, who is promised to Diego but in love with the dashing Zorro. She never suspects, of course, that her betrothed is actually the hero of her dreams.

For Tyrone Power, *The Mark of Zorro* became the first in a series of successful swashbucklers, including *The Black Swan* (1942) and *Captain from Castille* (1947). For Linda Darnell, it was proof that she could wear glamorous costumes gracefully, and that no close-up could find a flaw in her alabaster complexion. Under the always expert direction of Rouben Mamoulian, she capably handles the light comedic moments of romantic sparring with Power, and musters suitable outrage at learning what her family has been doing to the locals. But the role is blandly written and, through no fault of her own, Darnell emerges as the least interesting presence in the picture. Better parts lay ahead, beginning in 1946 with *My Darling Clementine* and culminating in *Forever Amber* (1947). The switch from shrinking violets to assertive vixens allowed Linda Darnell to play off her beauty as a means to an end, and not just an end in itself.

HOTEL FOR WOMEN
Directed by Gregory Ratoff; Written by Kathryn Scola and Darrell Ware, based on a story by Scola and Elsa Maxwell; Produced by Darryl F. Zanuck; Music by Elsa Maxwell

Cast
Ann Sothern (Eileen Connelly), LINDA DARNELL (MARCIA BROMLEY), James Ellison (Jeff Buchanan), Jean Rogers (Nancy Prescott), Lynn Bari (Barbara Hunter), June Gale (Joan Mitchell), Elsa Maxwell (Mrs. Tilford)

THE MARK OF ZORRO
Directed by Rouben Mamoulian; Written by John Tainton Foote, Garrett Fort and Bess Meredyth, based on the novel *The Curse of Capistrano* by Johnston McCulley; Produced by Raymond Griffith; Music by Alfred Newman

Cast
Tyrone Power (Don Diego Vega/Zorro), LINDA DARNELL (LOLITA QUINTERO) Basil Rathbone (Captain Esteban Pasquale), Gale Sondergaard (Inez Quintero), Eugene Pallette (Fra Felipe), J. Edward Bromberg (Don Luis Quintero)

BETTE DAVIS (1908-1989)

FIRST APPEARANCE: *Bad Sister* (Universal, 1931)

A STAR IS BORN: *Of Human Bondage* (RKO, 1934)

The battles waged by Bette Davis against the studio system were heroic, and the victories she achieved have immeasurably improved the actor's lot in Hollywood. However, when examining the rich body of work we now have from one of the movies' most dynamic actresses, one can't help but be selfishly glad that the system was in place for most of her early career. Because Davis began a new project just weeks after her last one was finished, she completed an astonishing 41 films in the 1930s alone. Which, among such treasures as *Dangerous* (1935), *Jezebel* (1938), and *Dark Victory* (1939), would no longer exist had Davis won her battle right away?

The conflict between traditional procedure and revolutionary change, engaged by Bette in her career, was first brought to her attention as a young girl growing up in Lowell, Massachusetts. Bette's father, Harlow Davis, was a strict disciplinarian, whose Victorian approach to child rearing was not given to open displays of affection. Her mother, Ruthie Fervor Davis, was a painter, photographer and public speaker who dismissed the restrictions placed on her sex by polite society. Their divorce in 1918 surprised no one who knew the family.

Bette and her sister Bobby lived with their mother, moving frequently and taking jobs after school to supplement Harlow's alimony payments. Bette's desire for a theatrical career began in her early teens, after she attended a performance of Ibsen's *The Wild Duck*. At the Mariarden Dance School in New Hampshire, she made her stage debut as a dancing fairy in *A Midsummer Night's Dream*. Bette's mother encouraged her daughter's aspirations, and in 1929 Bette made her New York stage debut in *The Earth Between*.

In early 1930, Davis agreed to a screen test for Samuel Goldwyn, though she had little interest in motion pictures. The test was a failure, and Bette gladly returned to the stage. But when her next play, *Solid South*, closed after just 31 performances, she accepted a second screen-test offer, this time from Universal. A few days later, Bette was under contract, and on her way to California to play the lead in the comedy *Strictly Dishonorable*, based on a play by Preston Sturges. She would not appear on Broadway again for twenty years.

Her first days in Hollywood were not pleasant--Bette fought hard to reject a name change to Bettina Dawes, which she thought sounded like "Between the Drawers," and then she was rejected for the role that brought her under contract. Universal chief Carl Laemmle deemed her "not sexy enough" for *Strictly Dishonorable*, and she was cast instead as the good girl in a bad movie entitled *Bad Sister*.

Acutally, neither of the two sisters in the film are all that bad, but one, Marianne Madison, is temporarily blinded by her love for a con man named Corliss (Humphrey Bogart). Marianne helps Corliss obtain a letter of endorsement with her rich father's signature, which is then used to bilk local merchants out of a fortune. They leave town together, but Corliss quickly dumps Marianne in a seedy motel and takes off with the money. She returns home, thoroughly ashamed, and finds true love with a wealthy man-about-town (Bert Roach).

As Marianne's sister Laura, Bette Davis has the lesser role and is called upon to do little more than convey her love for the handsome physician Dick Lindley (Conrad Nagel), who loves her sister but later changes his mind. *Bad Sister* has a terrific cast and more story than one would expect to fit into a 68-minute running time, but for all its passions restrained and expressed, there's never any real fire. Bette plays a sweet, simple girl, plainly dressed, but the eyes that would later speak volumes in better films are not yet the windows of her character's soul. "Lugubrious" was the opinion of the *New York Times*, for both Bette and the film. If it shows up on the late show, however, try to catch the scene in which Laura changes the diaper of a baby girl. Unbeknownst to Bette, a baby boy was used in the scene, and when she removes the diaper her surprised reaction is very funny.

The role that launched Bette Davis, Mildred Rogers in the film adaptation of Somerset Maugham's *Of Human Bondage*, is as far from Laura Madison as can be imagined. She made seventeen films between her debut and her starmaker, among them such minor gems as *The Man Who Played God* (1932) and *Three on a Match* (1932), but Davis's searing portrayal of a manipulative and cruel hash-slinging waitress was still seen as a revelation from a proficient but unremarkable contract player.

Englishman Philip Carey (Leslie Howard), a Paris art student turned London medical student, meets Mildred at the restaurant where she works, and is inexplicably intrigued by her odd beauty and guttural manner. She tolerates his attentions, but shows no outward sign that his affection is mutual. Indeed, after he chides her for dating someone else, and vows never to see her again, Mildred snaps, "Good riddance to bad rubbish!" and walks away without a backward glance.

Philip, however, cannot stay away, even after his obsession causes him to fail his medical exams, even after Mildred marries for money, and after he is offered love from another woman with a kinder heart and gentler nature. So when Mildred's husband leaves her broke and pregnant, and she shows up on Philip's doorstep, he once again falls under her spell, only to be used and discarded.

Bette Davis only got the role after RKO's leading ladies wanted no part of such a scheming, vicious character. Davis was undaunted by concerns over her Hollywood persona or typecasting, and attacked the role with unbridled intensity. Even in those rare moments when Mildred attempts to be obeisant, her speech is rapid, brittle, angry. Late in the film, when Philip refuses to be dragged into Mildred's web a third time, her ferocious response became the first great Bette Davis moment; "You cad! You dirty swine!" she screams at Howard, who played the soul tortured by romance as well as anyone, "It made me sick when I had to let you kiss me. I only did it because you begged me...and after you kissed me, I used to wipe my mouth! *Wipe my mouth!*"

Virtue is rewarded in Maugham's story--Philip recovers from his obsession and meets a woman worthy of his love, while Mildred suffers an appropriately grisly end. Hollywood doesn't work the same way--Bette Davis did not receive an Academy Award nomination after *Of Human Bondage* was released to unanimous raves. "My failure created a scandal that gave me more publicity than if I had won it," said Davis later. Her victory the following year for *Dangerous* (1935) was widely perceived as a face-saving correction for the oversight.

BAD SISTER
Directed by Hobart Henley; Written by Raymond L. Schrock, Tom Reed and Edwin Knopf, based on the novel *The Flirt* by Booth Tarkington; Produced by Carl Laemmle, Jr.

Cast
Conrad Nagel (Dick Lindley), Sidney Fox (Marianne), BETTE DAVIS (LAURA), ZaSu Pitts (Minnie), Humphrey Bogart (Corliss), Bert Roach (Wade Trumbull)

OF HUMAN BONDAGE
Directed by John Cromwell; Written by Lester Cohen, based on the novel by W. Somerset Maugham; Produced by Pandro S. Berman; Music by Max Steiner

Cast
Leslie Howard (Philip Carey), BETTE DAVIS (MILDRED ROGERS), Frances Dee (Sally Athelny), Reginald Owen (Thorpe Athelny), Kay Johnson (Norah), Reginald Denny (Harry Griffiths)

DORIS DAY (1924-   )

FIRST APPEARANCE: *Romance on the High Seas* (Warner Bros., 1948)

A STAR IS BORN: *Romance on the High Seas*

Her name doesn't spring to mind when lists of great movie musical stars are compiled; likewise she is seldom mentioned among the great light comediennes. Doris Day, who remained among the top two or three American box-office attractions for most of her career, is underappreciated now, but through the efforts of such longtime fans as critic Roger Ebert, her reputation as one of the best-loved and most genuinely talented actresses of the fifties and sixties is gradually being restored.

Part of the problem, certainly, is the absence of a defining role among the thirty-nine she played, and the less then stellar material in which she was cast. But if her filmography is short on classics it is long on cheerful musicals and romantic comedies that are sustained by Day's spirit and charm. She was equally adept in more serious roles, as in *The Man Who Knew Too Much* (1956) and *Midnight Lace* (1960), but it was her moments at the microphone, when her warm, tender voice caressed a ballad with a purity unmatched by any singer in the musical's Golden Age, that are most indelible.

Doris von Kappelhoff was born in Cincinnati, Ohio. She was named after actress Doris Kenyon by her mother, Alma Sophia. Her father Frederick was a church organist, choir master, violin teacher, and clearly the source of Doris's musical gifts. After her parents separated in 1936, Doris moved with her mother and brother to Evanston, Illinois.

From the age of four, when she sang "I's Gwine Down to the Cushville Hop" in a Cincinnati Masonic hall, Doris dreamed of a career in show business. In Evanston she studied dance and won a tap contest with a partner named Jerry Doherty. As Doherty & Kappelhoff they earned other dates and joined a touring company and seemed on their way until Doris's right leg was crushed in an automobile accident. Confined to hospitals for fourteen months, Doris began singing through her rehabilitation, and landed a job on the radio show *Karlin's Karnival*. Barney Rapp, a band leader and nightclub owner, heard her rendition of "Day After Day" and offered her a club date at $25 a week. He also advised a name change, so Kappelhoff was replaced by Day, from the song that launched her career. "I'm glad you didn't catch me singing the *Gotterdammerung*," she told Rapp.

Doris Day toured throughout the 1940s with the bands of Bob Crosby, Fred Waring and Les Brown. But it was her performance of "Embraceable You" at a Hollywood party that caught the attention of composer Jule Styne. The movie *Romance On the High Seas*, score by Styne and Sammy Cahn, was in jeopardy after its star Judy Garland dropped out and replacement Betty Hutton became pregnant. Styne suggested to director Michael Curtiz that he interview Doris for the role. Curtiz arranged a screen test and was impressed enough to cast the first-time actress in the film's most prominent role.

Romance On the High Seas is a pretty dumb movie about a married couple whose mutual mistrust sets the stage for a succession of silly misunderstandings and mistaken identities. Elvira Kent (Janis Paige) suspects her husband Michael (Don DeFore) of having an affair with his secretary. She pretends to leave for a South American cruise, but sends nightclub singer Georgia Garrett (Doris Day) in her place so she can spy on her mate. Michael, meanwhile, isn't crazy about the idea of his wife cruising alone, and hires detective Peter Virgil (Jack Carson) to follow her. Of course, Peter ends up following Georgia, and they fall in love. Ninety-nine minutes later explanations are made and two happy couples embrace before the fadeout.

Although fourth-billed, Doris performs five songs, has over twice the screen time of leading lady Janis Paige, and clearly emerges as the picture's star. All of the reasons she was so beloved and busy in Hollywood are here; her natural acting instincts and timing with a comic line, her wholesome good looks and radiant smile, and her easygoing personality--more down home than uptown, though her attempts to act posh on the cruise are the only funny moments in the movie. Jack Carson is an engaging foil, Oscar Levant turns up as a cynical piano player (no kidding), and the others supply what's needed to keep the gossamer plot moving.

Busby Berkeley is credited with choreographing the musical numbers, but don't expect a lot of geometric figures formed by the feathered legs of a hundred chorus girls. The Styne-Cahn score is comprised of six clinkers and one gorgeous, Oscar-nominated gem. "It's Magic" became one of Doris's signature songs, a multi-million seller and the movie's only highlight. "No one who has seen it can ever remember the cast or the plot of *Romance On the High Seas*," wrote George Walsh in an essay on Doris, "yet, equally, no one can ever forget the moment when Doris Day first sings 'It's Magic.' Her rendition of it transforms the movie. To think of a comparable moment in other musicals one has to think of Judy Garland--"The Boy Next Door' from *Meet Me in St. Louis* or 'The Man That Got Away' in *A Star is Born.*

Romance set the pattern for "happy pictures about happy people," which Doris said is what the public wanted and what she spent most of her career providing. Honky tonk singer Georgia Garrett is a saucier character than the bright, optimistic all-American girl she would come to personify in *On Moonlight Bay* (1951) and so many others, but even when she's winking at sailors the effect is more sweet than seductive. "Doris Day was one of the most popular stars the cinema has produced," George Walsh wrote, "because of her very real acting skill, her versatility, and her ability to synthesize for millions of people a particular kind of dream."

ROMANCE ON THE HIGH SEAS

Directed by Michael Curtiz; Written by Julius J. Epstein, Philip G. Epstein and I.A.L. Diamond, based on a story by S. Pondal Rios and Carlos A. Olivari; Produced by Alex Gottlieb; Music by Sammy Cahn, Jule Styne, Ray Heindorf and Oscar Levant

Cast
Jack Carson (Peter Virgil), Janis Paige (Elvira Kent), Don DeFore (Michael Kent), DORIS DAY (GEORGIA GARRETT), Oscar Levant (Oscar Farrar)

JAMES DEAN (1931-1955)

FIRST APPEARANCE: *Fixed Bayonets* (20th Century-Fox, 1951)

A STAR IS BORN: *East of Eden* (Warner Bros., 1955)

No one in the century-old history of motion pictures left us with more unfinished business than James Dean. However dubiously one might view the ghoulish Dean death cult, or the cynical marketing of the actor as an icon of adolescent angst, it is undeniable that there was, in his all too brief career, something genuine to get excited about.

James Byron Dean was born in Marion, Indiana, and lived in the nearby town of Fairmount for the next four years. In 1935 he moved with his family to Santa Monica, California, after his father's job was transferred. The loss of his mother, Mildred, when Jimmy was nine years old, was a tragedy from which he never fully recovered. He returned to Fairmount, at his father's insistence, to live with an aunt and uncle. In 1949, Dean graduated from Fairmount High School and moved back to Los Angeles, hoping to become an actor. He attended UCLA for awhile, and made his dramatic television debut in 1951. As a favor to his agent, Rogers Brackett, director Samuel Fuller agreed to give Dean a small part in his next film, *Fixed Bayonets*.

The film is set during the Korean War; a U.S. Army regiment, stationed on a remote mountaintop, is ordered to begin a strategic retreat. A small rear guard, under the command of Lt. Gibbs (Craig Hill) is left behind to hold the line. Gibbs is killed in battle, as are the next two officers in the chain of command. Corporal Denno (Richard Basehart), a quiet, sensitive soldier who has never fired his rifle in combat, is next in line. Fighting self-doubt and the incredulity of his men, Denno successfully completes the mission.

Fixed Bayonets is indeed James Dean's film debut, but his appearance is so brief that one almost has to take the reference books' word for it. Even the most dedicated Dean fan will have difficulty spotting him in a cast of identically-clad extras, whose mud and snow-covered features are further obscured by helmets and hooded jackets. At one point during production, Dean was given the line "It's a rear guard coming back," which would have simplified the search, but the line was cut before the film was released. However, it does provide a clue as to when he makes his appearance. Near the end of the film, the surviving members of Denno's platoon rejoin the regiment, and parade single-file through the center of the frame. James Dean is seventh in this solemn parade. His head bowed, his eyes blank, he is there and gone in less than five seconds.

There are some exciting moments in *Fixed Bayonets*, but the tension is undercut by long, dull stretches and performances that vary from credible to superficial. All of the action is studio-bound, but director Fuller and cinematographer Lucien Ballard accomplish wonders with indoor sets.

Dean was given bit parts in two more films, *Sailor Beware* (1951) and *Has Anybody Seen My Gal?* (1952), but found more success in numerous television anthology series and on the Broadway stage, where he played Louis Jourdan's homosexual houseboy in *The Immoralist* (1954). Paul Osborn, who was then working on the screenplay for *East of Eden*, saw Dean in the play and brought him to the attention of director Elia Kazan. He was deemed perfect for the role of Cal Trask, by both Kazan and *East of Eden* author John Steinbeck.

The film covered only the last one-fourth of the novel, which focused on the relationship between Adam Trask (Raymond Massey) and his two sons, Aron (Richard Davalos) and Cal. Cal, a distant, moody teenager, discovers that his mother (Jo Van Fleet), whom Adam had insisted was dead, is actually alive and running a brothel. With her help, he recoups all the money his father lost in a failed business venture. Despite his often churlish behavior, Cal yearns for his father's approval, and for the same affection he sees lavished on his straight-arrow brother. But when Cal gives the money to his father as a birthday present, his offering is rejected. Shattered, he lashes out at his brother, by revealing the secret about their mother.

When Dean first showed up on the Warner Bros. lot, the film crew thought he was a stand-in for the real star. But before the film premiered, industry screenings had produced a powerful buzz about James Dean. Reviews compared him to Marlon Brando, sometimes unfavorably, but most agreed that Kazan had discovered a remarkable new star. The *Hollywood Reporter* critic was especially prophetic in his praise; "He is that rare thing, a young actor who is a great actor, and the troubled eloquence with which he puts over the problems of misunderstood youth may lead to his being accepted by young audiences as a sort of symbol of their generation."

Rebel Without a Cause might be Dean's signature role, but his best motion picture performance can be found in *East of Eden.* Some credit for this belongs to Elia Kazan, who knew exactly how to motivate, and sometimes manipulate, the naturally gifted but still undisciplined actor. In the scene when Cal vents his rage in his father's ice house by hurling blocks of ice down a chute, Dean was unable to lift the blocks until Kazan made a derogatory remark about his acting. Later, after Dean sounded unconvincing in the scene when Cal speaks to Aron's girlfriend, Abra (Julie Harris), through her bedroom window, Kazan got him drunk on Chianti, and that did the trick.

The similarities between Dean's upbringing and that of Cal are obvious, and cannot be ignored in assessing his performance. The loss of a mother at an early age, and the search to fill the void left by her absence, was an emotional button that Kazan did not need to push. "Talk to me, father!" Cal pleads early in the film, "I gotta know who I am! I gotta know what I'm like!" Dean's searing portrayal in this scene, and his raw, primal moan after Cal is rebuffed by his father at the birthday party, have resonated with alienated teenagers ever since.

FIXED BAYONETS
Directed and written by Samuel Fuller; Produced by Jules Buck; Music by Roy Webb

Cast
Richard Basehart (Cpl. Denno), Gene Evans (Sgt. Rock), Michael O'Shea (Sgt. Lonergan), Richard Hylton (Wheeler), Craig Hill (Lt. Gibbs)..JAMES DEAN (G.I.)

EAST OF EDEN
Directed and produced by Elia Kazan; Written by Paul Osborn, based on the novel by John Steinbeck; Music by Leonard Rosenman

Cast
Julie Harris (Abra), JAMES DEAN (CAL TRASK), Raymond Massey (Adam Trask), Richard Davalos (Aron Trask), Burl Ives (Sam), Jo Van Fleet (Kate)

OLIVIA DE HAVILLAND (1916-   )

FIRST APPEARANCE: *Alibi Ike* (Warner Bros., 1935)

A STAR IS BORN: *Captain Blood* (Warner Bros., 1935)

The path to stardom was not long or arduous for Olivia de Havilland; a confident Warner Bros. introduced her to the public in a series of leading roles, and after *A Midsummer Night's Dream* (1935) no one questioned her right to be there. What followed was a distinguished, scandal-free career reknowned for reliable performances of ladylike refinement.

Olivia and her sister Joan (actress Joan Fontaine) were born in Tokyo, Japan of British parents. The blueblooded de Havilland ancestry dates back to the twelfth century, and accounts for the patrician qualities that were observable in both sisters. Their father Walter Augustus de Havilland was a Cambridge-educated English professor. Their mother, Lillian, had studied at London's Royal Academy of Dramatic Art, and encouraged her daughters' interest in the theater. Lillian wanted the girls to be raised in England, and when Walter refused he divorced her and married his Japanese housekeeper. The de Havilland women ended up settling in the village of Saratoga, about fifty miles south of San Francisco, California.

A fondness for "let's pretend" in grammar school was the first sign that Olivia might pursue an acting career. After graduating from high school, she was offered the role of Puck in the Saratoga Community Theatre production of *A Midsummer Night's Dream*. That same summer, the Austrian director Max Reinhardt was in California to launch a version of the same play at the Hollywood Bowl. Reinhardt's assistant was invited to attend the Community Theatre production, and was impressed enough by Olivia to suggest that she audition for Reinhardt. Olivia was hired to understudy actress Jean Rouverol in the role of Hermia, but when Rouverol dropped out to accept a movie offer, Olivia was given the part.

She earned favorable reviews, and remained with the play throughout its national tour. When Warner Bros. offered Reinhardt the chance to adapt his production for the screen, he talked Olivia into postponing her plans to attend college so she could make the film. The studio insisted on signing the attractive eighteen-year-old actress to a long-term contract, and Olivia reluctantly agreed. She thoroughly enjoyed the filmmaking experience, but was not as pleased when she was ordered immediately into a second project of a considerably lesser pedigree.

A Midsummer Night's Dream was released in November of 1945 after a sufficient period of advance publicity. *Alibi Ike*, her second film, did not require the same special handling; Warners knew the film had little chance of scoring beyond the small but loyal following of its star, comedian Joe E. Brown, so Olivia's sophomore effort was tossed into theaters in July, a couple of weeks after it was finished.

Brown plays the title character, a simple-minded farm boy with extraordinary baseball skills. His offbeat world-view tries the patience of his manager, but attracts the eye of Dolly Stevens, the team owner's wife's sister. Ike is kidnapped by racketeers who have placed a big bet on the other team, but he escapes in time to win the big game and escort Dolly down the aisle.

Alibi Ike is typical of the two or three low-rent offerings that Joe E. Brown made for Warners' 'B' unit throughout the 1930s. Brown's genial jerk persona, a story from Screenwriting 101 and a few recycled silent film bits were all the ingredients necessary for a modest moneymaker. If this one rates a half-star higher in some movie guides, it is due to the reliable support of talented journeymen like Roscoe Karns and William Frawley, and the debut of a pretty young actress who was just passing through the programmer ranks.

Olivia de Havilland is first seen about twelve minutes into the film; she is seated in the stands, watching Ike mow down the visitors with his wacky pitching style. Why this sweet, fresh-faced eighteen-year-old would pursue a romance with a clownish, middle-aged dimwit ballplayer is a valid question that the script cannot answer, but if one makes allowances there is a certain awkward charm to their relationship. If Olivia was disappointed at being pushed into a role that only required her to look pretty and demure, her sentiments are not discernible.

After *A Midsummer Night's Dream* elevated her into the "faces to watch" category, de Havilland appeared opposite James Cagney in *The Irish In Us* (1935), and then was cast in *Captain Blood*. The film is now remembered as the star-making vehicle of Errol Flynn, and is reviewed in the Flynn chapter. *Captain Blood* became one of Warners' biggest 1935 grossers, and Flynn's zestful performance in the title role transformed him into Hollywood's preeminent swashbuckler. But the film was also de Havilland's breakthrough, and the first of six films in which she would capture Flynn's heart.

Too often, de Havilland's crowdpleasing team-ups with Errol Flynn are dismissed as less important than her Oscar-winning dramatic performances as a plain, timid spinster in *To Each His Own* (1947) and *The Heiress* (1949). But as the feisty Arabella Bishop in *Captain Blood*, de Havilland does far more than lend adoring support to the hero. Here, as in *The Adventures of Robin Hood* (1938) and *Dodge City* (1939), she plays strong, self-assured women who play the dominant role in their romantic relationships. Whether it was seventeenth-century Jamaica, England in the middle ages or the American old west, de Havilland seemed at home in any historical period. In 1939 she would add the Civil War south to her time travels in *Gone With the Wind*, but the landmark status of that film aside, I like her much better in *Captain Blood*. It's the first evidence of her ability to bring a level of class to westerns and action films that is not only gone now, it is no longer even attempted.

ALIBI IKE
Directed by Ray Enright; Written by William Wister, based on a story by Ring Lardner; Produced by Edward Chodorov; Music by Leo F. Forbstein

Cast
Joe E. Brown (Frank X. Farrell), OLIVIA DE HAVILLAND (DOLLY STEVENS), Roscoe Karns (Cary), William Frawley (Cap), Joseph King (Owner), Ruth Donnelly (Bess)

CAPTAIN BLOOD
Directed by Michael Curtiz; Written by Casey Robinson, based on the novel by Rafael Sabatini; Produced by Hal B. Wallis; Music by Erich Wolfgang Korngold

Cast
Errol Flynn (Dr. Peter Blood), OLIVIA DE HAVILLAND (ARABELLA BISHOP), Lionel Atwill (Col. Bishop), Basil Rathbone (Captain Levasseur), Ross Alexander (Jeremy Pitt), Guy Kibbee (Hagthorpe)

ROBERT DE NIRO (1943-   )

FIRST APPEARANCE: *The Wedding Party* (Ajay, 1969)

A STAR IS BORN: *The Godfather, Part II* (Paramount, 1974)

Robert De Niro is the consummate "Method" actor. Unfazed by stardom and uninterested in the demands of celebrity, he cares only about achieving total immersion of his own personality within a performance. Through exhaustive preparation and sometimes startling manipulation of his physical appearance, De Niro becomes lost so completely in his characters that it took longer than it should have for anyone to notice the actor inside the role.

He was born in New York City and raised, after his parents' divorce, in the Lower East Side section of the city known as "Little Italy." The neighborhood would prove an ideal training ground for the roles he played for Martin Scorsese in *Mean Streets* (1973) and *Goodfellas* (1990). At the age of ten he enrolled in Saturday morning acting classes at Manhattan's New School for Social Research, but his interest soon waned, as it did for any type of formal education.

De Niro's life changed when he began attending classes taught by famed acting coach Stella Adler. After years of workshop presentations and Off Off Broadway productions, he met film studies graduate student Brian de Palma. De Niro accepted a supporting role in a student project at Sarah Lawrence College, produced, directed and written by De Palma and starring fellow student Jill Clayburgh. Production began on *The Wedding Party* in 1963, and was not completed until 1967. Two years later, the film was released in a handful of theaters to disastrous reviews.

The story centers on the upcoming nuptials of wealthy WASP socialite Josephine Fish (Jill Clayburgh) and her working-class fiance` Charlie (Charles Pfluger). Two days before the marriage, the couple and their family and friends gather at the posh estate of Josephine's parents, where Charlie starts having second thoughts. After trying unsuccessfully to find a polite escape, he runs out of the house, but is dragged back in time for the ceremony.

The grainy black and white photography and choppy editing tries to pass for we-meant-to-do-that effect, but ends up just looking cheap. It would have been as anonymous today as almost every student film, but *The Wedding Party* lucked into a reputation by containing the debuts of both Robert De Niro (billed as "Denero") and Jill Clayburgh, and by being an early credit for director Brian de Palma, who at this point was influenced more by *Laugh-In* than Alfred Hitchcock. *Laugh-In* was more coherent, however, than this loosely scripted, uninvolving muddle.

De Niro plays Cecil, an antisocial lout and friend of the groom, who first tries to talk Charlie out of getting married, and then changes his mind just when Charlie is ready to back out. Sporting a buzz cut and a cheap suit, he makes the most of his featured supporting role. All the performances are fine, in fact, it's the characters and the writing that are deficient. It's hard to judge anyone's ability in a vehicle this poor.

De Niro appeared in two more De Palma efforts, *Greetings* (1968) and *Hi, Mom!* (1970), and then played a psychotic killer for Roger Corman in *Bloody Mama* (1969). In his first major project, De Niro's portrayal of a dying baseball player in *Bang the Drum Slowly* (1973) brought critical raves.

It is tempting to select *Mean Streets* as De Niro's career-making film; it was his first collaboration with Martin Scorsese, the director with whom he is now most closely associated, and his first on-screen exploration of his New York Italian-American roots. Critics adored *Mean Streets* and pegged both Scorsese and De Niro as important new talent, but the film's caustic mix of street language and violence kept the public away.

De Niro next went into *The Godfather, Part II*, and the difficult position of playing a character for which Marlon Brando had already earned an Academy Award. In Francis Ford

Coppola's hugely successful sequel to Oscar's Best Picture of 1972, flashbacks to the early years of Vito Corleone (De Niro) are intercut with the efforts of Michael Corleone (Al Pacino) to govern his father's criminal empire.

De Niro performs the entire role in Italian, which he delivered in the dialect he learned during a research trip to Sicily. He doesn't imitate Brando's interpretation, but in the occasional face-rubbing mannerism and the trace of rasp in his voice, he manages to suggest the character played by Brando, without appearing derivative. Throughout production, Coppola was urged to drop the flashbacks, which differ completely in content and tone from Michael's story, and interrupt the flow of the main narrative. When *Godfather, Part II* became the only sequel to ever win a Best Picture Academy Award, and De Niro was named Best Supporting Actor (the only time two actors earned Oscars for the same role), such concerns were forgotten, despite the fact that they were not without some validity.

THE WEDDING PARTY
Produced, directed and written by Brian De Palma, Cynthia Munroe and Wilford Leach; Music by John Herbert McDowell

Cast
Jill Clayburgh (Josephine Fish), Charles Pfluger (Charlie), Valda Setterfield (Mrs. Fish), Raymond McNally (Mr. Fish), Jennifer Salt (Phoebe), John Braswell (Rev. Oldfield), Judy Thomas (Celeste), Sue Ann Converse (Nanny), John Quinn (Baker), ROBERT DE NIRO (CECIL)

THE GODFATHER, PART II
Directed by Francis Ford Coppola; Written by Francis Ford Coppola and Mario Puzo; Produced by Francis Ford Coppola, Gary Frederickson and Fred Roos; Music by Nino Rota and Carmine Coppola

Cast
Al Pacino (Michael), Robert Duvall (Tom Hagen), Diane Keaton (Kay), ROBERT DE NIRO (VITO CORLEONE), Talia Shire (Connie), John Cazale (Fredo)

MARLENE DIETRICH (1901-1992)

FIRST APPEARANCE: *Der Kleine Napoleon* (Union-Film, 1923)

A STAR IS BORN: *The Blue Angel* (UFA-Film/Paramount, 1930)

No prototype existed for Marlene Dietrich's success. When she first captivated audiences in *The Blue Angel*, Dietrich was not a variation on any other popular actress; the way she prowled across a stage on the most famous legs in the world (pre-Betty Grable), the way she smoked a cigarette, the way she wore a man's tuxedo, flaunting her androgynous sex appeal, the way she sang, a husky moan that is so easily parodied and yet, in its original form, is so enticing; it all seemed so daring, even dangerous, and utterly original. Exactly what she had, though immediately apparent, is hard to define and impossible to imitate. Actresses of subsequent generations have been dubbed "the next Harlow," or "the next Marilyn," but another Dietrich has never been found.

Several Dietrich biographies have been written, all attempting to set straight records that have been skewered since Paramount sent out the first press release about their new discovery of 1930. Even the place of her birth is difficult to verify, though most sources have settled on Schoneberg, Germany as correct. Maria Magdalene Dietrich was the second daughter born to Louis Erich Otto Dietrich, an officer in the Royal Prussian Police, and his wife, Wilhelmina. Louis Dietrich died when Maria and her sister Elisabeth were still young, and Wilhelmina married another officer soon after.

It was Maria's stepfather, Edouard von Losch, who first noticed her musical talent. She began piano and violin lessons at an early age, and by 1921 had progressed enough to be accepted in Berlin's State musical academy. When her career as a concert violinist was ended by nerve damage in her wrist, Maria set her sights on acting. She received permission from her mother to audition for the great producer-director Max Reinhardt's theatre company, but only if she did not use the von Losch name. So it was Marlene Dietrich who auditioned for Reinhardt, and it was Marlene Dietrich who was turned down for her lack of experience.

After playing a chorus role in a traveling revue, Dietrich auditioned again for Reinhardt in the spring of 1922, and this time she was accepted. After appearing in just three Reinhardt productions, her movie career began with an offer from director Georg Jacoby. The film, released under the title *Der Kleine Napoleon* and several others, was a historical comedy about the amorous adventures of Napoleon Bonaparte's little brother.

Jerome Bonaparte (Paul Heidemann) is made King of the newly created country of Westphalia. While gathering beautiful women to fill his court, he notices Charlotte (Antonia Dietrich), the niece of his Police Minister. Charlotte marries Georg (Harry Liedtke), a courier who stays in Westphalia after he meets Charlotte, but Jerome does not give up easily. Georg is jailed, but eventually Napoleon appears to reunite the young lovers and chastise his brother.

Marlene Dietrich worked only a few days on her single-scene appearance as Kathrin, Charlotte's maid. The role consisted of aiding Charlotte in escaping Jerome by disguising herself as a peasant and fleeing her country retreat. She got the part on looks and, some sources claim, her flirting with director Jacoby, but Marlene was not impressed at all with her appearance when she first saw the film. "I look like a potato with hair!" she exclaimed. Copies of the film still exist, and only confirm Dietrich's assessment. The temptress of *The Blue Angel* is hard to find beneath Kathrin's ill-fitting servant's costume and starched linen bonnet.

She progressed into ingenue roles on the stage, played the occasional bit part on the screen, then took a year off after marrying Rudolf Sieber, a production assistant on one of her early films. When Dietrich returned to acting, she was forced to start over from the extra ranks. It was another Max Reinhardt production, the musical *Liegt in der Luft* (*It's In the Air*) (1928) that reignited her career. By 1929, when she starred in the play *Zwei Krawatten* (*Two Neckties*), she was well-known in Germany and Austria. Josef von Sternberg attended a performance, and arranged for Dietrich to audition for his next film, *The Blue Angel*. After an arduous session in which Dietrich sang in both English and German, she was given the pivotal role of Lola-Lola.

Lola-Lola is a dance hall girl, whose scandalous costumes and provocative performances are the only topic of conversation at the boys' high school. Dr. Immanuel Kath (Emil Jannings), the stern, middle-aged professor of English literature, becomes frustrated with his students' inattention, and pays a visit to the cabaret where Lola performs. Kath is stunned by her beauty and by her immodest changing of costumes while he stands in her dressing room. Lola effortlessly seduces the mild-mannered teacher, abides his affection for a time, and then discards him, after he has sacrificed his career and his reputation. Reduced to humiliating appearances as a clown in Lola's cabaret, he takes his own life.

Rightly hailed as "one of the most horrific studies of human degradation on filmic record" by the *Motion Picture Guide*, *The Blue Angel* is arguably one of the twenty greatest films ever made. No serious student of the cinema has not watched this extraordinary masterpiece at least twice. Although best-remembered now for Dietrich's overtly sexual--bordering on erotic--rendition of "Falling in Love Again," the film is anything but a musical. It is a dark story of obsession, a harrowing examination of Professor Kath's unstoppable self-destruction, all for the capricious attention of a woman whose sensuality is exhibited in every word and every movement. "I am Dr. Immanuel Kath, professor at the high school," he haughtily announces when first meeting Lola. "Then you should know enough to remove your hat," she replies, and already the battle he had prepared for is over, and he has lost.

Emil Jannings is unforgettable as the doomed professor, and Dietrich stopped the heartbeat of the world with her dazzling magnetism. Under von Sternberg's tutelage, she played the character like a force of nature, causing destruction without calculation or conscience. Everything you need to know about Marlene Dietrich is in *The Blue Angel*. The film not only made her a star, it also charted her course in Hollywood--variations on Lola-Lola make up a sizable percentage of her career.

DER KLEINE NAPOLEON
AKA So Sind die Manner, Napoleon's Kleiner Bruder
Directed by Georg Jacoby; Written by Georg Jacoby and Robert Liebmann

Cast
Egon Von Hagen (Napoleon), Paul Heidemann (Jerome Bonaparte), Harry Liedtke (Georg von Melsungen), Antonia Dietrich (Charlotte)...MARLENE DIETRICH (KATHRIN)

THE BLUE ANGEL
Directed by Josef von Sternberg; Written by Robert Liebmann; Produced by Erich Pommer; Music by Friedrich Hollander and Robert Liebmann

Cast
Emil Jannings (Professor Immanuel Rath), MARLENE DIETRICH (LOLA-LOLA), Kurt Gerron (Kiepert), Rosa Valetti (Guste)

KIRK DOUGLAS (1916-   )

FIRST APPEARANCE: *The Strange Love of Martha Ivers* (Paramount, 1946)

A STAR IS BORN: *Champion* (Screen Plays/United Artists, 1949)

Eyes fixed in an intense stare, a firmly-set chin stamped with its trademark cleft, a snarling voice that must force its way through clenched teeth, and a wiry body poised like a tightened spring. That's the way most fans remember Kirk Douglas, who established his place in the Hollywood firmament with characters of passionate temperament whose driven natures sometimes threatened their sanity. To say that he played Vincent van Gogh in *Lust for Life* (1956) in much the same way he played the title role in *Spartacus* (1960) is not a criticism but a compliment; Douglas was perceptive enough to detect the similariities between two seemingly disparate men who lived centuries apart. He chose his roles with comparable, consistent expertise throughout his five-decade career.

The only son among seven children, Kirk Douglas was born Issur Danielovitch in Amsterdam, New York. He worked a variety of jobs from his high school days, both to help his family and to earn money for college tuition. He acted in school plays, but his first exposure to real show business came during a class field trip to Albany, where Katharine Cornell was appearing in *The Barretts of Wimpole Street.* In 1935, under the name Isadore Demsky, he entered St. Lawrence College in Canton, New York. He was class president, president of the college dramatic group, and a star wrestler.

After graduating in 1939, Douglas studied for two years at the American Academy of Dramatic Arts, and appeared on Broadway in minor stage roles before enlisting in the Navy. Upon his discharge in 1944, he resumed his fledgling career on stage and in radio serial programs. A supporting performance in Broadway's *The Wind is Ninety* (1945) prompted the offer of a movie contract with Hal Wallis, along with a personal recommendation from his former Academy classmate, Lauren Bacall.

In *The Strange Love of Martha Ivers*, Douglas makes a most impressive debut among seasoned professionals and one beguiling scene-stealer. It's the story of a secret shared by two children in Iverstown; on a dark and stormy night, Martha Ivers kills her abusive aunt during a fit of rage. Walter O'Neil, a timid boy who witnesses the murder, supports Martha's claim that an intruder is to blame. Years later, Martha (Barbara Stanwyck) and Walter (Douglas) are married. It is made clear that Walter's proposal, though elicited by love, was delivered with the threat of exposure, and that she accepted only to keep her secret safe. Enter Sam Masterson (Van Heflin), Martha's old boyfriend, who was also in the Ivers mansion on the night of the crime. His return to Iverstown triggers a web of plots, counterplots and deception too complex to outline, culminating in a terrible, explosive climax.

The Strange Love of Martha Ivers is a superb gothic drama that packs more Grand Guignol into its first ten minutes than most films generate from start to finish. Barbara Stanwyck and Van Heflin are as good as it gets in this kind of material, but Lizabeth Scott walks off with the film as the unforgettable Toni Marachek, a hard-luck ex-con who falls for Sam.

Kirk Douglas holds his own with Stanwyck in one of her great tough girl roles, playing somewhat against the persona he would later develop. District Attorney Walter O'Neil is a bespectacled, henpecked alcoholic who remains tormented by the memory of his childhood lie, compounded by the fact that an innocent man was executed for the murder of Martha's aunt. The challenge for Douglas, who is naturally adept at acting tough, is in playing a character who must act tough at work, but who remains at heart the scared little kid he was all those years ago. At those moments when Walter's vulnerability surfaces, Douglas plays cowardice with the same riveting intensity that he brought to the brave and the bold.

He earned promising reviews, and began a string of memorable supporting appearances in such films as *Out of the Past* (1947) and *A Letter to Three Wives* (1949). The first starring role he was offered was that of Midge Kelly, a sadistic, ruthless boxer, in the gritty drama *Champion*. Playing such a compassionless character was something of a risk at that stage of his career, but Douglas threw himself into the part and earned an Academy Award nomination and his entree` into the ranks of leading men.

Kelly is a drifter with a grudge against the world that has beaten him down since childhood. He takes up boxing as a last resort, and becomes a champion by channeling all his bitterness into his upper cuts, and believing that every fight is a fight for respectability. But wealth and fame cannot remove the chip on Midge's shoulder. Corrupted by a woman (Marilyn Maxwell, as quintessential blond poison) and by the seedy elements of the sport, he remains a shallow, selfish, angry young man.

Boxing always seems to make a good movie subject, especially in black and white, which heightens the metaphors of the glaring lights and dark shadows. *Champion* was an obvious inspiration for *Raging Bull* (1980), and contains a musical training montage that predates *Rocky* (1976) by twenty-seven years. The script did not dilute the unsavoriness of the character or the fight game as created by Ring Lardner, Mark Robson's direction is fast-paced and supporting performances are top-notch. And any film about boxing with a technical advisor named Mushy Callahan must be authentic.

Anchoring the film is Kirk Douglas who, besides showing off his chiseled physique and athleticism, must play a boorish character who never changes, and make him not only interesting, but sympathetic. He pulls it off in the film's final scenes; Midge seems doomed to defeat in the climactic championship bout, but at the last possible minute he rises from the canvas and, possessed by a berserker rage, pummels his opponent into submission with a flurry of devastating blows. Then, in the locker room after the fight, Midge's fury refuses to subside and, defiant to the last, he collapses, dead, on the hard concrete floor. At that moment we cannot help but feel sorry for him because, no matter how many friends and relatives he had mistreated through the years, Midge's most tragic victim is himself.

THE STRANGE LOVE OF MARTHA IVERS
Directed by Lewis Milestone; Written by Robert Rossen, based on the story *Love Lies Bleeding* by John Patrick; Produced by Hal B. Wallis; Music by Mikos Rozsa

Cast
Barbara Stanwyck (Martha Ivers), Van Heflin (Sam Masterson), Lizabeth Scott (Toni Marachek), KIRK DOUGLAS (WALTER O'NEIL), Judith Anderson (Mrs. Ivers)

CHAMPION
Directed by Mark Robson; Written by Carl Foreman, based on the story by Ring Lardner; Produced by Stanley Kramer; Music by Dimitri Tiomkin

Cast
KIRK DOUGLAS (MIDGE KELLY), Marilyn Maxwell (Grace Diamond), Arthur Kennedy (Connie Kelly), Paul Stewart (Tommy Haley), Ruth Roman (Emma Bryce), Lola Albright (Mrs. Harris)

MICHAEL DOUGLAS (1944-   )

FIRST APPEARANCE: *Hail, Hero!* (Cinema Center/NGP, 1969)

A STAR IS BORN: *The China Syndrome* (Columbia, 1979)

Michael Douglas built a successful career on playing characters who were, in his own words, "generally humane, morally responsible guys." And then he wiped out his wholesome image with *Wall Street* (1987), *Fatal Attraction* (1987) and *Falling Down* (1993). Hindsight now suggests that Douglas played all the nice guy roles early on only because they were the best of what was offered. Since *Wall Street* he now explores his darker side as often as he exposed his backside in *Basic Instinct* (1992). If there is a theme to Douglas's seasoned work, which began with *The China Syndrome*, it is a tendency toward films that reflect current events and public concerns.

He was born in New Brunswick, New Jersey, the eldest of two sons born to Kirk and Diana Douglas. The family moved to Hollywood soon after, but when Kirk's acting career took off and Diana's didn't, the resulting tension led to a divorce in 1950. Michael remained with his mother and grew up primarily in Westport, Connecticut. Although he was an indifferent student, Douglas completed his secondary education at Wallingford's prestigious Choate School. He was accepted by Yale but opted instead for the University of California at Santa Barbara, where he promptly flunked out in his freshman year. He was later readmitted, and after changing his major to drama he became a more dedicated student.

Douglas appeared in numerous campus productions, received his B.A. in 1968 and moved to New York to continue his theatrical education. He studied with Sanford Meisner at the Neighborhood Playhouse, and received good reviews for his television debut in a 1969 *CBS Playhouse* production entitled *The Experiment*. The role led to an offer to appear in *Hail, Hero!*, the first feature film from CBS's newly-organized Cinema Center production company.

Based on the novel by John Weston, *Hail, Hero!* is a sincere but very talky generation gap drama. Idealistic college student Carl Dixon (Douglas) decides to leave school and "love the enemy" into submission in Vietnam. He goes home first to tell his right wing, super-patriotic family of his plan. Carl, his intolerant father (Arthur Kennedy) and his self-possessed mother (Teresa Wright) are caricatures more than characters. The best performance belongs to Peter Strauss, also in his film debut, as the chip-off-the-old-block son who eventually grows to understand brother Carl's convictions. The very first scene, in which Douglas performs some matador shtick with a truck full of Mexican ranchhands, is a good litmus test for the entire film; if you find it charming, you'll probably enjoy what follows. if you find it stupid, as I did, you might as well stop the VCR.

For his part, Douglas spends a lot of time talking to flowers and animals, and annoying everyone else with his hippie-dippy philosophical claptrap. "Everybody's so worried about how long hair is," he whines, "nobody seems to care how long wars last." It doesn't help that his voice sounds like it was subjected to helium before every scene. Douglas does what he can to make us like Carl despite such deep thoughts. It's not the type of performance that would damage a burgeoning career, but it's not much of a boost either.

He continued to work steadily in other, equally forgettable films, including *Adam at 6 A.M.* (1970) and *Summertree* (1971). A guest-spot on the TV series *The F.B.I.* impressed producer Quinn Martin enough to sign Douglas as Karl Malden's sidekick for the police drama *The Streets of San Francisco*. He remained with the series for four years and raised his Hollywood stock considerably with three Emmy nominations. He left in 1975 after purchasing the movie rights to the book *One Flew Over the Cuckoo's Nest* from his father. Douglas coproduced the film, which won the Oscar that year for Best Picture.

After appearing in *Coma* (1978), Michael Douglas retreated behind the camera once again to produce *The China Syndrome*. But when Richard Dreyfuss upped his price to play crusading TV news cameraman Richard Adams, Douglas decided to cut the budget by playing the role himself.

Adams accompanies reporter Kimberly Wells (Jane Fonda) to the Ventana Nuclear Plant as the movie opens. Their intent is an innocuous story about nuclear power, but during the visit an accident occurs in the control room. Richard surreptitiously films the frantic activity as engineer Jack Godell (Jack Lemmon) successfully prevents a major disaster, but because Richard's act was illegal the TV station refuses to run the footage. The plant covers up the severity of the incident, but Godell continues to dig until he uncovers inferior welding that should prevent Ventana from reopening. Jack's boss ignores his warnings, so Jack calls Kimberly and attempts to go public.

The China Syndrome benefited from the dark serendipity of the Three Mile Island crisis, which unfolded just weeks after the film was released. The timing certainly increased business at the box office, but the movie should have performed well even if Pennsylvania had not almost disappeared. James Bridges' taut direction and a trio of strong lead performances invigorate a truly unnerving suspense film that builds to a chilling climax. The intelligent script deals not only with utilities and government agencies that encourage profit over public safety, but also the frail egos and situational ethics of the television news media, and the conceit of protest groups who undermine their cause with foolish theatrics.

With his beard and shoulder-length hair Michael Douglas looks more like a hippy here than he did in *Hail, Hero!* Despite his grating habit of saying nu-cue-lar, this was the performance that changed Douglas from a producer/actor to an actor/producer.

HAIL, HERO!
Directed by David Miller; Written by David Manber, based on the novel by John Weston; Produced by Harold D. Cohen; Music by Jerome Moross

Cast
MICHAEL DOUGLAS (CARL DIXON), Arthur Kennedy (Albert Dixon), Teresa Wright (Santha Dixon), Peter Strauss (Frank Dixon)

THE CHINA SYNDROME
Directed by James Bridges; Written by Mike Gray, T.S. Cook and James Bridges; Produced by Michael Douglas

Cast
Jane Fonda (Kimberly Wells), Jack Lemmon (Jack Godell), MICHAEL DOUGLAS (RICHARD ADAMS), Wilford Brimley (Ted Spindler), Peter Donat (Don Jacovich)

RICHARD DREYFUSS (1947-   )

FIRST APPEARANCE: *Valley of the Dolls* (20th Century-Fox, 1967)

A STAR IS BORN: *American Graffiti* (Universal, 1973)

Very few actors ever experience the kind of winning streak that Richard Dreyfuss enjoyed throughout the 1970s. Beginning with his starmaking performance in *American Graffiti*, Dreyfuss followed up with *The Apprenticeship of Duddy Kravitz* (1974) and two back-to-back Steven Spielberg blockbusters, *Jaws* (1975) and *Close Encounters of the Third Kind* (1977). *The Goodbye Girl* (1977) brought him an Academy Award for Best Actor.

Dreyfuss' strength is an effortless audience identification, achieved largely from the fact that he looks less like a movie star than the guy next to us in the theater; through his characters we have experienced the end of adolesence (*Graffiti*), love and romance (*Goodbye Girl*), death (*Whose Life Is it Anyway?*--1981) and the afterlife (*Always*--1989), not to mention spaceships and giant sharks. His reactions to the mundane and the extraordinary always seem to ring true, and any actor with that kind of gift can never be counted out.

Born and raised in Brooklyn, New York, Dreyfuss' offbeat upbringing was typified by his father's abrupt announcement, in February of 1956, of "Let's get the hell out of here." Their apartment was sold, their furniture was sold, and the Dreyfusses (dad, Richard and one brother and sister) were off to Europe for six months. After returning to New York they travelled cross country via 1949 Cadillac to Los Angeles, were Dreyfuss' father found work as a corporation lawyer. Although he had appeared in Hebrew School stage productions from earliest childhood, Richard never was possessed by the burning desire to perform. But while attending Beverly Hills High School he joined the Gallery Theatre troupe, and at San Fernando State College he majored in theatre arts before getting expelled over an argument with a professor.

As a conscientious objector to the Vietnam draft, he served two years of alternate service on the night shift at a hospital, while finding occasional work on television in such series as *The Mod Squad*, *Room 222* and *The Big Valley*. He was invariably cast, in his own words, as "the kind of guy Sally Field wouldn't go out with." He played bit parts in two 1967 films, *Valley of the Dolls* and *The Graduate*, and while the latter certainly looks better as a debut on a filmography, *Valley of the Dolls* beat it to the theaters by one week and must be considered his first film appearance. A bit of bad luck there, but just as Dreyfuss' few fleeting moments in *The Graduate* did nothing to assure that film's success, his bit part as a call boy at a Broadway theatre was in no way responsible for *Valley of the Dolls'* full-blown failure.

You could not bring a trashy novel to life more accurately than this laughably overheated adaptation of Jacqueline Susann's tale of three young women who are chewed up and spit out by show business. Neely (Patty Duke) becomes the biggest star in Hollywood until her drug habit lands her in a sanitarium; Jennifer (Sharon Tate) marries an up-and-coming singer who is later diagnosed with an incurable disease. She appears in skin flicks to pay his medical bills. Anne (Barbara Parkins) is a wholesome small town waif who arrives in New York and takes a job as a secretary. She is discovered by a cosmetics firm and becomes a famous model, but heads back home after watching her friends Neely and Jennifer self-destruct.

The movie is awful, but its litany of hilariously bad dialogue and scenery-chewing performances can be very entertaining if you're in the right mood. Good thing, because Dreyfuss' appearance comes 120 minutes into the 130 minute film. He walks briskly through the backstage area of a theater in an ugly brown sweater, and then delivers the line that all call boys must--"Five minutes, Miss O'Hara! Five minutes!" The part lasts twenty-five seconds, but that's long enough to concede that Sally Field probably wouldn't have anything to do with him.

He graduated to supporting roles in *Hello Down There* (1969) and *Dillinger* (as Baby

Face Nelson--1973), and then joined a cast of young actors who were all bound for stardom in *American Graffiti*. The film was an unlikely contender to become one of the decade's most successful productions--director George Lucas, whose previous filmmaking experience consisted of one student project at USC, shot *American Graffiti* in 25 days on a budget of $750,000. The biggest name in the cast was Ronny Howard, and that was only because he was Opie. The list of unknowns included Dreyfuss, Charles Martin Smith, Cindy Williams, Candy Clark, Mackenzie Phillips, Harrison Ford and Suzanne Somers. As enjoyable as the film is on its own merits, one of the treats in watching *Graffiti* now is the early appearances of these now famous faces.

The story is set in a small California town during one eventful late summer night in 1962. Recent high school graduates Curt Henderson (Dreyfuss), Steve (Howard), and Laurie (Williams) contemplate their future as they visit one last time the haunts of their past. Curt is a sensitive, shy intellectual who spends the night searching for a beautiful blonde in a white Thunderbird (Somers). Steve enthusiastically discusses his plans for college and career, but winds up staying in town to marry Laurie. Curt's wish to "stay 17 forever" ends with the sunrise, and he leaves town for a university.

American Graffiti is composed of touching, amusing vignettes that capture perfectly the last great time to be a teenager in America, and the last days of innocence before Kennedys were shot and Vietnam made headlines. Although the film was set less than ten years before its date of release, it was bathed in a warm nostalgia of music and malt shops that still comforts like a *Donna Reed Show* rerun. *Graffiti* also gets the credit for spawning TV's *Happy Days*, and for George Lucas getting the green light to shoot *Star Wars* (1977).

Curt is Dreyfuss' first Everyman character, and one of his most poignant. His search for the dream girl is both funny and sad, and his epiphany during an audience with the teenager's deity Wolfman Jack is perhaps the most indelible moment in a movie bursting with such treasures.

VALLEY OF THE DOLLS
Directed by Mark Robson; Written by Helen Deutch and Dorothy Kingsley, based on the novel by Jacqueline Susann; Produced by David Weisbart; Music by Johnny Williams, Andre Previn and Dory Previn

Cast
Barbara Parkins (Anne Welles), Patty Duke (Neely O'Hara), Paul Burke (Lyon Burke), Sharon Tate (Jennifer North), Susan Hayward (Helen Lawson)...RICHARD DREYFUSS (CALL BOY)

AMERICAN GRAFFITI
Directed by George Lucas; Written by George Lucas, Gloria Katz and Willard Huyck; Produced by Francis Ford Coppola and Gary Kurtz

Cast
RICHARD DREYFUSS (CURT HENDERSON), Ronny Howard (Steve), Paul LeMat (John), Charles Martin Smith (Terry), Cindy Williams (Laurie), Candy Clark (Debbie), Mackenzie Phillips (Carol), Wolfman Jack (Himself), Harrison Ford (Falfa), Suzanne Somers (Blonde in T-Bird)

FAYE DUNAWAY (1941-   )

FIRST APPEARANCE: *The Happening* (Columbia, 1967)

A STAR IS BORN: *Bonnie and Clyde* (Warner Bros., 1967)

Dorothy Faye Dunaway has the audacious elegance, penetrating eyes and perfectly sculpted cheekbones of a 1940s screen goddess. Combined with her aptitude for characters who conceal profound insecurities beneath a cool, composed facade, her casting as Joan Crawford in *Mommie Dearest* (1981) seemed ideal. The script did her in that time, but Dunaway's combination of surface elegance and inner turmoil lent themselves perfectly to such modern-day classics as *Bonnie and Clyde, Chinatown* (1974) and *Network* (1976).

Dunaway was a military brat, born in the small town of Bascom, Florida and educated at army schools in Texas, Arkansas, Utah, and Mannheim, Germany. After her parents divorced, she returned to Florida with her mother, and dedicated herself anew to the ballet, tap, piano and voice lessons she had picked up sporadically while moving around the world. Her decision to become an actress became resolute after Dunaway played the title role in a University of Florida production of *Medea*. "Of all the people who ever came in with such specific goals she was by far the most determined," said her drama director.

After transfering to Boston University, Dunaway played the lead in Arthur Miller's *The Crucible*, under the direction of Broadway veteran Lloyd Richards. Richards introduced Dunaway to producer Robert Whitehead, whose Broadway production of *A Man for All Seasons* was about to lose its leading lady. In 1962, just three weeks after her graduation from Boston University, Faye Dunaway made her professional debut in a play that was already a phenomenal success.

More distinguished theater work followed, from off-Broadway to Lincoln Center. Her performance in a play entitled *Hogan's Goat* (1965) led to her casting as a bored rich girl who helps engineer a kidnapping in the film *The Happening*. The story follows the exploits of four Miami beach bums on a weekend road trip, whose search for female companionship turns deadly when they stumble into an unlikely kidnapping. Before the dust settles there are skirmishes with the mob, the FBI and the IRS.

The film fluctuates between a satire on contemporary society, and a broad, slapstick farce that borrows elements from "Beach Party" movies and the Keystone Kops. The impressive cast is led by Anthony Quinn as a mafia hood turned respectable hotelier, George Maharis, Martha Hyer and Milton Berle. But the bizarre, barely coherent storyline moves too quickly for its own good, and even this talented company seems at a loss to keep up. Dunaway's debut notwithstanding, the film is best remembered today for its title song, performed by The Supremes.

Poor reviews for the film were shared by Dunaway, though the criticism fell more on her casting than on her performance as a flirtatious coed named Sandy. "Newcomer Faye Dunaway, though stunning to view and essaying her role with `elan, is too womanly seductive for a teenybopper role," wrote *Variety*. The *New York Times* dismissed the film and Dunaway, describing her as "a carbon copy of Jane Fonda."

The notices were not much better for her second film, Otto Preminger's *Hurry Sundown*. But a successful audition for producer Warren Beatty and director Arthur Penn won Dunaway the role that launched her career--Bonnie Parker in *Bonnie and Clyde*. This seminal '70s film, controversial for both its revisionist history and its graphic violence, purported to tell the actual story of the most notorious outlaws of the early 1930s. At the video store, the film might be filed under drama, action, true story, love story or classic, and all of the above would be correct.

Beyond the known fact that Bonnie Parker and Clyde Barrow were two bored hicks with a natural talent for crime, there's little truth in this stylized, romanticized portrayal of the duo as victims of circumstance in the Great Depression, who became folk heroes by robbing the banks that had foreclosed on the houses and farms of the poor. The benevolent acts attributed to them in the movie, such as allowing a downtrodden farmer to keep the money he just withdrew from a targeted bank, were actually borrowed from stories surrounding other infamous criminals, such as John Dillinger and Baby Face Nelson.

The truth is that Bonnie and Clyde were probably the least lovable of this century's better-known bandits but, as played by Beatty and Dunaway, their demise in a hail of bullets seems almost tragic.

Bonnie remains Dunaway's best performance; the actress who conveys sophistication by just entering a room faced a challenge in playing a naive farm girl, who is instinctively clever but amoral. Her amazing first scene tells us everything we need to know about the character; she flits around her room, bursting with pent-up energies and desires that have no means of release--until she sees handsome Clyde Barrow outside her window, trying to hotwire her mother's car. She joins him for a Coke and an armed robbery, because it's more exciting than anything else she had planned that day. It becomes clear that she could have learned any trade as quickly as she takes to crime, which became the first opportunity to present itself. "We're not gonna have a minute's peace!" Clyde tells her after they become wanted; "You promise?" she asks, excitedly.

THE HAPPENING
Directed by Elliot Silverstein; Written by Frank R. Pierson, James D. Buchanan and Ronald Austin, based on a story by Buchanan and Austin; Produced by Jud Kinberg; Music by De Vol, songs by Eddie Holland, Lamont Dozier and Brian Holland

Cast
Anthony Quinn (Roc Delmonico), George Maharis (Taurus), Michael Parks (Sureshot), Robert Walker, Jr. (Herby), Martha Hyer (Monica Delmonico), FAYE DUNAWAY (SANDY), Milton Berle (Fred)

BONNIE AND CLYDE
Directed by Arthur Penn; Written by David Newman and Robert Benton; Produced by Warren Beatty; Music by Charles Strouse

Cast
Warren Beatty (Clyde Barrow), FAYE DUNAWAY (BONNIE PARKER), Michael J. Pollard (C.W. Moss), Gene Hackman (Buck Barrow), Estelle Parsons (Blanche)

IRENE DUNNE (1904-1990)

FIRST APPEARANCE: *Leathernecking* (RKO, 1930)

A STAR IS BORN: *Cimarron* (RKO, 1931)

In *The Awful Truth* (1937) and *My Favorite Wife* (1940), Irene Dunne's refined beauty, effortless class and endearing mischievous streak were perfectly matched with those of her costar, Cary Grant. Dunne, who was equally at home in musicals, dramas and westerns, was a contender for "First Lady of Hollywood" status, between the reigns of Norma Shearer and Greer Garson. She retired from movies in the early 1950s, no longer first but always a lady.

Born in Louisville, Kentucky, Irene Dunne enjoyed a privileged upbringing of private schools and voice and piano tutors. After a year's study at a music conservatory, she was hired as a music and art teacher at an Indiana high school. She earned a one-year scholarship at the Chicago Musical College, and when her training was completed she set out for New York, hoping to join the divas on the Metropolitan Opera stage, but was rejected for being "too young, too inexperienced, and too slight."

Dunne returned to the Chicago Musical College, and between classes she started auditioning for musical comedies. She graduated with honors in 1926, and made her Broadway debut in 1927 in a play entitled *Yours Truly*. She was "discovered" in an elevator by impresario Florenz Ziegfeld, and after a terrific audition Dunne landed the role of Magnolia in Ziegfeld's production of *Show Boat*. After 72 weeks of rave reviews and packed houses, movie studio representatives became a fixture at her dressing room door.

She signed with RKO in 1930, and was cast immediately into *Leathernecking*, the film adaptation of the popular 1928 Richard Rodgers-Lorenz Hart stage musical *Present Arms*. But Hollywood didn't quite have the hang of musicals yet; hampered by static camera movement and devoid of the Busby Berkeley choreography that distinguished the stage version, *Leathernecking* was a less than ideal debut for Dunne's talents.

The frothy story follows the ever-escalating attempts of a Marine private (Eddie Foy, Jr.) to win the heart of Delphine (Dunne), a hard-to-get socialite. Stealing an officer's uniform doesn't work, so he fakes a shipwreck to win her sympathy, but once again his plan backfires. Inevitably, Delpine drops her protestations after a couple of love songs, and the soldier's realization that sincerity works better than deception. Two Rodgers and Hart songs, "You Took Advantage of Me" and "A Kiss for Cinderella," and Dunne's performance of "Careless Kisses," are the highlights of this well-intentioned failure.

Six months later, Dunne tested for and won the lead opposite Richard Dix in the sprawling western *Cimarron*. The film won the Academy Award for Best Picture in 1931, and remained the only western to be so honored until *Dances With Wolves*, 59 years later. It is also the only Best Picture winner that is, at times, almost unwatchable today. *Cimarron*'s best scene, a recreation of the great Oklahoma land rush, comes right after the opening credits, and even that scene was done better in 1925's *Tumbleweeds*. After that, it's two hours of dull, stodgy melodrama, with occasional moments of finesse and beauty.

Among the settlers barreling into Oklahoma to claim his share of two million first come, first serve acres is Yancey Cravat (Dix), scholar, statesman, preacher and crack shot, the kind of man who would help civilize the wild west. After settling in the boomtown of Osage, Yancey sends for his wife, Sabra (Dunne), and together they publish the territory's first newspaper. But seven years later, Yancey gets the urge to settle another frontier, and Sabra stays behind.

The film follows the fate of the Cravats through forty years of triumphs, tragedies and long separations. Richard Dix, a popular leading man in movies before the coming of sound, is still using the broad gestures and exaggerated reactions that served him well in silents; Dix has a rich, booming voice that works well in the big scenes, such as Yancey's sermon at the first church services in Osage, but he doesn't tone it down for more intimate scenes, and the result is rather ungraceful.

At first, Irene Dunne seems in danger of losing the picture to the inspired vamping of Estelle Taylor, who plays Sabra's sometime rival for Yancey's affection. But slowly, gradually, Sabra's struggle to maintain a semblance of decorum and refinement in untamed territory takes on resonance. Sabra's reputation ultimately eclipses that of her husband; Yancey's insatiable wanderlust leaves him frail and penniless, and his wife becomes one of America's first women in Congress. Her stirring speech after the election is Irene Dunne's first magic movie moment, but it's a long time coming, and we're still a long way from the divine Dunne of *Magnificent Obsession* (1935), *Show Boat* (1936) and *The Awful Truth* (1937).

LEATHERNECKING
Directed by Eddie Cline; Written by Alfred Jackson and Jane Murfin, based on the play *Present Arms* by Herbert Fields, Richard Rodgers and Lorenz Hart; Music by Oscar Levant, Rodgers and Hart

Cast
IRENE DUNNE (DELPHINE), Ken Murray (Frank), Louise Fazenda (Hortense), Ned Sparks (Ned Sparks), Eddie Foy, Jr. (Chick)

CIMARRON
Directed by Wesley Ruggles, Written by Howard Estabrook, based on the novel by Edna Ferber; Produced by William LeBaron

Cast
Richard Dix (Yancey Cravat), IRENE DUNNE (SABRA CRAVAT), Estelle Taylor (Dixie Lee), Nance O'Neil (Felice Venable)

ROBERT DUVALL (1931-   )

FIRST APPEARANCE: *To Kill a Mockingbird* (Universal, 1962)

A STAR IS BORN: *The Great Santini* (Orion, 1979)

"By now," wrote *New York* magazine in 1981, "Robert Duvall must be fed up with being 'rediscovered' with each new film he makes." The progression from character actor to leading man encompassed nearly twenty years of Duvall's professional life, and though he's been called "America's Olivier," the title refers only to the consistent quality and versatility of his work, and not the matinee idol looks that made Olivier a movie star as well as an actor. Indeed, Duvall's looks seem to change with every role, and he is able to bury himself so deeply into a character that he has never shown the public a recognizable personality of his own.

Robert Duvall was a Navy brat, the son of Rear Admiral and Mrs. William Howard Duvall. He was born in San Diego, but raised in a variety of cities where his father was stationed. The exposure he acquired to various lifestyles, cultural mannerisms and regional dialects would prove invaluable in his later career. However, it wasn't until he entered Principia college in Elsah, Illinois, that Duvall changed his focus from social studies to acting. After graduation he studied in New York for two years with Sanford Meisner, and met two other struggling young actors named Gene Hackman and Dustin Hoffman. Duvall's roomate was Robert Morse, who would win a Tony Award in *How to Succeed in Business Without Really Trying.* Surrounded by talent, Duvall proved himself worthy of their company with his performance in Horton Foote's play *The Midnight Caller* (1961). Foote, who was then adapting Harper Lee's novel *To Kill a Mockingbird* for the screen, insisted the young actor be cast in the film as Boo Radley.

The film became one of the most intelligent, fully-realized adaptations of a classic novel to ever emerge from Hollywood, a true classic in every sense, and a winner with critics, audiences, the book's readers and its author, who praised it as "a beautiful and moving motion picture." Gregory Peck stars as widowed attorney Atticus Finch, of Macomb County, Alabama. He is assigned to defend a black man accused of raping a white woman, and although he casts considerable doubt on the guilt of his client, the racist jury places prejudice ahead of logic. Although Atticus loses the case, he reaffirms the profound love and respect of his two bright, inquisitive children, Scout (Mary Badham) and Jem (Phillip Alford). Peck deservedly won an Oscar for his exemplary performance, and casting down to the incidental walk-ons is impecccable.

Duvall appears only at the very end of the film as Boo Radley, a reclusive, mentally ill young man who has been designated the neighborhood Boogey Man by Macomb's townfolk. But even though some citizens would happily shoot him on sight, Boo emerges to save the lives of the two Finch offspring, at which time they learn another lesson about the folly of prejudice and fearing the unknown. The film did nothing for Duvall's career, but his pale, wan appearance, unkempt shock of blond hair, hesitant movement and hunched-over, insecure pose tells us without a word of dialogue all we need to know about the tragic life of Boo Radley.

For the remainder of the 1960s, Duvall divided his time between the New York stage, where he won plaudits in Arthur Miller's *A View From the Bridge* (1965) and *Wait Until Dark* (1966), and films, including *Bullitt* (1968) and *True Grit* (1969). Throughout the 1970s he built a reputation a a reliable supporting player, most notably in *M*A*S*H* (1970) and *The Godfather* (1972). By the end of the decade his name was known to the frequent moviegoer, in the same way that Edward Arnold and Ward Bond were known to audiences of past generations. But in 1979, Duvall reached new prominence with his first lead role, as Bull Meechum, a gung ho Marine Corps airman, in *The Great Santini.*

The film is more a character study than a story-driven drama, with Duvall painting a fascinating portrait of a soldier without a war to fight, who treats his children as if they were raw recruits at boot camp. His competitive nature and fanatical need for authority are tested by his oldest son Ben (Michael O'Keefe), who has turned eighteen and wants out of the service. When father and son battle, on the driveway basketball court, in front of their home, both know that the contest is not just about basketball. Their stormy relationship is solidified, but doomed to be short-lived.

Duvall's challenge here is to make Bull Meecham more than General Patton stationed in the South Carolina suburbs. Despite his harsh discipline, his childish refusal to admit defeat after losing at one-on-one to Ben, and his crazy aerial stunts that enrage his Marine superiors, Bull Meecham is a man who loves his wife (Blythe Danner) and his children, and believes he must test those he loves to prepare them for life. Yes, he can be arrogant and cruel, calling everyone "sports fan" and bouncing a basketball off his son's head to goad him into a game. But he can make us laugh, too, and though his social skills are suspect his skills and heroism as a military man are not.

This was the performance that should have brought Duvall the Academy Award, that he actually won four years later for *Tender Mercies* (1983). The same year that *The Great Santini* was released, Duvall essayed a different, but equally provocative military figure as Lt. Colonel Billy "I love the smell of napalm in the morning" Kilgore, in Francis Ford Coppola's *Apocalypse Now*. Although the two films combined could not even outgross *The Amityville Horror* in 1979, they improved the quality of the scripts that arrived on Robert Duvall's doorstep. After 1979, his name still might not sell tickets, but moviegoers now knew that at least one character in the film would be interesting to watch.

TO KILL A MOCKINGBIRD
Directed by Robert Mulligan; Written by Horton Foote, based on the novel by Harper Lee; Produced by Alan J. Pakula; Music by Elmer Bernstein

Cast
Gregory Peck (Atticus Finch), Mary Badham (Scout), Phillip Alford (Jem), John Megna (Dill Harris), Brock Peters (Tom Robinson), James Anderson (Bob Ewell)...ROBERT DUVALL (ARTHUR "BOO" RADLEY)

THE GREAT SANTINI
Directed and written by Lewis John Carlino, based on the novel by Pat Conroy; Produced by Charles A. Pratt; Music by Elmer Bernstein

Cast
ROBERT DUVALL (BULL MEECHAM), Blythe Danner (Lillian Meecham), Michael O'Keefe (Ben Meechum), Lisa Jane Persky (Mary Anne Meechum), Julie Ann Haddock (Karen Meechum), Brian Andrews (Matthew Meechum)

CLINT EASTWOOD (1931-)

FIRST APPEARANCE: *Revenge of the Creature* (Universal, 1955)

A STAR IS BORN: *A Fistful of Dollars* (Jolly/Constantine/Ocean, 1964)

Why is it when an actor doesn't say much, like Clint Eastwood, they give him grief, but when an actor doesn't say anything, like Holly Hunter in *The Piano* (1993), they give an Oscar? The characters that made Eastwood a star, The Man with No Name (in three Sergio Leone westerns) and Inspector Harry Callahan, were impassive, unflappable men of few words, and the actor who portrayed them has been ridiculed for his lack of emotion. This is like criticizing Dudley Moore's performance in *Arthur* (1981) because he slurred his speech.

Clint Eastwood has been called the last great movie star, because audiences know him so well that they are able to read his thought processes on screen. When, as Dirty Harry, his eyes narrow to a ferocious squint, everybody in the movie theater knows that a bad guy is about to go down. The squint, like Bogart's twitch of the mouth, is the type of trademark mannerism that only real movie stars acquire, and no one since Eastwood has developed anything as definitive. In Europe, Eastwood is rightly regarded as an icon, but he is also respected as an auteur of remarkable insight into American archetypes. When *Unforgiven* (1992) won the Academy Award for Best Picture, he finally earned the same regard at home.

Clint Eastwood was born in San Francisco, and grew up in several different towns in northern California. His family settled in Oakland after Clint Sr. became an executive with the Container Corporation of America. At Oakland Technical High School, Clint Jr. was a basketball star, and after graduation he worked as a lumberjack in Oregon. He was drafted in 1951, and served his country by teaching other soldiers to swim at Fort Ord in California. Two years later he used his G.I. bill to study business administration at Los Angeles City College. A friend who worked as a cameraman at Universal Studios told Eastwood he had the lean, mean good looks of a matinee idol, and after a screen test Universal agreed. Once under contract, however, Eastwood was cast in a series of low-budget programmers, starting with *Revenge of the Creature*.

A sequel to the popular *Creature From the Black Lagoon* (1954), *Revenge* has the same producer and director, but a different cast except for Nestor Paiva as Lucas, the boat captain who leads another expedition into the Gill-man's backyard. After being captured by well-meaning but clueless scientists, the creature is once again attracted to a swimsuit-clad female (Lori Nelson), but his amphibian intellect is keen enough to realize that he's no match for John Agar. The creature escapes from his cage and returns to his undersea home.

When the action shifts from the Amazon to a Florida laboratory, that's the time to start looking for the unbilled Clint Eastwood; he plays a bumbling lab assistant who calls the head scientist over when one of his test rats is missing. He then reaches in the pocket of his lab coat and finds the lost rodent. "Now how'd he get in there?" says the stiff, mannered Eastwood, with all the comic timing of Richard Nixon. After that the chief returns to real science and Clint is gone for good. The film itself pales in comparison to *Creature From the Black Lagoon*, but it's still better than the final installment of the trilogy, *The Creature Walks Among Us* (1956).

After similarly undistinguished roles in such forgotten fare as *Tarantula* (1955) and *Francis in the Navy* (1955), Eastwood was cast as cowhand Rowdy Yates in the CBS television series *Rawhide*. After seven years of driving cattle on the small screen, he spent his 1964 summer vacation in Spain at the invitation of director Sergio Leone. Leone had tried unsuccessfully to interest Henry Fonda, James Coburn and Charles Bronson in the lead role of an enigmatic drifter in a low-budget "spaghetti western." Eastwood was intrigued by the script, a reworking of the Japanese film *Yojimbo* (1961), and the free trip to Europe, and when Leone realized he wasn't going to do any better he cast the TV actor as the serape-wearing, cheroot-smoking "Man With No Name."

The film, *A Fistful of Dollars*, revitalized a genre that had begun to look a little tired in the turbulent sixties. Leone's direction, which juxtaposed extreme close-ups with graphic, unrelenting violence, was enriched immeasurably by Ennio Morricone's score, which incorporated gunshots and hoofbeats into the musical soundtrack. The result was a western that looked different, sounded different and felt different from anything born in Hollywood. The straight-shooting hero exemplified by John Wayne was usurped by the antihero played by Eastwood, who scorned law and morality and acted out of self-promotion, not altruism. The bare-bones plot of *A Fistful of Dollars* has the Man With No Name riding into a bordertown that is controlled by two warring gangs, and playing the rivals against each other until they have been eliminated. He then shoots whoever's left and rides away with money from both sides.

Eastwood cashed a $15,000 paycheck for the role that made him an international star. He made the role his own by selecting The Man With No Name's distinctive garb himself, and subtracting most of his lines from the script. This decision ushered in the jokes that pursue him to this day, but it was the right decision. He was supposed to be a mysterious, mythical figure, and anyway the dialogue was always the weakest element in spaghetti westerns, so the less said, the better.

A Fistful of Dollars is the most uneven of Leone's westerns--there are times when you're not sure what, if anything, is going on, but even the most uneventful scenes are so highly stylized that it doesn't really matter. After topping the box office across Europe, the film opened in America to scathing reviews (the *New York Times* called Eastwood's character "a morbid, amusing, campy fraud"), but again proved immensely popular with the public. Two sequels, *For A Few Dollars More* (1965) and *The Good, the Bad and the Ugly* (1967), verified Eastwood's magnetism and transformed him into the most popular star in the world. "He is living proof," wrote Norman Mailer, "of the maxim that the best way to get through life is cool."

REVENGE OF THE CREATURE
Directed by Jack Arnold; Written by Martin Berkeley, based on a story by William Alland; Produced by William Alland; Music by Herman Stein

Cast
John Agar (Clete Ferguson), Lori Nelson (Helen Dobson), John Bromfield (Joe Hayes), Nestor Paiva (Lucas)...CLINT EASTWOOD (LAB TECHNICIAN)

A FISTFUL OF DOLLARS
Directed by Sergio Leone; Written by Sergio Leone, Duccio Tessari, Victor A Catena and G. Schock, based on the film *Yojimbo* by Akira Kurosawa; Produced by Arrigo Colombo and Giorgio Papi; Music by Ennio Morricone

Cast
CLINT EASTWOOD (THE MAN WITH NO NAME), Marianna Koch (Marisol), John Wells (Ramon Rojo), Pepe Calvo (Silvanito)

MIA FARROW (1946-   )

FIRST APPEARANCE: *John Paul Jones* (Warner Bros., 1959)

A STAR IS BORN: *Rosemary's Baby* (Paramount, 1968)

Early in her career, Mia Farrow's rail-thin, gossamer appearance typecast her in a series of fragile, virginal roles. But it was her ten-year professional and personal collaboration with Woody Allen that comprises her creative peak. The thirteen films in which she appeared under Allen's direction offered a variety of complex characters that other actresses could only dream about, from the gum-snapping mafia moll in *Broadway Danny Rose* (1984), to the abused wife who escapes her troubles at the movies in *The Purple Rose of Cairo* (1985). The Allen-Farrow partnership has since dissolved, seemingly forever, which is the best news Diane Keaton's had in years. But Farrow was a talented, intriguing actress before she met Woody, and even without her once-reliable source of quality material, there is no reason she cannot be so again.

Mia, born Maria de Lourdes Villiers Farrow, was the daughter of writer-director John Farrow and actress Maureen O'Sullivan. Her godparents were gossip columnist Louella Parsons and director George Cukor, which should have guaranteed good parts and good press throughout her career. She lived with her six siblings in a separate wing of her parents' Hollywood estate, a popular gathering place for the show business rich and famous. Before her twelfth birthday, Mia had survived a serious bout with polio and a period of sustained analysis.

In 1959, the Farrow family went to Spain, where John Farrow had been hired to direct the historical drama *John Paul Jones*. Jones, America's first great naval hero, had a life that sounds perfect for film adaptation; after killing a crewman while still in the English army, Jones fled to the American colonies to escape trial. There, encouraged by Patrick Henry, Jones' sympathies turn toward the cause of the colonists. He joins the American navy and wins several decisive victories before the colonies gain their independence. He is then sent to Russia to assist the navy of Catherine the Great.

John Paul Jones again raises the question of why most films about the American Revolution fail so miserably. In this case the answer is obvious--Robert Stack's stiff performance in the title role, and dialogue that sounds as if it emerged from the school play performed by Miss Crabtree's third-grade history class. The film's only merits are interior set design (the Declaration of Independence signing and other famous moments look like John Singleton Copley paintings come to life), Charles Coburn's performance as Ben Franklin, and a cameo by Bette Davis as Catherine the Great. But my favorite scene is Jones' stroll through Paris' Tuileries Gardens--if you look closely, you can see automobiles whizzing by in what is supposed to be eighteenth-century France.

All of John Farrow's children were given bit roles in the film, most of them in the background of a brief scene at about the forty-minute mark, in which Jones meets the commodore of the American navy just before being assigned a ship. Thirteen-year-old Mia stands on the dock with three of her siblings. The appearance is so brief that other sources can be forgiven for listing *Guns at Batasi* (1964) as her official debut.

Mia continued her undergraduate education in both England and Beverly Hills, and then began her acting career officially in an Off-Broadway production of *The Importance of Being Earnest*. Vivien Leigh, who attended the play to see a friend in the cast, was impressed enough with Mia's performance to bring her to the attention of 20th Century-Fox. The studio signed her for *Peyton Place*, a new television series that ran from 1964 to 1969, and became something of a national phenomenon. Mia stayed for only two seasons, but her popular portrayal of ingenue Allison MacKenzie launched her career. When she married Frank Sinatra in 1966, her name appeared in headlines worldwide.

Because she was already as famous as any actress in the country, *Rosemary's Baby* was not so much a star-maker as it was a confirmation of Farrow's talent, and the first proof that she could transfer her television success into features. As the movie opens, Rosemary Woodhouse (Farrow) and her husband Guy (John Cassavettes) move into a New York apartment building with a notorious, sordid history. Unconcerned with the supernatural legends, the young couple settle in and plan to start a family. But Guy, a struggling actor, quickly falls under the influence of a coven of witches that congregate in the next apartment, after he is promised success in his career in exchange for Rosemary's baby.

Ira Levin's bestselling book, one of the most unique horror stories ever imagined, is adapted with kinky aplomb by Polanski. There are no monsters jumping from the shadows in Levin's definition of horror; the action takes place mostly in daylight, not the dead of night, and in the heart of a big city, not a lonely, isolated mansion. And the face of evil is not sinister and ugly, but cordial and benign--who could be frightened by Ruth Gordon and Ralph Bellamy?

Anchoring the entire film is Mia Farrow, whose sweet, angelic appearance made her victimization in a Satanic plot even more horrific. The role of Rosemary was a grueling one that required intelligence, sincerity, sex appeal, and believability in both a variety of standard domestic situations and in the most bizarre of circumstances. The film's best scene might be when Rosemary realizes that her husband and her new friends are not what they seem; "All of them. All in it together," she says in a trembling voice, while standing in a phone booth on a busy New York street in the middle of the afternoon. By paralleling Rosemary's feelings of physical claustrophobia in the phone booth with the horrifying sensation of evil closing in on her from every direction, Polanski creates a moment of terror worthy of Hitchcock. After the baby is born and Rosemary must make a fateful decision, Farrow imbues the scene with sadness, tenderness and horror at the same time.

"Mia Farrow is quite marvelous," raved the *New York Times*, "pale, suffering, almost constantly on screen in a difficult role that requires her to be learning for two hours what the audience has guessed from the start." Ruth Gordon deservedly won an Oscar for her supporting effort, but Farrow, inexplicably, did not even receive a nomination.

JOHN PAUL JONES
Directed by John Farrow; Written by John Farrow and Jesse Lasky, Jr., based on the story *Nor'wester* by Clements Ripley; Produced by Samuel Bronston; Music by Max Steiner

Cast
Robert Stack (John Paul Jones), Bette Davis (Catherine the Great), Marisa Pavan (Aimee de Tellision), Charles Coburn (Ben Franklin), Macdonald Carey (Patrick Henry), Peter Cushing (Captain Pearson)...MIA FARROW (EXTRA)

ROSEMARY'S BABY
Directed and written by Roman Polanski, based on the novel by Ira Levin; Produced by William Castle; Music by Krzystof Komeda

Cast
MIA FARROW (ROSEMARY WOODHOUSE), John Cassavettes (Guy Woodhouse), Ruth Gordon (Minnie Castavet), Sidney Blackmer (Roman Castavet), Ralph Bellamy (Dr. Saperstein)

SALLY FIELD (1946-   )

FIRST APPEARANCE: *The Way West* (United Artists, 1967)

A STAR IS BORN: *Norma Rae* (20th Century-Fox, 1979)

    Women who are gloriously cute grow to hate that particular adjective because they hear it all their lives. Sally Field once described herself, with some derision, as having "a cutesy, smiley, all-American, girl-next-door face," and no doubt about it, she seems to have emerged from the womb waving pom-poms and eating apple pie. A petite 5'3", with brown Shirley Temple curls surrounding chipmunk cheeks and freckles, Field's indefatigable cuteness proved more curse than blessing in her search to be taken seriously as an actress. As a result, her journey from television's *Gidget* to an Oscar win for *Norma Rae* lasted fourteen years.
    She was born in Pasadena, California to pharmacist Richard Field, who left home when she was four, and his wife Maggie, a former contract player at Paramount. After the divorce Sally moved in with her grandmother while Maggie worked full-time. Old movies, especially those with Carole Lombard or Jean Arthur, were a welcome escape from her unsettled early childhood. In 1953, Maggie married Jock Mahoney, a former movie Tarzan and the star of TV's *Yancy Derringer*. Sally moved back home and got along famously with her new stepdad, who certainly encouraged her affection for acting and for the movies.
    As a teenager she hit the beach every day after school, which turned out to be ideal training for her first professional job. A casting director for Screen Gems Television plucked Sally from a summer acting workshop at Columbia Studios and invited her to audition for the lead in *Gidget*, a TV spinoff of the popular drive-in movie series. The character, dubbed Gidget by her surfing pals from the words "girl" and "midget," was first played by Sandra Dee and in subsequent movies by Deborah Walley and Cindy Carol. Sally beat out 75 hopefuls for the role, but the series was clobbered in the ratings by *The Beverly Hillbillies* and cancelled after one year.
    Field landed guest roles in other shows and then further delayed her plans for college after landing her first feature film. *The Way West* was a competent western with enough stars and scenery to maintain interest despite some slow stretches and some godawful songs. The story follows a wagon train of tenderfoot Easterners led by Senator William Tadlock (Kirk Douglas) that departs Independence, Missouri in 1843, destination Oregon. Among the travelers are Dick Summers (Robert Mitchum), a scout with failing eyesight, dirt farmer Lije Evans (Richard Widmark), his foxy wife Rebecca (Lola Albright) and awkward son Brownie (Michael McGreevey), and Mercy McBee (Field), a teenage girl with raging hormones.
    The train is endangered by raging rivers, attacking Indians, buffalo herds, Mercy's dalliance with frustrated newlywed Johnnie Mack (Michael Witney), and Tadlock's battles with Lije over leadership of the group, and over Lije's wife. Field, who receives "Introducing" billing in the credits, appears in the very first scene. It's a memorable debut--Mercy, legs apart and bare feet dangling off the back of a covered wagon, directs a seductive smile toward the captivated Brownie. *The New York Times* review called her a "saucy, sexy youngster," and though she never quite nails the prairie accent she is clearly an actress worth watching. The $5 million film was panned by critics, and barely grossed a million and change.
    After an unsuccessful screen test for the Katharine Ross role in *The Graduate* (1967), Sally Field returned to television as Sister Bertrille in *The Flying Nun*. It was one of the dumbest series in the history of the medium, but to be fair Field graced the role with undiminished perkiness, and it lasted three years. During that time Sally married her high school sweetheart in 1968, and gave birth to a son (while playing a nun!) in 1969. A second son, Elijah, was born in 1972. After five more made-for-TV movies and another series (the short-lived *The Girl With Something Extra*), Field fired her agent and her manager, divorced her husband and redoubled her efforts to break into movies. Her supporting role in *Stay Hungry* (1975) received

good notices, but when more scripts didn't follow it was back to television.

Field's brilliant performance as a woman with multiple personalities in *Sybil* (1977) brought her an Emmy as Best Actress and the respect she had craved for so long. A phone call from Burt Reynolds revived her film career--and her love life--with *Smokey and the Bandit*, which was second only to *Star Wars* at the box office in 1977. Her collaboration with Reynolds continued with *The End* (1978) and *Hooper* (1978), and while she seemed to find a niche in Burt's passenger seat, director Martin Ritt was trying without success to cast the title role in *Norma Rae*. He was turned down by Jane Fonda, Jill Clayburgh and every other 'A' list actress, but when Field offered herself he was hesitant. It was only after Ritt watched *Sybil* that he gave her a chance.

The film is a searing depiction of strained labor relations in a small southern town. Field is in practically every scene as Norma Rae Winston, a divorced mother of two who allies herself with a New York labor organizer (Ron Leibman) in an attempt to force the textile mill where she works into accepting a union. The film's avoidance of cliche`, especially in the relationship between Field and Leibman, is refreshing. Instead of the obligatory romance, they acknowledge temptation but part with only a kind word and a handshake. Though the "smoldering" of their characters remained unfulfilled, wrote the *New York Times*, Field communicates their longing "with the sensitivity that only great actresses possess."

Norma Rae is no Joan of Arc leading her people into the light; she drinks too much, sleeps around, and joins the union cause with great reluctance. But once she's in, her passion for justice and fiery determination are relentless, and culminate in the film's most famous scene; after being dismissed, Norma stands on a table with a hastily drawn sign that simply reads UNION, and shuts down the entire plant. The film was released in March, and Field's performance became the yardstick by which others would be measured that year. At the end of December, no one had come close. She won every major accolade from critics and film festivals, including the Academy Award.

THE WAY WEST
Directed by Andrew V. McLaglen; Written by Ben Maddow and Mitch Lindemann, based on the novel by Alfred Bertram Guthrie, Jr.; Produced by Harold Hecht; Music by Bronisalu Kaper and Mack David

Cast
Kirk Douglas (Sen. William J. Tadlock), Robert Mitchum (Dick Summers), Richard Widmark (Lije Evans), Lola Albright (Rebecca Evans), Michael Witney (Johnnie Mack), Stubby Kaye (Sam Fairman), SALLY FIELD (MERCY MCBEE)

NORMA RAE
Directed by Martin Ritt; Written by Irving Ravetch and Harriet Frank, Jr.; Produced by Tamara Asseyev and Alex Rose; Music by David Shire

Cast
SALLY FIELD (NORMA RAE), Beau Bridges (Sonny), Ron Liebman (Reuben), Pat Hingle (Vernon), Barbara Baxley (Leona)

ERROL FLYNN (1909-1959)

FIRST APPEARANCE: *In the Wake of the Bounty* (Expeditionary Films, 1933)

A STAR IS BORN: *Captain Blood* (Warner Bros., 1935)

Errol Flynn is one of the select few actors to personify a motion picture genre. As John Wayne is *the* western hero, and James Cagney is *the* gangster, Errol Flynn is indisputably *the* swashbuckler. His dashing good looks, acrobatic prowess and proficient swordsmanship were ideally employed in a succession of Warner Bros. classics, including *Captain Blood* (1935), *The Adventures of Robin Hood* (1938) and *The Sea Hawk* (1940). But where John Wayne also had his *Quiet Man* (1952) and Cagney his *Yankee Doodle Dandy* (1942), Flynn struggled outside of his specialty. He earned good notices for *Gentleman Jim* (1942) and *The Sun Also Rises* (1957), but it was frustrating to Flynn, an underrated actor throughout his career, that he never found the audience approval elsewhere that he received playing pirates, rebels and rogues.

It seems fitting that Flynn, who spent so much of his career on clipper ships, was born in the seaport of Hobart, Tasmania, to an Australian marine biologist, and his wife, the daughter of a sea captain. Errol was a troublemaker from the start, who was expelled from as many schools in England and Australia as his distinguished father could convince to take him. He tried government service in 1927, but his days as a cadet didn't last any longer than his days as a student. By the age of twenty, the restless Flynn had worked as a shipping clerk, a plantation overseer, a gold miner, a schooner captain, and a newspaper columnist.

From this diverse plethora of experience, it was a two-month expedition on his schooner that unintentionally launched Errol Flynn's career as an actor. A documentary filmmaker named Herman Erben hired Flynn to sail up the Sepik River in New Guinea, so Erben could shoot some footage of the headhunter tribes that lived along the shore. Erben also took some photos of Flynn at the helm, and two years later these pictures were noticed by Charles Chauvel, a producer and director of Australian films. Chauvel offered Flynn the role of Fletcher Christian in a movie entitled *In the Wake of the Bounty.* Flynn worked for three weeks on the film, in his own words, "without the least idea of what I was doing, except I was supposed to be an actor." The result is a strange hybrid that devotes fifty percent of its running time to a sketchy, incongruous account of the famous mutiny led by Fletcher Christian against Captain Bligh (Mayne Lynton), and fifty percent to documentary footage of the actual locations in Tahiti and Pitcairn Island where the Bounty sailed.

Chauvel's forte` is clearly the latter; the interviews with Christian's descendants and the descriptions of everyday life on Pitcairn are well-handled. The Bounty story (first told on film in a 1916 Australian silent) seems to have been mixed in to draw a bigger audience than documentaries usually receive. Lynton as Bligh is barely competent, but the performances of the Bounty crew are way over the top. Each sailor has just one or two lines, and they were obviously determined to make them count by packing a semester of acting lessons into every sentence. Flynn, who dons a blond wig to play Fletcher Christian, emerges best simply because he is called upon to say the least. His inexperience is obvious, however, and like his crewmates he overemotes every line with unintentionally amusing results.

Flynn was intrigued by show business after this experience, but he was unable to find any other jobs in the field in Australia (which is not surprising based on the evidence of his first attempt). Undaunted, he left for England in 1933 and joined a repertory company in Northampton where, over the next eighteen months, he would learn his craft. His suave, handsome features and engaging personality were enough to convince the Warner Bros. studio in Teddington, England, to put him under contract without a screen test. Three days later, the studio gave Flynn the lead role in *Murder at Monte Carlo* (1935), and he was judged impressive enough for a promotion to the Hollywood lot.

After small roles in *The Case of the Curious Bride* (1935) and *Don't Bet on Blondes*

(1935), Flynn was selected, after a screen test, to replace the ailing Robert Donat in the title role of *Captain Blood*. The studio gambled further in casting Olivia de Havilland, also unknown, opposite Flynn. But the gamble paid off when *Captain Blood* became the first great Hollywood swashbuckler since Douglas Fairbanks sheathed his sword.

Flynn plays Peter Blood, an English physician sold into slavery in Jamaica after he comes to the aid of an enemy of the King. He escapes with a band of other slaves and takes to the high seas, quickly earning a reputation as a ruthless buccaneer. His heart, however, remains on the island with the governor's attractive niece (de Havilland). *Captain Blood* marked the beginning of several long-term relationships that would flourish throughout Flynn's career; it was the first of six films to costar Flynn and de Havilland, who both became stars after *Blood* was released. It was the first of six Flynn films scored by the great Erich Wolfgang Korngold, and the first of seven epic adventures directed by Michael Curtiz. Three years later they would all reunite, along with *Captain Blood* costar Basil Rathbone, for *The Adventures of Robin Hood*, one of the best action movies ever made.

Anyone who has seen *In the Wake of the Bounty* can only marvel at Flynn's progress after just three films. He is poised and confident, not just in the dueling and daredevil sequences but also in the more subdued first hour, in which Peter Blood is captured and forced into a life of servitude. During a courtroom confrontation early in the film, he eloquently protests his death sentence, and Flynn dispels any notion that he is "just" an action movie hero. Once Peter becomes Captain Blood it is adventure all the way, right up to the wonderful final scene in which the former slave becomes governor of Jamaica. His gleeful "Good morning, Uncle!" to the man who once owned him, and who must now welcome him to the family, is as memorable a Flynn line as "Welcome to Sherwood, my lady!"

The resounding success of *Captain Blood* ushered in a new era of swashbucklers, the best of which starred Errol Flynn. It will amaze anyone who marveled at his exuberance and athletic ability on screen to learn that he was turned down for service in World War II, due to a combination of heart trouble, recurrent malaria, and a degree of tuberculosis. Flynn's attempts to prove worthy of his heroic persona in his private life almost certainly fueled his hedonistic excesses, which left him burned out at age forty, and dead at age fifty.

IN THE WAKE OF THE BOUNTY
Directed, produced and written by Charles Chauvel

Cast
Mayne Lynton (Captain Bligh), ERROL FLYNN (FLETCHER CHRISTIAN), Victor Gourier (The Blind Fiddler), John Warwick (Young), Patricia Penman (Isabella)

CAPTAIN BLOOD
Directed by Michael Curtiz; Written by Casey Robinson, based on the novel by Rafael Sabatini; Produced by Hal B. Wallis; Music by Erich Wolfgang Korngold

Cast
ERROL FLYNN (DR. PETER BLOOD), Olivia de Havilland (Arabella Bishop), Lionel Atwill (Col. Bishop), Basil Rathbone (Captain Levasseur), Ross Alexander (Jeremy Pitt), Guy Kibbee (Hagthorpe)

HENRY FONDA (1905-1982)

FIRST APPEARANCE: *The Farmer Takes a Wife* (20th Century-Fox, 1935)

A STAR IS BORN: *The Farmer Takes a Wife*

If John Wayne is the embodiment of the American spirit for political conservatives, it is Henry Fonda who most symbolizes all that's good and noble from the liberal perspective. In films such as *Young Mr. Lincoln* (1939), *The Grapes of Wrath* (1940) and *The Ox-Bow Incident* (1943), Fonda's projection of honest, homespun integrity has come to represent, in the words of director Joshua Logan, "a synthesis of all the heroes of Mark Twain, Bret Harte, James Fenimore Cooper, Hawthorne, Poe, and Irving."

Henry Jaynes Fonda was born in Grand Island, Nebraska, and raised nearby in Omaha. His modest midwestern upbringing fits the profile for the characters he would later portray, but the Fonda family tree actually has its roots in fifteenth-century Italian nobility. The first Fondas came to the United States long before the thirteen colonies were established, and settled in an upstate New York town that bears their name.

At the age of ten, Henry wrote the winning entry in a short story contest, and set his sights on becoming a writer. After graduating from Omaha Central High School in 1923, he enrolled as a journalism major at the University of Minnesota. He lasted two years, and then dropped out to follow the advice of family friend Dorothy Brando, who encouraged him to become an actor. She would later offer the same advice to her son, Marlon. Fonda played juvenile leads at the Omaha Community Playhouse, and then set out for New York in 1928. The $100 he brought didn't last long, and after Broadway proved less than welcoming he turned to summer stock.

In 1929, after working as actor, director and stage manager with various touring troupes, Fonda made his Broadway debut in a walk-on part in the play *The Game of Love and Death*. But it was not until 1934 that he received his first significant notice, playing comedy skits opposite Imogene Coca in the play *New Faces*. Movie producer Walter Wanger sent him an invitation to Hollywood, but Fonda had no interest in the movies and demanded $1000 a week, which he figured would cancel the offer instantly.

But Wanger agreed to Fonda's terms, and a contract calling for two films a year was negotiated. In 1934, he received the best reviews of his career in the Broadway production of *The Farmer Takes a Wife*. Although the play ran just thirteen weeks, it was purchased by 20th Century-Fox, and Henry Fonda reprised his stage role in his film debut.

Today, the film is not remembered as one of Fonda's best, and the 1953 musical remake with Betty Grable is a more popular video rental. It may seem an odd choice, then, as the movie that made Henry Fonda a star. A more logical choice, looking back on the actor's fifty years in film, would seem to be Fonda's definitive portrayal of America's greatest president in *Young Mr. Lincoln*; his previous assignment was playing second banana to Don Ameche in *The Story of Alexander Graham Bell* (1939), and he followed *Young Mr. Lincoln* with the classics *Drums Along the Mohawk* (1939) and *The Grapes of Wrath*.

But however convincing the film may seem as a turning point in Fonda's career, *Young Mr. Lincoln* was actually his 19th film. In the previous eighteen, including *The Farmer Takes a Wife*, Fonda was never lower than third-billed. By the time he played Lincoln, he had already appeared opposite Bette Davis in two films, including *Jezebel* (1938), with Barbara Stanwyck in *The Mad Miss Manton* (1938), and with Tyrone Power in *Jesse James* (1939). He wasn't always *the* star, but his name was well-known to audiences, a status that did indeed begin after the critical raves for *The Farmer Takes a Wife*.

The story is set in the New York farm lands of the 1850s; Dan Harrow (Fonda) dreams of owning his own farm, and gets a job on a boat to raise money for his future. As the boat sails up through the Erie Canal, Dan falls in love with the cook, Molly Larkins (Janet Gaynor). After

Dan wins a boat in a lottery, Molly is certain he will give up the rather dull lifestyle of a farmer and remain on the river, but Dan is steadfast in his desire to work the soil. After he runs from a fight with Molly's former boss (Charles Bickford), their relationship is severed. The happy ending has Dan agreeing to fight and winning by knock-out, and then plowing the fields of his dream with Molly by his side.

Both Gary Cooper and Joel McCrea were offered Fonda's role which, like the choice of Victor Fleming as director, is an indication of the film's A-list status at the studio. Gaynor was top-billed as a result of her status as Fox's biggest female star, but Henry Fonda had the film's principal role, and established immediately all of the elements in the trademark Fonda persona; "Mr. Fonda is a tall, lanky young man with a boyish face, a low voice and a quiet manner particularly effective," observed the *New York Sun*. "One of his most outstanding assets is his appearance of sincerity." The *New York American* echoed the *Sun*'s sentiments and confirms his elevation to leading man after only one performance--"Henry Fonda's day dawns...He dominates the scene and emerges from his film debut a certain success, and one of the really important contributions of stage to screen within the past few seasons."

THE FARMER TAKES A WIFE
Directed by Victor Fleming; Written by Edwin Burke, adapted from the play by Frank B. Elser and Marc Connelly, and the novel *Rome Haul* by Walter D. Edmonds; Produced by Winfield R. Sheehan

Cast
Janet Gaynor (Molly Larkins), HENRY FONDA (DAN HARROW), Charles Bickford (Jotham Klore), Slim Summervillle (Fortune Friendly), Andy Devine (Elmer Otway)

JANE FONDA (1937-)

FIRST APPEARANCE: *Tall Story* (Warner Bros., 1960)

A STAR IS BORN: *Cat Ballou* (Columbia, 1965)

The subject of politics is unavoidable when discussing Jane Fonda, for by her own assertion she chooses films to support the causes she believes in. Although she will always have a faction of detractors, Fonda's personal agenda has not impeded her status as a popular and bankable star. What is more impressive is her emergence from sex kitten roles into more serious material, a turnaround made by other actresses but not with the same ease or totality of transition. Fonda's journey from boy toy in *Barbarella* (1968) to homefront victim of Vietnam in *Coming Home* (1978) must have seemed intractable at one time, even in a fur-lined spaceship.

Jane Seymour Fonda was the first child born to Henry Fonda and his second wife, Frances Seymour. Jane lived and traveled in privilege from her New York City birthplace to Hollywood and back, as the demands of her father's career dictated. Although her childhood was generally a happy one, her mother's confinement to a mental hospital was a traumatic event. Frances Fonda committed suicide in 1953; Jane and her brother Peter were told that she died of a heart attack but, one year later, Jane learned the truth from a movie gossip magazine.

Henry Fonda did not encourage his children to make acting a family business, but he also did not object when Jane made her stage debut in a small role opposite her father, in a production of *The Country Girl* at the Omaha Community Playhouse in Omaha, Nebraska. In the summer of 1956, while attending Vassar College, Jane became an apprentice actress at the Cape Playhouse in Dennis, Massachusetts. She dropped out of Vassar a year later, when education began interfering with her active social life.

Party time stopped when Fonda enrolled in Lee Strasberg's Actors Studio. "He saw a tremendous amount of talent in me," she said of Strasberg, "which absolutely changed my life. Nobody had ever told me I was good at anything." If Strasberg gave her confidence, it was director Joshua Logan who gave her a job; Fonda made her Broadway debut in *There Was a Little Girl* (1959), and her film debut in *Tall Story*, both directed by Logan.

In *Tall Story*, she plays perky co-ed June Ryder, who enrolls in Custer University solely to meet and marry basketball star Ray Blent (Anthony Perkins). Her onslaught of enticement as cheerleader, classmate and constant companion have the outgunned Blent proposing marriage before the semester is over. Act two introduces a moral dilemma, when corrupt gamblers offer Blent a bribe to throw a game, just when he is desperate for money to build a lovenest for his new bride.

Change the names and faces in *Tall Story* and you've got a *Dobie Gillis* episode. As a coy sex comedy it is not very funny or very sexy, but there's a corny sweetness to the performances of Fonda and Perkins. Perkins, just months before finding immortality as Norman Bates in *Psycho* (1960), could still make his bookish demeanor and awkwardness around women endearing; Fonda, who makes her first movie entrance by running down two professors with her bicycle, is a fetching campus tease, and it's amusing to watch the future feminist set the cause back fifty years with lines like, "I came to college for the same reason every girl did--to get married." Fonda also reveals a pleasant singing voice, when she duets with Perkins on "Cuddle Up a Little Closer."

Fonda's career continued through short-lived Broadway plays like *The Fun Couple* (1962), and a series of box-office disasters now long forgotten. Disappointed at her lack of progress, she made a series of films in Paris for director Roger Vadim, whom she married in 1965, and was dubbed "La BB Americaine" by the continental press.

Cat Ballou, her first American film in three years, was also the first indication that Jane

Fonda might be more than America's answer to Bardot. In this clever, and occasionally hilarious, western spoof, Fonda plays Catherine Ballou, a young schoolteacher whose father is being driven off the family farm by the standard western villains. She attempts to hire a gunfighter for protection, but what she gets is Kid Shelleen (Lee Marvin), a broken-down drunk with the shakiest six-shooter in town. When her father is killed, Catherine escapes to plot revenge with Shelleen and two other wanted men.

Jane Fonda actually ranks third on the list of reasons to watch *Cat Ballou*, behind Lee Marvin's Academy Award-winning performance and the balladeering of on-screen narrator Nat King Cole. But the film was a huge hit, and the infectious quality in Fonda's portrayal of a wide-eyed innocent who becomes intoxicated by the life of an outlaw was well-received. The mature phase of her career did not begin until *Klute* (1971), but films like *Cat Ballou* began the reassessment of Jane Fonda as a fresh and exciting new screen personality. "She has," wrote Stanley Kauffmann, "the hum of that magnetism without which acting intelligence and technique are admirable but uncompelling."

TALL STORY
Directed and produced by Joshua Logan; Written by Julius J. Epstein, based on the play by Howard Lindsay and Russel Crouse; Music by Cyril J. Mockridge

Cast
Anthony Perkins (Ray Blent), JANE FONDA (JUNE RYDER), Ray Walston (Leo Sullivan), Marc Connelly (Charles Osman), Anne Jackson (Myra Sullivan)

CAT BALLOU
Directed by Elliot Silverstein; Written by Frank Pierson and Walter Newman, based on the novel by Roy Chanslor; Produced by Harold Hecht; Music by Frank DeVol, Mack David and Jerry Livingston

Cast
JANE FONDA (CAT BALLOU), Lee Marvin (Kid Shelleen/Tim Strawn), Michael Callan (Clay Boone), Dwayne Hickman (Jed)

HARRISON FORD (1942-   )

FIRST APPEARANCE: *Dead Heat on a Merry-Go-Round* (Columbia, 1966)

A STAR IS BORN: *Star Wars* (20th Century-Fox, 1977)

Harrison Ford is clearly on course for one of those career achievement Oscars, presented to actors in their declining years whose individual performances never seemed worthy of awards of excellence, but when viewed *en masse* constitute a legacy of astounding quality. His films have made more money than those of any other actor in history, but Ford's essential contribution to their success always seems overshadowed. Instead, people remember the amazing stunt sequences in the Indiana Jones trilogy, the special effects in the *Star Wars* trilogy, the production design in *Blade Runner* (1982). Ford's name may have been above the title in *The Fugitive* (1993), but Tommy Lee Jones won the critic's plaudits and the Academy Award.

Ford is not reknowned as an actor, but he should be. More than that, as a re-actor he is the best in the business. All of his finest non-action moments on screen are priceless reactions-- whether he is gazing upon snakes in *Raiders of the Lost Ark* (1981) or the breasts of Kelly McGillis in *Witness* (1985), Harrison Ford's face always reflects his emotions with the clarity of a mirror.

He was born in Chicago, Illinois and raised in the Windy City suburbs of Park Ridge and Morton Grove. His family had a marginal connection to show business--Ford's grandfather was a vaudevillian and his father, an advertising executive, did some radio acting and voiceovers for commercials--but Harrison's interest in performing did not emerge until his junior year at Wisconsin's Ripon College. He found a release from his intense shyness and a sense of responsibility and purpose on the stage, and after a season of summer stock in Wisconsin he left for Hollywood.

Ford was performing in a Laguna Beach production of *John Brown's Body* when he was spotted by a Columbia Pictures talent scout and signed to a $150-a-week contract. His film debut was a bit part in *Dead Heat on a Merry-Go-Round*, a dull caper movie starring James Coburn in his super-cool *Our Man Flint* mode. Coburn plays a con man who concocts an elaborate scheme to rob the bank at the Los Angeles Airport. There's an unexpected twist at the end, but it's not enough to redeem the rest of the movie. Ford, unbilled, appears at about the thirty minute mark, as a bellboy in a swank hotel. "Paging Mr. Ellis!" he proclaims repeatedly, in a hideous green bellboy uniform but (lucky for him) without the little matching hat. Ford's most popular characters are nondescript guys who are capable of exceptional deeds. Here, at the outset of his career, he just looks nondescript.

Columbia thought so too, and dropped him after eighteen months. Universal Pictures was next to take a chance, allowing Ford to continue his string of minor roles in low-priority films and guest spots on such television series as *Gunsmoke* and *Ironside*. When parts were scarce he worked as a carpenter, remodeling houses and building cabinets and furniture.

A small role in the megahit *American Graffiti* (1973) was the first worthy showcase for Ford's talent, and led to better roles in *The Conversation* (1974) and the TV movie *Dynasty* (1976). However, his principal occupation remained carpentry until George Lucas cast the still unknown actor as maverick starship captain Han Solo in a pet project called *Star Wars*. In its first year of release *Star Wars* grossed a record $300 million, and turned Ford, Mark Hamill and Carrie Fisher into overnight celebrities and, since all three had profit-sharing clauses in their contracts, overnight millionaires.

Part fairy-tale, part outer space western, *Star Wars* told the story of a ruthless galactic empire and the small band of rebels who fight for a better universe. Han Solo is a reluctant recruit in the rebel cause, motivated to act only by the promise of money. But in the final scene, when he rescues Luke Skywalker (Hamill) and clears a path for Luke's destruction of the empire's newest super-weapon, Han is motivated by a higher purpose.

It's a challenge to hold the viewer's eye in a big, flashy action movie, but Ford makes it look effortless. Han's devoted friendship with his hirsute copilot Chewbacca, his derision of the droids and obvious affection for Princess Leia (Fisher), hidden beneath a veneer of smart-aleck machismo, all remain as vivid in the memory as lightsabre duels and Darth Vader's asthma. Of the human characters in *Star Wars* Han Solo seems the most complex and interesting, but only because Ford gave him shadings that were not in the script. "He's a wry hero, but he's a real one, exuding just that quiet, sardonic masculinity that made stars like Bogart and Gable at once larger than life and down to earth." wrote *Newsweek*'s David Ansen, in a review of *Blade Runner* that sums up Ford's appeal in all of his films. Han Solo is the first archtypical Harrison Ford character--resourceful, self-assured, but improvising his heroics every step of the way.

DEAD HEAT ON A MERRY-GO-ROUND
Directed and written by Bernard Girard; Produced by Carter DeHaven III; Music by Stu Phillips

Cast
James Coburn (Eli Kotch), Camilla Sparv (Inger Knudsen), Aldo Ray (Eddie Hart), Nina Wayne (Frieda Schmid), Rose-Marie (Margaret Kirby)

STAR WARS
Directed and written by George Lucas; Produced by Gary Kurtz; Music by John Williams

Cast
Mark Hamill (Luke Skywalker), HARRISON FORD (HAN SOLO), Carrie Fisher (Princess Leia), Peter Cushing (Grand Moff Tarkin), Alec Guinness (Obi-Wan Kenobi)

JODIE FOSTER (1962-   )

FIRST APPEARANCE: *Napoleon and Samantha* (Disney, 1972)

A STAR IS BORN: *Taxi Driver* (Columbia, 1976)

Legions of young blond starlets are pawed by their costars off-screen in their first movie, but Jodie Foster had a particularly rough debut--she was only nine years old, and her costar was a full-grown lion. The film was *Napoleon and Samantha*, an underrated and under-remembered Disney adventure, and in it Foster already displays the odd but appealing hybrid of child and adult qualities that captivated directors, who described her in 1977 as "14 going on 40."

Jodie Foster achieved her first appearance and her starmaking performance before her thirteenth birthday. So much of her story was still to come; graduation with honors from Yale University, admission into a select club of actresses to earn two Academy Awards, and the unfortunate, uncontrollable linking of her name with an assassination attempt on President Ronald Reagan. But whether the headlines were flattering or devastating, Foster handled the fallout with the level-headed reserve and class that are apparent in so many of her movie characters.

She was born Alicia Christian Foster, but the "Jodie" nickname took precedence from earliest childhood. Her father Lucius, an air force officer and Yale graduate, was not around to see that childhood. He divorced Evelyn Foster before Jodie was born. When the child support payments for Jodie and her three older siblings dried up, Evelyn tried to get her children jobs in commercials. She had worked for awhile as a public relations person for a Hollywood producer, and used the connection to secure auditions for Jodie's brother, Buddy. A Coppertone commerical was looking for kids, and three-year-old Jodie tagged along with mom and Buddy. The director was impressed--with Jodie. She was already speaking in full sentences, and was able to read lines like a pro. Jodie got the job and many more, becoming the breadwinner for the Foster clan when most kids are getting ready for kindergarten.

She would soon be a familiar face on numerous sixties and seventies TV shows, including *My Three Sons, Mayberry R.F.D.* and *The Partridge Family*. In 1972, she graduated to features in *Napoleon and Samantha*. The title twosome are best friends growing up in rural Oregon, whose lives take an exciting turn when Napoleon's grandfather (wonderfully played by Will Geer) adopts an aging lion from a traveling circus. When grandpa dies Napoleon (Johnny Whitaker) worries about ending up in an orphanage, and leaves home with Samantha (Foster) and his lion. Their only ally is an amiable mountain man played by Michael Douglas, who was then more of a newcomer to the business than nine-year-old Foster.

Napoleon and Samantha was one of dozens of excellent live-action Disney films released in the shadow of the studio's animated classics, and is everything that wholesome family entertainment should be. Whitaker, best known for his role on TV's *Family Affair*, was a prominent child star of the time and it's easy to see why. Foster's Samantha is smart and pragmatic, though she admits (with great reluctance) an occasional fear of the dark. "(Jodie's) success was just at the beginning of women's liberation, and she kind of personified that in a child," said her mother, "She had a strength and uncoquettishness." When Napoleon repeats his grandfather's dying words to Samantha, about going off to a far better place, the level-headed Samantha replies "That's very beautiful, Napoleon, but who's going to take care of you now?"

The lion, named Major, proved less gentle than his reputation when he almost mauled Foster. After a spell in the hospital she resumed her career with more TV work and a memorable bit in *Alice Doesn't Live Here Anymore* (1975). *Alice* director Martin Scorsese remembered Jodie when he began casting *Taxi Driver*, a brooding psychological drama following the descent of social outcast Travis Bickle (Robert DeNiro) into violent madness.

Scorsese creates a quiet, dreamlike atmosphere for Travis's deranged existence, heightened by Bernard Herrmann's extraordinary jazz score. The result is a singularly beautiful film about the ugliness of modern urban society.

The role of Iris, a pre-teen prostitute whom Travis attempts to "save," contains only two substantial scenes, but Foster delievered in those moments a haunting portrayal of lost youth that earned her an Oscar nomination. One invariably expects characters like this to be played by actresses in their twenties who could pass for teenagers. It is Foster's conspicuous pre-adolescence--she was just four years older here than as the adorable moppet of *Napoleon and Samantha*--that makes her performance all the more chilling. It would be unsettling to watch anyone of her then-thirteen years playing overtly sexual scenes, and Jodie Foster accentuates the lurid novelty of the situation by bringing out the innocence that exists beneath Iris's tough talk. Like Samantha, she pretends to be mature and in control, but deep down she is still afraid of the dark.

NAPOLEON AND SAMANTHA
Directed by Bernard McEveety; Written by Stewart Raffill; Produced by Winston Hibler; Music by Buddy Baker

Cast
Michael Douglas (Danny), Will Geer (Grandpa), Arch Johnson (Chief of Police), Johnny Whitaker (Napoleon), JODIE FOSTER (SAMANTHA)

TAXI DRIVER
Directed by Martin Scorsese; Written by Paul Schrader; Produced by Michael and Julia Phillips; Music by Bernard Herrmann

Cast
Robert DeNiro (Travis Bickle), Cybill Shepherd (Betsy), JODIE FOSTER (IRIS), Peter Boyle (Wizard), Harvey Keitel (Sport), Albert Brooks (Tom)

CLARK GABLE (1901-1960)

FIRST APPEARANCE: *Forbidden Paradise* (Famous Players-Paramount, 1924)

A STAR IS BORN: *A Free Soul* (MGM, 1931)

Long before Elvis Presley swiveled out of Tupelo, the title of "King" had already been bestowed upon Clark Gable. It originated with an off-hand reference from Spencer Tracy, who was trying to get to work through a mob of Gable fans--"Long live the king!" he yelled as he finally cleared the MGM gates. Columnist Ed Sullivan heard about the incident and sponsored a poll among his readers to choose a king and queen of Hollywood. Sure enough, Tracy was right--King Gable was officially crowned in 1938, one year before his portrayal of Rhett Butler in *Gone With the Wind* (1939). Myrna Loy, Gable's costar that year in *Test Pilot* and *Too Hot to Handle*, was selected as Queen.

William Clark Gable was born in Cadiz, Ohio, the only child born to William and Adelaide Gable. Adelaide died from epilepsy before her son's first birthday, and young William was sent to live with his grandparents for five years. After his father remarried the family moved to Hopedale, Ohio. Gable's stepmother Jennie Dunlap was a perceptive, liberated woman who accepted Clark's inherent independence and allowed him a long leash. His six-foot frame and chiseled physique were in place when Gable was fourteen, and he broke a few hearts when he left high school two years later for a job in a tire factory in nearby Akron. On a day off he visited the Music Hall and saw a production of *Bird of Paradise*. Fascinated by the make-believe world of the theatre, he took a second job--without pay--as a backstage call boy.

When his stepmother died, Gable was ordered back home by his father and put to work in the oil fields. He left after one miserable year, and would not speak to his father again for ten years. His love for the stage undiminished, Gable hooked up with theatre groups in Kansas City and later Oregon, where he met his first wife Josephine Dillon. Dillon was a Broadway veteran and an accomplished director and teacher and, when she moved to Hollywood in 1924, "Billy" Gable, fourteen years her junior, followed. She taught him how to act, suggested he use his middle name instead of William or Billy, and used her connections to get him jobs as an extra in silent films.

The first of these was an uncredited bit as a soldier in Ernst Lubitsch's *Forbidden Paradise*. Pola Negri starred as the Czarina of a mythical European kingdom who is rescued from revolutionaries by a young officer (Rod La Rocque). He falls in love with her, but after she jilts him he joins the revolutionaries in another attempted overthrow. The rebels are captured, but the monarch spares her former lover from execution. So fleeting was Gable's appearance that even the actor himself could not recall it in detail. "I worked a few days, and couldn't seem to find out what it was all about, he said. "I was in a hot uniform, held a sword, and got five dollars a day."

Forbidden Paradise was a hit, and revived the career of screen vamp Pola Negri. It didn't do a thing for Gable, however, who followed up with similarly nondescript roles in *The Merry Widow* (1925) and *The Plastic Age* (1925). He left the movies to play a more substantial role on stage in *The Copperhead*. Producer Lionel Barrymore chewed out the still green Gable at every turn, but the two emerged friends and remained so until Barrymore's death. In 1930, Gable received his first good reviews playing a desperate criminal in the Los Angeles production of *The Last Mile*. Barrymore arranged a screen test at MGM, and although the test was judged a failure Gable was on his way. He was offered supporting roles, mostly in gangster movies and westerns, always as a leering, brutish bad guy.

Roles in *The Painted Desert* (1931) and *Night Nurse* (1931) found him again playing villains, but women in the audience responded to his virile sex appeal and cheered him no matter how rotten his characters behaved. Metro-Goldwyn-Mayer took note of the phenomenon and reconsidered their first evaluation. Clark Gable signed a two-year contract at $350 a week, played his first romantic lead opposite Joan Crawford in *Laughing Sinners* (1931), and then landed the role that began his ascent to the royal throne.

A Free Soul seems a musty old morality play now, but the performances of Norma Shearer, Lionel Barrymore and Clark Gable breathe fire into the emotional morass. Shearer plays Jan Ashe, the free-spirited daughter of brilliant attorney Stephen Ashe (Barrymore). Jan falls for one of her father's clients, racketeer Ace Wilfong (Gable), and breaks her engagement to the courtly polo player Dwight Winthrop (Leslie Howard). Jan becomes Ace's mistress (or in the vernacular of the time, "she went to his place and stayed there"), but realizes her mistake after Ace becomes abusive. When Dwight learns what's going on he kills Ace, but Stephen successfully defends him in court. In an impassioned closing statement he blames himself and his alcoholism for Jan's behavior, and then collapses to the floor, dead.

Director Clarence Brown was impressed by the raw power of the scenes in which Gable manhandled Shearer. When MGM production chief (and Shearer's husband) Irving Thalberg saw the footage he ordered Brown to increase the violence even further. The plan was to further emphasize Ace's cruelty so that audiences wouldn't sympathize with him. It didn't work; in a harbinger of *Gone With the Wind*, Leslie Howard's straight arrow hero could not compete with Gable's roguish charm. "It was Clark who made villains popular," said Shearer. "Instead of the audience wanting the good guy to get the girl, they wanted the heavy to win her."

Shearer, cast effectively against her spotless ladylike image, was top-billed, and Barrymore won an Oscar for his performance, but it was fifth-billed Clark Gable who stole the picture. When he pushed lovely Norma into a chair, revealing the ladykiller's dark side and growling "Sit down and take it and like it!", a new type of movie hero was born. When the swooning sounds from America's moviehouses reached MGM, the studio tore up Gable's contract and raised his salary to $1150 a week. The next year, 1932, found Gable appearing in lead roles opposite Greta Garbo and Jean Harlow. For the next eleven years he was a fixture in the annual list of top ten box-office stars.

FORBIDDEN PARADISE
Directed by Ernst Lubitsch; Written by Agnes Christine Johnston and Hans Kraly, based on the play *The Czarina* by Lajos Biro and Melchoir Lengyel

Cast
Pola Negri (Catherine, the Czarina); Rod La Rocque (Captain Alexis Czerny), Adolphe Menjou (Chancellor) Pauline Starke (Anna)...CLARK GABLE (SOLDIER)

A FREE SOUL
Directed by Clarence Brown; Written by John Meehan, based on the novel by Adela Rogers St. John and the play by Willard Mack; Produced by Irving Thalberg; Music by William Axt

Cast
Norma Shearer (Jan Ashe), Leslie Howard (Dwight Winthrop), Lionel Barrymore (Stephen Ashe), CLARK GABLE (ACE WILFONG)

GRETA GARBO (1905-1990)

FIRST APPEARANCE: *Peter the Tramp* (Sweden, 1922)

A STAR IS BORN: *The Torrent* (MGM, 1926)

Greta Garbo received more publicity by avoiding publicity than any other movie star in history. It was not a marketing ploy, but it might as well have been--the more she wanted to be alone, the more everybody wanted to drop in for a visit.

Garbo's withdrawn, world-weary film persona combined with her self-imposed solitude away from Hollywood to create the "Garbo mystique" for which the actress is now as famous as for her sparse but distinguished filmography. Contemporary critics scoffed at Garbo's aloof manner--"Mystery?" wrote *Photoplay* in 1930, "She may be thinking the most profound of thoughts. She may be wondering if her herring will be chopped properly for dinner."--but then as now, devoted fans rallied to her defense. Fifteen thousand angry letters poured into *Photoplay*'s office after that snide observation, along with a few packages that were forwarded to the bomb squad. There was evidently something about Greta Garbo that connected with audiences on a deeper level than movie stars usually reach.

Her status as the patron saint of the separated lovers and the casualties of an apathetic society was confirmed when she said goodbye to show business--and meant it--after filming *Two-Faced Woman* in 1942. Garbo would never sail on the Love Boat, trade quips with Johnny Carson or take a bow at a film industry tribute. For the next 48 years, though she received scripts until the day of her death, Garbo never found a role that she couldn't successfully resist.

Greta Gustaffson grew up in Stockholm, the youngest of three children born to an unskilled laborer and his wife. Greta's father died when she was fourteen, forcing the children prematurely into the workforce. During her tenure as a salesgirl in the department store Paul U. Bergstrom's, a director of advertising films with the imposing name of Captain Ragnar Ring arranged to film a short subject entitled *How Not to Dress*. Greta, who had modeled hats as part of her counter duties, was asked to model dresses in a small comic role. In 1922, Ring used the teenage shopgirl again in a short which he produced for the Co-operative Society of Stockholm's Bakery Department. Greta's role in the film, *Our Daily Bread*, amounted to stuffing herself with cookies and cream puffs. The experience was nothing to quit her day job over, but Greta did just that after learning that Erik Petschler, a well-known director of feature films, was in the store. She presented herself to Petschler, recited a poem she learned in school, and asked for a role in whatever movie he was working on at the time. Petschler, more impressed with her bravado than any star quality she might have already possessed, granted her request.

The film was *Luffar-Peter*, translated as *Peter the Tramp*, a slapstick comedy about a pompous army fire officer whose uniform is stolen by a tramp while he skinny-dips with the mayor's three daughters. Greta played one of the daughters, who was also named Greta. "We have received no impression whatever of her capacity," wrote the magazine *Swing* in its review, "It pleases us, though, to have the opportunity of noting a new name in Swedish films and we hope to have a chance to mention it again." Modest praise at best, but enough to convince Greta that show business was her life. She earned a scholarship at the Royal Dramatic Theatre of Stockholm and met Mauritz Stiller, the foremost figure in Sweden's film industry. Stiller took special interest in Greta, and cast her in the principal role of Countess Elizabeth Dohna in his four-hour epic romance *The Saga of Gosta Berling* (1923). Now billed as Greta Garbo, she was hailed as a promising new star.

While Garbo went next into *The Joyless Street* (1925), Stiller was being wooed by MGM boss Louis B. Mayer. The director agreed to sign with Mayer only if his protege` was hired as well, and Mayer reluctantly complied. Greta was given a three-year contract, and orders to lose weight. In 1925, Garbo started filming *The Torrent*, and Mayer was already doubtful about her chances. "If she's a success, I'll give you the finest watch you've ever seen," he told Stiller, who was not assigned to direct the film but continued to coach her day and night. Stiller's devotion fueled persistent rumors that his relationship with Garbo was more than professional, but of course Garbo never confirmed or denied.

The Torrent was a tepid melodrama; young lovers Leonora (Garbo) and Rafael (Ricardo Cortez) are separated by Rafael's domineering mother. Leonora leaves their small Spanish village for Paris, where she becomes a celebrated opera singer. Years later she returns to Spain, but Rafael is still controlled by his mother and marries another woman. Heartbroken, Leonora resumes her career, and leaves the village forever. But when Mayer and MGM production head Irving Thalberg saw the first rushes from the film, they immediately tried to renegotiate Garbo's contract--upwards. The consensus was that Garbo was no great shakes in person, but a strange metamorphosis transpired when she appeared before the cameras. Suddenly her plainish Nordic face looked ravishing, and her languorous eyes glowed with a hypnotic force. To pinpoint and define her distinctive allure has been a challenge to scholars and critics ever since, but clearly it did not rely on material or costars to emerge. Garbo's magnetism and her natural instincts as an actress instilled the most commonplace role with passionate grandeur, and when she would later get the plum parts--Anna Karenina, Mata Hari--she made good scripts better, and challenged cinematographers to find an angle that would not make her look exquisite.

Despite her husky voice and pronounced accent, Garbo effortlessly survived the transition to talking pictures. Her performances in such classics as *Anna Christie* (1930), *Queen Christina* (1933), *Camille* (1936) and *Ninotchka* (1939) earned her a special Academy Award in 1954, but by then Garbo had long since left Hollywood, never to return.

PETER THE TRAMP
Directed, written and produced by Erik Petschler

Cast
Erik Silverjalm (Fire Lieutenant), Erik Petschler (Petter), GRETA GARBO (Greta Nordberg)

THE TORRENT
Directed by Monta Bell; Written by Dorothy Farnum, based on the novel *Entre Naranjos* by Vincente Blasco-Ibanez

Cast
Ricardo Cortez (Don Rafael Brull), GRETA GARBO (LEONORA), Gertrude Olmsted (Remedios)

AVA GARDNER (1922-1990)

FIRST APPEARANCE: *We Were Dancing* (MGM, 1942)

A STAR IS BORN: *The Killers* (Universal, 1946)

Ava Gardner was the ideal choice to become Hollywood's Hemingway heroine; a woman of intoxicating beauty, who complemented the "man's man" characters created by Ernest Hemingway, sharing their lust for life, and masking the same insecurities that drove their creator. After *The Killers* made her a star, Gardner starred in two more adaptations of Hemingway works, *The Snows of Kilmanjaro* (1952) and *The Sun Also Rises* (1957). They rank, along with the stylistically similar *Mogambo* (1953), among the too-few highlights of a career that rarely saw material of equal caliber.

Ava Lavinnia Gardner was a Christmas Eve baby, born into a farming family of seven that could not afford to exchange gifts. Their farm in Smithfield, North Carolina, was lost when Ava was only two, forcing her father, Jonas, to turn to sharecropping. Ava enjoyed a carefree, happy childhood, despite schoolyard taunts about her family's financial straits. After graduating high school, she received a loan from her older brother that allowed her to attend Atlantic Christian College.

She studied to be a secretary, but her plans changed after a trip to New York City. Commercial photographer Larry Tarr, who was married to Ava's sister Beatrice, took some pictures of 18-year-old Ava, and placed one of them in the window of his Fifth Avenue studio. A Loews Theatre executive suggested that Tarr send the photos to MGM, and to his amazement the studio was interested in giving Ava a screen test.

She arrived in Hollywood in 1941, with a seven-year contract and not a whit of acting experience. Between lessons in diction, acting and make-up, Gardner posed for hundreds of cheesecake stills that made her semi-famous before her first motion picture. Assigned to the extra ranks, she walked through a dozen films before her billing improved to something other than "Girl."

In *We Were Dancing*, Gardner makes her debut in a superfluous scene set in a hotel lobby. Wearing slacks and a silk blouse, she can be seen walking slowly across the lobby, oblivious to the admiring glances of Melvyn Douglas. The film was a comeback vehicle for Norma Shearer, who had passed on both *Gone With the Wind* (1939) and *Mrs. Miniver* (1942), but could not resist playing Polish princess Vicki Wilomirsky in this adaptation of Noel Coward's comedy of manners, *Tonight at 8:30*. It was a decision Shearer would later regret; after the film's disappointing box-office performance, the former queen of MGM made just one more movie before quitting the business.

Gardner, meanwhile, married the number-one movie star in the world, Mickey Rooney, but it did not improve her selection of roles. Sixteen months later, her resume` growing with forgotten appearances in B-minus movies like *Joe Smith, American* (1941), *Kid Glove Killer* (1941) and *Hitler's Madman* (1942), she divorced Rooney. Ava Gardner was now a well-known celebrity, but still untested as an actress.

Finally, in 1945, Gardner played her first lead role in *Whistle Stop* (1945). The film, for which she was loaned out from MGM to United Artists, was a modest hit, but MGM showed no interest in building upon the buzz about Ava that resulted. Instead, she was loaned once again, this time to Universal for *The Killers*. The Hemingway short story that provided the premise was played out in the film's first ten minutes, but the final 90 minutes opened up the enigmatic source material with remarkable flair.

Two hit men walk into a diner and announce their intention to kill a Swede named Ole Andreson. The killers leave after the Swede doesn't show. A young boy runs to warn Ole of what has happened, but the Swede is tired of running and chooses to stay and accept whatever fate has in store. Hemingway stopped there, but screenwriters Anthony Veiller and (uncredited) John Huston added a backstory that traced the Swede's life from adolesence to the night of the killers' visit.

When Ole (Burt Lancaster) first meets Kitty Collins (Ava Gardner), he is a promising boxer who is on the fence between a life of integrity and a life of vice. The sight of Kitty, wearing a slinky black dress and seductively crooning "The More I Know of Love, The Less I Know," takes the decision out of his hands. Once he is hooked, the Swede serves a prison sentence to cover her involvement in a jewel theft, and after his release he joins her and a small gang of hoods in planning a payroll heist. Kitty insists that once the job is done she and the Swede will start a new life, but instead she disappears with the gang's leader, Big Jim Colfax (Albert Dekker). A few more twists play out before The Swede comes to accept his folly, and Kitty gets her comeuppance.

"I'm poison to myself and everyone around me," says Kitty at one point, and that's as good a description as any of the character. For Ava Gardner, however, Kitty was the chance to prove that four years of acting lessons had paid off. A cool temptress, at least on the surface, Kitty uses her feminine allure the way Big Jim uses a pistol. But when her scheme unravels, she becomes hysterical, reverting to the vulnerable child she tried so hard to conceal. Gardner owns every scene she's in, and sings well enough to question MGM's decision to dub her voice in *Show Boat* (1951).

The sensuality that Ava Gardner conveyed so casually was often squandered in later films, in which smoldering was the only prerequisite for the job. When the roles were mediocre, as in the empty costumer *Knights of the Round Table* (1953), Gardner seemed completely out of her element. But when the material played to her natural strengths, as in *The Killers*, she made good movies better.

WE WERE DANCING
Directed by Robert Z. Leonard; Written by Claudine West, Hans Rameau and George Froeschel, based on the play *Tonight at 8:30* by Noel Coward; Produced by Robert Z. Leonard and Orville O. Dull; Music by Bronislau Kaper

Cast
Norma Shearer (Vicki Wilomirsky), Melvyn Douglas (Nicki Prax), Gail Patrick (Linda Wayne), Lee Bowman (Hubert Tyler), Marjorie Main (Judge Sidney Hawkes)...AVA GARDNER (GIRL)

THE KILLERS
Directed by Robert Siodmak; Written by Anthony Veiller and John Huston, based on the story by Ernest Hemingway; Produced by Mark Hellinger; Music by Miklos Rozsa

Cast
Edmond O'Brien (Jim Reardon), AVA GARDNER (KITTY COLLINS), Albert Dekker (Big Jim Colfax), Sam Levene (Lt. Sam Lubinsky), Virginia Christie (Lilly Lubinsky), John Miljan (Jake), Vince Barrett (Charleston), Burt Lancaster (The Swede)

A
FIRST APPEARANCES
PHOTO GALLERY

James Cagney in *Sinner's Holiday*

Cary Grant in *This is the Night*

Bette Davis in *Bad Sister*

Humphrey Bogart in *A Devil With Women*

Clockwise from top, left: Charleton Heston in *Dark City*; Julie Andrews in *Mary Poppins*; Gene Kelly in *For Me and My Gal*

Clockwise from top, left: Abbott and Costello in *One Night in the Tropics*; Spencer Tracy in *Up the River*; Gregory Peck in *Days of Glory*; Peter O'Toole in *The Savage Innocents*; Richard Widmark in *Kiss of Death*; Paul Newman in *The Silver Chalice*; Warren Beatty in *Splendor in the Grass*

Clockwise from top, left: Jane Russell
in *The Outlaw*; Lauren Bacall in *To Have
and Have Not*; Jessica Lange in
King Kong

Clockwise from top, left: Doris Day in *Romance on the High Seas*; Esther Williams in *Andy Hardy's Double Life*; Maureen O'Hara in *Jamaica Inn*; Claudette Colbert in *For the Love of Mike*; Jane Fonda in *Tall Story*; Anne Bancroft in *Don't Bother to Knock*; Katharine Hepburn in *A Bill of Divorcement*

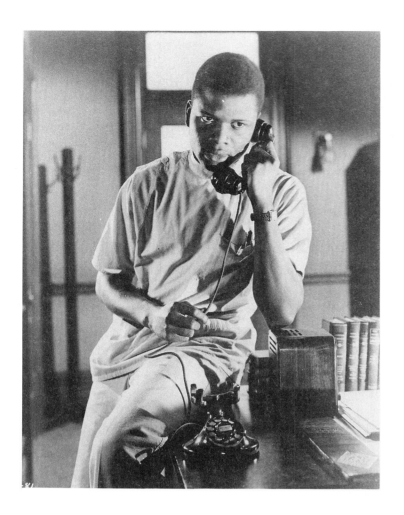

Clockwise from top, left: Sidney Poitier in
No Way Out, Barbra Streisand in *Funny Girl*,
Kirk Douglas in *The Strange Love of Martha
Ivers*

Clockwise from top, left: Elvis Presley in *Love Me Tender*, Jack Lemmon in *It Should Happen to You*, Elizabeth Taylor in *There's One Born Every Minute*, Faye Dunaway in *The Happening*, Olivia de Havilland in *Alibi Ike*, Burt Lancaster in *The Killers*, Joanne Woodward in *Count Three and Pray*

Clockwise from top, left: Fred Astaire in
Dancing Lady; Greer Garson in *Goodbye,
Mr. Chips*; Henry Fonda in *The Farmer Takes
a Wife*

Clockwise from top, left: Ronald Reagan in *Love Is On the Air*, Irene Dunne in *Leathernecking*, Linda Darnell in *Hotel for Women*; Charlie Chaplin in *Making a Living*; Jerry Lewis in *My Friend Irma*, Gene Tierney in *The Return of Frank James*, Tyrone Power in *Tom Brown of Culver*

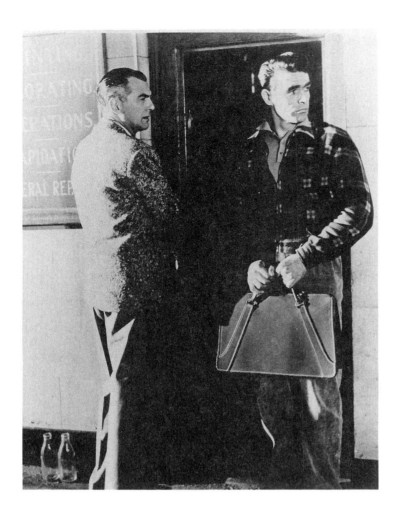

Clockwise from top, left: Sean Connery in
No Road Back; Michael Douglas in *Hail, Hero!*;
Marlon Brando in *The Men*

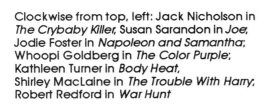

Clockwise from top, left: Jack Nicholson in
The Crybaby Killer, Susan Sarandon in *Joe*,
Jodie Foster in *Napoleon and Samantha*;
Whoopi Goldberg in *The Color Purple*;
Kathleen Turner in *Body Heat*,
Shirley MacLaine in *The Trouble With Harry*;
Robert Redford in *War Hunt*

JOHN GARFIELD (1913-1952)

FIRST APPEARANCE: *Footlight Parade* (Warner Bros., 1933)

A STAR IS BORN: *Four Daughters* (Warner Bros., 1938)

John Garfield, Hollywood's first antihero, was an actor ahead of his time; his portrayals of angry, socially underprivileged young men are a clear forerunner to the rebels of the next generation played by Marlon Brando and James Dean. Garfield's brusque demeanor usually masked a gentle, noble inner soul that would usually surface before the closing credits, often in an act of self-sacrifice.

He was born Julius Garfinkle on New York's lower East Side, and raised in the Bronx. The loss of his mother at the age of seven turned Julius into a bitter, felonious child who was expelled from several different schools. The authorities ordered that he attend a special school for problem children, and under the tutelage of its strict headmaster, Julius turned his life around. He took up boxing, and became proficient enough to rank as a semifinalist in a Golden Gloves tournament. Outside the ring, he studied oratory and drama at the Heckscher Foundation dramatic school. In 1928, while still a student, he appeared in the school's production of *A Midsummer Night's Dream*.

After playing a variety of small parts with a repertory group, Julius joined the newly-formed Group Theater Acting Company, changed his name to Jules Garfield, and worked as an apprentice during their 1930-31 season. His first role came in the road company production of *Counselor at Law*, and he was later engaged to play the same role on Broadway opposite Paul Muni. In between plays, Garfield visited California, and appeared as an extra in *Footlight Parade*. He then returned to Broadway where he was in far greater demand.

The film, set in the 1920s, begins as producer Chester Kent (James Cagney) is informed that talking pictures are threatening to put stage musicals out of business. Chester decides to create "prologues," live stage shows to be performed in movie theaters before the start of the feature. The new venture is successful, but is threatened by a rival producer who steals many of Kent's ideas. Like *Singin' In the Rain* (1952), *Footlight Parade* is a musical with an uncommonly strong storyline between songs, that presents an accurate look at how the advent of talkies put a lot of people out of work. The entire movie is a build-up to three spectacular Busby Berkeley numbers, played back-to-back in the final half-hour, but Cagney's energetic performance does not make it a chore to get there.

The last and best of the three numbers, "Shanghai Lil," features Cagney in the song-and-dance chores opposite Ruby Keeler, Dorothy Lamour and Ann Sothern somewhere among hundreds of chorus girls, and the first film appearance of John Garfield. The number begins with Cagney entering a waterfront bar, "lookin' for his Shanghai Lil." After a brawl clears out the bar, Cagney reappears in a sailor suit "borrowed" from another customer. What follows is three quick shots in rapid succession of other sailors, checking to see if the coast is clear. Garfield, peering out from over a barrel, is on for about two seconds.

Even when Garfield finally did decide on a motion picture career, he refused to leave the theater entirely. His contract with Warner Bros., signed in 1938, specified that he be allowed to do one play every year. Warners first cast Garfield in *Four Daughters*, an unassuming little domestic drama that unexpectedly turned into a mini-franchise for the studio. It's the kind of sweet-natured film about a loving family that might seem too sentimental for a modern audience, but it's our loss if we can no longer be moved by such sentiment.

The talented Lane sisters, Rosemary, Priscilla and Lola, were joined by Gale Page in portraying the four Lemp girls; Claude Rains plays their father and musical teacher. Felix Deitz (Jeffrey Lynn), a handsome, carefree young bachelor, arrives in town and charms all four sisters, but falls in love with Ann (Priscilla Lane). Felix is later joined by his friend Mickey Borden (Garfield), whose dark disposition is in complete contrast to that of Felix and the wholesome, happy Lemp family. Mickey's slovenly, cynical ways are gradually softened by the Lemp sisters, especially Ann. But when she accepts Felix's proposal, Mickey is convinced that the fates have once more conspired against him. The story then takes some unexpected turns that are best discovered without prior knowledge.

Garfield's colorful portrayal of the moody Mickey Borden was a star turn that came out of nowhere, and caught critics expecting him to conform to the conventions of a genteel melodrama completely off-guard. When Ann offers to help Mickey rent a room, he replies, "Make sure it's on the other side of the railroad track--I can't breathe this clean air." The Lemps' kindly aunt then asks Mickey if he'd like a cup of tea; "You needn't look so noble," he sneers, "Tea is only a little hot water." What is most haunting is Mickey's laughter, which sounds forced and unnatural, as if it's so rarely used that it needs practice.

Four Daughters was a Best Picture nominee that spawned three sequels, and John Garfield was nominated for Best Supporting Actor. His performance was described by the *New York Times* as "the most startling innovation in the way of a screen character in years."

FOOTLIGHT PARADE
Directed and produced by Lloyd Bacon, William Keighley and Busby Berkeley; Written by Manuel Seff and James Seymour; Music by Harry Warren, Al Dubin, Sammy Fain and Irving Kahal

Cast
James Cagney (Chester Kent), Joan Blondell (Nan Prescott), Ruby Keeler (Bea Thorn), Dick Powell (Scotty Blair), Guy Kibbee (Silas Gould)...JOHN GARFIELD (SAILOR IN "SHANGHAI LIL" NUMBER)

FOUR DAUGHTERS
Directed by Michael Curtiz; Written by Julius J. Epstein and Lenore Coffee, based on the novel *Sister Act* by Fannie Hurst; Produced by Hal B. Wallis; Music by Max Steiner

Cast
Claude Rains (Adam Lemp), May Robson (Aunt Etta), Priscilla Lane (Ann Lemp), Lola Lane (Thea Lemp), Rosemary Lane (Kay Lemp), Gale Page (Emma Lemp), Jeffrey Lynn (Felix Deitz), JOHN GARFIELD (MICKEY BORDEN)

JUDY GARLAND (1922-1969)

FIRST APPEARANCE: *Pigskin Parade* (20th Century-Fox, 1936)

A STAR IS BORN: *The Wizard of Oz* (MGM, 1939)

The emotional intensity that Judy Garland could summon in song has no peer. A joyful lyric became a festival of unbridled ecstasy; when the words were sad, Garland imparted them with such desperation and longing that they became the stuff of epic tragedy. Her filmography is composed almost entirely of musicals--*The Clock* (1945) and *Judgment at Nuremberg* (1961) are the notable exceptions--in which the passion in her vocals added depth to the characters she played. *The Wizard of Oz* would have been a classic fantasy without "Over the Rainbow," but Garland's rendition revealed and deepened the pathos in the orphaned Dorothy's desire to find happiness and security. Because Dorothy's search was more successful than Judy's, the song that became her signature grew ever more poignant with the passage of time.

Frances Ethel Gumm was the youngest of three daughters born to Frank Gumm, a singer, and his wife Ethel, a pianist. The Gumms operated a movie theater in Grand Rapids, Michigan, and would often perform a live show before the feature began. At the age of two, Frances walked out onto the stage where her sisters were singing, and launched into a rendition of "Jingle Bells," the only song she knew. From that day on, "Baby Gumm" was part of the act.

The Gumms toured vaudeville intermittently, and by the time they moved to Lancaster, California in 1926, the Gumm Sisters had become local celebrities. They performed on KFI Radio's *The Kiddie's Hour*, and in a 1929 short subject entitled *The Big Revue*. Frances was still known as Baby Gumm when the act played Chicago's Oriental Theatre in 1933 where, at the suggestion of George Jessel, the Gumms became the Garlands. Two years later, Frances changed her first name as well, choosing "Judy" from a song by Hoagy Carmichael.

During an August, 1935 engagement at the Cal-Neva Lodge in Lake Tahoe, Judy's parents hired an agent for their youngest, and a few weeks later Garland was singing "Zing Went the Strings of My Heart" for Louis B. Mayer at an MGM audition. Mayer was impressed with the thirteen-year-old's vocal ability, and soon Judy was attending classes on the MGM lot with Mickey Rooney and Deanna Durbin.

One of the most famous short subjects ever made is *Every Sunday* (1936), in which Garland's and Durbin's performances doubled as competition for a contract. MGM only wanted one teenage singer on their roster, and the decision to keep Judy and release Deanna has been scrutinized ever since. It is possible that Mayer's actual choice was Durbin, and his order was miscommunicated. Deanna became a star overnight at Universal, while Judy waited another year to make her MGM debut.

She did, however, appear in the 20th Century-Fox film *Pigskin Parade*. MGM endorsed the idea as a chance to gauge her talent and audience appeal without having to spend any money. It was the last time Garland would be loaned out in her career. The stars of the film were Stuart Erwin and Patsy Kelly, but the supporting cast is more fun to watch--Judy, Betty Grable, Tony Martin and Alan Ladd all make early-career appearances.

The story is ignited by the type of silly misunderstanding that always occurs in musicals; Yale University plans to invite the University of Texas to play football, but by mistake the invitation goes out to tiny Texas State, where by coincidence they've just hired new football coach Slug Winters (Jack Haley). Winless in two years, the newly-inspired Texas State recruits farm boy quarterback Amos Dodd (Erwin) and starts winning games. The climactic football game would have been more exciting if the teams weren't clad in almost identical uniforms, making it impossible to tell them apart.

Judy, ninth-billed and fourteen years-old at the time of her debut, plays Amos's kid sister

Sairy Dodd. Barefoot, wearing a ragged dress and long pigtails that suggest she wandered in from a Pippi Longstocking audition, a surprisingly plump Judy announces in a thick southern accent, "I'm Sairy Dodd and I kin sing--wanna hear me?" She has to ask three times before somebody finally agrees to listen.

Pigskin Parade may have been Garland's first film, but she was a seasoned veteran of stage and radio, and in the three songs she performs, she shows a polished performer's instincts and clear signs of the diva she was to become. While belting out "The Balboa" and "The Texas Tornado" with remarkable power, she is already facing the audience head on, feet spread apart, and throwing her arms open wide with dynamic flourish. On the romantic ballad "It's Love I'm After," which she inexplicably sings to fans in a football stadium prior to a game, her control is not yet precise, but when Judy unleashes a last note that could reach the back row of the stadium without electronic amplification, there is no doubt that the maturity of her talent at age fourteen is phenomenal.

MGM thought so too, but it took them awhile to find the right project to prove it. She turned sixteen while waiting for a movie, and was finally granted a solo number in *Broadway Melody of 1938*. Her performance of "You Made Me Love You" to a photo of Clark Gable was the highlight of the film, and Judy was seldom out of work again. After a series of minor (but worth seeing) musicals with Mickey Rooney, including *Thoroughbreds Don't Cry* (1937) and *Love Finds Andy Hardy* (1938), Judy became the studio's third choice to play Dorothy Gale in their lavish production of *The Wizard of Oz*. When Shirley Temple and Deanna Durbin proved unavailable, Judy received the plum assignment.

There's not much that hasn't been documented about *The Wizard of Oz*; all the backstage Munchkin difficulties, casting changes (from Buddy Ebsen to Jack Haley in the Tin Man role, Frank Morgan playing the Wizard after Ed Wynn turned it down), even the fact that "Over the Rainbow" was almost cut because some executive felt it "slowed the movie down," are stories known to every film lover. Annual television showings and multi-generational appeal make a convincing case for *Wizard* as the film seen by more people than any motion picture in history.

Although different actors were considered for every major role, no one else is now imaginable other than Garland, Haley, Ray Bolger as the Scarecrow, Bert Lahr as the Lion, Billie Burke as the Good Witch and Margaret Hamilton as the Wicked Witch of the West. Judy Garland won a special Academy Award for "outstanding performance as a screen juvenile." She was obviously not the ten-year-old envisioned by Baum in the *Oz* books, but Judy's ability to convincingly *act* the part of a child, even while singing with the voice of an adult, is perhaps the one element of excellence in the film that is most often overlooked.

PIGSKIN PARADE
Directed by David Butler; Written by Harry Tugend, Jack Yellen and William Conselman, based on a story by Arthur Sheekman, Nat Perrin and Mark Kelly; Produced by Bogart Rogers; Music by Lew Pollack and Sidney Mitchell

Cast
Stuart Erwin (Amos Dodd), Patsy Kelly (Bessie Winters), Jack Haley (Slug Winters), Johnny Downs (Chip Carson), Betty Grable (Laura Watson), Arline Judge (Sally Saxon), Dixie Dunbar (Ginger Jones), Anthony Martin (Tommy Barker), JUDY GARLAND (SAIRY DODD)

THE WIZARD OF OZ
Directed by Victor Fleming; Written by Noel Langley, Florence Ryerson and Edgar Allen Woolf, based on the novel by L. Frank Baum; Produced by Mervyn LeRoy; Music by Harold Arlen, E.Y. Harburg, others.

Cast
JUDY GARLAND (DOROTHY), Ray Bolger (The Scarecrow), Bert Lahr (The Cowardly Lion), Jack Haley (The Tin Man), Billie Burke (Glinda), Margaret Hamilton (The Wicked Witch)

GREER GARSON (1908-   )

FIRST APPEARANCE: *Goodbye, Mr. Chips* (MGM, 1939)

A STAR IS BORN: *Goodbye, Mr. Chips*

Greer Garson always seemed to have the audience on her side from the moment she appeared on screen. Garson herself, a rare combination of patrician poise and girl-next-door sincerity, deserves most of the credit for this, but MGM boss Louis B. Mayer was also responsible for stacking the deck in her favor. From the moment Mayer spotted Garson on a London stage in 1938, he guided her career with an almost paternal dedication. Mayer chose all of her movie roles until his death, and it was under his tutelage that Greer Garson became the queen of MGM in the years during and after World War II.

Born in County Down, Ireland, Greer Garson grew up planning to be a teacher, but her first steady employment after graduating with honors from the University of London was in the office of an advertising agency. Acting in local theatre productions was only a hobby at first, but eventually led to an association with the venerable Birmingham Reperatory Theater. Garson debuted in the 1932 production *Street Scene*, and remained with the company for two years. In 1934 she made her London debut in *The Tempest*, and in the next four years she played lead and featured roles in a variety of plays, including *Golden Arrow* (opposite Laurence Olivier), and *Mademoiselle*, directed by Noel Coward.

During one of his frequent trips to London, Louis B. Mayer added Garson to the MGM stable of stars after watching her performance in the play *Old Music*. That was the easy part. The hard part was finding a suitable film in which to debut his discovery. One year later Garson was about ready to give up and return to London when the studio acquired the rights to film James Hilton's novel *Goodbye, Mr. Chips*.

Charles Chipping (Robert Donat) arrives at the hallowed Brookfield School for Boys to begin his first year of teaching in 1870, and is promptly intimidated and ignored by his boisterous students. Determined to prove himself, he uses harsh discipline to gain his students' respect. He remains a capable if not very popular instructor until his fortieth birthday, when during a holiday in Vienna he meets and falls in love with Katherine, another British traveller. They return together to Brookfield, and almost immediately "Mrs. Chips," as she comes to be known, brings out the compassion for his students that Chipping always had, but never knew how to express. Tragically, Katherine dies in childbirth, and the baby does not survive either. Mr. Chips remains at Brookfield, where over the next four deades he becomes as revered an institution as the school itself.

Donat was exceptional as Chips, aging convincingly from a novice young teacher to an 83-year-old patriarch. The role of Katherine was much smaller but pivotal; it is she who awakens romantic love in the shy, insecure Chips, and inspires him to earn his students' regard with affection instead of discipline. Hilton describes the character in the book as "captivating and lively...(she) soon had Chips, the boys and the masters worshipping at her feet."

Greer Garson ably fit this exalted profile. "Her Katherine is one of the nicest people we would hope to meet anywhere," wrote the *New York Times*. "When she dies, we hate to have the picture continue without her." Truer words were never written in the *Times*--only the best of movies could survive the departure of such a delightful character. It seems perfectly natural that Chips would practically propose marriage to Katherine at their first meeting-he sees her through the mist on a mountaintop, and is instantly smitten with her red-haired beauty and Irish charm. Garson's impeccable diction imbues the British accent that most Americans automatically equate with refinement with warmth and compassion. *The New Yorker* defined her persona as "the shop girl's vision of a great lady, (which) made her an incontestable star in a decade that required a staunch, wholesome ideal."

Robert Donat's performance was chosen over Clark Gable's portrayal of Rhett Butler in

Gone With the Wind for the Best Actor Academy Award in 1939. Greer Garson received a Best Actress nomination, the first of seven she would collect over the next 21 years. Louis B. Mayer said that Garson "embodied the very essence of decency and good living," and continued to cast her in genteel roles; at age 32 she convincingly played the teenage heroine of *Pride and Prejudice* (1940), and had hits with *Blossoms in the Dust* (1941) and *Random Harvest* (1942). Her Oscar-winning performance as the title character in *Mrs. Miniver* (1942) had historical implications that transcended drama; one can only speculate how influential the film was in swaying American public opinion about entering World War II, but Winston Churchill said it was more important to the British cause than the combined efforts of six troop divisions.

Garson would occasionally play against her wholesome image (1949's *That Forsyte Woman*) but was content with the perception of her created by Mayer and treasured by audiences who needed such images in the trying times when their country was at war; "If you are going to be typed," she said, "there are worse molds in which you can be cast."

GOODBYE, MR. CHIPS
Directed by Sam Wood; Written by W.C. Sheriff, Claudine West, Eric Maschwitz and Sidney Franklin, based on the novella by James Hilton; Produced by Victor Saville; Music by Richard Addinsell

Cast
Robert Donat (Charles Chipping), GREER GARSON (KATHERINE ELLIS), Terry Kilburn (John/Peter Colley), John Mills (Young Peter Colley), Paul Henreid (Max Staefel), Judith Furse (Flora)

MEL GIBSON (1956-   )

FIRST APPEARANCE: *Summer City* (Avalon, 1977)

A STAR IS BORN: *Mad Max* (AIP-Filmways, 1979)

Action movie heroes with a difference have been Mel Gibson's specialty since he first donned black leather to play an angry guy named Max. High-speed car chases that end in fiery crashes were the hook for the *Mad Max* series, but what began as Roger Corman-esque quickies for the drive-in crowd gradually evolved into one man's search for the recovery of his soul. In the *Lethal Weapon* series, Gibson's Sgt. Riggs was a brooding, suicidal recluse, not the standard maverick hunk with a quip to follow every fight. If Gibson could add layers of complexity to guys who usually just drive fast and shoot straight, it should not have surprised anyone that he could play Hamlet without anyone laughing. He was even better in *The Man Without a Face* (1994). His portrayal of a disfigured recluse with a shady past ranks among the best performances anyone's given in the 1990s. But when you're labeled "The Sexiest Man Alive" by *People* magazine, it's an uphill battle for respect.

Articles that hailed Gibson as the hottest Australian export since the kangaroo didn't dig very deep in their research. Mel Columcille Gibson was born and raised in Peekskill, New York, the sixth of eleven children. Mel is *not* short for Melvin, as Gibson quickly points out in interviews, and Columcille is Gaelic for "dove of the church." Gibson's father Hutton worked in a variety of jobs, from railroad brakeman to computer programmer to plumber. After a winning streak on *Jeopardy*, he moved his family to Sydney, Australia to keep his sons out of Vietnam. Mel attended Catholic school, worked at Kentucky Fried Chicken for extra money, and showed no interest in acting or any other career. After high school, Mel's sister enrolled him in the National Institute of Dramatic Art at the University of New South Wales. "I was goofing off all my life, so I thought why not get paid for it?" he told *Redbook*. He auditioned with a scene from *King Lear*, and was one of only twenty students to be accepted.

In 1977, after appearing in various stage productions, Gibson earned a paltry $20 paycheck for his film debut in *Summer City*. From the looks of the movie, that may have been ten percent of the budget. His character, Scollop, is one of four hooligans who stumble through a drunken weekend at an Aussie beach in the 1950s. About halfway in, following scene after scene of this moronic quartet swilling beer and sexually harrassing every female they see, there is a shot of roaring ocean waves and gathering storm clouds, the director's subtle way of foreshadowing danger. Sure enough, Boo (the group's leader) seduces a fifteen-year-old girl and then brags about sleeping with the fiancee' of his pal, Sandy. Sandy overhears and grabs a rifle, but the girl's father kills Boo first. Dad then goes after the others, but Sandy is still armed and blows him away. Not exactly Frankie and Annette, mate.

If you were going to pick the one person in *Summer City* most likely to get another job in movies, the first answer (after "none of the above") would not be Gibson, who would finish near the bottom. Playing a blonde for the first and last time, he has the smallest of the four lead roles as the shy, quiet, slightly-less-obnoxious-than- the-rest surfer who does little more than observe the plot unfolding. His big dramatic moment occurs when Scollop discovers the dead body of Boo and breaks into tears. Gibson's attempt at heart-wrenching waterworks actually recalls Stan Laurel after he is bopped on the head by Oliver Hardy's bowler.

Fortunately, director George Miller had spotted Mel Gibson at drama school and cast him anyway in *Mad Max*. Although Miller wasn't aiming much higher than the *Summer City* creative team, his innovation as a filmmaker transformed a standard chase movie into something like art. *Mad Max* returned over $100 million on a $300,000 investment, and outgrossed *Star Wars* in Australia. Gibson became an international star overnight, despite the fact that his voice was dubbed in the few prints that reached America via an apathetic distributor.

The story, set "A few years from now," opens with police officer Max pursuing an escaped cop killer known as the Night Rider. When the Rider is killed, his allies exact revenge by brutally murdering Max's wife and son. Max, who had already expressed his frustration at following the rules in a time of near-anarchy, abandons law and order completely and wipes out the Rider's gang.

It's a bare bones plot, padded out by gratuitous nudity, but George Miller's flair for the creative angle in the bread-and-butter action scenes elevates *Mad Max* above the usual 'B' movie mix. The opening chase is a definite attention-getter, and the last stand of Max's family is superbly shot. Mel Gibson's performance is impaired by the dubbing that resulted from concern over his Australian accent, but his emotions and reactions clearly register in several dramatic moments. Gibson was allowed to speak in *The Road Warrior* (1981), the *Mad Max* sequel in which George Miller's vision of a post-apocalyptic society reaches fruition. Vehicular mayhem was in the spotlight once again, but thanks to Gibson, Max's spiritual journey became as intrinsic to the film as the climactic chase.

SUMMER CITY
Directed by Christopher Fraser; Written and produced by Phil Avalon; Music by Phil Butkis

Cast
John Jarrat (Sandy), Phil Avalon (Robbie), Steve Bisley (Boo), MEL GIBSON (SCOLLOP), James Elliot (Father), Debbie Forman (Caroline)

MAD MAX
Directed by George Miller; Written by George Miller and James McCausland, based on a story by Miller and Byron Kennedy; Produced by Byron Kennedy; Music by Brian May

Cast
MEL GIBSON (MAX), Joanne Samuel (Jessie), Hugh Keays-Byrne (The Toecutter), Steve Bisley (Jim Goose), Roger Ward (Fifi Macaffee), Vince Gil (Night Rider)

WHOOPI GOLDBERG (1950-   )

FIRST APPEARANCE: *The Color Purple* (Warner Bros., 1985)

A STAR IS BORN: *The Color Purple*

Whoopi Goldberg does not have the standard name, look, or manner of a movie star, but she had enough faith that there would be a place in Hollywood for an artist with her amazing, innovative gifts. Goldberg's strange, wonderful journey from a caustic, iconoclastic one-woman company on the fringe of New York theater in *The Spook Show* (1983), to America's sweetheart in *Sister Act* (1992) is an encouraging sign that talent, in whatever form, will always be embraced.

Raised in the Chelsea housing project of Manhattan, the childhood of Whoopi Goldberg, who was born Caryn Johnson, sounds like a made-for-TV movie with Cicely Tyson. Her father abandoned the family before she was out of diapers, forcing her mother to work long hours as a nurse to support her daughter. Caryn's education was hampered by dyslexia, and she dropped out of high school and into drug use before finishing the ninth grade. What rescued her from becoming another tragic statistic was a lifelong fascination with theater and motion pictures. She began performing at the age of eight, and never considered another career.

In her late teens, she stopped taking drugs, married her drug counselor, and gave birth to a daughter. In 1974, after the marriage dissolved, Caryn moved to San Diego. Part-time jobs as a bricklayer and a mortuary cosmetologist helped pay the bills while she pursued her dream of performing. She joined an improvisational theater group, and changed her name to Whoopi (after the cushion) Goldberg. After moving to Berkeley, she honed her acting skills and developed a personal repertoire of thirteen different characters, including a male junkie, a nine-year-old black girl who dreams of being white, and a surfer chick who is distraught over an unwanted pregnancy. In 1983, she performed all her characters in *The Spook Show*, a one-woman tour de force that earned rave reviews when it premiered in San Francisco.

Goldberg took the show across America and through Europe, before moving into a tiny off-Broadway theater in New York. After attending a performance, director Mike Nichols took the show to Broadway. A few months later, Goldberg gave a command performance of the show in Los Angeles for Steven Spielberg, Quincy Jones, and Alice Walker, the author of the Pulitzer Prize-winning novel *The Color Purple*. In addition to her regular act, she also slipped in a parody of Spielberg's *E.T.* (1982) called *Blee Tee*. The director was impressed enough to offer her the lead in his film adaptation of Walker's novel.

By the time we first see Goldberg in the film, we have already met her character, Celie, as a teenage girl who is raped by her father, and who gives birth to two children that are promptly given away. Albert (Danny Glover) is attracted to Celie's sister, Nettie, but when she rejects his advances, Albert marries Celie and refuses to let her see Nettie anymore. Nettie writes letters, but Albert intercepts them before they get to Celie. His mistreatment of his wife culminates with his invitation to another woman, singer Shug Avery (Margaret Avery) to move into their home.

Though they seem to have nothing in common, Celie and Shug form a devoted friendship (that evolves into far more in the book). Celie draws strength from her relationship with Shug and with Sofia (Oprah Winfrey), the wife of Albert's oldest son, whose tragic fate is revealed in a powerful subplot. Many years later, Celie finds the letters from her sister that her husband had concealed, and learns that Nettie is working as a missionary in Africa, and is raising Celie's two children. She summons the courage to leave her husband, and takes a job as a seamstress. When Nettie returns from Africa, the two estranged sisters are reunited after nearly forty years.

The Color Purple arrived in theaters amidst heavy speculation, much of it negative.

Fans of the book who were familiar with Spielberg's filmography were certain that the mix was a recipe for disaster--*Midnight Express* animated by Walt Disney. Such reverence for a writer is so rare in Hollywood that it's tempting to label the criticism as just another opportunity to bring the most successful director in history down a few pegs. The establishment had the last laugh by stiffing the film on all eleven of its Academy Award nominations, but nothing or nobody could dim the brilliance of Whoopi Goldberg's performance.

The word-of-mouth on her stage show had just started to reach the Hinterlands via *Entertainment Tonight*, so there were expectations attached to Goldberg's novelty-store name as well, though as yet no one was exactly sure what they were. Whether Spielberg delivered all the richness of the source material is debatable, but a better Celie than Goldberg could not be imagined. Playing a woman who is scared to show her feelings, speak too loudly, or dream too grandly, Goldberg must convey Celie's longing for her family, and her indomitable spirit, with a minimum of dramatic gesture. Rarely has facial expression played a more important role than dialogue in the depiction of a character, as it certainly does here. When Celie smiles, first in a pivotal scene with Shug Avery and later when she reads the letters from her sister, it's a smile that is so well-deserved that one cannot help but be moved. "The affirmation at the end of the film is so joyous," wrote Roger Ebert, "that this is one of the few movies in a long time that inspires tears of happiness, and earns them."

THE COLOR PURPLE

Directed by Steven Spielberg; Written by Menno Meyjes, based on the novel by Alice Walker; Produced by Steven Spielberg, Kathleen Kennedy, Frank Marshall, Quincy Jones, Jon Peters and Peter Guber; Music by Quincy Jones

Cast
Danny Glover (Albert), WHOOPI GOLDBERG (CELIE), Margaret Avery (Shug Avery), Oprah Winfrey (Sofia), Willard Pugh (Harpo), Akousa Busia (Nettie), Adolph Caesar (Old Mister), Rae Dawn Chong (Squeak)

BETTY GRABLE (1916-1973)

FIRST APPEARANCE: *Happy Days* (Fox, 1929)

A STAR IS BORN: *Down Argentine Way* (20th Century-Fox, 1940)

When Betty Grable's name is mentioned, the first image formed does not emerge from one of her sixty motion pictures, but from a photo taken by Frank Powolny in 1943 that became the most famous pin-up of World War II. Wearing a one-piece swimsuit and matching pumps, Grable smiles in a sexy over-the-shoulder pose that now holds a permanent place in American popular culture. That this one image is still so predominant doesn't say much for the quality of her filmography; although Grable was a top-ten draw at the box office from 1941 to 1951, the splashy 20th Century-Fox Technicolor musicals that brought her fame are formula-laden vehicles that tend to blur in retrospect.

Ruth Elizabeth Grable, born in St. Louis, Missouri, was the daughter of a former amateur actress who saw in Betty a second chance to enter the world of show business. Lillian Grable, in the grasp of full stage mother hysteria, enrolled Betty in voice lessons, dance lessons and saxophone lessons before the little girl had entered kindergarten. In 1929, Lillian felt she had learned her lessons well enough to move to Hollywood. Before it was discovered that she was underage, Betty was signed by Fox to a $50-a-week stock contract, and given a chorus spot in three of the studio's early musical efforts.

Most sources list *Let's Go Places*, released on December 30, 1929, as Betty Grable's film debut, but *Happy Days* was released one week earlier, and though you haven't a chance of finding her in the chorus, Grable does appear in one of the musical numbers. The movie is an excuse to bring together every star on the Fox lot, including Will Rogers, Janet Gaynor, Warner Baxter, George Jessel, Rex Bell, Victor McLaglen and Edmund Lowe, who appear either in cameos or as part of the climactic song and dance finale. The impetus is provided by the beloved old Colonel Billy Batcher (Charles E. Evans), whose celebrated show boat is threatened with drydock unless his plucky future daughter-in-law Margie (Marjorie White) can convince all the entertainers who got their start on the boat to put on a benefit revue.

The curtain opens on a chorus of over seventy men and women, identically costumed, and wearing a wig and blackface make-up for a number called "Minstrel Memories." The camera, which wasn't very mobile in the early talkies, stays well back in order to fit everyone into the frame and, as a result of the heavy make-up and lack of close-ups, it is impossible to spot Grable in the crowd. And if you think you're enough of an authority on Betty to identify her legendary million dollar legs, think again. She was just thirteen years old at the time, and the chorus wears slacks anyway. Those who can view minstrel shows in the context of their time might enjoy *Happy Days*, though admittedly it's tough to get beyond the offensive surface.

Fox released Grable when they learned her age, but she continued to work steadily, first as a "Goldwyn Girl" and later at RKO Studios in a variety of 'B' movie comedies and musicals. Minor chorus roles in two 1936 Fred Astaire-Ginger Rogers films, *The Gay Divorcee* and *Follow the Fleet*, comprise the meager highlight of her first decade in motion pictures. The big break came when Alice Faye, the reigning queen of 20th Century-Fox in 1940, was forced by illness to withdraw from her next project, *Down Argentine Way*. Betty, who was once again under contract at the studio where her career began, was cast in her place. After thirty-two films, she received her first lead role by default.

She plays Glenda Crawford, wealthy socialite and member of the horsey set. At an equestrian event in New York she meets Ricardo (Don Ameche), a handsome Argentinian who agrees to sell Glenda one of his father's prize horses. But when he later discovers that her last name is Crawford, he calls off the sale, remembering his father's lifelong hatred for the Crawford family. When Glenda follows Ricardo back to Argentina, he can no longer deny his affection for her, and together they attempt to halt his father's vendetta.

Down Argentine Way was an energetic beginning to the Grable dynasty at Fox, which brought $100 million into the studio's coffers and immeasurable cheer to millions of Americans during difficult times. You won't remember much from the film after it's over, but it is hard to look away while it's on. "If you're lucky enough to see a mint print of the picture, the Technicolor will bang your eyes out," raved the *Motion Picture Guide*, and the laserdisc certainly qualifies. Like all the Betty Grable musicals, this one is about beautiful people wearing beautiful clothes, singing and dancing to take people's minds off the war overseas, and if the product is sometimes deficient, the packaging could not be more sumptuous.

Carmen Miranda, she of the fruit salad hat, makes her film debut here, and there's a dazzling athletic dance by the Nicholas Brothers that is by far the best moment in the film. Grable's all-American beauty and natural ebullience compensates for a performance that can fairly be assessed as only adequate, though she sings well on the title song and "Two Dreams Met" opposite Don Ameche. As a dancer she is even better, and there is reason to believe, as many Grable fans do, that had she ever been allowed to costar with Fred Astaire or Gene Kelly she might have been taken to another level. However, she was too valuable a commodity to ever be loaned out to MGM, which made such dream team-ups impossible.

HAPPY DAYS
Directed by Benjamin Stoloff; Written by Sidney Lanfield and Edwin Burke; Music by Con Conrad, Sidney Mitchell, Archie Gottler, L. Wolfe Gilbert, Abel Baer, others.

Cast
Marjorie White (Margie), Charles E. Evans (Colonel Billy Batcher), Richard Keene (Dick), Stuart Erwin (Jig)...BETTY GRABLE (CHORUS)

DOWN ARGENTINE WAY
Directed by Irving Cummings; Written by Darrell Ware and Karl Tunberg, based on an idea by Rian James and Ralph Spence; Produced by Darryl F. Zanuck; Music by Mack Gordon, Harry Warren, Gene Rose, Al Dubin, Jimmy McHugh, others.

Cast
Don Ameche (Ricardo Quintana), BETTY GRABLE (GLENDA CRAWFORD), Carmen Miranda (Herself), Charlotte Greenwood (Binnie Crawford), J. Carroll Naish (Casiano), Henry Stephenson (Don Diego Quintana)

CARY GRANT (1904-1986)

FIRST APPEARANCE: *This is the Night* (Paramount, 1932)

A STAR IS BORN: *Topper* (MGM, 1937)

"Everyone wants to be Cary Grant. I want to be Cary Grant."

--Cary Grant

Even Grant himself had to admit the truth; the public persona of Cary Grant--on screen and to some extent off-screen--was a role played to perfection, as were so many others, by one Archibald Leach of Bristol, England. And in retrospect, it seems obvious that no one could be born with the genes for that much easy, confident charisma, urbane sophistication, sly sense of humor and self-effacing charm.

Andrew Sarris accurately labeled him "the most gifted light comedian in the history of the cinema," and for the most part Grant was content to remain within the genre in which his prowess is unequaled. Occasionally he would test his versatility with successful ventures into drama (*Penny Serenade*--1941, *None But the Lonely Heart*-- 1944), suspense (*Suspicion*--1941, *Notorious*--1946) and adventure (*Gunga Din*--1939). Always his audience gladly followed, for Cary Grant was a personality larger than life, and a force above genre and material. Whatever it is that makes a movie star more than an actor or a celebrity, Cary Grant had more of it than anyone else.

His story began on the poor side of Bristol, where Elias Leach married Elsie Kingdon in 1898, and Elsie gave birth to a son in 1899. The child died of menengitis two days before his first birthday, and Elsie never fully recovered from the loss. When Archie was born in 1904, she was determined that nothing would endanger his well-being. Her single-minded devotion to her son became so obsessive that Elias, fearing for Elsie's mental health, had her committed to an institution. Archie would not see his mother again for twenty years.

Life at home went from unhappy to intolerable when father and son moved in with Elias's less-than-welcoming mother. Archie found solace at the Bristol Hippodrome, a popular music hall. He was there so often that the manager gave him a job as a message-runner. When Bob Pender's Knockabout Comedians played the Hippodrome, the naturally-athletic Archie talked his way into joining the troupe at age fourteen. He remained with Pender for two years, but after a lengthy tour of America, he chose not to return with them to England.

At age nineteen, with five years of stage experience in which he tumbled and cartwheeled every night but never spoke a line, Archie Leach left the rapidly-dying vaudeville circuit for the legitimate stage. In 1927, four years after the boat for Bristol left New York, Archie had worked his way up from boardwalk barker at Coney Island to a role in the Broadway operetta *Golden Dawn*. Next up was the musical *Boom Boom*, which lasted just 72 performances but led to screen-test offers at Paramount for Archie and his costar, Jeanette MacDonald. Jeanette got a contract, Archie was sent back to Broadway.

Four more years of steady work convinced Paramount to offer Archie a small role as one of four sailors chasing Anna Chang in the one-reel short *Singapore Sue* (1931). *Singapore Sue* was shot in one week, but was not released for over a year, by which time Cary Grant was already an up-and-coming star. Chronologically this is his first film appearance, and his only credit under the name Archie Leach.

It was a meeting with Paramount production chief Benjamin Schulberg, the man who discovered Clara Bow and Gary Cooper, that led to another screen test, this time with happier results. Archie Leach was given a five-year contract at Paramount and a name change to Cary Grant--Cary from the character Cary Lockwood that he had played on stage in *Nikki* (1931), Grant just because he liked the sound of it.

Grant made eight movies in the first year of his contract, beginning with *This is the Night*, a strained bedroom farce in which three men and two women mix and match their affections in Venice. Grant plays Stephen, an Olympic javelin thrower who discovers his wife Claire (Thelma Todd) making time with rich bachelor Gerald Grey (Roland Young). Before the situation can turn violent, Gerald's friend Bunny West (Charles Ruggles) arrives bearing two tickets to Venice. Gerald tries to cover by claiming to be married, and offering to join Stephen and Claire in Italy. Bunny helps by hiring a struggling actress (Lily Damita) to play his wife. In Venice, while Stephen attempts to keep an eye on Gerald, he finds himself attracted to his "wife." Complications, as they say, ensue. Grant hated the movie and his performance (which is dictated by the frenetic nature of the material), but his handsome features, and the musical inflection in his distinctive British accent were praised in reviews. *Variety* tagged him as a "potential femme rave."

Some of Grant's early films are memorable, but primarily for the performances of others--Marlene Dietrich in *Blonde Venus* (1932), Mae West in *She Done Him Wrong* (1933), Katharine Hepburn in *Sylvia Scarlett* (1936). For the next five years, he was consistently better than the bemused straight men and suave, tuxedo-clad playboys he was forced to play. Frustrated, Grant bought out his Paramount contract and became one of Hollywood's only free agents. After 27 films he was still an up-and-coming actor, looking for the movie that would establish him as a major box-office draw. He found it during a conversation with his neighbor, Hal Roach.

In *Topper* (1937), the famous Cary Grant persona blossoms. His character, George Kerby, is a rich, happy-go-lucky millionaire who perishes with his wife Marion (Constance Bennett) in a car crash. As spirits, they must teach the stuffy, henpecked banker Cosmo Topper (Roland Young) how to have fun, before being allowed entry into Heaven. Grant is completely in his element here, mischievously interrupting Topper's bank directors' meeting the way a ten-year-old would pester a substitute teacher; while Topper drones on about profits and losses, Kerby tries to write his name upside-down and backwards. "It can't be done," he announces to the board, oblivious to the proceedings, before joining his wife for another day's revels. The beleaguered Topper cannot help but admire George's pleasure-seeking lifestyle, and under his ghostly influence he loosens up.

Roland Young, forced to act opposite thin air when the Kerbys are not visible, earned an Oscar nomination for a performance that grows more impressive with every viewing. Constance Bennett is a perfect complement for Grant, playing the role of both love interest and sparring partner that would be inhabited in later films by Irene Dunne and Rosalind Russell. Few, however, could equal the slinky, sexy Bennett in trading whimsical quips with the master. As for Cary Grant, he followed up his new wave of success in *Topper* with *The Awful Truth* (1937), *Bringing Up Baby* (1938), *Holiday* (1938) and *Gunga Din* (1939).

THIS IS THE NIGHT
Directed by Frank Tuttle; Written by Avery Hopwood and George Marion, Jr., based on the play *Naughty Cinderella* by Hopwood; Music by Ralph Rainger

Cast
Lily Damita (Germaine), Charlie Ruggles (Bunny West), Roland Young (Gerald Grey), Thelma Todd (Claire) CARY GRANT (STEPHEN)

TOPPER
Directed by Norman Z. McLeod; Written by Jack Jevne, Eric Hatch and Eddie Moran, based on the novel *The Jovial Ghosts* by Thorne Smith; Produced by Hal Roach; Music by Edward Powell and Hugo Friedhofer

Cast
Constance Bennett (Marion Kerby), CARY GRANT (GEORGE KERBY), Roland Young (Cosmo Topper), Billie Burke (Henrietta Topper), Alan Mowbray (Wilkins)

MELANIE GRIFFITH (1958-   )

FIRST APPEARANCE: *Night Moves* (Warner Bros., 1975)

A STAR IS BORN: *Body Double* (Columbia, 1984)

"I must have been a hard child to raise, a difficult and headstrong kid." So reflected Melanie Griffith on her childhood, which was unique even by Hollywood standards. Her mother was actress Tippi Hedren, the last of Alfred Hitchcock's icy blond heroines and the star of *The Birds* (1963) and the underrated *Marnie* (1964). When Melanie was six, Hitchcock sent her a toy coffin with a replica of her mother in it. Whether the director was retaliating after Hedren spurned his advances, or merely indulging his macabre sense of humor, it was the kind of present that is hard to forget. Griffith still recalls the experience with disgust; "Even then, I knew that was really sick."

Hedren was not without eccentricities of her own. She imported lions, tigers and other big cats to her California ranch, and treated them like members of her family. A pet leopard, Buster, slept on Griffith's bed. She grew up feeding and taking care of the animals, and as the wild beasts became domesticated, Melanie herself started to walk the wild side. At age fourteen she visited her mother on the set of *The Harrad Experiment* (1973), and met 22-year-old Don Johnson. They began dating, and when Melanie was sixteen they moved in together. Two years later they were married; two months after that they split up.

Griffith began appearing in movies with no intention of building a career. She supposedly appears in some background shots in *The Harrad Experiment*, a soft-porn exploitationer masquerading as social commentary, but I couldn't see her. Griffith's first genuine movie role was in Arthur Penn's *Night Moves*, one of the most cynical of the seventies "anti-genre" films. Gene Hackman stars as Harry Moseby, a former pro football player turned private detective. Moseby is hired by faded 'B' movie starlet Arlene Iverson (Janet Ward) to find her missing sixteen-year-old daughter Delly (Griffith). He tracks her from Los Angeles to the Florida Keys, where she has moved in with her stepfather. Harry suspects that there's more to this case than a runaway teenager, but by the time he confirms his suspicions it is too late to act on them.

The "anti-genre" films borrow a scenario from Hollywood's golden age and point out how the world has changed since the genre was fashionable. Hackman's character wants to be Sam Spade, but his life consists of one dull job after another. At home Harry's choice of career is ridiculed by his wife (Susan George), but still he dreams of the big case. When it comes, he is too distracted by his wife's infidelity to realize it. The film's clever title refers to the knight on a chessboard, which like Harry's case never moves in a straight line. Harry is actually better at chess than detective work--unlike Sam Spade he's a step behind all the way, and doesn't uncover the truth until Delly and her stepfather are both dead. "I didn't solve anything," he admits, "it just fell in on top of me."

Griffith, at age seventeen, was so nervous when she filmed her first scene that director Arthur Penn had to literally hold her by the hips and move her toward her marks. The little girl voice and one-Twinkie-away-from-Rubenesque body, both of which she still has, are apparent in her debut, as is her natural beauty. Half her screen time is spent in various stages of undress, which was probably the key to her casting. Griffith's inexperience at line-reading is clearly visible, but she was adequate enough to be called "an appealing talent" by *Variety*.

Following *Night Moves*, Griffith was to appear opposite her mother in *Roar*, a jungle adventure with a heavy wildlife preservation message. While filming in 1977, she was mauled by a lion. Eleven years in the making, *Roar* was finally released in 1981, and was mauled by critics. Meanwhile, Griffith served time in made-for-TV movie Hell (1981's *She's In the Army Now* and others) and then spent the next three years living up to her party girl reputation. When she tried to resume her career, the reaction was "You're a problem, you drink too much, you do drugs," she recalled in a *Newsweek* interview; "It was like, OK, yes, I have done all those things, but...I've got a whole lot to give."

She got her chance in *Body Double* (1984), Brian De Palma's homage to (or rip-off of, depending on your perspective) Alfred Hitchcock's *Rear Window* (1954), and *Vertigo* (1959). The story begins when an unemployed actor named Jake (Craig Wasson) housesits for a friend and begins watching Gloria, his beautiful neighbor, through a high-powered telescope. When Gloria appears to be murdered, Jake investigates and uncovers an elaborate scheme in which he has unwittingly played a major role. Griffith plays Holly Body, an adult movie star with a mysterious connection to the murdered woman. Like Griffith herself, who was again called upon to play several nude scenes, Holly is hired for her body but is smart enough to use the users for all they're worth. The role wasn't much on paper, but Melanie Griffith made it memorable with a savvy, street-smart performance.

Body Double was trashed by many reviewers for its Hitchcock lineage, but it does have its moments; the Beverly Hills mall sequence unfolds with a balletic movement of actors and cameras, and the grisly murder by power drill of Gloria, which understandably caused walkouts at previews, is nonetheless a textbook on evoking horror. Both scenes are punctuated by Pino Donaggio's wonderful score, and are not hampered by the simplistic dialogue that is the film's greatest fault. But even the bad notices praised Griffith, describing her as "Billie Dawn in a punk hairdo" and lauding her "perfectly controlled comic performance" (*New York Times*). After receiving an Oscar nomination for *Working Girl* (1988), Griffith would actually play Billie Dawn opposite Don Johnson (whom she has since married and divorced again) in a 1993 remake of *Born Yesterday*.

NIGHT MOVES
Directed by Arthur Penn; Written by Alan Sharp; Produced by Robert M. Sherman; Music by Michael Small

Cast
Gene Hackman (Harry Moseby), Susan Clark (Ellen Moseby), Jennifer Warren (Paula), Janet Ward (Arlene Iverman), MELANIE GRIFFITH (DELLY GRASTNER)

BODY DOUBLE
Directed and produced by Brian De Palma; Written by Brian De Palma and Robert J. Avrech (based on a story by De Palma); Music by Pino Donaggio

Cast
Craig Wasson (Jake), MELANIE GRIFFITH (HOLLY BODY), Gregg Henry (Sam), Deborah Shelton (Gloria), Guy Boyd (Jim McLean)

GENE HACKMAN (1931-)

FIRST APPEARANCE: *Mad Dog Coll* (Columbia, 1961)

A STAR IS BORN: *The French Connection* (20th Century-Fox, 1971)

Through hard work, and taking what seems like every part he was offered, Gene Hackman built a reputation as a resourceful, versatile character actor. Ten years after his film debut, *The French Connection* turned Hackman into an Academy Award-winning leading man, but it did not alter his work ethic--Hackman kept taking everything as if he still needed to build a resume`. Many actors with his credentials complete one film every eighteen months, but Hackman has appeared in two or three movies a year since the 1970s; lead roles, supporting roles, comedies, westerns, action, romance--his pure professionalism and total absence of discernible technique fit seamlessly into any project.

Time magazine described Eugene Alden Hackman as "a sort of blue-collar actor, slightly embarrassed about art but avid about craft." Hackman's blue-collar childhood began in San Bernadino, California, and continued in Danville, Illinois, where his father and grandfather worked for the local newspaper. His parents separated when he was thirteen, and Gene remained with his mother. In 1947, while still in high school, he felt an urge to see the world that looked so inviting in the movies that played at the local cinema. He left home to join the Marine Corps, lying about his age to get accepted. After serving in China, Japan and Hawaii, Hackman was discharged in 1952 and, having earned a high school equivalency diploma in the service, he enrolled in journalism classes at the University of Illinois.

He flirted with careers as a disc jockey and a commercial artist, before moving to California to study acting at the Pasadena Playhouse. His first professional experience came on the off-Broadway stage, in a play called *Chaparral* (1958). It was his portrayal of Cass Henderson in the comedy *Any Wednesday* (1964) that established Hackman's Broadway reputation. By that time, he had already made a very quiet film debut in the very noisy gangster film *Mad Dog Coll*.

The film was based on the life of Vincent Coll (John Davis Chandler), a severely abused kid who grew up angry, and became a vicious killer who challenged crimelord Dutch Schultz (Vincent Gardenia) for control of New York's Harlem territory. The script is filled with inaccuracies, not the least of which is the fact that it was Schultz's men who put an end to Coll's killing spree, and not the police as depicted in the film. But *Mad Dog Coll* succeeds more through style than substance anyway. A plot that seems ripped from a Jim Thompson paperback, explosive bursts of violence, a jazzy, bongo-drum score--you'd swear it was a Roger Corman production.

John Davis Chandler snarls lines like "From now on, I'm king in this town!" with the same twisted smile that Richard Widmark sported in *Kiss of Death* (1947). Jerry Orbach and Brooke Hayward also appear, but the biggest name in the cast is Telly Savales, who plays a tough but compassionate police detective who tries unsuccessfully to set Coll straight. About twenty minutes into the film, you'll see Gene Hackman as a beat cop who accompanies Savales in staking out Coll's apartment. When the gangster appears Telly grills him to no avail, while Hackman looks on. After Coll leaves, Savales turns to Hackman and says, "Sure as I'm standin' here, there goes tomorrow's headline." Gene nods solemnly and looks as if he's about to say something, but remains mute as the scene concludes.

He got to talk in his second film, but had to wait three years for the opportunity (*Lilith*-- 1964). Hackman's first significant credit was his supporting performance in *Bonnie and Clyde* (1967), as Clyde's gregarious brother Buck Barrow. Pauline Kael called the Oscar-nominated portrayal "a beautifully controlled performance, the best in the film." This launched his film career in earnest, and led to well-received appearances in *Downhill Racer* (1969) and *I Never Sang for My Father* (1970).

The role that took Hackman to the next level, New York City narcotics detective Popeye Doyle in *The French Connection*, only became his after passing through the hands of Jackie Gleason, Steve McQueen and Peter Boyle. Hackman spent several weeks riding in a squad car with Eddie Egan, the real-life detective whose exploits inspired the movie, to prepare for the part.

The story, told without subplots or detours, follows a large shipment of heroin from Marseilles, France, to New York City. Doyle and his partner Buddy Russo (Roy Scheider) follow a known high-level drug dealer, and uncover the plan by Alain Charnier (Fernando Rey) to sell the shipment. After days of surveillance they capture the drugs, but Charnier escapes.

Director William Friedkin is one of the very best at capturing the sounds, rhythm and soul of a big city. New York becomes another character in the film during several long sequences with little or no dialogue, set in all hours in all neighborhoods, from the most celebrated landmarks to the most sinister back alley frontiers. The most famous of these is the hair-raising chase sequence that ranks with the most unique and spectacular chases every conceived.

Popeye Doyle is the kind of unsympathetic antihero that was in vogue during the early 1970s, and Hackman spares no energy in trying to make him likable. The brutal, arrogant, racist Doyle is just one short step up the social ladder from the low-life cokeheads he arrests; after chasing Charnier's hitman, risking the lives of numerous innocent bystanders, Doyle shoots him in the back. His obsessive approach to casework has, we are told, already resulted in the death of one fellow officer, and when it happens again Popeye shows no remorse.

The French Connection was Oscar's Best Picture of 1971, and also earned awards for Best Direction, Best Script and Best Editing. Gene Hackman won his first Academy Award for Best Actor. Twenty-one years later, he would again win an Oscar as another sadistic law enforcement officer in Clint Eastwood's *Unforgiven* (1992).

MAD DOG COLL
Directed by Burt Balaban; Written and produced by Edward Schreiber, based on material by Leo Lieberman; Music by Stu Phillips

Cast
John Davis Chandler (Vincent Coll), Neil Nephew (Rocco), Brooke Hayward (Elizabeth), Joy Harmon (Caroline), Jerry Orbach (Joe), Telly Savales (Lt. Dawson), Vincent Gardenia (Dutch Schultz)...GENE HACKMAN (COP)

THE FRENCH CONNECTION
Directed by William Friedkin; Written by Ernest Tidyman, based on the book by Robin Moore; Produced by Philip D'Antoni; Music by Don Ellis

Cast
GENE HACKMAN (JIMMY "POPEYE" DOYLE), Fernando Rey (Alain Charnier), Roy Scheider (Buddy Russo), Tony Lo Bianco (Sal Boca)

TOM HANKS (1956-   )

FIRST APPEARANCE: *He Knows You're Alone* (MGM/UA, 1980)

A STAR IS BORN: *Splash* (Touchstone, 1984)

He's the next Cary Grant. He's the next Jimmy Stewart. He's the next Jack Lemmon. Actually he's not, but hyperbolic critics and p.r. types have compared Tom Hanks to everyone but Mary Pickford since his breakthrough in *Splash*. What he is, in reality, is the first popular, marketable leading man in the 1980s to draw an audience without carrying a machine gun or exposing his backside. "I guess I come off in movies as a guy who you wouldn't mind hanging around with," he told *Rolling Stone* magazine, and that's a more accurate explanation for his success than any talk about second comings of past generation's legends. Hanks looks like an ordinary guy and is usually cast that way, though the characters he plays often find themselves in the most extraordinary situations.

Tom Hanks was born in Concord, California, but by the time he was ten he had lived in a dozen different states. After his parents' divorce Tom went with his older brother and sister to live with their father, whose job as a chef kept the family on the move. His mother remarried three times and his father remarried twice, which left Tom with enough step-siblings to fill an elementary school. After finally settling in Oakland, California, Hanks attended Skyline High School and began participating in theatrical productions, which proved an ideal outlet for his quick sense of humor and nervous energy. He graduated in 1974 and enrolled at Charbot College in the nearby town of Hayward. His decision to become an actor was confirmed after he watched a performance of *The Iceman Cometh* at the Berkeley Repertory Theatre. "I came out of the theatre enthralled with what those people had done that night," he said in 1976. "And I wanted to do something in the theatre, something as immediate and personal as that."

In 1976, Hanks transferred to California State University in Sacramento, studied acting, and spent three summers with the Great Lakes Shakespeare Festival. In 1980 he left to try his luck in New York City, but countless auditions yielded only one offer-- a small role in a sloppy, disjointed slasher film entitled *He Knows You're Alone*.

The plot--Amy (Caitlin O'Heaney) is being stalked by a knife-wielding maniac one week before her wedding. She is helped (but not much) by a cop obsessed with the case ever since his bride-to-be became the killer's first victim. Seventh-billed Hanks plays Elliot, an amiable college psychology major who tells his friend Amy that the stalker exists only in her head. He has a couple of nondescript scenes about halfway through, and then disappears without explanation. The best performance in the film belongs to future soap opera diva Patsy Pease, who unfortunately is knocked off early on.

Any idiot can make a person jump in a darkened theater with a sudden move and a musical cue; to do so with subtlety, style and creativity is a more difficult trick. *He Knows You're Alone* aspires to nothing but the lowest common denominator, and like every film of its ilk it breaks every rule of common sense to scare the audience. I really hate movies like this.

It got better for Tom Hanks later in 1980 when he was cast with Peter Scolari in the ABC television series *Bosom Buddies*. The show was cancelled two years later, but its sophomoric wit and pop culture references hold up well, and it's not surprising that both Scolari and Hanks have worked steadily ever since. Director Ron Howard remembered Hanks from a guest spot he did on *Happy Days*, and invited him to audition for the film *Splash*. He tried out for a supporting role but wound up playing the lead in a movie that became one of 1984's surprise hits.

Allen Bauer (Hanks) is a vegetable merchant who is dumped by his girlfriend after a stormy relationship. He is drawn to Cape Cod, where his life had twice before been saved by a mysterious woman (Daryl Hannah) who turns out to be a mermaid. He meets her again in New York, where she has been arrested for indecent exposure (on land, of course, a mermaid's fin changes into human legs). Love blossoms instantly, as our mermaid takes the name Madison (from a street sign) and begins adjusting to life on the surface. Everything seems wonderful, except for the fact that Madison can only stay on land for six days, Allen doesn't know that she's a mermaid, and a wacko scientist who does know (Eugene Levy) is out to reel her in.

Splash is sometimes silly and a bit uneven, but Ron Howard's upbeat direction catches most of the loose ends before they can damage the clever storyline. This was Daryl Hannah's breakthrough as well, and since the film's most memorable scenes are all Madison's--the dinner date at which she devours a lobster, shell and all, her attempts to learn English by watching television--she garnered most of the critical praise. Tom Hanks had to play straight man, and fight to be noticed on the screen opposite a beautiful blonde with a tail fin. Not an easy task, but Hanks' reactions to Hannah's hijinks are priceless, and his shocked but resigned remark upon learning the truth-- "Okay...so...she's a fish..."--is the film's best line. *Splash* established him as comedian, romantic lead, and a guy in movies you wouldn't mind hanging around with.

HE KNOWS YOU'RE ALONE
Directed by Armand Mastroianni; Written by Scott Parker; Produced by George Manasse, Robert Di Milia and Nan Pearlman; Music by Alexander and Mark Peskanov

Cast
Don Scardino (Marvin), Caitlin O'Heaney (Amy), Elizabeth Kemp (Nancy), Tom Rolfing (Killer), Lewis Arlt (Gamble), Patsy Pease (Joyce) TOM HANKS (ELLIOT)

SPLASH
Directed by Ron Howard; Written by Lowell Ganz, Babaloo Mandel and Bruce Jay Friedman, based on a story by Friedman and Brian Grazer; Produced by Brian Grazer; Music by Lee Holdridge

Cast
TOM HANKS (ALLEN BAUER), Daryl Hannah (Madison), Eugene Levy (Walter Kornbluth), John Candy (Freddie Bauer), Dody Goodman (Mrs. Stimler), Shecky Greene (Mr. Buyrite)

JEAN HARLOW (1911-1937)

FIRST APPEARANCE: *Moran of the Marines* (Paramount, 1928)

A STAR IS BORN: *Hell's Angels* (United Artists, 1930)

She was a genuine free spirit who packed three marriages, thirty-six films and a lot of living into twenty-six years, but the public image of Jean Harlow, the brassy platinum blonde hailed as the first sex symbol of talking pictures, still managed to outrun reality. Harlow had two Hollywood careers in a timespan that could barely accommodate one; after first achieving a hollow sort of notoriety as a screen-scorching seductress, she found more genuine, lasting success in comedy, often by mocking the type of sluttish glamour-girl roles that first brought her fame.

The real Jean Harlow was a stunning Kansas City beauty who married Mont Clair Carpenter in 1908, and three years later gave birth to a girl, Harlean Harlow Carpenter. Harlean wanted to be a star. So did Jean, and since her marriage was never happy she divorced her husband and, in 1922, set off with her daughter for Hollywood. But although Jean's good looks were undiminished at age thirty-four, she realized her chances were slim at a time when most leading ladies were in or barely out of their teens. Harlean, contrarily, was too young, though signs of star quality were already apparent. Her white blonde hair, deep green eyes, and tendency to sashay rather than walk, caused a minor sensation at the Hollywood School for Girls.

When their money ran out, mother and daughter returned to Kansas City and later moved to Chicago, where Harlean dropped out of school and, at the age of sixteen, married a wealthy businessman named Chuck McGraw, and moved into his lavish home in Beverly Hills. In the spring of 1928, Harlean accompanied a friend to the Fox Studio, where executives paid more attention to her. Later, at a party, friends bet Harlean that she wouldn't have the guts to take the letters of introduction she received from the executives to casting directors. Although her desire to become an actress had waned since childhood, she took the bet. To her amazement, offers began arriving within a few days. In 1928, Beverly Hills socialite Harlean McGraw, using her mother's name of Jean Harlow, was paid seven dollars and a box lunch for appearing in the comic-action film *Moran of the Marines*. She arrived at the studio in designer clothes and an expensive roadster, the most affluent extra in show business.

Moran of the Marines starred heartthrob Richard Dix as a Navy attache` who fights bandits in China and romances a Marine Corps General's daughter (Ruth Elder). Jean can be glimpsed in the background of a restaurant scene. She sits facing the camera at a table for six, wearing a black dress and holding a cigarette. Another film, *Honor Bound*, has been designated by one source as Harlow's actual debut. Its date of release, April 19, 1928, would support this theory, since *Moran of the Marines* was not released until October 13 of the same year. However, the film is believed lost and there is no photographic evidence to prove Harlow's appearance as an unbilled extra. Because her presence in *Moran* is incontestable, the film has been named here as her debut.

Harlow subsequently signed with the Hal Roach studio and played numerous bit parts, including a memorable lingerie-clad stroll through the Laurel and Hardy short *Double Whoopee* (1929). Meanwhile, somewhere across town, Howard Hughes was already two years into production on *Hell's Angels*, a World War I epic that he hoped would become one of the greatest silent films ever made. When talking pictures made the silents obsolete, he was forced to reshoot the film and add dialogue. The problem was leading lady Greta Nissen, a Norweigan actress with a prominent accent. The role had to be recast and Hughes, who had already poured $2 million into the project, wanted to recast it cheap. Enter Jean Harlow, now divorced, living back with her mother, an unproven unknown who would work for $100 a week. That was good enough for Hughes.

The story follows two brothers who leave Oxford University to join the British Royal Flying Corps when "the war to end all wars" begins. Roy Rutledge (James Hall) loves Helen (Harlow), a wanton temptress who feigns loyal devotion while seducing his brother Monte (Ben Lyon). The brothers reconcile before taking on a dangerous mission that lands them both in a German prison camp. Roy is forced to kill the shellshocked Monte before he can reveal information of an upcoming attack, and is then executed for his action.

By the time Hughes had finished *Hell's Angels*, he had shot 2.5 million feet of film, spent $3.8 million, and lost three pilots in tragic accidents. The result is a movie with spectacular aerial action sequences and many fine individual scenes, that is done in by a stilted pace and dialogue that was obviously first-draft. Technically, the film was a triumph, especiallly in a marvelously-staged attack on a German dirigible, and an early Technicolor sequence that constitutes the only color footage of Jean Harlow. But money could not buy good reviews, especially for Hughes' bargain-priced discovery. "Jean Harlow is plain awful," wrote the *New Yorker*, echoing the sentiments of many others. But *Variety*, while also acknowledging the shortcomings of her performance, was not surprised that she had rocketed to stardom anyway; "this girl is the most sensuous figure to get in front of a camera in some time. She'll probably always have to play these kind of roles, but nobody ever starved possessing what she's got."

Harlow's line-readings are flat, even when uttering the now-immortal come-on, "Would you be shocked if I put on something more comfortable?". And at the end of her first scene, you can just catch her looking off-camera for the "cut" signal. "I know I'm the worst actress in pictures," she said in 1931, "but I can learn, and I will." It didn't happen right away; in her next few roles, Harlow was not surrounded by the sumptuous production values of *Hell's Angels*, rendering her inexperience and downright ineptitude all the more obvious. But after a series of flops Harlow bounced back in *Red-Headed Woman* (1932), and established the brassy comedic persona that took her back to the top.

MORAN OF THE MARINES
Directed by Frank Strayer; Written by Linton Wells, Agnes Brand Leahy, Sam Mintz and Bay Harris

Cast
Richard Dix (Michael Moran), Ruth Elder (Vivian Marshall), Roscoe Karns (Swatty), Brooks Benedict (Basil Worth), E.H. Calvert (General Marshall)...JEAN HARLOW (EXTRA)

HELL'S ANGELS
Directed by Howard Hughes, Marshall Neilan and Luther Reed; Written by Harry Behn, Howard Estabrook and Joseph Moncure March, based on a story by March and Marshall Neilan; Produced by Howard Hughes; Music by Hugo Riesenfeld

Cast
Ben Lyon (Monte Rutledge), James Hall (Roy Rutledge), JEAN HARLOW (HELEN), John Darrow (Karl Arnstedt), Lucien Prival (Baron von Kranz)

GOLDIE HAWN (1945-   )

FIRST APPEARANCE: *The One and Only, Genuine Original Family Band* (Disney, 1968)

A STAR IS BORN: *Cactus Flower* (Columbia, 1969)

Is Goldie Hawn the giggling, jiggling blonde on the *Laugh-In* reruns, or is she the actress/producer regarded as one of the smartest, savviest businesswomen in Hollywood? Both sides are true reflections of her personality, and what is most refreshing is how she has embraced rather than outgrown her younger self. Even today, when she speaks seriously in talk show appearances about the shortage of roles for women, there will escape from Goldie a twinkle in her eye and an infectious laugh, and once again she is the girl dancing in a white bikini with "Dangerous Curves Ahead" tattooed on her thigh. And then it is gone, and the mature, intelligent woman returns. The incongruity of the two sides of Goldie would make Dr. Jekyll jealous.

Her unusual but oh-so-appropriate name sounded hand-picked by an agent, but Goldie Jeanne Hawn was named after her great-aunt. She was born in Washington, D.C. and raised in Takoma Park, Maryland. Her father, Edward Rutledge Hawn, was a professional musician who played a variety of instruments in society bands at White House and embassy affairs. But it was Goldie's mother Laura who encouraged her daughter to study music, tap dancing and ballet. "When I decided to go into show business, no one disagreed," she told the *New York Post* in 1969, and after taking part in community and school dramatic productions (and graduating high school), Goldie danced in choruses at the New York World's Fair's Texas Pavilion and in summer stock musicals. She also worked as a go-go dancer at a Manhattan disco and at the Desert Inn Hotel in Las Vegas.

Goldie was plucked from the chorus of an Andy Griffith television special in 1967 and signed by the mighty William Morris Agency. She appeared in the short-lived 1967 sitcom *Good Morning World*, and then became the most "massively loved" personality on television (as one reporter raved) in the groundbreaking hit *Laugh-In*. The high-pitched laugh that made her famous was provoked by the show's creators as often as possible, usually by slipping dirty words into her cue cards.

Prior to her debut on *Laugh-In*, Goldie made her film debut in Disney's musical *The One and Only, Genuine Original Family Band*, the true story of a nineteenth-century Partridge Family with a dream of performing at the 1888 Democratic convention. Walter Brennan, Buddy Ebsen and Lesley Ann Warren lead a strong cast that also includes Kurt Russell, Goldie's future paramour. Goldie's character is listed only as "Giggly Girl," which would make a great title for her autobiography. She appears as one of the featured dancers in the "West of the Wide Missouri" number near the end of the film. It's a crowded scene but you can't miss her; she is wearing a pea-green dress, has a couple of close-ups and one line of dialogue--"I think you're sweet"--which she gushes to John Davidson. She also giggles a couple of times, hence the name of her character.

The movie has the feel of a Main Street, U.S.A. parade at Disneyland--happy and wholesome, but bland. The score by veteran Disney composers Richard and Robert Sherman is okay in context but a far cry from their *Mary Poppins* triumph (then again, Lesley Ann Warren is no Julie Andrews). Still, Brennan and company all play the nicest people you'd ever want to meet, and because of that *The One and Only, Genuine Original Family Band* is nigh impossible to dislike. It did nothing for Goldie Hawn, who had become a star already by the time the film was released. She dances well, and that's all she was asked to do.

Goldie was still a fixture on *Laugh-In* when her second film, *Cactus Flower*, opened in 1969. This time she was third-billed and stealing scenes from real movie stars Walter Matthau and Ingrid Bergman. She plays Toni Simmons, a cute young Greenwich Village bohemian who

124

has an affair with lothario dentist Dr. Julian Winston (Matthau). Julian's not married but to avoid commitment to Toni he tells her that he has a wife and three kids. After Toni threatens suicide he agrees to marry her, but Toni will only say "I do" if she first clears it with Julian's wife. The trapped dentist convinces his staid nurse (Bergman) to pose as Mrs. Winston, and of course a variety of complications ensue, not the least of which is Julian's discovery that his nurse looks a lot better out of her uniform.

At first Toni seems an extension of the dizzy blonde Goldie was playing on *Laugh-In*, but beneath her wide-eyed, open-mouthed blank stare there is a character of sweetness and heart, who somehow maintains her innocence while playing a mistress. Her sense of right and wrong is almost childlike--in Toni's world, it is okay to marry the man you're having an affair with, as long as you get his wife's permission. Goldie's sensitive and sexy performance won the Oscar for Best Supporting Actress, and the lion's share of critical praise in *Cactus Flower's* otherwise mixed reviews. "It is mainly the emerging sweetness and perceptions of (Hawn's) character...that gives the picture its persuasive luster and substance," wrote the *New York Times.*

Which is not to say that Walter Matthau is not his usual reliably engaging self, and that Ingrid Bergman, her remarkable beauty undiminished at age 53, is not absolutely delightful. Nurse Stephanie Dickinson (the "cactus flower" of the title who blooms before Matthau's eyes) is one of the least celebrated Bergman performances, but her comic timing is as flawless as Goldie's, and their shared dance in a swinging sixties nightclub is a wonderful movie moment.

THE ONE AND ONLY, GENUINE ORIGINAL FAMILY BAND
Directed by Michael O'Herlihy; Written by Lowell S. Hawley, based on the book by Laura Bower Van Nuys; Produced by Bill Anderson; Music by Richard M. and Robert B. Sherman

Cast
Walter Brennan (Grandpa Bower), Buddy Ebsen (Calvin Bower), John Davidson (Joe Carder), Lesley Ann Warren (Alice Bower), Janet Blair (Katie Bower), Kurt Russell (Sidney Bower)...GOLDIE HAWN (GIGGLY GIRL)

CACTUS FLOWER
Directed by Gene Saks; Written by I.A.L. Diamond, based on the play by Abe Burrows, adapted from the French play by Barillet and Gredy; Produced by M.J. Frankovich; Music by Quincy Jones

Cast
Walter Matthau (Julian Winston), Ingrid Bergman (Stephanie Dickinson), GOLDIE HAWN (TONI SIMMONS), Jack Weston (Harvey Greenfield), Rick Lenz (Igor Sullivan)

SUSAN HAYWARD (1918-1975)

FIRST APPEARANCE: *Hollywood Hotel* (Warner Bros., 1937)

A STAR IS BORN: *Adam Had Four Sons* (Columbia, 1941)

Susan Hayward began her motion picture career in 1937 by being rejected for the most coveted role in film history, that of Scarlett O'Hara in *Gone With the Wind*. It was the first of several false starts for Hayward, who is to be admired as much for her dedication as for her talent.

She was good-natured--in public, at least--about her rocky path to stardom, calling herself "God's gift to the lower part of the double-bill." Hayward paid her dues playing supporting roles in movies good and bad (mostly bad) and, in the late 1930s, appeared poised to become a character actress. The forcefulness of her screen personality and extravagance of her mannerisms led to comparisons with Bette Davis, and typecasting as vixens and Jezebels who met appropriately grisly ends while the leading lady lived happily ever after. Physical abuse wasn't exactly the greatest niche, but she did it proud, trading on the contrast between her waif-like beauty and the ferocity of her characters--no one was ever drowned, burned, stoned, beaten or fried in the electric chair quite like Susan Hayward. The one role that would have ideally utilized both her angelic and feral qualities was the one that got away--Scarlett O'Hara.

Hayward, born Edythe Marrener to a working-class family in Brooklyn, was a fighter from her first days of life, demonstrating the perseverence that would serve her well in Hollywood. As a young girl barely out of diapers she was run over by a car, and told by doctors that she probably would never walk again. Six months later, she walked. The desire to be an actress began at birth, she said, but when the school play-drama club route didn't work she turned to modeling. Her voluptuous figure and gorgeous red hair (which consistently earned top honors in the forties whenever actress body parts were rated in fan magazines) graced dozens of print advertisements. One of the ads was spotted by director George Cukor, who was then searching for Scarlett. Hayward's screen test for *Gone With the Wind* got her a contract with Warner Bros., and a film debut in the musical *Hollywood Hotel* (1937).

Busby Berkeley directed Dick Powell and the usual cast of thousands in this predictably cornball story of a young saxophonist (Powell) who becomes an overnight sensation. *Hollywood Hotel* was the last in a string of successful, gargantuan Warners musicals that sacrificed plot for spectacle, which proved to be a winning formula with Depression-era audiences. The outstanding score includes Johnny Mercer's "Hooray for Hollywood," Rodgers and Hart's "Blue Moon," and performances by the Benny Goodman orchestra featuring Gene Krupa and Lionel Hampton.

Susan Hayward was billed as "Starlet at Table," which is a good clue to the size of her role. She can be glimpsed about forty minutes into the film, in a moment that lasts scant seconds. Warner Bros. apparently felt Hayward looked enough like a starlet to play one, but they were not willing or able to make her one. She was dropped by the studio after three more films.

While Hayward toiled in the Hollywood trenches, Ingrid Bergman had become a star after her first American film, the 1939 romance *Intermezzo*. Her next film, *Adam Had Four Sons*, was set in New York in the early 1900s. She played Emilie Gallatin, the devoted governess to the Stoddard family--Adam (Warner Baxter), Molly (Fay Wray), and their four sons. The Stoddards are devastated and divided by the death of Molly, the failure of Adam's business, and the outbreak of World War I. Susan Hayward played Hester, a deceitful tart who marries one of Adam's sons and tries to seduce two others before receiving her comeuppance from the virtuous Emilie.

The movie was accurately labeled an "antique tearjerker" by the *New York Times*, but

Hayward turns up the temperature with her first scene, invading the home and hearth of the Stoddards and cutting through their polite manners with a machete. It was her first role as a villainess, and she played it with such venomous glee that it threatened to define the rest of her career. Critics said her "stunning" performance was "quite as outstanding as Miss Bergman's exemplary one." (*Richmond News Ledger*).

Adam Had Four Sons was a noteworthy launch, but one that Hayward could not follow up. She remained trapped in third- and fourth-billed roles, and would not play the lead until *Hit Parade of 1943*, two years and seven films after *Adam*. Her career was again revived after her superb, Oscar-nominated performance in *Smash Up--The Story of a Woman* (1947), in which she played a nightclub singer who descended into alcoholism. But Hayward's ratio of hits to flops would not improve until the fifties, when she starred in *The Snows of Kilmanjaro* (1952) and *I'll Cry Tomorrow* (1955), but was still not immune to disasters like *The Conqueror* (1956), in which she played a Tartar temptress opposite an absurdly miscast John Wayne as Ghengis Khan. In 1958, two decades after her arrival in Hollywood, Susan Hayward received an Academy Award for her performance in *I Want to Live*. It was a long overdue moment of triumph for one of the movies' most tenacious performers.

HOLLYWOOD HOTEL
Directed by Busby Berkeley; Written by Jerry Wald, Maurice Leo and Richard Macauley; Produced by Hal B. Wallis; Music by Richard W. Whiting, Johnny Mercer, Richard Rodgers, Lorenz Hart and Phil Baxter

Cast
Dick Powell (Henry Bowers) Rosemary Lane (Virginia Stanton), Lola Lane (Mona Marshall), Hugh Herbert (Chester Marshall), Ted Healy (Fuzzy)...SUSAN HAYWARD (Starlet at Table)

ADAM HAD FOUR SONS
Directed by Gregory Ratoff; Written by William Hurlbutt and Michael Blankfort, based on the novel *Legacy* by Charles Bonner; Produced by Robert Sherwood

Cast
Ingrid Bergman (Emilie Gallatin), Warner Baxter (Adam Stoddard), SUSAN HAYWARD (Hester), Fay Wray (Molly), Richard Denning (Jack), Johnny Downs (David), Robert Shaw (Chris), Charles Lind (Phillip)

RITA HAYWORTH (1918-1987)

FIRST APPEARANCE: *Cruz Diablo* (Columbia quota, 1935)

A STAR IS BORN: *Blood and Sand* (20th Century-Fox, 1941)

Life magazine called Rita Hayworth "The Love Goddess" in a 1948 article, after she played a series of fiery femme fatales in such films as *Blood and Sand* and *Gilda* (1946). Movie screens in the 1940s were graced by a cornucopia of alluring actresses, but none could match Hayworth's aggressive sensuality, which she used to fulfill a man's every desire, or to break him into tiny pieces. "Instead of attempting to convey wanton lust with just her eyes or even her entire face," observed *Blood and Sand* director Rouben Mamoulian, "she used her entire body to do it--and do it with an animal grace that no actress I have ever known has come close to equaling."

The fires that Hayworth could light with a penetrating glance seemed real, but the "Love Goddess" image was a manufactured one, belonging to a movie star who was largely manufactured herself. Born Marguerita Carmen Cansino, Rita's Mexican heritage was hidden beneath make-up, hair color, and an electrolysis treatment that lifted her hairline. She was transformed from an ethnic seductress in her early, forgotten screen appearances to an all-American beauty whose pin-up popularity rivaled that of Betty Grable.

Her father, actor Eduardo Cansino, met and married her mother Volga Haworth while she was working as a Ziegfeld showgirl. Marguerita, their first child, was born and raised in New York, and at the age of four she made her Carnegie Hall debut with "The Dancing Cansinos," a vaudeville act that her father had performed in since his teenage years. In 1926, they appeared in *La Fiesta*, a Vitagraph ten-minute short subject about traditional dance forms around the world. At the end of the Cansinos' number, eight-year-old Rita can be seen doing a few flamenco twirls and clicking a pair of miniature castanets. Although she did not make many musicals in her subsequent career, Hayworth still gets some votes as Fred Astaire's best dancing partner based on their work in *You'll Never Get Rich* (1941) and *You Were Never Lovelier* (1942).

In 1929, the Cansinos moved to Hollywood, where Eduardo opened a dancing school at the corner of Sunset and Vine. When business dropped off during the Great Depression, Eduardo reformed The Dancing Cansinos, this time with fourteen-year-old Rita in a featured role. During a tour through Mexico, Rita was spotted by director Fernando de Fuentes, and persuaded to appear in a film called *Cruz Diablo*. She performed a street dance outside a bullring, and was paid a few pesos for her unbilled contribution. The film was released in 1935 in Spanish-speaking countries and in the few U.S. theaters that screened Mexican films.

Cruz Diablo is not listed in any encyclopedia of film, and may be lost forever. Rita later commented that she had never watched the movie, and knew of no one who had seen it and recognized the future sex symbol when she was "just another dirty-faced Mexican kid."

That same year--1935--The Dancing Cansinos performed at Mexico's Caliente Club, where Rita was noticed by a vice-president of the Fox Film Corporation. After a screen test she was signed up, and after a few acting lessons Rita Cansino was cast in a dance sequence in the Spencer Tracy film *Dante's Inferno* (1935). As Rita Cansino she appeared in ten films, all bottom-of-the-bill programmers. When Fox merged with 20th Century Films, the new bosses canceled Rita's contract. In 1937, Columbia Pictures picked her up and changed her name to Hayworth, a variation on her mother's maiden name. Fan mail poured in after her appearance in *Only Angels Have Wings* (1939), but Columbia couldn't turn Hayworth into a star. The magic happened when she was loaned out, ironically to 20th Century-Fox, for *Blood and Sand*.

Tyrone Power stars as Juan Gallardo, the son of a great matador who dreams of following in his father's footsteps. He rises to the top of his profession in Madrid, then returns home to Seville to marry his childhood sweetheart, Carmen (Linda Darnell). But Juan loses his wealth, fame and happiness after succumbing to the charms of Dona Sol (Hayworth), a heartless enchantress.

Blood and Sand was first filmed in 1922 with Rudolph Valentino and Nita Naldi. It doesn't happen often, but in this case the second version clearly outclasses the first; Technicolor was never so glorious as when Power first dons the garb of the matador, and the colors practically jump off the screen. Director Rouben Mamoulian saw Spain the way El Greco and Goya did, and even though the film crew only got as far as Mexico City, the sumptuous cinematography deservedly won an Oscar.

Valentino and Power generate roughly the same degree of suave Latin charm, but Hayworth's Dona Sol has no equal. Watching her performance, its hard to believe she only got the part after Carole Landis turned it down, and sixteen other candidates were tested. "The moment I saw Rita Hayworth walk I knew I had my Dona Sol," said Mamoulian. She was a dancer, so naturally I expected her to be graceful, but she had something more than that--a feline sort of movement that was subtle and insinuating--exactly the kind of animation I imagined Dona Sol would possess."

Juan first sees Dona Sol in a church, just before he enters the bullring. Instead of smiling at the sight of a beautiful woman, Juan sees the predatory expression on her face and looks frightened--as well he should. "If this is death in the afternoon," says an onlooker, pointing to the bullring, "then she is death in the evening." Juan is doomed the moment he ignores his first instinct, and accepts an invitation to her villa.

During one of their trysts, she playfully imitates a matador and he becomes a bull, a game symbolic of their relationship. When they embrace, Juan kneels at her breast, and Dona grabs him by the hair and pulls him up, relishing her total domination over "the First Man of Spain." As they are about to kiss the doorbell rings, and Dona twirls on her heel, says "Excuse me" in a polite, even tone, and walks away. Hayworth executes this instant evaporation of feigned passion magnificently. After 31 films, she had finally arrived.

Blood and Sand holds up as well as Hayworth's performance, educating as it entertains about the cult of the matador and its fascinating rituals. The sport is rightly portrayed as graceful and elegant, but also barbaric, just like Dona Sol.

CRUZ DIABLO
Directed by Fernando de Fuentes

<u>Cast</u>
Ramon Pereda...RITA HAYWORTH (GIRL)

BLOOD AND SAND
Directed by Rouben Mamoulian; Written by Jo Swerling, based on the novel by Vincente Blasco Ibanez; Produced by Darryl Zanuck; Music by Alfred Newman

<u>Cast</u>
Tyrone Power (Juan Gallardo), Linda Darnell (Carmen Espinosa), RITA HAYWORTH (DONA SOL), Anthony Quinn (Manolo de Palma), J. Carol Naish (Garabato), John Carradine (Nacional)

AUDREY HEPBURN (1929-1993)

FIRST APPEARANCE: *Nederlands in 7 Lessen* (Dutch Independent, 1948)

A STAR IS BORN: *Roman Holiday* (Paramount, 1953)

Audrey Hepburn starred in only twenty films from 1953 to 1993, but her place in the pantheon is secure; Hepburn's portrayals of Princess Anne (*Roman Holiday*), Sabrina Fairchild (*Sabrina*, 1954), Sister Luke (*The Nun's Story*, 1959), Holly Golightly (*Breakfast at Tiffany's*, 1961) and Eliza Doolittle (*My Fair Lady*, 1964) are treasured by generations of audiences. She won an Academy Award and a Tony Award three days apart in 1954, and would later achieve another unique distinction by receiving Oscar nominations for playing both a nun and a prostitute.

But after completing *Wait Until Dark* in 1967 and garnering her fifth Oscar nomination, Hepburn went into semi-retirement to devote more time to her family, and the type of on-location charity work for UNICEF that is not always covered on *Entertainment Tonight*. As a child in the Nazi-occupied Dutch town of Arnhem, she experienced first-hand the horrors of war and the pangs of starvation, and never forgot the kindness of relief workers who assisted her family after Holland was liberated. When UNICEF called, the choice between helping children facing similar hardships or headlining another movie was made without hesitation or regret. But though Audrey left Hollywood, her status as the epitome of class, style and elegance remained, unassailable by time, age or absence from the public eye. "In a cruel and imperfect world," wrote Rex Reed, "she is living proof that God could still create perfection."

Born in Belgium, Edda Kathleen Hepburn van Heemstra was a quiet, shy little girl who developed a strong affection for music and dance at a very early age. Her dream of a career in ballet helped sustain Edda through the divorce of her parents, the desertion of her father, and the hardships of living under Nazi rule in the Dutch city of Arnhem. Her studies never culminated with the lead in *Swan Lake*, but they were directly responsible for her introduction to movies.

Director Charles Hugenot van der Linden was about to begin work on a British-Dutch travelogue in 1948, and was looking for an attractive and sophisticated young woman to play a KLM stewardess, who would introduce the movie. Accompanied by coproducer H.M. Josephson, van der Linden visited the ballet class of Madame Olga Tarassova, hoping that one of her students would possess the combined qualities of beauty, charm and refinement they were seeking. Both men singled out 18-year-old Audrey, "the tall, thin girl with the eyes," as van der Linden recalled describing her, as the ideal choice. Hepburn happily accepted their offer, and completed her part in *Nederlands In 7 Lessen* in just three days. It was the only film she appeared in prior to changing her name from Edda van Heemstra. It is unknown as to whether any copies still exist.

In 1951, Audrey Hepburn received both the title role in the Broadway show *Gigi* and the lead role opposite Gregory Peck in *Roman Holiday*, while her resume' contained only limited experience in both media; on the stage, she had danced in the chorus of the musical *High Button Shoes* in London; at the movies she played bit parts in a string of British farces, and can be seen briefly at the beginning of *The Lavender Hill Mob* (1951). It was Colette, the author of *Gigi*, who discovered Hepburn and cast her on sight for the play. The day after *Gigi* closed its successful run of 219 performances, Hepburn flew to Italy to being filming *Roman Holiday*.

As the movie opens Princess Anne is nearing the end of a highly publicized tour of European capitals. In Rome, she begins to rebel against her restricted, regimented schedule. The doctor gives her a sedative, but that night she hops into the back of a delivery truck and escapes her luxurious confinement. The sedative starts to take effect, and the princess is soon asleep on a public bench. She is found by Joe Bradley (Peck), an American newspaper reporter stationed in Rome. Once he realizes his good fortune, Joe promises his editor an exclusive interview. Anne spends a delightful day with Joe and his friend Irving, who surreptitiously snaps photos of the princess to accompany Joe's story. But by day's end the reporter and the princess have fallen in love, and Joe cannot bring himself to betray her. At a press conference held the following day, Anne is shocked to see Joe and Irving among the press corps. He conveys the message that her secret is safe.

The role of Princess Anne showcased Audrey Hepburn's regal bearing, aristocratic voice and chic fashion sense in a way that blurred the distinction between actress and role. Though it would merely be the first of many memorable performances, the image of Hepburn as a beautiful European princess would prove indelible. It was at Gregory Peck's insistence that Audrey receive equal billing at the top, and after the film opened no one questioned the decision; Audrey received worldwide acclaim and a trophy case full of awards, including the Oscar and the Golden Globe. The film itself was a huge critical and popular success, and remains one of the most delightful romantic-comedies ever made.

NEDERLANDS IN 7 LESSEN
Directed, produced and written by Charles Hugenot van der Linden and H.M. Josephson

Cast
AUDREY HEPBURN (KLM AIR HOSTESS), Wam Heskes, Han Bents van den Berg, Koos Koon

ROMAN HOLIDAY
Directed and produced by William Wyler; Written by Dalton Trumbo; Music by Georges Auric

Cast
Gregory Peck (Joe Bradley), AUDREY HEPBURN (PRINCESS ANNE), Eddie Albert (Irving Radovich), Tullio Carminati (Gen. Provno)

KATHARINE HEPBURN (1907-   )

FIRST APPEARANCE: *A Bill of Divorcement* (RKO, 1932)

A STAR IS BORN: *A Bill of Divorcement*

Any summation of Katharine Hepburn's life and career, whether attempted in one paragraph or a three-hundred page book, always seems to fall back on a single word-- *independence*. In most of her films she was strong, spirited, plain-speaking (also more plain-looking than most screen stars, though her angular features had a unique, patrician radiance), and possessed of a no-nonsense intelligence. A progression has been noted by some chroniclers that begins with Hepburn as the first "free woman" on screen throughout the 1930s. After being labeled box-office poison she left films, but returned in *The Philadelphia Story* (1940) playing a parody of her earlier roles. Thus began the "taming" of Hepburn which continued throughout the fifties and sixties and culminated with *On Golden Pond* (1981), in which she settled into passive domesticity.

It's a theory. But whether viable or not, her independence off-screen has never wavered. Despite sixty years in the business, Hepburn is not a symbol of Hollywood or the movies, because she refused to play the games of either one. She is, however, a symbol of excellence in the acting craft, as her still-record four Academy Awards and twelve nominations attest.

Katharine Houghton Hepburn was born in Hartford, Connecticut, the second of six children raised in an atmosphere of near total freedom by Dr. Thomas Norval Hepburn, a noted surgeon, and his crusading suffragette wife, Katharine. Young Kate is clearly the offspring of a father who stressed self-sufficiency and physical fitness (Kate was fond of wrestling and the trapeze), and a mother who marched on Washington demanding the right to vote and unrestricted birth control. Acting was in the mix as well, but it was only after Kate's brother Tom was killed in a freak accident that she threw herself into performing with a local stock company, as both therapy and a means to forget.

In 1924, she attended Bryn Mawr, where her interest in dramatics intensified. After graduation Hepburn joined a stock company run by Edward Knopf, who would later become a producer at MGM. When Knopf landed his first play on a New York stage, he gave Kate a small role. After ten days of rehearsal, she replaced the leading lady, but on opening night Hepburn rushed through her lines with such a nervous flurry that she was fired after one performance.

From 1928 to 1932 Hepburn worked steadily in a number of plays on and off-Broadway. Frequent clashes with writers and directors often prevented her from finishing the run, but when she did make it on stage the reviews were enthusiastic. In March of 1932, Hepburn opened as the Amazon Queen Antiope in *The Warrior's Husband*, which ran 83 performances and brought Hollywood knocking at her stage door. Since she had no interest in movies, Hepburn demanded $1500 a week, an unheard-of salary for a newcomer. But RKO met her price after viewing her screen test, and Kate found herself on a train headed for Los Angeles.

Before she arrived her first project had already been determined. John Barrymore was signed to star in the film adaptation of Broadway's *A Bill of Divorcement*, a David O. Selznick production to be directed by George Cukor. Barrymore's Hillary Fairfield was a family man who returned from World War I in severe shellshock, and was confined to an asylum. His wife Meg (Billie Burke) makes plans to remarry after fifteen years of waiting, but on the eve of her wedding Hillary returns, back in his right mind and overjoyed to be home. The pivotal role of Sydney Fairfield, the fiery daughter that Hillary has never seen, was coveted by such luminaries as Norma Shearer and Irene Dunne, but after Cukor saw Hepburn's screen test he insisted she play the part.

Sydney sympathizes with her mother's difficult situation, but she is glad to be reunited with her father. Her joy turns to sorrow when a doctor reveals that Hillary's insanity is genetic, and that the condition could exist in Sydney and any children she might have. Devastated by the news, she sends her fiance` away and remains home to take care of her father.

A Bill of Divorcement was the first of several Hepburn-Cukor collaborations, and is the least successful of their efforts, but it still launched Hepburn into the ranks of leading ladies. She was top-billed in her next film, *Christopher Strong* (1933), and never looked back. "Katharine Hepburn...is both beautiful and distinguished, and seems definitely established for an important cinema career," wrote the *New York Herald Tribune*. Most of the Hepburn trademarks are already apparent--a free-spirited character who calls the shots in life and romance, and speaks her mind at a rapid clip. The Hepburn pipes were described as "harsh" and "grating" by *The London Times*, but her sharp, nasal New England-formed voice was ideal for socialites like Sydney. It raised a fuss because Hepburn was simply unlike anything audiences had heard--or seen--before. "Half Botticelli page and half bobbed-hair bandit," was the *New Yorker's* slant.

Despite the stuffiness and staginess of the plece, *A Bill of Divorcement* is saved by its cast. Hepburn's performance, Billie Burke, and John Barrymore, possibly at his best but certainly at his most restrained, all elevate a standard melodrama. When Hillary buries his head in his wife's lap and begs to be taken back into his own home, prepare to be moved.

A BILL OF DIVORCEMENT
Directed by George Cukor; Written by Howard Estabrook and Harry Wagstaff Gribble, based on the play by Clemence Dane; Produced by David O. Selznick; Music by Max Steiner

Cast
John Barrymore (Hillary Fairfield), Billie Burke (Margaret Fairfield), KATHARINE HEPBURN (SYDNEY FAIRFIELD), David Manners (Kit Humphrey), Elizabeth Patterson (Aunt Hester)

CHARLTON HESTON (1923-   )

FIRST APPEARANCE: *Dark City* (Paramount, 1950)

A STAR IS BORN: *The Greatest Show on Earth* (Paramount, 1952)

Motion picture epics in glorious Technicolor, breathtaking Cinemascope and stereophonic sound comprise only one facet of Charlton Heston's resume`; but *The Greatest Show on Earth*, *The Ten Commandments* (1956), *Ben Hur* (1959) and *El Cid* (1961) are so colossal in scope and enduring in popularity that they always grab the lead in any assessment of his career. Actually, Heston's filmography is impressively diverse, encompassing an equal distribution of hero and villain roles, and an uncommercial, independent movie for every larger-than-life saga.

Charlton Carter was born in Evanston, Illinois, the son of Lilla and Russell Carter. The name Heston came from Lilla's second husband, whom she married when Charlton was still young. The family moved to St. Helens, Michigan, a town with a population of less than two hundred. There, Charlton first discovered acting, and made his stage debut at the age of five by playing Santa Claus in a school play. After a decade of rural life, the Hestons returned to the northern suburbs of Chicago, where Charlton attended high school and earned a scholarship to Northwestern University, He majored in theater, and played lead roles in several college productions.

After three years in the Air Force, Charlton Heston moved to New York with his wife, Lydia, and began his professional career with Katharine Cornell's acting company. In 1947, he appeared on Broadway in *Antony and Cleopatra*, and for the next two years he worked steadily in *Studio One* and other television anthology series. Producer Hal Wallis saw one of Heston's television appearances, and signed the 27-year-old actor to a contract with Paramount.

Most sources list *Dark City* as Heston's film debut, and such is the case here. However, he appeared in two amateur films prior to *Dark City*, both of which were released theatrically after Heston's subsequent stardom; *Peer Gynt*, a feature-length silent, was made when Heston was sixteen. And in 1950, just prior to signing with Paramount, he played Marc Antony in a sixteen-millimeter film version of *Julius Caesar*, with the lofty budget of $11,000.

Top-billed in *Dark City*, his official debut, Heston plays Danny Haley, a hard-bitten con man who lures naive businessman Arthur Winant (Don DeFore) into a rigged card game. Winant commits suicide after being wiped out, and his psychotic brother comes to town seeking revenge. He kills Danny's associates one by one, but Danny defeats him after a vicious struggle. As the film ends, Danny seems ready to turn his life around.

There are only two reasons to watch *Dark City*, a minor film noir where nothing happens that is not easily foretold; the first is Lizabeth Scott, who is always worth watching when she plays a hard-luck woman who falls for the wrong man. The second is the humorous casting of Jack Webb and Harry Morgan, costars of *Dragnet*, as members of Danny's criminal gang.

Heston's performance is adequate to the material, but never transcendent. Granted, his character is supposed to be tightly-wound, and cognizant of the importance to his livelihood of keeping his emotions in check. But among the gang of thieves he ostensibly leads, Danny is the only one who realizes how aimless and pathetic his life has become, and there is no subtext beneath his cynicism to reflect this understanding. Instead, Heston conveys only Danny's bitterness, with a ready smirk and a defiant slouch.

Cecil B. DeMille, however, was impressed with Heston's formidable screen presence, a trait that would be essential for his next cinematic extravaganza. *The Greatest Show on Earth* was the director's salute to the circus, made with the full cooperation of the Ringling Bros. Barnum & Bailey troupe; DeMille, the most ringmaster-like of filmmakers, packed four different stories, dozens of actual circus acts (including two of the century's greatest clowns, Emmett

Kelly and Lou Jacobs), and a documentary on circus production into 150 minutes of screen time, and the challenge for the film's cast was not getting lost amidst the dazzling glitz and spectacle.

Heston plays Brad, the boss of the big top, whose affection for star aerialist Holly (Betty Hutton) must often take a back seat to the business of running the show. Holly is none too pleased about this, and starts making time with Sebastian (Cornel Wilde), the circus's new star attraction. Subplots involving sexy, flirtatious elephant trainer Gloria Grahame and her jealous partner, the sinister past of Buttons the clown (Jimmy Stewart), and two hoods running crooked carnival games on the midway all share the spotlight and bend, but do not break, the indomitable spirit of the circus folk, who brave all this plus a devastating trainwreck and never miss a performance.

As in *Dark City*, Heston plays a resolute man who suppresses his feelings for the good of his business. He is the voice of authority and reason, the middle man between the fantasy world of the performers and the cold, hard reality of the circus owners and accountanats. His mission is more noble this time, but the effect on his loved ones is no less harmful. It is Brad's determination and drive that keeps the circus running, and although there were bigger stars in the cast, including Jimmy Stewart at his most genial and the always emphatic Betty Hutton, it is Heston's performance that holds this long, rambling busy movie together.

The Greatest Show on Earth won the Academy Award for Best Picture in 1952, and launched Charlton Heston into an assocation with the motion picture epic that still endures. No matter how enormous the sets, or how many extras populate the background, he always seems up to the task of taking charge and taking care of business.

DARK CITY
Directed by William Dieterle; Written by Larry Marcus and John Meredyth Lucas, based on a story by Marcus; Produced by Hal B. Wallis; Music by Franz Waxman

Cast
CHARLTON HESTON (DANNY HALEY), Lizabeth Scott (Fran), Viveca Lindfors (Victoria Winant), Dean Jagger (Captain Garvey), Don DeFore (Arthur Winant), Jack Webb (Augie), Ed Begley (Barney), Harry Morgan (Soldier)

THE GREATEST SHOW ON EARTH
Directed and produced by Cecil B. DeMille; Written by Frederic M. Frank, Barre Lyndon and Theodore St. John, based on a story by Frank, St. John and Frank Cavett; Music by Victor Young, songs by various composers

Cast
Betty Hutton (Holly), Cornel Wilde (Sebastian), CHARLTON HESTON (BRAD), Dorothy Lamour (Phyllis), Gloria Grahame (Angel), James Stewart (Buttons)

DUSTIN HOFFMAN (1937-   )

FIRST APPEARANCE: *The Tiger Makes Out* (Columbia, 1967)

A STAR IS BORN: *The Graduate* (Embassy, 1967)

"With his short stature, hook nose, beady eyes and unkempt hair, he looks like a loser, and it is precisely because of that loser image. . .that the younger generations have made him a winner," wrote *Parade* magazine of Dustin Hoffman, after Hoffman became a star overnight in *The Graduate*. Backhanded compliments were a prevalent part of Hoffman's rave reviews, which praised him as the "anti-star hero" who "looks least like such heroes as Gregory Peck, John Wayne and William Holden." If such assessments suggested a limited future, Hoffman proved how versatile a loser image could be, when it is backed by a dedication to the acting craft that borders on the fanatical, but that often produces astonishing results.

Acting seemed a natural career choice for Dustin Hoffman, who was born and raised in Los Angeles, and whose father was a prop man at Columbia Pictures. He played Tiny Tim in his junior high school's production of *A Christmas Carol*, but his height (or lack thereof) kept him out of most high school plays. After one year at Santa Monica City College and two years of acting classes at the Pasadena Playhouse, he set out to conquer New York City. Seven years later, he was still trying.

Hoffman finally attracted some attention in 1964, playing a crippled German transvestite in a workshop-theater production of the black comedy *Harry, Noon and Night*. He earned more good reviews in other productions, winning both an Obie and a Drama Desk Award for off-Broadway achievement. In October of 1966, Hoffman was released from the hit play *Eh?*, so he could make his movie debut in *The Tiger Makes Out*.

The film was an expanded adaptation of a one-act, two character play, that should have been left the way it was. Eli Wallach stars as a disgruntled postal worker who declares a one-man war on his crooked landlords and the New York City housing authority. To attract attention to his cause, he kidnaps a suburban housewife (Anne Jackson), but is surprised to find that she agrees with most of his beefs against society. He lets her go and returns to his home.

The Tiger Makes Out has not aged well, but Dustin Hoffman is not around long enough to be tainted by its tired anti-establishment diatribes. As "Hap," one of a pair of beatnik lovers who pop up halfway into the running time, Hoffman's debut lasts about 45 seconds.

At about the same time, director Mike Nichols had acquired the film rights to a little-known book entitled *The Graduate*, and had already cast Anne Bancroft and Katharine Ross in two of the three principal roles. Robert Redford was Nichols' first choice for the main character, Benjamin Braddock. Described in the book as handsome, blond and athletic, Redford seemed ideal for the role. But it was Dustin Hoffman, ten years older than the Benjamin of the book and the antithesis of the WASP-y character described by author Charles Webb, who was able to best capture the youthful bewilderment that Nichols wanted.

As the film opens, Benjamin has returned from college, to spend the summer at his parents' Los Angeles home before starting graduate school in the fall. At a party to celebrate his academic achievements, Benjamin is nearly seduced by Mrs. Robinson (Bancroft), the wife of his father's law partner. At first he resists, but eventually he gives in to temptation. After meeting the Robinsons' daughter, Elaine, Benjamin learns the difference between lust and true love. Elaine is repulsed when she finds out about the affair, but he tracks her down, on her wedding day to someone else. Despite having concluded the ceremony, she runs off with Benjamin.

It's fair to say that not much was expected of *The Graduate*; Nichols paid only $1000 for the film rights, the adaptation was written by the untested Buck Henry (who appears in the film as the desk clerk in the Taft Hotel), and Hoffman, whose salary was $17,000, had less than one minute of movie experience to his credit. It didn't matter. *The Graduate* became the number-one hit of 1968, and grossed the third highest box-office receipts in Hollywood history. The film received near-unanimous critical adoration, and seven Academy Award nominations, including Best Picture and acting nominations for Dustin Hoffman, Katharine Ross and Anne Bancroft. The score, written by Paul Simon and performed by Simon and Garfunkle, swept the Grammy Awards and has never left the radio.

More than twenty-five years after its release, *The Graduate* is now hailed as one of the most important films of the 1960s, and also one of the most entertaining. Several scenes remain fresh in the memory, no matter how much time has passed--Ben's seduction, the "plastics" scene, Benjamin being greeted by every employee at the Taft Hotel, after telling Elaine he had never been there before, and the incredible, climactic scene at the church, when Benjamin fends off the hordes of angry relatives with a cross, which he then uses to bar the door. It should be too much, but in context the dramatic escape of Benjamin and Elaine plays just right.

Mike Nichols won the Oscar for his stylish direction, which owes much to the cinematography of Robert Surtees. Incorporating underwater imagery with exhilarating, swooping pans and meticulously framed angles, *The Graduate* is one of very few films that actually inspires favorite camera shots discussions among non-movie buffs.

If Dustin Hoffman was nervous at all about his first starring role, his insecurity was incorporated perfectly into that of the character. Benjamin Braddock became a symbol of his generation, and Hoffman fashioned an unforgettable portrait of a boy who, in the words of *Newsweek,* "was caught in the full panic of self-discovery, and dragged kicking and screaming into manhood."

THE TIGER MAKES OUT
Directed by Arthur Hiller; Written by Murray Schisgal, based on his play; Produced by George Justin; Music by Milton Rogers

Cast
Eli Wallach (Ben Harris), Anne Jackson (Gloria Fiske), Bob Dishy (Jerry Fiske), John Harkins (Leo). . .DUSTIN HOFFMAN (HAP)

THE GRADUATE
Directed by Mike Nichols; Written by Calder Willingham and Buck Henry, based on the novel by Charles Webb; Produced by Lawrence Turman; Music by Dave Grusin, songs by Simon and Garfunkle

Cast
Anne Bancroft (Mrs. Robinson), DUSTIN HOFFMAN (BENJAMIN BRADDOCK), Katharine Ross (Elaine Robinson), William Daniels (Mr. Braddock), Elizabeth Wilson (Mrs. Braddock), Buck Henry (Room Clerk)

WILLIAM HOLDEN (1918-1981)

FIRST APPEARANCE: *Prison Farm* (Paramount, 1938)

A STAR IS BORN: *Golden Boy* (Columbia, 1939)

Roguishly handsome William Holden specialized in flawed characters who won the audience's affection despite their shortcomings. "In enshrining the philosophy of 'Never apologize, never explain,'" wrote film historian John Baxter, "(Holden) epitomized the engagingly unreliable drinking pal or feckless nephew to whom one lends money, confident that the loan will be neither repaid nor--more importantly--resented."

William Holden was born William Franklin Beedle, Jr. in the small town of O'Fallon, Illinois, and raised in Pasadena, California. A dutiful son and obedient student, William played Rip Van Winkle in a sixth-grade school play, and found the experience enjoyable, though not necessarily the beginning of a future career. He seemed destined to follow his father into the family chemical and fertilizer-analysis business, but after studying chemistry at Pasadena Junior College, his aptitude for science proved insufficient.

In 1937, at the age of nineteen, William and a friend embarked on a cross-country road trip that concluded in New York City, where he attended several plays and became stagestruck. He returned to college, enrolled in a radio drama course, and appeared in a workshop theater production of an original play about Marie Curie. William's performance as Madame Curie's 80-year-old father was witnessed by a talent scout for Paramount Pictures, who invited him to the studio for a screen test. "Sorry," replied William, "I have to take an exam tomorrow."

But a week later he did the screen test, and was signed to a $50-a-week contract. His last name was changed to Holden, after a friend of the Paramount executive who signed him up, and he was assigned to a group of other newcomers known as "The Golden Circle," which included such future stars as Susan Hayward and Robert Preston. Holden's first screen appearance amounted to less than a minute in a men-behind-bars programmer entitled *Prison Farm*.

A cast of reliable character actors, including Lloyd Nolan, J. Carrol Naish, Marjorie Main and John Hart, play out a familiar story about a loser (Nolan) who may be wrongly accused of a robbery, getting sent up the river and tortured by an abusive guard (Naish). Nolan's crisis is solved in a scant 67 minutes, which is more than enough. Once he's incarcerated, watch the corners of the screen during the inevitable rock-pounding scenes, and you'll see William Holden making little ones out of big ones.

Holden next went into the Betty Grable comedy *Million Dollar Legs* (1939), which was set on a college campus. During the graduation ceremony scene, he uttered his first line, "Thank you," while accepting a diploma. His break came when Columbia Pictures began searching for an unknown to play the lead in *Golden Boy*, a film based on Clifford Odets' Broadway play. Studio chief Harry Cohn wanted John Garfield for the role, but director Rouben Mamoulian saw "an indefinable quality" in Holden, and fought to acquire his services. Cohn eventually relented, and Holden took the bus across town to play one of the most coveted movie roles of the year.

The "Golden Boy" in the title is Joe Bonaparte, a promising young violinist who turns to prizefighting to earn money for his musical education. It soon becomes apparent that Joe's talent in the ring is almost as prodigious as his talent as a musician. His manager suspects that Joe is holding back in his fights, to prevent serious injury to his hands. Enter Lorna Moon (Barbara Stanwyck), a femme fatale who goads Joe into abandoning his dreams of the concert stage. After discovering he has been set up by her charms, Joe channels his outrage into his next fight; he kills his opponent, and breaks his hand. Now washed-up as a violinist and as a boxer, Joe is consoled by Lorna, who realizes that she truly loves him after all.

Despite William Holden's outstanding performance in his first significant role, *Golden Boy* is Barbara Stanwyck's film, and this is one of her best black widow characters; Stanwyck is mesmerizing when she taunts Joe into throwing his life away, and she plays Lorna's ultimate conversion with remarkable, understated tenderness. As Joe's manager, Adolphe Menjou is the personification of the corrupt boxing world, and Lee J. Cobb has some wonderful moments as Joe's devoted father.

Innocence and naiveté are not the personality traits that come to mind when discussing William Holden, so it's surprising that, even at this early stage of his career, he is so effective as a young idealist, whose gentle nature is destroyed by the cold, cruel world. He looks convincing as a boxer and a violinist, though he had no experience in either field before shooting began. Stanwyck, already a film veteran, was a tremendous help to the 21-year-old novice film actor, working long hours with him to help create the character, and ordering that Holden's best takes--not hers--be added to the final cut. Reviews of the film and Holden's performance were mixed--The *New York Times* berated him for "exaggerated recoils, lip-bitings and hand-clenchings"--but both have aged gracefully, and *Golden Boy* has earned its place on the "Classics" shelf of the video store.

PRISON FARM

Directed by Louis King; Written by Eddie Welch, Robert Yost and Stuart Anthony, based on the story by Edward V. Westrate; Music by Boris Morros

Cast

Lloyd Nolan (Larry Harrison), Shirley Ross (Jean Forest), John Howard (Dr. Roi Conrad), J. Carrol Naish (Noel Haskins), Porter Hall (Chiston R. Bradby). . . WILLIAM HOLDEN (PRISONER)

GOLDEN BOY

Directed by Rouben Mamoulian; Written by Lewis Meltzer, Daniel Taradash, Sarah Y. Mason and Victor Heerman, based on the play by Clifford Odets; Produced by William Perlberg; Music by Victor Young

Cast

Barbara Stanwyck (Lorna Moon), Adolphe Menjou (Tom Moody), WILLIAM HOLDEN (JOE BONAPARTE), Lee J. Cobb (Mr. Bonaparte)

ANTHONY HOPKINS (1937-   )

FIRST APPEARANCE: *The Lion in Winter* (Avco Embassy, 1968)

A STAR IS BORN: *The Silence of the Lambs* (Orion, 1991)

By his aristocratic refinement and mastery of acting technique, Anthony Hopkins clearly belongs to the tradition of great British stage actors, whose classical training is most often utilized by Hollywood in film biographies of English monarchs, and other *Masterpiece Theater* subjects. But Hopkins has refused to be kept within such narrow parameters; he has taken roles in made-for-TV movies that would be considered slumming by his fellow members of London's National Theatre, and has appeared in kinky horror films such as *Audrey Rose* (1977) and *Magic* (1978). Hopkins' willingness to play against type paid off when he returned to the horror genre in 1991 with *The Silence of the Lambs*, a blockbuster hit that rejuvenated his career and brought him an Academy Award.

An only child born in the small town of Port Talbot in South Wales, Anthony Hopkins was an awkward, unpopular kid who was shipped off to boarding school to improve his grades and his social skills. However, because he came from blue collar stock, the snobbish students at his new school shunned him, and his adolesence proved no more fulfilling than his childhood. After leaving school, Hopkins became interested in acting after joining a Y.M.C.A.-sponsored theater group. His interest remained undiminished after he served his two-year national service requirement, and he joined the student body of the Royal Academy of Dramatic Art. From 1961 to 1963, Hopkins studied the traditional methods in class and the Stanislavsky "Method" on the side.

Hopkins made his London stage debut in a 1964 production of *Julius Caesar*, and in 1966 he joined the National Theatre after passing an audition for Sir Laurence Olivier. He remained a member of the company until 1973, garnering a reputation for versatility and excellence. During his association, Hopkins was allowed frequent leaves of absence to accept movie offers, beginning in 1968 with *The Lion in Winter*, a perfect vehicle for his film debut.

Writer James Goldman did the adaptation himself of his extraordinary play, which takes place in the castle of England's King Henry II (Peter O'Toole) on Christmas Eve, 1183. Henry's estranged wife Eleanor of Aquitaine (Katharine Hepburn), who has been confined to her own castle under king's orders, is released to spend the holiday with her husband and their three sons, all of whom expect to be Henry's heir.

The Lion in Winter is the most enjoyable history lesson ever conceived; you need a scorecard to keep track of the plots and plans hatched by this very dysfunctional family, in which every alliance is temporary and the line between love and hate has never been thinner. O'Toole and Hepburn are magical together, and Goldman's Oscar-winning script produced as many quotable lines as a Shakespeare play. Tragedy and farce might seem like strange bedfellows, but both are served up here in generous doses.

Hopkins plays Richard, Eleanor's choice for the throne. In a family that does not hide its ambition, Richard is the most determined to rule of Henry's three cold-hearted, power-hungry offspring. "I am a constant soldier, a sometime poet, and I *will* be king," vows the Lion-Hearted Richard, who was as good as his word. Hopkins holds his own in several standout scenes with Katharine Hepburn and, like all the best British actors, he can carry off a medieval haircut and the chain mail look with authority. *The Lion in Winter* is also the film debut of Timothy Dalton, who plays the teenage king of France.

In the twenty-plus years that followed his debut, Hopkins compiled an impressive list of credits in a wide variety of projects on stage, in movies and on television. The most memorable would include his TV movie portrayals of Bruno Hauptmann in *The Lindbergh Kidnapping Case* (1976), and Adolf Hitler in *The Bunker* (1981). On the big screen he played a repressed but more humane Captain Bligh in *The Bounty* (1984), but there were already too many Bounty movies so no one paid much attention. He also triumphed in one of his many carefully constructed portrayals of a refined English gentleman in the delightful *84 Charing Cross Road* (1987).

But it was *The Silence of the Lambs* that brought Anthony Hopkins a level of recognition far beyond what he already achieved. Jodie Foster stars as FBI trainee Clarice Starling, who is assigned to the team of agents attempting to catch a serial killer known as "Buffalo Bill." The Bureau believes that Dr. Hannibal "the Cannibal" Lecter (Hopkins), another serial killer serving a life term for crimes too disgusting to describe, could provide information that would hasten Bill's capture. Clarice meets with Lecter, who will only cooperate if she will reveal information about her personal life. The stakes are raised in their game of *quid pro quo* when Lecter escapes from his cell.

Hopkins brings many superb qualities to his portrayal of Lecter, but his best decision is in not falling into the trap of getting us to like him. Lecter bullies and insults Clarice in a maddeningly condescending tone; his penetrating stare burrows into her soul, exposing all of its secrets and insecurities. His intent is not just sadistic--he craves the intellectual exercise of dissecting her past, and Hopkins brilliantly conveys Lecter's joy in causing Clarice discomfort, and offering his clues about Buffalo Bill in the form of another puzzle to test her wits and her mettle.

And just when his soft-spoken charm has us convinced that he's just a lovable eccentric, Lecter reveals the savage tendencies that landed him in maximum security. He kills without conscience, and desecrates his victims with grisly pleasure. But Hopkins is just too good, too delightful, to inspire only repulsion. How else can one explain the laughter, and even the applause, provoked by the film's final scene and Lecter's ghoulish double-entendre--"I'm having a friend for dinner?" Cannibalism has never been so well-received.

THE LION IN WINTER
Directed by Anthony Harvey; Written by James Goldman, based on his play; Produced by Martin Poll; Music by John Barry

Cast
Peter O'Toole (King Henry II), Katharine Hepburn (Eleanor of Aquitaine), Jane Merrow (Princess Alais), John Castle (Prince Geoffrey), Timothy Dalton (King Philip), ANTHONY HOPKINS (PRINCE RICHARD), Nigel Terry (John)

THE SILENCE OF THE LAMBS
Directed by Jonathan Demme; Written by Ted Tally, based on the book by Thomas Harris; Produced by Kenneth Utt, Edward Saxon and Ron Bozman; Music by Howard Shore

Cast
ANTHONY HOPKINS (HANNIBAL LECTER), Jodie Foster (Clarice Starling)

ROCK HUDSON (1925-1985)

FIRST APPEARANCE: *Fighter Squadron* (Warner Bros., 1948)

A STAR IS BORN: *Magnificent Obsession* (Universal, 1954)

Rock Hudson was a capable actor who worked well in a variety of movie genres, but rarely with the magnificence of virtuosity for which screen legends are celebrated. Traditionally, such skills would dictate assignment to the ranks of the character actors, but Hudson was so handsome that one cannot blame Hollywood for grooming him as a leading man. He learned his craft on the screen, sometimes clumsily, but with movies like *Giant* (1956), *Written on the Wind* (1956) and *Pillow Talk* (1959), Hudson eventually earned the stature that was thrust upon him.

Born in Winnetka, Illinois, Roy Scherer, Jr. watched his father leave home, and the family finances evaporate in the Great Depression, all before his eighth birthday. From the age of ten, he worked to help support his mother and her second husband, with whom he never got along. Roy tried out for plays in high school, but his inability to memorize lines kept him out of most productions. He joined the Navy in 1944, and returned to Winnetka after his discharge to work in a succession of odd jobs. Still determined to become an actor, he spent $25 on a photography session, and then sent the photos with a resume` to various producers and directors.

Hard to believe, but the plan worked. In September of 1947, Henry Willson, a talent scout for the Selznick Studio, invited Roy Scherer in for an interview. First order of business was a name change, and Willson chose for Roy the name "Rock" from the Rock of Gibraltar, and "Hudson" from the Hudson River. He then shopped his discovery to various studios, to underwhelming reaction. According to some sources, a screen test Hudson filmed for 20th Century-Fox was later shown to acting classes as a perfect example of how not to do it.

Willson introduced Hudson to director Raoul Walsh, who put the neophyte actor under contract, and invested $9000 in his living expenses and acting lessons. Hudson made his film debut in Walsh's *Fighter Squadron*, a standard World War II aviation film. It was not a distinguished showcase; the aerial combat scenes, usually the highlight of a movie like this, never generate much in the way of excitement, and the performances, music score, and even Walsh's direction are strictly earthbound.

A squadron of central casting military types features Edmond O'Brien as the dedicated squad leader and Robert Stack as the stoic, pensive second-in-command. Hudson first appears as an unnamed airman twenty minutes into the film, and he can be glimpsed in all the group scenes set at the base watering hole. His big moment comes at about the one-hour mark, when he was to deliver the line, "Pretty soon, you'll have to get a bigger blackboard," a reference to the squad's method for keeping track of downed enemy planes. However, he had a little trouble with the last two words, which kept coming out "bligger backboard." Thirty-eight takes later, he still hadn't nailed the line, which was finally changed to "Pretty soon, you'll have to get smaller numbers."

It was an inauspicious beginning, to say the least, but in 1949 Universal Pictures bought Hudson's contract from Raoul Walsh, and signed the still not-quite-actor at $125 a week. Six years and twenty-eight films later, Hudson had worked his way up from bit parts to romantic leads, and was enthusiastically anticipating the start of production on *Magnificent Obsession*, a remake of the 1935 film that made a star of Robert Taylor. He fractured his collarbone two weeks before beginning the role that he hoped would become his breakthrough, and had to convince his doctors and the studio that his performance would not be affected.

Hudson plays Bob Merrick, a frivolous millionaire playboy who is seriously injured in a motorboat accident of his own causing. A machine used to save his life was also needed across town to revive a beloved doctor after a heart attack. Merrick survives, but the doctor dies. Merrick later learns what has happened and seeks out the doctor's wife, Helen Phillips (Jane Wyman). His crude attempts at compensation are spawned only by a desire to ease his conscience and date the attractive Mrs. Phillips, but bring only further tragedy. While fleeing from his advances, Helen is hit by a car, and blinded for life. Merrick is inspired by a friend of Dr. Phillips to change his ways; he courts Helen under an assumed name, and dedicates his life to helping others. He becomes a surgeon, and through a set of circumstances that somehow seem believable at the time, he performs the operation that restores Helen's eyesight.

Magnificent Obsession is a thoroughly shameless melodrama, but director Douglas Sirk was as good at presenting these types of three-Kleenex box stories as anyone, and he knew exactly how to present Rock Hudson to best advantage. Hudson first worked with Sirk on *Has Anybody Seen My Gal?* (1952), and together they would make a total of eight films, many of which brought out a depth in Hudson that was not always palpable. Depth was not an issue here, however; irresistable on one level, almost laughable on another, *Obsession*'s unabashed manipulation of the emotions does not require subtlety. The performances of Hudson and Wyman float gracefully along amidst Technicolor travelogue backdrops, and a raft of violins that punctuate every dramatic flourish. The execution is slick and sure, and audiences loved Hudson's every anguished gaze, that the beautiful but sightless Wyman could not return. The film earned $5 million at the box office, and established Rock Hudson as Universal's top star.

FIGHTER SQUADRON
Directed by Raoul Walsh; Written by Seton I. Miller and Martin Rackin; Produced by Seton I. Miller; Music by Max Steiner

Cast
Edmond O'Brien (Maj. Ed Hardin), Robert Stack (Capt. Stu Hamilton), John Rodney (Col. Bill Brickley), Tom D'Andrea (Sgt. Dolan), Henry Hull (Brig. Gen. Mike McCready)...ROCK HUDSON (SOLDIER)

MAGNIFICENT OBSESSION
Directed by Douglas Sirk; Written by Robert Blees and Wells Root, based on the novel by Lloyd C. Douglas and the screenplay by Sarah Y Mason, Finley Peter Dunne and Victor Heerman; Produced by Ross Hunter; Music by Frank Skinner

Cast
Jane Wyman (Helen Phillips), ROCK HUDSON (BOB MERRICK), Barbara Rush (Joyce Phillips), Agnes Moorehead (Nancy Ashford), Otto Kruger (Rudolph)

JENNIFER JONES (1919-   )

FIRST APPEARANCE: *The New Frontier* (Republic, 1939)

A STAR IS BORN: *The Song of Bernadette* (20th Century-Fox, 1943)

Seldom has there been such strong audience identification between actor and role as existed after Jennifer Jones played Bernadette Soubirous in *The Song of Bernadette*. Jones' only previous credits had been a minor 'B' western and a Dick Tracy serial, both of which she made four years earlier and under her real name of Phyllis Isley. Jennifer Jones was introduced to the world within her exquisite Oscar-winning performance as Bernadette, and the saintly attributes of the character were subsequently ascribed to her portrayal. When Jones divorced husband Robert Walker less than a year after the film's release, the public reacted with shocked disappointment--it was like discovering that John Wayne was a communist. Rather than retreat and apologize, Jones instead shattered her virginal image completely with a lusty performance in *Duel in the Sun* (1946). Once freed of her first impression, Jennifer Jones alternated saints (*Portrait of Jennie*--1948) and sinners (*We Were Strangers*--1949) in an impressive filmography that is long overdue for upgraded assessment.

Phil and Flora Mae Isley were the owners, operators and stars of the Isley Stock Company acting troupe, which toured the south central states performing popular dramas for ten cents a ticket. It was not surprising then when their daughter Phyllis, born in Tulsa, Oklahoma, would desire to become an actress. By the age of ten she was working the ticket booth and the concessions tent, but her stage debut came in school when she played a peppermint stick in a Christmas play.

After attending junior college in Oklahoma, Phyllis enrolled in the drama department of Northwestern University, and then tranferred one year later to the New York Academy of Dramatic Arts. She appeared in various summer stock productions, but returned to Oklahoma after being offered her own dramatic program on radio. *The Phyllis Isley Radio Theatre* debuted in 1938 and lasted thirteen weeks. She married actor Robert Walker in 1939, and together they left Tulsa for Hollywood to break into the movies. They were rejected separately and as a unit by all the major studios, but Phyllis was signed by low-rent Republic Pictures for six months at $75 a week. Before the ink on her contract was dry she was cast in a Three Mesquiteers programmer called *The New Frontier*.

From 1935 to 1943, The Three Mesquiteers appeared in 51 bottom-of-the-bill features. John Wayne was a founding member of the trio, and *The New Frontier* was his final appearance as a Mesquiteer before he became a star in *Stagecoach* (1939). Such was the dearth of ideas at Republic that the film's title had already been used on another film four years earlier. To avoid confusion, the video release has been retitled *Frontier Horizon*.

The tired plot pits ranchers in New Hope Valley against a government plan to flood the valley to build a new dam. The Mesquiteers mostly stand around and do nothing while the two sides argue, but take action when the offer to relocate the ranchers is revealed to be phony. The swindlers are sent to jail and the residents of New Hope are moved to greener pastures. Phyllis Isley, who looks as if she just returned to the old west from Christophe of Beverly Hills, plays Celia Braddock, the plucky granddaughter of the settlement's founder. She spent just five days on the film, and plays the small supporting role as well as it can be played, though she obviously used a double for the riding scenes. John Wayne and fellow Mesquiteers Raymond Hatton and Ray "Crash" Corrigan try to arouse some excitement, but even at a scant 55 minutes the film seems padded out. True-blue movie lovers, however, will feel a nice twinge when the youthful Wayne and the soon-to-be Jennifer Jones share a dance in a too-brief scene.

That same year Phyllis Isley appeared as Dick Tracy's secretary in Republic's serial *Dick Tracy's G-Men* (1939), and then recognized a dead end when she saw it and managed to get released from her contract. She and Robert Walker moved to New York, where Walker found work in radio dramas while Phyllis raised their two children. In 1941, she auditioned for a film adaptation of the play *Claudia*, and though she lost the part she gained the attention of the film's producer, David O. Selznick. Selznick signed Phyllis to a seven year contract and changed her name to Jennifer Jones. One year later, she was chosen from two thousand hopefuls for the lead in *The Song of Bernadette*.

In 1858, fourteen-year-old Bernadette Soubirous sees a vision of a beautiful lady in white religious garb in a grotto near her home in Lourdes, France. She is branded a lunatic by the local authorities and a heathen by the church, but eventually the intensity of her faith begins to win converts. Guided by "the Lady," Bernadette uncovers a spring in the grotto, and when a blind man washes his face in the waters his sight is restored. The news travels quickly through Europe, and the church is forced to take Bernadette seriously. She enters a religious order and spends several years in uncelebrated solitude before succumbing to tuberculosis. She is later canonized as Saint Bernadette.

Jones' performance is not of the flamboyant type that generally wins Oscars. As Bernadette she speaks calmly and quietly, with very little gesturing or mannerism. She develops the portrayal from within, relying almost solely on facial expression to communicate Bernadette's sincerity and devotion. Director Henry King recalled watching audition footage of several actresses interpreting the scene in which Bernadette first sees "the Lady." "All of the other girls looked," he said, "Jennifer actually *saw*." Watching the film, one can almost sympathize with the public's sadness at learning that Jones was only Bernadette for 156 minutes. The image of her kneeling before the grotto in prayer is as indelible as movie moments get.

THE NEW FRONTIER
AKA Frontier Horizon
Directed by George Sherman; Written by Betty Burbridge and Luci Ward; Produced by William Berke; Music by William Lava

Cast
John Wayne (Stony Brooke), Raymond Hatton (Rusty Joslin), Ray Corrigan (Tuscon Smith), PHYLLIS ISLEY [JENNIFER JONES] (CELIA)

THE SONG OF BERNADETTE
Directed by Henry King; Written by George Seaton, from the novel by Franz Werfel; Produced by William Perlberg; Music by Alfred Newman

Cast
JENNIFER JONES (BERNADETTE SOUBIROUS), Charles Bickford (Dean Peyramale), William Eythe (Antoine Nicolau), Vincent Price (Prosecutor Dutour), Lee J. Cobb (Dr. Dozous), Gladys Cooper (Sister Vauzous), Linda Darnell ("the Lady")

BORIS KARLOFF (1887-1969)

FIRST APPEARANCE: *The Dumb Girl of Portici* (Universal, 1916)

A STAR IS BORN: *Frankenstein* (Universal, 1931)

    Boris Karloff's performance as Dr. Frankenstein's monster is one of those magical mergers of actor and role that are afforded legendary status. As with Dracula and Tarzan, the role of the monster has been played by many actors (over fifteen at last count), but remains associated with only one. If such fame is a blessing it can also be a curse, but Karloff, now forever linked with horror, at least was able to play a variety of memorable roles within the genre, in such classics as *The Mummy* (1932), *The Old Dark House* (1932) and *The Man Who Lived Again* (1936).

    Born in Dulwich, England, and raised in the London suburb of Enfield, young William Henry Pratt did not seem to have the makings of a future cinema star. He was tall, gangly, bowlegged, and spoke with a stammer and a lisp. Still, acting intrigued him, because his older brother George had appeared in a few local stage productions. William was the youngest of ten children, and among his siblings only George had a kind word for the shy, awkward, youngest member of the family.

    In a play at the Enfield parish church, William played a demon king, a harbinger of roles to come. He made it through the prestigious Uppingham public school with only average grades and, after a brief stint at the University of London, sailed for Canada in May of 1909. In between a variety of odd jobs, he tried to find work as an actor. In 1910, at the age of twenty-two, he received an offer from The Jean Russell Players, a stock company in Vancouver. Before reporting for duty, William Henry Pratt changed his name to Boris Karloff. His stay lasted until the company's theater was destroyed in a tornado.

    For the next five years, Karloff joined any repertory company with an opening, including one that brought him to Hollywood. He began to knock on studio doors, hoping that the movies might offer more steady employment. He started with five-dollar-a-day extra work in a number of silent films, many of which have gone unrecorded on his filmography. However, the first time Karloff appeared on screen was definitely in 1916's *The Dumb Girl of Portici*, an adaptation of the opera *La Muette de Portici*. Today, the very thought of turning an opera into a silent film sounds ludicrous, but actually the practice was rather common; *Carmen*, *La Boheme* and *Samson and Delilah* all found their way from the stage of the Met to the soundstages of Hollywood in the days before *The Jazz Singer*.

    Portici tells the story of a poor, backward peasant girl, played by the great ballerina Anna Pavlova, who finds love in seventeenth-century Naples as the people of the town revolt against oppressive Spanish rule. Only one copy of the film is known to exist, and those who have seen it report disappointment at the overwrought performances by all the leads, especially Pavlova, and the stunning decision to limit the legendary dancer to a few rudimentary steps. According to the book *Dear Boris*, it is impossible to ascertain the extent of Karloff's role as an extra with any certainty, however author Cynthia Lindsay singles out one stone-throwing peasant, or a soldier holding back crowds during the insurrection, as the most likely candidates. Because extras were sometimes used in more than one scene, it is possible that both parts were played by Karloff.

    Three years would pass before Boris would again appear on screen; during the 1920s he divided his time between bit roles and driving a truck for a construction company. In 1930, Karloff appeared in the Los Angeles production of the prison drama *The Criminal Code*, and was offered the chance to reprise his role the following year in Howard Hawks' film adaptation. From then on, he was in demand. *The Criminal Code* was one of eighteen films in which Karloff appeared in 1931. Others include *Five Star Final* with Edward G. Robinson, the Laurel and Hardy short *Pardon Us*, and a horror film called *Frankenstein*.

There were silent versions of Mary Shelley's novel before, and dozens of sequels and remakes after, but James Whale's 1931 classic is a touchstone not only for film adaptations of *Frankenstein* but for the entire horror genre. Colin Clive stars as the brilliant but slightly deranged Dr. Henry von Frankenstein, whose successful attempt to create life in a laboratory spawns a brief reign of terror in a small German village. The doc learns his lesson after his creation kills his assistant (Dwight Frye as Fritz, not Igor, as some might expect) and a small child, and attacks his fiancee` (Mae Clarke). Angry torch-carrying villagers corner the monster inside an old windmill, and set it ablaze. The monster was supposedly killed, but after *Frankenstein* added $12 million to Universal's coffers for a $250,000 investment, he somehow found his way out for the sequel.

Colin Clive, his jubilant cries of "It's alive! It's alive!" now as central to the legend as Karloff's grunts, became the movies' quintessential mad scientist, although in quieter moments the egomaniacal doctor becomes more coherent. Why, he wonders, can't the big questions of life and death be asked and answered by man? His creation is meant to provide the answer. *Frankenstein* thus becomes a spiritual fable, a warning against man attempting to usurp the role of God. It can also be seen as an examination of a dysfunctional parent-child dynamic; Henry says at one point he works so hard at his experiments to win his distant father's respect, but then makes the same parental mistakes with the monster, a new life that he brings into the world and then callously discards. So while the horror emerges partly from the supernatural, it is actually rooted in the very real fears of a helpless, confused child, separated from his parents. No wonder that so many children, like the little girl in the movie who invites the monster to play, sensed a kindred spirit in the seven-foot behemoth. His death-screams as he burns in the windmill would not be so affecting had Karloff not captured the monster's childlike quality.

It is this aspect of Frankenstein's monster that is so unforgettably-realized by Karloff's performance. Underneath layers of make-up, a misshapen headpiece, and a costume weighing sixty-five pounds, enough to make any sort of performance a challenge, he was able to make the monster terrifying, yet sympathetic. The film runs a scant seventy minutes, and of that Boris Karloff is on screen for only about thirty minutes. Rarely has so monumental an impression been made in so short a time. His billing was a question mark ("? as the Monster"), but word got out of the man beneath the make-up, and Karloff was rarely out of work again.

THE DUMB GIRL OF PORTICI
Directed by Lois Weber and Phillips Smalley; Written by Lois Weber, based on the opera by Daniel Francois Espirit

Cast
Anna Pavlova (Fenella), Rupert Julian (Masaniello), Wendworth Harris (Duke of Arcos), Douglas Gerrard (Alphonso), John Holt (Conde)...BORIS KARLOFF (EXTRA)

FRANKENSTEIN
Directed by James Whale; Written by Garrett Fort, Francis Edwards Faragoh, John L. Balderston and Robert Florey, based on the novel by Mary Shelley; Produced by Carl Laemmle, Jr. Music by David Brockman

Cast
Colin Clive (Dr. Frankenstein), Mae Clarke (Elizabeth), John Boles (Victor), BORIS KARLOFF (THE MONSTER), Edward Van Sloan (Dr. Waldman), Dwight Frye (Fritz)

DIANE KEATON (1946-   )

FIRST APPEARANCE: *Lovers and Other Strangers* (Cinerama Releasing Corporation, 1970)

A STAR IS BORN: *Annie Hall* (United Artists, 1977)

In the Hall of Fame of great motion picture lines, the phrase "La de dah" is certainly among the more peculiar inductees. But to those who watched the frazzled Annie Hall unleash the expression with profound assertion, in a desperate attempt to extend a conversation that wasn't much to begin with, the words are forever etched in the memory.

As a defining moment in the career of Diane Keaton, the "La de dah" scene is surprisingly apt. The character of Annie Hall was based on Keaton (real name: Diane Hall), and Annie's feelings of displacement and insecurity were not unfamiliar to Diane. "She is always afraid she is never going to work again," said her longtime companion Woody Allen, "She worries that she hasn't earned her success." But she did continue to work, advancing from broad caricatures in Allen's early comedies to sobering portrayals in *Reds* (1981) and *Mrs. Soffel* (1984), and finally settling into more conventional terrain (1988's *Baby Boom*, 1992's *Father of the Bride*) with undiminished zest. Her name may not open a movie anymore, but her presence still makes any movie worth a look.

Diane Hall had a typical middle-class suburban upbringing in the Highland Park area of Los Angeles. The family had a television, but preferred to put on their own plays in the living room. Diane's love of performing began while appearing alongside her brother Randy and sisters Dorrie and Robin in everything from "Bonnie and Clyde" to "Peter Pan." She was a below-average student, more out of boredom than ineptitude, and attended college sporadically (Orange Coast and Santa Ana) primarily to gain entry into their summer stock programs.

Before graduation, Diane moved to New York and earned a scholarship with the Neighborhood Playhouse School of the Theater. Since Equity already had a Diane Hall on its union books, she used her mother's maiden name of Keaton for her first professional job, in a small off-Broadway musical called *Hair*. The play moved to Broadway in April of 1968, and Diane was promoted to the lead female role. For the record, she did not strip on stage. She next auditioned for Woody Allen's *Play it Again, Sam*, landing both the role and the writer. The play debuted in February of 1969, received excellent reviews and ran for a year.

Keaton's stage credentials helped her win a role in the film adaptation of the play *Lovers and Other Strangers*, a seriocomic look at events before and during the wedding of two young lovers (Michael Brandon and Bonnie Bedelia). Keaton plays Joan, the estranged wife of Brandon's brother who causes a mild commotion at the reception. A good cast-- Bedelia, Bea Arthur, Anne Jackson, Cloris Leachman, Gig Young and others--play Neil Simonesque characters, but without Simon's wit or heart. One or two sweet moments, such as when the newlyweds-to-be check into the bridal suite the night before their wedding, are not enough to salvage this cynical, episodic misfire, best remembered now for its Oscar-winning song "For All We Know." Keaton's scenes, occurring about an hour into the running time, are overwritten like most of the film, and in reading inane lines about how a book on Spain broke up her marriage, she shows no discernible sign of breakout talent.

Diane received no mention in reviews, but she did receive an introduction to producer Al Ruddy, who screen tested her for *The Godfather* (1972). She was again lost in a large crowd, but a Best Picture Oscar winner always looks good on a resume`. That same year she reprised her stage role in the film version of *Play It Again, Sam*. She was well-received in Woody Allen's *Sleeper* (1973) and *Love and Death* (1975), but away from Allen her career sputtered in the dismal *I Will, I Will...For Now* (1976) and *Harry and Walter Go to New York* (1976).

In 1977, Diane Keaton turned thirty, and turned into something of a phenomenon. *Annie Hall* brought her stardom, an Academy Award for Best Actress, and the cover of *Time* Magazine, which described her as "the most interesting actress in the American cinema." The film, a thinly-disguised dramatization of Keaton's seven-year relationship with Woody Allen, also transformed its writer-director from outrageous comedian to a brilliant auteur. Nothing in Allen's previous work had prepared the world for such a personal, insightful examination of modern love, which was hailed as a watershed for its creator. *Annie Hall* was part confession, part therapy session and part love letter, all delivered with enough one-liner gems to satisfy Allen's comedy following.

The Allen-Keaton romance was as strange in truth as it was in fiction. He was a short, intellectual nerd who still bore all the attributes of his Brooklyn Jewish upbringing; she was a tall California WASP who bordered on glamorous. For the reaction of Keaton's family to their relationship, one need only watch *Annie Hall*, and the scene in which Alvy Singer (Allen) meets Annie's parents and the formidable Grammy Hall. The entire film is made more intriguing by such voyeuristic disclosures of their off-screen relationship.

Because we're dealing with a writer's depiction of his ex-girlfriend, Annie Hall became one of the most psychoanalyzed characters in movie history. Did Annie-Diane simply outgrow Alvy-Woody's neuroses and death obsession? Was it a *Pygmalion* partnership without a happy ending? Does Annie use Alvy, however unwittingly, to advance her career? Keaton offered her summation in an interview with Gene Siskel; "I see Annie Hall as basically stupid. Maybe unformed and innocent is better. And I think Woody may have seen a little of that in me."

Keaton's vibrant, quirky performance established her as both actress and sex symbol; critic Richard Schickel swooned over her "dizzying grin that spreads and resonates like the sound of trumpets blown at dawn by celestial heralds." For the first time, we also got to hear Keaton's engaging singing voice, though it's used to better advantage in *Radio Days* (1987). Annie Hall's wardrobe of multi-layered, unisex earth tones started a major international fashion trend, that has thankfully now subsided.

LOVERS AND OTHER STRANGERS
Directed by Cy Howard; Written by Renee Taylor, Joseph Bologna and David Zelag Goodman, based on their play; Produced by David Susskind; Music by Fred Karlin, song "For All We Know" by Fred Karlin, Robb Wilson and Robb Royer

Cast
Gig Young (Hal Henderson), Bea Arthur (Bea Vecchio), Bonnie Bedelia (Susan Henderson), Anne Jackson (Cathy), Harry Guardino (Johnny), Michael Brandon (Mike Vecchio), Richard Castellano (Frank Vecchio)...DIANE KEATON (JOAN)

ANNIE HALL
Directed by Woody Allen; Written by Woody Allen and Marshall Brickman; Produced by Charles H Joffe

Cast
DIANE KEATON (ANNIE HALL), Woody Allen (Alvy Singer), Tony Roberts (Rob), Carol Kane (Allison), Paul Simon (Tony Lacey), Colleen Dewhurst (Mom Hall), Janet Margolin (Robin), Shelley Duvall (Pam), Christopher Walken (Duane Hall)

GENE KELLY (1912-1996)

FIRST APPEARANCE: *For Me and My Gal* (MGM, 1942)

A STAR IS BORN: *For Me and My Gal*

    Gene Kelly and Fred Astaire are unquestionably the greatest dancers in movie history, but what is less celebrated is their enormous impact on how dance should be presented on film. It was Astaire who insisted that his entire body appear in the frame and that his performances should be presented with a minimum of editing, two valuable lessons in preserving dance's aesthetic grace that are completely ignored today. Kelly arrived in Hollywood ten years later and used Astaire's postulate as a launching pad. As a dancer, choreographer and director, he pushed the envelope constantly throughout the next two decades, and introduced more innovative ideas for the movie musical than anyone on either side of the camera. His characters were usually working-class types who danced in t-shirts, baseball uniforms and raincoats, which offered a nice contrast to Fred Astaire's white tie and tails elegance.

    Eugene Joseph Kelly of Pittsburgh, Pennsylvania was one of five children born to Columbia Gramaphone executive James Patrick Kelly and his wife Harriet, an actress with a local stock company. He took dancing lessons as a young boy, which made him an object of derision among classmates, but at Peabody High School he redressed the balance by also excelling in football, basketball and hockey. After graduation he entered Pennsylvania State College, but the Great Depression dwindled the family finances and Gene was forced to return home. He taught gymnastics at a YMCA camp for a year, and then resumed his education at the University of Pittsburgh.

    Gene Kelly's first real taste of show business was a nightclub act he performed with his brother Fred. Their success in amateur contests helped support the family. Gene also taught dance lessons at fifty cents an hour, and his classes quickly outgrew the Kelly cellar and led to the establishment of the Gene Kelly School of the Dance. In 1933 he graduated college, opened a second school, and continued to perform for larger crowds in clubs.

    In 1938, Kelly left his family in charge of the schools and set out for Broadway. Almost immediately he landed a small role in *Leave It to Me*, the show in which Mary Martin performed "My Heart Belongs to Daddy." He worked steadily in such musicals as *Diamond Horseshoe* before landing the title role in *Pal Joey*. The show opened in 1940, and Kelly was hailed as the best young leading man on Broadway. The *New York Times* even lauded his ability to "raise dancing several notches as a theater art." After another triumph in 1941's *Best Foot Forward*, Kelly was signed to a movie contract by David O. Selznick, who tried to steer the dancer into a career in dramatic roles. Although Kelly would later prove himself an accomplished actor, most notably in *Inherit the Wind* (1960), he knew it was musicals that offered the greater opportunity. Fortunately, Selznick sold his contract to MGM, the home of the movie musical, and in his first assignment Kelly was cast opposite Judy Garland in a bit of tune-filled nostalgia entitled *For Me and My Gal*.

    This was Garland's first name-above-the-title feature and was clearly her showcase throughout; she played Jo Hayden, a singer who teams with dancer Harry Palmer (Kelly) in the hope of breaking out of a chintzy vaudeville circuit and playing New York's famous Palace. Jo and Harry become lovers as well as partners, but their plans for marriage and for stardom are put on hold by World War I.

    Kelly's character was originally conceived as a selfish, conniving rat, so much so that preview audiences wanted Garland to wind up with George Murphy, who played Jo's first partner. Director Busby Berkeley wanted Murphy to play Kelly's role, and was hostile toward the newcomer throughout production. But Kelly had an ally in Judy Garland, who sided with him

150

against Berkeley on the set, and another in Louis B. Mayer, who ordered extensive reshooting to make Harry Palmer a more sympathetic character. Kelly's natural charm was better served by these changes, and audiences approved. *For Me and My Gal* turned a tidy $4 million profit, and boosted the careers of both Kelly and Garland to new heights.

The title song is performed with a low-key graceful soft shoe by the two stars, and is easily the film's best moment. The final half-hour becomes a bit bombastic, with Garland belting every World War I song ever written and Kelly driving through artillery fire in war-torn France. But when the lovers are reunited and "For Me and My Gal" is reprised before the closing credits, the excesses are forgiven and forgotten.

For someone who had "raised dancing several notches as a theatre art," Kelly isn't challenged much by the routines in his film debut. In subsequent films, however, he would shatter the boundaries of the movie musical. Kelly was the first to combine live action and animation (1945's *Anchors Aweigh*) the first to film a musical on location (1949's *On the Town*), and the first to tell an entire story on film using only dance (1957's *Invitation to the Dance*).

FOR ME AND MY GAL
Directed by Busby Berkeley; Written by Richard Sherman, Fred Finklehoffe, Sid Silvers, Jack McGowan and Irving Brecher, based on the story by Howard Emmett Rogers; Produced by Arthur Freed; Music by Edgar Leslie, F. Ray Goetz, George W. Meyer, Roger Edens, others

Cast
Judy Garland (Jo Hayden), George Murphy (Jimmy K. Metcalf), GENE KELLY (HARRY PALMER), Marta Eggerth (Eve Minard)

GRACE KELLY (1929-1982)

FIRST APPEARANCE: *Fourteen Hours* (20th Century-Fox, 1950)

A STAR IS BORN: *Rear Window* (Paramount, 1954)

One of the joys of moviegoing in the 1950s was watching the icy Grace Kelly slowly melt. In six of the eleven films she made in her brief career, there comes a moment when the reserved Kelly, always beautiful but seemingly unapproachable, abandons her heavenly visage for more earthly pursuits. The romantic highlight in *Mogambo* (1953), *To Catch a Thief* (1955) and *The Swan* (1956) is a kiss that unleashes a torrent of pent-up passion that, as one reviewer commented, "gave vent to the undercurrents her performance to that point had implied."

Grace Kelly was born into a working-class Irish-Catholic family that had already produced a Pulitzer Prize-winning playwright and an Olympic gold medalist. Her father, John Brendan Kelly, was a bricklayer who ran a formidable campaign for mayor of Philadelphia, and almost ran for the U.S. Senate. Competition and accomplishment were encouraged, and with nine siblings Grace had to fight to be noticed. However, she preferred to play fantasy games with dolls than battle for position in the family. When she joined the East Falls Old Academy Players at age eleven, she decided that acting was what she wanted to do.

In 1947, Kelly enrolled in New York's American Academy of Dramatic Arts. She found success as a model, enough to pay her school tuition, but happily quit when acting roles were offered. During one thirty-month stretch, Grace Kelly appeared in sixty television dramas, as everything from a chorus girl to Abraham Lincoln's wife. In 1949, she nearly made her film debut after director Gregory Ratoff saw her in a stock company stageplay, and insisted she play the role of an Irish immigrant girl in *The Taxi*. However, the producer voted thumbs down on her screen test, and Ratoff was overruled. Kelly, who felt her future was on the stage, was unfazed by the rejection. She debuted on Broadway in *The Father* (1949), but after the play closed she accepted an offer from movie producer Sol Siegel, to take a small role in the suspenseful drama *Fourteen Hours*.

It's the story of a young man named Robert (Richard Basehart) who steps out onto the ledge of his hotel room window, sixteen stories above New York City. For the next fourteen hours, a traffic cop (Paul Douglas) tries to talk him in, with the help of Robert's overprotective mother (Agnes Moorehead), absentee father (Robert Keith) and loving girlfriend (Barbara Bel Geddes). Gradually we learn more about Robert, and why he is contemplating suicide, while on the street below cynical New Yorkers form betting pools on the time of the jump, and gripe about the resulting traffic jam.

The fourteen hours that Robert spends on the ledge are compressed into a tight, exciting ninety minutes by director Henry Hathaway. Richard Basehart looks uncannily like James Dean, and his portrait of tortured, dysfunctional adolesence only augments the resemblance. Casting down to the smallest roles is excellent, and overall the film paints a seemingly accurate picture of how a crisis of this sort affects those directly involved and those just passing by.

Grace Kelly first appears in the back of a cab about fifteen minutes after the opening credits. Stuck in traffic, she walks to her attorney's office to finalize her divorce. She sees Robert on the ledge through the window, and remains in the crowd throughout the day, where she is later joined by her husband. The subplot is left unresolved, but in a scene cut from the film, they reexamine their relationship and call off the divorce. Kelly is a chic blonde dressed in black, but beyond that nothing more can be discerned.

When Kelly was offered *High Noon* (1952), she was still dead set against becoming a movie star, but the quality of the script and of the personnel involved convinced her to step before the camera again. She received good notices, but her minor role did not constitute a breakthrough. Said producer Stanley Kramer, "You certainly couldn't have foreseen how far, and how fast, she'd go." Kelly happily returned to New York, but before a month had passed Hollywood was calling again, this time with an offer from John Ford to play the second female lead in *Mogambo* (1953). After much soul-searching, she left for Africa knowing full well that her future, like it or not, was in the movies.

Steven Englund's excellent biography *Grace of Monaco* correctly notes that while *Mogambo* and *Dial M For Murder* (1954), Kelly's next film, were well-received, they did not launch the Grace Kelly phenomenon; "she does a nice job," was all the enthusiasm the *New York Times* could muster for Kelly's work in the latter. But after *Rear Window* was released, *Life* magazine raved, "It won't be long before this attractive kid will be the Number One feminine box-office attraction in the world." Grace Kelly's billing was gradually elevated in the film's publicity to the same level as that of star James Stewart and director Alfred Hitchcock. *Life's* prediction proved accurate, and Kelly never ranked lower than third among box-office favorites for the remainder of her film career.

Kelly plays society dame Lisa Fremont, a classy, beautiful fashion plate who has fallen in love with scruffy news photographer L.B. "Jeff" Jeffries (Stewart). Jeff, confined to his apartment with a broken leg, takes to watching the neighbors, and begins to suspect that a murder has been committed in one of the buildings across the courtyard. The Hitchcock touch transforms this simple premise into one of the most suspenseful films ever made.

Lisa is a sheltered, rich, utterly feminine character, graced with what Hitchcock described as "sexual elegance." Kelly was an ideal choice, and her first appearance is breathtaking; the closer Hitchcock zooms in with his camera, the more flawless she appears. "If only she were ordinary," laments Jeff. "She's too perfect. She belongs to that rarefied atmosphere of Park Avenue."

Jeff shows a callous condescension toward Lisa's lifestyle, and is only slightly aroused by her beauty. When Lisa tries to dazzle Jeff with a series of outfits that are all potential *Vogue* covers, he'd rather look out the window. But when Lisa begins to assist Jeff in solving the mystery, she takes on an added dimension in his eyes. The first time he looks upon her with genuine affection is when she helps to set a trap for the murderer.

The emergence of Lisa's adventurous spirit draws the audience closer to her as well. Kelly's aristocratic charm was apparent long before she became Princess Grace of Monaco, but in those moments when breeding won't help, she becomes Gracie Kelly from Philly, and her nervous smile while standing inside a killer's room only makes her more beloved to Jeff, and to us.

FOURTEEN HOURS
Directed by Henry Hathaway; Written by John Paxton, based on the story *The Man On the Ledge* by Joel Sayre; Produced by Sol Siegel; Music by Alfred Newman

Cast
Paul Douglas (Dunnigan), Richard Basehart (Robert Cosick), Barbara Bel Geddes (Virginia), Debra Paget (Ruth), Agnes Moorehead (Mrs. Cosick), Robert Keith (Mr. Cosick), Jeffrey Hunter (Danny), GRACE KELLY (MRS. FULLER)

REAR WINDOW
Directed and produced by Alfred Hitchcock; Written by John Michael Hayes, based on the story by Cornell Woolrich; Music by Franz Waxman

Cast
James Stewart (L.B. "Jeff" Jeffries), GRACE KELLY (LISA FREMONT), Wendell Corey (Detective Thomas Doyle), Thelma Ritter (Stella), Raymond Burr (Lars Thorwald)

DEBORAH KERR (1921-   )

FIRST APPEARANCE: *Major Barbara* (Rank/United Artists, 1940)

A STAR IS BORN: *The Hucksters* (MGM, 1947)

Even in the earliest phase of her film career, Deborah Kerr projected a semblance of modesty and maturity. It is not quite accurate to say that she supplanted Greer Garson at MGM as the studio's ideal English gentlewoman, but Kerr certainly shared Garson's innate qualities of elegance and refinement. Her penchant for characters with Victorian morals was occasionally interrupted by more adventurous portrayals, as in *King Solomon's Mines* (1950), and most memorably in *From Here to Eternity* (1953). The sight of the normally tightly-wrapped Kerr frolicing in the surf with Burt Lancaster unquestionably turned up the heat on an already sexy scene.

Deborah Jane Kerr-Trimmer was born in Helensburgh, Scotland, and raised in Sussex and later Somersetshire. She attended school only until the age of fifteen, at which time she left to pursue a career on the stage. Her first goal was to be a dancer, and toward that end she spent one year at the famous Sadler's Wells Ballet School in London. But once she turned eighteen Kerr saw more opportunity, and more longevity, in acting. In 1939 she played walk-on parts with a repertory company, and supported herself by reading children's stories over the British Broadcasting Network.

Her career began in earnest in 1940, although her first film appearance in Michael Powell's *Contraband* ended up on the cutting room floor. A few months later, however, she met producer Gabriel Pascal, who sensed a "spiritual" quality in Kerr that was just right for the role of Salvation Army worker Jenny Hill in the film adaptation of George Bernard Shaw's 1905 play *Major Barbara*. Wendy Hiller stars as heiress Barbara Undershaft, who turns her back on the family munitions business to join the Salvation Army. Barbara is eventually reunited with her eccentric, estranged father Andrew (Robert Morley), and it is their good-natured discussions of religion, capitalism and ethics that comprise the greater part of the film.

These verbal exchanges, ping-ponging between the whimsical and the solemn, are as profound and eloquent as any in the movies, but those seeking more from their video rentals than debate might get bored. *Major Barbara* is also too long at 135 minutes, and contains too many superfluous scenes early on. Chances are you'll know where it's going an hour before it gets there. But the cast is impeccable, especially the wondrous Wendy Hiller, Rex Harrison and Robert Morley, who at age thirty-two plays the father of twenty-eight-year-old Hiller, and is utterly convincing.

Deborah Kerr, seventh-billed, has only one scene of note, when the impressionable Jenny Hill is accosted by an ill-tempered dockworker whose girlfriend has joined Major Barbara's crusade. She is appropriately spiritual, as Pascal had hoped, but the part doesn't call for much else.

Kerr appeared in eight more films over the next seven years, among them *Love on the Dole* (1941) and *The Life and Death of Colonel Blimp* (1943), ·in which she played three different roles and earned praise from critics for "a charm that is both physical and intellectual." (*New Movies*). As her British films were released in the United States, Deborah Kerr gradually became known to the American public and, in 1942, the *Motion Picture Herald* listed her as a "star of tomorrow." Louis B. Mayer, who was always on the lookout for stars of tomorrow, bought out Kerr's British contract at a cost of $200,000, and brought the actress to MGM. She signed a seven-year contract and was cast in her American debut opposite Clark Gable in *The Hucksters*.

Gable played Vic Norman, an advertising whiz who returns from the war eager to get back in the trade. His first assignment is to convince Kay Dorrance (Kerr), a distinguished military widow, to endorse Beautee Soap. Before he can even begin his sales pitch, however, Kay accepts his offer, mostly for the money but also because she is attracted to Vic. Gradually, their relationship becomes serious, though Vic is not above being distracted by sexy chanteuse Jean Ogilvie (Ava Gardner). But as his affection for Kay grows into love, he begins to recognize the shallowness of his lifestyle, and the corruption in his profession. Eventually he must make a choice between Kay and a megabuck-paying job.

The Hucksters defies easy description, consisting as it does of equal parts comedy, drama, and romance, with a couple of musical numbers thrown in as well. Audiences liked the mix enough to make the film Gable's first post-war hit. Excellent support came from Sydney Greenstreet as the deranged president of Beautee Soap (the radio commercials for the product are hilarious), Keenan Wynn as a hack comedian, and Ava Gardner, in one of her best performances, as a sultry nightclub singer.

Deborah Kerr seemed to have chemistry with all her leading men, but the match with Gable worked particularly well because their personas are so opposite; in *The Hucksters*, Gable, as usual, plays the fast-talking operator and ladykiller, while Kerr remains genteel, honest and chaste. It is only after both of them surrender a little ground that love between them is possible. Kerr's sophistication, combined with what *Hucksters* costar Adolphe Menjou describes at one point as " a lot of *oomph*," impressed the New York Film Critics enough to earn their Best Actress award. When her last British film, *Black Narcissus* (1947), followed *The Hucksters* into American theaters within one month, Deborah Kerr justified MGM's boast in the film's advertising that "Kerr rhymes with star."

MAJOR BARBARA
Directed by Gabriel Pascal, Harold French and David Lean; Written by Anatole de Grunwald and George Bernard Shaw, based on the play by Shaw; Produced by Gabriel Pascal; Music by William Walton

Cast
Wendy Hiller (Major Barbara Undershaft), Rex Harrison (Adolphus Cusins), Robert Morley (Andrew Undershaft), Emlyn Williams (Snobby Price), Robert Newton (Bill Walker), Sybil Thorndike (The General), DEBORAH KERR (JENNY HILL)

THE HUCKSTERS
Directed by Jack Conway; Written by Luther Davis, Edward Chodorov and George Wells, based on the novel by Frederic Wakeman; Produced by Arthur Hornblow, Jr.; Music by Lennie Hayton

Cast
Clark Gable (Victor Norman), DEBORAH KERR (KAY DORRANCE), Sydney Greenstreet (Evan Llewellyn Evans), Adolphe Menjou (Mr. Kimberly), Ava Gardner (Jean Ogilvie), Keenan Wynn (Buddy Hare), Edward Arnold (Dave Lash)

ALAN LADD (1913-1964)

FIRST APPEARANCE: *Once In a Lifetime* (Universal, 1932)

A STAR IS BORN: *This Gun For Hire* (Paramount, 1942)

It is doubtful that any major star played as many bit parts starting out as Alan Ladd. After ten years in Hollywood, he still received "Introducing" billing on *This Gun For Hire*, the film that made him famous. His enigmatic, amoral character--a contract killer who only does the right thing at the last possible moment, set the tone for a career of bad guys who weren't all bad, and good guys who weren't all good.

Born in Hot Springs, Arkansas, Alan Walbridge Ladd moved to Hollywood before the age of ten, by which time his father had died, and his mother had remarried. Poor but not destitute, the Ladds made use of the paychecks Alan earned in his teenage years by selling newspapers and jerking sodas. As a swimmer and diver he set records at North Hollywood High School and, in 1931, he was named diving champion of the west coast. Ladd became interested in theater at about the same time, and played principal roles in several school productions. Before graduation, he was invited to join a group of "discoveries" that Universal Studios hoped to groom into stars. It was during this unfulfilling early phase of his career that he made his inauspicious film debut.

Not that *Once In a Lifetime* is a bad film; actually, it's a very clever send-up of the panic that gripped Hollywood after silent films were replaced by talkies. Jack Oakie plays George Lewis, one of three New York vaudevillians who try to scam the movie studios by opening a voice training school for fading silent stars. After George inadvertently insults a big wheel movie producer, the twisted logic of the movie business labels him a genius, and he is hired as a motion picture supervisor.

The film was adapted from a play written by Moss Hart and George S. Kaufman, who were able, without ever having worked in the industry, to capture all the movie character types that were just beginning to become cliches`. Oakie leads a spirited cast that also includes Sidney Fox, who plays a variation of the role later played by Jean Hagen in *Singin' In the Rain*.

As for Alan Ladd, you'll have to wait for the scene in which George Lewis presents the results of his first studio assignment, and turns a worthless script into a hit film. Look fairly quickly for the projectionist at the screening--that's Alan Ladd, whose few moments on screen did not convince Universal that he was star material. Ladd, along with Tyrone Power, was dropped from the program.

After two years as a "grip," Ladd quit and enrolled in the Bard Dramatic School, where for the second time he was "discovered." Both MGM and RKO expressed interest, which resulted in more forgettable appearances; Ladd played a college student in *Pigskin Parade* (1936), a sailor in *Hold 'em Navy* (1937), and the reporter with the pipe in the last ten seconds of *Citizen Kane* (1941).

Finally, his luck changed after meeting Sue Carol, who started as his agent and later became his wife. Ladd achieved a minor breakthrough with his role as a British fighter pilot in *Joan of Paris* (1942), which led to his successful audition for *This Gun for Hire*. After viewing the first day's rushes of Ladd's performance, Paramount Pictures signed him to a contract. As filming continued, the focus was gradually shifted away from the romance between nightclub entertainer Ellen Graham (Veronica Lake) and her policeman boyfriend (Robert Preston) and toward the relationship between Ladd and Lake, whose chemistry here made the film a hit and led to three more cinematic teamings--*The Glass Key* (1942), *The Blue Dahlia* (1946) and *Saigon* (1948).

As the film opens, Philip Raven carries out the job he received from Willard Gates, a corrupt pharmaceuticals executive who is selling poison gas to America's enemies--kill two employees who can blow the whistle. Raven then collects his fee, only to discover that the cash payment is made in marked bills, and the police are after him. Instead of escape, he prepares to visit Gates to collect his money and his revenge. The clever killer eludes the authorities with the help of Ellen Graham, with whom he is thrown together by chance on a train to New York. Ellen has been hired by the government to seduce a confession out of Gates, and convinces Raven to handle the situation her way.

Philip Raven, a brooding lost soul, without a friend or a conscience, is hardly the type of character that transforms actors into matinee idols. But something in Ladd's presence intrigued moviegoers, especially women, who sent him 3000 letters just three weeks into the film's release. His blond hair dyed black to match his character's name, Ladd brought an enigmatic magnetism to Raven that made an audience hope for his ultimate conversion. When Ellen shows him the first kindness he's known in his life, Raven's half-smile is for him the equivalent of a jump for joy. He dies happier than he ever lived, after experiencing for the first time what it's like to be accepted by another human being.

Veronica Lake, of the arched eyebrows and monotoned delivery, was never better than when matched with Alan Ladd. A diminutive but perfectly-proportioned 5' 5", Ladd had to look up to most of his leading ladies but, at 5'2", Lake was just the right size, and her tough-girl persona was ideal for playing off Ladd's would-be heroes who never got a break.

ONCE IN A LIFETIME
Directed by Russell Mack; Written by Seton I. Miller, based on the play by Moss Hart and George S. Kaufman; Produced by Carl Laemmle, Jr.

Cast
Jack Oakie (George Lewis), Sidney Fox (Susan Walker), Aline MacMahon (May Daniels), Russell Hopton (Jerry Hyland) ZaSu Pitts (Miss Leighton)...ALAN LADD (PROJECTIONIST)

THIS GUN FOR HIRE
Directed by Frank Tuttle; Written by Albert Maltz and W.R. Burnett, based on the novel *A Gun for Sale* by Graham Greene; Produced by Richard M. Blumenthal; Music by David Buttolph

Cast
Veronica Lake (Ellen Graham), Robert Preston (Michael Crane), Laird Cregar (Willard Gates), ALAN LADD (PHILIP RAVEN), Tully Marshall (Alvin Brewster)

HEDY LAMARR (1914-   )

FIRST APPEARANCE: *Geld Auf Der Strasse* (Sasca-Film, 1930)

A STAR IS BORN: *Algiers* (United Artists, 1938)

Ed Sullivan called her "the most beautiful woman of the century" when the century wasn't even half over. Hedy Lamarr was certainly among the most breathtaking of the screen goddesses, but she always seemed too refined for the accustomed cheesecake publicity. In photos she rarely smiled--her expression was often aloof, even haughty, and her dark eyes, usually cast heavenward, were sad and reflective. Swimsuit shots just didn't seem appropriate, and very few were ever attempted. How ironic, then, that Lamarr's most prominent contribution to the movies was being the first actress to walk naked across the screen in a commercially distributed film.

Hedwig Eva Maria Kiesler was born in Vienna, Austria. Her father was a prominent bank manager, her mother a concert pianist who abandoned her career after Hedy was born. The Kieslers' only child was brought up in luxurious surroundings, and educated by private tutors in language, culture, ballet and music. When she wasn't observing parties at the family mansion that were RSVP'd by the crowned heads of Europe, Hedy was trying out her Italian, Hungarian and English while touring the continent with her parents. Ten years at a Swiss finishing school was not the best preparation for a theatrical career, so when Hedy announced her plan to become an actress she transfered to a dramatic school in Berlin. She studied for one year under director Max Reinhardt, and became engaged to a German count, but homesickness brought her back to Vienna. When Hedy broke her engagement, the count killed himself.

In 1930, sixteen-year-old Hedy slipped into the studio of Sascha-Film, which was in the process of filming its first sound picture, *Geld Auf der Strasse* ("Money on the Street"). She just wanted to look around, but like a bad dime store novel that life often imitates, Hedy was spotted by director Georg Jacoby, who figured it couldn't hurt to have a beautiful girl in the background, and cast her in the bit part of a customer in a nightclub. If you can find a copy of the film, that's Hedy (billed as Hedy Kiesler) in the black evening gown, sitting at a table with the film's stars Georg Alexander and Lydia Pollmann.

More small parts in European films followed, but the first Hedy Lamarr credit that everyone knows about is *Ecstasy* (1933). The film, made in Czechoslovakia, was a melodrama about marital infidelity in which Hedy appeared nude at a time when nude scenes were as rare as slasher films. *Ecstasy* was banned in Germany, denounced by the Pope, and only released in the U.S. with the controversial footage removed. Hedy married the super-rich, super-possessive Friedrich Mandl that same year, who would attempt unsuccessfully to buy up and burn every print of the film.

By 1937, Hedy felt trapped in a loveless marriage and frightened over the rise to power of Adolf Hitler. Disguised as a servant, she escaped from her husband's grip and made her way to London, where she met a talent agent who introduced her to MGM boss Louis B. Mayer. Mayer was conducting an unofficial European talent search which had already added Greer Garson to the MGM fold; he knew about *Ecstasy*, and practically called Hedy a porno actress before reluctantly offering her $125 a week for six months. Hedy was insulted at his offer and his demeanor and left for New York, unaware that Mayer was booked on the same ship. During the voyage they patched things up and Hedy signed a more lucrative contract. Hedy Kiesler became Hedy Lamarr, a name chosen by Mayer after silent screen star Barbara LaMarr. She also learned to put up with Americans pronouncing her first name Hedd-y, instead of the correct Hay-dee.

While MGM decided how best to debut their new discovery, Charles Boyer saw Hedy and pleaded with the studio to lend her out for *Algiers*, United Artists' scene-for-scene remake of the French film *Pepe Le Moko* (1937). The studio agreed, in exchange for Boyer's appearance opposite Greta Garbo in MGM's *Conquest* (1937).

In *Algiers*, Boyer plays the notorious jewel thief Pepe Le Moko, who has fled the French authorities for refuge in a shady section of Algeria known as the Casbah. He is safe as long as he stays put, but Pepe cannot resist the charms of a French tourist named Gaby (Lamarr). When he follows her into town he is arrested, and when he runs to get a closer look at her ship as it sails away, he is gunned down.

Gaby was not a vamp role for Lamarr, though the character is often described that way. As much as Pepe is attracted to her beauty, he also sees in her all the cosmopolitan elegance of Paris that does not exist in the Casbah, and it is this reminder of his former life that proves too much for Pepe to resist. Boyer is perfectly cast as the suave Le Moko, and Lamarr is fine in her American debut. Her exchanged glances with Boyer tell the love story better than the dialogue, and were the main reason for the film's huge success. Hedy's line-readings were understated and unemotional, which was appropriate for the character, but in assessing her work most viewers probably shared the conclusion of the *New York World-Telegram* ; "Hedy Lamarr gives a vivid and forthright performance. But whether she is a good actress or not will make practically no difference at all once you get an eyeful of her brunette beauty." This would be the testimony on most of her career.

James Wong Howe's masterful, film noir style cinematography also contributed much to *Algiers'* excellence, and actually made the backlot settings look like the real thing. Howe also knew exactly how to light and photograph Hedy. Her part-in-the-middle hairstyle was emulated by women across the country. The film also spawned a classic line that was never actually said-- "Come wit me to de Casbah," supposedly spoken by Pepe Le Moko to Gaby. He had no reason to say it, though, because they were both already there. Pepe Le Pew, however, did say the line in several less serious features.

GELD AUF DER STRASSE
AKA Money on the Street
Directed by Georg Jacoby; Written by Rudolf Oesterreicher, based on a play by Oesterreicher and Rudolf Bernauer; Produced by Nikolaus Deutsch; Music by Stephan Weiss and Peter Herz

Cast
Georg Alexander (Peter Paul Lutz), Leopold Kramer (Emil Reimbacher), Lydia Pollman (Dodo)...HEDY KIESLER [LAMARR] (YOUNG GIRL)

ALGIERS
Directed by John Cromwell; Written by John Howard Lawson and James M. Cain; Produced by Walter Wanger; Music by Vincent Scott, Mohammed Igorbouchen and Ann Ronell

Cast
Charles Boyer (Pepe Le Moko), HEDY LAMARR (GABY), Sigrid Gurie (Ines), Joseph Calleia (Slimane), Gene Lockhart (Regis), Johnny Downs (Pierrot), Alan Hale (Grandpere)

BURT LANCASTER (1913-1994)

FIRST APPEARANCE: *The Killers* (Universal, 1946)

A STAR IS BORN: *The Killers*

The virtue of self-control, and the vice of controlling others, are the most striking traits in the characters played by Burt Lancaster. He showed stoic self-control when facing racism in *Jim Thorpe--All American* (1951) and years of confinement in *The Birdman of Alcatraz* (1962). Exhibiting a darker side as gossip columnist J.J. Hunsecker in *Sweet Smell of Success* (1957), he controlled an entire city with the wave of his pen; in his Oscar-winning role as *Elmer Gantry* (1960), he achieved the same objective with eloquence and charm.

Lancaster's square-jawed face and brawny physique were intimidating on screen, but there was usually an intellectual side to the men of action he played, on either side of the law, that made them doubly-formidable. His accomplished performances in a wide variety of roles and genres helped Lancaster to avoid typecasting, and to age as gracefully as any actor ever has before the cameras. In later years, he played characters that recalled the powerful men he once inhabited, who yearn to recapture their former prestige; the aging low-level mobster in *Atlantic City* (1981), and the baseball player whose career ended after one game in *Field of Dreams* (1989) rank with his best work.

He never played an English aristocrat, but Burton Stephen Lancaster can trace his ancestry back to Britain's royal house of Lancaster. Burt, however, was born in the East Harlem section of New York City, and raised a commoner. At the age of sixteen, he entered New York University on an athletic scholarship, and excelled at basketball, boxing, baseball, track and gymnastics. After two years, he left college and joined the Kay Brothers Circus. Lancaster earned three dollars a week as an acrobat, touring with carnivals, vaudeville shows, and circuses (including Ringling Brothers) from 1932 to 1939.

Lancaster was drafted into the army in 1942. In 1945, during a discharge furlough in New York, he met stage producer Irving Jacobs in an elevator, and was invited to read for the part of a tough sergeant in the play *A Sound of Hunting*. The play lasted only five weeks, but that was long enough for Lancaster to receive seven offers from Hollywood. He signed a two-picture deal with producer Hal Wallis, and was set to begin work on *Desert Fury*, but the script was not yet ready. Instead, he made his debut as "The Swede," in an offbeat combination of film noir and *Citizen Kane* (1941), entitled *The Killers*.

Like *Kane*, the film begins with the death of its central character, an unassuming gas station attendant known as The Swede, then works backward to trace his life story and uncover the meaning of his enigmatic last words--"I did something wrong...once." That job falls to insurance investigator Jim Reardon (Edmond O'Brien), who travels to the New York neighborhood where The Swede grew up, and interviews his former best friend, and his first love.

The Swede, it turns out, was an amateur boxer with more determination than talent, who was lured into a life of crime by the flashy mobster Big Jim Colfax (Albert Dekker). At one of Colfax's parties, The Swede is mesmerized by the beautiful Kitty Collins (Ava Gardner), Big Jim's girlfriend, who convinces him to take part in an elaborate armored car robbery, with the promise that she will leave Colfax after the job is done. Instead, she double-crosses The Swede, and Colfax assigns two hit men to kill the naive dupe. The Swede leaves town and tries to start his life over, but eventually Colfax's men track him down and kill him. Jim Reardon lures the killers into a trap, and then attempts to bring Big Jim and Kitty to justice.

The Killers is a hard-boiled, hard-hitting crime drama that never fulfills the promise of its first scene, the only one to be adapted faithfully from the Ernest Hemingway story that provided the title. Still, under Robert Siodmak's direction, the murder mystery unfolds at a brisk pace, and benefits from the casting of Lancaster and Ava Gardner, who also became a star with this film.

Lancaster's screen presence is already powerful in his debut. His combination of brute force and wistful melancholy, likened by *Entertainment Weekly* to "a Stallone who could do George Bernard Shaw," is in evidence in his portrayal of The Swede. Edmond O'Brien actually has the most screen time, but Lancaster's presence is palpable from his first appearance, in which he is seen only in shadow. The pivotal moments in The Swede's life, of temptation, desperation and, ultimately, acceptance of his folly and his fate, are what linger most in memory.

THE KILLERS

Directed by Robert Siodmak; Written by Anthony Veiller and John Huston, based on the story by Ernest Hemingway; Produced by Mark Hellinger; Music by Miklos Rozsa

Cast
Edmond O'Brien (Jim Reardon), Ava Gardner (Kitty Collins), Albert Dekker (Big Jim Colfax), Sam Levene (Lt. Sam Lubinsky), Virginia Christine (Lilly Lubinsky), John Miljan (Jake), Vince Barrett (Charleston), BURT LANCASTER (SWEDE)

JESSICA LANGE (1949-)

FIRST APPEARANCE: *King Kong* (Paramount, 1976)

A STAR IS BORN: *The Postman Always Rings Twice* (Paramount, 1981)

If any actress seems heir to the exemplar of regal beauty and cool, brainy elegance set by Grace Kelly during her brief stay in Hollywood, it is Jessica Lange. Surprisingly, however, the blond ice princess that Kelly immortalized is the one type of character that Lange has yet to tackle. She emerged as one of the premier leading ladies of the 1980s after earning simultaneous Oscar nominations for the comedy *Tootsie* (1982) and the dramatic biopic *Frances* (1982). She won for *Tootsie*, and Lange has since won plaudits playing downtrodden farm folk (*Country*--1984), an eccentric Southern belle (*Crimes of the Heart*--1986) and even a brunette (*Sweet Dreams*--1985). But if someone doesn't cast her in a remake of *To Catch a Thief* (1955) pretty soon, it will be a monumental loss.

A native of rural Minnesota, Jessica Lange moved eighteen times growing up, but wound up attending high school back where she started near the town of Cloquet. As a child she was fascinated with Hollywood and "obsessed with *Gone With the Wind*," according to a *Rolling Stone* interview. One summer when she was sick in bed she practiced Melanie's death scene for hours at a time, but the drive to turn her performing instincts into a career did not take hold until much later. Although Lange was the star of the senior class play, it was a scholarship in art that brought her to the University of Minnesota. A few months later she dropped out to travel the world with Spanish photographer Paco Grande, whom she would eventually marry. Lange so loved Paris during the couple's visit in 1968 that she moved there in 1971, which began a long separation from her husband that led to divorce.

It was during her two years in Paris that Lange first began to study acting, first via mime with Edienne DeCroux, the legendary teacher of Marcel Marceau, and then at the Opera Comique where she performed as a dancer. She returned to America in 1973 and settled into a Bowery flat in New York City. Modeling jobs for the Wilhelmina agency paid the bills, and it was one of her glossies on file that ended the sideshow-like talent search for the heroine of *King Kong*, conducted by veteran Hollywood huckster Dino De Laurentiis.

De Laurentiis' remake of the 1933 classic departed somewhat from its familiar storyline; this time the voyage to Skull Island is prompted by a search for oil, led by petroleum company executive Fred Wilson (Charles Grodin). Paleontology professor Jack Prescott (Jeff Bridges) sneaks aboard the ship to warn Wilson about possible dangers on the island. Jessica Lange plays Dwan, a budding actress who is pulled from a lifeboat after her party boat sinks. Once the island is found, what follows is more or less identical to the '33 model.

The movie had a great poster, depicting Kong with one foot on each of the World Trade Center's twin towers fending off Air Force F-15s just like his ancestor swatted down bi-planes. As the suspense builds steadily throughout the film's rousing first half, *King Kong* appears to be worthy of its advertising. But then we see the big ape for the first time, and realize that all De Laurentiis bought for $24 million was a guy in a monkey suit, filmed before a backscreen just like Frankie Avalon's surfing scenes in *Beach Blanket Bingo* (1965). When that happens, the illusion is shattered and the film collapses.

Lange was compared unfavorably to Fay Wray, which is unfair because she wasn't playing the same character. Dwan is a ditz, pure and simple, and Lange plays her that way. She had two strikes against her with the "model-turned-actress" label, but if her ability did not fully surface in *King Kong* it is because acting, quite frankly, was not what she was hired to do. The proof is a shameless montage of Dwan walking around the ship flirting and giggling in shorts and a cut-off t-shirt, and then taking a shower for no other reason than viewer titillation. Lange spends most of the film in clothes that are either see-through or shredded, and generates prurient interest to the tenth power.

Dwan's repartee` with Kong ("Nice monkey...I'm a Libra, what sign are you?") is dreadful, but no actress could play these scenes and make them work, or emerge unscathed from their backlash--Lange did not appear in another movie for two years after *King Kong*'s release. She had one unexpected supporter in Pauline Kael, who also derided Dwan's one-liners as "so dumb that the audience laughs and moans at the same time," but observed that "when Jessica Lange says them she holds the eye, and you like her, the way people liked Carole Lombard." And Lange's performance is easily more credible than that of Charles Grodin, who chews scenery the way Kong chews explorers. The best moment in the film is when the giant ape squashes him like a bug. Only Jeff Bridges emerges with his dignity intact.

After her *Kong*-induced hiatus, Lange returned to the screen as the "Angel of Death" who haunts the workaholic hero of *All That Jazz* (1979), and as a suburban housewife in the disappointing comedy *How to Beat the High Cost of Living* (1980). But it was another remake, *The Postman Always Rings Twice*, that turned the corner in her career, though like *King Kong* the film ran a poor, distant second to its predecessor.

David Mamet's script is more faithful to the James M. Cain novel than the 1946 version, which was restricted by prevailing standards of sex and violence. Lange and Jack Nicholson play the roles made famous by Lana Turner and John Garfield; Cora Papadakis (Lange) runs a California roadside diner with her much-older husband Nick (John Colicos). She has an affair with Frank Chambers (Nicholson), a drifter hired by Nick, and together they kill her husband. They are tried but acquitted of the murder, but their relationship is strained by guilt and distrust, and ultimately ends in tragedy.

Both Mamet's script and Bob Rafelson's direction are lifeless, and the film is so visually dull that one wonders why they bothered to use color film. It's not a very good movie, but Jessica Lange is very good in it, as is Jack Nicholson. Lange was chosen from one hundred actresses by Rafelson, who was struck by her frank, natural sexuality. Unlike Lana Turner, whose first appearance in a white two-piece swimsuit is forever seared into memory, Lange de-glamourizes for the part; her Cora looks like the Depression-era hashslinger that Cain described, but all her banked-up sensuality is still conspicuous. It is released in a controversial, highly-charged sex scene that makes *Basic Instinct* look like *The Bells of St. Mary*.

Lange's ability to suggest murder with the slightest hint of a smile, and her willingness to play raw physical scenes that are shockingly graphic for a mainstream film did not go unnoticed even by critics who trashed the movie. "She made the transitions between the winsome side of Cora and the manipulative side with the natural ease of a polished actress, which she has clearly become," wrote the *New York Daily News*. One writer ranked Lange above Kathleen Turner in *Body Heat* (1981) and Rachel Ward in *Against All Odds* (1984), declaring that "she has no female equal in contemporary film noir." She would return to the genre, belatedly but with even better results, in *Night and the City* (1992).

KING KONG
Directed by John Guillermin; Written by Lorenzo Semple, Jr., based on a screenplay by James Creelman and Ruth Rose, from a concept by Merian C. Cooper and Edgar Wallace; Produced by Dino De Laurentiis; Music by John Barry

Cast
Jeff Bridges (Jack Prescott), Charles Grodin (Fred Wilson), JESSICA LANGE (DWAN), John Randolph (Captain Ross)

THE POSTMAN ALWAYS RINGS TWICE
Directed by Bob Rafelson; Written by David Mamet, based on the novel by James M. Cain; Produced by Charles Mulvehill and Bob Rafelson; Music by Michael Small

Cast
Jack Nicholson (Frank Chambers), JESSICA LANGE (CORA PAPADAKIS), John Colicos (Nick Papadakis), Michael Lerner (Katz), Anjelica Huston (Madge)

STAN LAUREL (1895-1965) AND OLIVER HARDY (1892-1957)

FIRST APPEARANCE: *Lucky Dog* (Metro, 1917)

A STAR IS BORN: *Do Detectives Think?* (Hal Roach-Pathe, 1927)

Stan Laurel and Oliver Hardy did not make their film debut as a team. Long before their names became linked together in the pantheon of great comedians, both were under separate contract to the Hal Roach Studio and were enjoying busy--if not particularly stellar-- careers.

Laurel, born Arthur Stanley Jefferson, learned his craft in vaudeville and the music halls of his native England, where he understudied Charlie Chaplin in the Fred Karno Theatrical Troupe. When Chaplin left the stage for Hollywood in 1913 Laurel did the same, making his solo debut in the MGM two-reeler *Nuts in May* (1917). Oliver Norvelle Hardy came to Hollywood via Harlem, Georgia, where he was born and raised in a decidedly non-show business family (unlike his future partner, whose father was a well-known theatrical impresario in England). After abandoning the study of law, Hardy opened a movie theater in Georgia, and was so intrigued by the new art form that he decided to try his luck on the other side of the screen. He was signed by the Florida-based Lubin Company, and first appeared in the forgotten short *Outwitting Dad* (1913).

Hardy's rotund, moonfaced appearance made his casting as a comic villain inevitable. He played the "heavy," literally and figuratively, in dozens of shorts starring Billy West, and later in a couple of Buck Jones westerns. Stan Laurel, however, was the protagonist in his films. He usually played a hard-luck working man, but his screen persona was far more aggressive (and sometimes downright nasty) than it would become after his teaming with Hardy.

There are sufficient grounds to nominate several different two-reeler comedies as the first appearance of Laurel and Hardy. Although the team was created at the Hal Roach Studio, the pair actually appeared together for the first time in 1918's *Lucky Dog*, five years before either comedian had signed with Roach. In their first shared scene, Hardy plays a thug who holds up Laurel at gunpoint. The pairing was purely accidental, and when both men finished their roles they resumed their individual careers. In 1926, Laurel and Hardy appeared in separate scenes along with Charley Chase and many other Hal Roach contract players in *Forty-Five Minutes from Hollywood*. It was the first of six two-reelers in which they were featured.

At the time there was no real precedent for two-man teams as a film commodity. All of the recognized greats in the early days of movie comedy--Chaplin, Buster Keaton, Harold Lloyd--worked alone. This seems the only possible explanation as to why it took Hal Roach so long to recognize their potential. Like Astaire and Rogers in the next decade, it was apparent that Laurel and Hardy were better together than apart. As they started to instinctively gravitate together in *Slipping Wives* (1927) and *Sailors Beware* (1927), the decision was made to bill them as a unit.

Putting Pants on Phillip (1927) was their first true team effort, but it was in *Do Detectives Think?* (1927) that the characters most commonly associated with Laurel and Hardy first appear; Ollie the pompous would-be leader of the pair, Stanley the well-meaning innocent. They play private detectives hired to guard a judge who has been threatened by a fearsome escaped convict, and of course they capture the crook by sheer luck. As they exchange and fumble with their now trademark bowler hats, one can see the birth of something magical. Their chemistry would fully blossom in such classic shorts as *Big Business* (1929), and the Oscar-winning *The Music Box* (1932).

Laurel and Hardy were the only silent era comedians to become even more popular with the coming of sound, which they first embraced in *Unaccustomed As We Are* (1929). Their precise vocal inflections, their catch phrases ("This is *another* fine mess..."), Hardy's exasperated sigh at Laurel's ineptness, and Stanley's uncontrollable whimpering were added to their already-formidable comic arsenal. The team's feature film debut was in *Hollywood Review of 1929*, in which they traded lines with Jack Benny. For the next twenty years they set the standard for every comedy team that followed in both features (1933's *Sons of the Desert*, 1937's *Way Out West*) and two-reelers, which they continued to make throughout the thirties. After *Atoll K* (1952), their last film as a duo, they retired from show business, only to be rediscovered by a new generation in *The Golden Age of Comedy* (1958) and *Laurel and Hardy's Laughing Twenties* (1965) documentaries of the silent era compiled by producer Robert Youngson.

LUCKY DOG
Directed by Jess Robbins; Produced by Gilbert M. Anderson

Cast
Florence Gilbert...STAN LAUREL, OLIVER HARDY

DO DETECTIVES THINK?
Directed by Fred Guiol; Written and produced by Hal Roach; Titles by H.M. Walker

Cast
STAN LAUREL, OLIVER HARDY, James Finlayson, Viola Richard, Noah Young, Frank Brownlee, Will Stanton, Charley Young, Charles A. Bachman

BRUCE LEE (1940-1973)

FIRST APPEARANCE: *Golden Gate Girl* (Golden Gate, 1941)

A STAR IS BORN: *Enter the Dragon* (Warner Bros., 1973)

More than twenty years after his death at the age of thirty-three, Bruce Lee is still the preeminent symbol of excellence in the martial arts genre. Through his charisma as an actor and his artistry as an athlete, he elevated chop-socky cinema to a level it had never reached before, and has yet to achieve since.

Jun Fan Lee was born in San Francisco, California, and moved to Hong Kong with his family before his first birthday. He was given the name Bruce by the doctor who delivered him. Lee's father, Li Hoi Chen, was a popular actor and opera singer in China, who was performing in San Francisco when his son was born. Before they returned home, Chen appeared in the first feature-length Chinese talking picture ever made in San Francisco's Chinatown. A baby was needed for one scene, and Chen just happened to have a son who could play the part.

Golden Gate Girl tells the story of a curio shop owner in Chinatown whose daughter (Tso Yee Man) falls in love with the star of an operatic troupe (Wong Hok Sing). Disowned by her stern father, she marries the singer but dies in childbirth after returning to China. The child grows into the image of her mother (and is played by the same actress), and eventually reconciles with her grandfather. Li Hoi Chen appears as one of the performers in the opera, and Bruce Lee, not yet one year old, makes his film debut as a baby girl.

Chen would later discourage his son's interest in show business, but Bruce appeared in bit parts and supporting roles in over twenty Chinese films, earning the nickname "Little Dragon." In several films, including 1958's *The Orphan*, he was cast as a tough street kid who never backed down from a fight. The role was one that Bruce also played away from the screen--he was the Chinese boxing champion of his high school, and was eager to prove his skills on any volunteers.

At the age of eighteen, Lee moved to Washington, attended college and met his future wife, Linda Cadwell. He opened a martial arts school in Seattle, where he taught his self-developed fighting style of "jeet kune do," loosely translated as the "way of intercepting fists." Lee would later open two more schools in Oakland and Los Angeles, but all the while he hoped to get back into show business. His martial arts skills won him the role of Kato in the short-lived television series *The Green Hornet* (1966-67), and a small but memorable role as a hitman in *Marlowe* (1969). He was offered a contract by MGM and Warner Bros., but chose instead to sign with Hong Kong producer Raymond Chow. The three films Lee made with Chow during their two-year collaboration, *Fists of Fury* (1971), *The Chinese Connection* (1972) and *Return of the Dragon* (1973), broke all box-office records in Asia and the Far East.

Lee's Hong Kong films were released in the United States after *Enter the Dragon*, the movie that made him an international star, and still the best martial arts movie ever made. *Enter the Dragon* follows the same formulaic story of a hundred other genre entries, but corrects the inferior production values of standard chop socky fare. The action is almost non-stop, and for the first time the fight scenes that do not include Lee are also worthwhile, thanks to a cast of kung fu all-stars including Jim Kelly, John Saxon, Yang Sze, the "Chinese Hercules," and Angela Mao Ying, the genre's greatest lady martial artist.

Lee's character, also called Lee, is hired by the British government to infiltrate the island stronghold of Master Han (Shih Kien), a drug trader and white slaver, who recruits assassins for his operation through a martial arts tournament. Lee has a personal stake in the assignment--his sister was attacked by Han's operatives, and chose suicide over serving their cause.

No need for in-depth analysis here--the plot is only necessary to put Lee in a position of defending himself from as many adversaries as possible. What happens next is every action scene from his previous films multiplied by ten. It is violent, to be sure, but there is also a balletic grace to Lee's fighting style, and his speed and agility are astonishing. Even those who would dismiss the entire martial arts genre as shoddy and formulaic cannot help but acknowledge his mastery of technique. Between battles, Bruce Lee displays a powerful screen presence that would certainly have given him a fighting chance at other types of roles outside his specialty. His smile was one of the most disarming in movies, whether used in relaxed moments with friends, or to mock an opponent just before a fight. The intense ferocity of his stare could wither most challengers before the first punch was thrown.

We can only speculate on what might have been, had Bruce Lee not died suddenly of a cerebral edema under what many still insist are mysterious circumstances; *Enter the Dragon* should have been the starting point of a career in which Lee carried the martial arts film to greater heights. Instead, it serves only as an elegy of the genre's brightest star.

GOLDEN GATE GIRL
Directed by Esther Eng; Written by Moon Quan

Cast
Tso Yee Man (The Girl), Wong Hok Sing (The Boy), Moon Quan (The Father), Liu Nom (Salesman), Luk Won Fee (The Cook)...BRUCE LEE (BABY)

ENTER THE DRAGON
Directed by Robert Clouse; Written by Michael Allin; Produced by Fred Weintraub and Paul Heller, in association with Raymond Chow; Music by Lalo Schifrin

Cast
BRUCE LEE (LEE), John Saxon (Roper), Jim Kelly (Williams), Shih Kien (Han), Bob Wall (Oharra), Angela Mao Ying (Su-Lin), Yang Sze (Bolo)

VIVIEN LEIGH (1913-1967)

FIRST APPEARANCE: *Things Are Looking Up* (Gaumont British, 1935)

A STAR IS BORN: *Gone With the Wind* (MGM, 1939)

In the early nineteenth century, the rousing tales of Rudyard Kipling seduced many a British subject to seek their fortune in exotic India. Among them was Ernest Richard Hartley, an actor who moved to Calcutta and established a theater troupe to entertain soldiers and their families. Hartley met and married Gertrude, a fellow Britisher who couldn't wait to leave India. Ernest promised they would do so, but after their daughter Vivian was born in Darjeeling he changed his mind and joined the Indian cavalry.

The Hartleys were stationed in Ootacamund, where at age three Vivian recited "Little Bo Peep" in full costume to an audience of army wives, and received good notices for her stage debut. Gertrude, a devout Roman Catholic, insisted that her daughter receive a religious education, so at age seven Vivian entered a convent near central London. Fellow student Maureen O'Sullivan became a confidante, and after a rough first term she grew to love the serenity of the convent and the special attention she received from the nuns, who thought her the most beautiful child they had ever seen, but expressed some concern over her frontier spirit.

After four years Vivian rejoined her parents and traveled the European continent, completing her education sporadically at various religious institutions. Maureen O'Sullivan had become famous in Hollywood, and Vivian dreamed of doing the same. She entered the Royal Academy of Dramatic Arts in London, which delighted her thespian father but worried mom to no end. At eighteen Vivian met Herbert Leigh Holman, a barrister thirteen years her senior. They married in 1930, and had a daughter one year later. Holman didn't want any wife of his working in the theater, especially when there was a child to raise. Vivian dutifully abandoned her studies, but then she went back, exhibiting Ernest Hartley's capricious nature and his inherent love for performing.

One look at Vivian at age twenty and it would hard to imagine her anywhere else but on a stage. Her alabaster skin, alluring grey-green eyes, long, graceful neck and tiny waist were the stuff that dreams are made of, and she was a naturally gifted actress who could play Shakespeare and pantomime with equal elan`. Her striking good looks led to an offer to appear in a low-budget film comedy called *Things Are Looking Up*, and despite the insignificance of the role she happily accepted. The movie was a showcase for Cicely Courtneidge, who played the dual role of a teacher at a private girls school and her twin sister, a trick rider in the circus. When the teacher elopes her sister steps in and unexpectedly earns a promotion to headmistress. Vivian spent three weeks making the film, in which she played one of the schoolgirls and uttered one line--"If you are not made headmistress, I shan't come back next term!" Her character was not given a name, but she can be seen throughout the film in classroom scenes and in several close-ups which almost certainly drove the plot from the minds of male viewers.

She dropped the "Holman" and was billed as Vivian Leigh, but when she hired an agent after the film was released he suggested another change--to April Morn. Names were obviously not this guy's specialty, but he did open doors for the rising starlet, and Vivian did the rest. She was fourth-billed in *The Village Squire* (1935), which was made in six days and forgotten in three, and then played the female lead in *Gentleman's Agreement* (1935), a lightweight comedy with no connection to the 1947 film of the same title. That same year she appeared on stage in the play *Green Sash* and received her first favorable reviews. Sydney Carroll, the drama critic for the *Sunday Times*, suggested another name change--to "Vivien" with an "e", which he thought was more feminine. This time, she agreed.

In her next play, *The Mask of Virtue*, Leigh made full use of her seductive charms in the role of a scheming temptress. Her performance generated front page stories, heralding Vivien Leigh as the "fame in one night" girl. She signed a 50,000 pound film contract, and starred in *Fire Over England* (1937) and *A Yank at Oxford* (1938), while triumphing on stage in *Henry VIII, A Midsummer Night's Dream* and, in 1937, a production of *Hamlet* opposite future husband Laurence Olivier.

Meanwhile, back in Hollywood, producer David O. Selznick was in the midst of spending over two years and $50,000 in his search for Scarlett O'Hara. Leigh had read *Gone With the Wind* in 1937, and when the movie was announced she thought herself perfect for the role of its tempestuous heroine. Her agent sent a photo and some clippings to Selznick's office, where they landed on the desk of New York representative Kay Brown. Brown cabled Selznick that Leigh had possibilities, but Selznick tabled the news and went off to audition Tallulah Bankhead. One year passed, and while Leigh remained busy on the London stage she was still determined to play Scarlett. When she discovered that Selznick's brother Myron was the Hollywood agent for Laurence Olivier, who was now her steady companion, the couple sailed for America. Myron was instantly convinced that the search was over, and introduced Vivien to his brother. "I took one look and knew she was right," said David O. Selznick, and the rest, as they say, is history.

Anyone who loves movies has already seen *Gone With the Wind* at least twice, and anyone who doesn't isn't reading this book, so a plot synopsis is unnecessary. The film is a milestone in the history of motion pictures, and its cast, particularly Leigh and Clark Gable, is now beyond criticism. Of Vivien Leigh, who was unknown in America before the film's release, the *New York Times* wrote "[Her] Scarlett is so beautiful she hardly need be talented, and so talented she need not have been so beautiful. No actress, we are sure, was as perfectly suited for the role." Leigh won the Oscar for Best Actress, but she would appear in just eight more films over the next 26 years.

THINGS ARE LOOKING UP
Directed by Albert de Courville; Written by Stafford Dickens and Con West, based on a story by Albert de Courville and Daisy Fisher; Produced by Michael Balcon

Cast
Cicely Courtneidge (Cicely/Bertha Fytte), Max Miller (Joey), William Gargan (Van Guard)...VIVIEN LEIGH (STUDENT)

GONE WITH THE WIND
Directed by Victor Fleming; Written by Sidney Howard, based on the novel by Margaret Mitchell; Produced by David O. Selznick; Music by Max Steiner

Cast
Clark Gable (Rhett Butler), VIVIEN LEIGH (SCARLETT O'HARA), Leslie Howard (Ashley Wilkes), Olivia de Havilland (Melanie Hamilton)

JACK LEMMON (1925-   )

FIRST APPEARANCE: *It Should Happen to You* (Columbia, 1954)

A STAR IS BORN: *Mister Roberts* (Warner Bros., 1955)

Jack Lemmon's father worked in minstrel shows until a particularly hostile audience hit him in the head with a bottle. After that he retired from showbiz for good, but fortunately his son was not discouraged by this oft-told family story. Jack's father John would later rise to the vice-presidency of the Doughnut Corporation of America, and was personally responsible for introducing the doughnut to Great Britain. Jack, who was christened John Uhler Lemmon III, was born in Newton, Massachusetts and made his stage debut at age four, in an amateur production of *Gold in Them Thar Hills*. His only line was "The dam's bust."

Jack was a frequently ill child who underwent ten operations before his teenage years. In school, his classmates delighted in denigrating Jack's full name ("Jack, U. Lemmon!"), so Jack set out to earn laughs in a less embarrassing way. He starred in several school plays and entertained with his talent at the piano, which also provided solace during the civil but prolonged break-up of his parents.

He entered Harvard in 1943, where his already polished skills as an actor and musician made him well-liked. His studies were interrupted for seven months by the Naval Cadet Corps, but when World War II ended he resumed his plans for a career in the theater. Lemmon joined a stock company called the North Shore Players, where he met Roddy McDowall, whose mother was the company's manager. He finished school--barely--and immediately left Boston for New York with a lot of confidence and $300 from his father. One year later, when the senior Mr. Lemmon came to visit, he found his son living in near poverty, barely supporting himself with piano playing jobs in bars and restaurants. Impressed by Jack's tenacity, he moved his son into a decent apartment and started sending him money every month.

After a handful of stage credits, Jack Lemmon made his first important breakthrough as "Bruce" on the NBC radio drama *The Brighter Day*. He spent a year on the series at $75 a week, then joined the cast of *The Road of Life*. The next stop was television, where he piled up an impressive list of credits on the *Kraft Music Hall* and several dramatic anthologies. But ironically it was back on the stage where Lemmon earned his invitation to Hollywood; in 1953 he appeared in a revival of *Room Service*, which lasted just long enough for Lemmon to be spotted by a talent manager for Columbia Pictures. He was offered a supporting role in *It Should Happen to You*, a Judy Holliday vehicle written by Garson Kanin and directed by George Cukor. No fool he, Lemmon jumped at the chance to make his film debut in such prestigious company.

Holliday plays Gladys Glover, an out-of-work model who dreams of standing out above the crowd. She invests her life savings in renting a large billboard in New York's Columbus Circle, on which she has her name written in huge letters. The company that usually buys that space every summer offers her six other billboards if she surrenders the Columbus Circle location, which she does, and soon Gladys is on her way to becoming a national celebrity. Lemmon plays Pete Sheppard, a small-time documentary filmmaker who warns Gladys that fame is a double-edged sword.

This delightful movie is Miss Holliday's from start to finish, but Lemmon deserves credit just for keeping up. Pete is a sprightly, affable city boy, an average Joe who is content with what life has to give; if any persona is dominant in Lemmon's diverse filmography, this is probably it. With a good part, a good cast and a good movie, Lemmon seems to begin his film career in full stride--he even gets to play the piano and duet with Judy on "Let's Fall in Love."

It Should Happen to You was a hit, and Lemmon (after resisting a name-change order from Columbia boss Harry Cohn) was reteamed with Holliday in the memorably titled *Phfft!*

(1954), and then appeared in the musical *My Sister Eileen* (1955). Offers were arriving steadily now and it was inevitable that sooner or later Lemmon would tackle a role that would transform him into a popular leading man. As so often happens in Hollywood, though, luck and coincidence were principal players. Years earlier Lemmon filmed a failed screen test for John Ford's *The Long, Gray Line* (1955), a movie that was eventually made with Tyrone Power. Ford saw the test much later and agreed that Lemmon was wrong for the movie, but thought he was perfect for the pivotal role of Ensign Pulver in Ford's next project, *Mister Roberts*. Ford later dropped out of the film and was replaced by Mervyn LeRoy.

As with his film debut, Lemmon was once again working in first-rate material and surrounded by excellence. Henry Fonda reprised the role of Mister Roberts from the Broadway stage, James Cagney played the tyranical Captain of the cargo ship Reluctant, and William Powell, in the last film of his sterling career, played the genial ship's doctor. The story is set in the closing days of World War II; Mister Roberts yearns to see some real action, but the Captain resents Roberts' popularity with the crew and refuses to approve his transfer. Finally he blackmails Roberts into unquestioning obedience by threatening to withhold a long-overdue shore leave for the entire ship. There's a lot more going on, but *Mister Roberts* is ill-served by a standard plot synopsis. The movie's strength is in its wonderfully-realized characters, and several individual scenes that range from broadest comedy to deepest tragedy.

Fonda is perfect as the soft-spoken American hero archetype Doug Roberts, and Cagney is brilliant as a man thoroughly corrupted by power who delights in creating fear and intimidation. Jack Lemmon has the flashiest role in the piece; Roberts describes Pulver as incredibly likable, but also "the most hapless, lazy, disorganized and lecherous person I've met in my life." It is Lemmon who carries nearly all the film's lighter moments, which happen to be the best moments in the film. These include Pulver's first meeting with the captain, his destruction of the laundry room with a homemade firecracker, and the classic final scene in which he hurls the captain's beloved palm tree into the ocean. Lemmon makes a difficult, near-instantaneous shift from heartbreak when he learns of Roberts' death to comic-outrage when he confronts the captain, shouting "What's all this crud about no movie tonight?" to an exasperated Cagney. Lemmon's peers recognized this career-making portrayal with an Academy Award for Best Supporting Actor.

IT SHOULD HAPPEN TO YOU
Directed by George Cukor; Written by Garson Kanin; Produced by Fred Kohlmar; Music by Frederick Hollander

Cast
Judy Holliday (Gladys Glover), JACK LEMMON (PETE SHEPPARD), Peter Lawford (Evan Adams III), Michael O'Shea (Brod Clinton)

MISTER ROBERTS
Directed by John Ford and Mervyn LeRoy; Written by Joshua Logan and Frank S. Nugent, based on the play by Logan and Thomas Heggen; Produced by Leland Hayward; Music by Franz Waxman

Cast
Henry Fonda (Lt. Doug Roberts), James Cagney (Captain), JACK LEMMON (ENSIGN FRANK THURLOWE PULVER), William Powell (Doc), Ward Bond (C.P.O. Dowdy), Betsy Palmer (Lt. Ann Girard)

JERRY LEWIS (1926-   )

FIRST APPEARANCE: *My Friend Irma* (Paramount, 1949)

A STAR IS BORN: *My Friend Irma*

Is Jerry Lewis an auteur of unique vision, or a second-rate burlesque goofball? The answer may depend on what country you're in. In Europe, and particularly France, Lewis is embraced as "Le Roi de Crazy," a comic genius whose childlike cinematic persona is not only beloved, but studied by cinephiles as a peer of Charlie Chaplin and Buster Keaton. In America, Lewis has a loyal cult of devotees`, but his antics are more commonly dismissed as infantile silliness, lacking in any of the subtext that separates great comedians from clowns.

Newark, New Jersey-born Jerry Lewis made his first entrance on a stage at the age of five, when he sang "Brother, Can You Spare a Dime?" in the showroom of a Borscht Belt hotel, where his father worked as master of ceremonies. Young Joseph Levitch adopted the stage name of his parents, Danny and Mona Lewis, and dreamed of becoming a movie star. By the time he entered New York's Irvington High School, he had already begun to formulate a wacky alter-ego that earned him the nickname "Id," short for "Idiot." Lewis left school after the tenth grade to try out his first nightclub act, in which he would comically mouth the lyrics to songs played on an off-stage phonograph. In 1942, the act went over big at Brown's Hotel in New York, where Lewis worked during the day as a bellboy.

Lewis toured with the routine, and during a run at the Glass Hat in New York City he met and befriended singer Dean Martin. In July of 1946, Lewis was playing Atlantic City when one of the entertainers on the bill suddenly quit. He suggested that the owner hire Martin. Both performed separately and successfully but, on July 25, 1946, they decided to discard their usual act and improvise routines together. The mix of patter, slapstick and music that emerged was an immediate hit, and the team of Martin and Lewis was born. Eight months later, they were playing the prestigious Copacabana, and their salaries had soared from $350 to $5000 a week.

Producer Hal Wallis brought the boys to Hollywood, and signed them to a movie contract with Paramount Pictures. Their debut came in *My Friend Irma*, a seemingly indestructible piece of material that was successful on radio, television and in motion pictures. The premise remained the same in any medium; Irma Peterson, a lovable dumb blonde (Marie Wilson), shares an apartment with Jane Stacey (Diana Lynn), a more level-headed career girl. Jane aspires to marry her rich boss, Richard Rhinelander (Don DeFore). Irma's beau is a shifty con man known only as Al (John Lund), for whom any respectable job is anathema.

In the 1949 film, two more characters were added; Steve Baird (Dean Martin), a struggling singer, and his peculiar pal Seymour (Lewis). Al discovers Steve at his day job, and becomes his manager. With Rhinelander's backing, he successfully launches Steve's career in show business. Seymour tags along, mostly because he would be unable to function on his own.

Irma's name is in the title but she's a secondary character in the film, and it's actually just as well. Marie Wilson's dumb blonde schtick has not aged well, and barely provokes a smile, much less any real laughs. Diana Lynn, Irma's "straight woman," is the most appealing member of the cast, and Martin's crooning constitutes the closest thing to a highlight. However, it was Jerry Lewis that made the strongest impression on critics and audiences; "There just hasn't been anything like him on land, sea or celluloid." (*Los Angeles Examiner*); "This freakishly built and acting young man...has a genuine comic quality. His idiocy constitutes the burlesque of an idiot, which is something else again. He's the funniest thing in it." (*New York Times*)

Every type of routine Martin and Lewis attempt from their rather limited pallette has been done better by other teams, and all Lewis proves to me here is that comedy is subjective. I didn't laugh once at his simian appearance, his "seal impressions," his rubber-faced comic tantrums, his exaggerated, screeching New York accent or his spastic contortions. In fact, I found them tasteless and not a little embarrassing. But to dismiss him as appealing only to the smallest child or the smallest intellect would be to offend the Lewis loyal, who glean something ingenious in the behavior of his grown-up kid persona.

A sequel, *My Friend Irma Goes West* (1950), was actually a little better, but neither film is likely to win any converts to the Lewis cult. He became as famous as you can get right here, but the movies that built his international reputation came after the break-up of Martin and Lewis. These include *The Bellboy* (1960) and *The Errand Boy* (1961), both of which he also directed, and *The Nutty Professor* (1963), glorified in the cult as his masterpiece, and perhaps the only Jerry Lewis film that even non-fans would agree achieves excellence.

MY FRIEND IRMA
Directed by George Marshall; Written by Cy Howard and Parke Levy, based on the radio show created by Howard; Produced by Hal Wallis; Music by Roy Webb, Ray Evans and Jay Livingston

Cast
John Lund (Al), Diana Lynn (Jane Stacey), Don DeFore (Richard Rhinelander), Marie Wilson (Irma Peterson), Dean Martin (Steve Baird), JERRY LEWIS (SEYMOUR)

CAROLE LOMBARD (1908-1942)

FIRST APPEARANCE: *A Perfect Crime* (Dwan Associates, 1921)

A STAR IS BORN: *Twentieth Century* (Columbia, 1934)

Any book worth reading about Carole Lombard will turn over several of its pages to the saber-witted quotations of its subject. There are scores of legends about Lombard and her fertile, ribald sense of humor, so many in fact that one wonders why she didn't find her true Hollywood calling until the forty-fifth of her sixty-four film appearances. The only reason I can offer is that Lombard at her best could never be captured unedited in the movies of the day.

"She was the only woman I ever knew who could tell a dirty story without losing her femininity," said Mitchell Leisen, her director on *Hands Across the Table* (1935). Like Mae West and Jean Harlow, Carole Lombard combined beauty with a spirited, liberated outlook that was ahead of its time. Lombard, however, could also tone down the brass and project a softer side, as she did opposite Shirley Temple in *Now and Forever* (1934) and in the classic soaper *Made for Each Other* (1939).

Carole Lombard grew up as Jane Alice Peters in Fort Wayne, Indiana, the youngest of three children. Hers was a comfortable, middle-class childhood composed of dancing lessons, chasing after her two older brothers, and weekly trips to the movies. Jane's life changed after her mother divorced her father, and moved with the children to Los Angeles. Jane attended drama school, but her motion picture debut had its roots in her oddball friendship with Benny Leonard, a boxing champion who lived in the neighborhood. Tomboy Jane took boxing lessons from the champ, and Jane loved to test her skills by scrapping with boys and girls alike.

Allan Dwan, one of the most prolific directors of both the silent and sound eras, happened to catch one of twelve-year-old Jane's streetfights, and cast her as the tough little sister of hero Monte Blue in *A Perfect Crime*. Blue plays Wally Griggs, a mild-mannered bank messenger who concocts a scheme to get rich by pretending to steal $25,000 in bonds. After being captured he successfully sues the city for false arrest when the bonds are found. *A Perfect Crime* is today believed lost, but various sources record that Jane appears in three scenes, which she filmed in three days. Production stills from the film depict Jane as a petite, wide-eyed child in a plaid dress. The film received favorable reviews, but after its release Jane resumed her life as a typical teenager.

In 1924, she filmed a screen test for Charlie Chaplin's *The Gold Rush* (1925), but lost the part to Georgia Hale. However, Chaplin liked her enough to arrange a contract for Jane, now sixteen, with 20th Century-Fox. She changed her name under studio orders to Carol Lombard, and played bit parts for the next year, but Fox decided that she was not star material and let her contract lapse without renewal. A serious car accident kept her out of commission for six months, and when she returned to work it was as a "Bathing Beauty" for Mack Sennett in a series of two-reel slapstick comedies.

Carol Lombard survived the transition from silents to talkies, but was still a relative unknown when she signed a seven-year contract with Paramount in 1930. She was billed accidently as "Carole" for her first Paramount release, *Fast and Loose* (1930), and decided to keep the change. Lombard was featured in five films in 1931 and five more in 1932, playing everything from librarians to prostitutes, but her best-known role was still as Mrs. William Powell, after their 1931 marriage. "There is no one else on the screen who has had more consistently bad pictures than I," Lombard told *Movie Mirror* magazine, and she was probably right; during one stretch, she appeared in seventeen consecutive flops.

Finally, her breakthrough came after director Howard Hawks selected Carole for *Twentieth Century*, the film adaptation of the popular stage farce by Ben Hecht and Charles MacDonald. John Barrymore starred as grandiose Broadway director Oscar Jaffe, who plucks lingerie model Mildred Plotka (Lombard) out of a department store and transforms her into acclaimed actress Lily Garland. When their personal relationship blows up, Lily heads for Hollywood and greater stardom, while Oscar directs one disaster after another. When the ex-lovers inadvertantly wind up on the same cross-country train, Oscar sees his chance to lure Lily back to the stage and salvage his career.

Twentieth Century was filmed in five weeks, and during that time, according to Lombard biographer Robert D. Matzen, "Carole learned more about acting that she had in the past ten years put together. Under the tutelage of Hawks and Barrymore she *became* Lily Garland exactly as ordered." The critics agreed; "When you see her, you'll forget the rather restrained and somewhat stilted Lombard of old," raved *Shadowplay*. "You'll see a star blaze out of this scene and that scene, high spots Carole never dreamed of hitting."

The film, now rightly hailed as a classic screwball comedy, is a tour de force for John Barrymore, who brings new meaning to the phrase "larger than life" with his magisterial performance. His entire body trembles with excitement as he hurls commands and caustic remarks with the force of a human steamroller. As Lily, Lombard starts out sweet and demure, but after her time with Oscar she becomes a female version of the temperamental impresario. In their battle royals on the train, she matches every ballistic outburst he unleashes--the scene in which Oscar explains the staging of the Passion Play to Lily reaches heights of inspired lunacy that were not approached again until *The Lion in Winter* (1968).

For Carole Lombard, whom Barrymore called "probably the greatest actress I have ever worked with," *Twentieth Century* was the jump-start that had eluded her for a decade. "I knew that all those years of striving had brought me to my goal," she told *Movie Mirror*. "At last, I could call myself an actress."

A PERFECT CRIME
Directed and written by Allen Dwan, from a story by Carl Clausen

Cast
Monte Blue (Wally Griggs), Jacqueline Logan (Mary Oliver), Stanton Heck (Big Bill Thaine), JANE PETERS [CAROLE LOMBARD] (WALLY'S SISTER)

TWENTIETH CENTURY
Directed and produced by Howard Hawks; Written by Ben Hecht and Charles MacArthur, based on their play

Cast
John Barrymore (Oscar Jaffe), CAROLE LOMBARD (LILY GARLAND), Roscoe Karns (Owen O'Malley), Walter Connolly (Oliver Webb), Ralph Forbes (George Smith)

SOPHIA LOREN (1934-   )

FIRST APPEARANCE: *Quo Vadis?* (MGM, 1951)

A STAR IS BORN: *The Gold of Naples* (Gala/DCA, 1957)

Sophia Loren, Brigitte Bardot and Catherine Deneuve are the only actresses to gain widespread popularity in America before appearing in an English-speaking film. Sex appeal, it would seem, needs no translation; whether dubbed or subtitled, when Sophia sashayed down an Italian avenue in *The Gold of Naples*, she achieved first-name recognition around the world. But even after she was brought to Hollywood in *Boy on a Dolphin* (1957), Loren continued to find better roles and greater success in the cinema of her native Italy. In 1961, she became the first actress to win an Academy Award in a foreign-language film (*Two Women*). In the process, observed *Time* magazine, "She has rewritten the canons of beauty." The Hollywood standard in the 1950s was not yet open to darker skin, even if it was as slight as Sophia's olive complexion. It would not be accurate to say that Sophia broke the color barrier, but she certainly put a few dents in it.

The city of Pozzuoli, Italy has been described as the main entrance to Hades, because of the noxious fumes and vapors that emerged from nearby volcanic activity and two polluted lakes. To this squalid port town young Sofia Scicolone returned with her mother Romilda after being born out of wedlock in Rome. World War II pushed the financially-strapped family closer to poverty; Sofia would later recall long periods of starvation, and watching her mother beg in the streets for bread and cheese.

When Sofia was thirteen, she emerged from the shadow of her beautiful blond sister Maria, and rendered her old nickname of *Stuzzicadenti*--"toothpick"--obsolete. When she was fourteen, she turned down a marriage proposal from her gym teacher, and was a runner-up in the Queen of the Sea beauty contest. The 25,000 lire prize money (about $40) was spent on drama lessons, and young Sofia was ready to break into movies. In July of 1949 Sofia and her mother visited the Cinecittà Studios, colloquially known as Hollywood-on-the-Tiber. One of the films in production was *Quo Vadis?*, a gargantuan epic about Nero's Rome that required thousands of extras. Sofia was noticed among the throng of hopefuls by an assistant director, and both she and her mother were given walk-on roles.

Quo Vadis? was made at a time when the movies had been thrown into a panic by television, and tried to compete with the new medium by staging spectaculars that would lure the audience away from Milton Berle. The story of Marcus (Robert Taylor), a Roman soldier torn between his loyalty to the empire and his love of Lygia (Deborah Kerr) a Christian slave, played second fiddle to Nero's destruction of Rome by fire, and his unleashing of the lions in a packed Colisseum that was not cheering for the Christians. The movie's best moments are its biggest, but the great epic films also impress in their more intimate scenes, and here *Quo Vadis?* just misses, though the performances of Taylor and Kerr are proficient enough, and Peter Ustinov is splendid as the snivelling, whining Nero.

Rex Reed, in his usual compassionate manner, wrote that Sophia Loren began her career "as one of ten thousand slave-girl extras with no talent, no training and no range." Alan Levy's book *Forever Sophia* relates how Sophia was interviewed by director Mervyn LeRoy, who considered giving her a small speaking role. "Do you speak any English?" he asked. "Yes," she replied. "Where did you learn your English?" he asked next. "Yes," she replied again. "How old are you?" asked LeRoy. "Yes," said Loren. LeRoy laughed, and sent the pretty fourteen-year-old back with the slaves. She appears in the background of the frame, over Deborah Kerr's shoulder, in the banquet scene at which Marcus tells Lygia that he is now her master. Don't expect to catch it on the first viewing, and on video it is even more difficult-- one can barely make out the blank stare on her face. Explained Sophia later, "I was trying to see where the camera was."

176

You will, however, have no trouble at all spotting Sophia in Vittorio De Sica's *L'Oro Di Napoli*, aka *The Gold of Naples*. In fact, you probably won't notice anyone else while she's on screen. By 1957, she had signed a contract with producer Carlo Ponti, who chose her films, chose her roles, and taught her to handle the glare of celebrity. She changed her name to Sofia Lazzaro and then, during the filming of *Africa Under the Sea* (1953), to Sophia Loren, at the request of the film's producer. Ponti was twenty years older than Sophia and married, facts that landed his guidance of her career in the gossip columns of every Italian newspaper. It was indeed proven that their relationship was personal as well as professional when they were married in 1966.

The Gold of Naples is a collection of six unrelated story vignettes, a familiar style of filmmaking in Italy. The U.S. release included only four of the stories, including Loren's, which is entitled "The Ring". She is billed only as "The Wife," opposite Giacomo Furia as "The Husband," but during the segment her character is called Sophia. It's a pedestrian account of an unfaithful pizza baker's wife who loses her wedding ring, supposedly in the dough of a pizza, only to recall leaving it in the room of her lover. Try to avoid dubbed prints of the film, because the voice used for Loren is too thin for the voluptuous, formidable woman on screen. For some reason, other cast members are dubbed with a cockney accent, which dilutes all the Neapolitan flavor.

In the final scene, Loren takes what *Time* magazine called "a long, unforgettable walk in the rain through the streets of the city, drinking the applause of venal eyes." Wearing a low-cut white blouse that clings tighter with every drop of rain, Loren strides proudly, large, almond-shaped eyes flashing, swinging her arms and hips with an exaggerated flair and pushing awestruck men out of her way. Sophia's fifteen minutes on screen offer little evidence of a vital new talent, but one cannot deny that she makes an impression. Raved the smitten *Time* critic, "Sophia's self-congratulating look seemed to say 'Look at me, I'm all woman and it will be a long time before you see such a woman again."

QUO VADIS?
Directed by Mervyn LeRoy; Written by John Lee Mahin, S.N. Behrman and Sonya Levien, based on the novel by Henryk Sienkiewicz; Produced by Sam Zimbalist; Music by Miklos Rozsa

Cast
Robert Taylor (Marcus Vinicius), Deborah Kerr (Lygia), Leo Genn (Petronius), Peter Ustinov (Nero), Abraham Sofaer (Paul)...SOPHIA LOREN (SLAVE GIRL)

THE GOLD OF NAPLES
Directed by Vittorio De Sica; Written by Cesare Zavattini, Vittorio De Sica and Giuseppe Marotta, based on the novel by Marotta; Produced by Dino De Laurentiis; Music by Alessandro Cicognini

Cast
"The Ring"--SOPHIA LOREN (THE WIFE), Giacomo Furia (The Husband), Alberto Farnese (The Lover), Paolo Stoppa (The Widower)

MYRNA LOY (1905-1994)

FIRST APPEARANCE: *Pretty Ladies* (MGM, 1925)

A STAR IS BORN: *The Thin Man* (MGM, 1934)

Myrna Loy waited eighty-eight years to receive an Academy Award, but what's even more astounding is that, after a storied career that encompassed 123 films, Loy was never even nominated for the industry's biggest prize. Wait a minute, you say, not even for *The Thin Man*? For *Evelyn Prentice* (1934)? For *The Best Years of Our Lives* (1946)? Not even. The woman who epitomized impeccable style and class for a generation of moviegoers accepted this egregious oversight with her trademark grace, and if the slight is understandable it is only because Loy made acting look so easy. "Hers is a talent easily taken for granted, seeming so assured and effortless," observed critic Frank Thompson; "but this only heightens the delightful sense of discovery that comes whenever she directs her wry and beautiful countenance toward the camera."

A cattle ranch in Raidersburg, Montana, was home to Myrna Williams for the first seven years of her life. Her first name was chosen by her father, David, from the name of a town he had seen on a train. In 1912, the Williamses moved to the city of Helena, where Myrna enjoyed a childhood busy with rough and tumble, tomboy activity. At the age of eleven she took the Universal Studios tour during a family vacation, and decided to become an actress. Her classmate back in Helena, Johnny Mack Brown, shared her aspirations, and later became a popular movie cowboy.

An epidemic of influenza took the life of Myrna's father in 1918, and she moved with her mother to Los Angeles. At Venice High School, fifteen-year-old Myrna modeled for a statue entitled *Aspiration*, that still stands in front of the school. After graduating she made several show business contacts at the Horsley Dance Studio, where she worked part-time as a teacher. One of them was photographer Henry Waxman, who arranged a screen test for Myrna with Rudolph Valentino. In her autobiography, Myrna remembered the test as a disaster, but she continued to hang around the casting bureaus at different studios hoping for another chance.

She got a job modeling costume tests at MGM for actress Kathleen Key, a supporting player in *Ben-Hur* (1926), and director Fred Niblo was impressed enough with Myrna to offer her a bit part in several crowd scenes. Word-of-mouth about Myrna's poise and good looks led to another extra role in MGM's *Pretty Ladies*, which was actually released first, and thus became her official debut.

The film was a backstage romance/musical, clearly inspired by the Ziegfeld Follies. The stars were ZaSu Pitts and Tom Moore, but *Pretty Ladies* is more famous now for the chorus appearances of Myrna Loy (billed as Myrna Williams) and Joan Crawford, who was still using the name Lucille LeSueur.

In an era when chorus girls tended toward the zaftig side, the svelte, brunette Myrna is not hard to spot in the line. In the "Japanese Garden" number, she is the first girl on the bridge. In a later scene, Loy wears what appears to be an Egyptian handmaiden costume, complete with Cleopatra wig.

Soon after the release of *Pretty Ladies*, Myrna changed her last name to Loy, a suggestion from a writer who felt it matched the exotic qualities of her appearance. She progressed from bit parts to small speaking roles, and achieved her first notoriety playing a succession of vamps and foreign temptresses in silent films. With no one at the studio actively promoting her, Loy spent years being shuffled between second- and third-lead roles and walk-ons. For such journeyman players, the ascension to stardom is usually unanticipated by the brass, who then adopt a "we knew it all along" attitude after the fact.

For Myrna, the breakthrough came in MGM's *The Thin Man*, in which she was cast over Louis B. Mayer's objections. Shot in just twelve days, this adaptation of Dashiell Hammett's detective mystery was deigned a minor project that hoped to benefit from the pairing of Loy with William Powell, after their well-received collaboration in *Manhattan Melodrama* (1934). The results went far beyond anyone's expectations; *The Thin Man* introduced one of the screen's most inspired pairings, and became one of 1934's most popular films.

Powell and Loy play Nick and Nora Charles, a wealthy, urbane, deliriously happy married couple who get mixed up in the disappearance of an inventor, and the murder of his secretary. Nick, a retired detective, reluctantly takes the case, much to the delight of his wife, who tries to help figure out whodunnit. After wading through a wacky gathering of suspects and onlookers (including Maureen O'Sullivan and Cesar Romero), Nicky schedules a dinner party to announce the murderer's identity, at which Nora utters the immortal double entendre`, "Waiter, would you please serve the nuts?"

The teaming of Powell and Loy was magical. "There was this feeling of rhythm, of complete understanding, and an instinct of how each of us could bring out the best in the other," Loy once said. Their sophisticated style and witty, playful banter were an idealized expression of marital love. Loy's beguiling, completely feminine charm was as enticing as any of the legendary screen goddesses, yet she could still be one of the boys. And it's not every actress that can make her first entrance with a face-forward pratfall, as Loy does here, and recover her grace and decorum in an instant. Her past specialties of gypsies, tramps and thieves were instantly obliterated in favor of a newer, better on-screen persona; when Nora learns that the obviously inebriated Nick has had six martinis, she doesn't berate him; she orders five more to catch up. From that moment on, she was, and would always be, the perfect wife. "She had a good time, always," was Loy's simple but flawless assessment of Nora's outlook, and no one could have better conveyed the character's infectious *joie de vivre*.

The Thin Man became the first of a six-film series, and the only one in which the actual "thin man" appeared. The title refers to one of the suspects, played by Edward Ellis, not Nick Charles. Subsequent Nick and Nora films successfully captured the unpretentious, carefree spirit of the original, even when the script was less than cooperative.

PRETTY LADIES
Directed by Monta Bell; Written by Alice D.G. Miller, based on the story by Adela Rogers St. John

Cast
ZaSu Pitts (Maggie Keenan), Tom Moore (Al Cassidy), Ann Pennington (Herself), Lilyan Tashman (Selma Larson)...MYRNA LOY (CHORUS GIRL)

THE THIN MAN
Directed by W.S. Van Dyke; Written by Albert Hackett and Frances Goodrich, based on the novel by Dashiell Hammett; Produced by Hunt Stromberg

Cast
William Powell (Nick Charles), MYRNA LOY (NORA CHARLES), Maureen O'Sullivan (Dorothy Wynant), Nat Pendleton (Lt. John Guild), Minna Gombell (Mimi Wynant), Cesar Romero (Chris Jorgenson), Edward Ellis (Clyde Wynant)

BELA LUGOSI (1882-1956)

FIRST APPEARANCE: *A Leopard* (Star Film, 1917)

A STAR IS BORN: *Dracula* (Universal, 1931)

Backstage at Broadway's Fulton Theatre, in October of 1927, Bela Lugosi could be heard chanting "I am Dracula! I <u>am</u> Dracula!" while gazing into a full-length mirror, just prior to every performance of the play that was adapted into the film that made him famous. Had he really been Dracula, of course, he would not have seen his reflection, but that doesn't mean the mantra didn't work--for generations of moviegoers, Bela Lugosi *is* indeed Dracula.

His success came with a price; the black, satin cape he labored so hard to wear with pride did not come off easily. Lugosi encouraged his association with Dracula so fervently that the public no longer accepted him in other roles. So he donned the cape again and again, in two *Dracula* films, on stage in 1943, 1947 and 1951, and to play an assortment of other vampiric menaces in lesser films, the nadir being his brief, infamous, final screen appearance as the Ghoul Man in *Plan 9 From Outer Space* (1959). When he died, he was buried in his cape.

In 1930, the publicity department at Universal Studios must have been thrilled to discover that Lugosi, star of their soon-to-be-released film *Dracula*, was actually born in Lugos, a Hungarian town just fifty miles from Transylvania. Bela Blasko was a banker's son who was under parental orders to get a good education and become a lawyer, or to join his father in the bank. The plan fell apart after Bela watched the performance of a touring company of actors. He left school at the age of eleven and traveled three hundred miles, mostly by foot, to search for acting jobs in the town of Resita. His earliest recorded role was in the 1902 play *Ocskay Brigaderos*. After using and abandoning several stage names, he settled on Lugosi, from the town in which he was born.

Lugosi played a wide variety of roles in Hungary, from singing parts in operettas to the lead in *Romeo and Juliet*, and by 1913 he was playing supporting parts in the Hungarian Royal Theatre and the National Theatre of Budapest. He fought in the first World War from 1914 to 1916 and then, unhappy with the small roles and smaller paychecks offered by the National Theatre, he entered the five-year-old Hungarian film industry.

Hoping to cash in on Lugosi's pre-war matinee idol status, Star Film cast him in *A Leopard*, as a rakish aristocrat who romances the daughter of a member of the landed gentry. Lugosi hoped that the exposure he received in the film would lead to better stage roles, but just in case the fallout was negative he used the name Arisztid Olt. The film is believed lost and details are sketchy, but photos show a dapper Lugosi wearing a dark blazer, striped tie and trilby hat, and appearing to successfully woo a blond waif clad in, believe it or not, a black cape.

Political instability cut short his film career in Hungary, so Lugosi continued to make movies in Germany. At the age of 38, he left for America without money or a passport, hoping to continue his career. Granted asylum as a political refugee, he soon established a theatrical company of other Hungarian expatriates living in New York City. In 1922, their production of *The Tragedy of Man* was attended by producer Henry Barton, who subsequently cast Lugosi in the off-Broadway melodrama *The Red Poppy*. The play closed in six weeks, but Lugosi's American stage career was underway. After five years of steady work, he won the lead role in *Dracula*.

After forty weeks on Broadway and a national tour that played to packed houses, Lugosi was somewhat surprised that he was not Universal's first choice for the film adaptation. When he was finally chosen over such candidates as Conrad Veidt and Paul Muni, the studio paid him just $500 a week, on a film budgeted at $400,000. Most of the money was spent on extraordinary, elaborate sets, which were beautifully photographed by Karl Freund under the direction of Tod Browning. No one, with the later exception of Mario Bava, ever got more atmosphere out of a dry ice machine and a few well-placed shadows.

Dracula the film is better than *Dracula* the novel, which tends to forget about its main character for dozens of pages at a stretch. Universal wisely opted to take its story from the stageplay rather than Bram Stoker's text; Count Dracula leaves his Transylvanian castle to take up residence in London. Professor Van Helsing (Edward van Sloan, splendidly reprising his Broadway role), becomes the vampire's adversary after discovering his true nature. They battle for the lives and souls of Mina Seward (Helen Chandler) and her finace` John Harker (David Manners), with Van Helsing's knowledge of vampire lore finally winning the day.

Lugosi owns the title role from his first appearance, when he stands motionless in the bowels of his huge, forbidding castle, eyes piercing through the fog, the expression on his hawk-like face indecipherable, but still unsettling after all these years. Lugosi breaks every rule of motion picture acting; his movements are either overly deliberate or broad and sweeping. His line-readings are delivered with a thick Slavic accent and have an unnatural cadence, stemming from Lugosi's discomfort with English. When asked to join a doomed guest at his castle for a drink, he responds "I never drink. . .wine" in a way that sounds at first like he's stepping on the joke. Definite flaws anywhere else, but since Lugosi is playing a monster in human form, his cryptic approximation of natural speech and movement makes the character all the more strange and otherworldly.

At forty-nine years old, with thirty years in show business behind him, Bela Lugosi became a star. Had he accepted the next role offered to him, that of Frankenstein's monster, his stature would now be unsurpassed in the horror film genre. But Lugosi turned down the part, which made a star out of Boris Karloff. His reason-- "anybody can moan and grunt."

A LEOPARD
Directed by Alfred Deesy

Cast
Peter Konrady, BELA LUGOSI (ARISTOCRAT), Ila Loth, Klara Peterdy, Anna Goth

DRACULA
Directed by Tod Browning; Written by Garrett Fort, based on the play by Hamilton Deane and John Balderston and the novel by Bram Stoker; Produced by Carl Laemmle, Jr.; Music by Petr Illich Tchaikovsky and Richard Wagner

Cast
BELA LUGOSI (COUNT DRACULA), Helen Chandler (Mina Seward), David Manners (John Harker), Dwight Frye (Renfield), Edward van Sloan (Van Helsing), Francis Dade (Lucy Weston)

SHIRLEY MACLAINE (1934-)

FIRST APPEARANCE: *The Trouble With Harry* (Paramount, 1955)

A STAR IS BORN: *Some Came Running* (MGM, 1958)

     Shirley MacLaine's cropped hairstyle and bangs have practically become a trademark, but MacLaine sported long, curly red tresses when she arrived in New York with dreams of a career on Broadway. These were ordered cut, despite her protests, for a job in the chorus of her first show. Apparently she's adjusted to the style now, as it hasn't changed much in the past 30 years, but the story is significant as one of the first and last times MacLaine was forced into a career decision that was not her own. "It turns out that the egg-beater hairdo is the front for a well-oiled thinking mechanism" said Frank Sinatra, her recruiter into the legendary Rat Pack. That "mechanism" steered her into classics such as *The Apartment* (1960), *Sweet Charity* (1969) and others, and also inspired best-selling books on philosophy. She did follow up her Oscar-winning performance in *Terms of Endearment* (1983) with a role in *Cannonball Run II* (1984), but even the best mechanisms have the occasional glitch.

     Young Shirley Maclean Beaty (yes, Warren's sister) grew up in Virginia exhibiting both tomboy and feminist inclinations before her tenth birthday. Her parents, traditional Southerners, were taken aback by their daughter's outspoken manner, and the relationship was frequently strained. Shirley started ballet lessons at age four, primarily to strengthen her weak ankles, but she instantly fell in love with dancing and stayed in class for the next decade. A ballet career became unthinkable when she grew to five feet seven inches (six feet *en pointe*), which had her towering over male partners who could only lift her after a nutritious breakfast.

     But Shirley was a trouper--at age sixteen her ankle snapped and broke minutes before she was to dance the fairy godmother role in the *Cinderella* ballet. She went on anyway, performed the role and only then went to the hospital. She didn't walk again for four months. Such perseverence deserved a reward, and Shirley got one with an offer to tour in the European company of *Oklahoma*. She said yes, but her father insisted that she turn it down and finish high school. After graduation she moved to New York, dropped the "Beaty" from her name, and spent what little money she had on singing and dancing lessons while working to lose her Southern accent.

     Producer George Abbott noticed MacLaine in the chorus of his musical *The Pajama Game*, and chose her to understudy the star, Carol Haney. In grand *42nd Street* tradition, Haney broke her leg and MacLaine went on in her place. Her triumphant performance brought a slew of job offers, including one from an associate producer for Alfred Hitchcock. The Master of Suspense was casting a comedy called *The Trouble With Harry*, and knowing that it was not what the public expected from him he was trying to cast it cheap, to offset the anticipated low box-office turnout.

     The press noted with equal parts admiration and skepticism MacLaine's rapid rise from Broadway understudy to the female lead in a Hitchcock movie, and waited to judge the result. *The Trouble With Harry* was and remains a curious film, in which a corpse named Harry turns up in a small Vermont town and the residents calmly debate how best to handle the situation. The blase` attitudes of the townfolk is Hitchcock spoofing much of his own work, in which the discovery of a corpse always leads to mayhem. MacLaine, as the deceased's ex-wife Jennifer Rogers, deftly assumes the detatched, bemused outlook required of the cast (which includes John Forsythe, Edmund Gwenn and Jerry Mathers, but not as the Beaver), and it might have been a star-making performance had anyone actually gone to see the movie. The middle of the fifties was not a good time for black comedy ("mild and mellow merriment" was about all the enthusiasm critics could muster) but the film seems much better today. "Miss MacLaine impresses despite the handicap of some high school, amateur mannerisms, which manage to get by here but will need correction for the future." wrote the *New York Times*.

Her next film, *Artists and Models* (1955), was a tepid Dean Martin-Jerry Lewis vehicle that did not enhance her resume`. She played an Indian princess in the Oscar-winning *Around the World in 80 Days* (1955), but MacLaine was lost in the crowd of forty-some celebrity cameos. Her career holding pattern continued through *Hot Spell* (1958) and *The Matchmaker* (1958), but that same year MacLaine landed the role that brought her newfound respect as a dramatic actress and the first of her five Oscar nominations. The film was *Some Came Running*, Vincente Minnelli's expose` of smoldering passion in a small Indiana town. MacLaine plays Ginny, a giddy, kindhearted prostitute who attaches herself to part-time writer Dave Hirsh (Frank Sinatra). Dave only tolerates Ginny when he's drunk, but marries her out of spite after being rejected by a refined schoolteacher (Martha Hyer) who is only interested in his writing. When a jealous former boyfriend of Ginny's tries to shoot Dave, she takes the bullet.

The easy chemistry MacLaine generates with pals Sinatra and costar Dean Martin is immediately apparent. It was Sinatra and Minnelli who saw Shirley on *The Dinah Shore Show* and convinced MGM that she was perfect for Ginny. The studio didn't think she was sexy enough, but a screen test directed by Minnelli himself convinced the executives otherwise. Reviews praised the two veteran Rat Packers (though Sinatra lays on the tortured writer stuff a bit thick), but singled out Shirley for "her touching, unforgettable portrait of the crude, pathetic little floozy who falls in love with Frank" (*Los Angeles Mirror*). It's an amazing performance-- watching Ginny smile after every casual debasement from Dave, and revel in the slightest acknowledgment of her existence is heartbreaking, but MacLaine then breaks into a drunken, off-key rendition of "After You're Gone" and turns the tragedy into high comedy. Even after several repeat viewings, her death scene never becomes easier to watch.

Both MacLaine and Martha Hyer deserved the Oscars they did not get, but it was Ginny that landed Shirley on the cover of *Time* magazine the following year, which praised her as "the brightest face, the freshest character and the most versatile new talent in Hollywood." Shirley MacLaine would go on to set some kind of record for prostitute portrayals (seven at last count), but of all the characters she's played in forty films, she still lists Ginny as her favorite role.

THE TROUBLE WITH HARRY
Directed and produced by Alfred Hitchcock; Written by John Michael Hayes, based on the novel by John Trevor Story; Music by Bernard Herrmann

Cast
Edmund Gwenn (Capt. Albert Wiles), John Forsythe (Sam Marlowe), SHIRLEY MACLAINE (JENNIFER ROGERS), Mildred Natwick (Miss Graveley), Mildred Dunnock (Mrs. Wiggs), Jerry Mathers (Arnie Rogers)

SOME CAME RUNNING
Directed by Vincente Minnelli; Written by John Patrick and Arthur Sheekman, based on the novel by James Jones; Produced by Sol C. Siegel; Music by Elmer Bernstein (song "To Love and Be Loved" by Sammy Cahn and James Van Heusen)

Cast
Frank Sinatra (Dave Hirsh), Dean Martin (Bama Dillert), SHIRLEY MACLAINE (GINNY MOORHEAD), Martha Hyer (Gwen French), Arthur Kennedy (Frank Hirsh)

THE MARX BROTHERS:
GROUCHO (1890-1977), HARPO (1888-1964)
AND CHICO (1887-1961)

FIRST APPEARANCE: *The Cocoanuts* (Paramount, 1929)

A STAR IS BORN: *The Cocoanuts*

There were actually five, not three, and their names were Leonard, Adolph, Julius, Milton and Herbert. Cinephiles know that Leonard became Chico, Adolph became Harpo, and Julius became Groucho, and most fans might remember Milton as Zeppo, but only the most fervent Marxists will come up with Herbert's *nom de plume* of Gummo, so given because of his preference for gumshoes. They were all part of the comedy team at one time, but never simultaneously. Gummo retired to join the army during World War I, and Zeppo left after the first five Marx movies. At the risk of sounding harsh, it wasn't a great loss. Both of the lesser-known brothers functioned ostensibly as straight men, and as the definitive team of legend (Groucho, Harpo, Chico) proved, the Marx Brothers didn't need a backboard for their hyperkinetic routines--unless you count Margaret Dumont.

The brothers Marx were born and raised in a tough, poor neighborhood of New York City. Their father was an unhappy tailor whose boredom on the job did not generate many repeat customers. Show business was inherited from their mother's side of the family--Minnie Marx's father was a magician, her mother played the harp (and passed her fondness for the instrument down to grandson Adolph), and her brother Al Shean was a popular vaudeville performer.

It is ironic that Groucho was considered the most obedient of the brood, and then developed the most aggressive and nasty of the brothers' comic personas. Pop psychologists have traced the turnabout to the lack of affection he received from Minnie. Chico was her favorite, despite his compulsive gambling and skirt-chasing (his name is pronounced Chick-o, and referred to his success with chicks). Harpo and Chico could almost pass for twins in their teen years, which made it easier for Chico to pawn his brother's harp to make a bet on a horse (which he did). All three shared an interest in music (Chico was an ingenious piano player, Groucho played the guitar), and a lack of interest in formal education. Harpo never made it to the third grade.

Groucho was the first to try show business; at age fifteen he joined a singing group called the Leroy Trio. During a performance in Colorado, his partners disbanded the act without telling him, and stole his share of the profits. Undaunted, he continued to experiment with different acts, and even appeared in the bit part of an office boy in the 1906 film *The Man of Her Choice*. The first Marx family act debuted in 1907, consisting of Groucho, Gummo and a girl singer. Their billing as The Three Nightingales was changed to Four after Harpo joined, at his mother's urging. Still primarily a singing act, they toured the smaller vaudeville houses from New York to Chicago. Chico joined in 1910, and a change was made from music to comedy. The clown-like names they used were inspired by a comic strip character named Sherlocko, the Monk.

The first successful Marx venture was *Fun in Hi Skule*, in which Groucho (wearing his trademark mustache for the first time) played a German teacher with an exaggerated accent, Harpo and Chico played unruly students, and Gummo served as straight man. The follow-up, *Home Again*, was written by Al Shean, and became their entree` into the legendary Palace Theater. Their fast-paced, unique comic style, composed of equal parts verbal and physical lunacy, was quickly becoming famous, and their tendency to ad lib half the show every night brought audiences back for several performances. Zeppo replaced Gummo in 1917, and in

1920 the brothers starred in a silent short subject called *Humorisk*, which they financed themselves. After a disastrous sneak preview, the film was destroyed.

The Marx Brothers debuted on Broadway in *I'll Say She Is!* (1924); the lines flew faster, the situations grew more outlandish. Their follow-up, *The Cocoanuts*, ran from 1925 to 1928. Irving Berlin provided the music, and Margaret Dumont made her first appearance as Groucho's favorite target. *The Cocoanuts* was adapted for the screen in 1929. After years of stage performances the Marx Brothers had refined their personae, material and timing to perfection, resulting in a confident and polished film debut. Still they tried to ad lib, but it proved difficult because codirector Robert Florey's laughter was picked up by the primitive sound recording equipment. After numerous ruined takes Florey was banished to a sound-proof booth with the cameraman, and was forced to direct with hand gestures.

The plot has something to do with Groucho running a financially-troubled Florida hotel, but anyone who watches a Marx Brothers movie for the plot probably reads *Playboy* for the articles. *The Cocoanuts* is not among the more mature examples of the team's manic immaturity, and its pace is slowed somewhat by the inability of the sound-proof booth-bound cameras to move with any fluency, forcing the actors to deliver their lines standing still. But the film does have Margaret Dumont being romanced and ripped to shreds by Groucho, and two classic Marx routines that stand up to anything in *Duck Soup* (1933) or *A Night at the Opera* (1935). The first has Groucho explaining a set of blueprints to Chico, and pointing out a viaduct, prompting Chico to ask "Why a Duck?". The comedy mileage they get out of one bad pun is remarkable. The second highlight is set at a land auction conducted by Groucho, in which Chico continually tops his own worthless bids. The scene builds until it becomes almost unendurably funny.

In between there are the musical interludes that would become a regular feature of every Marx Brothers film. This batch is among the worst (Berlin on a *very* off day), but are easily fast-forwarded away on homevideo, leaving only Groucho, Harpo, Chico and that immortal question, "If you got a duck, why-a-no chicken?"

THE COCOANUTS
Directed by Robert Florey and Joseph Santley; Written by Morrie Ryskind, based on the play by Ryskind and George S. Kaufman; Produced by Walter Wanger; Music by Irving Berlin

Cast
Groucho Marx (Mr. Hammer), Harpo Marx (himself), Chico Marx (himself), Zeppo (Jamison), Mary Eaton (Polly Potter), Margaret Dumont (Mrs. Potter)

WALTER MATTHAU (1920-   )

FIRST APPEARANCE: *The Kentuckian* (Hecht-Lancaster/United Artists, 1955)

A STAR IS BORN: *The Fortune Cookie* (Mirisch/United Artists, 1966)

The gallant men and women who place the big plastic letters on theater marquees will forever be grateful to Walter Matuschanskayasky, for having the compassion to change his name before breaking into movies.

The Matuschanskayasky family emigrated to America from Lithuania in 1920, and settled like many of their countrymen in the lower east side of New York City. Walter's father, a Russian orthodox priest, deserted his family when Walter was three, compelling his mother to work in one of the infamous sweatshops in the city's garment district. Walter and his brother Harry spent their preschool days in the Daughter of Israel Nursery, where Walter got his first taste of performing in a religious play.

As a teenager, he worked the concession stands at various off-Broadway theaters, and by getting to know some of the actors he developed an interest in performing, and was allowed to play minor roles in plays like *The Dishwasher* (1934), for fifty cents a performance. Walter's enthusiasm for the stage ripened in high school, but after graduating in 1939 he worked in every business but show business. In April of 1942, after stints as a lumberjack, baseball coach and oven-cleaner, Walter Matuschanskayasky enlisted in the Air Force to fight Nazis. He earned six battle stars, and served in the same squadron as Colonel Jimmy Stewart. Though he never got to know Stewart well, the association was enough to rekindle Walter's dream of performing. In 1944 he left the service and used his G.I. Bill to enroll in the Dramatic Workshop of the New York School for Social Research. Among his classmates were Rod Steiger, Eli Wallach, Harry Belafonte and Tony Curtis.

After graduation Walter Matthau landed a small role in Broadway's *Anne of a Thousand Days* (1948), and progressed to lead roles in *Twilight Walk* (1951) and several television dramatic anthologies. In 1955 he earned his first glowing stage notices in *Will Success Spoil Rock Hunter?* opposite Jayne Mansfield, and also made his film debut in a dull western called *The Kentuckian*.

Matthau played Sam Bodine, a surly tavern owner in the town of Humility, who clashes with travelling frontiersman Eli Wakefield (Burt Lancaster). Wakefield is on his way to Texas with his young son, and stops in Humility to visit his brother. When the pretty schoolteacher (Diana Lynn) takes a liking to Eli, Sam ventilates his jealousy with a bullwhip. "I'm gonna cut that buckskin off you," snarls Matthau in his first scene, his face contorted in a permanent evil smirk. He would later call it "a ridiculous part" that he accepted only for the money. The film is amiable but stagnant, despite Lancaster's best efforts as both star and director.

Walter Matthau worked steadily in films both good (*Charade*--1963) and awful (*Ensign Pulver*--1964) for the next ten years. After he appeared in *Fail Safe* (1965), the *Los Angeles Times* called him the best character actor in America. That same year, at age 44, he graduated from the ranks of the third-billed after landing the role of Oscar Madison in Neil Simon's Broadway hit *The Odd Couple*. Matthau won the Tony Award for Best Actor, and would reprise the role in a hit film version, with Jack Lemmon replacing Art Carney as Oscar's annoying roomate Felix Unger. It would have been his big movie break, had another plum role not come along first.

In Billy Wilder's *The Fortune Cookie* (1966), Matthau plays "Whiplash Willie" Gingrich, a conniving shyster who never met an ambulance he didn't chase. Jack Lemmon plays Willie's brother-in-law Harry, a television cameraman who is accidently pummeled while covering a football game. His injuries aren't serious but Willie smells money, and files a million-dollar lawsuit against the team and the stadium. Harry wants to blow the whistle, but agrees to the scheme in the hope of winning back his golddigging ex-wife. It was Lemmon who recommended

Matthau for the role, and when Matthau later asked why he would offer him such a wonderful part, Lemmon replied "Don't you think it's about time?" They were friends from that day on.

The rumpled suit and slouched posture look of the cynical downtrodden, which Matthau wore so well in many of his best roles, achieves its zenith here. He appeared more downtrodden than usual after suffering a heart attack during production. But when he returned to set seven weeks later and thirty pounds lighter, Matthau was able to flawlessly recapture Whiplash Willie's dynamic corruptness. "Matthau is leering, sneering, sniggering, swaggering, popping his optics, slopping his chops and generally behaving like the Nero of the Nuisance Claims Division," wrote *Time* in its rave review. The scene in which he tries to talk, cajole, bribe and bully his brother-in-law into litigation is a tour de force that earned Matthau the Oscar for Best Supporting Actor.

THE KENTUCKIAN
Directed by Burt Lancaster; Written by A.B. Guthrie, Jr., based on the novel by Felix Holt; Produced by Harold Hecht; Music by Bernard Herrmann

Cast
Burt Lancaster (Eli Wakefield), Dianne Foster (Hannah), Diana Lynn (Susie), John McIntire (Zack), Una Merkel (Sophie), WALTER MATTHAU (SAM BODINE)

THE FORTUNE COOKIE
Directed and produced by Billy Wilder; Written by Billy Wilder and I.A.L. Diamond; Music by Andre Previn

Cast
Jack Lemmon (Harry Hinkle), WALTER MATTHAU (WILLIE GINGRICH), Ron Rich (Luther "Boom Boom" Jackson), Cliff Osmond (Mr. Purkey), Judi West (Sandy Hinkle)

STEVE McQUEEN (1930-1980)

FIRST APPEARANCE: *Somebody Up There Likes Me* (MGM, 1956)

A STAR IS BORN: *The Magnificent Seven* (United Artists, 1960)

Steve McQueen was able to convey a sense of natural superiority without any perceptible effort to do so. Sometimes it seemed like arrogance, but usually McQueen projected confidence just short of arrogance, thus turning a potential defect into an admirable quality. Other actors, such as Roger Moore and Robert Vaughn, also had this attribute, but usually it came packaged in a wealthy character with impeccable breeding, who attends wine tastings in tailored formalwear and identifies the origin of every bottle after one sip. But only McQueen, through the controlled movements of his wiry physique, the icy stare of his pale blue eyes, and the calm, soft-spoken tone of his voice, could project this same superior bearing in blue collar roles.

McQueen's early years were so turbulent, and so infrequently discussed by the actor, that even his place of birth is unconfirmed. The best evidence designates Indianapolis, Indiana as the city where Terence Stephen McQueen entered the world (the year 1930 is also uncertain), with a move to Slater, Missouri following in short order after the separation of his parents. Four years later his mother remarried, and they moved with his stepfather to California. McQueen started public school but wound up in reform school after several run-ins with the authorities.

When he was fifteen, he ran away to join a tanker sailing to the West Indies. McQueen jumped ship when it returned to Texas and got a job in the oilfields, then left to become a barker in a traveling carnival. In April of 1947 he enlisted in the Marines, and was discharged three years later with a newfound sense of discipline and responsibility. McQueen moved to New York City's Greenwich Village, where he was exposed to music, culture, and, as he told the *Saturday Evening Post*, "a way of life where people talked out their problems instead of punching you." For the first time he considered becoming an actor.

McQueen used his G.I. Bill to attend dramatic school, and became one of five out of two thousand applicants to be accepted by the Actors Studio. He spent three years learning his craft, and made his debut in a 1952 summer stock production of *Peg o' My Heart*. He appeared throughout the early fifties in minor television roles, and first gained attention in 1956 after replacing Ben Gazzara in the Broadway production of *A Hatful of Rain*. He was considered for the lead role in the Rocky Graziano biopic *Somebody Up There Likes Me*, but lost the part to Paul Newman. However, director Robert Wise liked McQueen enough to give him a smaller role.

Somebody Up There Likes Me is an excellent look at boxer Rocky Graziano's rise from the slums of New York to become one of the most successful and ferocious boxers to ever step into a ring. The film made a star out of Paul Newman, which probably didn't make Steve McQueen very content with his consolation-prize role. About nine minutes into the film, you'll see McQueen for the first time as Fido, one of Rocky's childhood friends and fellow troublemakers. He is bent over a pool table sizing up a shot, with a cigarette dangling from his mouth, looking every inch the tough young punk with a dim future. He can be seen in the background of the next few scenes, in which Rocky's gang robs the back of a truck, fences the merchandise, and rumbles with their crosstown rivals.

Steve McQueen would wait another three years for his breakthrough, which occurred not in the movies but on the television series *Wanted: Dead or Alive* (1956-1959). His portrayal of bounty hunter Josh Randall was atypical of the western heroes that were all over television in the late fifties; pragmatic and unemotional, he would do his job with a minimum of moralizing and snappy patter, and then hit the road in search of another paycheck. The series ran three successful years, but did not raise McQueen's stock as a leading man in features. In his next film, he starred opposite a malicious mass of red jello in *The Blob* (1958).

After forgotten appearances in *Never Love a Stranger* (1958) and *The Great St. Louis Bank Robbery* (1959), McQueen was cast with a field of up-and-coming actors in John Sturges' *The Magnificent Seven*. The film was a westernization of Akira Kurosawa's classic Japanese epic *The Seven Samurai* (1954), which told the story of a small village that is repeatedly ravaged by a gang of bandits. The villagers hire professional warriors to put a stop to the attacks. It is sacrilege to say that *The Magnificent Seven*, which transports the saga to rural Mexico and replaced the samurai with cowboys, is an even better film, but which one would you rather watch again?

As Vin, one of the first to be recruited to the villagers' cause, McQueen establishes his primary screen persona of a cool, capable professional. Actually, the "cool" factor in this film is clear off the scale--witness the entrance scenes of McQueen, Yul Brynner, James Coburn and Robert Vaughn, four of the super-suave Seven. Some film commentators have described Vin as motivated only by money, and indifferent toward the people he is hired to protect, but this simply isn't true. Vin's first act early in the film is to ride shotgun on a hearse, to escort a deceased Indian to a dignified burial over the objections of a bigoted community. There wasn't any money in that. Later, he is seen sharing his food with the starving Mexicans, and although he chastises Brynner because "a hired gun can't afford to care too much," Vin admits that he is guilty of the same offense.

Yul Brynner was the only established star in the cast, having already won an Oscar for *The King and I* (1956). But when *The Magnificent Seven* deservedly became a global hit, McQueen was launched along with Coburn (even though he spoke less than twenty words in the entire film) and Charles Bronson. The film is still among the most beloved westerns ever made, and its exhilarating score by Elmer Bernstein has entered the popular culture.

SOMEBODY UP THERE LIKES ME
Directed by Robert Wise; Written by Ernest Lehman, based on the book by Rocky Graziano and Rowland Barber; Produced by Charles Schnee; Music by Bronislau Kaper and Sammy Cahn

Cast
Paul Newman (Rocky Graziano), Pier Angeli (Norma), Everett Sloane (Irving Cohen), Eileen Heckart (Ma Barbella), Sal Mineo (Romolo), Harold J. Stone (Nick Barbella)...STEVE MCQUEEN (FIDO)

THE MAGNIFICENT SEVEN
Directed and produced by John Sturges; Written by William Roberts, based on the film *The Seven Samurai*; Music by Elmer Bernstein

Cast
Yul Brynner (Chris), Eli Wallach (Calvera), STEVE MCQUEEN (VIN), Horst Buchholz (Chico), Charles Bronson (O'Reilly), Robert Vaughn (Lee), Brad Dexter (Harry Luck), James Coburn (Britt)

LIZA MINNELLI (1946-)

FIRST APPEARANCE: *In the Good Old Summertime* (MGM, 1949)

A STAR IS BORN: *The Sterile Cuckoo* (Paramount, 1969)

Her mother was Judy Garland and her father was Vincente Minnelli, and talent was considered a birthright for Liza Minnelli. No question that the genes were first-rate, but casting her success as inevitable conveniently forgets all the offspring of famous parents who tried and failed--what happened to Chastity Bono's birthright? Still it's an understandable explanation; Liza has clearly inherited her mother's ability to command a stage and belt a song with dramatic flourish, as well as her paralyzing stagefright. She also has her father's innate sense of how to package music and choreography to maximum effect.

Frank Sinatra was the first visitor to the maternity ward after Liza was born, and her first friends were Charlie Chaplin's children. The parties at her parents' Beverly Hills home brought out half of Hollywood and, before she was ten, Liza had joined Judy Garland as part of the entertainment. When she did it again on stage at the Palace Theatre, the applause contained for her the same lifeforce that her mother craved. She was exposed to the volatile side of show business as well; her parents divorce in 1951, her mother's drug-induced mood swings, the multiple, unexpected remarriages of Judy and Vincente (she first learned about her mother's nuptials with Sid Luft on the evening news) and the shuffling back and forth between them every six months.

Liza watched her father direct Fred Astaire in *The Band Wagon* (1953), and decided she would become a dancer. She started taking classes, and practiced at home using many of her mother's routines. But a childhood spent in constant adjustment to new surroundings, new siblings and the ever-present instability of Judy Garland would inevitably take its toll. At the age of 13 she weighed 165 pounds, and had few friends outside of Lana Turner's daughter Cheryl Crane, with whom she once offered to exchange mothers.

In 1961 Liza attended the New York High School for the Performing Arts, later immortalized in the 1980 film *Fame*. She had already shifted her career goal from dancing to acting, and would sing whenever a teacher or classmate would ask. At age sixteen she spent one term at the Sorbonne in Paris, but then left school for good, with her mother's reluctant permission, to hopefully break into the family business. She began by avoiding Hollywood and the long shadows of her parents and setting her sights on Broadway. Liza auditioned for and won a secondary role in *Best Foot Forward* (1963), but her lineage would not allow a normal, steady rise to success. While still appearing in her first show, seventeen-year-old Liza was appearing on the talk show circuit and her mother's television show, and later on stage with Judy at a now-famous London Palladium performance. Such early, massive exposure did not allow Liza the luxury of learning her craft in private. Fortunately, she didn't need time.

In 1965 she won a Tony Award for *Flora, the Red Menace*, recorded her first album and headlined sold-out concerts. She played Albert Finney's amorous secretary in the disappointing *Charlie Bubbles* (1968) and reviewers called it a poised film debut. Actually, her first appearance in movies was at the age of two in the final scene of *In the Good Old Summertime*, a musical remake of *The Shop Around the Corner* (1940). Judy Garland and Van Johnson starred in this slight but tune-filled fluff with all the MGM gloss still working its magic. Just before the closing credits, Judy holds up a little girl with black curls and a white dress. The face, especially the large almond-shaped eyes, is unmistakably Liza's.

Liza's next film after *Charlie Bubbles* was *The Sterile Cuckoo*, a quirky coming-of-age at college drama based on the popular book by John Nichols. After reading the book Liza thought herself ideal for the role of Pookie Adams, and first-time director Alan J. Pakula saw box-office appeal in her rising celebrity for a potentially hard-sell film. The story centers on Pookie, a boisterous, mercurial waif who grafts herself to Jerry, a shy, quiet etymology student

(Wendell Burton) during a long bus trip. Romance blossoms between the two complete opposites, but eventually Pookie's constant patter and possessive nature become too much for Jerry, who ends the relationship. When the film was released Liza's performance was described as "perfect" by Pauline Kael, and received an Oscar nomination for Best Actress (she lost to Maggie Smith in *The Prime of Miss Jean Brodie*).

In her portrayal of a girl with an unhappy homelife who talks and talks and talks, grabbing the spotlight to mask her insecurity, we may be seeing something of Liza as well, which adds an intriguing element to a sometimes disagreeable character. The movie itself is better in its individual moments than as a whole--Pookie's line before her first sexual experience--"Okay, Valentino, hit it" caps a sweetly awkward scene, and when the lovers part it is sad but expected, though there is the feeling that both partners are leaving a little better off than they were before.

There was no music in *The Sterile Cuckoo* outside of its theme, the cloying "Come Saturday Morning" played ad nauseum, and it was not until *Cabaret* (1972) that Liza Minnelli found a role that merged her abilities as actress and musical performer, and earned her the Oscar she missed three years earlier.

IN THE GOOD OLD SUMMERTIME
Directed by Robert Z. Leonard; Written by Samson Raphaelson, Francis Goodrich, Ivan Tors and Albert Hackett, based on the play by Miklos Laszlo; Produced by Joe Pasternak; Music by George Stoll, Fred Fisher, George Evans, Ren Shields, others

Cast
Judy Garland (Veronica Fisher), Van Johnson (Andrew Larkin), S.Z. Sakall (Otto Oberkugen) Spring Byington (Nellie Burke)...LIZA MINNELLI (BABY)

THE STERILE CUCKOO
Directed and produced by Alan J. Pakula; Written by Alvin Sargent; Music by Fred Karlin

Cast
LIZA MINNELLI (POOKIE ADAMS), Wendell Burton (Jerry), Tim McIntire (Charlie Schumacher), Elizabeth Harrower (Landlady)

ROBERT MITCHUM (1917-   )

FIRST APPEARANCE: *Hoppy Serves a Writ* (United Artists, 1943)

A STAR IS BORN: *The Story of G.I. Joe* (United Artists, 1945)

The best actors do not show any conscious effort to act. Robert Mitchum takes the process one step further-he seems to show no conscious effort to do much of anything. The laconic Mitchum, who drifted into his career almost by accident, specialized in playing world-weary cynics, some of whom still fight the good fight, despite outward apathy over who's going to win. His brooding screen persona worked even better from the opposite side of the law, especially in *Night of the Hunter* (1955) and *Cape Fear* (1962).

Born in Bridgeport, Connecticut, Robert Mitchum moved to South Carolina when his father took a job in the Charleston Navy Yard. When Robert was two years old, James Mitchum was killed in a gruesome accident, after becoming trapped between the couplings of two freight cars. When his mother was forced to take a job, Bob was sent to live with an aunt and uncle. It was a tough first five years on the planet.

Mitchum's older sister, Julie, developed an interest in show business after winning fifteen dollars singing in an amateur contest. Robert's talent seemed to be writing, after one of his poems was published in a local newspaper. Like many writers, he grew up a loner, and made few friends at Haaren High School in Philadelphia, where the family had relocated after his mother's remarriage. Mitchum developed a reputation for being sullen, crude, and possibly dangerous; he broke his nose in a fight at the age of fourteen, and was later expelled.

He left home in 1932, spent time in hobo jungles and in jail on vagrancy charges. When his family moved once more, to California, Robert returned home. Still uncertain about his future, he followed Julie into the Players Guild of Long Beach, a local theater group, and was surprised to discover his natural talent at acting. In his spare time he continued to write, and at one point he earned money creating comedy routines for a female impersonator.

In May of 1942, Mitchum talked his way into an audition with Harry "Pop" Sherman, producer of the Hopalong Cassidy film series. Shannon looked at Mitchum's 6-foot 2-inch height, imposing frame, lazy stare and drooping eyelids, and saw in him the perfect outlaw. *Hoppy Serves a Writ* became the first of eight Cassidy films in which Mitchum appeared between 1942 and 1943.

The film was a typical entry in the series, and is notable only as Mitchum's debut, and the last of the Cassidy films to be based on an original story by the character's creator, Clarence Mulford. Hoppy (William Boyd) plays a Texas sheriff chasing a gang of bandits led by Tom Jordan (Victor Jory) out of Oklahoma and back into his jurisdiction.

Mitchum, sporting a shaggy mustache and beard, plays Rigney, a member of Jordan's gang. Most of his scenes are on horseback, which is significant because the horse played a pivotal role in Mitchum's casting; *Hoppy Serves a Writ* was already in production before Mitchum met with Harry Sherman. The actor who was first cast as Rigney was thrown repeatedly from the horse, and was later killed in an accident on the set. Mitchum took over the role, and was thrown three times by the ill-tempered bronco. Refusing to surrender, he got up, slapped the horse in the jaw, and climbed back on. After that, the horse behaved.

Eventually, the job offers increased and the roles improved. He appeared in twenty films in 1943 alone, most of them sixty minute programmers. In 1944 he played leading roles in both *Nevada* and *West of the Pecos*. His break came with a chance meeting on Sunset Boulevard with director William Wellman, who was then casting *The Story of G.I. Joe*. The pivotal role of Lieutenant Walker was as yet uncast, though Gary Cooper and several other top stars had expressed their interest. Wellman appraoched Mitchum on the street, tapped him on the shoulder and asked him to audition.

Wellman's instincts proved accurate--Mitchum delivered a spectacular reading, and earned his only Academy Award nomination for his performance in what is still considered by many to be the best World War II movie ever made. Burgess Meredith plays journalist Ernie Pyle, whose efforts to tell the story of the regular soldiers, the G.I. Joes, are played out as he accompanies a platoon of infantrymen in Italy. After several skirmishes most of the platoon, including Lt. Walker, are killed during an assault on a mountain held by the Germans.

The combat scenes are terrific, but the film's strength is its examination of the day-to-day lives of men under fire, who stoically perform their duties knowing that every day might be their last. Among the many moving stories that emerge from the platoon is one soldier's search for a phonograph, to play a record he received from his wife and child. The most powerful moment is Mitchum's final scene; after his death, the body of Lt. Walker is hoisted onto the back of a mule, as his devastated troops look on. With no time to grieve for their fallen leader, it is back to the battlefield to conquer another precious mile of ground.

The air of authority that Robert Mitchum imparts without a line of dialog has rarely been used better. Unable to reveal his own fears, or his revulsion at having to lead his platoon into mortal danger over and over, Lt. Walker instills bravery and confidence, and becomes a hero in the eyes of his men. The scene in which Walker must write letters to the mothers of the soldiers who were killed tests the lieutenant's determination to keep his emotions in check, which turns out to be yet another losing battle.

Mitchum was so convincing as a military hero that the U.S. army drafted him, just weeks before *The Story of G.I. Joe* was released. He was granted a hardship discharge eight months later, and found himself being hailed back in Hollywood as the movies' newest male star.

HOPPY SERVES A WRIT
Directed by George Archainbaud; Written by Gerald Geraghty, based on characters created by Clarence E. Mulford; Music by Irwin Talbot

Cast
William Boyd (Hopalong Cassidy), Andy Clyde (California Carlson), Jay Kirby (Johnny Travers), Victor Jory (Tom Jordan), George Reeves (Steve Jordan)...ROBERT MITCHUM (RIGNEY)

THE STORY OF G.I. JOE
Directed by William Wellman; Written by Leopold Atlas, Guy Endore and Philip Stevenson, based on the book by Ernie Pyle; Produced by Lester Cowan; Music by Ann Ronell and Louise Applebaum, songs by Jack Lawrence and Ann Ronell

Cast
Burgess Meredith (Ernie Pyle), ROBERT MITCHUM (LT. WALKER), Freddie Steele (Sgt. Warnicki), Wally Cassell (Pvt. Dondaro), Jimmy Lloyd (Pvt. Spencer), Jack Reilly (Pvt. Murphy)

MARILYN MONROE (1926-1962)

FIRST APPEARANCE: *Scudda Hoo, Scudda Hay* (20th Century-Fox, 1948)

A STAR IS BORN: *Niagara* (20th Century-Fox, 1953)

The public figure, the private woman, the frustrated sex symbol, the talented actress, the tragic loss; there is nothing about Marilyn Monroe that hasn't been documented, dissected, or guessed at. Her place in the history of Hollywood, popular culture and even the womens' movement remain topics of debate thirty years after her death. What do we know for sure? Marilyn Monroe progressed from bit player to star to icon within her lifetime. She did so primarily as a result of her intense sex appeal, which seemed amplified before a movie camera. "The luminosity of that face!" said Billy Wilder; "There has never been a woman with such voltage on screen, with the exception of Garbo." While she projected sex from without, she radiated trust, naivete` and innocence from within. "She's half-child," said Cary Grant, "but not the half that shows." When we hear the name "Marilyn," she is still the woman that pops into our heads. And she left us much too soon.

Norma Jeane Mortenson was born in Los Angeles, California, and raised in a succession of foster homes. Thomas Mortenson, her father, disappeared before she was born, and was killed in a motorcycle accident in 1929. Gladys Baker, her mother, had a history of mental illness in her family, one that Marilyn feared would affect her as an adult. Because Gladys spent half her time in institutions, Norma Jeane was made a ward of the county at the age of five.

After two years in an orphanage, she moved in with an elderly aunt, and attended junior high and high school in Westwood, California. She married a soldier at age sixteen, and went to work in a defense factory while her husband served overseas. One day at work, Norma Jeane was spotted by an army publicist, and asked to pose for some pin-ups. This led indirectly to a modeling career and then, in 1946, to a screen test with 20th Century-Fox. She was signed to a one-year contract, transformed from brunette to blonde, and given the name of Marilyn Monroe, which was selected by her agent from his admiration for actress Marilyn Miller.

Her first role was to be a glorified walk-on in the horribly-titled *Scudda Hoo, Scudda Hay*, an unpleasant drama about a boy and his two mules. Most of her tiny role was excised from the final cut, but enough survived for the film to officially be called her debut. June Haver was top-billed, as the love interest of an alienated teenager (Lon McCallister), who buys a pair of mules from their owner (Tom Tully) and, with the help of an old muleskinner (Walter Brennan), whips them into shape. The film's title is a call that is used to train the stubborn animals.

Just before the one-hour mark, there's a scene set on the banks of a river, where Haver and friends plan to take a dip. Marilyn filmed two scenes, one in which she says "hello" to June Haver, and another in which she is seen paddling up the river in a canoe with another girl. But all you'll see is Haver on the dock flirting with two male admirers, as a canoe floats downstream in the back left corner of the frame. Marilyn is in the boat, but it's so far in the background that you'll have to take my word for it.

So here's a film that snips footage of Marilyn Monroe to spend more time on mules. There is very little to recommend, what with Tom Tully's constant yelling, Brennan's repeated deep thought "Yes sir, them's mules, all right," and a romance that requires a depth of feeling that neither Haver nor McCallister can muster. On the paltry plus side, there's a cute little girl performance from Natalie Wood, as the smartest character in the film.

Despite the unprecedented amount of books and articles written about Marilyn Monroe since her death, there is still no clear consensus as to which of her films conveyed the mantle of stardom. The post-mortem coverage unfailingly mentions the small, showy roles she played in *The Asphalt Jungle* (1950) and *All About Eve* (1950), but these are judged as far more important now than they were at the time. Even after playing a lead role in *Don't Bother to*

Knock (1952), Marilyn was not bringing people into theaters with her name or her face.

I've chosen *Niagara*, primarily because the two previous films in which she played supporting roles (*Monkey Business* and *O. Henry's Full House*, both from 1952) still leave some doubt as to her status. But she was top-billed in *Niagara*, an obvious showcase for her abilities, and her impact upon moviegoers was compelling. It's possible to build a case for an earlier film, but from *Niagara* on there was no doubt about Marilyn's popular appeal.

She played Rose Loomis, the unfaithful wife of a neurotic husband (Joseph Cotten), whom she plots with her lover to kill during their stay at a honeymoon hotel near Niagara Falls. Rose befriends another couple, Polly and Ray Cutler (Jean Peters and Casey Adams), for the sake of establishing an alibi, but Rose's plan goes awry when her husband survives the attack. There's an exciting chase at the end; when the story is set at Niagara Falls, you can be sure that somone is going to go over the falls, or be rescued from the edge at the last minute. *Niagara* has both.

The situations and characters are straight out of film noir, which would usually mean shooting in black and white. But the sole purpose of the film, every scene, every camera angle, every light, was to present Marilyn Monroe as irresistible. The making of a sex symbol began with her first appearance, in which Rose, supposedly nude, writhes in bed under a thin, white sheet. So color film was needed, if only to immortalize the tight, shiny red dress that Marilyn poured herself into during one of the longest and most famous bounce-walks in cinema history--116 feet of film. When she passes three couples on a dancefloor, the guys freeze in their tracks, and no suspension of disbelief is required.

Her performance as Rose wavers--she is surprisingly more convincing as a hard-bitten harlot who could plot her husband's death, than she is as the soft-spoken, concerned wife that Rose pretends to be. The required "performance within a performance" was still beyond Marilyn's grasp at this stage of her career, but after eighteen films she had taken her first step toward immortality.

SCUDDA HOO, SCUDDA HAY
Directed and written by F. Hugh Herbert, based on the novel by George Agnew Chamberlain; Produced by Walter Morosco; Music by Cyril Mockridge

Cast
June Haver (Rad McGill), Lon McCallister (Snug Dominy), Walter Brennan (Tony Maule), Anne Revere (Judith Dominy), Natalie Wood (Bean McGill), Tom Tully (Roarer McGill)...MARILYN MONROE (GIRL IN CANOE)

NIAGARA
Directed by Henry Hathaway; Written by Charles Brackett, Walter Reisch and Richard Breen; Produced by Charles Brackett; Music by Sol Kaplan

Cast
MARILYN MONROE (ROSE LOOMIS), Joseph Cotten (George Loomis), Jean Peters (Polly Cutler), Casey Adams (Roy Cutler)

DEMI MOORE (1962-   )

FIRST APPEARANCE: *Choices* (Oaktree, 1981)

A STAR IS BORN: *About Last Night* (Tri-Star, 1986)

Esquire called Demi Moore "The Last Pin-up," and in recent years she has become almost as famous for her evocative cover appearances on *Vanity Fair* and other magazines as she has for her film roles. It's not that Moore is that much more enticing than other actresses of her generation, though she would probably rank in most male moviegoers' top five. What sets her apart is attitude; in these politically correct times Demi Moore may be the only star of any significant status who would actively covet pin-up status, and accept the distinction without threatening a lawsuit.

The name Demi was taken from a beauty magazine by her mother, Virginia Guynes. "I don't know if it was the name of a hair product or a make-up." Moore told *Vanity Fair.* She was born in Roswell, New Mexico, but her stepfather Danny's advertising job kept the family on the road for most of her childhood. Virginia and Danny married and divorced twice, and after the final split Virginia took fifteen-year-old Demi and her younger brother Morgan to West Hollywood. Two years later, Dan Guynes committed suicide. Moore has since become estranged from her mother, who posed nude for a skin magazine in 1993, and has had only occasional contact with her biological father.

The woman who would one day coax a million bucks from Robert Redford for a night of romance in *Indecent Proposal* (1993) was an unusually skinny child with a damaged right eye that took two operations to straighten out. She was often forced to wear a patch over the eye, which did not make her nearly biannual entry into a new school any easier. "Being uncomfortable was normal," she told an interviewer in 1992. After the move to West Hollywood she began attending Fairfax High School, but dropped out at sixteen--"It was the best choice at the time," she recalled. Nastassia Kinski was a neighbor in her apartment building, and Moore would occasionally help her read scripts. For the first time, as she watched Kinski's career blossom, she began considering a similar career move. She started acting classes, but didn't last any longer there than she did at Fairfax. " I came at this from guts, and on-the-job training," she said. Secretarial jobs and an explicit layout in *Oui* magazine helped pay the bills until she landed her first acting assignment.

Choices has been repackaged for videocassette release as a Demi Moore vehicle, but actually the film is about high school senior John Carluccio (Paul Carafotes), who is torn between becoming a football player and a concert violinist. His life is further complicated by a hearing disability that could keep him off the team and out of the orchestra. I suppose it's possible to make a good movie from that, but it doesn't happen here. With its plodding pace and heavy-handed script, *Choices* makes the *ABC Afterschool Specials* look like *The Shakespeare Plays.*

Performances are atrocious across-the-board, with the exception of Dennis Patrick as the busybody administrator who bans John from football. I could buy Demi Moore as a high school senior, but not as the kid sister of a senior, which is what she plays here. As Carri, John's jailbait girlfriend, Moore's seductive, sandpapery voice is deeper than that of her leading man. It's a small, undistinguished supporting role of little relevance to her subsequent career.

Her first significant break came in 1982 on the soap opera *General Hospital*, where she played the Lois Lane-like reporter Jackie Templeton. Daytime television's rigorous schedule provided Moore with solid training, and a role in the spin-off soap spoof *Young Doctors in Love* (1982). She returned to playing the nymphet in *Blame It on Rio* (1984), but it was *St. Elmo's Fire* (1985) that brought Moore her first memorable role, a three-year romance with Emilio Estevez, and membership in the trendy Brat Pack.

About Last Night was Demi Moore's graduation from the Pack and into leading lady status. The film was an adaptation of David Mamet's play *Sexual Perversity in Chicago*, and though it was rewritten for the screen much of Mamet's trademark ear for the poetry in gritty urban dialogue survived intact. Rob Lowe plays Danny, a worker at a Chicago grocery wholesaler. He meets Debbie (Moore), an art director for an advertising agency, at a softball game. The film follows their relationship from first meeting to first date to first you-know-what, followed by disagreement and drifting apart. But Mamet does not allow his cynicism to win out this time--Danny and Debbie meet again by chance, and a tentative reconciliation begins.

The film has all the universal truths about love and relationships down pat, coupled with the kind of up-to-the-minute outlook on the state of how we live today that John Hughes achieves in his high school movies. Everything in *About Last Night* looks right, sounds right and feels right, and the performances of Lowe and Moore are no exception. "There isn't a romantic note (Moore) isn't required to play in this movie, and she plays them all flawlessly," raved Roger Ebert. She also proved adept at comedy--Debbie's reaction to Danny's presenting her with a drawer in his apartment, which exemplifies his idea of commitment, keys the film's best scene.

Chicago has rarely been captured in such loving detail as it is here, a by-product no doubt of the midwestern residency of Mamet, scripter Tim Kazurinsky and costar Jim Belushi. There is one image of snow gently falling on an elevated train platform that is somehow indescribably beautiful. There is nudity and sex as well, but it's not the part of the film that leaves the strongest impression. Demi Moore's best scenes are all "G"-rated, and ultimately that's what separates an actress from a pin-up.

CHOICES
Directed by Silvio Narrzano; Written by Rami Alon; Produced by Alicia Rivera Alon and Rami Alon; Music by Christopher L. Stone

Cast
Paul Carafotes (John Carluccio), Steve Nichols (Chris), Victor French (Mr. Carluccio), Dennis Patrick (Dr. Bowers), DEMI MOORE (CARRI)

ABOUT LAST NIGHT
Directed by Edward Zwick; Written by Tim Kazurinsky and Denise DeClue, based on the play *Sexual Perversity in Chicago* by David Mamet; Produced by Jason Brett and Stuart Oken; Music by Miles Goodman, John Oate, Cynthia Weil, Bob Seger, J.D. Souther, Karla Bonoff, others

Cast
DEMI MOORE (DEBBIE), Rob Lowe (Danny), James Belushi (Bernie Litko), Elizabeth Perkins (Joan), George DiCenzo (Mr. Favio)

EDDIE MURPHY (1961-   )

FIRST APPEARANCE: *48 Hours* (Paramount, 1982)

A STAR IS BORN: *48 Hours*

Had it not been for Eddie Murphy, *Saturday Night Live* probably would have never made it to 1990. The brilliantly innovative series faltered after the departure of the original cast, but when Murphy emerged as a talent equal to any of the Not-Ready-For-Prime-Time-Players, the reputation of *Saturday Night Live* as a television training ground for tomorrow's movie stars was established. The possibility of discovering another Eddie Murphy, already realized to some extent with the success of Dana Carvey, has been enough to sustain the series through more than one shaky season.

Murphy created several memorable characters on *SNL*, but the one that has served him best on the big screen has been the fast-talking, streetwise commentator on the world outside his Brooklyn neighborhood, which he first developed as a stand-up comic. Whether he's playing a criminal in *48 Hours*, a policeman in *Beverly Hills Cop* (1984) or a con man in *The Distinguished Gentleman* (1993), Murphy plays the fish-out-of-water formula so deftly that he always ends up owning the aquarium.

There wasn't much to laugh about in Eddie Murphy's childhood--his parents divorced when he was three, and his father Charles, a police officer and amateur comedian, died five years later. But, as is so often the case with comics, humor became a mechanism against difficult times. Murphy received an extra year of class clown training when he was forced to repeat the tenth grade, but before he was seventeen his comedic skills were earning him $300 a week at Manhattan comedy clubs. After being voted the "most popular" boy in his high school graduating class, Murphy enrolled at Nassau Community College to study theatre. A few months later, the NBC network held auditions for the second incarnation of *Saturday Night Live*. Back in the tenth grade, Murphy had announced that he was going to be "bigger than Bob Hope." This was his chance to prove it.

Murphy was hired, mostly to play supporting roles in sketches featuring fellow cast members. But when one particularly dull broadcast ended five minutes early, Murphy was asked to fill the gap, and woke up the studio audience with a sanitized version of his stand-up routine. An amazed *Rolling Stone* critic called the impromptu spot "a masterful performance," and suddenly Eddie Murphy was doing his own skits. Only Murphy and Joe Piscopo returned for the next season, and together they led the series into its second successful era. After viewing tapes of Murphy from the show, director Walter Hill sent him the script for *48 Hours*. The role of smooth, small-time thief Reggie Hammond seemed so tailor-made for Murphy that Hill never contacted another actor.

Hammond is in jail, serving a three-year stretch when he is visited by police detective Jack Cates (Nick Nolte). Two vicious cop killers are at large, and Reggie might know something about their whereabouts. Cates gets Reggie released for 48 hours, during which time he will help find the killers. If successful, he can stay sprung. Cates, a hard-bitten, cynical grizzly bear, doesn't like the idea and lets Reggie know it at every possible opportunity. But both men learn to trust each other after their partnership is tested under fire.

When we first see Murphy he is recreating one of his *Saturday Night Live* creations--a nasty but hilarious impression of Stevie Wonder. What has doomed many of the films made by *SNL* alumni is a tendency to stay in that mode, abandoning story for a series of sketches designed to showcase a performer's strengths. *48 Hours* does not fall into this trap; director Hill keeps the emphasis on action instead of comedy, and by teaming the rookie with seasoned pro Nick Nolte, who seems to work well with just about everyone, there is no pressure on Murphy to carry the film. But the script does give him one scene to show off, and Murphy turns it into the movie's best moment.

After Reggie brags that he can handle himself in any situation, Jack calls his bluff and unleashes his new partner in a country-western bar to question its redneck clientele. The bartender sneers at Reggie and with undisguised malice offers him a "Black Russian." Reggie smiles, laughs, and then after a perfectly-timed pause he fires his glass through the mirror behind the bar. "I'm your worst nightmare--a nigger with a badge," he announces at the beginning of a smashing tirade, as the astonished urban cowboys look ready to wet their blue jeans. He gets his information, and the grudging respect of his partner.

"Sometimes an actor becomes a star in just one scene...in *48 Hours*, it happens to Eddie Murphy," wrote Roger Ebert in his rave review. The film earned $5 million in one week, and became one of 1982's biggest hits. A sequel, *Another 48 Hours* (1990), reunited Hill, Murphy and Nolte, but no one on either side of the screen seemed to care.

48 HOURS
Directed by Walter Hill; Written by Roger Spottiswoode, Walter Hill, Larry Gross and Steven E. de Souza; Produced by Lawrence Gordon and Joel Silver; Music by James Horner

Cast
Nick Nolte (Jack Cates), EDDIE MURPHY (REGGIE HAMMOND), Annette O'Toole (Elaine), Frank McRae (Haden), James Remar (Ganz)

PAUL NEWMAN (1925-   )

FIRST APPEARANCE: *The Silver Chalice* (Warner Bros., 1954)

A STAR IS BORN: *Somebody Up There Likes Me* (MGM, 1956)

Paul Newman inherited the mantle of untamed male sex symbol that first elevated Clark Gable to stardom. "To think that after *Hud* (1963) and *Cool Hand Luke* (1967) I come off as the guy women would most like to go to bed with--it's frightening." he once said of his feminine appeal. But despite his public protestations every time some reporter gushes over his famous blue eyes, Newman has not exactly been adventurous in his attempts to break the mold. In thirty years of comedies, dramas and westerns, the Newman persona has remained within rather limited parameters. There were exceptions, such as *Rally 'Round the Flag Boys!* (1958), but none were critical or box-office hits. One Academy Award and six nominations, however, attest to his mastery of the sometimes brooding, sometimes likable rule-breaker who challenges the depth of a woman's love.

Born and raised in Cleveland, Ohio, Paul Newman enjoyed a refreshingly normal, scandal-free childhood. He moved through the school system with good grades and enrolled in Ohio's Kenyon College, which he left in 1944 to join the navy. Color-blindness kept him out of the officer-training program, but Newman served for two years as radioman on torpedo planes in the Pacific. He then returned to Kenyon and graduated in 1949 with a B.A. in English. He tried dramatics in college after football didn't work out, and performed in over a dozen campus plays. Now convinced that his future was as an actor, he joined the Woodstock Players in Woodstock, Illinois and gained more stage experience. After his father's death in 1950 Newman returned to Cleveland to run the family sporting goods store, but the call of the stage proved irresistible. He abandoned the business for the drama program at Yale University, and earned his Master's in 1952.

Newman quickly became a familiar face on all the television anthologies of the day, including a *Playhouse 90* production of *The Eighty-yard Run* in which he costarred with a young actress named Joanne Woodward. Their relationship blossomed after both were hired for the Broadway production of *Picnic* (1953). His performance as Alan Seymour brought a contract offer from Warner Bros., which he accepted. Newman moved to Hollywood in 1954, and Woodward joined him later that year, having signed a contract with 20th Century-Fox. They were married in 1958.

Paul Newman's first movie is one he would rather forget--in fact, it is one that I'm still trying to forget. *The Silver Chalice* was labeled one of the worst pictures of its decade by Newman himself, who claimed to be "horrified" and "traumatized" when he first watched it. When the film ran on TV he took out ads in newspapers to apologize. Of course, telling people not to watch something is the best way to guarantee a high rating, and Newman only succeeded in calling further attention to his unfortunate debut. Twenty years later, his performance earned the Golden Turkey Award for "Most Embarrassing Movie Debut of all Time."

The Silver Chalice is a rambling, aimless Biblical epic about a young sculptor named Basil (Newman), who is born into poverty but adopted by a wealthy patron. After his benefactor dies Basil is sold into Roman slavery, where his gifts as an artist are soon noticed. Eventually, he ends up in Jerusalem where he is commissioned to sculpt a receptacle for the chalice Jesus used at the Last Supper. This is a film from a major studio--Warner Bros.-with a then-considerable budget of $4.5 million, and to watch it now is to sit in utter amazement at how awful it is. If you survive the 135 minutes to the closing credits, you deserve a silver chalice yourself.

The only kind words critics directed at 29-year-old Newman was in noting his resemblance to Marlon Brando--in looks, not talent. "Paul Newman delivers his lines with the emotional fervor of a Putnam Division conductor announcing local stops," wrote the *New Yorker*. Other reviews were not as kind. However, Newman can take some solace in the fact that nothing he could have done would make this hackneyed film more tolerable, and that his is not the worst performance in the movie. For that distinction it's a toss-up between Herbert Rudley as the scenery-chewing villain Linus, and Jack Palance as the evil wizard Simon, whose costumes and pointy hats provide welcome, albeit unintentional, comic relief. Newman's worst sin is a tendency towards wooden line readings, which is matched by his leading ladies Pier Angeli and Virginia Mayo.

After the film's predictably disastrous release, Newman returned to Broadway for a well-received turn in *The Desperate Hours* (1955). Warner Bros. then ordered him back to Hollywood, where he was lent out to MGM to star in the film biography of boxer Rocky Graziano, *Somebody Up There Likes Me*. To prepare for the film, which he recognized instantly as far superior to his previous effort, Newman studied the real Graziano for two weeks, and worked out tirelessly in the gym. Once you get past the Perry Como title song, *Somebody Up There Likes Me* is an engrossing, unflinchingly honest biopic that traces Graziano's rise from juvenile delinquent to army deserter to jailbird. During a one-year stay in Leavenworth a physical instructor suggests to Rocky that he use boxing as a constructive outlet for his hatred and resentment. After his release Rocky begins a rapid climb to the Middleweight title, which he wins from Tony Zale on his second try.

Newman is convincing as an Italian street kid, complete with a heavy east-side New York accent and a medley of nervous twitches. He also captures Graziano's charging-bull fighting style. In a very classy gesture, Tony Zale plays himself and recreates his title loss in the film's thrilling climax. Eileen Heckart gives an Oscar-worthy performance as Rocky's mother, but the biggest surprise is Pier Angeli as Rocky's wife Norma. After fizzling alongside Newman in *The Silver Chalice*, Angeli delivers a sweet and sensitive performance that is dead center in most of the film's best moments. Maybe it was something in the togas.

THE SILVER CHALICE
Directed and produced by Victor Saville; Written by Lesser Samuels, based on the novel by Thomas B. Costain; Music by Franz Waxman

Cast
Virginia Mayo (Helena), Jack Palance (Simon), PAUL NEWMAN (BASIL) Pier Angeli (Deborra), Alexander Scourby (Luke), Joseph Wiseman (Mijamin), E.G. Marshall (Ignatius), Herbert Rudley (Linus), Lorne Greene (Peter)

SOMEBODY UP THERE LIKES ME
Directed by Robert Wise; Written by Ernest Lehman, based on the book by Rocky Graziano and Rowland Barber; Produced by Charles Schnee; Music by Bronislau Kaper and Sammy Cahn

Cast
PAUL NEWMAN (ROCKY GRAZIANO), Pier Angeli (Norma), Everett Sloane (Irving Cohen), Eileen Heckart (Ma Barbella), Sal Mineo (Romolo), Harold J. Stone (Nick Barbella)

JACK NICHOLSON (1937-)

FIRST APPEARANCE: *The Crybaby Killer* (Allied Artists, 1958)

A STAR IS BORN: *Easy Rider* (Columbia, 1969)

The elevation of Jack Nicholson from rebel oddity to the most significant American actor of his era mirrors the evolution of both American film and American society since 1970.

Nicholson spent the 1950s and '60s in low-budget exploitation films, where his quirky appeal and iconoclastic manner were ideally suited to the material. In the seventies, a wave of cynicism propelled by Vietnam and Watergate motivated major studios into exploring themes of corrupted authority and alienation, territory already familiar to the drive-in crowd. Nicholson's performance in *Easy Rider*, the first film to cross into the mainstream from the fringe genres, branded him as a dynamic anti-establishment hero. Since then, his selection of roles has been colorful and diverse, but usually he's still the non-conformist who derives great pleasure from shaking up the status quo.

Jack Nicholson was born in Neptune, New Jersey, and raised by his mother after the separation of his parents. He played the class clown all through school, and was among the most popular students in his high school graduating class. Nicholson passed on college and moved to Los Angeles in 1957. He took a job as an office boy in the animated cartoon department at MGM, and studied acting with a young resident troupe at the Players Ring Theatre. Among his fellow students were Michael Landon and Martin Landau.

Roger Corman, the legendary "King of the B's," whose ten-day shooting schedules and $30,000 budgets have made him one of the most prolific filmmakers in history, gave Nicholson his first break. *Cry Baby Killer* was cheap even by Corman standards--the film was completed for less than $7000 in the director's standard week-and-a-half timetable. Were it not for Nicholson's debut in the title role, it would surely be relegated to the same bargain bin as the auteur's 150 other releases.

Troubled youth was a favorite Corman topic, and Nicholson became one of his first James Dean wannabes to play a tortured, misundersood teenager. Jimmy Walker (Nicholson) is on a date when he is accosted by three tough hoods. Words are exchanged and punches thrown, a gun is pulled and then dropped, and Jimmy picks it up and starts shooting. After watching two of the bullies fall, a terrified Jimmy flees the scene, and takes hostages to avoid being captured. After a tense stand-off, Jimmy's girlfriend talks him into surrendering.

The ads screamed, "From Teen Rebel to Mad-Dog Killer!", two lies in one sentence. Jimmy is a good kid when the movie begins, he doesn't kill anyone, and after being assured that a self-defense plea will probably be successful, he happily turns himself in and reclaims his life. Such promotion was typical, however, for drive-in fare like *Cry Baby Killer*, a film with no higher aspiration than two or three decent weekends to amass a small profit, while Corman was already busy shooting another project.

Reviewers took little notice of the film or of Nicholson's performance, but after his star ascended many looked back curiously on his debut for any trace of the trademark Nicholson manner. There were flashes--brief flashes--of the charismatic actor within, most of them evident after Jimmy becomes a fugitive. His then-higher pitched voice did not snarl and slide the way it does now, and his line readings are either too excited or too sedate. However, there is a powerful, almost manic intensity in his eyes when he holds a gun on the hostages, that contrasts nicely with the character's clean-cut appearance.

Nicholson's next film, *Little Shop of Horrors* (1960), is one of Roger Corman's best-remembered works, but its cult following was slow to develop and didn't do much for Nicholson at the time. The balance of his sixties work is dominated by psychos, more troubled teenagers, and bit parts in bigger, though not necessarily better films like *Studs Lonigan* (1960). He also picked up a screenwriting credit on the Monkees movie *Head* (1968).

Easy Rider seemed like just another paycheck. Nicholson had made biker movies before (*Hell's Angels on Wheels*--1967), and it was not the type of genre from which stars are discovered. But timing is everything, and in the summer of 1969 a burgeoning counter-culture was looking for heroes. Critics trying to be hip mistook the amateurish *Easy Rider* for a bold, daring artistic achievement, and before anyone emerged from the purple haze the film won a prize at Cannes, and became one of the years' biggest hits. If you grew up with it, the film will always be a treasured memory, but those who know it only by reputation might be surprised to learn that it dates even worse than *Billy Jack* (1971).

Peter Fonda and Dennis Hopper play Wyatt and Billy, two California bikers who serve as middlemen in a drug deal, and use the profits to finance a cross-country trip to the Mardi Gras in New Orleans. Along the way they meet kindred spirits in a hippie commune, and are villified by the redneck residents of every town they pass through (though the town's women find them irresistable). They reach their destination, take a bad acid trip, and are then snuffed out in a sudden, senseless act of violence.

The first half, which consists almost solely of Fonda and Hopper riding their choppers through the desert, is made tolerable only by a soundtrack of classic songs by the Byrds, The Band and Steppenwolf, whose "Born to Be Wild," became a biker's anthem. Then Jack Nicholson appears as ACLU lawyer George Hanson, and joins the trip to New Orleans for a stretch. The character, who looks and dresses establishment but whose sympathies are with the rebels, is able to verbalize what director Hopper tries to suggest through images only. In an instant, the movie is upgraded from barely coherent to sincere and profound.

Vincent Canby described the character as "a full-blooded, almost Faulknerian character in a southern landscape otherwise inhabited by cartoon figures." "This used to be a hell of a country," says George as the film's best scene begins. He explains how the bikers represent a concept of freedom that most Americans will never taste. But don't tell them they're not really free, he warns, "or they'll start killing and maiming to prove that they are." His words prove tragically prophetic, not just for George but for his traveling companions.

Despite the visceral impact of the final scene, it's hard to work up much empathy for Wyatt and Billy, because the performances of Fonda and Hopper barely register. That Jack stole the movie is not an amazing accomplishment, since there wasn't much there to steal. But to deliver one speech in a biker flick and earn comparisons to Faulkner and an Academy Award nomination for Best Supporting Actor, that's something else entirely.

CRY BABY KILLER
Directed by Jus Addis; Written by Leo Gordon and Melvin Levy, based on a story by Gordon; Produced by David Kramarsky and David March; Music by Gerald Fried and Dick Kallman

Cast
Harry Lauter (Porter), JACK NICHOLSON (JIMMY WALKER), Carolyn Mitchell (Carole), Brett Halsey (Manny), Lynn Cartwright (Julie)

EASY RIDER
Directed by Dennis Hopper; Written by Peter Fonda, Dennis Hopper and Terry Southern; Produced by Peter Fonda; Songs by Bob Dylan, Carole King, Gerry Goffin, Mars Bonfire, others

Cast
Peter Fonda (Wyatt), Dennis Hopper (Billy), JACK NICHOLSON (GEORGE HANSON), Antonio Mendoza (Jesus), Phil Spector (Connection), Robert Walker, Jr. (Hippie Leader), Karen Black (Karen)

KIM NOVAK (1933-   )

FIRST APPEARANCE: *The French Line* (RKO, 1954)

A STAR IS BORN: *Pushover* (Columbia, 1954)

When Rita Hayworth stopped jumping when Columbia Pictures generalissimo Harry Cohn gave the order, Cohn issued an edict to manufacture another sex symbol. The job fell to Maxwell Arnow, the man who discovered Marilyn Monroe, and Arnow submitted for Cohn's approval another blonde named Marilyn, who was then appearing in the distant background of a tepid Jane Russell musical called *The French Line*. Columbia changed her first name to Kim, kept her last name of Novak, and launched her into the firmament with lead roles in *Pushover*, *Picnic* (1955) and *The Man With the Golden Arm* (1956). At the end of 1956, Kim Novak was the number one box-office star in the country. Even more impressive is how Novak, like Hayworth before, outgrew her sex goddess image and became a talented actress, who deserves as much credit for the classic status of *Vertigo* (1958) as Alfred Hitchcock and James Stewart.

Marilyn Pauline Novak, born in Chicago, Illinois, was a shy and socially awkward child from working class roots. Marilyn's aloof personality concerned her parents, who advised her to join the Fair Teen Club, a group begun by a department store to provide a meeting place for teenagers. Fashion shows were one of the club's activities, and eventually Marilyn overcame her shyness and participated. Her poise and beauty were noticed by a modeling school, who offered her a scholarship.

Novak attended college part-time and appeared as a model in fashion shows, magazines and an early television commercial. Two weeks after her arrival in Hollywood, she was chosen as one of fifteen models to appear in *The French Line*. If you think that's enough to make spotting her in the film simple, guess again. *The French Line* parades dozens of fashion models across the screen in several musical numbers, primarily to distract the viewer from the capable yet hardly stellar song-and-dance skills of Jane Russell.

Russell plays Mary Carson, a Texas oil heiress who can't find a fella, and decides that the best way to do so is to travel incognito on a transatlantic ocean liner under an assumed name. The plan works when she meets a French singer (Gilbert Roland), and after too many contrived complications to detail here they live happily ever after. It's the kind of bright, colorful froth that Doris Day did so well and so often, and benefits from an enthusiastic supporting performance by Mary McCarty as Russell's best friend. Russell's heaving bosom is poured into a succession of swimsuits and strapless evening gowns, and for some in the 1950s that was worth the price of admission.

The only confirmed Novak sighting in the movie occurs at about the seventy-five minute mark, during the "Any Gal from Texas" number. Before Russell's entrance, as a bewildered, red-jacketed waiter balances a silver tray in each hand, a succession of models pass two-by-two into the foreground. When the lyric "...cannot give a canape` away" is sung, that's Kim on the left, wearing a pink strapless formal. Is she also the girl in the orange shawl with her blonde hair under wraps at Madame Ferrelli's boutique? Or the buxom beauty in the low-cut blue dress in the "With a Kiss" number? Models flit this way and that at a fever clip, and Novak may well be in the backgrounds of more than one production number. But to freeze frame every possible sighting is to stretch the running time of *The French Line* well beyond its intended 102 minutes, and that's something you really don't want to do.

Such was the experience on her movie resume` when Kim Novak was promoted to the lead role opposite Fred MacMurray in the hardboiled police drama *Pushover*. Novak didn't think she was ready and the studio had reservations as well, but in the role of gangster moll Lona McLane, Novak not only captured her character's practice of using her looks at a weapon, she also conveyed a vulnerability that made Lona far more intriguing than the standard femme fatale.

The story must have been described as "*Rear Window* meets *Double Indemnity*" in pitch meetings. Police detective Paul Sheridan is assigned to trail Lona, the girlfriend of a hood suspected of stealing $200,000 in a daring daylight bank robbery. Paul falls hard for Lona, and for her scheme to run off with the stolen money. But from the moment their plan is hatched, it begins to unravel, as Paul is driven to desperate deeds to conceal his duplicity from fellow officers.

Pushover is a first-rate film noir that is carried by MacMurray's charisma, which works equally well no matter what side of the law he lands on, and the intensity of his on-screen relationship with Novak--the moves that Lona puts on Paul at their first meeting are so potent that they should be illegal. Though Lona became the first in a series of "smart blondes" that made Kim Novak the top motion picture discovery of the year, according to six magazines and the Hollywood Foreign Press Association, Novak's feline sensuality was rarely utilized this well again.

THE FRENCH LINE
Directed by Lloyd Bacon; Written by Mary Loos and Richard Sale, based on a story by Matty Kemp and Isabel Dawn; Produced by Edmund Grainger; Music by Walter Scharf, Andre Josef Myrow, Ralph Blaine and Robert Wells

Cast
Jane Russell (Mary Carson), Gilbert Roland (Pierre), Arthur Hunnicutt (Waco Mosby), Mary McCarty (Annie Farrell), Joyce McKenzie (Myrtle Brown)...KIM NOVAK (MODEL)

PUSHOVER
Directed by Richard Quine; Written by Roy Huggins, based on the story *The Killer Wore a Badge*, the novel *Night Watch* by Thomas Walsh, and the novel *Rafferty* by William S. Ballinger; Produced by Jules Shermer; Music by Arthur Morton

Cast
Fred MacMurray (Paul Sheridan), KIM NOVAK (LONA MCLANE), Phil Carey (Rick McAllister), Dorothy Malone (Ann), E.G. Marshall (Lt. Carl Eckstrom)

MAUREEN O'HARA (1921-   )

FIRST APPEARANCE: *Jamaica Inn* (Mayflower/Paramount, 1939)

A STAR IS BORN: *The Hunchback of Notre Dame* (RKO, 1939)

Maureen O'Hara was crowned the "Queen of Technicolor," and for most of us our first mental image of her is bathed in Technicolor's glowing, vibrant hues. It might be from *Sinbad the Sailor* (1947), *At Sword's Point* (1952) or *Against All Flags* (1952), three of her many roles as princess/prizes to be won by dashing swashbucklers in any historical era in which low-cut bodices were in vogue. But most likely our first thought of O'Hara places her opposite John Wayne, her favorite on-screen sparring partner and sweetheart, among the kelly green hills of Ireland in *The Quiet Man* (1952).

Born Maureen FitzSimons in Milltown, Ireland, O'Hara would exchange one quintessentially Irish surname for another at the request of Charles Laughton, her costar in both *Jamaica Inn* and *The Hunchback of Notre Dame*. As a child she wrote and performed plays in her backyard with her three sisters and two brothers, and at the age of five she made her official debut reading a poem between acts of a school play. From then on if there was an opportunity to perform, she was first in line. Maureen appeared on radio at the age of twelve, and was featured in neighborhood plays, pageants and festivals. At fourteen she enrolled in the Abbey Theatre School, and received numerous awards in dramatic contests, culminating in the All-Ireland Cup for her portrayal of Portia in *The Merchant of Venice*.

Immediately after her graduation, she was offered a leading role with the Abbey Players. Instead she moved to London at the invitation of an English film company. She screen-tested for a movie that was never completed, but the footage was brought to the attention of Charles Laughton, whose production company was casting a screen adaptation of Daphne du Maurier's novel *Jamaica Inn*. Eighteen-year-old Maureen was offered the feminine lead role of Mary Yelland.

The story is set on the rugged Cornwall coast of England in the mid-nineteenth century, where a band of pirates lure unsuspecting ships to their destruction, kill the crew and steal whatever can be carried away. Jem Trehearn, an investigator from Lloyd's of London, infiltrates the band at their lair in Jamaica Inn, but is discovered and sentenced to hang. He is rescued by Mary Yelland, who has come to Cornwall in search of her Aunt Patience. She is shocked to learn that Patience is married to one of the pirates. She and Jem flee the Inn and seek refuge in the manor house of the local squire, Sir Humphrey Pengallan, unaware that Sir Humphrey is actually the brains behind the pirate raids.

Jamaica Inn was directed by Alfred Hitchcock, and is one of the Master of Suspense's most underrated films. The pace is taut, the settings rich in Gothic atmosphere, and at the center is a delightfully over-the-top performance by Charles Laughton as Pengallan. Laughton and Hitchcock battled constantly over his interpretation of the role, and watching the film it is obvious who prevailed. The performance would have been more understated, and technically better, had Hitchcock triumphed, but it wouldn't have been as much fun.

For her part, Maureen O'Hara turned in a capable performance as the innocent party who is propelled into a world of violent intrigue, a trademark Hitchcock plot device. Although the reviews were negative, *Jamaica Inn* was a modest hit and O'Hara was on her way.

Her next film was *The Hunchback of Notre Dame*, in which she played Esmerelda to Charles Laughton's Quasimodo. Everybody knows the story, either from Victor Hugo's novel or any of the six film adaptations. Quasimodo is the deformed, brutish bell-ringer at Notre Dame Cathedral, circa the late 1400s. He falls in love with Esmerelda, a beautiful gypsy who is wrongly accused of murdering one of the king's soldiers. Quasimodo rescues her from the gallows but pays the ultimate price for his heroism. The lavish sets are packed to bursting with huge crowds, and for sheer spectacle this is superior to the classic Lon Chaney version or any of those that followed.

Laughton is actually more restrained as the hunchback than he was as the nobleman in *Jamaica Inn*. The incredible make-up job convincingly transforms him into a monster, but Laughton's touching performance restores the character's humanity. Maureen O'Hara's imposing 5'8" height further accentuated the obvious disparity between beauty and the beast, but as a character she is hard to pin down. The remarkable, sliding string arrangements of composer Alfred Newman actually provide more insight into the two sides of Esmerelda's gypsy passion than anything in the script; she seems to exist here only to fall victim to a series of captors, from the church to the hunchback to all the king's men.

But O'Hara was beautiful on screen even without Technicolor, the film was a huge success, and it launched her into better roles--though not always in better projects. O'Hara's early movies forced her to take a lot of abuse, but she would be at her best when she could give it back, especially to guys like the Duke who were not used to the receiving end.

JAMAICA INN
Directed by Alfred Hitchcock; Written by Sidney Gilliat, Joan Harrison, J.B. Priestley and Alma Reville, based on the novel by Daphne du Maurier; Produced by Erich Pommer and Charles Laughton; Music by Eric Fenby

Cast
Charles Laughton (Sir Humphrey Pengallan), MAUREEN O'HARA (MARY YELLAND), Leslie Banks (Joss Merlyn), Robert Newton (Jem Trehearne), Marie Ney (Patience Merlyn)

THE HUNCHBACK OF NOTRE DAME
Directed by William S. Dieterle; Written by Sonya Levien and Bruno Frank, based on the novel by Victor Hugo; Produced by Pandro S. Berman; Music by Alfred Newman

Cast
Charles Laughton (Quasimodo) MAUREEN O'HARA (ESMERELDA), Sir Cedric Hardwicke (Frollo), Thomas Mitchell (Clopin), Edmond O'Brien (Gringoire), Alan Marshal (Phoebus)

MAUREEN O'SULLIVAN (1911-)

FIRST APPEARANCE: *Song O' My Heart* (Fox, 1930)

A STAR IS BORN: *Tarzan, the Ape Man* (MGM, 1932)

She spoke dialogue from the pages of Dickens, Tolstoy and Austen, but "Me Jane, You Tarzan," or words to that effect, is Maureen O'Sullivan's sole contribution to great movie lines. A featured player from her movie debut, O'Sullivan found her best niche as Jane opposite Johnny Weissmuller's Tarzan in six tremendously popular films. Several actresses and Bo Derek have played the role since, but none were as successful or are as fondly remembered. Fearing typecasting, she used Tarzan as a bargaining chip to secure other roles, and since a new Tarzan film was like printing money in the 1930s, she got her wish. O'Sullivan appeared in such high profile MGM projects as *David Copperfield* (1935), *Anna Karenina* (1935) and *Pride and Prejudice* (1940), but the public's memories of her remain dominated by leg-revealing loincloths and elephant-driven elevators.

A winsome Irish lass from Boyle in County Roscommon, Maureen O'Sullivan moved frequently as a child, a result of her father's service in the Connaught Rangers, an elite military regiment. After Major John O'Sullivan was seriously injured in World War I, the family (Maureen, parents, one brother and three sisters) settled near Dublin. When she was twelve Maureen was sent for her education to the Convent of the Sacred Heart in London, where she made friends with ten-year-old Vivien Leigh and Gwen McCormack, the daughter of world-reknowned Irish tenor John McCormack, who would later star in Maureen's first film. She came in second behind Leigh in a Convent vote to determine the prettiest student, and was moved to tears by the recognition, "because I couldn't believe that anyone thought me pretty," she later told the *Chicago Tribune*.

In 1929, after she completed her education in Paris and returned to Dublin, Maureen's insecurity about her looks stopped her from auditioning for a part in the musical *Song O' My Heart*, which was then shooting exterior footage in Ireland. Several of her friends had already been interviewed, and some of them were cast as extras. Instead, Maureen went to a horse show where, as luck would have it, the film's director, Frank Borzage, was in attendance. He noticed O'Sullivan at a nearby table and personally offered her a small part in the film. After a screen test, he improved the offer to a supporting role. Fox executives were so impressed with her innocent charm and sophistication that they offered Maureen a contract before her first film was completed.

Song O'My Heart was intended as a vehicle to introduce John McCormack to American audiences. He plays Sean O'Callaghan, a tenor with a voice "that should be heard in the great capitals of Europe," who prefers to stay in his small Irish village, nursing a broken heart. Had McCormack signed with MGM, he might have had a movie career similar to Mario Lanza's; possessed of an incredible voice and a natural screen charisma, McCormack could have appeared in a string of lightweight musicals that would be worth the price of admission for his singing alone. In *Song O' My Heart*, he performs fifteen songs, including the magical "Rose of Tralee."

Maureen O'Sullivan is featured in a wholly unnecessary subplot that exists to pad the running time between songs. As Eileen O'Brien, she must see her true love Fergus (John Garrick) in secret, because her domineering aunt does not approve. Though she looks lovely and seems right at home in a symphony of lilting Irish accents, her performance is forced and awkward. O'Sullivan's inexperience is especially apparent in an early scene in which McCormack consoles her after another run-in with her aunt; when she finally confronts the bitter old woman, she cannot summon the required passion to play the scene.

Song O' My Heart was a hit, and O'Sullivan learned her craft on screen with supporting performances in three more 1930 films. In 1931, after being dropped from the Fox roster, she was signed by MGM to play Jane in *Tarzan, the Ape Man*. It was hardly the first film adaptation of the Edgar Rice Burroughs classic--Elmo Lincoln became the first movie Tarzan in 1918, just six years after Burroughs' original tale appeared in *All-Story Magazine*. Lincoln returned for two sequels, and was followed by Gene Pollar, Jim Pierce and Frank Merrill. Olympic swimming champion Johnny Weissmuller became Tarzan number five in Tarzan movie number eight, and instantly rendered all prior versions obsolete.

British explorers Henry Holt (Neil Hamilton) and James Parker (C. Aubrey Smith) are searching for the elephant's graveyard in Africa, when Parker's daughter Jane arrives unexpectedly to join the expedition. Tarzan helps them navigate a dangerous river, and becomes fascinated with Jane. He whisks her into the treetops for a closer look. She is frightened at first, but as they learn to communicate Jane senses the gentle nature beneath Tarzan's primitive facade. The explorers are ready to shoot Tarzan, but when they are abducted by a tribe of nasty dwarves it is the king of the jungle who leads a herd of elephants to the rescue. They find the elephant's graveyard, but Parker doesn't survive the trip. Henry returns to England, and Jane decides to remain with Tarzan.

The script uses only bits of the Burroughs story; Jane Porter from Baltimore becomes Jane Parker of London, but that's nothing compared to the makeover done on Tarzan. The civilized, erudite man among beasts described by his creator became an uncivilized man-ape with no knowledge of the world outside his jungle. When Weissmuller was understandably dubbed the perfect Tarzan by critics and audiences, his interpretation became the official one, and a prototype for all future attempts.

The progress made by Maureen O'Sullivan since *Song O' My Heart* is astonishing. She is exceptional here, playing Jane as a delightfully mischievous, giggling, giddy schoolgirl, who matures over the course of six films into a capable young woman who stands (and swings) by her man. She is sweet and funny and very sexy, and her chemistry with Weissmuller is as palpable as exists in any male-female team-up ever created in the movies. In *Tarzan, the Ape Man* and its even-better sequel, *Tarzan and His Mate* (1934), when Tarzan and Jane get acquainted up in the trees, the steam on screen isn't all jungle humidity.

SONG O' MY HEART
Directed by Frank Borzage; Written by Sonya Levien and Tom Barry; Produced by William Fox; Music by Charles Glover, C Mordaunt Spencer, William Kernell, James Hanley, Alfred Burns, William Michael Balfe, Albert Hay Malotte, others

Cast
John McCormack (Sean O'Callaghan), MAUREEN O'SULLIVAN (EILEEN O'BRIEN), John Garrick (Fergus O'Donnell), J.M. Kerrigan (Peter Conlon)

TARZAN, THE APE MAN
Directed by W.S. Van Dyke; Written by Cyril Hume and Ivor Novello, based on characters created by Edgar Rice Burroughs; Produced by Irving Thalberg

Cast
Johnny Weissmuller (Tarzan), MAUREEN O'SULLIVAN (JANE), Neil Hamilton (Harry Holt), C. Aubrey Smith (James Parker)

PETER O'TOOLE (1933-   )

FIRST APPEARANCE: *The Savage Innocents* (Paramount, 1960)

A STAR IS BORN: *Lawrence of Arabia* (Columbia, 1962)

Peter O'Toole is the master of the grand gesture. From *Lawrence of Arabia* on, he found his most successful niche as magniloquent monarchs (*The Lion in Winter*--1968) flamboyant aristocrats (*The Ruling Class*--1972), and less-pedigreed men with delusions of grandeur (*The Stuntman*--1980 and *My Favorite Year*--1982). Watching him play a charged moment with dramatic flourish is always a treat, but after a bombastic soliloquy and a swirl of his cape, O'Toole becomes no less interesting in relaxed moments. By finding a comedic spin in a serious scene, or choosing a slightly off-center reading for a standard line of dialogue, his reactions always carry a sense of wonder and novelty.

The son of a bookmaker, or "turf accountant" in Irish racetrack parlance, Peter Seamus O'Toole was born in the Connemara region of Ireland, and spent his early years on the road with his parents and older sister, Patricia. From County Kerry to Dublin to Lincolnshire, England the O'Tooles moved, before finally settling in Leeds, a northern English town with a large Irish population. At the age of six, Peter attended a performance of the operetta *Rose Marie*, and thought for the first time of becoming an actor.

He attended school intermittently, before quitting for good and joining the staff of the *Yorkshire Evening News* as a copyboy and photographer's assistant. In his spare time, he performed in amateur theatricals. In 1952, he earned a scholarship to study at the Royal Academy of Dramatic Art, and spent three years with the famed Bristol Old Vic repertory company. Seventy-three roles later, O'Toole opened in the West End play *The Long and the Short and the Tall* (1959), and won overnight fame and the Actor of the Year award from the London critics.

Movie offers followed, but O'Toole was wary of long-term Hollywood contracts, and instead made his film debut as a supporting player in *The Savage Innocents*. Directed and cowritten by Nicholas Ray, who made his reputation with *Rebel Without a Cause* (1955), this British production starts out as a documentary about Eskimo life in the great white north, and then shifts into more familiar Ray themes of intolerance and parochial distrust.

Amidst gorgeous arctic scenery (Canada standing in for the North Pole), and ponderous travelogue narration ("In the age of the Atom Bomb, they still hunt with bow and arrow"), Inuk the Eskimo (Anthony Quinn) hunts for food and longs for a wife. After a dull beginning, the movie picks up after Inuk accidentally kills a missionary over a cultural misunderstanding, and becomes a fugitive on the run.

Peter O'Toole is listed only as "1st Trooper," but the role is actually bigger than its billing. He first appears 80 minutes into the film, as one of two mounties who track and, eventually, capture Inuk. After his partner is killed, O'Toole's character is rescued by Inuk, and has a change of heart about his mission.

Anthony Quinn, the movies' foremost ethnic chameleon, is utterly convincing as Inuk, especially when expressing the eskimo's confusion at being apprehended for a crime he can hardly remember. A bearded Peter O'Toole, eyes burning with indignation, already shows signs of the rousing volatility that would captivate audiences in *Lawrence of Arabia*. His voice, however, was dubbed into a flat American type that does too much damage to what might have been a noteworthy debut. As a result, the critical praise for *The Savage Innocents* was not shared by O'Toole. The film was largely ignored by the public, and has practically disappeared since its initial release.

At the age of 27, O'Toole became the youngest leading man in the hundred-year history of the Shakespeare Memorial Theatre in Stratford-on-Avon. He appeared in Disney's 1960 production of *Kidnapped*, and received his first praise from film critics in *The Day They*

Robbed the Bank of England (1960), but stagework remained O'Toole's top priority, until David Lean made an offer he couldn't refuse.

O'Toole accepted the title role in *Lawrence of Arabia*, Lean's biography of British soldier/adventurer T.E. Lawrence, amid speculation that he was not yet ready to anchor a three-hour epic. Such concerns were dissolved on the day the film premiered. After beginning his motion picture career in the frozen tundra, Peter O'Toole became an international star in the blazing desert sands of Spain and Morocco.

Lawrence is a listless 29-year-old General Staff officer in Cairo, who is transferred at his request to Arabia. There, he leads an Arab rebellion against the ruling Turks, culminating in a surprise attack on the Turkish stronghold at the port of Aqaba. Eventually, Lawrence's exploits attract worldwide publicity, but his attempt to unite the warring Arab tribes into one nation is ultimately unsuccessful. He returns to England, where he lives in anonymity until his death in a motorcycle accident in 1935.

O'Toole spent months researching the role of T.E. Lawrence before filming began; he learned to ride a camel, familiarized himself with Bedouin culture, and became fluent in Arabic. Still, we never really get to know the character very well. He was a complex man, who attempted the impossible over and over, and won more often than he lost. The supreme self-confidence that led him to cross the Sinai Desert ("Why not?" he said before beginning, "Moses did."), alternated with moments of paralyzing self-doubt. At times his very sanity is questionable, which leaves open the question of whether his death was an accident or a successful suicide attempt.

That these questions are not answered is not a criticism of the script or O'Toole's performance, which is more effective for its enigmatic complexion. The distinguished cast includes Alec Guinness, Anthony Quinn, Omar Sharif, Claude Rains and thousands of caftan-clad extras, but even amidst these larger-than-life surroundings, O'Toole emerges larger still. David Lean, the master of the sweeping vista, deserves equal credit for the magnificence of *Lawrence of Arabia*, the winner of seven Academy Awards including Best Picture. Lean filmed the scorching desert so vividly that one moviegoer asked for seats on the shady side of the theater.

THE SAVAGE INNOCENTS
Directed by Nicholas Ray; Written by Nicholas Ray, Hans Ruesch and Franco Solinas, based on the novel *Top of the World* by Hans Ruesch; Produced by Joseph Janni and Maleno Malenotti; Music by Angelo Francisco Lavagnino

Cast
Anthony Quinn (Inuk), Yoko Tani (Asiak), Carlo Giustini (2nd Trooper), Marie Yang (Powtee), PETER O'TOOLE (1ST TROOPER)

LAWRENCE OF ARABIA
Directed by David Lean; Written by Robert Bolt and Michael Wilson, based on *The Seven Pillars of Wisdom* by T.E. Lawrence; Produced by Sam Spiegel and David Lean; Music by Maurice Jarre

Cast
PETER O'TOOLE (T.E. LAWRENCE), Alec Guinness (Prince Feisal), Anthony Quinn (Auda Abu Tayi), Jack Hawkins (Gen. Allenby), Jose Ferrer (Turkish Bey), Omar Sharif (Sherif Ali Ibn El Kharish)

LAURENCE OLIVIER (1907-1989)

FIRST APPEARANCE: *The Temporary Widow* (UFA, 1930)

A STAR IS BORN: *Wuthering Heights* (United Artists, 1939)

    Opera singers rarely sound convincing on tin pan alley standards, and prima ballerinas do not win line dancing contests, but Laurence Olivier, the greatest Shakespearian actor of his age, never appeared out of his element when removed from the rarified air of the classical stage. His performances as Henry V, Hamlet and Richard III represent the most mutually gratifying merger of Shakespeare and cinema, but Olivier also played swashbucklers, clowns and Nazi dentists, proficiently adapting his mastery of technique to characters of highbrow tragedy and lowbrow comedy.

    The son of a clergyman, Laurence Kerr Olivier was born in Dorking, Surrey, England, and was instructed in the ritual, literature and music of the church from an early age. When he was fifteen, Olivier made his first stage appearance at a 1922 Shakespeare festival at Stratford-on-Avon, playing Katharine in an all boys' performance of *The Taming of the Shrew*. Gradually, he began to gravitate away from the ministry and toward the stage; when he told his father of the decision to study acting, he received his blessing and generous financial support.

    Two years later, Olivier enrolled in London's Central School of Dramatic Art, followed by three years of apprenticeship at the Birmingham Repertory Theatre. Actor Ralph Richardson became his mentor, and under Richardson's tutelage a 19-year-old Olivier won raves in the title role of *Uncle Vanya*. After leaving the Birmingham troupe, he toured in a variety of plays in both New York and London. The year 1930 proved to be a turning point; Olivier appeared with Noel Coward and Gertrude Lawrence in an acclaimed production of *Private Lives*, and made his film debut in a German-made comedy entitled *The Temporary Widow*.

    Earlier in 1930, Olivier starred in the short film *Too Many Crooks*, as a young playboy who is dared by his fiancee` to break into a mansion. "If Laurence Olivier's future work is up to the standard he has set here, his appearance in the leading role of a more ambitious film is assured," wrote one review. *The Temporary Widow*, alas, was not that film. He plays Peter Bille, a struggling artist who is reported drowned in a boating accident. His wife, Kitty (Lilian Harvey), is accused of murder, until another man comes forward and confesses. The film's surprise twist (which will come as little surprise to any alert viewer) is Peter's return from the "dead," and his admission that he had faked his own death to stimulate interest in his paintings.

    Besides Olivier's debut, the only interesting aspect of *The Temporary Widow* was its simultaneous shooting in both German and English. Lilian Harvey starred in both productions, but Olivier appeared only in the English version. Dressed in a wide, double-breasted pinstripe suit and sporting a jaunty mustache, Olivier cuts a slightly smarmy but debonair, flamboyant figure as the crafty artist. He also plays the man who confesses to his murder. The film is a pleasant timekiller, nothing more, and Olivier gives a capable performance that was greeted as such by the critics.

    Olivier compiled an impressive list of stage credits throughout the 1930s, and also appeared in a number of less-than-impressive films. He looked upon movies as "a dull means of making money between interesting stage roles," and his lack of discretion in accepting scripts and paychecks is evident in films such as *Westward Passage* (1932), *Perfect Understanding* (1933) and *No Funny Business* (1934). But in 1939, a year in which the movies could do no wrong, Olivier was coaxed back to Hollywood to star in Samuel Goldwyn's production of *Wuthering Heights*. He still wasn't sold on the medium, but director William Wyler convinced Olivier that motion pictures were an art form that deserved his respect, and his best effort.

    The haunting love story of Heathcliff and Cathy, set on the barren Yorkshire moors of England, ends at chapter 17 of the Emily Bronte` novel, which will surprise anyone who reads the book after seeing the film. At the risk of defaming a classic work of literature, however, it was the right thing to do. The script by Ben Hecht and Charles MacArthur managed to condense the entire scope of Heathcliff and Cathy's doomed affair without sacrificing any of its depth or complexity.

Olivier and Merle Oberon, who had previously worked together in the comedy *The Divorce of Lady X* (1938), were ideally cast as Heathcliff and Cathy, who are played less here like Gothic archetypes and more like credible human beings. Cathy is a spoiled child even as an adult, whose attraction to the elegant life of the landed gentry triumphs over her true feelings for Heathcliff. And Heathcliff's inferiority complex over his heritage alternates with a fierce, endemic pride.

The inscrutable, brooding master of Wuthering Heights is "brilliantly played (with) wild tenderness" by Olivier, raved the *New York Times*. Framed by the ethereal, Academy-Award winning cinematography of Gregg Toland, who somehow captured the dark beauty of the Yorkshire moors in California's Conejo Hills, Olivier's dashing looks and tortured soul made him a matinee idol overnight, and his performance earned him an Oscar nomination. *Wuthering Heights* has been remade twice since this 1939 version, but the original remains unsurpassed in the splendor of its storytelling, and the beauty of its stars.

THE TEMPORARY WIDOW
Directed by Gustav Ucicky; Written by Karl Hartl, Walter Reisch and Benn Levy (based on the play *Hokuspokus* by Curt Goetz; Produced by Erich Pommer

Cast
Lilian Harvey (Kitty Kellermann), LAURENCE OLIVIER (PETER BILLE), Felix Aylmer (Public Prosecutor), Frederick Lloyd (Counsel for the Defense)

WUTHERING HEIGHTS
Directed by William Wyler; Written by Ben Hecht and Charles MacArthur, based on the novel by Emily Bronte`; Produced by Samuel Goldwyn; Music by Alfred Newman

Cast
Merle Oberon (Cathy Linton), LAURENCE OLIVIER (HEATHCLIFF), David Niven (Edgar Linton), Donald Crisp (Dr. Kenneth), Flora Robson (Ellen Dean), Hugh Williams (Hindley Earnshaw), Geraldine Fitzgerald (Isabella Linton)

AL PACINO (1940-   )

FIRST APPEARANCE: *Me, Natalie* (National General, 1969)

A STAR IS BORN: *The Godfather* (Paramount, 1972)

Al Pacino's portrayal of Michael Corleone in *The Godfather* and *The Godfather, Part II* illustrated what may be his greatest strength as an actor--the ability to play men of good conscience who fall prey to dark forces. Corleone was the archetype, but traces of the same moral battles are fought by Pacino's characters in *Dog Day Afternoon* (1979), *Sea of Love* (1985), and his Academy Award-winning portrayal of a bitter, blind military man in *Scent of A Woman* (1992).

Pacino was born in New York City, the only child of parents who divorced before he was two years old. The perils in their Bronx neighborhood prompted Pacino's mother to restrict her son from playing outside during the day. To cope with the isolation he staged one-man shows for his grandmother, often based on the movies he had seen the night before. The skills he developed in acting and mimicry landed him several lead roles in school plays, and a successful audition for the High School of the Performing Arts. But he dropped out, failing almost every course, at the age of seventeen.

In 1966, after a series of odd jobs that only intensified his desire to become an actor, Pacino was accepted for training at the Actors Studio. He made his debut in a Workshop production opposite James Earl Jones, and then appeared off-Broadway in a variety of roles. In 1967, he earned an Obie as Best Actor in an Off-Broadway production for his role in *The Indian Wants the Bronx*. Pacino made his Broadway debut in 1969, playing a psychotic junkie in *Does a Tiger Wear a Necktie?*. The play closed after 39 performances, but Pacino was singled out as a remarkable new discovery. He earned the Tony Award as Best Supporting Actor, and was named the "most promising new Broadway actor" in a *Variety* poll.

The performance also led to Pacino's movie debut, in a forgotten Patty Duke vehicle entitled *Me, Natalie*. The movie was made in New York, where Pacino's glowing reviews as a junkie prompted director Fred Coe to cast him in a similar role. Duke, just three years after her TV stint as identical cousins, plays Natalie Miller, an idealistic college student who drops out to "find herself" among the eccentrics in New York City's Greenwich Village. After working as a cocktail waitress in the colorfully named Topless-Bottomless Club, and having an affair with a married artist, she escapes her shallow surroundings and returns to her parents' home.

Besides Duke, who is worth watching even in the sappiest made-for-TV disease movie, other notable names attached to *Me, Natalie* include Martin Balsam, Elsa Lanchester and Nancy Marchand, who play supporting roles, and Henry Mancini, who contributed the score. The performances are sincere and effective, but the "innocent young girl in the big city" story is older than dirt, and A. Martin Zweiback's script adds nothing new to the model.

Pacino, as "Tony," plays what is little more than a walk-on. Look for him in the nightclub, dancing clumsily with an equally graceless partner. His memorable first words on the screen, "Do you put out?" is met with an outraged rebuke. "Listen," he replies, "somebody like you ought to be asking me!" He worked for one day on the film, and then happily returned to the New York stage.

It would be two years before Pacino made his second film, *The Panic in Needle Park* (1971), which once again cast him as a drug addict. Executives at Paramount Pictures, after viewing part of the film, consented to test Pacino for the role of Michael Corleone in *The Godfather*, though they were hoping to cast a "name" actor such as Warren Beatty or Jack Nicholson. Pacino's Sicilian ancestry certainly didn't hurt his chances. Two additional screen tests later, he won the role.

The Godfather, certainly one of the most prestigious films of the 1970s, has been called a treatise on the spiritual death of the American family, and a metaphor on the corruption of big business. Such lofty interpretations may be accurate, but there's as much pulp fiction as grand opera in the story of the Corleones, which made the film as popular with audiences as it was with the *cognoscente*.

Vito Corleone (Marlon Brando), the aging godfather of a prominent east coast mafia family, is gunned down by hit men from a rival clan. He survives the assassination attempt, and during his long recovery his sons, Sonny (James Caan), Fredo (John Cazale) and adopted son Tom Hagen (Robert Duvall) plot their revenge. Michael, Vito's youngest son, shunned the family business to join the military. But after his father is almost killed, Michael offers to even the score, knowing that his straight arrow reputation will make it easier to infiltrate enemy territory.

Michael's slow, subtle transition from a college-educated, dispassionate observer of his family's activities to a ruthless killer and godfather-in-training, gave Pacino the meatiest role in the film, and he stands out over one of the best casts ever assembled, including Oscar-winner Marlon Brando. Observed Pauline Kael, "Pacino has an unusual gift for conveying the divided spirit of a man whose calculations often go against his inclinations." The movie ends with the closing of a door; outside the door is Michael's wife, Kay (Diane Keaton), who no longer recognizes the man she married. On the other side is Michael, now bereft of the easy smile and animated mannerisms he displayed at the beginning of the film. Weary, expressionless, and looking much older than he did just one year ago, he assumes the reins of his father's empire.

ME, NATALIE
Directed by Fred Coe; Written by A. Martin Zweiback, based on a story by Stanley Shapiro; Produced by Stanley Shapiro; Music by Henry Mancini

Cast
Patty Duke (Natalie Miller), James Farentino (David Harris), Martin Balsam (Uncle Harold), Elsa Lanchester (Miss Dennison), Salome Jens (Shirley Norton), Nancy Marchand (Mrs. Miller)...AL PACINO (TONY)

THE GODFATHER
Directed by Francis Ford Coppola; Written by Mario Puzo and Francis Ford Coppola, based on the novel by Puzo; Produced by Albert S. Ruddy; Music by Nino Rota

Cast
Marlon Brando (Don Vito Corleone), AL PACINO (MICHAEL CORLEONE), James Caan (Sonny Corleone), Richard Castellano (Clemenza), Robert Duvall (Tom Hagen), John Cazale (Fredo Corleone), Diane Keaton (Kay Adams), Talia Shire (Connie), Abe Vigoda (Tessio)

GREGORY PECK (1916-   )

FIRST APPEARANCE: *Days of Glory* (RKO, 1943)

A STAR IS BORN: *Keys to the Kingdom* (20th Century-Fox, 1944)

He was the busiest leading man in Hollywood during World War II (which all the other leading men were off fighting), and quickly became a director's first choice for movies that required a champion of liberal reform. Gregory Peck was such a natural as a man of unflinching morality that he was rarely asked to cross the line into villainy, but when he did, as in *Duel in the Sun* (1946) and *The Gunfighter* (1950), the results were often fascinating.

Eldred Gregory Peck was born in La Jolla, California; after his parents' divorce he was raised primarily by his father, Gregory, and his maternal grandmother. He passed unremarkably through the public school system and then spent one year at San Diego State College. He dropped out, thought better of it and resumed his education, this time at the University of California at Berkeley. After appearing in campus productions of *Moby Dick* and *Anna Christie*, Peck abandoned his plans to become a doctor and changed his major to English and drama. In 1939, immediately after graduation, Peck set out for New York and spent the next two years doing graduate work of sorts at the Neighborhood Playhouse School of the Theater.

Numerous summer stock productions prepared Peck for a lead role in the drama *Morning Star* (1942), but after opening in previews he received "as bad a set of notices from the critics as it is possible for an actor to get," according to the *Saturday Evening Post*. By the time the play opened on Broadway, however, his performance had improved considerably, and the New York critics responded favorably. Two more Broadway shows, *The Willow and I* and *Sons and Soldiers*, followed in short order, and led to an offer from filmmaker Casey Robinson. Peck made his movie debut in *Days of Glory*, a project produced and scripted by Robinson, and intended by the studio as a test project to assess audience reaction to a cast of newcomers led by Peck and Tamara Toumanova, a former prima ballerina of the Ballet Russe de Monte Carlo.

When you hear the ponderous opening narration, you might want to shut off the VCR then and there--it's the right move. *Days of Glory* is a heavy-handed account of a small group of Russian guerillas led by Peck, who battle the Nazis in World War II. Robinson's adoration of the patriots' cause makes Leni Riefenstahl look subtle by comparison, and director Jacques Tourneur can breathe no life into the material, even when there is finally some action in the last reel.

The inexperience of the neophyte cast is obvious. The fact that you've never heard of Tamara Toumanova should explain her impact on the American movie landscape; the prima ballerina was not a prima actress, and after four more films she retired (and was so unknown that she's the only one who knew she retired). Gregory Peck didn't have a chance, but the film did establish the practice of casting him as an enemy of oppression. He certainly looks like a movie star, and that voice--deep, melodic, stage-trained but with a resonance that can't be taught--compels an audience to listen. When Vladimir (Peck) speaks to Nina (Toumanova) about his former life before the war, when he was a builder, and how he is now forced to destroy instead of build, you watch the passion in Peck's angular face and deep-set eyes and think about all the other (better) parts he should be playing. Abraham Lincoln is the first to come to mind.

Days of Glory was a real stiff of a movie that understandably flopped at the box office, but Peck found no shortage of work after its failure. Even before its release, Peck's agent "was a harried auctioneer presiding over the wildest bidding (among producers) Hollywood had ever seen," wrote *Collier's* magazine in 1945. When the dust cleared, Peck had signed contracts with 20th Century-Fox, MGM, RKO, and with producers Casey Robinson and David O. Selznick. Certainly part of the reason for this stampede can be attributed to the wartime shortage of stars, as even Peck himself acknowledged (a spinal injury rendered him ineligible for military service), but to imply that Peck's career was launched by default would be unfair. The war may have opened doors, but had Peck not proven himself he would have been sitting next to Tamara Toumanova on the train out of town.

In 1945, Peck began fulfilling the demands of his multitude of contracts; he appeared in three popular films; *Keys of the Kingdom*, which brought Peck the first of his five Academy Award nominations, *Valley of Decision* opposite Greer Garson, and the Alfred Hitchcock classic *Spellbound*. *Keys of the Kingdom* was released first; it was a return to the holy well for Fox after *The Song of Bernadette* (1943) filled the studio collection plates. Peck ages from eighteen to eighty in his portrayal of Father Francis Chisholm, a selfless priest who establishes a parish in China.

Chisholm has no congregation at all when he arrives in Tai Pan, and quickly discovers that the only converts are "Rice Christians," whose faith left them when the rice ran out. He overcomes indifference, derision, threats of violence and a military revolution in his quest to spread the good word. Eventually, his dedication, piety, and genuine affection for those in his care attract a number of followers. The movie does right by religion without trying to convert the audience, and amidst the heartwarming drama there are welcome doses of humor and adventure. Edmund Gwenn is excellent in support as Chisholm's mentor in the church, and when you see Roddy McDowall play Chisholm as a boy, you'll be surprised as how much he actually resembles a young Gregory Peck.

Peck secures his status as an actor of unforced integrity, but what is always so interesting about his good guy roles is the impression he conveys, through his imposing six-foot three-inch height and intense manner, that he could bust out at any time and smack somebody. In several films, including *Keys of the Kingdom*, Peck's characters call upon reserves of quiet strength to overcome their palpable dark sides, which gave an edge to their personalities that turned potentially-bland heroes into complex, intriguing human beings.

DAYS OF GLORY
Directed by Jacques Tourneur; Written and produced by Casey Robinson, based on a story by Melchoir Lengyel; Music by Constantin Bakaleinikoff

Cast
Tamara Toumanova (Nina), GREGORY PECK (VLADIMIR), Alan Reed (Sasha), Maria Palmer (Yelena), Lowell Gilmore (Semyon), Hugo Haas (Fedor)

KEYS OF THE KINGDOM
Directed by John M. Stahl; Written by Joseph L. Mankiewicz and Nunnally Johnson, based on the novel by A.J. Cronin; Produced by Joseph L. Mankiewicz; Music by Alfred Newman

Cast
GREGORY PECK (FATHER FRANCIS CHISHOLM), Thomas Mitchell (Dr. Willie Tullock), Vincent Price (Rev. Angus Mealy), Roddy McDowall (Francis, as a boy), Edmund Gwenn (Rev. Hamish MacNabb)

MICHELLE PFEIFFER (1958-   )

FIRST APPEARANCE: *Falling In Love Again* (O.T.A., 1980)

A STAR IS BORN: *Into the Night* (Universal, 1985)

"The beautiful face captures your attention," wrote *Vanity Fair*, "but what holds it is the measured tension in her performance--the disquieting balances of self-possession and self-abandonment." Michelle Pfeiffer's traffic-stopping radiance inevitably draws so much attention, that the challenge she faces in bringing an audience past that distracting surface and into the heart and soul of a character is formidable. She has met the challenge, and has carved out a place as one of the most versatile actresses of her generation.

Had she accomplished this only by choosing parts that deglamourize her appearance, as in *Married to the Mob* (1988) and *Frankie and Johnny* (1991), it would have been a Pyrrhic victory. But even when Pfeiffer is at her most desirable, as in the already classic scene from *The Fabulous Baker Boys* (1989) when she slinks across the top of a piano singing "Makin' Whoopee," the effect is more than just erotic. Pfeiffer brings her intelligence and her surprising vocal ability to the scene, and as we watch, transfixed, we are also watching an actress at work. From *Baker Boys* to *Dangerous Liaisons* (1988), *The Age of Innocence* (1993) to *Batman Returns* (1992), Pfeiffer's body of work is remarkable in its diversity.

She was raised with her three siblings in Midway City, a tiny spot on the map near Santa Ana in Orange County, California. "Michelle Mudturtle" was one of her many unflattering nicknames, which in a rare 1990 interview she admitted to deserving. "I was a rotten kid, just rotten. I was always in trouble." She frequently skipped school for the beach, appeared in no school plays, and only took theater courses to earn English credits that would hasten her departure from Fountain Valley High. By the age of eighteen Pfeiffer dropped out of community college and stenography school, and was working as a checkout girl in a Vons supermarket in El Toro. There, as she listened to a customer complain about the cantaloupes, she contemplated her future; "I was frustrated and aimless and asked myself, what are you going to do with you life? And the answer I came up with, the only thing I really wanted to do, was acting."

In 1978, Pfeiffer entered and won the Miss Orange County beauty pageant, and was signed by a talent agency that brought her modeling and television commercial assignments. After playing bimbo roles on two short-lived TV series, *Delta House* (1979) and *B.A.D. Cats* (1980), she made her film debut in *Falling in Love Again*, a forgotten romantic comedy starring Elliott Gould and Susannah York.

Gould plays Harry Lewis, a clothing store manager suffering from a midlife crisis. He reflects at length on his adolescent years spent in the Bronx, New York, the courtship of his wife Sue (York), and what happened to his dream of becoming an architect. Pfeiffer, sixth-billed, plays Sue in the flashbacks that comprise much of the film (Stuart Paul plays the young Harry). His dad works in a garment district factory, her dad owns the factory, and that's just one of the many cliches` that found their way into the script.

Falling in Love Again was produced, directed and cowritten by 21-year-old Steven Paul, who deserves points for chutzpah, but his filmmaking inexperience shows. Paul tries for a Neil Simon-esque combination of comedy and drama, wistful nostalgia for New York neighborhoods, and cheap shots at California. He's not even close. The flashbacks are the best part of the film, because we don't have to listen to Elliott Gould's annoying, self-pitying diatribes about the "good old days."

"I kind of learned how to act on screen," Pfeiffer said, and one look at her first performance proves it. She appears at about the twenty minute mark; her character is British, but her attempt at an accent is half-hearted at best. When her voice isn't cracking, it is drifting into what one critic described as "a flat, friendly Americanese edged with the self-protective hesitancy common to beautiful women who are tired of being hit on." But she looks angelic with her blonde hair coiffed in the classic 1940s style, and it's not a stretch to believe that teenage Harry would organize "the biggest scrap drive the Bronx has ever seen," which he does, just to win her hand.

Pfeiffer next played forgettable roles in *The Hollywood Knights* (1980) and *Charlie Chan and the Curse of the Dragon Queen* (1981). She won the lead role in *Grease 2* (1982), and although the film was a disastrous flop, she was already getting noticed. She did not appear in a genuine box-office hit until *The Witches of Eastwick* (1987), and was not embraced by the critics until *Married to the Mob* (1988), but Michelle Pfeiffer had already been the subject of enough articles with titles like "The Fabulous and Foxy Pfeiffer" to arouse public curiosity. Dazzled moviegoers, if they hadn't done so already, searched for her name in the credits of *Scarface* (1983), after her portrayal of a cocaine-addled mafia mistress.

"The first time I ever saw Michelle Pfeiffer on-screen was in *Into the Night*, an otherwise forgettable thriller," wrote *Newsweek* critic David Ansen. "I had never heard of her before, but the first words out of my mouth when the movie ended were 'Who *was* that girl?' It wasn't simply that she was beautiful; she was riveting, despite the standard femme fatale role...she was just getting started, but she was, at this early date, already a star."

Jeff Goldblum plays Ed Okin, a restless, depressed insomniac trapped in a failing marriage and a dead-end career. At the airport he meets mystery woman Diana (Pfeiffer), who lands on the hood of his car while fleeing from the Iranian secret police. Ed helps her escape and then tries to leave, but he is continuously drawn back to her side as the details of her plight are gradually revealed.

The film did only marginal business, but director John Landis has a knack for lightweight thrillers, and keeps the pace moving fast enough to successfully hide all the holes in the plot. *Into the Night* is slick, superbly photographed, and an intriguing look at the odd people and places that exist in Los Angeles after midnight. Landis packs the film with appearances by his fellow directors, including Roger Vadim, David Cronenberg, Jim Henson and Paul Mazursky. It's an inside joke that will mean nothing to the general public, but film buffs might find the game enjoyable. The movie's real appeal stems from its stars; Jeff Goldblum's bemused half-smile is just right for the bone dry brand of humor in Ron Koslow's script. In one scene, in which he negotiates with the Iranians, his deadpan delivery is hilarious.

Pfeiffer is entrancing as the cool, streetwise Diana, a good girl who's not as tough as she thinks. She wears a red leather jacket, t-shirt and jeans in what is probably, considering all the other cinephile references, an homage to James Dean in *Rebel Without a Cause* (1955). When Dean is on screen in *Rebel* you can't take your eyes off of him, and Pfeiffer's allure is just as powerful. Her beauty and Diana's charming personality are a potent combination--you'd need to go back to an early Audrey Hepburn performance for comparison. Although *Into the Night* is a long way from a classic, Pfeiffer makes you wish the film would never end, just so you could spend more time with her.

FALLING IN LOVE AGAIN
Directed and produced by Steven Paul; Written by Steven Paul, Susannah York and Ted Allan; Music by Michel Legrand

Cast
Elliott Gould (Harry Lewis), Susannah York (Sue Lewis), Stuart Paul (Young Harry), MICHELLE PFEIFFER (YOUNG SUE), Kay Ballard (Mrs. Lewis)

INTO THE NIGHT
Directed by John Landis; Written by Ron Koslow; Produced by George Folsey, Jr. and Ron Koslow; Music by Ira Newborn

Cast
Jeff Goldblum (Ed Okin), MICHELLE PFEIFFER (DIANA), Richard Farnsworth (Jack Caper)

MARY PICKFORD (1893-1979)

FIRST APPEARANCE: *Her First Biscuits* (Biograph, 1909)

A STAR IS BORN: *Tess of the Storm Country* (Famous Players, 1914)

Mary Pickford, "America's Sweetheart," was the first genuine movie star. A decade before talking pictures, she was as famous as any woman in the world. Pickfair, her Hollywood mansion, was America's Buckingham Palace, and Mary and her husband, Douglas Fairbanks, introduced the concept of cinema royalty. A child actress before the age of six, she used her unprecedented renown, and the 10,000 letters a week she received from devoted fans, to change the way movies were made, and the way that stars were treated. In 1916, Pickford signed a $1 million contract, an unheard-of sum for a film actress; she became an independent producer in 1918, and was a cofounder of United Artists in 1919.

She was born Gladys Smith in Toronto, Canada, and worked for awhile under the name Gladys Pickford, before becoming Mary Pickford as a teenager. Her entree` into show business originated from necessity, not desire; after Mary's father died when she was four, her mother played small parts in various theater stock companies to put food on the table for her three children. In 1898, Mary accompanied her mother to a Valentine Stock Company rehearsal of the play *Bootle's Baby*. The manager was looking for a child to play the title role, and five-year-old Mary volunteered to play the part.

She played many more roles for the company until 1902, when she left with her mother, sister and brother to go on tour with another play. For several years the Pickfords, as they were now billed, played one night stands across the United States, and Mary gradually began to emerge as the star of the family. Brimming with self-confidence, she interrupted a rehearsal of the Broadway play *The Warrens of Virginia* to request a try-out. Amused by her bravado, producer David Belasco granted her request, and was impressed with her audition. Mary opened in the play in 1907, and remained with Belasco for the next two years.

In April of 1909, Mary walked into the New York mansion occupied by Biograph Studios, recited her resume`, and was given a screen test by director David Wark Griffith. He offered her extra work at five dollars a day. She held out for ten and got it. The very next day, fifteen-year-old Mary Pickford played a ten-year-old girl in a slapstick comedy entitled *Her First Biscuits*.

Most silent films, especially those made before 1910, are lost forever, but fortunately, copies of *Her First Biscuits* still exist. Filmed in one day, the fifteen-minute short concludes with a mob of hungry actors voraciously eating a bad batch of biscuits, and then writhing with comic indigestion. Mary, wearing a linen and lace dress and a matching hat, can clearly be seen as one of the unfortunate biscuit eaters.

One day after her film debut, Mary was playing the lead role in Griffith's *The Violin Maker of Cremona*. Such was the nature of the business in 1909--actors, so insignificant that their names were not even listed in the credits, would switch from walk-ons to leads with no change in their status or their paycheck. When *Cremona* became a surprise hit, however, Griffith made certain that Mary would remain with the studio. At one point, he threatened to resign unless she received a raise to $40 a week.

Pickford spent the next three years at Biograph, where fans dubbed her "The Girl With the Curls" and, once her name was discovered, "Our Mary." Her star already on the rise, she joined the Famous Players Film Company in 1912. The films she made for Famous Players producer Adolph Zukor made her famous, but it would be inaccurate to single out one release that made the difference. *Hearts Adrift* (1914) is listed in some sources as her first real hit, but its success was dwarfed by her next film, *Tess of the Storm Country*.

Mary played the title character, Tessibell Skinner, a plucky squatter who falls in love with a divinity student, and discovers that his sister is pregnant out of wedlock. She takes the mother and child into her ramshackle home, and asserts that the child is hers to protect the mother's reputation. She is then branded a societal outcast and spurned by her lover, but after four reels of suffering everything works out in the fifth.

   Tess of the Storm Country, budgeted at $10,000, saved Zukor's studio from bankruptcy. The actress who began her career playing a baby at age five, and made her film debut as a teenager playing a ten year-old, moved audiences to tears as the young and innocent Tess. No adult woman before or since has been able to play a childlike waif with more sincerity, and without a trace of gimmickery. Hearts broke in theaters across the country when the illegitimate baby, deathly ill, is refused the rite of baptism by a minister; Tess storms into the church, and delivers the sacrament herself, and Mary was "America's Sweetheart" from that day on. The scene would have been even more powerful had director Edwin Porter gone in for a close-up at least once during the film.

   Tess was so successful that Pickford remade it in 1922, again playing the title role. Her performance in both versions is a wonder, but she is helped in the remake by its more fluid directing style, that brings the camera in closer to capture the desperation in her eyes, and the exquisiteness of her ringlet-framed face.

HER FIRST BISCUITS
Directed and produced by D.W. Griffth

Cast
Linda Arvidson, Marion Sunshine, Florence Lawrence, Mack Sennett, Harry Salter, Charles Inslee, John Compson, Harry Myers, MARY PICKFORD

TESS OF THE STORM COUNTRY
Directed and written by Edwin S. Porter, based on the novel by Grace Miller White; Produced by Adolph Zukor

Cast
MARY PICKFORD (TESS), W.R. Walters, Olive Fuller Gordon, David Hartford, Harold Lockwood, Lorraine Thompson, Louise Dunlap, Richard Garrick, Jack Henry

SIDNEY POITIER (1927-   )

FIRST APPEARANCE: *No Way Out* (20th Century-Fox, 1950)

A STAR IS BORN: *The Defiant Ones* (United Artists, 1958)

A door opened in Hollywood in 1950, when Sidney Poitier proved that an African-American actor could fill theaters in any American neighborhood. It would be another decade before more black actors reached the same status, so for awhile Poitier was tabbed as a representative of his race, a star whose performances were judged not just on quality of technique, but also on their social statement. That's a heavy burden, but Poitier accepted the responsibility unfairly thrust upon him, becoming an avatar of the black male in America and doing so with a level of class that is hard to find anywhere in Hollywood anymore.

Sidney Poitier was born in Miami, Florida, during the three months his Bahamanian parents had spent in the United States trying to sell tomatoes from their small farm on Cat Island. He grew up in near-poverty conditions in the Bahamas, spending his early years in a hut without running water. When he was eleven years old, the Poitiers lost their land and joined the swelling ranks of the dispossessed. They moved to New Providence Island, where Sidney quit school after eighteen months and supported himself with various manual labor positions. "Films taught me about other people, how to dial a telephone, geography, names of places, things I never knew before," he said of his youth, and also took note of a situation that he himself would later change; "I very rarely saw a Negro man when I was looking for myself."

His journey to stardom began when, after years of running with a wicked crowd, he was sent to Miami to live with his brother, Cyril. The arrangement quickly dissolved and Sidney set out for New York with $1.50 in his pocket. He joined the Army, but was discharged after one year and found himself back on the streets. In 1945, while searching for a job in the *Amsterdam (New York) News*, Poitier saw an "Actors wanted" announcement for the American Negro Theater. He auditioned and was rejected, but after several more attempts he negotiated a deal that allowed him to work as a janitor in exchange for acting lessons. He met Harry Belafonte, who became his best friend and whom he would understudy in several productions. Director James Light saw Poitier during one of Belafonte's off nights and offered him a small role in a Broadway production of *Lysistrata*. From 1946 to 1948, Poitier learned his craft in a variety of plays, from classics to broad comedies.

In 1949, Sidney Poitier first stepped before a camera for an Army Signal Corps documentary entitled *From Whom Cometh My Help*. Soon thereafter, Darryl Zanuck offered him $750 a week to star in *No Way Out*. Poitier eagerly accepted, and vowed that he "would never ever work in a film that was not cause for members of the Negro audiences to sit up straight in their seats."

Dr. Luther Brooks (Poitier), a young resident at a major metropolitan hospital, is called upon to treat a career criminal who is brought in by the police after an attempted robbery. The patient's brother, Ray Biddle (Richard Widmark), threatens Dr. Brooks if his treatment is unsuccessful. When the patient dies, Ray makes good on his threat by provoking a race riot, and escaping custody to exact his revenge.

No Way Out did not flinch in addressing questions about society's ability to accept black professionals. The racial epithets hurled by a poorly-educated lout like Biddle are insulting to Luther, but far more harmful are the similar views, expressed more subtly, by some of his patients and coworkers. Its candid chronicling of racism in America "made all previous efforts look like pussyfooting," wrote *Life* magazine, but may also have been responsible for the film's poor performance at the box office. The jubilance that followed the end of World War II had not yet subsided, and audiences were in no mood to see stories about America in which all was not right.

Richard Widmark is marvelous as an ignorant, hate-filled racist, in a performance that recalls in intensity his classic debut in *Kiss of Death* (1947). Linda Darnell, as the hard-bitten wife of Ray's brother, delivers her most effective dramatic performance. The phrase "quiet dignity" turned up in more than one assessment of Poitier's portrayal of Luther Brooks. In his first role he was already an attractive, charismatic presence on screen, with a vocal delivery that is almost evangelical in its passion. When he begs a black orderly to not join the riot about to take place, his plea for a peaceful solution to racial disharmony seems directed at everyone in the theater. Later, as Dr. Brooks treats the victims of the riot, the mother of a white patient spits in his face. Poitier registers shock, rage, and bitterness in rapid succession. You expect him to explode at any moment, but then he turns and walks away. It's the quietest moment in the film, and the most indelible.

Poitier was not under contract to any studio, and was thus open to any offer that was made. But there weren't many roles for black actors in the 1950s, and his career suffered accordingly. "I was exercising free choice over a fairly one-dimensional set of material. I didn't really have a wide range of offers." he said in a 1975 interview. Memorable work in *Cry, the Beloved Country* (1952) and *The Blackboard Jungle* (1955) emerged between a misguided Harlem Globetrotters biopic, *Go, Man, Go* (1954) and the drippy dog movie *Goodbye, My Lady* (1956).

The script for *The Defiant Ones* was gathering dust for two years in various studio storage houses, and director Stanley Kramer had to play producer as well to overcome resistance to its controversial subject matter and get the movie made. The result, completed in a grueling 31 days, received Oscars for its script and cinematography, a nomination for Best Picture, and the first ever Academy Award nomination for an African-American actor.

Two prisoners, Noah Cullen (Poitier) and Joe ("Joker") Jackson (Tony Curtis), escape from a southern chain gang while still shackled together. They cooperate while fleeing from the authorities, but during moments of respite a mutual prejudice threatens their uneasy truce. A friendship forms before the chains are at last removed, and both men must choose between loyalty and freedom.

When the symbolism is that far up front, subtlety goes out the window and the only option is to play the material with as much honesty and conviction as possible. *The Defiant Ones* is, for the most part, a gripping action film that is enriched by its social conscience. Stanley Kramer builds suspense superbly, especially in the Hitchcock-worthy scene when Noah and Joker try to slip into a small town after dark.

Tony Curtis had to insist that Poitier receive equal billing, which is disgraceful considering how equal their contributions are to the finished product. Although Poitier plays a convict, he has not broken his vow to only play virtuous roles. It is made clear that Noah acted in self-defense when he committed the murder that landed him in jail, and was not acquitted because the victim was white. Noah is smarter that Joker, more practical and more dependable. Poitier paints a vivid portrait of a courageous man of unbroken spirit, who accepts his inevitable recapture with cool-headed resignation, and a defiant song for his jailers.

NO WAY OUT
Directed by Joseph L. Mankiewicz; Written by Joseph L. Mankiewicz and Lesser Samuels; Produced by Darryl F. Zanuck; Music by Alfred Newman

Cast
Richard Widmark (Ray Biddle), Linda Darnell (Edie), Stephen McNally (Dr. Wharton), SIDNEY POITIER (DR. LUTHER BROOKS), Stanley Ridges (Dr. Moreland)

THE DEFIANT ONES
Directed and produced by Stanley Kramer; Written by Nathan E. Douglas and Harold Jacob Smith; Music by Ernest Gold

Cast
Tony Curtis (John "Joker" Jackson), SIDNEY POITIER (NOAH CULLEN), Theodore Bikel (Sheriff Max Muller), Lon Chaney (Big Sam), Claude Akins (Mac), Cara Williams (The Woman)

WILLIAM POWELL (1892-1984)

FIRST APPEARANCE: *Sherlock Holmes* (Goldwyn, 1922)

A STAR IS BORN: *The Last Command* (Paramount Famous Lasky Corp., 1928)

William Powell's voice--suave, aristocratic, impeccable in diction and instantly recognizable--had women swooning when Frank Sinatra was still in diapers. How surprising, then, that Powell had already become a popular star before the coming of sound. It was to be the actor's good fortune that he actually spoke the way audiences "heard" him in his many silent portrayals of charismatic villains.

Born William Horatio Powell in Pittsburgh, Pennsylvania, young Bill grew up in the nearby city of Allegheny. When he was nine his father, a banker, accepted a better job in Kansas City, Missouri, and the family was off to the midwest. Powell's intelligence and eloquence manifested themselves early, prompting dad to steer him toward a career in law. William went along with the idea until he started high school and successfully auditioned for his first play. After a few curtain calls and a stint in the Shakespeare Club, William Powell was convinced that he had the desire and the talent to pursue a career in acting. The next step was to convince his parents that the money they had set aside for his tuition to Kansas University should instead be handed over to the American Academy of Dramatic Arts in New York City. This he could not accomplish with all his gifts of articulation, but a favorite aunt was swayed and sent William $700 to pursue his dream--with instructions to pay it back with six percent interest.

Powell graduated the Academy in 1912 at the age of nineteen, and almost immediately he won a small part in the Broadway play *The Ne'er-Do-Well*. Throughout the next ten years he would work on the New York stage and in the occasional touring company, mostly playing villains. It was his performance as the heavy in the melodrama *Spanish Love* (1922) that got Powell noticed by film director Albert Parker. Parker was casting *Sherlock Holmes*, and thought Powell would be ideal as Forman Wells, one of Professor Moriarty's henchmen. It was not a well-drawn part, but the money was terrific compared to Broadway, and would finally allow Powell to pay back his very patient aunt.

Watching the great John Barrymore play Holmes helped Powell over his somewhat snobbish disdain of the "flickers", and he quickly came to realize that film acting carried its own set of skills, and offered even greater rewards without the requirement to memorize dialogue and rehearse for weeks. *Sherlock Holmes* was well-received by the public, who delighted in booing Gustav von Seyffertitz's masterful portrayal of Moriarty, and cheering for Barrymore's earnest, if somewhat inebriated, consulting detective. Powell appears in several scenes, mostly in the background, and subtly generates an effective air of menace.

After two more 1922 films, William Powell quit the stage for good. By 1925 he had appeared opposite the leading actors of the screen, including Marion Davies (*When Knighthood Was in Flower*), Lillian Gish (*Romola*) and Ronald Colman. After *Beau Geste* (1926) he appeared to be forever typecast as a villain, but the mold began to crack with *The Last Command* (1928), one of the best films about the film industry ever made.

Emil Jannings won the very first Academy Award for Best Actor after his portrayal of Grand Duke Sergius Alexander, cousin to Russia's almighty Czar and commander of the Imperial Army. After the Bolshevik Revolution, Alexander escapes to America, where he is reduced to appearing as an extra in movies. Powell plays Leo Andreyev, a Bolshevik leader who was once captured and interrogated by the Grand Duke. Later he also defects to the states, but with much greater success. Leo becomes one of Hollywood's top directors, and during a casting session for a film about the Revolution he recognizes the Grand Duke's photo. He casts Alexander, now a broken shell of a man, as a Russian general. After donning the uniform, the fallen leader imagines himself back in the motherland. He grabs a Russian flag and orders his troops into battle before succumbing to a heart attack.

While *The Last Command* clearly belongs to Jannings, the third-billed Powell dominates the opening scene and carries off the role of Alexander's nemesis memorably. The film's attempted parallel between directors and dictators, in a Hollywood every bit as heartless as Imperial Russia, is strengthened by Powell's Mephistophelian mustache and eyebrows, his swaggering walk, and the icy stare he fixes on the once-haughty commander. But Leo also knows that Alexander could have had him executed years earlier, and did not. Was this job offer just the exacting of revenge, or was he now returning the favor?

In the heartbreaking final shot, Leo cradles the dying general in his arms, and then drapes the Russian flag over his lifeless body. They were both patriots in their own way, and when the director's assistant regrets the loss only because Alexander was a great actor, Leo adds that he was also "a great man." For the first time Powell is able to transcend his villainy with compassion. Now the possibility of other roles opened to him, and when William Powell made his first full-talkie the following year it was as the hero--detective Philo Vance in *The Canary Murder Case* (1929). From there it was a short step to Nick Charles in *The Thin Man* (1934).

SHERLOCK HOLMES
Directed by Albert Parker; Written by Marion Fairfax and Earle Browne, based on the play by William Gillette and the stories of Sir Arthur Conan Doyle; Produced by F.J. Godsol

Cast
John Barrymore (Sherlock Holmes), Roland Young (Dr. Watson), Carol Dempster (Alice Faulkner), Gustav von Seyffertitz (Professor Moriarty)...WILLIAM POWELL (FORMAN WELLS)

THE LAST COMMAND
Directed by Josef von Sternberg; Written by John F. Goodrich, based on a story by Lajos Biro; Produced by B.P. Schulberg

Cast
Emil Jannings (Grand Duke Sergius Alexander), Evelyn Brent (Natascha), WILLIAM POWELL (LEO ANDREYEV)

TYRONE POWER (1914-1958)

FIRST APPEARANCE: *Tom Brown of Culver* (Universal, 1932)

A STAR IS BORN: *Lloyd's of London* (20th Century-Fox, 1936)

In his first three films, Tyrone Power was billed with a "Jr." on the end of his name, to distinguish him from his father, a popular stage actor. After *Lloyd's of London* made Power 20th Century-Fox's most sought-after leading man, the clarification was no longer necessary. Power's blend of brash cocksureness and sensitivity made him the only actor to rival Errol Flynn as Hollywood's preeminent swashbuckler, and also served him well during forays into the western (*Jesse James*--1939) and film noir (*Nightmare Alley*--1947).

The first Tyrone Power was born in 1798; he was a celebrated comedian on the stages of Dublin, Ireland, and one of the first European actors to tour the United States. Tyrone Power II was born and raised in London, and became a matinee idol in England and on Broadway. Tyrone Edmund Power III was born in Cincinnati, Ohio. His poor health prompted a family move to the more temperate climate of San Diego, California. At the annual mission play in San Gabriel, Ty made his acting debut as a Mexican lad named Pablo in *La Golondrina*.

In 1923 the Power family returned to Cincinnati, where Tyrone Sr. worked in both Shakespearian drama and silent films, and his son ushered at a movie theatre where he could watch his father on the screen. Encouraging his son's acting ambitions, Power Sr. enrolled his son in drama and diction classes, and secured him a spot with a Shakespearian troupe. In 1931, father and son went to Hollywood, where Ty Sr. was to appear in a film called *The Miracle Man*. He collapsed on the set, and died in his son's arms. Power Jr. chose to remain in Hollywood, and after personal pitches at every casting office in town, he was given a small role in William Wyler's *Tom Brown of Culver*.

Set in the Culver Military Academy of Indiana, and featuring many of the actual cadets in minor roles, *Tom Brown of Culver* is a vivid account of one boy's maturation from unruly kid into model cadet. Tom Brown, the name of the actor and the main character, is traumatized after learning that his father, whom he had believed to be a decorated war hero, has confessed to desertion from the military. Shame compels Brown to drop out of the Academy, but after receiving the support of his friends he returns, and not only graduates but manages to change his father's status with an honorable discharge.

Some critics found the film's attention to the minute detail of Academy life to be detrimental to the story, but actually these scenes create an air of authenticity that heightens the drama. Tyrone Power plays cadet Donald MacKenzie, one of the less sympathetic members of Brown's class. He can be spotted frequently throughout the movie, whenever the cadets gather for inspections or meals. Power appropriately underplays the stern, by-the-book MacKenzie.

He donned military garb once more as an extra in *Flirtation Walk*, and then joined the stable of up-and-coming hopefuls signed by Darryl Zanuck at 20th Century-Fox. When female moviegoers began noticing Power in the background of *Girls' Dormitory* (1936) and *Ladies in Love* (1936), Zanuck moved the bobbysoxers' latest idol onto the studio's fast track. *Lloyd's of London*, an elaborate costume drama directed by Henry King, was set to begin production with Don Ameche and Loretta Young, until Zanuck decided to replace Ameche with Power. Young balked at the switch, and was then replaced herself by Madeleine Carroll.

However, it was child star Freddie Bartholomew who was top-billed as young Jonathan Blake, an earnest boy who stumbles upon a planned act of piracy, and reports the information to Lloyd's, the famous London insurance firm. Blake is given an apprenticeship with the firm after his notification prevents the crime. Power then takes over as Blake, who develops into one of Lloyds' most prominent investigators. He falls in love with Lady Elizabeth Stacy (Carroll), the wife of a slimy aristocrat who becomes his enemy after Lloyd's refuses to bail out his gambling debts.

Napoleon's war with England places the company in dire straits; Lady Elizabeth offers financial support, over her husband's vehement objections. Lord Stacy tries to ruin Lloyds by spreading rumors that Lord Nelson's victory over the French at Trafalgar, as reported by Nelson's friend Blake, never happened. At the last moment, confirmation of the outcome arrives to save the company. Lord Stacy dies in a duel with Blake, who is then joined with Lady Elizabeth for the requisite tidy ending.

The film's budget--$850,000--was the largest ever approved by the studio, and every dollar ended up on the screen. Any connection between the events depicted in *Lloyd's of London* and real life is purely accidental; however, the sumptuous sets and costumes are so diverting, and the story floats along so deftly, that its historical accuracy doesn't really matter. No studio could match Fox at these kind of period pieces during the 1930s--some critics even suggested that Zanuck change the company name to "16th Century-Fox."

For the first time, Tyrone Power had his chance to engage in the kind of roguish romancing and adventuring that provoked sacks of fan mail from lovestruck females. When his smoldering eyes melt Lady Stacy's courtly reserve, hearts swooned in theaters across the country. "Not in a long time has there been a player as dynamic and promising as Tyrone Power," raved the *Los Angeles Examiner*. Blake's opposition to the pompous ruling class, personified by Sanders' Lord Stacy, is a clear precursor to his spirited escapades in his classic remake of *The Mark of Zorro* (1940).

TOM BROWN OF CULVER
Directed by William Wyler; Written by Tom Buckingham and Clarence Marks, based on the story by George Green and Dale Van Every; Produced by Carl Laemmle, Jr.

Cast
Tom Brown (Tom Brown), H.B. Warner (Dr. Henry Brown), Slim Summerville (Elmer "Slim" Whitman), Richard Cromwell (Bob Randolph III), Ben Alexander (Cpl. John Clarke), Sidney Toler (Maj. Wharton)...TYRONE POWER, JR. (DONALD MACKENZIE)

LLOYD'S OF LONDON
Directed by Henry King; Written by Ernest Pascal and Walter Ferris, based on the story by Curtis Kenyon; Produced by Kenneth MacGowan;

Cast
Freddie Bartholomew (Young Jonathan Blake), Madeleine Carroll (Lady Elizabeth Stacy), George Sanders (Lord Stacy), TYRONE POWER (JONATHAN BLAKE), Sir Guy Standing (John Julius Angerstein), C. Aubrey Smith (Old "Q"), Virginia Field (Polly)

ELVIS PRESLEY (1935-1977)

FIRST APPEARANCE: *Love Me Tender* (20th Century-Fox, 1956)

A STAR IS BORN: *Love Me Tender*

Elvis Presley made 31 movies, all of them bad. And yet, his influence on the motion picture industry is monumental. In the days before Elvis, a young performer would be groomed, nurtured, trained in skills other than the ones he arrived with, and ultimately introduced in a worthy project with able support from writers, directors, composers and a seasoned supporting cast. Elvis proved that such careful supervision was no longer necessary. In almost every film he was saddled with an awful script, a ridiculous role as a singing frogman or a rock and roll surgeon, worse than formula songs like "No Room to Rhumba in a Sports Car," and support from such distinguished thespians as Stella Stevens and Yvonne Craig. But the tremendous Presley following followed their idol into movie after movie. His collective films grossed over $180 million, and transformed nine schlock soundtrack albums into gold.

Once the studio bean counters realized that movies could be built around one hot commodity with a minimum of effort and still make money, the floodgates opened for every top-40 singer with blemish-free skin. Pictures were created for Pat Boone, Tommy Sands and Tab Hunter, all of which made even Elvis's films look like Fellini by comparison. And just when you thought those innocent days were over, Whitney Houston propels a bit of fluff called *The Bodyguard* (1993) into a $100 million-plus take at the box office. The King is dead, according to most reliable sources, but his legacy lives on.

Elvis Presley's life is practically the stuff of folk hero myth and legend; he was born in Tupelo, Mississippi to Vernon and Gladys Presley, and had his first singing experiences in the choir of the local church. On his twelfth birthday Elvis received a guitar, and the heavens thundered in approval. In 1949 the family moved to Memphis, where Elvis graduated high school and became a truck driver for the Crown Electric Company. In 1953, he paid $4 to make a primitive recording of "My Happiness" as a birthday present for his mother. Sam Phillips, the president of the Sun Record Company, heard the record and discovered what he had previously thought only existed in his fantasies--a handsome young white singer whose vocal style merged African-American blues with country and gospel. Phillips signed Elvis to the Sun label, where he recorded "That All Right, Mama," and about thirty more songs that would lay the foundation of rock and roll.

A wheeler-dealer named Thomas Parker, known as the Colonel, recognized Elvis's potential and signed him to a personal appearance tour. A talent scout for RCA caught Elvis's Nashville performance and convinced his company to buy out the Sun Records contract. By May of 1956, seven of RCA's fifteen best-selling albums were recorded by Elvis. That same year, Hal Wallis Productions signed Elvis to a seven-year movie contract. His first film was to be called *The Reno Brothers*, but was rechristened *Love Me Tender* after one of the King's biggest hits.

The story is set in the waning days of the Civil War. Elvis plays Clint Reno, the youngest of four brothers and the only one who does not serve in the Confederate cause. When all three siblings return the family is shocked--Vance Reno (Richard Egan) was rumored to be dead. Of course they're glad that he's not, but when Vance sweeps longtime girlfriend Cathy (Debra Paget) into his arms, he learns that Cathy and Clint are married. More trouble visits the household when a government marshall accuses the brothers of stealing a federal payroll.

"In the first scene of his movie debut, Elvis was seen deep in the frame laboriously dragging a plow." wrote critic Doug Tomlinson, "In retrospect we can only marvel at how prophetic that shot was considering the material he was convinced to drag through movie theatres for the next 14 years." Indeed, *Love Me Tender* was the first of countless poor decisions that ruined Elvis's movie career. One can only wonder what Twentieth Century-Fox was thinking--here they had an artist who had established himself on the cutting edge of an exciting new musical art form, and they cast him in a Civil War costume drama? Elvis still gives his public what it wanted--at a town picnic he takes the stage, guitar in hand, and performs "Let Me" with all the swivels and gyrations that brought swooning and below-the-waist censorship on *The Ed Sullivan Show*. But the performance is so obviously anachronistic that he might as well be wearing a white sequined jumpsuit.

The only other moment worth mentioning from the competent but lackluster *Love Me Tender* is Elvis's performance of the title song. The scene transcends the movie, and is one of his few film moments in which the King's enormous talent and charisma are allowed to fully shine. The opening number from *Jailhouse Rock* (1957) is another. He was actually a capable actor as well, especially from *King Creole* (1958) on, and on those rare occasions when Elvis worked with a skillful director (Michael Curtiz on *Creole*, Don Siegel on 1960's *Flaming Star*) he turned in a fine performance. My personal choice as the best from a weak field is *Viva Las Vegas* (1964), co-starring Ann-Margret at her most va-voom. But when *Love Me Tender* recouped its $1 million cost in its first three days of release, there was little incentive to set a higher goal for Elvis Presley's cinema forays.

LOVE ME TENDER
Directed by Robert D. Webb; Written by Robert Buckner, based on a story by Maurice Geraghty; Produced by David Weisbart; Music by Lionel Newman, W.W. Fosdick, George R. Poulton, Vera Matson and Elvis Presley

Cast
Richard Egan (Vance), Debra Paget (Cathy), ELVIS PRESLEY (CLINT), Robert Middleton (Siringo), William Campbell (Brett), Neville Brand (Mike Gavin)

RONALD REAGAN (1911-   )

FIRST APPEARANCE: *Love Is On the Air* (Warner Bros./First National, 1937)

A STAR IS BORN: *Knute Rockne--All American* (Warner Bros., 1940)

One could reasonably argue, without intending a cheap shot, whether Ronald Reagan *ever* really became a star. In 1937, he made his film debut with the 'B'-movie unit at Warner Bros., and stayed there for most of his thirty-year career. The overwhelming majority of Reagan's film work consisted of quickly-made programmers, definitely mediocre but hardly as inept as detractors and liberals would have us believe. You don't get to make 53 films in Hollywood without talent, and it was Reagan's breezy, good-natured persona that often made an otherwise dismal film bearable. He was a prolific, well-known, respected journeyman actor, but stardom is something else entirely.

Ronald Reagan was born in 1911 into a family of hard-working, occasionally hard-drinking Irish Democrats. He enjoyed a wholesome and happy small town childhood, first in Tampico, Illinois and later in nearby Dixon, which if you obey the speed limit is about two hours south of Chicago. He worked as a lifeguard from age fourteen to age 21, and the muscles he built rescuing drowners led to an athletic scholarship to Eureka College. There Reagan became a football hero who also excelled in the school's dramatic society.

After graduation Reagan combined his two loves--sports and performing--by becoming a sportscaster for an Iowa radio station. He later joined station WHO in Des Moines, where he broadcast dozens of football and baseball games to a national audience. In February of 1937, Reagan traveled to California with the Chicago Cubs to cover their spring training season. He had contemplated trying his luck in Hollywood since college, and decided that now was the time.

The ease with which Reagan broke into movies will certainly make current hopefuls sick; he first contacted a nightclub singer named Joy Hodges, whom he had known in Iowa. She introduced him to an agent, who was impressed enough to arrange for a screen test at Warner Bros.. Four days later, studio chief Jack Warner saw the test and liked it. Reagan was signed to a seven-year contract at $200 a week. Four months later, Ronald Reagan walked onto the set of his first film, *Love Is On the Air*. He was top-billed, but the 61-minute film was low priority even at Warners' 'B'-unit, and there was no detectable publicity push behind the studio's newest leading man.

Reagan, then 26, played radio announcer Andy McLeod, a good first role considering his earlier broadcasting experience. The film was a remake of the 1934 release *Hi, Nellie*, which you haven't heard of either. Reagan had the role first played by Paul Muni, a crusading journalist whose tirades against organized crime endangers both his job and his life. *Variety* dispensed mild praise for the film's "rapid-prancing pace" and "pleasant characters," but assessed Reagan's performance as "in and out."

Reagan went immediately into *Hollywood Hotel* (1937), Susan Hayward's film debut, and convincingly earned his paycheck and eventual raise to $500 a week by appearing in twenty films over the next three years. He made occasional forays into better films, notably *Dark Victory* (1939) with Bette Davis, but these were exceptions. So when Warners gave the go-ahead to a film biography of legendary football coach Knute Rockne, and cast Pat O'Brien in the title role, the brass was reluctant to cast Reagan in the small but important role of George Gipp. The fact that making the film and casting O'Brien was actually Reagan's idea did not prevent the studio from auditioning ten other actors--it was only after Reagan showed up with photographs of himself in his college football uniform, and mentioned his athletic scholarship, that he was allowed to test for the part. Pat O'Brien rehearsed with Reagan at the test, a magnanimous gesture that Reagan always appreciated, and never forgot.

Knute Rockne--All American (1940) traces the coach's story from childhood to his playing days at Notre Dame, to his choice of football over a promising career in chemistry. He became the head coach at Notre Dame in 1918, and revolutionized football with his use of the forward pass and offensive-defensive substitutions. His life was tragically cut short by a plane crash in 1931. Rockne's most famous player was half-back George Gipp, who died of pneumonia after a brief but brilliant career. In the film Gipp appears only in the middle third; he is at first cocky about his abilities--when the coach asks him to run with the ball, he asks "How far?". But under Rockne's influence he becomes a better person as well as a better player.

Ronald Reagan makes the most of his supporting turn, especially in Gipp's moving deathbed scene; "Someday when the team is up against it," he tells O'Brien as Rockne, "ask them to go in there with all they've got, and win just one for the old Gipper." It is certainly Reagan's best-remembered moment in the movies, and a big reason why the *New York Times* hailed the film as "one of the best biographical picturizations ever turned out."

Reagan's career received a major boost after *Knute Rockne--All American*. It is no coincidence that a few months later he was appearing opposite Errol Flynn and Olivia deHavilland in the 'A'-list movie *Santa Fe Trail* (1940) The momentum he had started to build in Hollywood might have continued had he not been drafted later that year.

LOVE IS ON THE AIR
Directed by Nick Grinde; Written by Morton Grant, based on a story by Roy Chanslor; Produced by Bryan Foy

Cast
RONALD REAGAN (ANDY MCLEOD), Eddie Acuff (Dunk Glover), Robert Barrat (J.D. Harrington), June Travis (Jo Hopkins)

KNUTE ROCKNE--ALL AMERICAN
Directed by Lloyd Bacon; Written by Robert Buckner; Produced by Hal B. Wallis; Music by Ray Heindorf

Cast
Pat O'Brien (Knute Rockne), Gale Page (Bonnie Rockne), RONALD REAGAN (GEORGE GIPP), Donald Crisp (Father Callahan) Albert Basserman (Father Nieuwland)

ROBERT REDFORD (1937-)

FIRST APPEARANCE: *War Hunt* (United Artists, 1962)

A STAR IS BORN: *Butch Cassidy and the Sundance Kid* (20th Century-Fox, 1969)

Robert Redford, Hollywood's only male blond bombshell, fervently fought against handsome prince typecasting by playing characters with flaws that seemed incongruous with his clean-cut, all-American appearance. In *Downhill Racer* (1969) he played an Olympic skier who was only graceful on the slopes; in *The Candidate* (1972), Redford was utterly convincing as a politician who is all image and no substance. From *The Great Gatsby* (1974) to *Indecent Proposal* (1993), Redford seems drawn to characters with a surface elegance that cannot conceal a complex, impersonal soul. *Ordinary People* (1980), his directorial debut, covered similar territory and earned Redford his only Academy Award.

Born Charles Robert Redford in Santa Monica, California, Redford excelled in sports and what passed for teenage rebellion among the 1950s suburban middle-class. But when his mother died when Bob was eighteen, he began to turn his life around. He attended the University of Colorado on a baseball scholarship, and developed an interest in art. He left school to study painting in Paris and Florence, but gave up the starving artist life in 1958 and returned to Los Angeles.

A desire to learn theatrical scenic design brought Redford to the American Academy of Dramatic Arts in New York. He studied acting to learn about the stage and make some contacts, but showed such remarkable natural ability that he was encouraged to continue as a student. Two years later, Redford made his Broadway debut with a one-line part in *Tall Story* (1959). He appeared in over thirty television dramas between 1960 and 1964, building a sufficient reputation to earn offers from Hollywood. He accepted a supporting role in *War Hunt*, a powerful drama about the Korean confilct and its devastating effect on both the soldiers who fought and the civilians who are left behind.

Private Roy Loomis (Redford) joins a squad on the front lines of the war, where his notions of heroism are shattered by the harsh reality of life under fire. Pvt. Endore (John Saxon) leads the squad in enemy kills, but his late-night stalking and murdering of every North Korean he sees seem irreconcilable with his adopting of Charlie, an eight-year-old Korean orphan. Loomis suspects that Endore may be mentally ill, after he threatens to kill Loomis for speaking to Charlie. When a cease-fire is declared, Endore takes Charlie and flees. Loomis and two others track them down to a bombed-out bunker where Endore, now completely insane, attacks his own men. He is killed in the fight, and Charlie runs off into no-man's land, an orphan once again.

Redford is just one among the host of future notables who play minor roles in *War Hunt*, including Gavin MacLeod, Tom Skerritt, Francis Ford Coppola, who drives one of the army trucks, and director Sydney Pollack, who would later direct Redford in four films. The film was shot in three weeks for just $250,000, but since there weren't any huge battle scenes the schedule and budget limitations are not liabilities. The performances are meant to carry the movie, especially those of John Saxon and Robert Redford, and they succeeded well enough to earn the film a "minor masterpiece" endorsement in several reviews.

Saxon is downright scary as Endore, and one can only wonder why he could not build on the glowing notices he received for his extraordinary portrayal. Redford, playing the less flashy role, succeeds in making Loomis more than a naive recruit who is, in the words of the *New Yorker*, "all thumbs and milkfed intentions." In the character's many introspective moments, his quiet foreboding sustains the tense atmosphere that doesn't subside until the closing credits.

A contract dispute with the producer and director of *War Hunt* kept Redford off movie screens until 1965. He returned to Broadway, and scored his first major triumph playing the lead in Neil Simon's *Barefoot in the Park* (1963). Movie lawsuits settled, he appeared in *Situation Hopeless--But Not Serious* (1965), *Inside Daisy Clover* (1966), *The Chase* (1966) and *This Property is Condemned* (1966) before starring in the film adaptation of *Barefoot in the Park* (1967) opposite Jane Fonda. It was Redford's first big screen hit and first name-above-the-title credit. But it was his next film, the instant classic *Butch Cassidy and the Sundance Kid*, that established Robert Redford as a leading man.

Paul Newman plays the fast-talking outlaw Butch Cassidy, Redford plays his fast-drawing partner, the Sundance Kid. Together with the "Hole in the Wall" gang, they pull off a daring series of train robberies and bank heists in the waning days of the "wild west." After their fame puts too many lawmen on their heels, Butch and Sundance head for South America and continue their crime spree. Finally cornered in Bolivia by hundreds of soldiers, they plan another move to Australia, knowing full well that their trail has already come to an end.

William Goldman's Oscar-winning script was a superb blend of comedy, action and pathos, historically accurate in the essentials but embellished in its portrait of the two most likable outlaws ever seen at the movies. Butch and Sundance aren't portrayed as heroes or antiheroes; they're simply skilled professionals whose trade happens to be against the law. They enjoy their work immensely, and accept both the rewards and the pitfalls of the business with gracious good humor.

Paul Newman had been a movie superstar for ten years when he played Cassidy, and Redford landed in the same league with this one performance. So exuberant was the chemistry between Redford and Newman that they are still remembered as a great acting team, though they would costar just once more (in 1973's *The Sting*). A tremendous box-office hit, *Butch Cassidy and the Sundance Kid* announced Redford's arrival as the dashing "Golden Boy" of the 1970s, an image he has fought against ever since.

WAR HUNT
Directed by Denis Sanders; Written by Stanford Whitmore; Produced by Terry Sanders; Music by Bud Shank

Cast
John Saxon (Pvt. Raymond Endore), ROBERT REDFORD (PVT. ROY LOOMIS), Charles Aidman (Capt. Wallace Pratt), Sydney Pollack (Sgt. Van Horn), Gavin MacLeod (Pvt. Crotty), Tommy Matsuda (Charlie), Tom Skerritt (Cpl. Showalter)

BUTCH CASSIDY AND THE SUNDANCE KID
Directed by George Roy Hill; Written by William Goldman; Produced by Paul Monash and John Foreman; Music by Burt Bacharach, Hal David

Cast
Paul Newman (Butch Cassidy), ROBERT REDFORD (SUNDANCE KID), Katharine Ross (Etta Place), Strother Martin (Percy Garris), Henry Jones (Bike Salesman), Cloris Leachman (Agnes)

BURT REYNOLDS (1936-   )

FIRST APPEARANCE: *Angel Baby* (Allied Artists, 1961)

A STAR IS BORN: *Deliverance* (Warner Bros., 1972)

"(Burt) Reynolds could probably become a more substantial and important actor if he were willing to experiment more frequently with more ambitious roles."

How tired Reynolds must be of hearing assessments like this one, expressed by critic James M. Welsh, which have dogged his career since *Smokey and the Bandit* (1977) transformed him into America's favorite good ol' boy. Like a fourth-grader with a teacher's note saying he could do better than straight 'C's if only he'd apply himself, Reynolds has been branded a wasted talent. But in the late 1970s and early 1980s, no other actor could even approach his box-office appeal. He worked hard and he worked often, churning out 25 films between 1975 and 1985. Some were better than others, but every one of them made money. The loyalty and devotion of millions of moviegoers does not impress the serious cinephiles, however, who apparently require an apology from Reynolds for choosing light comic crowdpleasers over more profound fare, simply becuase he has the ability to play them both.

Born in Waycross, Georgia, and raised in West Palm Beach, Florida, Burt Reynolds was a rebellious kid who would pay a painful price for his antics from his father, the chief of police. Although he appeared in school plays, Burt gave better performances on the football field, and dreamed of being drafted in the NFL. He was an All-Southern Conference halfback, but when a knee injury destroyed his chances at a professional career, he dropped out of Florida State College and drifted into a succession of odd jobs.

In New York, Reynolds' interest in acting was rekindled, and he returned to Florida and enrolled in the drama department of Palm Beach Junior College. In 1958, after two successful college productions, he was signed by an agent, and made his New York City stage debut in a revival of *Mister Roberts*. He also made his television debut that year in an episode of *M Squad*. Thus began a decade of steady work during which Reynolds described himself as "a well-known unknown."

It was, in fact, television that really made Reynolds a celebrity, first in the short-lived series *Riverboat* (1959), which was followed by dozens of guest spots in different shows and then a three-year run on *Gunsmoke* (1962-1965) as blacksmith Quint Asper. He later played the title role in two different police dramas, *Hawk* (1966) and *Dan August* (1970), which were both canceled after one season.

Reynolds also appeared in nine films throughout the 1960s, none of which seemed to indicate that he had any future as a movie star. "My movies were the kind they show in airplanes and prisons, because nobody can leave," he told the *New York Post*. The first of these was *Angel Baby*, a southern Gothic pseudo-true story about the crusade of evangelist Jenny Angel. Salome Jens plays Angel, who sees the light after a tent show faith healer (George Hamilton) restores her ability to speak. Hoke Adams (Reynolds), her long-time boyfriend, cannot understand her newfound religious conviction, but when he discovers the profit potential in faith-healing he becomes Jenny's "manager." After being exploited by Hoke she is labeled a fake, but Jenny silences the doubters by curing a lame child.

Hoke is not like the lovable lawbreakers Reynolds would later play in *The Longest Yard* (1974) or *Smokey and the Bandit*. He is a genuine bad guy, a selfish, small-town bully with no redeeming qualities, who cannot accept that his days of sinning with Jenny are over. When Jenny tries to make him understand how her life has changed, Hoke tries to brutally rape her. It's an effective performance, more controlled and more convincing than others in the cast (including Mercedes McCambridge, way, way over the top as Hamilton's fanatical wife). I am tempted to point out that Reynolds should have played more heavies, but the last thing he needs is more what-might-have-beens.

Angel Baby was at best an average drama, though far superior to other early Reynolds films such as *Navajo Joe* (1967) and *Shark!* (1969). To revive his stalled movie career Reynolds returned again to television, where in 1971 he displayed his sharp, self-depracating sense of humor in several memorable *Tonight Show* appearances with Johnny Carson. "The talk shows... changed everything drastically overnight," he told critic Roger Ebert. "Suddenly I have a personality. People have heard of me." This newfound fame culminated in 1972 with Reynolds' notorious nude appearance in *Cosmopolitan* magazine, and a lead role in John Boorman's harrowing adventure film *Deliverance*.

The story begins innocently enough when four buddies (Reynolds, Ned Beatty, Jon Voight and Ronny Cox), leave their comfortable suburban homes for a weekend of canoeing on a river deep in the Appalachian wilderness. But there is an unsettling feeling about the trip from the very first day, as the foursome discover that they have drifted into an alien world. Has there ever been a more eerie musical number in a movie than the performance of "Dueling Banjos" in *Deliverance*? When Cox finishes trading licks with a retarded mountain boy, whose expression grows into a moronic grin and then fades instantly into an otherworldly deadpan, it's the first sign that the city boys are out of their element, and from then on Boorman's direction is relentless. Beatty and Cox are attacked and sexually molested by two inbred backwoods slimeballs before Reynolds and Voight catch up. They kill one of the molesters and drive the other off. The rest of the trip is one long ordeal that changes each man forever.

Burt Reynolds' career was built on characters who are in total control of themselves and their environment. Lewis, his character in *Deliverance*, starts out the same way; he is clearly the ringleader, and as the river journey begins he laughs at the danger of the rapids. Later, after being stalked by a rifle-toting hillbilly and seriously injured when his canoe capsizes, Lewis's bluster disappears. Reynolds is always believable as a hero, but when he becomes helpless and can only shriek in agony as his broken body is dragged over miles of rough water, he paints a moving picture of a man's ultimate struggle to survive. Reynolds earned his last round of unanimous critical praise to date for his powerful performance. "The movie was Reynolds' own deliverance," wrote *Time* magazine. "Overnight, he became the Frog Prince of Hollywood."

ANGEL BABY
Directed by Paul Wendkos; Written by Orin Borsten, Paul Mason and Samuel Roeca, based on the novel *Jenny Angel* by Elsie Oaks Barber; Produced by Thomas F. Woods; Music by Wayne Shanklin

Cast
George Hamilton (Paul Strand), Mercedes McCambridge (Sarah Strand), Salome Jens (Jenny Angel), Joan Blondell (Mollie Hays), Henry Jones (Ben Hays), BURT REYNOLDS (HOKE ADAMS)

DELIVERANCE
Directed and produced by John Boorman; Written by James Dickey, based on his novel; Music by Eric Weissberg

Cast
Jon Voight (Ed), BURT REYNOLDS (LEWIS), Ned Beatty (Bobby), Ronny Cox (Drew), Billy McKinney (Mountain Man)

DEBBIE REYNOLDS (1932-   )

FIRST APPEARANCE: *June Bride* (Warner Bros., 1948)

A STAR IS BORN: *Singin' In the Rain* (MGM, 1952)

What June Allyson was to MGM in the 1940s, Debbie Reynolds was to the 1950s--a sweet, pretty, spunky all-American girl who lent her spirited charm to a string of merry musicals. Her singing and dancing were not world class, but she was proficient enough to keep up with the studio's best. *Singin' In the Rain* has brought her immortality, but Reynolds' considerable comedic skills were not deployed until *The Tender Trap* three years later, and her greatest individual triumph came over a decade after *Singin' In The Rain*, when she earned an Oscar nomination for her dynamic performance in *The Unsinkable Molly Brown* (1964).

El Paso, Texas was home to Marie Frances Reynolds until she was eight years old, when her father was transferred by the Southern Pacific Railroad to California. The family settled in Burbank, where Marie excelled in sports, Girl Scout activities, baton twirling at John Burroughs High School and French horn in the Burbank Youth Symphony Orchestra. In 1948, Marie won the "Miss Burbank" contest, where she first displayed the talent for impressions that remains a staple of her nightclub act. Her performance of "My Rockin' Horse Ran Away" as Betty Hutton helped clinch the tiara.

A Warner Bros. talent scout saw her in the contest, and after a screen test Reynolds was signed as a contract player. Jack Warner changed her name to Debbie, which did not go down well with Marie. "I don't know how he came up with Debbie," Reynolds told the *Saturday Evening Post* in 1964, "I think he saw a dog across the street and asked its name." No one would ever call Debbie a dog, but the expression was applicable to the treatment she received at Warner Bros. for eighteen months.

Her film debut was as an extra in *June Bride*, a very funny class comedy starring Bette Davis and Robert Montgomery. Davis is Linda Gilman, the editor of a woman's magazine who takes her staff to Indiana in the dead of winter to prepare a story on a June bride. Montgomery is Carey Jackson, a hard news veteran and former flame of Linda's who is transferred against his will to her magazine. His attempt to write a puff piece about young love blossoming in the midwest is complicated when the bride runs off with the groom's brother. In the end Linda gets her story and then retires to join Carey on an overseas assignment.

The dialogue is clever, razor sharp and surprisingly racy for the time. It's a familiar story-- cynical New Yorkers look down on Indiana hicks, but come to appreciate their unpretentious ways (see *Groundhog Day* [1993] for latest variation), but the cast makes it work one more time. Bette Davis's wonderful way with a sardonic line makes you wish she did a few more comedies, and Robert Montgomery gives one of his best smart-aleck performances. His head-first dive into the snow after overdosing on "apple cider" is hilarious.

As for Debbie, she appears on screen for about two seconds as one of the girlfriends of the bride's younger sister, Boo (Betty Lynn). At the wedding near the end of the film, when the camera is behind the minister facing the happy couple, she can barely be glimpsed in the front row of the guests, fourth from the left. Don't blink. After playing an only slightly more distinguished role in *The Daughter of Rosie O'Grady* (1950) Reynolds was fired by Warner Bros. and immediately hired by MGM. She played one memorable scene in *Three Little Words* (1950) and then won the hearts of critics and audiences with her rendition of "Aba Daba Honeymoon" with Carleton Carpenter in *Two Weeks With Love* (1950).

Singin' In the Rain seemed a natural, logical step in her career progression, a supporting role larger than her last and in a higher-profile production. The film's emergence into the most popular musical ever made transformed that step into a quantum leap. The songs and dances are all beloved and instantly recalled, and the story is unusually substantive for a musical. The film is set in Hollywood in the 1920s, when the coming of sound sends the moviemaking industry into a panic. Silent screen star Don Lockwood (Gene Kelly) is able to make the transition to talkies, but his costar Lina Lamont (Jean Hagen) has a voice that could shatter glass, and her career is in jeopardy. Don falls for struggling young actress Kathy Selden (Debbie Reynolds) and when Lina hears Kathy sing she insists that Kathy dub her vocals. Don cannot stand to see Lina take credit for Kathy's talent, and exposes the scam.

That's the basic idea, but *Singin' In the Rain* is so much more. It is Kelly dancing through puddles in the most famous moment in the movie musical genre; it is Donald O'Connor hurling himself over couches and into walls singing "Make 'em Laugh." And it is Debbie Reynolds, all of nineteen years old, tapdancing between Kelly and O'Connor in the joyous "Good Morning" number, and matching the veteran hoofers every step of the way. Her singing voice on the ballad "You Are My Lucky Star" was dubbed by Betty Royce, but the other vocals are hers, the moves are hers, and her radiant smile and bubbly personality, which is what sent Kelly into his romp through the raindrops in the first place, is an integral part of the movie's success.

The only drawback to Debbie's participation in *Singin' In the Rain* was MGM's subsequent reluctance to cast her in anything more challenging. She was stuck in the ingenue role for too long, but she broke through eventually and in retrospect it's a small price for such a large dose of movie magic.

JUNE BRIDE
Directed by Bretaigne Windust; Written by Ranald MacDougall, based on the play by Eileen Tighe and Graeme Lorimer; Produced by Henry Blanke; Music by David Buttolph

Cast
Bette Davis (Linda Gilman), Robert Montgomery (Carey Jackson), Fay Bainter (Paula Winthrop), Betty Lynn (Boo Brinker), Tom Tully (Mr. Brinker), Barbara Bates (Jeanne Brinker)...DEBBIE REYNOLDS (BOO's FRIEND)

SINGIN' IN THE RAIN
Directed by Gene Kelly and Stanley Donen; Written by Adolph Green and Betty Comden; Produced by Arthur Freed; Music by Nacio Herb Brown, Arthur Freed, Adolph Green and Betty Comden

Cast
Gene Kelly (Don Lockwood), Donald O'Connor (Cosmo Brown), DEBBIE REYNOLDS (KATHY SELDEN), Jean Hagen (Lina Lamont), Rita Moreno (Zelda Zanders), Cyd Charisse (Dancer), Madge Blake (Dora Bailey)

JULIA ROBERTS (1967-   )

FIRST APPEARANCE: *Blood Red* (Hemdale, 1986)

A STAR IS BORN: *Pretty Woman* (Touchstone, 1990)

The next time someone says they don't make movie stars like they used to, mention Julia Roberts. If they're honest, they'll surrender the argument. Gone forever is the era when stars were larger-than-life personalities who didn't look like anyone who lived in your neighborhood, but Julia brings a bit of that magic back. She is beautiful, yes, with a megawatt smile that outshines the New York City skyline, but her multifarious appeal goes well beyond physical appearance. That elusive, ephemeral star quality, a glow from within that makes a potent, personal connection between the viewer and the actor on the screen, is more tangible in her than anyone else in movies today. Audiences have agreed to the tune of over $500 million, the combined gross of a half-dozen movies that have made Roberts the first bankable actress of the 1990s.

She was the youngest of three children born in Smyrna, Georgia, to Walter and Betty Roberts, the operators of an actors workshop in Atlanta. It was not surprising to her family that Julia would inherit what Betty called "the family disease," but it was her brother Eric that broke through first after terrific performances in *King of the Gypsies* (1978) and *Star 80* (1983). Julia, meanwhile, was taking acting classes in New York, and paying the bills by modeling. In 1986, Eric signed on to a low-budget drama entitled *Blood Red*. As casting progressed on the less important roles, director Eric Masterson recalled in *People* magazine the day Roberts approached him with an offer; "I've got this sister. Is it O.K. if she *plays* my sister?"

Apparently it was, as Julia was cast as Maria Collogero in a movie seen by less people than the total population of her tiny hometown. Set in California's Napa Valley in the late 1800s, *Blood Red* follows the treacherous tactics used by evil railroad baron W.B. Berrigan to run a community of Sicilian immigrants off their farmland. But the "hard-headed grape growers," led by the idealistic Sebastiano Collogero (Giancarlo Gianinni), refuse to sell. The dispute turns violent, and after Sebastiano is killed his son Marco (Eric Roberts) swears vengeance--that's the Sicilian way.

To watch the smoldering eyes and buffed physique of Eric Roberts, who makes an effective rebel hero in *Blood Red*, is to wonder why his career did not survive the 1980s. The novelty of watching a real brother and sister play a brother and sister does not sustain the first half of this rather tedious film, but there is some fun to be had in watching Dennis Hopper, as Berrigan, trying out an awful Irish accent that he obviously learned from Lucky Charms commercials. After Sebastiano's murder, however, the film does pick up considerably, though the occasional Julia Roberts sighting has no bearing on this improvement. She is in the background of several scenes, but has just three discernible lines and no effect whatsoever on the unfolding of the plot. It's exactly the kind of no-damage role an untested actress might be allowed to play through nepotism. If you're watching the film to see her, the wait will be brief-- Julia appears just after the opening credits, and at occasional intervals throughout the first hour.

Mystic Pizza (1988), a wonderful, underrated coming-of-age film, brought Julia Roberts her first good reviews. As town flirt Daisy Araujo, she flaunted her natural sensuality, and stole every scene she was in. That led to a plum assignment as one of six modern-day southern belles in the seriocomic talkfest *Steel Magnolias* (1989). *People* rightly summed up the film as "a sappy, melodramatic *Terms of Endearment Goes South*," but Roberts was singled out for praise and an Academy Award nomination for Best Supporting Actress.

Steel Magnolias got her noticed, but in a pedigree crowd that included Sally Field, Shirley MacLaine and Dolly Parton, Roberts' greatest achievement was just keeping up. The jump from "faces to watch" to the select company of actresses who can open a movie happened with Roberts' next film, *Pretty Woman*. The old *Pygmalion* plot is brushed off once again, this time combined with an uplifting "money can't buy you love" twist that was as clear a signal as any that the '80s were over.

Roberts plays Vivian Ward, a Hollywood Boulevard hooker who pokes her head into the window of an expensive car driven by Edward Lewis (Richard Gere), a multi-millionaire corporate raider. Lewis needs directions back to Beverly Hills, and Vivian shows him the way for twenty bucks. Facing a week of business dinners and social engagements, he offers to buy her services as an escort. The symbolism in a romance between a corporate raider and a prostitute was not exactly subtle; "We both screw people for a living," says Lewis, just in case anybody missed it. But by the end of the movie Vivian has left the business, and Edward lets a fortune get away by choosing to help a struggling company rather than take it over. Their future is threatened by the tough facade that both have developed as an occupational requirement, but deep down they're really nice people, and they land inevitably in each other's arms in the kind of fairy tale ending that was in short supply at the time.

Pretty Woman became *the* date movie of 1990, and one of the biggest surprise success stories of the year. Richard Gere shows an unexpected flair for romantic comedy, but the film belongs to Julia, and it's been so long since moviegoers have seen her kind of magnetism that they can be forgiven for confusing it with brilliant acting. Still, Roberts proves herself a talented comedienne, and her performance is genuinely charming and delightful, as irresistible as the movie itself. When, after the Pygmalion transformation is complete, Vivian reappears in a stunning black cocktail dress, smiling a smile so wide that her face seems hardly able to contain it, we understand.

BLOOD RED
Directed by Peter Masterson; Written by Ron Cutler; Produced by Judd Bernard and Patricia Casey; Music by Carmine Coppola

Cast
Eric Roberts (Marco Collogero), Giancarlo Gianinni (Sebastiano), Dennis Hopper (W.B. Berrigan)...JULIA ROBERTS (MARIA COLLOGERO)

PRETTY WOMAN
Directed by Garry Marshall; Written by J.F. Lawton; Produced by Arnon Milchan and Steven Reuther; Music by James Newton Howard

Cast
Richard Gere (Edward Lewis), JULIA ROBERTS (VIVIAN WARD), Ralph Bellamy (James Morse), Jason Alexander (Philip Stuckey), Laura San Giacomo (Kit De Luca), Alex Hyde-White (David Morse)

EDWARD G. ROBINSON (1893-1973)

FIRST APPEARANCE: *Arms and the Woman* (Pathe`-Gold, 1916)

A STAR IS BORN: *Little Caesar* (First National/Vitaphone, 1931)

There were gangster movies before *Little Caesar*, but nobody paid much attention to them. It was Edward G. Robinson's riveting performance as Rico Bandello that made the tommy gun-toting, tough-talking, sharp-dressed gangster as popular with movie audiences as the cowboy, and established Warner Bros.' domination of the genre for the next twenty years.

"I was born when I came to America," Robinson would say when reflecting on his childhood, but he was actually born Emanuel Goldenberg in Bucharest, Rumania, and when he was nine he emigrated with his family to New York. Emanuel, or Manny as his brothers called him, first contemplated becoming a rabbi and then a lawyer, until he discovered acting in his junior year of high school. In 1910 he entered City College of New York, and the following year he earned a scholarship to the American Academy of Dramatic Arts. Advised to change his name to something more Anglo-Saxon, he chose Edward G. (to keep his initials) and added the "Robinson" on a whim.

It was Robinson's natural talent for ethnic dialects that first brought him to Broadway. In the play *Under Fire* (1915), he played a French soldier, a Belgian patriot, a German, and a Cockney Englishman. In subsequent plays he would appear as a Canadian and a Japanese, earning the nickname "the League of Nations."

He made his film debut as an extra in *Arms and the Woman*, a silent screen drama that is now best remembered for several documentary style scenes of New York in 1916. Mary Nash stars as Rozika, a Hungarian immigrant who loses her singing job at a rundown cafe` after her brother, Carl (Carl Harbaugh) kills a man during a brawl. Reduced to singing on street corners, she is lifted from the gutter by wealthy steel manufacturer David Fravoe (Lumsden Hare), who turns Rozika into a famous opera star. After World War I erupts in Europe, Carl is ordered by the anarchist group that sheltered him from the law to blow up Fravoe's munitions factory. Rozika tries to warn her husband, but is too late to prevent the destruction.

Arms and the Woman exists only in fragments today, but footage of Edward G. Robinson as a worker in Fravoe's factory has survived. He is only a face in the crowd, but is clearly visible in the scene when the workers gather around Fravoe; Robinson, standing right-center in the foreground of the frame, wears an all-dark suit and cap, and listens intently to the heated discussion in progress. Besides Robinson, only star Mary Nash emerged from the cast into a noteworthy career. She appeared opposite Shirley Temple in *Heidi* (1937), and played Katharine Hepburn's mother in *The Philadelphia Story* (1940).

Robinson served a brief stint in the Navy, and then returned to the Broadway stage. Seven years later, he appeared with Dorothy Gish, Richard Barthelmess and Mary Astor in *The Bright Shawl* (1923), which some sources list as his film debut. In 1927, Robinson played a gangster on stage in *The Racket*, and was heralded as a dynamic new Broadway star. It was during the play's Los Angeles run that Robinson was again wooed by the movies. He played tough bad guys in three 1930 releases, *Night Ride, Outside the Law* and *The Widow From Chicago*, but when *Little Caesar* was released it was still seen as a revelation.

The book by William R. Burnette elevated its mob leader, Cesare Enrico Bandello, into a classic villain in the tradition of Macbeth and Richard III--an intelligent but ruthless man, blinded by the ambition that ultimately leads to his destruction. The script was altered at Robinson's request to preserve the character as originally conceived, while satisfying the cheap-thrill requirements expected from a shoot-'em-up. The result was a prototype that cast a shadow over every gangster film that followed.

Rico and his partner Joe Massara (Douglas Fairbanks Jr.) join a gang led by Sam Vettori (Stanley Fields). Rico rises quickly through the ranks and eventually deposes Vettori as the gang's leader. After he is betrayed by Joe's girlfriend (Glenda Farrell), his power and success evaporate, but Rico, who has gunned down dozens of men with cold-blooded indifference, cannot bring himself to kill his friend. His moment of conscience proves fatal--Rico is reduced to living in flophouses, and he is branded a coward in the newspapers for failing to confront outspoken police lieutenant Tom Flaherty (Thomas Jackson). The story, planted by Flaherty, draws Rico out of hiding. After a brief last stand in a deserted street, the man dubbed "Little Caesar" dies in a hail of bullets.

Time magazine described Robinson's performance as "the supreme embodiment of a type." Director Mervyn LeRoy deserves an assist for his novel correction of Robinson's habit of blinking every time he fired a gun; the problem was solved by affixing transparent pieces of tape to the actor's eyelids. Rico's wide-eyed, intense stare during a fight gave the impression that he was not only comfortable with violence, he enjoyed it.

Under LeRoy's waste-no-time and take-no-prisoners direction, *Little Caesar* barrels through a lot of story in 77 minutes. Edward G. Robinson became a star at the age of 37, and gave every impressonist an addition to the repertoire with his snarling delivery. His dying words, "Mother of mercy! Is this the end of Rico?" have found their way into many a nightclub act.

ARMS AND THE WOMAN
Directed by George Fitzmaurice; Written by Ouida Bergere

Cast
Mary Nash (Rozika), Lumsden Hare (David Fravoe), H. Cooper Cliffe (Captain Halliday), Robert Broderick (Marcus), Carl Harbaugh (Carl)...EDWARD G. ROBINSON (Factory Worker)

LITTLE CAESAR
Directed by Mervyn LeRoy; Written by Robert N. Lee and Darryl Zanuck, Francis Edward Faragoh and Robert Lord, based on the novel by William R. Burnette; Produced by Darryl Zanuck; Music by Erno Rapee

Cast
EDWARD G. ROBINSON (CESARE ENRICO BANDELLO), Douglas Fairbanks Jr. (Jos Massara), Glenda Farrell (Olga Strassoff), William Collier Jr. (Tony Passa), Stanley Fields (Sam Vettori), Sidney Blackmer (The Big Boy)

GINGER ROGERS (1911-1995)

FIRST APPEARANCE: *Young Man of Manhattan* (Paramount, 1930)

A STAR IS BORN: *Flying Down to Rio* (RKO, 1933)

Say "Fred Astaire" in a game of word association, and the most frequent response will probably be "Ginger Rogers." A discussion of Astaire's many dance partners will exalt the grace of Rita Hayworth, the long-legged beauty of Cyd Charisse, the ballet training of Audrey Hepburn and the athleticism of Eleanor Powell, but with Ginger Rogers, an element of magic was created that transcends all the standard evaluations of dance. As a legacy that's not bad, but Rogers also earned a Best Actress Academy Award for her dramatic performance in *Kitty Foyle* (1940), and as a comedienne her blend of refinement and brass was the equal of Carole Lombard and Jean Arthur.

The marriage of Eddins and Lela McMath of Independence, Missouri was not a happy one, before or after the birth of their daughter, Virginia. When Lela left her husband and petitioned for divorce, Eddins kidnapped Virginia twice. After that, he was forbidden by law to see his family. When Virginia was five, Lela began a successful career as a screenwriter, prompting a move to New York City. The Fox Film Corporation was interested in grooming Virginia as a new child star, but her mother would not allow it, having witnessed first hand what happens to most child stars after they grow up.

Virginia's earliest ambition was to be a pianist, but after appearing at age eleven in an amateur production of *To a Wild Rose*, show business became another possibility. In 1925, she won an amateur Charleston contest, and formed an act with the two runners-up that was billed as "Ginger and her Redheads." The nickname "Ginger" had its origin in the way her baby cousin pronounced "Virginia," and became her professional name during the vaudeville tour that followed her contest victory. She stayed on the circuit until 1929, building a reputation as a talented singer, dancer and comedienne.

As Ginger Rogers, she made her Broadway debut in the musical *Top Speed* (1929), earning glowing reviews and a screen test offer from Paramount Pictures. She had earlier appeared in three 1929 short films, *Campus Sweethearts*, *A Night In a Dormitory*, and *A Day Of a Man of Affairs*, but made her feature film debut in the musical romance *Young Man of Manhattan*.

New York newspaper reporters Ann Vaughn (Claudette Colbert) and Toby McLean (Norman Foster) fall in love while covering the Gene Tunney-Jack Dempsey fight, but their whirlwind marriage after a brief courtship is soon on the rocks. Toby becomes jealous of Ann's success as a magazine writer, and finds solace with flighty socialite Puff Randolph (Ginger Rogers). When Ann is stricken blind after drinking tainted alcohol in Toby's apartment, Toby rushes back to her side. Ann recovers her eyesight, and reconciles with her husband.

Claudette Colbert and Norman Foster were top-billed, but Ginger Rogers and Charlie Ruggles, who plays Puff's occasional boyfriend, garnered most of the favorable notices. A brunette in her film debut, Ginger plays a slightly more lowbrow version of the sassy society girl who turned Fred Astaire's head in *Swing Time* (1936) and *Carefree* (1938). Her exclamation "Cigarette me, Big Boy!" became a catch-phrase, and her performance of "I've Got 'It' but 'It' Don't Do Me No Good" is as close to a highlight as exists in *Young Man of Manhattan*. "(Rogers) came within an ace of purloining the picture," wrote *Hollywood Filmograph*.

She followed her debut with a handful of equally undistinguished films, and then returned to Broadway, where she introduced the George Gershwin song "But Not for Me," in the musical *Girl Crazy* (1930). Fred Astaire, who was then appearing down the street in another musical called *Smiles*, was called in to help choreograph one dance routine, and it was then that he first met Ginger Rogers.

Ginger made nineteen films between 1930 and 1933. *Forty-Second Street* (1933) was the most successful, and it was Ginger's performance as "Anytime Annie" that RKO executives remembered when casting began on *Flying Down to Rio*. Dolores Del Rio and Gene Raymond were the stars, and Arline Judge was given the supporting role of Honey Hale. Then Fred Astaire was signed by RKO and joined the film, and Judge was replaced by Ginger Rogers. Thus began a partnership that would have no peer in the movie musical.

The barely-there story involves orchestra leader Roger Bond (Raymond), who takes his talented troupe to Rio to work at a large resort hotel. There, Roger tries to romance Latin beauty Belinha de Rezende (Del Rio) and fend off competition from the dashing Julio Rubeiro (Raul Roulien). In *Rio*'s one legendary scene, Honey Hale and Fred Ayres (Astaire) are seated in a nightclub when the band begins playing a rhumba-like dance called The Carioca. "We'll show them a thing or three," says Honey, as she and Fred join the dancers on stage.

It was the only number performed by Astaire and Rogers in the film, but critical and public response was instant and overwhelming. Even the finale, when a chorus line of blond bombshells (led by Ginger) dance on the wing of a bi-plane as it flies into Rio, could not supplant The Carioca as the film's most memorable moment. One year later, Astaire and Rogers reteamed in *The Gay Divorcee*, and their names were linked forevermore.

YOUNG MAN OF MANHATTAN
Directed by Monta Bell; Written by Robert Presnell and Daniel Reed, based on a novel by Katherine Brush; Music by Irving Kahal, Pierre Norman and Sammy Fain

Cast
Claudette Colbert (Ann Vaughn), Norman Foster (Toby McLean), GINGER ROGERS (PUFF RANDOLPH), Charles Ruggles (Shorty Ross)

FLYING DOWN TO RIO
Directed by Thornton Freeland; Written by Cyril Hume, H.W. Hanemann and Erwin Gelsey, based on a play by Anne Caldwell from an original story by Lou Brock; Produced by Lou Brock; Music by Vincent Youmans, Edward Eliscu and Gus Kahn

Cast
Dolores Del Rio (Belinha de Rezende), Gene Raymond (Roger Bond), Raul Roulien (Julio Rubeiro), GINGER ROGERS (HONEY HALE), Fred Astaire (Fred Ayres)

MICKEY ROONEY (1920-   )

FIRST APPEARANCE: *Not to Be Trusted* (Fox, 1926)

A STAR IS BORN: *A Family Affair* (MGM, 1937)

By the time he was five years old, Mickey Rooney had already gone through three different stage names. The quintessential show business kid, Rooney made his stage debut at the age of 17 months, and replaced Clark Gable as America's top box-office draw while still a teenager. His talent seems as limitless as his enthusiasm; as an actor, singer, comedian, dancer and musician, Rooney's obvious love for performing seems barely contained by the movie screen.

Joe and Nell Carter Yule were popular vaudeville entertainers, who appeared together in a musical act under the name Yule and Carter. Their son, Joe Yule, Jr., was born in Brooklyn, and spent his infancy backstage, on tour with his parents. While still in diapers, he donned a tuxedo, sucked on a big rubber cigar, and appeared on stage as a midget. He learned to sing when he learned to talk, and his rendition of "Pal of My Cradle Days" became part of the act.

After his parents separated in 1924, Joe Yule, Jr. moved to Hollywood with his mother, and began his film career by recreating his stage role as a midget in the two-reeler *Not to Be Trusted*. The storyline centered on a gang of criminals consisting of a con man, a burglar and a midget. Dressed in a curly blond wig and a velvet, Little Lord Fauntleroy suit, the midget pretends to be an orphan, who is taken in by a wealthy couple. Once inside their mansion, he helps the gang clean out the valuables.

At five years old, Joe Yule, Jr. was so convincing at playing a midget that he was treated like one on the set. Instead of using a fake cigar, the crew gave him an actual stogie. Nautious but undeterred, he played the scenes and was good enough to land another midget role in *Orchids and Ermine* (1927), his official feature film debut. But when casting calls for midgets proved to be few and far between, Yule tried acting his age, and it paid off in a series of popular short films based on a Fontaine Fox comic strip about a precocious tyke named Mickey McGuire. His mother wanted to change his name legally to Mickey McGuire, but when the character's creator objected, it was changed to Mickey Rooney.

From 1927 to 1932, Rooney appeared in 80 episodes of the McGuire series, and then appeared in a variety of films, most notably as Puck in *A Midsummer Night's Dream* (1935), before signing a contract with MGM in 1934. In between assignments, he attended school on the lot with Lana Turner, Deanna Durbin and Judy Garland.

A Family Affair was the third of six films Rooney made in 1937, and was not given much hope by the studio. The star, Lionel Barrymore, felt rather indignant about being ordered into a sixty-minute programmer, but dutifully honored his contract and was cast as Judge Hardy, patriarch of the Hardy family from the happy, small town of Carvel. Spring Byington played his wife, and Rooney played his eldest son, Andy.

The judge is in hot water as the movie opens; a Carvel citizens committee is outraged at the restraining order issued by Hardy to prevent construction of a new aqueduct. He faces more trouble at home when his daughter, Marian, arrives with news that her marriage is on the rocks. Through faith, and love, honesty, and the type of simple homespun common sense that is too often ridiculed in contemporary movies, all problems are solved and life in Carvel returns to its idyllic norm.

Shot in fifteen days, the film was released in April of 1937, and was considered such a non-event that *Variety* didn't even print a review. Critics who bothered to take notice found *A Family Affair* pleasant but unspectacular. Hard to tell, then, who was more shocked when the film earned over half a million dollars at the box-office, and became one of MGM's most popular films of the year. Audiences and exhibitors clamored for "another Hardy picture," and the studio obliged, though at the time sequels to successful movies were still rare occurrences.

Lewis Stone replaced Barrymore as Judge Hardy, Fay Holden assumed the role of Mrs. Hardy, and Ann Rutherford was added to the cast as Polly Benedict. Mickey Rooney was not replaced. In a handful of otherwise unremarkable scenes, he stole *A Family Affair* from Barrymore, and his role was expanded accordingly in future installments. The titles of later entries, such as *Love Finds Andy Hardy* (1938) and *Andy Hardy Gets Spring Fever* (1939) left no doubt as to who audiences were paying to see. The fifteen films in the series were a huge money-maker for MGM and, as a result of Mickey Rooney's infectious charm and energy, the name Andy Hardy has become a synonym for American teenager.

NOT TO BE TRUSTED
Directed by George E. Marshall; Written by Murray Roth, based on a story by Mabel Herbert Urner

Cast
Bud Jamison, MICKEY ROONEY

A FAMILY AFFAIR
Directed by George B. Seitz; Written by Kay Van Riper, based on the play *Skidding* by Aurania Rouverol; Produced by Lucien Hubbard and Samuel Marx; Music by David Snell

Cast
Lionel Barrymore (Judge Hardy), MICKEY ROONEY (ANDY HARDY), Cecilia Parker (Marian Hardy), Eric Linden (Wayne Trenton), Charley Grapewin (Frank Redmond), Spring Byington (Mrs. Hardy), Margaret Marquis (Polly Benedict)

JANE RUSSELL (1921-   )

FIRST APPEARANCE: *The Outlaw* (Howard Hughes/RKO, 1943)

A STAR IS BORN: *The Outlaw*

In her autobiography *My Path and My Detours*, Jane Russell wrote "I honestly feel sorry if *The Outlaw* publicity campaign was responsible for the young girls who decided that the only way to make it in show business was to shove out their bosom." Hollywood's "anything goes" atmosphere has been prevalent since the late 1970s, so it seems amazing now that Jane Russell's cleavage could be the principal attraction of more than one feature film. The publicity blitz that preceded *The Outlaw*'s premiere was built around photos of its star in a low-cut blouse, reclining in a haystack. These days, you can see more exposure on network television during the family hour, but back then the times had not yet a'changed, so *The French Line* (1954) could still make money by presenting Jane's bosom in 3-D, and *Underwater!* (1955) was promoted by photos of Jane wearing a swimsuit. To her credit, however, she did develop (no pun intended) into a capable actress, and on those rare occasions when Russell was offered quality material, such as *Gentlemen Prefer Blondes* (1953), more than her bustline rose to the occasion.

Jane Russell was born in Bemidji, Minnesota, near her grandparents' summer home. She moved with her parents to Canada and then to Glendale, California before her first birthday. Her father, an office manager for the company that made Woodbury Soap, was one of the lucky few who worked steadily throughout the Depression. Her mother was a retired actress with a few stage credits, including the road company of *Daddy Longlegs*. Both parents were devout Christians who instilled their values in Jane and her four younger siblings.

After graduating high school, Jane chose a dramatic school over her mother's choice of a finishing school, but spent most of her time at the bowling alley across the street. She later switched to an academy run by actress Maria Ouspenskaya. She was still vacillating between mild interests in acting and fashion design on the day her career unintentionally began. A friend of Jane's was offered a job posing for cheesecake photos. Jane accompanied her to the studio of photographer Tom Kelley, and was soon posing in swimsuits as well. Kelley used the photos to set up some screen tests, but Paramount thought Jane was "too tall," and Twentieth Century-Fox dismissed her as "unphotogenic." Since she had no burning desire to become an actress, Russell took the rejections in stride.

It was many weeks later that Levis Green, a casting agent for Howard Hughes, noticed the photos in Kelley's studio. Hughes was readying his production of *The Outlaw*, and was looking the right girl to play Rio, the fiery mistress of gunslinger Doc Holliday. Nineteen-year-old Jane screen-tested with the soon to be infamous haystack scene, in which Rio is raped by Billy the Kid. She beat out four other actresses for the role, but was only signed to a stock contract paying $50 a week.

The film is a wholly fictional account of the friendship between Billy the Kid (Jack Beutel) and Doc Holliday (Walter Huston), and their battles with Sheriff Pat Garrett (Thomas Mitchell). Although they meet after Billy steals Doc's horse, a mutual respect quickly surfaces. Rio tries to kill Billy for shooting her brother years earlier, but he survives only to be shot by Garrett. Rio is ordered by Doc to tend his wound, and they fall in love. Doc graciously steps aside, and helps them escape one step ahead of Garrett's posse.

The Outlaw was to be directed by the great Howard Hawks, but when Hughes was displeased with the rough footage he decided to direct the film himself. His inexperience and perfectionism combined to torture the cast with endless retakes. The scene in which Billy talks to Doc's grave was shot 103 times before Hughes was content. As a result, a routine western of the kind that Republic Pictures churned out in two weeks took nine months to complete. And even longer to release. The almighty Hays Office demanded eleven minutes of cuts, all of which involved Jane Russell. Her blouses were too low, and her method of "nursing" Billy back to health was a bit too overt. Hughes resisted the cuts for two years, but in 1943 he relented and *The Outlaw* finally opened in a few major cities (general release was delayed until 1946).

Billed as "The picture that couldn't be stopped," *The Outlaw* did turnaway business. Billboards of Jane Russell posing seductively carried the captions "Sex has not been rationed" and "What are the two reasons for Jane Russell's stardom?" Hughes's five-figure investment in advertising helped the film overcome disastrous reviews--"Beyond the sex attraction of Miss Russell's frankly displayed charms, picture, according to accepted screen entertainment standards, falls short," wrote *Variety*. *The New York Times* saved its most severe prose for Russell--"While she is undeniably decorative in low-cut blouses, she is hopelessly inept as an actress."

As more than one wag commented, the only thing flat about Russell was her performance. And though Rio was supposed to be a poor frontier trollop, she managed to make more costume changes than Diana Ross at Caesars Palace, which only drew more attention to the reason she was hired. Jack Beutel's lanky, rail-thin appearance and slow, genial Southern drawl were reminiscent of a young Jimmy Stewart, but his line-readings were not. Walter Huston emerged best as Doc Holliday.

Over forty years later, *The Outlaw*'s scandalous reputation persists. Its running time was 122 minutes, but most video prints run 95 minutes and do not include the excised scenes. Though interest in them now is more historic than prurient, these scenes remain the only reason to see the film.

THE OUTLAW
Directed and produced by Howard Hughes; Written by Jules Furthman; Music by Victor Young

Cast
Jack Beutel (Billy the Kid), JANE RUSSELL (RIO), Thomas Mitchell (Pat Garrett), Walter Huston (Doc Holliday), Mimi Aguglia (Guadalupe)

ROSALIND RUSSELL (1908-1976)

FIRST APPEARANCE: *Evelyn Prentice* (MGM, 1934)

A STAR IS BORN: *The Women* (MGM, 1939)

The one movie that I personally treasure above all others is *His Girl Friday* (1940). Howard Hawks' frenetic remake of *The Front Page* ranks with the best comedies ever made, and features unforgettable, take-no-prisoners performances from Cary Grant and Rosalind Russell. Hawks we know is a genius and Cary Grant can do anything, but Russell's performance is the one that grows more impressive with every repeat viewing. Her timing is absolutely flawless in breakneck scenes that would give a lesser actress whiplash. After rising to prominence a year earlier in *The Women, His Girl Friday* confirmed that Russell has no peer in playing a fast-talking, caustic career woman.

Born and raised in Waterbury, Connecticut, Rosalind was constantly fighting for attention among her six brothers and sisters. She was nicknamed "Railroad" by her father because of her "R.R." initials, but the name also fit her loud, outgoing, athletic personality. She was educated in Catholic schools, where she was a frequent source of mischief, and then enrolled in the American Academy of Dramatic Arts. After graduating in 1929, Russell gave herself five years to make it as an actress.

She talked her way into a position with a stock company based in the upstate New York town of Sarnac Lake, and after one season she made her Broadway debut in the musical comedy *Garrick Gaieties*. In 1934, a representative from Universal paid her way to Hollywood, where Russell was offered a contract after nine screen tests. She thought about signing, but at the last minute accepted a better offer from MGM. Her first assignment was a small ingenue role in *Evelyn Prentice*, a classy courtroom melodrama.

Workaholic attorney John Prentice (William Powell), successfully defends accused murderess Nancy Harrison (Russell), and collects more than a fee in return. His wife Evelyn (Myrna Loy) learns about the brief affair, and begins accepting lunch invitations from Lawrence Kennard (Harvey Stephens), a lovestruck poet. The Prentices reconcile, but then Kennard tries to blackmail Evelyn, and is found murdered.

Evelyn Prentice is a piquant little soap opera that is expertly played by Powell and Loy. This was their third joint venture, and once again they play a chic society couple, but don't expect the same playful sparks generated in *The Thin Man* (1934). Embroiled in illicit romance, blackmail and murder, the Prentices do not glide through their troubles like Nick and Nora Charles, but their level-headed lack of histrionics is just as refreshing. Loy's controlled desperation is especially moving, as is her breakdown during an exciting courtroom climax with an unexpected twist.

The film rates all of one paragraph in Rosalind Russell's 250-page autobiography, *Life is a Banquet*, which is a good indication of its impact on her career. Although fourth-billed, she appears only in three early scenes, and figures little in the main plot. Nancy Harrison is timid, vulnerable and soft-spoken, everything Russell was not, but she plays the unremarkable role proficiently. The only laughs in the film are provided by Una Merkel as Evelyn's fun-loving best friend, the kind of role that would be described as a "Roz Russell type" after *His Girl Friday*.

Russell settled comfortably into what she called the "second echelon" of MGM's roster, working steadily in some good films such as *The Citadel* (1938), but rarely to her best advantage. After twenty films, she saw her chance to finally play comedy in *The Women*, but MGM, who "tested everyone but Lassie and Mrs. Roosevelt" according to *Life is a Banquet*, did not send her a script. Russell fought hard for a chance and when it came, she joined the all-star cast after staggering director George Cukor with a dynamic presentation.

The film was written by two women--Anita Loos and Jane Murfin--and not one man appears on screen in the entire running time. A feminist statement? Not even close. Norma

Shearer and Joan Fontaine do play intelligent, refined ladies, but the rest, as played by Russell, Joan Crawford and Paulette Goddard among others, are gossips and golddiggers, made of brass and full of sass; "There's a word for you ladies," says Crawford late in the film, "but it is seldom used in high society, outside of a kennel."

In the opening credits, each character is depicted as a different member of the animal kingdom. Russell, as Sylvia Fowler, is a cat, and her catty behavior begins when she learns about the infidelity of a friend's husband. She is on the phone instantly dishing all the gory details to anyone who'll listen. When she flashes her new "jungle red" nail polish, another cohort says, "Looks like you've been tearing at somebody's throat."

There's a lot of taunting and backstabbing going on in *The Women*, but Sylvia is clearly the most shameless. She gets her comeuppance when she learns that her own husband has been cheating as well, and then meets the mistress during a divorce-induced trip to Reno. After a hair-pulling, clothes-ripping catfight, she is carried off in a fit of hysteria. Russell, a sophisticated brunette beauty in studio glamour photos, lets her tall, gangly frame flop all over the screen in this tremendous comic turn. Her voice exaggerated into a snide, guttural purr, she tears through pages of dialogue about who's doing what to whom, and then leans right into the other performers' faces and prods for dirt with all the subtlety of a trainwreck.

The Women was a hit in 1939 and has become a classic today, as hilarious now as it was fifty years ago. If the cast was not as outstanding, Russell would have walked off with the film, but Shearer, Crawford et. al. were not about to go quietly. Nobody, in fact, does anything quietly in *The Women*, which is what makes the movie so delightful.

EVELYN PRENTICE
Directed by William K. Howard; Written by Lenore Coffee, based on the novel by W.E. Woodward; Produced by John W. Considine, Jr.; Music by Oscar Raclin

Cast
Myrna Loy (Evelyn Prentice), William Powell (John Prentice), Una Merkel (Amy Drexel), ROSALIND RUSSELL (NANCY HARRISON), Harvey Stephens (Lawrence Kennard)

THE WOMEN
Directed by George Cukor; Written by Anita Loos and Jane Murfin, based on the play by Clare Boothe; Produced by Hunt Stromberg; Music by Edward Ward and David Snell

Cast
Norma Shearer (Mary Haines), Joan Crawford (Crystal Allen), ROSALIND RUSSELL (SYLVIA FOWLER), Mary Boland (Countess DeLave), Paulette Goddard (Miriam Aarons), Joan Fontaine (Peggy Day), Lucille Watson (Mrs. Moorehead)

WINONA RYDER (1972-   )

FIRST APPEARANCE: *Lucas* (20th Century-Fox, 1986)

A STAR IS BORN: *Heathers* (New World Pictures, 1989)

The first generation to follow the Brat Pack into Hollywood has not been as bountiful in breakout stars. Thus far, only the petite (five foot four), demure Winona Ryder has become a darling of critics and an audience favorite. She is also the only Generation X alumnus to successfully adapt to period pieces, such as *The Age of Innocence* (1993) and *Little Women* (1994), in which cutting edge sensibility is not a prerequisite. However, her strongest connection remains with her peer group; for a generation that seems made up entirely of outsiders, Ryder has become the outsider's outsider. Pretty but awkward, denouncing the chichi set yet wanting to join them, she has become, in the words of her *Reality Bites* (1994) costar Ben Stiller, "the poster girl of every Trekkie, every computer nerd, every information-superhighway addict, every comedyhead and every comic book collector."

Winona Horowitz was raised in Petaluma, California by bohemian parents--her mother runs a production company that specializes in filming births, her father sells books about the 1960s. Winona and her siblings, Sunyata, Jubal and Yuri, enjoyed a free-spirited childhood rich in left-wing intellectual wisdom (Timothy Leary is her godfather), but lacking in creature comforts. "My parents did what they were passionate about, and they didn't make money. And there were a lot of kids, so we lived with no electricity, no running water and no heating, except for a stove," she told *Rolling Stone*. "(They) compensated with amazing amounts of love and support, so I don't regret any of it."

Ryder was thirteen years old when a Hollywood talent scout spotted her at San Francisco's American Conservatory Theater. After being screen-tested and rejected for the lead role in *Desert Bloom* (1986), Ryder debuted in *Lucas*, a wonderful film that never found the audience it deserved. Writer-director David Seltzer's story of adolescent friendship and unrequited love benefited from a superb ensemble cast led by Corey Haim and then-newcomers Charlie Sheen, Courtney Thorne-Smith, and the luminous Kerri Green.

Lucas (Haim), a scraggly, intellectual fourteen-year-old, becomes infatuated with Maggie (Green), the pretty new girl in town. A friendship forms amid a summer filled with classical music concerts and tennis lessons. "I just wish fall would never start," Lucas says in one of the film's many bittersweet moments, because he knows that once school starts, Maggie will not be his alone anymore. Sure enough, she is drawn to the studly football player Cappie (Sheen), which inspires Lucas to join the team with amusing--and frightening--consequences.

About twenty minutes into the film, Winona Ryder appears as Rina, a quiet, plain girl who sits with Lucas at the "geek" table during lunch period. She has a crush on Lucas, but he only has eyes for Maggie. In several scenes with Corey Haim (who has never been better), the pint-sized Ryder already shows the poise of a veteran.

Supporting turns in *Beetlejuice* (1987) and *Great Balls of Fire* (1989) followed, and then Ryder played her first lead role in an offbeat, controversial comedy entitled *Heathers*. The title refers to the most popular, exclusive clique in Ohio's Westerburg High School, composed of three gorgeous girls all named Heather. Ryder plays Veronica Sawyer, a new recruit into the clique who enjoys the status but detests the way the Heathers flaunt their superiority. She starts dating J.D. (Christian Slater), a smooth-talking rebel who also resents the Heathers, and suggests murder as a solution to their smug attitude.

Beyond that I will not venture, because the delights of *Heathers* should be savored with as little prior knowledge as possible. The film captures perfectly the casual cruelty of the high school caste system, and has been accurately described as the definitive black comedy of Reagan youth lust and greed. It is a polar opposite to *Lucas*, an honest, gentle coming-of-age story; but as slick, sharp, raunchy and cold-blooded as it is, *Heathers*' satiric take on the quest for popularity is often just as genuine. Daniel Waters' brilliant script says more about the dangers of peer pressure than every public service announcement ever made.

As Veronica, Ryder sits at a better table in the cafeteria than she did in *Lucas*, and in the three years between films she has blossomed from wallflower to dazzler. As the only character in the film with a conscience, she must be in sync with the flip tone of the entire film ("Are we going to the prom, or to Hell?", she writes in her diary), yet still register shock and disgust at her actions. Sometimes the shift is instantaneous, as it is when Veronica and J.D. attend the funeral of two Westerburg students. In the midst of laughing at the hypocrisy of the mourners, she is stunned into silence by the tearful glance of a little girl. Most satires tend to sidestep such sobering moments, but *Heathers* has the guts--and the cast--to carry them off. Christian Slater also becomes a star with this movie, and the Heathers--Kim Walker, Shannen Doherty and Lisanne Falk--personify the heartless high school enchantresses that every boy remembers.

"With *Heathers*, Ryder entered her generation's circulatory system," wrote *Rolling Stone*. "Teenage life was twisted, and Ryder, more than any other actor or actress, was in on the joke." The film demands that she excel in caustic verbal combat, delirious farce, and gun-toting heroics, and Ryder never makes a false move. *Heathers* didn't receive much studio backing and earned a miniscule $1 million at the box office, but the film never really went away. Already an established cult hit and revival house favorite, video store word-of-mouth has made *Heathers* a popular rental with Baby Boomers and Generation X.

LUCAS
Directed and written by David Seltzer; Produced by David Nicksay; Music by Dave Grusin

Cast
Corey Haim (Lucas Blye), Kerri Green (Maggie), Charlie Sheen (Cappie Roew), Courtney Thorne-Smith (Alise), WINONA RYDER (RINA)

HEATHERS
Directed by Michael Lehmann; Written by Daniel Waters; Produced by Denise Di Novi; Music by David Newman

Cast
WINONA RYDER (VERONICA SAWYER), Christian Slater (J.D.), Shannen Doherty (Heather Duke), Lisanne Falk (Heather McNamara), Kim Walker (Heather Chandler)

SUSAN SARANDON (1946-   )

FIRST APPEARANCE: *Joe* (Cannon, 1970)

A STAR IS BORN: *Atlantic City* (Paramount, 1981)

From the 1980s on, any movie with Susan Sarandon has been worth checking out. Sarandon's unique, mature sensuality, heightened by her sly wit and unpretentious manner, was the spark that made *The Witches of Eastwick* (1986) and *Bull Durham* (1987) sizzle, and was the only saving grace of *White Palace* (1990) and *Light Sleeper* (1992). It took Hollywood ten years and twelve films to channel her erotic yet vulnerable persona into the right vehicle, but after *Atlantic City* she received every sexpot-over-30 role available. Before they became a trap, Sarandon proved in *Lorenzo's Oil* (1992) that she can also tone it down.

Susan Abigail Tomalin was born in New York City, the oldest of nine children, and raised in Edison, New Jersey. She described herself as "a very spacey child," which will surprise no one who has seen her work. Plays written and performed by kids in the neighborhood provided her first acting experience. After graduating high school she enrolled at Catholic University in Washington, D.C., where she majored in drama and earned her tuition working as a secretary in the theater department. She married fellow student Chris Sarandon, who pursued his own acting career after the couple graduated in 1968, while Susan pursued opportunities in modeling.

Susan accompanied her husband when he read for an agent, just to feed him lines in an audition scene, but to her surprise the agent asked them both to return in the fall. The Sarandons moved to New York, and before Susan had even resolved to pursue acting as a career the agent sent her on an audition for the movie *Joe*. After performing one improvisation for the producers, she was offered a prominent supporting role.

The film, released in 1970, was a generation gap drama revolving around the odd friendship between Joe (Peter Boyle), a blue-collar palooka with an intense loathing for the counterculture, and Bill Compton (Dennis Patrick), an affluent businessman who, in a fit of rage, kills his daughter's hippie boyfriend. He admits the deed to Joe in a bar, but instead of attempting blackmail Joe embraces Bill as a hero. Later, Bill's daughter Melissa (Sarandon) overhears her parents discussing the murder, and leaves home. Bill and Joe comb the hippie hangouts of Greenwich Village to locate her, and wind up at a marijuana party. They later discover that their wallets are gone, and trace the thieves to a commune outside the city. Brandishing a shotgun, Joe starts shooting the hippies, and Bill realizes that they must kill all of them to escape unseen. Bill guns down one girl as she flees the commune, before realizing that she is his daughter.

Peter Boyle and Dennis Patrick dig deeper than the cliches` and find some genuine humanity in their crude, unpleasant characters. Credit Norman Wexler's script as well, which received an Oscar nomination. If the "establishment" is represented by Joe, an Archie Bunker prototype with an "R" rating that allows for more colorful bigotry, the film is balanced enough to also portray the "lost generation" in an equally unflattering light.

Sarandon's is the first face you'll see when the film begins. She strolls the streets of New York City in an opening credits montage, and then disrobes right after her first entrance. Melissa Compton is one of Sarandon's most dependent, immature characters, but although she is the motivation for most of the story and the focal point of the final twist, the role is more of a plot device than a real human being. Sarandon's most resonant moment occurs early on, just after her gratuitous nude scene; she climbs into bed between her apathetic, junkie boyfriend and a Raggedy Ann doll. After a perfectly timed pause, she turns toward the doll for comfort and security.

Sarandon worked steadily throughout the 1970s in a series of forgettable films, though she did costar in the cult classic *The Rocky Horror Picture Show* (1975). Louis Malle's *Pretty Baby*

(1978) began her rediscovery by Hollywood, although the attention was generated as much by her undraped figure as it was by her performance. In 1980 she starred on Broadway in *A Coupla White Chicks Sitting Around Talking*, and earned the first flat-out raves of her career. "For those of us who associate (Sarandon) with dreary roles in dreary movies, the actress we see comes as a shock, wrote Frank Rich in the *New York Times*. "(She) is a rubber-faced comedienne with considerable resources of charm and craft."

Possessed of renewed confidence and a newfound critical respect, Sarandon reunited with director Louis Malle for *Atlantic City*. She played Sally Matthews, a clam-bar waitress who is studying to be a croupier in a casino. The film is more a series of character studies than a sustained, linear story; there is Burt Lancaster as Lou, a former small-time mobster on whom fate bestows one last chance to be the big-time operator he imagines himself to be. And there is Sarandon as Sally, a dealer forced to deal with a lot more than a deck of cards.

Even though the film ends happily, or at least with everyone better off than they were when the movie began, there is a profound sadness that pervades every frame. *Atlantic City* is populated by young people and old people, rich and poor, all with lives going nowhere. Sally is the only character in the film with no delusions of grandeur; like Atlantic City itself, she has been abused and neglected, but the casinos offer a hope of rebirth and the impetus to try again.

Once again, Susan Sarandon's most memorable scene contains nudity, but this time the credit for its impact belongs as much to Louis Malle as to Sarandon. Despite the American setting and the American cast, Malle directs in the style of European cinema, and that includes an artsy approach to sexuality. Sally, topless, stands before a window, slicing lemons and, to eradicate the smell of fish from her day's work, squeezing them over her arms and chest. The soft lighting, slow, languid camera movement and opera music on the soundtrack are so suggestive of continental filmmaking that you'll expect subtitles.

Sally has all the sensual qualities that first brought Sarandon to the public's attention, but this time they were just one aspect of the character and not a defining trait. As a result, Sarandon received an Academy Award nomination for Best Actress, and a much better selection of future projects.

JOE
Directed by John G. Avildsen; Written by Norman Wexler; Produced by David Gil; Music by Bobby Scott and Danny Meehan

Cast
Peter Boyle (Joe Currran), SUSAN SARANDON (MELISSA COMPTON), Dennis Patrick (Bill Compton), Audrey Caire (Joan Compton), K. Callan (Mary Lou Curran)

ATLANTIC CITY
Directed by Louis Malle; Written by John Guare; Produced by Denis Heroux; Music by Michel LeGrand

Cast
Burt Lancaster (Lou), SUSAN SARANDON (SALLY), Kate Reid (Grace), Michel Piccoli (Joseph), Hollis McLaren (Chrissie), Robert Joy (Dave)

ARNOLD SCHWARZENEGGER (1947-)

FIRST APPEARANCE: *Hercules in New York* (RAF-United, 1970)

A STAR IS BORN: *Conan the Barbarian* (Universal, 1982)

Terminator. Commando. Predator. Barbarian. Destroyer. The name above these titles is Arnold Schwarzenegger, who represents the actor as trademark. Schwarzenegger-brand movies promise good and evil in their most black and white manifestations, innocents that need protection, villains without conscience, special effects, explosions and larger-than-life action from a larger-than-life kinda guy. Analogous careers have been forged by the likes of Chuck Norris, Jean Claude Van Damme and Steven Seagal, but only Schwarzenegger appears to have the personality and versatility to segue into less combustible projects.

He was born in Graz, Austria, the son of the police chief, in a house without a telephone or indoor plumbing. Gustav Schwarzenegger would make his sons Arnold and Meinhard "earn their breakfast" every morning at 6 a.m. with fifteen minutes of rigorous calisthentics, which certainly laid the foundation for Arnold's drive and dedication toward physical fitness. Meinhard was likewise inspired and became a champion boxer before his death in a car accident at the age of 23.

"I did not want anything in my life to be little," Arnold said of his childhood dreams. "What I wanted was to be part of the big cause, the big skyscrapers, the big money, the big action." He started by making himself big, lifting weights and working out for hours every day. At the age of fifteen, he decided that he would one day win the Mr. Universe contest, and after a year in the Austrian army he began to collect bodybuilding titles all over Europe. In 1967, at the age of twenty, he became the youngest man ever to become Mr. Universe. In 1970 he scored an unprecedented triple by winning Mr. World, Mr. Universe and Mr. Olympia titles. When he retired from competition in 1980 the "Austrian Oak" had won more bodybuilding contests than anyone in history.

It was his chiseled physique that impressed Italian film producers enough to offer Arnold the title role in *Hercules in New York*. Schwarzenegger was not looking for movie stardom, but the chance to play a role made famous by his bodybuilding idol Steve Reeves was irresistible. He knew he had no acting ability, but figured if the producers didn't mind than he wouldn't either. The results, however, were so terrible that the film was never even released in the United States. But when Arnold became famous in *Conan the Barbarian* the footage was rediscovered, the title was changed to *Hercules Goes Bananas* (nasty, but undeniably appropriate), and thousands paid to watch poor Arnold learn his craft.

The film begins with Hercules dropping in on the Big Apple, defying Zeus's orders to stay away from earth. He is befriended by Pretzy (Arnold Stang), a nebbishy opportunist who enters Herc in weightlifting contests. Juno, who never liked her mighty stepson, saps the Prince of Power's strength so he will lose the contest, but Zeus takes pity on him and helps Hercules mop the floor with the contest's crooked promoters. After a tearful farewell to Pretzy, he returns to Olympus.

Schwarzenegger was billed as "Arnold Strong," since no one expected Schwarzenegger to become a household name. Who could blame them? And if Arnold had remained at this level, it never would have. Incompetence reigned on both sides of the camera, from director Arthur Allen Seidelman's complete inability to disguise the film's meager budget (Olympus looks like a two-star hotel) to the irritatingly non-stop diddle-diddle-diddle of the bouzouki music. As for our man Arnold, he looks confused most of the time, and takes his shirt off in nearly every scene, proudly displaying the reason he got the job. It's a male bimbo role all the way, and the dubbing of his voice kills any chance of his natural charisma coming through.

That charisma was effortless when Arnold played himself in the bodybuilding documentary *Pumping Iron* (1977). The *New York* magazine review noted that he "lights up the film like neon every time he comes on screen. (His) physical power is balanced by great humor and prodigious charm." The film was a surprise hit, and Schwarzenegger found in filmmaking another mountain to conquer. He played small roles in *Stay Hungry* (1976) and *The Villain* (1979) before finding the ideal vehicle for his still-developing talent.

Conan the Barbarian, the Hyborian Age hero of comic books and pulp fiction created by Robert E. Howard, was the perfect role for Arnold in stage one of his career. He had the muscles, he had the Teutonic intensity, he didn't have to talk much and when he did his accent would not be a liability. Stunt doubles were hard to find, though, so Arnold did everything himself during six months of production under a scorching Spanish sun.

The budget was spent on incredible production design and set decoration, which apparently left just a few dollars for the script, a barely fleshed-out adaptation of Howard's sword and sorcery tale. As a boy, Conan is orphaned when his parents are brutally murdered by Thulsa Doom (James Earl Jones), the powerful leader of a snake-worshipping cult. Conan escapes a sentence of slavery and gladiator-like battles to the death, and begins his journey for revenge. Along with sidekicks Subotai the Mongol (Gerry Lopez) and Valeria, Queen of the Thieves (Sandahl Bergman), he tracks Thulsa Doom to a fortress-like temple. After a vicious, blood-stained battle, Conan's broadsword finds Thulsa's neck.

John Milius, one of the best action film directors ever, clearly relishes the mandate of recreating the savagery of the source material, and gleefully sets all systems on overkill. The story is forgotten ten minutes after the credits and the clanging swords and severed limbs all tend to run together, but while it's on *Conan the Barbarian* is big, loud, dumb and loads of fun. Arnold happily bellowed Conan's favorite exclamation--"Crom!" in a lusty baritone, and withstood critics' exclamations of "Crap!" while the movie raked in $100 million worldwide. There were doubters and laughers while he stayed strong and silent in the *Conan* sequel and in *The Terminator* (1984), working up steadily to actual paragraphs of dialogue and then proving in *Twins* (1988) that he didn't need to kill anybody on screen to draw an audience. As this book is being written Arnold Schwarzenegger is the world's most popular movie star, and nobody's laughing now.

HERCULES IN NEW YORK
AKA Hercules Goes Bananas
Directed by Arthur Allan Seidelman; Written and produced by Aubrey Wisberg; Music by John Balamos

Cast
Arnold Stang (Pretzy), ARNOLD STRONG {SCHWARZENEGGER} (HERCULES), Deborah Loomis (Helen), Ernest Graves (Zeus), Tanny McDonald (Juno)

CONAN THE BARBARIAN
Directed by John Milius; Written by John Milius and Oliver Stone, based on the character created by Robert E. Howard; Produced by Buzz Feitshans and Raffaella De Laurentiis; Music by Basil Poledouris

Cast
ARNOLD SCHWARZENEGGER (CONAN), James Earl Jones (Thulsa Doom), Max Von Sydow (King Osric), Sandahl Bergman (Valeria), Gerry Lopez (Subotai), Mako (The Wizard)

FRANK SINATRA (1915-)

FIRST APPEARANCE: *Las Vegas Nights* (Paramount, 1941)

A STAR IS BORN: *Anchors Aweigh* (MGM, 1945)

"Frank Sinatra's voice *is* pop music history" wrote *The Rolling Stone Record Guide.* In the twentieth century no singer has had a more significant influence on the development of popular music, or how it should be performed. Frank Sinatra didn't need movies to be a star, but once his career was propelled in their direction he worked extremely hard to prove himself worthy of their interest. Unlike Elvis Presley, the only other musical superstar of Sinatra's level who went Hollywood, Sinatra actually gave a damn about his movies. He dutifully tolerated the early roles that required him to sing and then hit the road, and gradually progressed to films in which his performance was more important than the soundtrack album. Sinatra's dedication and professionalism were justly rewarded with an Academy Award for his compelling work as the hard-luck soldier Angelo Maggio in *From Here to Eternity* (1953).

Francis Albert Sinatra grew up in Hoboken, New Jersey idolizing Bing Crosby. He would later blend Crosby's mellow crooning style with Billie Holiday's jazz phrasing, and the note-bending techinque used by trombonist Tommy Dorsey, thus creating a sound that was officially dubbed "The Voice" as early as 1943. Sinatra's parents, particularly his mother Dottie, supported their son's interest in music, but their encouragement backfired somewhat when Sinatra quit school to pursue a singing career. After a few amateur contests he won a spot on Major Bowes, a national radio talent contest that was the *Star Search* of its day, though much more popular and without spokesmodels (radio, you know). Sinatra's big break came during a stint as the featured performer, and head waiter, at a New Jersey roadhouse called the Rustic Cabin, where he was discovered by trumpet player Harry James. He spent six months with James's band, and then joined up with Tommy Dorsey. He cut 84 songs with Dorsey, and tagged along with him to Hollywood for the orchestra's appearance in the low-budget 1941 musical *Las Vegas Nights.*

The lame plot about a vaudevillian family who inherit a fortune in Las Vegas, lose most of it at the gambling tables, then use the rest to start their own nightclub, only becomes watchable in its musical numbers. Sinatra performs only one song, but it's one of the most noteworthy of his career--"I'll Never Smile Again," which he recorded with Dorsey and the Pied Pipers vocal group, was his first number one record, and the number one song on the first music chart ever published by *Billboard* magazine.

Sinatra himself was not mentioned in the reviews, but the Tommy Dorsey Orchestra was well-received, and appeared in the MGM film *Ship Ahoy* the following year. Sinatra's contribution was increased to two songs, and this time the critics noticed. In 1942, he left Dorsey's band to become a soloist, and overnight he became a national rage. His two 1943 films, *Reveille with Beverly* and *Higher and Higher*, were preachings to the converted that again restricted Sinatra's role to singing. He finally read some dialogue in *Step Lively* (1944), but it was only after MGM put him under contract that Sinatra was given a chance (more like an order) to do more.

Anchors Aweigh (1945) was the film in which Sinatra became a movie star. His role as Clarence, a Brooklyn-born sailor who has trouble getting girls, required at least a modicum of acting ability, a dash of comedic timing, and the formidable challenge of tapdancing alongside Gene Kelly. It was the first role Sinatra could not have played simply by being Frank Sinatra.

The story wasn't any more sophisticated than the drippy *Las Vegas Nights*; Kelly and Sinatra are two sailors on leave in Hollywood, who both fall in love with the same girl (Kathryn Grayson). But the casting, the Academy Award-winning score and the legendary MGM luster make this a classic. Kelly's dance with Jerry the cartoon mouse is the showstopper, but his

Spanish swashbuckler number and his charming dance with a little Mexican girl are just as memorable. The songs are Sinatra's and Grayson's; his "I Fall in Love too Easily" and her "Jalousie" are highlights, but sadly they do not perform together. In his famous dance with Kelly, Sinatra matches his partner in acrobatic elan` as they leap across a row of beds with the kind of joyful abandon that only exists in MGM musicals.

"All the world knows Frank Sinatra can sing," wrote the *Motion Picture Herald*, "now it turns out he can act, too. His characterization of Kelly's shipmate is delightful." Rail-thin, clean-cut and handsome in a goofy sort of way, Sinatra is actually convincing as a guy who couldn't get a date, and if you weren't around in the forties you can't imagine how much of a stretch that was.

LAS VEGAS NIGHTS
Directed by Ralph Murphy; Written by Ernest Pagano, Harry Clork and Eddie Welch, based on a story by Pagano; Produced by William LeBaron; Music by Ruth Lowe, "Red" Bone, William LeBaron, Victor Jacobi, Frank Loesser, Burton Lane and Louis Alter

Cast
Phil Regan (Bill Stevens), Bert Wheeler (Stu Grant), Tommy Dorsey and his Orchestra (with, unbilled, FRANK SINATRA)

ANCHORS AWEIGH
Directed by George Sidney; Written by Isobel Lennart, based on a story by Natalie Marcin; Produced by Joe Pasternak; Music by Jule Styne and Sammy Cahn

Cast
FRANK SINATRA (CLARENCE DOOLITTLE), Gene Kelly (Joseph Brady), Kathryn Grayson (Susan Abbott), Jose Iturbi (Himself), Dean Stockwell (Donald Martin)

SISSY SPACEK (1949-   )

FIRST APPEARANCE: *Trash* (Cinema 5, 1970)

A STAR IS BORN: *Carrie* (United Artists, 1976)

Although she's won an Academy Award (in 1980 for *Coal Miner's Daughter*) and been nominated for two others, Sissy Spacek may be the most undervalued actress of her generation. She's contributed to this perception herself by playing to her natural strength--rural Southern waifs-- too often, by working infrequently (four years passed between *Crimes of the Heart* (1986) and *The Long Walk Home* (1990), and by lending her talent to unsavable projects (*Violets are Blue* [1986]). But Spacek can locate the soul of a character and project its contents, however complex, with crystal clarity. This ability separates gifted actresses from the merely talented, and I hope she will share it more often as she enters the mature phase of her career.

To look at Spacek now you would speculate that her childhood was spent in a small Southern town, and was filled with tomboy endeavors that gave way in high school to cheerleading and drama clubs. And you'd be close. Mary Elizabeth Spacek was born and raised in Quitman, Texas. She was renamed Sissy by her two older brothers, but didn't act like a sissy when she competed as a barrel-racer in rodeos. She entered Quitman High School, and was elected Homecoming Queen, but she was turned down after auditioning for her senior class play.

Spacek's first career aspiration was as a musician; she taught herself to play the guitar at the age of thirteen, and performed at school assemblies. In 1966, she spent a summer with her cousin, actor Rip Torn, and his wife, Geraldine Page, who introduced Spacek to the world of professional show business. After graduating from high school she tried to make it as a singer, and got her start by performing background vocals on television commercial jingles. She was booked three times on *The Tonight Show*, but cancelled every time due to stagefright.

Sissy Spacek was heard on screen a year before she was seen--her voice is on the soundtrack for the Andy Warhol film *Lonesome Cowboys* (1969). One year later she made her debut as an extra in another Warhol film, appropriately named *Trash.* Written and directed by Paul Morrissey, *Trash* is a half-scripted, half cinema verite` visit with a brain-fried heroin addict name Joe (Joe Dallasandro), and those who travel in his squalid social circle. The film actually received good reviews from Vincent Canby and Rex Reed, and is the closest the Warhol camp got to mainstream moviemaking. However, the action is still X-rated and would strike most audiences as vulgar, aimless and self-indulgent. Performances range from excellent (the female impersonator Holly Woodlawn as Joe's roommate) to dreadful (everybody else).

Fifteen minutes into what passes for the story, Joe walks his dog down a New York street. Just as he passes a barber shop with the word "Royal" on the window, a red-haired woman dressed in a black coat walks briskly through the frame. That's Sissy Spacek, but be prepared to hit the Freeze Frame button on your remote because the appearance lasts less than a second.

In 1972, after six months of acting classes at the Lee Strasberg Theatrical Institute, Spacek appeared opposite Lee Marvin and Gene Hackman in *Prime Cut*, the film that is usually listed as her official debut. In 1973 she gave her first great performance in *Badlands,* as the fifteen-year-old girlfriend of a teenage serial killer, played by Martin Sheen. *Badlands* and its stars received glowing reviews, but the film was a box-office failure.

Lesser roles in made-for-TV movies such as *Katharine* (1975) were well-received, but her breakthrough came as a result of working with her husband, Jack Fisk, as an art director and set decorator on the Brian De Palma film *Phantom of the Paradise* (1974). Two years later, Fisk was again hired to work with De Palma on a film adaptation of the Stephen King novel *Carrie.*

De Palma remembered Sissy and invited her to audition for a supporting role. After the audition, he gave her the lead.

Carrie White (Spacek) is a shy, awkward teenager who is constantly tormented at school, and is abused both physically and mentally at home by her fanatical mother (Piper Laurie). Carrie also happens to have telekinesis, the ability to move objects with her mind, which she unleashes with murderous ferocity after she is victimized by a cruel joke at the high school prom.

Carrie is not only the best of the "Based on Stephen King" movies, it is one of the best horror films of all time. De Palma's wonderfully ostentatious direction was well-suited to the source material, but most of the credit for the film's success belongs to Spacek. Academy Award nominations in the horror genre are a rarity, especially for films with graphic scenes of violence that do not project the image that the Academy likes to promote, but Spacek's performance was so dazzling that it could not be ignored.

In the opening scenes, Spacek conveys Carrie's alienation with heartbreaking emotion. She is confused and frightened when her powers manifest themselves, but is unable to share her feelings with anyone. And then, unexpectedly, a ray of sunshine enters her world when a popular, handsome boy asks her to the prom. The sequence leading up to Carrie's first date is superb; for the first time Carrie allows herself to be beautiful, smiles without shame and believes she has now been accepted by her peers. But when this too turns out to be another form of persecution, our sympathy is with her as she destroys the school. Even after Carrie has become a mass murderer, Spacek makes you feel her pain, and it is for her that we weep at the conclusion, not her victims. The final scene of the film may be the most shocking, audience-levitating jolt ever conceived.

"She responds splendidly to every mood and transformation the role requires: panicky, hysterical schoolgirl; wretched but sensitive daughter; the momentarily happy, glowing young woman at the prom; a maddened, bulging-eyed vessel of wrath; a contrite, concerned, tragic child," wrote Gary Arnold in the *Washington Post*. "It's been several years since a young American actress has been encouraged to make such an impact, and it's exhilarating to watch Spacek take advantage of this opportunity." She deserved to win that Oscar but so did its recipient, Faye Dunaway (for *Network*). However, Spacek did receive Best Actress honors from the National Society of Film Critics.

TRASH
Directed and written by Paul Morrissey; Produced by Andy Warhol

Cast
Joe Dallesandro (Joe), Holly Woodlawn (Holly), Jane Forth (Jane), Michael Sklar (Welfare Investigator), Geri Miller (Go-go Dancer)...SISSY SPACEK (EXTRA)

CARRIE
Directed by Brian De Palma; Written by Lawrence D. Cohen, based on the novel by Stephen King; Produced by Paul Monash; Music by Pino Dinaggio

Cast
SISSY SPACEK (CARRIE WHITE), Piper Laurie (Margaret White), Amy Irving (Sue Snell), William Katt (Tommy Ross), John Travolta (Billy Nolan), Betty Buckley (Miss Collins), P.J. Soles (Norma Watson)

SYLVESTER STALLONE (1946-)

FIRST APPEARANCE: *Bananas* (United Artists, 1971)

A STAR IS BORN: *Rocky* (United Artists, 1976)

It sounds like a Jackie Collins novel; a tough Italian kid from the mean streets of Hell's Kitchen, New York, overcomes tremendous adversity and a scandalous past to become the highest paid actor in Hollywood.

There is a tangible connection between Sylvester Stallone's early years and the environment of his most famous creation, Rocky Balboa. He's so good at playing the dumb but likable palooka that a lot of people think Stallone really *is* a dumb but likable palooka. But the off-screen Stallone, a soft-spoken, erudite, Armani-clad chap with a refreshingly self-deprecating sense of humor, seems a very different person from the kid who was tossed into Devereux Manor Hall, a high school for boys with learning and social adjustment disabilities.

Young Sylvester Stallone began his east coast tour of underprivileged neighborhoods at age five, when his family moved from Hell's Kitchen to the worst section of Maryland. His parents divorced when he was fifteen, prompting a move to Philadelphia with his mother (and if you've seen her managing lady wrestlers on the GLOW circuit, you can imagine what life at home was like). Sly was booted out of fourteen schools in eleven years, but managed to get accepted to the American College in Switzerland on an athletic scholarship. There he began to turn his life around, and develop an interest in writing and performing. He returned to the U.S., joined the drama department at the University of Miami, and was told to give up any hope of a career in performing.

After stints as a lion cage cleaner at the zoo and an usher at New York's Baronet Theater, Stallone finally broke into showbiz in two revealing roles; he appeared nude in the off-Broadway drama *Score*, and followed up with a supporting role in the stag film *Party at Kitty and Studs* (1967). The film was later renamed *The Italian Stallion* to capitalize on Stallone's subsequent celebrity. His first feature film appearance was in the Woody Allen comedy *Bananas*, in which he kept his clothes on but didn't get his name in the credits. Stallone's debut occurs in a two-minute scene ten minutes into the film; Woody, as Fielding Mellish, is riding the subway when he is accosted by two leather-jacketed hoods (Stallone and another unbilled actor). The sequence is performed, silent movie-like, with barrelhouse piano accompaniment and without dialogue.

Bananas contains some of the funniest scenes in any Woody Allen film, including Howard Cosell's play-by-play call of a political assassination. Stallone's contribution was not among the memorable, but he was a good enough as a thug to get more work in the next few years in *The Lords of Flatbush* (1974) and *Capone* (1975). He also sold a television script, and continued to work on screenplays. After watching a boxing match on TV in which Muhammad Ali had more trouble than expected with an unknown fighter named Chuck Wepner, legend has it that Stallone sat down and wrote *Rocky* in three days. He began presenting himself and the script to producers as a package deal. He was offered $200,000 for the script, on condition that the title role be given to an established star. Though he was nearly broke, Stallone turned down the offer. After numerous rejections he convinced United Aritsts to take a chance, and the rest is history. *Rocky* raked in sixty times its production cost, and won the Oscar for Best Picture of 1976.

When we first meet Rocky Balboa he is a beaten down club fighter who works part time collecting payments for a loan shark. Life takes a sudden, thrilling turn with Apollo Creed, the heavyweight boxing champion of the world, offers to give a title shot to an unknown fighter on July 4, to prove that America is still the land of opportunity. Rocky is chosen because of his "Italian Stallion" nickname, and it's time to cue the thrilling Bill Conti theme music, as Rocky begins training for his final chance at glory. The fight quickly escalates into a war, with Creed winning a split decision. Rocky also raises his fist in triumph, as he hears the cheers of the crowd for what should be the first and last time. The final, oft-parodied shot, of Rocky bellowing "A-dree-ennnnnel" as his geeky girlfriend climbs though the ropes and into his arms, is one of the great choke-up scenes in movies, set up beautifully by the rest of the film and striking just when the audience is already emotionally drained from watching the fight. It was the last perfect moment in a film that never takes a wrong turn.

Witty scribes have subsequently lambasted Stallone for making the same movie four more times, but the fact is that as sequels go *Rocky II, III* and *V* are outstanding entertainments, and even *Rocky IV* has its moments. There is real character development throughout the series, and Stallone's performance never wavers from perfection. With Rocky and Rambo, Stallone has created (not just with performance but with screenwriting and direction) two of the most popular movie heroes in history. If he never makes another good movie (which these days seems entirely possible) he will have already done what few in his profession have accomplished.

BANANAS
Directed by Woody Allen; Written by Woody Allen and Mickey Rose; Produced by Charles H. Joffe and Jack Grossberg; Music by Marvin Hamlisch

Cast
Woody Allen (Fielding Mellish), Louise Lasser (Nancy), Carlos Montalban (General Vargas), Natividad Abascal (Yolanda)...SYLVESTER STALLONE (unbilled, hood)

ROCKY
Directed by John G. Avildsen; Written by Sylvester Stallone; Produced by Irwin Winkler and Robert Chartoff; Music by Bill Conti, Carol Connors, Ayn Robbins and Frank Stallone, Jr.

Cast
SYLVESTER STALLONE (ROCKY BALBOA), Talia Shire (Adrian), Burt Young (Pauly), Carl Weathers (Apollo Creed), Burgess Meredith (Mickey), Thayer David (Miles Jergens)

BARBARA STANWYCK (1907-1990)

FIRST APPEARANCE: *Broadway Nights* (First National, 1927)

A STAR IS BORN: *Ladies of Leisure* (Columbia, 1930)

Barbara Stanwyck was always praised as a natural actress--as if she ever had the chance to be anything else. There wasn't time for formal training in Stanwyck's tumultuous childhood, but the toughness and street sense she developed through years of tragedy and rejection were used to good advantage in her film career. Stanwyck had the legs and the smile for cheesecake photos, but her hardboiled, penetrating gaze sent the message that she was not just smart, but smarter than you. In the best of her eighty films she was the intellectual equal of any man, but her looks and cunning made her superior. Seduction was never more predatory--or more inviting.

Stanwyck was born Ruby Stevens in Brooklyn, New York. When she was just two years old her mother Catherine was killed in a freak accident after stepping off a trolley car. Her father, devastated, left for Panama to work on the Canal, abandoning Ruby, her brother, and her four sisters. The children were doled out to foster homes, many of them less than inviting. Ruby spent the summers of her eighth and ninth years traveling with her sister Mildred, who had become a dancer and chorus girl. She fell in love with the footlights, and at age sixteen was dancing herself in the Ziegfeld Follies of 1923.

Ruby developed her acting ability by being courteous to customers in her other job at a department store, a difficult role with the chip that remained on her shoulder. It was enough to land a role in the 1926 Broadway play *The Noose*. The name Barbara Stanwyck was created by her director, Willard Mack, from an old program for the play *Barbara Frietchie*, starring Jane Stanwyck. One can only wonder how close she came to becoming Jane Frietchie.

The Noose was a hit, and Stanwyck was offered a screen test at New York's Cosmopolitan Studios by producer Bob Kane. Her film debut was as a dancer in *Broadway Nights*, one of those broken-heart-for-every-lightbulb melodramas that were a dime-a-dozen in the silent era. Lois Wilson and Sam Hardy play nightclub performers whose careers are derailed by Hardy's gambling. Wilson goes on to solo stardom, and pulls her old flame out of the gutter for the inevitable happy ending. Stanwyck was not challenged or amused by her formulaic fifth-billed role, and returned to the stage. Her debut along with that of Sylvia Sidney make *Broadway Nights* important now, but all copies are believed lost.

When the coming of sound drove many superstars with squeaky voices into premature retirement, Hollywood looked to Broadway for actors who could deliver lines without breaking glass. Stanwyck was lured back to films by United Artists, but her next two efforts, *The Locked Door* and *Mexicali Rose* (both 1929) were flops. Columbia Pictures called next, and Stanwyck used the emotional, final scene from *The Noose* as her screen test. In it, she pleads for the executed body of the man she loved after he is condemned to die by the state. Columbia president Harry Cohn and director Frank Capra raved over the test, but by then Stanwyck had had enough. Her upbringing had left her slow to trust, and after two false starts in movies she was feeling jerked around. After Capra cast her as the lead in *Ladies of Leisure*, she approached the project with caution, but quickly recognized the quality of the material and the professionalism of her director.

Capra gave Stanwyck her first real lessons in film performance; he modulated her stage technique, trusted her impeccable instincts, and adapted to her tendency to peak on first takes. "Stanwyck doesn't act a scene. She lives it." Capra said. "Her best work is the result--not of timing and rehearsing and study--but of pure feminine reaction."

Stanwyck played Kate Arnold, a golddigging party girl who accepts a ride from a straight-arrow society heir named Jerry. As they become an item Kate begins to recognize the shallowness of her existence and tries to turn her life around. But when Jerry's mother refuses to bless their marriage Kate removes herself from the picture with dire results (bad girls still weren't reformable in 1930). "Stanwyck Triumphs" was the headline of the *New York Times* review, and it was echoed even by the notices that had mixed feelings about the film. She is downright vulgar in the first scene, hitting up Jerry for both a cigarette and a flask in the first minute of their acquaintance. Her reformation is played with heartbreaking depth and sincerity.

Columbia offered Barbara Stanwyck an exclusive contract, but she was still wary of commitment and instead negotiated a non-exclusive deal with both Columbia and Warner Bros..Her respect for Capra led to three more collaborations, culminating in the classic *Meet John Doe* (1941), in which she once again played a scheming opportunist who rediscovers her humanity through the kindness of an unpretentious man.

BROADWAY NIGHTS
Directed by Joseph C. Boyle; Written by Forrest Halsey, based on a story by Norman Houston; Produced by Robert Kane

Cast
Lois Wilson (Frannie Fanchette), Sam Hardy (Johnny Fay), Louis John Bartels (Baron), Phillip Strong (Bronson), BARBARA STANWYCK (DANCER)

LADIES OF LEISURE
Directed by Frank Capra; Written by Jo Swerling, based on a play by David Belasco and Milton C. Gropper

Cast
BARBARA STANWYCK (KATE ARNOLD), Marie Provost (Dorothy), Ralph Graves (Jerry), Lowell Sherman (Bill), George Fawcett (Father), Nance O' Neill (Mother)

JIMMY STEWART (1908-   )

FIRST APPEARANCE: *Murder Man* (MGM, 1935)

A STAR IS BORN: *Mr. Smith Goes to Washington* (Columbia, 1939)

Kindness, decency, and honesty are the words that spring to mind to describe Jimmy Stewart. He's an actor who can never be caught acting, because the integrity of his characters seems to emerge instinctively from the man who inhabits them. He has been beset by the corrupt privileged class in two Frank Capra classics, ruthless gunslingers in a series of Anthony Mann westerns, and assorted spies and murderers in four Alfred Hitchcock thrillers, but in the films of Jimmy Stewart, there is no force known to civilization that can stand long against a simple man of virtue.

He was born James Maitland Stewart in Indiana, Pennsylvania, but his mother, Elizabeth, called him "Jimsy," and his father Alexander called him "Jimbo." Informality thus joined community spirit, faith, and a strong sense of family as defining traits of Stewart's formative years. He worked in the family hardware store, joined the local Boy Scout troop and, while his father served in the First World War, wrote and performed a number of patriotic plays.

Jimmy was an above-average student and star athlete, but acting did not present itself as a life goal until after he entered Princeton University in 1928. While earning a B.S. in architecture, Stewart appeared in several school productions with fellow student Joshua Logan, whose directing credits would later include *Mister Roberts* (1955) and *South Pacific* (1958). Logan tried to entice Stewart into foregoing his post-graduate studies and committing to the stage. After many difficult weeks of deliberation, Stewart wrote to his parents, explaining his decision to leave college.

He appeared in two Broadway plays in 1932, *Carrie Nation* and *Goodbye Again*, and satisfied his curiosity about the cinema with an appearance in the Warner Bros. two-reeler *Art Trouble* (1934). But in 1935, MGM offered him a contract, and Jimmy Stewart left the New York stage and moved next door to Greta Garbo in a Brentwood farmhouse with his east-coast pal Henry Fonda, who had already gone Hollywood.

Stewart's first assignment was in the fast-talking newspaper drama *Murder Man*, as a cub reporter named Shorty. Spencer Tracy stars as Steve Gray, nicknamed the "Murder Man" for his coverage of every major murder case for the *New York Daily Star*. When a financier with ties to organized crime is killed in the backseat of his chauffeur-driven roadster, Gray uses Sherlock Holmes-like deductions to assist the police. His testimony in court lands the victim's business partner on death row, even though Gray knows the man is innocent. It's not a surprise that the newsman eventually comes forward to solve the case, but there are a couple of unexpected twists in the solution that make *Murder Man* a better than standard programmer.

This was the first and last teaming of Tracy and Stewart, the two actors now most associated with working-class heroes but, sadly, they share only a couple of scenes and there is little interaction between them; Steve gives orders, Shorty carries them out, and then joins the crowd of reporters who stand in awe of Steve's instincts. Stewart's best scene has him trying to talk Steve into cancelling his vacation to interview the condemned man. Although *Murder Man* can hardly be credited with setting the pattern, the lanky Stewart is already playing self-effacing straight arrows with a strong sense of duty.

MGM paraded their latest acquisition through a wide-ranging variety of roles in fifteen films over the next three years; Stewart sang to Eleanor Powell in *Born to Dance* (1936), played a murderer captured by Nick Charles in *After the Thin Man* (1936), and cleaned the sewers of Paris in *Seventh Heaven* (1937). He was already a leading man, but Stewart's ascent to stardom followed his appearance in a pair of Frank Capra classics: *You Can't Take It With You*, Oscar's Best Picture of 1938, and *Mr. Smith Goes to Washington* (1939), a film that many still consider Stewart's finest moment. Despite the formidable cast of *You Can't Take It With You*,

Stewart has several individual moments to shine, and he does so wonderfully. His "regular guy" persona is now honed to perfection, and his performance is the reason that he was even cast in *Mr. Smith*. But the impact of *Mr. Smith Goes to Washington* on Jimmy Stewart's career cannot be understated, and gets the nod here.

Jefferson Smith is a freshman senator who learns a difficult lesson about the realities of politics, but never abandons his noble ideals. His education is shared by the viewer, who would like to think, as Jeff does, that our government operates with the same elegance and dignity as the monuments that Smith gazes lovingly on during his first tour of Washington, D.C.. We feel Jeff's pain when his beliefs are beset by cynicism, even when it comes in the pretty packaging of Jean Arthur. The challenge of remaining true to himself and his convictions, in the face of laughter, derision and even personal threats, seems insurmountable. Jeff's struggle for democracy in a place where it should already exist is as inspiring as any fight for a cause ever depicted on film. And Jimmy Stewart, from the moment he appears as leader of his hometown "Boy Rangers," through his search for guidance at the foot of Abraham Lincoln, to his anguished collapse on the Senate floor, is unforgettable.

Gary Cooper was considered first for the role of Jefferson Smith, but how could the tall, broad-shouldered Cooper ever look as frail as Stewart in the film's most indelible moment-- Jeff's twenty-three hour, one-man filibuster after being victimized by a smear campaign; "You all think I'm licked," he whispers in a hoarse voice, battling exhaustion and illness. "Well, I'm not licked, and I'm going to stay right here and fight for this lost cause even if the room gets filled with lies. . .Somebody will listen to me." the entire country listened, despite grumblings from the real U.S. Senate that the film was defamatory. If *Mr. Smith Goes to Washington* were required viewing for every elected official, how much better would America work today?

MURDER MAN
Directed by Tim Whelan; Written by Tim Whelan and John C. Higgins, based on a story by Whelan and Guy Bolton; Produced by Harry Rapf; Music by William Axt

Cast
Spencer Tracy (Steven Gray), Virginia Bruce (Mary Shannon), Lionel Atwill (Capt. Cole), Harvey Stephens (Henry Mander), Robert Barrat (Robbins), JIMMY STEWART (SHORTY)

MR. SMITH GOES TO WASHINGTON
Directed and produced by Frank Capra; Written by Sidney Buchman, based on the book *The Gentleman From Montana* by Lewis R. Foster; Music by Dimitri Tiomkin

Cast
Jean Arthur (Saunders), JIMMY STEWART (JEFFERSON SMITH), Claude Rains (Sen. Joseph Paine), Edward Arnold (Jim Taylor), Guy Kibbee (Gov. Hubert Hopper)

MERYL STREEP (1949-   )

FIRST APPEARANCE: *Julia* (20th Century-Fox, 1977)

A STAR IS BORN: *The Deer Hunter* (Universal, 1978)

     Meryl Streep became the premier American motion picture actress in the 1980s, and the most impressive part of her ascension was the fact that no critic, no audience and no other actress ever rose to challenge the distinction. Such choices have always seemed impossible; who could select from Bette Davis, Joan Crawford and Katharine Hepburn in the 1940s? Who would choose in the fifties between Audrey Hepburn and Deborah Kerr, or in the sixties from such diverse talents as Faye Dunaway, Julie Christie and Jane Fonda? But Streep's anointment as the most significant actress of her generation was simply incontestable.

     Over a decade later Meryl Streep still had first choice of blue chip scripts, which she exercised in an almost calculated attempt to display her gift in as diverse an assortment of characters and films as possible. The emphasis has been on tragic heroines, as in *Sophie's Choice* (1982) and *Silkwood* (1983), in which Streep is able to best subjugate her physical features completely within character and to employ her mastery of foreign and regional dialects. But as technically meticulous as these performances are, there was also a human, emotional power to her work that amplified its intensity beyond what any classroom technique could provide. Only the exquisiteness of her performances gave crossover appeal to such esoteric offerings as *The French Lieutenant's Woman* (1981) and *Plenty* (1985). Yet she could also elevate *Falling in Love* (1984), a glorified made-for-TV soaper, by sheer expertise, and though it was not a challenge or a showcase, it was wonderful to see her smile and laugh in *Defending Your Life* (1991).

     She was born into well-to-do circumstances in Basking Ridge, New Jersey in 1949, though interviewers who believe everything she says write down 1951. She took operatic voice lessons at age twelve, a serious pursuit for a serious child. "At seven," she said, "I looked like a forty-year-old." Streep's first acting assignment was to cover up her insecurity when high school began. She played it well enough to become a cheerleader and Homecoming Queen. At Vassar she majored in drama, looking every inch the cool, prim WASP that would rather discuss Kierkegaard than go bowling. Her sense of humor, then and now, was always ready to deflate such assumptions with a self-effacing joke or a cut-up Zsa Zsa Gabor impression.

     At the Yale School of Drama, Meryl Streep finished her graduate studies and played the lead in several school productions. In 1976, her portrayal of a poor white-trash Southerner in *27 Wagons Full of Cotton* went to Broadway's Phoenix Theater and earned Streep a Tony nomination. She built a distinguished resume` on stage performing Shakespeare, Chekov and Tennessee Williams, which led to her being considered for the title role in the film *Julia*. The producers wanted Streep, but director Fred Zinnemann held out for Vanessa Redgrave and convinced the moneymen that an unknown in the lead might be risky. Instead, Streep was given the role of Anne-Marie, an affluent friend of playwright Lillian Hellman (Jane Fonda).

     Hellman tells the story in flashback of her long friendship with Julia, an heiress who joins the European resistance movement in World War II. Forty-five minutes into the film, Hellman is greeted in a restaurant by Anne-Marie, who congratulates her on the success of her play. Later, the two women sit at a bar and discuss Julia's adventures. A brunette Streep conveys the blissful ignorance of a flighty, shallow socialite who can't understand why a rich girl like Julia would waste her life fighting fascism. Her role was originally much larger, but it was dismantled in the editing room before the film was released. It might have been her first great performance, but since two tiny scenes are all that survived the cut you shouldn't look for magic yet. *The Motion Picture Guide*'s assertion that Streep "showed the radiance that has taken her to the top of her craft" is reflex praise.

     That same year Streep played a small role in the television movie *The Deadliest Season.*

The following year she won an Emmy for the miniseries *Holocaust*, and an Oscar nomination for *The Deer Hunter*. The film is a long, too long, unrelentingly bleak, nightmarish journey to hell and back; hell is Vietnam, and the travelers are three blue-collar types in a Pennsylvania steel town played by Robert De Niro, Christopher Walken and John Savage. De Niro saw Streep in *The Cherry Orchard* at Lincoln Center, and suggested her for the role of Linda, the girlfriend of Walken's character, who winds up with De Niro after Walken does not return from the war.

It was not a star-making part on paper, but this time Streep had enough time to build a fully-realized character who personified the heartbreak and confusion of those who lost loved ones in a war without winners. In the final scene, Linda gathers at a funeral with survivors of the fight--and the homefront--for an devastating, impromptu chorus of "God Bless America." "Her character in *The Deer Hunter* could have been a deaf-mute," wrote Streep biographer Nick Smurthwaite, "but by the time Streep had finished with her, Linda was an integral part of the meaning of the film, a poignant reminder that war also scars those left behind." The top of her craft begins here.

JULIA
Directed by Fred Zinnemann; Written by Alvin Sargent, based on the story by Lillian Hellman; Produced by Richard Roth; Music by Georges Delerue

Cast
Jane Fonda (Lillian Hellman), Vanessa Redgrave (Julia), Jason Robards (Dashiell Hammett), Maximilian Schell (Johann), Hal Holbrook (Alan Campbell), Rosemary Murphy (Dorothy Parker), MERYL STREEP (ANNE-MARIE)

THE DEER HUNTER
Directed by Michael Cimino; Written by Deric Washburn, based on the story by Washburn, Cimino, Louis Garfinkle and Quinn K. Redeker; Produced by Barry Spikings, Michael Deeley, Michael Cimino and John Peverall; Music by Stanley Myers

Cast
Robert De Niro (Michael), John Cazale (Stan), John Savage (Steven), Christopher Walken (Nick), MERYL STREEP (LINDA), George Dzundza (John), Chuck Aspregen (Axel)

BARBRA STREISAND (1942-   )

FIRST APPEARANCE: *Funny Girl* (Columbia, 1968)

A STAR IS BORN: *Funny Girl*

During an interview on the television series *20/20*, Barbra Streisand was asked how she defined herself professionally. Surprisingly, she listed "actor" and "director" first, and added "singer" only after being prompted by the interviewer. She is the only person in the world to rank her achievements in that order. Certainly Streisand has accomplished much as an actress, but the roles for which she was best-suited and for which she will always be best-remembered are those that also utilized her musical gifts. Some of Streisand's best acting is actually done in song, whether there's a movie camera around or not. The power and range of her two-octave tessitura climbs emotional peaks not ascended since Judy Garland, and it is this talent for raising a standard lyric of lost love to operatic levels of tragedy that is her crowning achievement. If you don't count the classical sopranos--and maybe even if you do--Streisand's is the voice of the century.

Barbara Joan Streisand was born in Brooklyn, New York. Her father, an English teacher, died when she was just fifteen months old. From the age of four Barbara planned to be an actress, and she pursued her goal with the single-minded determination that would become her defining non-show business trait. At age fourteen she worked at a summer theater in Malden, New York, and after graduating high school in 1959 she left home to become a star. When she was advised to change her name to something that would look better on a marquee, Streisand responded by keeping her surname and dropping an "a" from Barbara.

Her sense of humor (see last sentence), non-conformity and off-the-scale chutzpah helped her win a talent contest and earn a job at a Greenwich Village bar. She worked her way up to nightclubs and local TV appearances. After a one-performance run in the 1961 off-Broadway production *Another Evening With Harry Stoones*, Barbra was booked into the prestigious Blue Angel. Producer David Merrick saw her and gave her the part of lonely secretary Miss Marmelstein in *I Can Get it For You Wholesale* (1962). It was Streisand's performance that kept the mediocre musical running for nine months.

Barbra was everywhere in 1963--selling out concerts, recording albums that soared to number one on the strength of hit singles like "Happy Days are Here Again," and singing on television with everyone from Bob Hope to Judy Garland, whose duet with Barbra on "Happy Days" was not conceived as a passing of the torch, though it so obviously was. *Look* magazine called her "the most talked-about, sought-after performer in many, many years." From a plethora of offers she then chose to return to Broadway for *Funny Girl*, a musical biography of Fanny Brice. Streisand won a Tony for her performance, and an invitation to appear in the film adaptation.

Fanny Brice is still her signature role, though the actual character that emerged in both the play and the film is a lot more Barbra than Fanny. *Funny Girl* established Streisand's film persona throughout the sixties and seventies--a fast-talking, near hyperactive go-getter who still exhibits the badges and the scars of her Brooklyn Jewish upbringing. She's no fashion model and she knows it, but her insecurity does not stand in the way of career success and a relationship with a handsome Gentile. She starts out thrilled that he even notices her, but ends up leaving him in the end when he proves not to be on her level either intellecutally or morally. It was a mold Streisand did not convincingly break until *Yentl* (1983).

As the movie opens Fanny is desperate to escape her life on New York's lower East Side and into the magical world of the theatre (sound familiar?). She fails as a chorus girl, provoking unintentional laughter during a roller skating routine, but her antics are noticed by a handsome, notorious gambler named Nicky Arnstein (Omar Sharif). He introduces Fanny to the great Flo Ziegfeld (Walter Pidgeon), who hires her for his famous Follies. On stage she breaks the Ziegfeld tradition of beauty and glamor by appearing in a bridal gown, pregnant. Although he is outraged by her insubordination, Ziegfeld cannot help but notice that she's become the hit of the Follies. He gives her carte blanche to develop new material. Fannie and Nicky are married, but as she rises to stardom he falls on hard times. Nicky loses all of their money and is sent to jail for a year after trying to get even in a phony bond deal.

Rumor had it that Streisand made her directorial debut along with her movie debut on *Funny Girl*, but William Wyler is the director of record and he (or whoever) did a commendable enough job to receive an Academy Award nomination. The movie's only technical fault is that it's too long, probably resulting from an attempt to recapture everything that was in the play. They had Barbra, and that was really enough. She won the Oscar that year, tieing with Katharine Hepburn in *The Lion in Winter*. Over the course of two-and-a-half hours she performs half of her first greatest hits album ("People", "My Man," "Second Hand Rose"), and displays flawless comedic timing and a contagious sense of joy. Classic musical moments have been scarce since Gene Kelly jumped through puddles in 1952, but *Funny Girl* contains one for the ages; Fanny sings "Don't Rain on My Parade" while racing through New York to join Nicky on a cruise ship. The song continues from train station to train to taxi and finally to the deck of a tugboat, where Barbra (captured in a spectacular helicopter shot) belts the song's defiant creed with enough power to light the Big Apple skyline.

FUNNY GIRL
Directed by William Wyler; Written by Isobel Lennart, based on the musical by Jule Styne, Bob Merrill and Isobel Lennart; Produced by Ray Stark; Music by Jule Styne, Bob Merrill, Fred Fisher, Billy Rose, others)

Cast
BARBRA STREISAND (FANNY BRICE), Omar Sharif (Nick Arnstein), Kay Medford (Rose Brice), Anne Francis (Georgia James), Walter Pidgeon (Flo Ziegfeld)

ELIZABETH TAYLOR (1932-   )

FIRST APPEARANCE: *There's One Born Every Minute* (Universal, 1942)

A STAR IS BORN: *National Velvet* (MGM, 1944)

At the tender age of twelve, when Elizabeth Taylor first entranced movie audiences in *National Velvet*, she was already on her way to setting one of the standards by which American beauty would be measured. Taylor's successful transition from child star to leading lady may have been eased by the maturity of her appearance and manner at an early age. "As a child in the Hollywood limelight," wrote biographer Jerry Vermilye, "she faced movie cameras with the cool assurance of a pro and the uncanny facial beauty of an adult."

Elizabeth Rosemond Taylor was born in London to American parents, who were traveling in Europe on business. After spending seven years in England, the Taylors returned to the United States in 1939, just before Europe was engulfed in World War II. Elizabeth's father, Frances, was hired to manage an art gallery in the Beverly Hills Hotel, and Elizabeth was enrolled in Beverly Hills' Hawthorne School.

Sara Taylor, Elizabeth's mother, decided that her adorable daughter ought to be in pictures, and so did the father of one of her classmates, who was a producer at Universal Pictures. Elizabeth was signed to a contract, and although her song and dance skills were minimal she was groomed as a successor to Deanna Durbin. The plan was short-lived, as was Taylor's career at Universal. She was dropped from the roster after just one film, a nearly forgotten comedy called *There's One Born Every Minute*.

At sixty minutes, the movie barely qualifies as a feature, but that still doesn't explain why *Variety*, the *New York Times* and every other major newspaper did not even bother to print a review. Taylor's own recollections of the film were so vague that she referred to it in her memoirs by its working title, *Man or Mouse*; "I played a beastly child who slung rubber bands at ladies' bottoms," was Taylor's only comment on her movie debut.

There's One Born Every Minute was a screwball comedy about the mayoral campaign of pudding manufacturer Lemuel Twine (Hugh Herbert). When Vitamin Z is discovered in Twine's pudding, sales skyrocket and his victory seems assured. But the town's corrupt political boss, Lester Cadwalader (Guy Kibbee), pronounces the story to be a fraud, hoping to keep Twine out of office. But when Twine exposes Cadwalader as the real fraud, he clears his name and wins the election.

Nine-year-old Elizabeth Taylor plays Twine's daughter, Gloria. Her cuteness and wide-eyed charm are obvious, but having her play against that image as a pixie hellion doesn't always work. Her vocal duet with Carl "Alfalfa" Switzer surely brought any thoughts of Taylor as the next Deanna Durbin to a screeching (and I mean screeching) halt.

There's One Born Every Minute was originally intended as a vehicle for W.C. Fields, but when the deal collapsed so did the studio's interest. Hugh Herbert was a less-than-adequate substitute, and except for a few slow burns from Edgar Kennedy and the appearance of a Little Rascal, there is little to recommend.

A chance meeting between Frances Taylor and Samuel Marx, an MGM studio executive, led to Elizabeth's casting in *Lassie Come Home* (1943). After brief appearances in *Jane Eyre* (1944) and *The While Cliffs of Dover* (1944) she campaigned (with help from her mother) for the role of Velvet Brown in *National Velvet*. MGM had owned the movie rights to the 1935 novel by Enid Bagnold for five years, but had been unable to cast the title role. Taylor, still a relative unknown, was given the part after demonstrating her equestrian skills, and embarking on a weight-gaining, height-stretching program to allay the studio's fears that she was too frail-looking to play the rambunctious Velvet.

The story is set in Sussex, England, where Velvet wins a high-spirited horse named "The Pie" in a village raffle. Mi Taylor (Mickey Rooney), a vagabond teenager who works for

Velvet's father, is amazed at the horse's speed and jumping ability, but is more astonished when Velvet announces her intention to enter The Pie in the Grand National, England's most prestigious horse race. "A big dream for a little girl," cautions her mother (Anne Revere), but eventually Velvet's passion and determination make believers of the entire village.

Fifty years after its release, *National Velvet* remains one of the greatest family films ever made. Flawless in the conversion of its source material, the movie is a perennially popular video rental, capable of captivating any age group. Every word in every line of the script was chosen with the utmost care, making *Velvet* as enchanting to listen to as it is to watch. The performances--Donald Crisp as Velvet's father, Angela Lansbury, Mickey Rooney, and especially Oscar-winner Anne Revere as Mrs. Brown, project a tender sincerity as warm as the Technicolor world where their characters reside.

Elizabeth Taylor was third-billed, though her performance carries the film. MGM expected the popularity of Mickey Rooney and of the Bagnold novel to sell tickets but, after seeing the film, critics and audiences were only talking about the twelve-year-old girl who was already more Ava Gardner than Shirley Temple. Her performance did not contain evidence of a prestigious dramatic talent, comparable to, say, Patty Duke in *The Miracle Worker* (1962), but when Velvet's face gets, in Mi's words, "all lighted up," the screen glows with Taylor's beauty, charm and vibrance. "Her face is alive with youthful spirit," wrote Bosley Crowther in the *New York Times*, "her voice has the softness of sweet song and her whole manner in this picture is one of refreshing grace." *National Velvet* was only the fifth entry in a filmography that would encompass over fifty motion pictures and two Academy Awards, but it remains, arguably, Elizabeth Taylor's finest two hours on screen.

THERE'S ONE BORN EVERY MINUTE
Directed by Harold Young; Written by Robert B. Hunt and Brenda Weisberg, based on the story *Man or Mouse* by Robert B. Hunt; Produced by Ken Goldsmith

Cast
Hugh Herbert (Lemuel P. Twine), Peggy Moran (Helen Barbara Twine), Tom Brown (Jimmie Hanagan), Guy Kibbee (Lester Cadwalader), Edgar Kennedy (Mayor Moe Carson)...Carl "Alfalfa" Switzer (Junior Twine), ELIZABETH TAYLOR (GLORIA TWINE)

NATIONAL VELVET
Directed by Clarence Brown; Written by Theodore Reeves and Helen Deutsch, based on the novel by Enid Bagnold; Produced by Pandro S. Berman; Music by Herbert Stothart

Cast
Mickey Rooney (Mi Taylor), Donald Crisp (Mr. Brown), ELIZABETH TAYLOR (VELVET BROWN), Anne Revere (Mrs. Brown), Angela Lansbury (Edwina Brown), Juanita Quigley (Malvolia Brown)

SHIRLEY TEMPLE (1928-   )

FIRST APPEARANCE: *War Babies* (Educational Films, 1932)

A STAR IS BORN: *Little Miss Marker* (Paramount, 1934)

There are child stars, and then there is Shirley Temple. A separate classification is required, because no other silver screen tyke before or since can even approach her legacy.

In the 1930s, Shirley Temple was the most popular star in Hollywood, and the most famous child in the world. At the age of seven, she starred in eight films and received an Academy Award. She was the youngest performer to grace the cover of *Time* magazine, and her entry in *Who's Who* was longer than Greta Garbo's. From 1935 to 1938, she was ranked number one at the box office by the *Motion Picture Herald*, an achievement that was never equaled. At her peak, during an unbroken run of twenty-seven hit films, Shirley sold more dolls than Cabbage Patch (saving the Ideal Toy Company from bankruptcy in the process), and more dresses--copies of her film wardrobe--than Givenchy. On her eighth birthday she received 135,000 presents from five continents; and she could afford to send everyone a "thank you" note because, in 1938, her income was the seventh highest in the world.

Temple's more substantial accomplishments are not as easily measured by statistics. When the Great Depression was at its most depressing, movies offered escape and solace to millions of Americans as they never had before. The stories told in Shirley Temple movies, of one little girl overcoming hardship with a smile and a song, were simplistic, to be sure, but Shirley's perseverence, optimism and pluck were exactly what was needed at the time. In addition, Shirley's capacity to charm and befriend everybody she met in her movies offered a hopeful vision of racial and class harmony that still, sadly, has not come to pass. As critic Maryann Oshana observed, "Wrapped up in a little girl were all the ideals that Americans cherished but seldom practiced."

Born in Santa Monica, California, Shirley Jane Temple was an exceptionally pretty child who was, though anyone who saw her on film would find it hard to believe, uncommonly introverted. Sent to a dance school to overcome her shyness, she was noticed by Charles Lamont, a producer of one-reel comedies called *Baby Burlesks*. The *Burlesks* were takeoffs on famous movies, with all the parts played by precocious tots wearing oversized diapers. The job paid ten dollars a day for four days, a good salary for an adult during the Depression. Shirley hid underneath a piano while Lamont looked for new talent, and after observing a class he said, "I'll take the one under the piano."

At the age of four, Shirley's show business career began in *War Babies*, a kiddie version of *What Price Glory?* (1926). She played Charmaine, the Dolores Del Rio role, and spoke her first words on screen, "Mais oui, mon cher!" in French. She dances for the soldiers in Buttermilk Pete's Cafe, wearing an off-the-shoulder dress and a flower in her hair, and then two-times her boyfriend for a guy with a lollipop.

Shirley's performance is not the best in the piece--as of yet she is not acting as much as just repeating words she was told to memorize. But she was still two years shy of kindergarten, so let's give her a break. Years later, the adult Shirley Temple actually singled out the *Burlesks* as "the best things I ever did," but it's hard to justify such high praise when comparing these primitive one-reelers to Shirley's performance of "On the Good Ship Lollipop" in *Bright Eyes* (1934), or her magnificent step dance with Bill Robinson in *The Little Colonel* (1935).

Stand up and Cheer (1934) marks the beginning of Temple's rise to stardom. Near the end of this otherwise lackluster musical, she sings "Baby Take a Bow," and walks off with the picture. So overwhelming was the critical and public reaction to her performance that theaters added her name to the marquee, despite the fact that she was only on screen for about fifteen minutes. Twentieth Century-Fox signed her to a contract with her mother's blessing, just as Shirley's next film, *Little Miss Marker*, was released.

It would be the first of many film adaptations for Damon Runyon's story of a little girl who is left with bookie Sorrowful Jones (Adolphe Menjou) as a marker to cover her desperate father's horseracing wager. The girl's father commits suicide that night, and "Markie" (Temple) is informally adopted by Sorrowful and his band of underworld cronies. Because Shirley had not yet become a national treasure, she is allowed here to play a feisty moppet who picks up the lingo of the gamblers and gives it back. This edge to her character and the other denizens of Runyon's world separate *Little Miss Marker* from the more treacly Temple vehicles that would follow.

In her performance of one song, "Laugh You Son-of-a-Gun," and her delivery of lines like "Aw, lay off me," with an adorable pout, Shirley has improved considerably since her appearance in the *Burlesks*. At the ripe old age of five, the impossibly cute Temple displays polished comic timing and acres of charm, without ever seeming artificial. "If she were forty years old and on stage all her life, she wouldn't have had the time to learn all she knows about acting," said costar Adolphe Menjou, referring not just to Shirley's ability to play a scene, but to control it; "She knows all the tricks," he said. "She backs me out of camera, blankets me, crabs my laughs. Don't ask me how she does it."

From *Little Miss Marker* on, Shirley Temple's name went above the title. But the thirties gave way to the forties, times changed, Shirley grew up, and her phenomenal popularity gradually declined until, in 1949, she hung up her tap shoes for good. "It was sad that the spark lasted only to a certain age," said Allan Dwan, the director of three Temple films, "But if Shirley Temple was only a moment in movie history, it was a great moment."

WAR BABIES
Directed by Charles Lamont; Written and produced by Jack Hays

Cast
Georgie Smith (Soldier), Eugene Butler (Soldier), SHIRLEY TEMPLE (CHARMAINE)

LITTLE MISS MARKER
Directed by Alexander Hall; Written by William R. Lipman, Sam Hellman and Gladys Lehman, based on the story by Damon Runyon; Produced by B.P. Schulberg; Music by Ralph Rainger

Cast
Adolphe Menjou (Sorrowful Jones), Dorothy Dell (Bangles Carson), Charles Bickford (Big Steve), SHIRLEY TEMPLE (MISS MARKER), Lynn Overman (Regret)

GENE TIERNEY (1920-1991)

FIRST APPEARANCE: *The Return of Frank James* (20th Century-Fox, 1940)

A STAR IS BORN: *Laura* (20th Century-Fox, 1944)

Kind words for Gene Tierney performances were hard to find in the 1940s. Even *Laura*, perhaps the quintessential film noir, was praised in every detail but Tierney's interpretation of the title role. She earned an Academy Award nomination for *Leave Her to Heaven* (1945), but *Time* magazine's reviewer was not impressed-- "No amount of strenuous plot trouble seems to jar Gene Tierney's smooth deadpan."

It doesn't seem that way now. *Heaven Can Wait* (1943) began an unbroken streak of wonderful Tierney vehicles, that get a better reception now than when they were first released; *Laura*, *A Bell for Adano* (1945), *Leave Her to Heaven*, *Dragonwyck* (1946), *The Razor's Edge* (1946) and *The Ghost and Mrs. Muir* (1947) are all now classics or cult favorites, and reason enough to reexamine the Gene Tierney legacy. Either we've just grown accustomed to her amazing face, equally enticing and enigmatic in the chiaroscuro of *Laura* or the stunning Technicolor of *Leave Her to Heaven*, or the critics of the day were dead wrong.

Born to Howard and Belle Tierney in Brooklyn, New York, the second of three children, Gene Elizabeth Tierney received her unusual first name after her mother's beloved late brother. The family moved to Green Farms, Connecticut, before Gene was a teenager, where she attended the classy St. Margaret's School. The Tierneys enjoyed a respected social position, but without the wealth that usually accompanies the lifestyle.

In 1938, during a family sightseeing tour of the west coast, Gene was plucked from a Warner Bros. studio tour by director Anatole Litvak with the immortal line "You oughta be in pictures." The seventeen-year-old debutante filmed a screen test the next day, and her heart-shaped face, penetrating green eyes, high cheekbones, cool elegance and natural gentility overwhelmed any questions of whether she could act. Her father forbade Gene from signing the contract that was offered, but when the passage of time did not deter her desire to become an actress, he accompanied his daughter on a tour of agents' and producers' offices in New York.

Gene Tierney made her stage debut in *Mrs. O'Brien Entertains* in February of 1939. The play closed on Broadway after 37 performances, but Tierney's performance was praised. She was signed by Columbia Pictures, but returned to New York after six months of inactivity. After receiving the best reviews of her life in the play *The Male Animal* (1940), Hollywood again came calling. This time she signed with 20th Century-Fox, and within days was on the set of her first film, *The Return of Frank James*.

In this dreary sequel to *Jesse James* (1939), Henry Fonda reprises his role as Jesse's brother Frank. He takes up the trail of Jesse's killers, concealing his search by planting a report of his death with newspaper editor Tom Grayson (Jackie Cooper). Eleanor Stone (Tierney), the mayor's daughter and a fledgling journalist, wants to get the real story, but after discovering that Frank is still alive she offers her help in finding the killers.

This was director Fritz Lang's first western, but one should not blame his inexperience for the film's failure, because the material just wasn't there. Henry Fonda is fine as always, but Tierney was described as "singularly mannered and colorless" by the *New York Times*, and in this case the critique was accurate. Tierney's frequent costume changes betray the decorative nature of the role, and her performance is a flurry of Scarlett O'Hara voice inflections and mannerisms. In 1940, she was named "Worst Actress" by the *Harvard Lampoon*.

There was nowhere to go but up, and Tierney did indeed improve with each subsequent film. Her career is a textbook example of steady, gradual ascent through the Hollywood ranks, which makes the selection of one film as a turning point particularly tough. *Laura* seems the obvious choice, but by 1944 Tierney had already appeared on the cover of

Life and played lead roles in three films. In his autobiography, director Josef von Sternberg takes credit for launching Tierney in *The Shanghai Gesture* (1941), but the film was actually panned by critics and a box-office flop. She worked with John Ford in *Tobacco Road* (1940) and Tyrone Power in *Son of Fury* (1942), but both films were designated as low priority programmers at Fox.

So we're back to *Laura*, which is no more valid than any other selection, but at least it sounds right. *Laura*, too, was a 'B' movie; Tierney costarred with Dana Andrews, who was then unproven as a leading man, and Clifton Webb, who had never made a movie before. But the chemistry was magic between the leads and director Otto Preminger, and the film was immeasurably enriched by the cinematography of Joseph La Shelle, and an exquisite theme, composed in a long weekend by David Raksin, that played under almost every scene.

Andrews, as detective Mark McPherson, investigates the violent death of Laura Hunt (Tierney) by interviewing her friends and relatives. He learns a great deal about her from newspaper columnist Waldo Lydecker (Webb), who was Laura's benefactor, and her fiance` Shelby Carpenter (Vincent Price). McPherson becomes obsessed by a portrait of Laura that hangs in her home, and as the case progresses he finds himself, uncontrollably, falling in love with a dead woman. More happens, but for the benefit of those who haven't seen the film, I'll stop here.

Gene Tierney, whose beauty had an aristocratic, unapproachable mystique, was perfect as the ultimate of unapproachable lovers. La Shelle's photography won an Oscar, Webb earned a nomination for Best Supporting Actor, and *Laura* made several "ten best" lists and a vault of money for Fox. This level of prestige and accomplishment was rare for a 'B' movie, but one viewing of the unforgettable *Laura* is all that's needed to understand its success.

THE RETURN OF FRANK JAMES
Directed by Fritz Lang; Written by Sam Hellman; Produced by Darryl F. Zanuck; Music by David Buttolph

Cast
Henry Fonda (Frank James), GENE TIERNEY (ELEANOR STONE), Jackie Cooper (Tom Grayson), Henry Hull (Major Rufus Cobb), John Carradine (Bob Ford)

LAURA
Directed and produced by Otto Preminger; Written by Jay Dratler, Samuel Hoffenstein, Betty Reinhardt, Ring Lardner, Jr. and Jerome Cady, based on the novel by Vera Caspary; Music by David Raksin and Johnny Mercer

Cast
GENE TIERNEY (LAURA HUNT), Dana Andrews (Mark McPherson), Clifton Webb (Waldo Lydecker), Vincent Price (Shelby Carpenter), Judith Anderson (Ann Treadwell)

SPENCER TRACY (1900-1967)

FIRST APPEARANCE: *Up the River* (Fox, 1930)

A STAR IS BORN: *San Francisco* (MGM, 1936)

"Learn your lines." was the only advice Spencer Tracy dispensed to aspiring actors. He was not the type to ask, "What's my motivation?" before a scene, but when "Action!" was called, every word Tracy spoke sounded more from his heart than from the script. Tracy's "non-Method" Method drew praise from dedicated students of the acting craft like Sir Laurence Olivier, who declared, "There is great truth in everything Spencer Tracy does."

Born and raised in Milwaukee, Wisconsin, Spencer Bonaventure Tracy was a reluctant student, who finished his undergraduate education only because his father demanded it. After a six-month stint in the Navy, Tracy faced a choice between joining his father's trucking business, or going to college. He enrolled at Ripon College in 1921 as a pre-med student, and became a star on the debating team. The confidence he gained in public speaking prompted him to try out for the commencement play. While touring east coast colleges in a series of debates, Tracy was accepted into the acting program at Sargent's School in New York City, where he was reunited with his old friend from Milwaukee, Pat O'Brien. "It sounds like a silly idea to me," wrote his father in a letter, "but if you have your mind set on it, I'll go halfway with you."

When the tuition money arrived from home, Tracy and O'Brien moved into a lodging house, studied their craft, and skipped meals to pay the rent. Tracy made his professional stage debut as a robot in the 1923 science-fantasy *R.U.R.*. He toured with several stock companies over the next three years, appeared in two George M. Cohan productions, and received his first *New York Times* rave as a convict in the prison drama *The Last Mile* (1930). John Ford attended a performance and offered Tracy a lead role in a prison picture he was preparing entitled *Up the River*.

The film is almost forgotten now, which is somewhat surprising considering it contains the feature film debut of Spencer Tracy (he appeared in two Vitaphone shorts earlier in the year, *Taxi Talks* and *The Hard Guy*), and the second feature appearance of Humphrey Bogart. The two young actors, who forged a lifelong friendship on the set, share many scenes that will make a cinephile smile, but they can only do so much with a script that vacillates uncomfortably between comedy and melodrama.

Steve (Bogart) returns to his small hometown after being released from jail, and is back walking the straight and narrow when a former cellmate shows up, and threatens to expose Steve's criminal past unless he helps out in a swindling scheme. Steve turns for help to his best friends, St. Louis (Tracy) and Dannemora Dan (Warren Hymer), who break out of jail to come to his rescue. After restoring Steve's reputation, they return to their cells.

The film belongs more to Bogart, whose shy, unassuming "Oh, gee, guys" portrayal is a far cry from the tough guy persona that made him famous. Tracy, however, has already found his most enduring character type; St. Louis is a remorseless criminal, but he's also a cheerful operator who can request a cell with a Southern exposure, and spend a carefree afternoon trading riddles with the warden's little daughter. His one big dramatic speech, when St. Louis talks Steve out of killing the blackmailer, is not delivered with the subtle underplaying that would become one of Tracy's trademarks.

The Fox Studio offered Tracy a long-term contract before *Up the River* was released, but Tracy insisted on first returning to Broadway and finishing the run of *The Last Mile*. He made thirteen more films at Fox without any notable success, and then signed with MGM in 1935. There, his fortunes turned with the weeks-apart release of two box-office hits the following year. Fritz Lang's *Fury* cast Tracy as an innocent man wrongly imprisoned for kidnapping, who is nearly killed by a mob that burns down the jail. The buzz that began after Tracy's turbocharged performance was amplified after his supporting role in *San Francisco*, the studio's biggest moneymaker of the year.

Tracy and Clark Gable, whose collaboration proved so popular that they would be reteamed for *Test Pilot* (1938) and *Boom Town* (1940), play childhood friends who end up on opposite sides of the law; Tim Mullin (Tracy) becomes a priest, Blackie Norton (Gable) a nightclub owner hailed as "King of the Barbary Coast." The friendship survives until the arrival of Mary Blake (Jeanette MacDonald), a pretty songbird who dreams of a career in opera, but signs a contract with Blackie to stay out of poverty. She falls for her boss, but Father Tim cannot stand by and let her be corrupted by Blackie's influence.

A miniseries worth of action, music and drama culminates in a ten-minute earthquake sequence that out-dazzles the disaster flicks of the 1970s. After wandering through the rubble, a reformed Blackie is reunited with Mary, and reconciled with Father Tim.

San Francisco is a love letter to the Golden Gate city, that brought Spencer Tracy the first of his nine Academy Award nominations. "You're the only actor I know who can bring humanity to the part of Father Mullin" said director W.S. Van Dyke to Tracy; the Gable-MacDonald romance is spotlighted until the ground begins to rumble, but Tracy, as the voice of reason and virtue, is the beacon of light in the gaudy, bawdy days before the quake, and a personification of the drive and determination that would be necessary to rebuild a bigger and better city by the bay.

UP THE RIVER
Directed by John Ford; Written by Maurine Watkins and William Collier, Sr.; Produced by William Fox; Music by Joseph McCarthy and James F. Hanley

<u>Cast</u>
SPENCER TRACY (ST. LOUIS), Warren Hymer (Dannemora Dan), Humphrey Bogart (Steve), Claire Luce (Judy), Joan Lawes (Jean)

SAN FRANCISCO
Directed by W.S. Van Dyke; Written by Anita Loos, based on a story by Robert Hopkins; Produced by John Emerson; Music by Edward Ward, songs by Bronislau Kaper, Walter Jurmann, Gus Kahn, Ted Healy

<u>Cast</u>
Clark Gable (Blackie Norton), Jeanette MacDonald (Mary Blake), SPENCER TRACY (FATHER TIM MULLIN), Jack Holt (Jack Burley), Ted Healy (Matt)

JOHN TRAVOLTA (1954-   )

FIRST APPEARANCE: *The Devil's Rain* (Bryanston, 1975)

A STAR IS BORN: *Saturday Night Fever* (Paramount, 1977)

John Travolta became a superstar in the 1970s by playing street smart and book dumb teenage wiseacres with a facade of machismo to safeguard a sensitive, vulnerable soul. Compare and contrast his Vinnie Barbarino from the TV series *Welcome Back, Kotter*, Tony Manero from *Saturday Night Fever* (1977) and Danny Zucco from *Grease* (1978), all of whom are variations on a rather limited theme. No question that Travolta is great at finding the heart in greasers and delinquents--*Fever* brought him an Oscar nomination as Best Actor--but there wasn't much room to grow in that typecast, and Travolta's subsequent attempts to do so have been almost entirely unsuccessful. *Pulp Fiction* (1994) proved he has the talent to make it as a mature leading man, but only by avoiding formula roles (*The Experts, Look Who's Talking,* 1989) that could just as well be played by Tony Danza.

The youngest of six children, John Travolta was born and raised in Englewood, New Jersey, where he studied acting with his mother, Helen. His father Sal built a theater in the basement, complete with curtains, where the children would perform musicals for an audience consisting of mom and dad. All six kids expressed interest in acting as a career, but only John began to land roles outside of the basement. In his early teens he appeared in commercials and summer stock, and at the age of sixteen he quit school completely to concentrate on his career. Agent Bob LeMond signed Travolta after spotting him in a New Jersey dinner theater, and it wasn't long before he had moved to California and won the role of Kenickie in the touring company of *Grease,* the show that also launched the careers of Barry Bostwick, Jeff Conaway and Richard Gere.

In 1975, Travolta made his film debut in *The Devil's Rain*, a below-average horror film with an above-average cast. Ernest Borgnine plays Jonathan Corbis, the leader of a cult of devil-worshippers. In the 1700s, one of Corbis's followers steals the book in which is written the names of all the doomed souls pledged to Satan. Corbis cannot deliver these souls without the book, which remains hidden from him for two hundred years. Finally, he tracks it down to the descendant of its original abductor. The climax, which is the only reason to pay attention, is a memorable gross-out scene in which Corbis and his followers melt away in an unholy rainstorm, and in more graphic detail than Margaret Hamilton did in *The Wizard of Oz.* There is also a great overacting duel when Borgnine bellows "Open wide the gates of Hell!" while a helpless William Shatner recites The Lord's Prayer in his inimitable grandiose style.

Travolta plays Danny, who appears in two scenes; about halfway into the film he attacks Tom Preston (Tom Skerritt), the book's guardian, and later he is among the melted masses dissolving into jello. Travolta is fifth-billed on the video box, although he is unrecognizable behind a black hood and gobs of monster make-up.

Also in 1975, Travolta played a small role in *Carrie* and then joined the cast of *Welcome Back, Kotter* as Barbarino, one of the four "sweathogs" who made life miserable for schoolteacher Gabe Kotter (Gabe Kaplan). The series became a huge hit, especially among teenagers, but only Travolta was able to parlay his newfound popularity into a career in movies.

Saturday Night Fever is the first film that should be included in the seventies time capsule. In addition to the obvious disco craze that *Fever* helped create, the film is packed with visual and verbal allusions to other icons of the decade, from Farrah Fawcett to Rocky Balboa. Travolta himself, clad in his white suit and gold chains, was elevated to similar status through his terrific portrayal of Tony Manero.

At home, Tony is considered a failure for not following his brother into the priesthood. He works at a dead-end job in a paint store for near minimum wage, and is repulsed at the prospect of remaining a stockboy all his life. He lives for Saturday night and the moments he spends on the dance floor, the only place where he is respected and admired. One night at the disco he meets Stephanie (Karen Lynn Gorney), a girl from the neighborhood who escaped to Manhattan. Tony jilts Annette, his usual dance partner (Donna Pescow) and teams with Stephanie to enter a dance contest. In the film's most telling scene, a Puerto Rican couple is robbed of first prize in the contest because of racism. The real world and its problems have now invaded Tony's sanctuary, and he realizes that it's time to grow up. After giving the other couple the trophy, he apologizes to Stephanie for his constant, clumsy attempts at seduction and makes plans to follow her into Manhattan and into a new life.

Travolta's looks--the hair, the smile, the walk--had women fainting in the aisles. The character of Tony was based on a real Italian-American dancer named Vincent, whose story was told in a *New York Magazine* article entitled "Tribal Rites of the New Saturday Night." 2001 Odyssey, the disco seen in *Saturday Night Fever*, is the same one where Vincent ruled the dance floor. "You're a cliche` going nowhere on the way to no place," Stephanie tells Tony, and Tony knows it. Travolta poignantly conveys Manero's desire to find the same high he feels in the disco somewhere else in his life. In his cruel treatment of Annette and his immature need for the adoration he receives while dancing, Tony does not always emerge as a sympathetic character. He ultimately gains our admiration by recognizing his faults and working to correct them.

The film's soundtrack is one of the best of the past two decades, and became the most atrocious oversight for Academy Award nomination since Paul Simon was snubbed for *The Graduate* in 1967. The dancing has aged better than you might expect as well, and it's refreshing to watch John Badham's direction and Lester Wilson's choreography before MTV ruined dance on film with its mandatory three-second cuts. Travolta's superb solo, shot in one continuous take, provoked applause in movie theaters two decades ago, and remains the epitome of seventies cool.

THE DEVIL'S RAIN
Directed by Robert Fuest; Written by Gabe Essoe, James Ashton and Gerald Hopman; Produced by James V. Cullen; Music by Al De Lory

Cast
Ernest Borgnine (Corbis), Eddie Albert (Dr. Richards), Ida Lupino (Mrs. Preston), William Shatner (Mark Preston), Keenan Wynn (Sheriff Owens), Tom Skerritt (Tom Preston)...JOHN TRAVOLTA (DANNY)

SATURDAY NIGHT FEVER
Directed by John Badham; Written by Norman Wexler, based on an article by Nik Cohn; Produced by Robert Stigwood; Music by Barry, Robin and Maurice Gibb, David Shire, others

Cast
JOHN TRAVOLTA (TONY MANERO), Karen Lynn Gorney (Stephanie), Barry Miller (Bobby C.), Joseph Call (Joey), Paul Pape (Double J), Donna Pescow (Annette)

KATHLEEN TURNER (1954-)

FIRST APPEARANCE: *Body Heat* (Warner Bros., 1981)

A STAR IS BORN: *Body Heat*

With her first film, *Body Heat*, and quite possibly with her first entrance in that film, Kathleen Turner became the *femme fatale* of the 1980s. The easy comparisons were Ava Gardner and Barbara Stanwyck; advanced cinephiles saw in Turner's portrayal of Matty Walker shades of Gloria Grahame and Lizabeth Scott, women famous for characters who used their long-haired, long-legged sexuality as a weapon. It was a sizzling debut for the former soap opera star, and one that provided a niche that a less adventurous actress would have exploited in *Body Heat 2* and a few other clones. Instead, Turner successfully broke her temptress image with successful ventures into domestic drama and romantic comedy.

She was born in Springfield, Missouri, the third of four children, and by the age of sixteen she had lived in Canada, Cuba, Washington, D.C., Venezuela and England. Her father was a Foreign Service officer who dismissed her dreams of becoming an actress. He died one week before Kathleen graduated from the American School in London. She planned to study drama in the land of Shakespeare, but instead returned to America and enrolled in Southwest Missouri State University. Turner was thrown out of her dorm after writing "Better to reign in hell than serve in heaven" on the *Thought for the Day* bulletin board, and eventually transferred to the University of Maryland.

She graduated from the dramatic arts program in 1977, and headed for New York to become famous. What she became was a waitress, who landed the occasional role in an off-off Broadway production. Perseverence led to a nine-month stint in the Broadway play *Gemini*, and the role of Nola Aldrich in the NBC soap opera *The Doctors*. That job lasted over a year, and then her agent saw the script for *Body Heat*. He knew it was perfect for Kathleen, but the film's casting director was not returning his calls. The producers wanted a major, bankable star to play Matty, but Turner's agent was persistent and she was finally allowed to audition. Writer-director Lawrence Kasdan recalled that she was the first actress to read his lines exactly as he had imagined them.

The film was Kasdan's homage to classic film noirs, particularly *Double Indemnity* (1944). There was no attempt to hide the roots of *Body Heat*'s style and substance, but the classic noir elements--shadows cast through venetian blinds, ceiling fans, the use of black and white images to suggest good and evil, the Raymond Chandler-esque dialogue, the jazzy, seductive saxophone-heavy score by John Barry--were paraded out with such priority that the film edges dangerously close to send-up. Pauline Kael summed it up as "a '40's pastiche that verges on camp but takes itself straight."

The story is set in hot, steamy Miranda, Florida, where attorney Ned Racine (William Hurt) meets the beautiful and married Matty Walker (Turner) at a band concert and unsuccessfully tries to pick her up. Sparks fly again at their second meeting, and a torrid affair begins, during which Matty laments over her loveless marriage to a wealthy businessman (Richard Crenna). Together they conjure a successful scheme to kill her husband, but as the investigation continues Ned realizes that Matty has set him up. She collects a large inheritance, fakes her own death and leaves the country. Ned is convicted of the murder and sent to prison.

Accepted limits on movie sexuality have risen considerably since the heyday of film noir, and Kasdan accordingly turns up the heat on Ned and Matty's affair. "You shouldn't wear that body," Ned tells Matty at their first meeting, but later he changes his mind. The graphic lovemaking scenes are memorable for their ferocity and abandon. When Turner lures Ned to his own doom with a voice that is pure Lauren Bacall, she exudes more animal sex appeal while fully clothed than Sharon Stone in *Basic Instinct* (1993), or Madonna in her entire life.

280

William Hurt is just right as the powerless fall guy, and the casting is impeccable down to Ted Danson as Ned's tapdancing lawyer and soap opera diva Kim Zimmer as Matty's lookalike friend Mary Ann, who unwittingly plays a role in Matty's plans.

     Body Heat was labeled derivative, and not without reason, but that doesn't answer the question of whether it's any good. The performances are perfect, the script has the one predictable twist plus the additional, less obvious twist that distinguishes better noir, the direction is energetic and obviously affectionate. Most movie buffs inevitably sport a smile of nostalgic recognition watching the story unfold, while those unfamiliar with the form will discover that all of its tricks and treats still work. The film was not a big box-office hit, but it made Turner a star and still rents well at video stores. There were even *Body Heat* fan clubs for awhile, in which satin sheets and wind chimes became the equivalent of the water pistols and toast carried by the *Rocky Horror Picture Show* crowd. I think they have all disbanded now, but the memory of Kathleen Turner, sitting on a barstool in a slit skirt and blowing cigarette smoke in seductive circles, lingers on.

BODY HEAT
Directed and written by Lawrence Kasdan; Produced by Fred T. Gallo; Music by John Barry

Cast
William Hurt (Ned Racine), KATHLEEN TURNER (MATTY WALKER), Richard Crenna (Edmund Walker), Ted Danson (Peter Lowenstein), J.A. Preston (Oscar Grace), Mickey Rourke (Teddy Lewis), Kim Zimmer (Mary Ann Simpson)

LANA TURNER (1921-1995)

FIRST APPEARANCE: *A Star Is Born* (David O. Selznick/United Artists, 1937)

A STAR IS BORN: *Ziegfeld Girl* (MGM, 1941)

It is the most famous "discovery" story to emerge from Hollywood; a teenage Lana Turner is sipping a soda at Schwab's Drug Store when she is spotted by Billy Wilkerson, publisher of *The Hollywood Reporter*. "How would you like to be in pictures?" Wilkerson asks. Turner accepts the offer and becomes a star, and Schwab's becomes a landmark for movie buffs. The problem is that Turner was cutting a class at Hollywood High when destiny struck, and Hollywood High is a good two miles away from Schwab's, and therefore could not possibly have been the discovery site. When Turner's memory failed, a new search nominated the Top Hat Malt Shop, located across the street from the high school at the corner of Sunset and Highland, as the most likely spot of the event. The truth came too late to save the Top Hat, which is now a Texaco. Schwab's, once bereft of its starmaking reputation, bit the dust as well.

If Lana Turner's place of birth remains debatable, it is incontestable that Julia Jean Turner was born in Wallace, Idaho. Her father Virgil, an insurance salesman, moved the family to various California cities in his search for work. At the age of 36, he was killed during a robbery attempt, a case that remains unsolved. Julia, who preferred the nickname "Judy," was shuffled off to Modesto and later to Los Angeles by her mother, Mildred. Money was tight-- sometimes days went by without food--when fifteen-year-old Judy transferred to Hollywood High. "She was the most incredibly beautiful girl we had ever seen," recalled classmate Nanette Fabray. "Even the teachers stared at her. She'd walk down the hall, looking straight ahead while all the other kids gawked at her."

In January of 1936, after ninety days of sophomore studies, Judy skipped a typing class for the malt shop, where she had become a regular. The soda jerk knew her well enough to arrange an introduction for Billy Wilkerson on that fateful day. She thought it was a pick-up, until he produced a business card and an invitation for her and her mother to visit his office.

Judy was 5' 3", with auburn shoulder-length hair, gray-blue eyes and a curvaceous, bodacious figure. Clearly Wilkerson believed her stunning beauty was enough, even though she had never even played a tree in a school play, and had no interest in acting whatsoever. But in the days of the studio system, a comely lass could be nurtured from extra to bit player to supporting player to star, while learning her craft like an apprentice in any other trade. It is fitting then that Turner's first moment of note on screen (in 1937's *They Won't Forget*) was one of pure physical allure, played without a word of dialogue. The problem with this scenario is that it gives too little credit to Turner; there were and always will be a lot of pretty girls in California, but not many could have learned their lessons as well. By the time of *The Postman Always Rings Twice* (1946) she had proved a gifted student; when she made *The Bad and the Beautiful* (1952), Lana Turner had become a fine actress.

Wilkerson brought Judy to a talent agency owned by Zeppo Marx and introduced her to a 21-year-old vice president named Henry Willson. It was Willson who changed her name to Lana and introduced her to the studio bosses, after getting permission from her Hollywood High principal. David O. Selznick hired Turner as a extra for $25, and she made her first appearance in his 1937 release *A Star is Born*. Ninety minutes into the film, a fight breaks out at Santa Anita racetrack between has-been celebrity Norman Maine (Frederic March) and his bitter, former publicity man (Lionel Stander). Sixteen-year-old Lana is among the crowd (which also includes Carole Landis) that gathers to watch the brawl. She appears in the foreground for about ten seconds, dressed in a blue coat and brown hat, and is only shown from the back (not one of Selznick's brighter decisions). Stars Janet Gaynor and Frederic March were Oscar-nominated, and the film holds up well against the Judy Garland musical of 1954 and the bombastic Barbra Streisand vehicle of 1976.

A case could be made for *They Won't Forget*, Lana's second film, as her star-making vehicle. Her role as murder victim Mary Clay ran its course in the first twelve minutes, but before departing Turner sashays across the screen in a tight sweater, high heels and a saucy black beret, saying nothing but communicating a great deal. Gasps and whistles filled America's moviehouses, and overnight Lana Turner was christened the "Sweater Girl" in fan magazines. But the moment did more for sweater manufacturers than for Lana's career.

Ziegfeld Girl was not Turner's first starring role, but it was her first assignment on MGM's 'A' list. After appearing in the programmers *Dancing Co-Ed* (1939) and *Two Girls on Broadway* (1940), Lana now found herself reporting for work on the same project as Busby Berkeley, Judy Garland, Jimmy Stewart, Hedy Lamarr, Tony Martin, Jackie Cooper and Eve Arden. Metro thought she was ready, and the critics agreed--"Lana Turner--and I couldn't have been more surprised--actually does some effective acting." wrote the *Cleveland Press*, and their amazement was echoed in reviews across the country.

The story follows the lives of three young women from different walks of life who become Ziegfeld girls; Susie (Garland), a showbiz veteran in her early twenties, leaves her father's vaudeville act to join the Follies; Sandra (Lamarr), the wife of a brilliant but penniless concert violinist, joins the show against her husband's wishes; Sheila (Turner) is plucked from the elevator of a New York department store and onto the stage; When the Ziegfeld Follies closes one year later, Susie has her name in lights as a rising star, and Sandra returns to her husband's side as he embarks on a concert tour. Sheila, after leaving her boyfriend Gil (Jimmy Stewart) for a rich society playboy, descends from Park Avenue to Skid Row in an alcoholic fog.

As the only Ziegfeld girl gone bad, Turner had (by a fraction) the biggest role, and carried all the heavy-duty drama scenes. She matches up well with Jimmy Stewart, and as her character succumbs to the corrupt temptations of fame and money Turner still manages to convey the inherent--though distracted--goodness of a girl who learns that the ups and downs of life are more severe than the ones in an elevator. The musical numbers, especially Garland's "I'm Always Chasing Rainbows," are most rapidly recalled, but the dramatic high point is Turner's and she plays it beautifully. Late in the film, a deathly ill Sheila drags herself back to the theater to watch Susie's first solo performance. When the pain becomes unbearable she leaves her seat and approaches the stairs from the balcony. In her delirium, she imagines herself back on stage, walking down a lavish marble staircase in an opulent costume. The plastic showgirl smile returns as she gracefully descends the steps, staggering occasionally, and collapsing at the bottom, while inside the show goes on. Melodramatic, to be sure, but Sheila's departure is certainly the most vivid manifestation of Lana Turner's arrival.

A STAR IS BORN
Directed by William A. Wellman; Written by Dorothy Parker, Alan Campbell and Robert Carson, based on the story by Carson and William A. Wellman; Produced by David O. Selznick; Music by Max Steiner

Cast
Janet Gaynor (Esther Blodgett), Frederic March (Norman Maine), Adolphe Menjou (Oliver Niles), Andy Devine (Danny McGuire), Lionel Stander (Libby)...LANA TURNER (EXTRA AT SANTA ANITA BAR)

ZIEGFELD GIRL
Directed by Robert Z. Leonard; Written by Marguerite Roberts and Sonya Levien, based on a story by William Anthony McGuire; Produced by Pandro S. Berman; Music by Roger Edens, Gus Kahn, Nacio Herb Brown, Joseph McCarthy, Harry Carroll, others

Cast
James Stewart (Gilbert Young), Judy Garland (Susan Gallagher), Hedy Lamarr (Sandra Kolter), LANA TURNER (SHEILA REGAN), Tony Martin (Frank Merton), Jackie Cooper (Jerry Regan), Ian Hunter (Geoffrey Collis), Edward Everett Horton (Noble Sage), Eve Arden (Patsy Dixon)

JOHN WAYNE (1907-1979)

FIRST APPEARANCE: *Brown of Harvard* (MGM, 1926)

A STAR IS BORN: *Stagecoach* (United Artists, 1939)

John Wayne has become more of a wild west icon than Wyatt Earp, Bat Masterson or any of the historical figures who were actually there. This is somehow fitting for an era that was always more myth than reality anyway; our affection for the period has been shaped almost entirely by the Western movie genre, and John Wayne, its most recognizable symbol, has become the idealization of the American cowboy's rugged individualism, resourcefulness and heroism.

Wayne's sincerity on screen, his strongest trait as an actor, stems from his reverent belief in the value system of his film persona. In the 1960s, his high-profile, right-wing conservatism was the subject of scorn in some circles, and for awhile threatened to extend to a revisionist backlash against his films. But today, the name John Wayne has become a synonym for American patriotism, in a way that transcends politics. Observed film critic Andrew Sarris, "He has come to embody even for his ideological foes the survival of certain vestigal virtues-- bravery, loyalty, stoicism in the face of pain, loss, and even death--in a world reduced to mealy-mouthed relativism."

He looked right at home midst the vast plains and craggy, geometric buttes of Monument Valley, Utah, but John Wayne was actually born in the small town of Winterset, Iowa. Marion Michael Morrison is the name on his birth certificate, and "Duke" is the nickname he picked up at the age of six, after moving with his family to Glendale, California. Glendale's firemen called the boy Duke after his dog, a large Airedale with the same name. He was an above-average student and a football star at Glendale Union High School, but his application to attend the U.S. Naval Academy at Annapolis was rejected. Disappointed, he accepted a football scholarship to the University of Southern California.

John Wayne's film debut came about as a result of an arrangement between USC football coach Howard Jones and western movie star Tom Mix. In exchange for good seats to Trojan home games, Mix gave bit parts in Fox movies, with pay, to several members of the team. In 1926, Wayne received $7.50 to serve as the stunt double for Francis X. Bushman in *Brown of Harvard*.

The film chronicles the exploits of Harvard underclassman Tom Brown (William Haines), and his attempts to romance his professor's daughter (Mary Brian), while helping his alma mater beat rival Cambridge in rowing and football. The climactic football game combined actual footage of a Harvard-Cambridge contest with shots of actors Haines and Bushman supplying the heroics. In one scene, Bushman's character, Bob McAndrews, dashes almost one hundred yards before being tackled from behind. John Wayne's job was to do some of the running (when being filmed from the back), and to take the hit and go down.

The USC team appeared in another film, *The Drop Kick*, one year later, but Wayne's decision to become an actor was made when he saw Tom Mix drive onto the campus in a fancy, expensive car; "It was right there and then," he told *Time* magazine, "I told myself this was a good business for me to be in." Wayne worked as an extra and a stuntman, impressing director John Ford on the set of *Men Without Women* (1930) with his derring-do and work ethic. The friendship that developed was instrumental in Wayne's progression from bit player to supporting player to leading man.

He paid his dues in a seemingly endless series of "B" westerns, and achieved a minor sort of fame as a member of the "Three Mesquiteers" in one of Republic Pictures' most popular serials. Throughout the 1930s, Wayne appeared in over sixty interchangable horse operas. Only *The Big Trail* (1930) stands out above the throng, but it could not elevate the Duke to stardom. For this reason, John Ford's decision to cast his friend in *Stagecoach* did not sit well with producer Walter Wanger, who wanted Gary Cooper to play the role of the Ringo Kid. Wanger finally agreed to the casting only after Ford promised that Claire Trevor would receive top billing.

Stagecoach was hailed upon its release as a touchstone in the evolution of the western, and remains a popular term paper subject for film students. Ostensibly, it's a straightforward tale of a stagecoach from Tonto, New Mexico, bound for Lordsburg, that must carry eight passengers through hostile Indian territory. Among the travelers are an alcoholic doctor (Thomas Mitchell, who earned an Academy Award for his performance), a prostitute (Trevor), a Southern gentleman (John Carradine), a gruff banker (Berton Churchill) and a refined soldier's wife (Louise Platt). During the journey they are joined by the Ringo Kid (Wayne), an outlaw on the trail of the men who killed his father and brother. But beneath the surface, Dudley Nichols' literate script examined the conflicting and consenting dynamics between the characters--male and female, North and South, highbrow and lowbrow, valiant and cowardly, and how those dynamics change as the trip progresses. Because they are presented as more than targets for Apache arrows, the viewer's concern for their welfare is intensified when the shooting begins.

As *Stagecoach* became a template for the genre in its characters, flawless cinematography and editing of action sequences, the Ringo Kid became a template for the film persona most associated with John Wayne; a strong, independent man of imposing height and build, who lives by a moral code that doesn't always conform to the law of the land. He is respectful toward women, but awkward and timid when it comes to romance. Ringo's marriage proposal to the prostitute Dallas, delivered with head bowed and voice wavering, is the kind of quiet, poignant moment that was not found in westerns before John Ford.

John Wayne's entrance scene seems deliberately designed to introduce a significant new presence in the genre; a long zoom shot emanating from the moving stagecoach closes rapidly on a figure in the distance. Wayne looks larger than life as he forces the stagecoach to a halt with a gesture. He stands, legs apart, a saddle slung over his shoulder, twirling a Winchester rifle. "Looks like you've got another passenger," he tells the driver (Andy Devine), and western movies would never be the same.

BROWN OF HARVARD
Directed by Jack Conway; Written by A.P. Younger and Donald Ogden Stewart, based on the play by Rida Johnson Young

Cast
Jack Pickford (Jim Doolittle), Mary Brian (Mary Abbott), Francis X. Bushman (Bob McAndrews), Mary Alden (Mrs. Brown), William Haines (Tom Brown)...JOHN WAYNE (STUNT DOUBLE FOR FRANCIS X. BUSHMAN)

STAGECOACH
Directed by John Ford; Written by Dudley Nichols, based on the short story *Stage to Lordsburg* by Ernest Haycox; Produced by Walter Wanger; Music by Richard Hageman, W. Franke Harling, Louis Gruenberg, Leo Shuken and John Leipold

Cast
Claire Trevor (Dallas), JOHN WAYNE (THE RINGO KID), John Carradine (Hatfield), Thomas Mitchell (Dr. Josiah Boone), Andy Devine (Buck), Donald Meek (Mr. Peacock), Louise Platt (Lucy Mallory), George Bancroft (Curly), Berton Churchill (Hanry Gatewood), Tim Holt (Lt. Blanchard)

SIGOURNEY WEAVER (1949-   )

FIRST APPEARANCE: *Annie Hall* (United Artists, 1977)

A STAR IS BORN: *Alien* (20th Century-Fox, 1979

Time magazine called her "Dom Perignon in a town built to sell Dr. Pepper," but Sigourney Weaver can be a Pepper too. Few other actresses are able to move with such ease from the mainstream to the art houses and back without (pardon the expression) alienating either audience. Weaver elevates genre films (1984's *Ghostbusters*, 1986's *Aliens*) with her regal grace and the respectful, carefully considered approach she instills in otherwise conventional roles; conversely, she makes the esoteric more approachable by bringing out the universal emotions that are evident even in the most austere, ambiguous characters (1983's *The Year of Living Dangerously*, 1986's *Half Moon Street*).

Sigourney's father, Sylvester "Pat" Weaver, is famous for a lot more than producing a monster-slaying daughter; in the 1950s Weaver was the president of the NBC television network, and is responsible for creating both *Today* and *The Tonight Show.* Sigourney, who answered to Susan Weaver until age fourteen, frequently visited the *Today* set and played with J. Fred Muggs, which provided good training for *Gorillas in the Mist* (1988). Her theatrical yearnings were passed down from mother Elizabeth Inglis, an actress trained at London's Royal Academy of Dramatic Arts, and a featured performer in such films as *The 39 Steps* (1935) and *The Letter* (1940). There was comedy timing in the genes as well from Uncle "Doodles" Weaver, the vocalist on several classic Spike Jones recordings.

"I was a privileged, pampered, sheltered child," said Weaver of her genteel upbringing. The family lived in an apartment in New York's Sutton Place once owned by Marion Davies. She attended Chapin, Brearley, Ethel Walker (if you have to ask. . .), and ballroom dancing classes at the Colony Club. She was a debutante twice at separate coming out parties. Her parents indulged Susan's becoming Sigourney after she read *The Great Gatsby*, her three weeks of potato peeling at an Israeli kibbutz and her living in a treehouse with a boyfriend while attending Stanford University. Their only wish was that Sigourney, or "S" as they called her after the name change, would steer clear of an acting career. Pat Weaver called show business "a crooked, awful enterprise, notable for hustles and heartbreak."

Sigourney pleased her folks by studying for a doctorate in English and planning to teach literature, but then she got bored and left Stanford for the Yale School of Drama. There she met playwright Christopher Durang, and played lead roles in several of his offbeat comedies. Weaver made her Broadway debut in 1974's *The Constant Wife*, and received a Tony nomination for her performance opposite William Hurt in *Hurlyburly* (1984).

Her first movie was *Annie Hall*, Oscar's Best Picture of 1977 and arguably Woody Allen's most beloved film. Weaver appears near the end, as the date of Allen's character Alvy Singer, but to see her you'll need 20-20 vision and one of those RCA televisions with an "Ultra Zoom" button on the remote. The scene lasts only ten seconds and does not contain dialogue.

The following year she appeared in an Israeli military drama called *Madman*, opposite Oscar-winner F. Murray Abraham. But it was *Alien*, Ridley Scott's science fiction suspense thriller, that established Sigourney Weaver as an actress worth watching. As Warrant Officer Ripley, second in command on the mineral tanker ship *Nostromo*, Weaver essays a character who is sexy, clever and tough all at the same time. The story borrows elements from Hitchcock, Howard Hawks's *The Thing* (1951) and every haunted house film ever made, but the actual inspiration was a schlock fifties sci-fi programmer called *It! The Terror From Beyond Space* (1958). The Nostromo's seven-member crew are ordered to investigate the remains of a derelict spacecraft, and are attacked by a ferocious creature. The alien returns with them to their ship, and kills the crew one by one. Ripley, the last survivor, assures the audience that Victoria's Secret is still in business in the high-tech future, and then blows the creature out into space.

Lingerie-clad women have been attacked by monsters in movies as far back as *King Kong* (1933); usually they end up killed and eaten, or rescued by one or more guys with names like Dirk Squarejaw. Not so with Ripley, whom Weaver has dubbed "Rambolina" after her exploits in *Alien* and its two sequels. "I structured the character after Henry V and the women warriors of classic Chinese literature," she told *Time*, and by playing the part seriously, without the wink to the audience that most movie action heroes can't resist, she creates one of the more memorable female protagonists of the seventies.

The alien itself was inspired by the artwork of Moebius and H.R. Giger, and may be the most terrifying creature imagined and built by special effects. Director Ridley Scott heightens the tension by filming the alien mostly in shadow, and maneuvering the creature and a reputable cast of character actors through a seemingly endless series of dark, claustrophobic hallways. The password is atmosphere, and Scott lays it on with relish.

Weaver reprised her role in *Aliens* (1986), a thrill ride of a movie that earned her an Oscar nomination as Best Actress. Ripley was finally killed in *Alien 3* (1992), but not without one hell of a fight.

ANNIE HALL
Directed by Woody Allen; Written by Woody Allen and Marshall Brickman; Produced by Charles H. Joffe

Cast
Woody Allen (Alvy Singer), Diane Keaton (Annie Hall), Tony Roberts (Rob), Paul Simon (Tony Lacey)...SIGOURNEY WEAVER (ALVY'S DATE OUTSIDE THEATER)

ALIEN
Directed by Ridley Scott; Written by Dan O'Bannon, based on a story by O'Bannon and Ronald Shusett; Produced by Gordon Carroll, David Giler and Walter Hill; Music by Jerry Goldsmith

Cast
Tom Skerritt (Dallas), SIGOURNEY WEAVER (RIPLEY), Veronica Cartwright (Lambert), Harry Dean Stanton (Brett), John Hurt (Kane), Ian Holm (Ash), Yaphet Kotto (Parker)

RAQUEL WELCH (1940-)

FIRST APPEARANCE: *Roustabout* (Paramount, 1964)

A STAR IS BORN: *One Million Years B.C.* (Hammer/20th Century-Fox, 1966)

There was a time when a starlet could sign a movie contract without a single ounce of acting ability, and then be coached and developed until she was qualified, or until she was famous enough for her inability to not matter. Raquel Welch, who arrived just as the studio system was on life support, was the last product of this procedure. She never played a substantial role, or developed a screen personae more significant than a walking pin-up. Of the 25 films Welch made in her heyday, the only ones worth seeing are those that were not built around her puffed-up brunette 'do and well-endowed figure. *Fantastic Voyage* (1966), *The Last of Sheila* (1973) and *The Three Musketeers* (1974) all succeeded with (despite) Raquel in a supporting role. Her star vehicles were all disastrous, though *Fathom* (1967) and *Kansas City Bomber* (1972) almost qualify as guilty pleasures. Welch did prove surprisingly impressive in a couple of made-for-TV movies in the 1980s, but today's Hollywood is not as patient; Bo Derek's failure to follow up *10* (1979) was a clear signal that beauty alone would no longer sustain a career.

Raquel Tejada was the first of three children born in Chicago, Illinois to a Bolivian father and American mother. The family moved to La Jolla, California when Raquel was two years old. As a teenager she was a cheerleader at La Jolla High and the winner of several beauty pageants, and such titles as "Miss Photogenic." When she was eighteen, Raquel married classmate James Welch and had two children, Damon and Tahnee. The marriage was never happy, and ended in 1963. She then decided to pursue her lifelong dream of performing, and it may surprise many to learn that she actually earned a dramatic scholarship to San Diego State College. After one year she dropped out, but remained active in local theatre groups and the La Jolla Playhouse. After a stint as the weather girl on a local TV station, Raquel Welch moved to Hollywood, where she found work as a model and as a walk-on bombshell in burlesque sketches on *The Red Skelton Show*.

Her movie debut consisted of one unbilled minute at the very beginning of *Roustabout*, a typically dopey Elvis Presley vehicle. This time the King plays a love 'em and leave 'em wanderer who takes a job at a financially-strapped carnival owned by Barbara Stanwyck. He sings the usual batch of lousy songs, but somehow the carnival is still saved. Raquel, wearing a blue dress and with her dark tresses shorter than we're used to seeing, plays one of four college students who watch Elvis perform at a nightclub. He sings "Poison Ivy League," a satiric slap at fraternities that lands him in hot water, but by then you've seen the last of Raquel. She has one line--"How come they call this place a teahouse, dear?" Stanwyck adds some class, and Teri Garr can be spotted dancing in the "Carny Town" number, but *Roustabout* never rises above the mundane.

She played another bit part in *A Swingin' Summer* (1965) and then hooked up with a talent agent and future second husband Patrick Curtis, who brought her to the attention of producer Saul David at Twentieth Century-Fox. She was second-billed in Fox's *Fantastic Voyage*, an outstanding science fiction adventure with Oscar-winning special effects, and then mesmerized the European paparazzi during a tour of the continent. By 1966 Raquel had appeared on over one hundred magazine covers, and was selected along with Robert Redford as a "Star of Tomorrow" by the *Motion Picture Herald*. The prediction was accurate-- even before her next film, *One Million Years B.C.*, was released, photos of Raquel in her skimpy cavegirl bikini had appeared in newspapers around the world, and posters of her emerging from the prehistoric surf were on the doors of every boys dormitory in the country.

The film was a remake of *One Million B.C.* (1940) starring Carole Landis and Victor Mature. After a voiceover intro that sounds like every earth science filmstrip you ever sat through in eighth grade, we meet Tumak of the Rock People (John Richardson), who is banished from his tribe after a fight with his father. After wandering in the desert he is rescued from a giant snapping turtle by Loana of the Shell People (Welch). Tumak and Loana become an item, but their love is tested when war breaks out between their tribes. After an earthquake decimates the ranks of both sides, the Rock People and the Shell People opt for peaceful coexistence.

The stop motion creations of the great Ray Harryhausen effectively break the monotony of grunting and growling that comprise the film's dialogue, but this is the first time that Harryhausen's effects are overshadowed by the special effects of a human being--Raquel's flowing blond hair, olive complexion and voluptuous figure, exposed just within the limits of the film's rating. The *New York Times* called her "a marvelous, breathing monument to womanhood," and with press like that you don't need dialogue. Good thing too, since Raquel's consisted of three words--"Tumak!" "Akita!" (which means "help") and "Serron!" (which means "giant bird"). The huge dinosaurs and spiders and lizards are all well and good (Loana's abduction by a pterodactyl is superbly conceived), but in the end it is Raquel's assets that turned *One Million Years B.C.* into a modest and much-publicized hit.

ROUSTABOUT
Directed by John Rich; Written by Paul Nathan, Anthony Lawrence and Allan Weiss, based on a story by Weiss; Produced by Hal B. Wallis; Music by Joseph L. Lilley, Jerry Leiber, Mike Stoller, Fred Wise, Randy Starr

Cast
Elvis Presley (Charlie Rogers), Barbara Stanwyck (Maggie Morgan), Joan Freeman (Cathy Lean), Leif Erickson (Joe Lean)...RAQUEL WELCH (COLLEGE GIRL)

ONE MILLION YEARS B.C.
Directed by Don Chaffey; Written by Michael Carreras, based on a story by Mickell Novak, George Baker and Joseph Frickert; Produced by Michael Carreras; Music by Mario Nascimbene

Cast
RAQUEL WELCH (LOANA), John Richardson (Tumak), Percy Herbert (Sakana), Robert Brown (Akhoba)

RICHARD WIDMARK (1914-   )

FIRST APPEARANCE: *Kiss of Death* (20th Century-Fox, 1947)

A STAR IS BORN: *Kiss of Death*

Although his career spanned over fifty films in five decades, Richard Widmark never topped the impact he made in his first film appearance. As Tommy Udo, the giggling, psychotic mobster in *Kiss of Death*, he earned his only Academy Award nomination, and set a new standard for movie brutality.

A native of Sunrise, Minnesota, Widmark traveled with his family throughout the midwest as a youth, before settling at last in Princeton, Illinois, where he attended high school and excelled in both football and the dramatic club. He gave the commencement address at the 1932 graduation ceremony, and in the fall he began attending Lake Forest (Illinois) College on a full scholarship. After graduating in 1936, he remained with the college as a drama instructor.

Following two years of teaching, Widmark went to New York to meet up with a former classmate, who gave him a part in the radio series *Aunt Jenny's Real Life Stories*. Thus began a decade-long career of playing a variety of roles on such popular dramas as *March of Time* and *Cavalcade*. He made his Broadway debut as a young Army Air Corps lieutenant in the comedy *Kiss and Tell* (1943). But the movies had been his real objective from the time he worked as a doorman at a theater just to see every film that made it to Princeton, Illinois.

Finally, at the age of 33, Widmark achieved his dream after he was cast in Henry Hathaway's *Kiss of Death*. At first, Hathaway thought that Widmark looked too well-bred and intellectual for the part of a savage killer, until he discovered that the actor's natural intelligence and confidence only made the villain more intimidating.

Recollections of the film always return to the exploits of Tommy Udo, but *Kiss of Death* is primarily about the troubles of Nick Bianco (Victor Mature), a small-time hood with a wife and two young daughters. After trying unsuccessfully to go straight, Nick pulls another robbery and is caught before he's out the door. Now facing a long sentence, he is devastated at the thought of not seeing his children grow up. The district attorney (Brian Donlevy) senses something decent within Nick, and offers him another chance--turn state's evidence in exchange for a reduced sentence. Nick refuses, but after his wife commits suicide and the two girls are sent to an orphanage, he reconsiders.

Bianco is given parole, but in return he must help the state form a case against Tommy Udo, a mobster with a particular hatred for squealers. He does his job and Tommy is arrested, but the D.A.'s case doesn't hold up. Nick, now remarried, realizes that the psychotic Udo will be coming after him--and his family. The police offer protection, but Nick decides to deal with the threat himself.

What separates good films from great ones is how quickly they are able to draw an audience into the story. *Kiss of Death* prompts almost instantaneous involvement. In the first scene Nick and his gang hold up a jewelry store on the top floor of a skyscraper. They tie up the salesmen and make their escape by elevator, but as they slowly descend from the 24th floor, one of the clerks begins crawling toward the alarm button. From then on, we're hooked.

Widmark's first appearance comes early on, when Udo, who temporarily shares a cell with Bianco, grumbles about being incarcerated "just for choppin' the ears off of some guy's head." But the scene that has passed into cinema legend comes later, when Tommy enters the apartment of a mob snitch, intending to silence him permanently, but finds only his quarry's mother (Mildred Natwick) at home. A twisted grin falls upon the face of the killer, as he stalks the frail, wheelchair-bound woman. And then, quick as a flash, he ties her arms with a lampcord, and pushes her wheelchair down a flight of stairs.

Before you realize what he's going to do, it's over. There's no long build-up to the act, which has little bearing on the main plot, but the reverberations of Tommy's assault are felt all

290

through the film. Even today, when movies like *The Texas Chainsaw Massacre* (1974) and *Friday the 13th* (1980) wallow in the most graphic depictions of violence imaginable, Udo's depravity is still shocking, because he so clearly enjoys his handiwork. Later, at the final confrontation between Tommy and Nick Bianco, the tension is electric when Tommy smiles and tells Nick, "I'm gonna enjoy meetin' your family." Widmark lets the line slide out, with a snarl in his deep voice that is broken by high-pitched, sadistic laughter. Fans of the camp classic television series *Batman* cannot miss the similarities between Widmark and Frank Gorshin, who obviously patterned his portrayal of The Riddler on Tommy Udo.

Richard Widmark would lend an intriguing presence to many more film noirs, such as *Night and the City* (1950) and *Pickup on South Street* (1954). Although he successfully avoided the sort of typecasting that plagued Anthony Perkins after *Psycho* (1960), he would occasionally return to the type of role that earned him overnight fame, most memorably as Sidney Poitier's nemesis in *No Way Out* (1950).

KISS OF DEATH
Directed by Henry Hathaway; Written by Ben Hecht and Charles Lederer, based on a story by Eleazar Lipsky; Produced by Fred Kohlmar; Music by David Buttolph

Cast
Victor Mature (Nick Bianco), Brian Donlevy (D'Angelo), Coleen Gray (Nettie), RICHARD WIDMARK (TOMMY UDO), Karl Malden (Sgt. William Cullen)

ESTHER WILLIAMS (1923-   )

FIRST APPEARANCE: *Andy Hardy's Double Life* (MGM, 1942)

A STAR IS BORN: *Bathing Beauty* (MGM, 1944)

"I can't sing, I can't dance, I can't act," she said unapologetically, but Esther Williams could swim, dive, and smile underwater, and that was enough to make her a sensation at the home of the Hollywood musical. She earned approximately $80-90 million for MGM between 1944 and 1955, appeared on fifteen fan magazine covers a year (more than any other performer), and was ranked in 1949 as the number eight money maker in movies, and the biggest female star behind Betty Grable.

The youngest of five children, Esther Jane Williams was born in Inglewood, California, and learned to swim during one of the family's frequent trips to the beach. When she was eight a playground swimming pool opened across the street from her home, and Esther took a job counting locker room towels to earn extra swimming time. She joined the Los Angeles Athletic Club at the age of fifteen, and was told by a swimming coach that she had the potential to be a champion.

Two years later, Esther won every race she entered in the 1939 Women's Outdoor Nationals, set a record for the 100-meter breast stroke and earned a spot on the U.S. Olympic team. But when the 1940 Summer Games in Helsinki were cancelled because of World War II, she returned to the University of Southern California and to modeling sportswear at a Los Angeles I Magnin's. Then she was asked to jump back in the water--not for gold medals, but for show business.

Today the films of Esther Williams seem a whimsical anomaly, but lavish aquatic stage shows were actually quite popular in the 1930s and '40s, and the movies simply elaborated and amplified what was possible on a stage, just as they were already doing to song and dance on dry land. it was an offer from Billy Rose's Aquacade that had Esther swimming in San Francisco with Johnny Weissmuller four times a day (five times on weekends) for eight months. Hollywood scouts saw the Aquacade and offered Esther a contract, but she opted to return to I Magnin's. One year later Louis B. Mayer tried again, this time easing Esther's fears about having never acted before by promising six months of lessons and preparation. This time she accepted, and it was off to the classrooms of Metro-Goldwyn-Mayer.

When the six months were up, Esther filmed a screen test with Clark Gable and was sent to the town of Carvel for her first assignment. As any movie buff knows, Carvel was home to the Hardy family, who were featured in MGM's most beloved film series. *Andy Hardy's Double Life* (1942) was the thirteenth entry, and as usual it's Mickey Rooney mugging through ninety wonderful minutes of carefree entertainment. Esther played Sheila Brooks, college psychology major and houseguest of Andy's longtime girlfriend Polly Benedict (Ann Rutherford). She helps Polly teach the flirtatious Andy a lesson by manipulating him into a marriage proposal.

The Hardy series was MGM's favorite place to launch new female contract players, and Esther was the last of a graduating class that included Judy Garland, Lana Turner and Donna Reed. She first appears in a white two-piece bathing suit (Andy is understandably dazzled) and it isn't long before Esther is in the Benedicts' Olympic-sized backyard pool--nothing fancy yet, though, just a couple of underwater spins and a wet kiss for Rooney. Sheila Brooks was the type of role that Esther would play most often--a self-assured, independent woman who took charge of her romantic relationships. She actually could act, not enough to play Camille perhaps but certainly well enough to handle the elementary plot twists of the musicals that would make her famous.

Andy Hardy's Double Life also contains typically fine performances from Mickey Rooney, Lewis Stone as the Hardy patriarch, and a virtuoso medley of '40's slang ("trick a chicken", "clincheroo") that Andy must amusingly translate for his father. The film was a hit like all previous entries, and after playing a small, dry role in *A Guy Named Joe* (1943) Esther was given a movie of her own. Just to play it safe, however, MGM also threw in Red Skelton, Basil Rathbone, Janis Paige and the orchestras of Harry James and Xavier Cugat.

In *Bathing Beauty*, Esther plays Caroline Brooks (Sheila's sister?), who breaks her engagement with musician Steve Elliott (Skelton) over a misunderstanding concocted by Elliot's boss (Rathbone). Steve follows Caroline to the all-girl college where she works, and manages to gain admittance as a student. So much for the script. Skelton's antics in ballet class are good for a laugh, and two great big bands kick out some catchy tunes. Musical numbers like "Loch Lomond--You Take the High Note" didn't make the cut for *That's Entertainment* (1974) but they have a silly, infectious exuberance that is irresistible. Esther is sometimes lost in a crowd as the story unfolds, but she takes center stage amid fountains and fire in the climactic water ballet, which combines her athletic grace with all the glitz of a Las Vegas revue multiplied by ten. They would become even more elaborate in later films such as *Neptune's Daughter* (1949) but this remains one of her best. Watching the unique little slice of history created by Hollywood's Mermaid is still a kick, sweetly nostalgic and also a little sad, because you know this sort of thing will never happen again.

ANDY HARDY'S DOUBLE LIFE
Directed by George B Seitz; Written by Agnes Christine Johnson; Music by Daniele Amifitheatrof

Cast
Lewis Stone (Judge Hardy), Mickey Rooney (Andy Hardy), Fay Holden (Mrs. Hardy), Cecilia Parker (Marian Hardy), Ann Rutherford (Polly Benedict), ESTHER WILLIAMS (SHEILA BROOKS)

BATHING BEAUTY
Directed by George Sidney; Written by Dorothy Kingsley, Allen Boretz, Frank Waldman and Joseph Schrank, based on a story by Kenneth Earl and M.M. Musselman; Produced by Jack Cummings; Music by Johnny Green, Arthur Freed, Gus Arnheim, Abe Lyman, J. Camacho, Noro Morales

Cast
Red Skelton (Steve Elliot), ESTHER WILLIAMS (CAROLINE BROOKS), Basil Rathbone (George Adams), Bill Goodwin (Willis Evans), Ethel Smith (Organist)

ROBIN WILLIAMS (1952-   )

FIRST APPEARANCE: *Can I Do It Till' I Need Glasses?* (National-American, 1977)

A STAR IS BORN: *Moscow on the Hudson* (Columbia, 1984)

In the late 1970s, comedy clubs became the new breeding ground for motion picture talent. Steve Martin, Eddie Murphy, Billy Crystal and Richard Pryor all began their careers doing stand-up before making a successful, if not always graceful, transition to features. But the valedictorian of class clowns is Robin Williams, a two-time Academy Award nominee who has proven equally effective in dramatic performances as he has in recreating on film the mercuric, stream-of-consciousness routines that have made him this generation's certified (certifiable?) comic genius.

Robin Williams was born in Chicago, Illinois, and raised on a twenty-acre estate in Bloomfield Hills, Michigan. He had two older stepbrothers from the previous marriages of both parents, but the difference in their ages did not make them steady companions. Robin spent much of his childhood looking to relieve the loneliness in a thirty-room house where his father was seldom seen. He would create characters and plays, sometimes with the help of the two thousand toy soldiers who fought epic battles in the Williams basement. In his later childhood, the family moved frequently; during an eight-year period Robin was the new student at six different schools. His sense of humor proved invaluable in turning awkward situations to his advantage. At Redwood High School in Marin County, California, he was voted "Most Humorous" and "Least Likely to Succeed."

His classmates were half right. Williams won a full scholarship to the Julliard School in New York City, and for the next three years he studied drama and speech, while scribbling notes about comic characters and skits that he would try out on weekends as a performing mime. He followed a girlfriend to San Francisco before the completion of his studies, and decided to remain on the west coast after the relationship dissolved. In the summer of 1976, on "open mike night" at the Comedy Store in Los Angeles, Robin Williams was promoted from amateur comic to paid professional. He became a regular at the club, and was spotted by producer George Schlatter. He joined the cast of a short-lived revival of *Laugh-In*, and appeared in *America 2-Night* and *The Richard Pryor Show*, before making an inauspicious film debut in *Can I Do It Till I Need Glasses?*

In and around 1977, a mini-wave of sophomoric "sketch movies" crept into theaters, inspired by the television success of *Saturday Night Live*. A few, like *Kentucky Fried Movie* (1977), hold up well, but most were embarrassing disasters. *Can I Do It...*is one of the worst. Freed from the restrictions of television, the film took the *SNL* concept into 'R' rated territory, but its use of nudity and profanity are a poor substitute for talent and wit. Only Robin Williams still had a career after its release, and he almost had the good fortune to escape any long-term association with the movie. His two scenes were cut before the original release, but after *Mork and Mindy*, they were hastily replaced.

In both of the scenes in which he appears, straight man Williams (!) sets up feeble punch lines better than they deserve. In the first, about 35 minutes into the film, he plays a prosecuting attorney in a courtroom sketch; "Is it true, Mrs. Frisbee, that last summer you had sexual intercourse with a red-headed midget in a thunderstorm, while riding nude in the sidecar of a Kawasaki motorcycle...on the night of July 14?" "Hmm," replies Mrs. Frisbee, "could you repeat that date?" Cue the wah-wah fadeout music, and fade to black. Fifteen minutes later Williams reappears for an even worse (and unprintable) exchange outside a gynecologist's office.

There is no question that Robin Williams' ascent to stardom did not begin at the movies. In a February, 1978 guest appearance of the TV show *Happy Days*, Williams played a genial but confused alien who introduced himself as "Mork from Ork." The phenomenal response to the character led to the spinoff series *Mork and Mindy*, which proved an ideal showcase for Williams' improvisational skills. The sixty million viewers who tuned in every week also turned out to watch Williams at sold-out personal appearances at the kind of venues that usually played host to touring rock bands and sporting events. Williams then returned to the movies, but success was not immediate. His first three post-spaceman attempts, *Popeye* (1980), *The World According to Garp* (1982) and *The Survivors* (1983) were ambitious failures that baffled 'em in Peoria and sputtered at the box office.

His first popular hit, *Moscow on the Hudson*, was also the first definite sign that Mork from Ork was an actor with much more to offer than manic flights of comic inspiration. Williams plays Vladimir Ivanoff, a musician who defects from the pre-Glasnost Soviet Union. The gentle, soft-spoken Vladimir makes a rough adjustment to life in New York, passing through stages of ecstasy, disillusionment, fear, homesickness and then, finally, contentment. His journey is the movie.

Only Robin Williams' background has classified *Moscow on the Hudson* as a comedy in video store filing systems. While there are a few of the expected fish-out-of-water sequences played for laughs, such as Vladimir's first trip to a supermarket, the film is primarily in the liberal-patriotic Frank Capra tradition, in which the hero must pass through several arduous trials before his oft-stated faith in America is rewarded.

Williams speaks perfect phonetic Russian in the film's first half-hour, which wisely lets us get to know Vlad in his homeland, so we'll care more about what happens to him after he leaves. The theme isn't that much different from *Mork and Mindy*, but this time the role calls for quiet desperation, subtlety and restraint, none of which were associated with Williams at the time. However, he delivers an Oscar-caliber performance.

CAN I DO IT TILL I NEED GLASSES?
Directed by I. Robert Levy; Written by Mike Calley and Mike Price; Produced by Mike Callie; Music by Bob Jung

Cast
Roger Behr, Debra Klose, Moose Larkon, Walter Olkewicz, Jeff Doucette, Roger Peltz, Vic Dunlop, Patrick Wright, Sara, ROBIN WILLIAMS

MOSCOW ON THE HUDSON
Directed and produced by Paul Mazursky; Written by Paul Mazursky and Leon Capetanos; Music by David McHugh

Cast
ROBIN WILLIAMS (VLADIMIR IVANOFF), Maria Conchita Alonso (Lucia Lombardo), Cleavant Derricks (Lionel Witherspoon), Alejandro Rey (Orlando Ramirez)

DEBRA WINGER (1955-   )

FIRST APPEARANCE: *Slumber Party '57* (Cannon, 1977)

A STAR IS BORN: *Urban Cowboy* (Paramount, 1980)

If the versatile Debra Winger has a particular specialty on screen, besides dying at the end of sentimental tearjerkers, it is in her thoughtful portrayals of hearty, working-class women. The rough-and-tumble, trailer park vixens she played in *Urban Cowboy, An Officer and a Gentleman* (1982) and *Cannery Row* (1982) did not aspire to escape their surroundings, if they could find happiness and security within them. Winger plays professional women, as in *Black Widow* (1986) with the same rugged tenacity. Although she is not a classic beauty, there is an earthy sensuality to Winger that works best when she inhabits characters of humble origin and unpretentious candor.

Mary Debra Winger was the youngest of three children both to Robert and Ruth Winger of Cleveland, Ohio. When she was six the family moved to Van Nuys, California where Mary, an energetic, independent child, participated in every school play. After graduating high school in 1971, a newfound interest in her Jewish heritage inspired Mary to visit Israel, where she worked on a kibbutz and spent three months training with the Israeli army. Back in the United States a year later, she attended California State University at Northridge, and worked part time at the Magic Mountain Amusement Park. On New Year's Eve, 1973, she was thrown from a moving truck, which left her partially paralyzed and blind in one eye for several months.

Years later, she would tell *People* magazine that the accident "propelled me into doing what I wanted to do." Winger left college a year before earning a degree in sociology, and started taking acting lessons. She appeared in repertory theater productions throughout the San Fernando Valley, and behind a counter singing "Hold the pickle, hold the lettuce" in a popular Burger King commerical. She achieved a breakthrough, of sorts, in 1977, with a recurring role as "Wonder Girl" on the television series *Wonder Woman*, and her first feature film role in *Slumber Party '57.*

American Graffiti (1973) and the TV series *Happy Days* had made 1950s nostalgia trendy, and the opportunistic makers of *Slumber Party '57* hoped to take advantage of the fad, while baiting adults with all the naughty stuff that Fonzie couldn't do on television. The result is a shallow, sex-obsessed exercise in soft porn that is no better acted or directed than the hardcore variety. Even the plot sounds straight out of a Ginger Lynn vehicle--six nubile high school girls each recall their first sexual experience, depicted in flashback, at a slumber party. Not for once is the fifties setting believable, no matter how many Jerry Lee Lewis songs are played on the soundtrack.

Winger, sad to say, does not emerge from the muck with any more dignity than the rest of the cast. As "Debbie", she is third to tell her tale, which begins when a college preppie named Bud picks her up in a white Thunderbird. At a roadside mini-mart, he fights off three biker thugs before claiming his prize. Winger appears throughout in skimpy lingerie, and occasionally topless. The overall effect is more sad than provocative, especially when one considers how many actresses, with or without talent, are forced to start this way. Little can be said of her "performance"--she reads lines with mock enthusiasm, giggles a lot, and tries to act dumber than she is.

Minor roles in *Thank God It's Friday* (1978) and *French Postcards* (1979) followed, and then Winger beat out two hundred hopefuls to star opposite John Travolta in *Urban Cowboy.* Like *Slumber Party '57, Urban Cowboy* was made to capitalize on a craze, in this case country music and western fashion. The timing was perfect, and with Travolta riding a wave of superstardom after *Saturday Night Fever* (1977) and *Grease* (1978), the film's success was almost inevitable.

Travolta plays Bud, a factory laborer who moves to Texas to find work. On his first night in town Bud's aunt and uncle take him to Gilley's, the legendary honky tonk, where Bud becomes attached to the cowboy lifestyle. At the club he meets Sissy (Winger), a tomboy charmer whom Bud marries after one of the oddest courtships in movie history. The marriage rapidly dissolves, and Bud seeks solace with a cowboy groupie (Madolyn Smith), while Sissy moves in with a shady ex-con who works at the honky tonk (Scott Glenn).

Much of the action in *Urban Cowboy* revolves around Gilley's bar and its mechanical bull, which allows would-be rodeo riders to test their skills. After the film was released, every country bar in America ordered one of the bulls, and if the manufacturer has any class he should have sent a handsome royalty to Debra Winger. Clad in an orange tank-top and skin-tight blue jeans, Winger straddles the bull and performs an erotic, gymnastic, slow-motion ride that made her a household name. "I never intended it to be sexual," she told critic Gene Siskel. "All I thought was that I was making Bud jealous by how good I was riding the bull." When she dismounted, Bud wasn't the only one with a raised temperature. Although her "ride" was easily the film's most memorable scene, Winger brings more than sex appeal to the character. Sissy is a naive hick who tries to be a dutiful wife, but doesn't think ahead much before or after her marriage. Winger finds some nobility in the uncultured cowgirl, and she's the only one in the movie who has the accent down right.

Though the whole urban cowboy movement is a bygone fad--even Gilley's has closed its doors--a perceptive script has kept *Urban Cowboy* from aging. When Bud starts to care more about riding a mechanical bull than keeping his wife or his job, the title becomes ironic instead of heroic, which is a smarter statement that you'd expect from a movie like this. It also helps that the music of Mickey Gilley, Johnny Lee, Bonnie Raitt and others still sounds terrific.

SLUMBER PARTY '57
Directed by William A. Levey; Written by Frank Farmer; Produced by John A. Ireland, Jr. and William A. Levey; Music by Miles Goodman

Cast
Noelle North (Angie), Bridget Holliman (Bonnie May), DEBRA WINGER (DEBBIE), Marry Ann Appleseth (Jo Ann) Rainbeaux Smith (Sherry), Janet Wood (Smitty)

URBAN COWBOY
Directed by James Bridges; Written by James Bridges and Aaron Latham, based on a story by Latham; Produced by Robert Evans and Irving Azoff; Music by Ralph Burns

Cast
John Travolta (Bud), DEBRA WINGER (SISSY), Scott Glenn (Wes), Madolyn Smith (Pam), Barry Corbin (Uncle Bob), Brooke Alderson (Aunt Corene)

JOANNE WOODWARD (1930-   )

FIRST APPEARANCE: *Count Three and Pray* (Columbia, 1956)

A STAR IS BORN: *The Three Faces of Eve* (20th Century-Fox, 1957)

All stars are not actors, and all actors are not stars. Brooke Shields proves the former point, Joanne Woodward the latter. Woodward's accomplishments as an actress are formidable and unquestioned, yet she has never really attained movie star status. It's not just the lack of tabloid copy about her private life, and her absence from the talk show circuit and the Hollywood party scene; the fact is, despite an Academy Award and four decades of critical adoration, Woodward's name will never draw a crowd or open a movie.

One gets the feeling she could not care less. "I'd rather have a small role that I feel would be good for me than star in a part unsuited for me. I think I'd even risk studio suspension to turn down a role I felt wasn't right," she said in 1958. "I believe in what James Dean said-- 'You can turn down a picture morally, if not legally.'" Over thirty years later she remains steadfast in her avoidance of good career moves. Woodward is content to remain an unassuming Connecticut housewife who occasionally takes time out from her various political interests to add another distinguished and uncommercial credit to her resume`.

She was born in Thomasville, Georgia, the second child born to Elinor and Wade Woodward, a school administrator. Her mother was a movie buff and shared her enthusiasm with Joanne, who dreamed of being an actress from earliest childhood. Her parents divorced while Joanne attended high school in Greenville, South Carolina, where she appeared in a number of plays and spent her free time modeling and memorizing the encyclopedia.

After two years at Louisiana State University, Woodward worked in summer stock and then enrolled in New York's Neighborhood Playhouse of the Theatre. Her first professional job was in an episode of the television series *Penny*. She progressed to larger roles in other programs, including *Omnibus* and *Studio One* and, in 1953, she understudied both Kim Stanley and Janice Rule in the Broadway show *Picnic*. During the 477-performance run Woodward made fifty appearances.

Actor Dick Powell watched Joanne on a TV show called *Interlude*, and praised her to Twentieth Century-Fox. The studio signed Woodward to a seven year contract, and then lent her to Columbia for what would become her film debut. In the Civil War-era drama *Count Three and Pray*, Woodward found one of her least effective roles as a backwoods wildcat who poses a constant challenge to a novice preacher.

Luke Fargo (Van Heflin), an infamous hellraiser and skirt-chaser, sees the light during the war and returns home to build a church. Lissy (Woodward) is a squatter in the parsonage who refuses to leave. Luke allows the orphaned teenager to stay, which starts rumors flying throughout the town. Of course, someone eventually cleans the girl up and Luke makes an honest woman of her. He is also able to overcome his scandalous past and the corrupt machinations of local big shot Yancey Huggins (Raymond Burr, at his nastiest).

This one starts slow and grows on you as it goes. It's worth a look not so much for Woodward but for Heflin's earnest performance, and the smaller townsfolk roles well-filled by Phil Carey and Jean Willes. While there really isn't a "typical" Woodward character type, the first that comes to mind certainly wouldn't be a cussing, cigar-smoking white-trash girl who can skin a squirrel with her teeth. Woodward has one of those faces that radiates integrity, and try as she might it cannot be erased. Also she's 25 here, playing an eighteen-year-old who supposedly could pass for fifteen. She is no more successful at reverting to adolesence than the cast of *Beverly Hills 90210*.

The following year Woodward returned to television in a variety of roles, and played the lead in the short-lived Broadway drama *The Lovers*. Then, in 1957, Fox offered her the title role in *Three Faces of Eve*, and Woodward found an ideal showcase for her considerable talent.

Eve White is an introverted, unhappy wife and mother with a multiple personality disorder. As Eve Black, she becomes a flamboyant, flirtatious party girl; as Jane, she is level-headed, poised and perceptive, an intermediate between the two Eves. Her insensitive, poorly-educated husband (David Wayne) thinks "a good whipping" will cure her, and her psychiatrist (Lee J. Cobb) wants to help, but isn't sure how. After years of therapy, he uncovers the root cause of Eve's illness and is able to merge her three personalities.

The role of Eve is an obvious acting showcase, but what impresses most is the subtlety of Woodward's performance, and the film's corresponding choice of restraint over sensationalism. Alastair Cooke's introduction lends a documentary feel to the proceedings, and what follows is an almost clinical study of Eve's disorder. The drama, never forced, flows naturally from the Q and A sessions between Eve and her psychiatrist, and the fascinating nature of her malady. You just know that if the film were remade today every facet would be more exaggerated.

Woodward superbly creates three separate personalities without histrionics or scenery-chewing. She deservedly won the Academy Award for a performance which *The New York Times* praised for its "superlative flexibility and emotional power." Light years away from "Disease of the Week" movies made for TV, *The Three Faces of Eve* remains a compelling portrait of mental illness.

COUNT THREE AND PRAY
Directed by George Sherman; Written by Herb Meadow; Produced by Ted Richmond; Music by George Duning

Cast
Van Heflin (Luke Fargo), JOANNE WOODWARD (LISSY), Phil Carey (Albert Loomis), Raymond Burr (Yancey Huggins), Allison Hayes (Georgina Decrais), Nancy Kulp (Matty), Jean Willes (Selma)

THE THREE FACES OF EVE
Directed, written and produced by Nunnally Johnson, based on a book by Corbett H. Thigpen, M.D. and Hervey M. Cleckley, M.D.; Music by Robert Emmett Dolan

Cast
JOANNE WOODWARD (EVE), David Wayne (Ralph White), Lee J. Cobb (Dr. Luther)

LORETTA YOUNG (1913-   )

FIRST APPEARANCE: *The Only Way* (Famous Players-Lasky, 1917)

A STAR IS BORN: *The Devil To Pay* (United Artists, 1930)

Loretta Young was rarely absent from movie screens between 1917 and 1953, but it is very difficult to determine exactly when she progressed from a welcome, reliable presence to an esteemed leading lady. Young was an audience favorite from the early thirties, when she appeared in the first of seven frothy programmers with Douglas Fairbanks, Jr.. "Serious" cinema devotees` saw her as a lovely, saucer-eyed set decoration, but were forced to upgrade their assessment in the forties after she won an Oscar for *The Farmer's Daughter* (1947). In the fifties, after Young had finally added a handful of gems to her mediocre filmography, she parlayed her popularity and her reputation as one of the more down-to-earth, friendly stars in the Hollywood firmament into success on television in the long-running *Loretta Young Show* (1953-1961).

After the separation of her parents, three-year-old Gretchen Michaela Young moved with her mother Gladys, two older sisters and brother from Salt Lake City, Utah to Hollywood. Gladys secured a loan from the Catholic church to start a boardinghouse in downtown Los Angeles, but one year later the business was in desperate financial trouble. It was Ernest Traxler, Gladys's brother-in-law and an assistant director at the Famous Players-Lasky film studio, who first suggested that the beautiful Young sisters could be bit players and extras in the movies. Gladys agreed, and within days Ernest picked up Gretchen from her backyard playground and introduced her to director George Melford, who was then shooting a film called *The Only Way*. Melford examined the four-year-old tot and said "Wash her face and bring her back tomorrow."

Gretchen played her one scene in the film on an operating table, where her performance consisted of crying piteously. She earned $3.50 for the day, and the nickname "Gretch the Wretch," after her sisters grew tired of her yammering about becoming a star. For the next four years Gretchen and her siblings appeared in a variety of films, including Rudolph Valentino's *The Sheik* (1921), in which they played a quartet of Arab children. Gladys had now begun to worry about show business as a career for her kids, and sent the girls off to school at the Ramona Convent in Alhambra. It didn't last--they had all genuinely enjoyed the experience of movie-making, and were eager to return. Gretchen's two older sisters resumed their careers--Betty Jane graduated from extra to contract player at Paramount, and changed her name to Sally Blane. Polly Ann was also getting parts and, in 1927, she received a call from director Mervyn LeRoy to read for a role in the comedy *Naughty But Nice*. But Gretch the Wretch took the call and decided to go to the audition herself.

LeRoy was amused and impressed by the kid's audacity, but no way could he cast fourteen-year-old Gretchen as the ingenue. He gave her another part in the movie, however, and it was *Naughty But Nice* that began her trek toward stardom. She met actress Corinne Griffith, studied her technique and followed her around like a pint-sized Eve Harrington for months. Griffith suggested "Loretta" as a replacement for Gretchen, which she thought "sounded too Dutchy", and arranged for a screen test. The test was successful, and Loretta Young left school after finishing the eighth grade to become a contract player at First National.

She played the female lead opposite Lon Chaney in *Laugh Clown Laugh* (1928), only her third film under contract. After *The Squall* (1929), her first talkie, Loretta Young was always top- or second-billed. *The Devil To Pay* (1930), Young's eighteenth film since *Naughty But Nice* just three years earlier, gets the nod (if any single Young film can claim the status) as her starmaking effort for its across-the-board success with both critics and audiences, and Young's ability to hold her own (at the still tender age of sixteen) with a cast that was clearly superior (Ronald Colman, Myrna Loy) to any in her previous work.

Colman plays Willie Leeland, a rich playboy pleasure-seeker who falls on hard times just before meeting gorgeous socialite Dorothy Hope (Young). Dorothy is engaged to a Grand Duke, who actually has less money than Willie. When the Duke is exposed through Willie's investigation, Dorothy breaks the engagement and ends up with Willie for the obligatory happy ending. Colman owned the film but, for the first time, Loretta Young was lauded in the reviews--"continually helpful and sufficiently smart in smart surroundings," wrote *Variety*.

Young's patrician elegance and cultivated voice were ideally suited to upper crust roles like Dorothy, and in *The Devil To Pay* she also shows a talent for romantic comedy that might have been advanced by Ronald Colman. She had a crush on her costar during production, and he encouraged the infatuation only to help her through their scenes together. They remained friends for years, but it was mere months later that Loretta married Grant Withers, her co-star in *The Second-Floor Mystery* (1930).

THE ONLY WAY
Directed by George Melford

Cast
Fanny Ward, Theodore Roberts...LORETTA YOUNG (crying child)

THE DEVIL TO PAY
Directed by George Fitzmaurice; Written by Benjamin Glazer and Frederick Lonsdale, based on the play by Lonsdale; Produced by Samuel Goldwyn; Music by Alfred Newman

Cast
Ronald Colman (Willie Leeland), LORETTA YOUNG (DOROTHY HOPE), Florence Britton (Susan Leeland), Frederick Kerr (Lord Leeland), Paul Cavanagh (Grand Duke)

MORE FIRST APPEARANCES

Versatile character actor **Don Ameche** launched his film career with a challenging dual role, playing two sons of an Austrian bell-ringer in *Sins of Man* (1936). Two years later, he became one of 20th Century-Fox's most popular stars by battling Tyrone Power for the affections of Alice Faye in *Alexander's Ragtime Band* (1938). **Jean Arthur** played a bit part in *Cameo Kirby* (1930), before establishing her sassy but sweet screen persona in Frank Capra's classic *Mr. Deeds Goes to Town* (1936). Singing cowboy **Gene Autry** made the transition from radio to film with *In Old Santa Fe* (1935), and after starring in the serial *The Phantom Empire*, he began his career as a headliner in the Republic western *Tumbling Tumbleweeds* (1935).

Saturday Night Live made **Dan Aykroyd** a star; he appeared in one film before joining the show, an awful Canadian comedy entitled *Love at First Sight* (1974). A SNL sketch turned feature film, *The Blues Brothers* (1980), was his first big-screen hit. Tough guy **Ernest Borgnine** was introduced to movie audiences as Hu Chang, an Asian thief, in the routine adventure film *China Corsair* (1951). Four years later, he softened his image, became a star and earned an Academy Award by playing the title role in *Marty* (1955). **Clara Bow**, the "It" girl, debuted in the film *Beyond the Rainbow*, now sadly lost, before starring in the film that gave her her nickname, *It* (1927). **Jeff Bridges** was just a baby when he was carried onto the screen in *The Company She Keeps* (1950). Twenty-one years later, he convincingly played a high schooler in Peter Bogdanovich's haunting *The Last Picture Show* (1971).

Matthew Broderick followed up his film debut in *Max Dugan Returns* (1983) with the huge hit *WarGames* (1983). **Charles Bronson** was for awhile the most bankable action star in Hollywood. Under the name Charles Buchinsky, he made his film debut (as did Lee Marvin) as an enlisted man in the lightweight comedy *You're In the Navy Now* (1951). He played his first starring role in the Roger Corman shoot 'em up, *Machine Gun Kelly* (1958). **Yul Brynner**, who costarred with Bronson in the classic western *The Magnificent Seven* (1960), first appeared, with a full head of hair, as a ruthless drug trafficker in *Port of New York* (1949). He became a star on the Broadway stage in *The King and I*, and established his film career in 1956 with the same role.

As Ellen McRae, **Ellen Burstyn** made her film debut in the Tony Curtis-Debbie Reynolds comedy *Goodbye Charlie* (1964). She earned an Oscar nomination as Linda Blair's mother in *The Exorcist*, but received a bigger boost after starring in *Alice Doesn't Live Here Anymore* (1974). You'll have to pay close attention to catch **James Caan**'s brief walk-on role in *Irma La Douce* (1963), his film debut. Together with Al Pacino, he became a star as one of the Corleone boys in *The Godfather* (1972). Ballerina/gamine **Leslie Caron** needed but one dance near the Seine with Gene Kelly to achieve stardom in her first film, *An American in Paris* (1951). Gorgeous **Julie Christie** played a stripper named Babette in the comic heist film *Crooks Anonymous* (1963), before making international waves and winning an Oscar as the star of *Darling* (1965), still cited by some sources as the definitive 1960s movie.

Montgomery Clift's sensitive, brooding rebel persona opened the door to Hollywood for Marlon Brando and James Dean. He made his first two films simultaneously; *The Search* (1948) was released first, but *Red River* (1948), in which Clift went toe-to-toe with John Wayne, made him a star. He-man **James Coburn** played an outlaw in the Randolph Scott western *Ride Lonesome* (1959). His first starring role came in the James Bond pastiche *Our Man Flint* (1966). **Joseph Cotten** joined his fellow Mercury Players in *Citizen Kane* (1941), his film debut, but made his first significant impact on movie audiences as Uncle Charley, the Merry Widow Murderer, in Alfred Hitchcock's *Shadow of a Doubt* (1943).

Crooner **Bing Crosby** appeared in two 1930 shorts, *Two Plus Fours* and *Ripstitch the*

Tailor, before making his feature debut in *King of Jazz* (1930). In 1944, he was the number one male box-office star and an Academy Award winner after playing Father O'Malley in *Going My Way*. After starring in the short-lived television series *Operation Petticoat*, **Jamie Lee Curtis** began her film career as a terrorized babysitter in *Halloween* (1978). Brooklyn-born **Tony Curtis** debuted as a gigolo in the violent film noir *Criss Cross* (1949), and found stardom as a slimy public relations leech in *Sweet Smell of Success*. **Catherine Deneuve** played a minor role in *Les Collegiennes* (1962), before starring in a delightful French homage to classic American musicals entitled *The Umbrellas of Cherbourg* (1964). Distinguished British actor **Robert Donat** made his first film appearance in *Men of Tomorrow* (1932), a romantic drama set at Oxford University. His swashbuckling role in *The Count of Monte Cristo* made him a star.

Forced to choose between Judy Garland and **Deanna Durbin**, MGM chief Louis B. Mayer decided on Garland, and was certain he made a mistake after Durbin went to Universal and became an overnight sensation in her first film, *Three Smart Girls* (1936). **Douglas Fairbanks**, the movie's first great action hero, got his career off to a running, jumping start in *The Lamb* (1915). Though he was already well-known when he made *The Mark of Zorro* (1920), his first movie as a costumed adventurer was a tremendous box-office success. **Alice Faye** was a chorus girl in the Broadway show *George White's Scandals*. When the musical became a movie in 1934, Faye won the female lead role and became a star in her feature debut.

As Joan Burfield, Olivia de Havilland's sister **Joan Fontaine** made her first film appearance in the Joan Crawford vehicle *No More Ladies* (1935). Alfred Hitchcock didn't want Fontaine for his classic Gothic drama *Rebecca* (1940), but producer David O. Selznick wisely overruled the rejection. **Glenn Ford** was the star of his movie debut, the intriguingly-titled *Heaven With a Barbed Wire Fence*, but became a star by romancing Rita Hayworth in *Gilda* (1946). Television made **James Garner** a star, but his 40-film career contains no shortage of notable work. Debuting as a soldier in *Toward the Unknown* (1956), he made his first big-screen splash as tycoon *Cash McCall* (1959).

Janet Gaynor, the first-ever Academy Award winner for Best Actress, played supporting role to a natural disaster in her film debut, *The Johnstown Flood* (1926), and starred one year later in the touching romance *Seventh Heaven* (1927). Playing a sleazy pimp in *Report to the Commissioner* (1975) did not stop **Richard Gere** from achieving major ladykiller status in the 1970s, especially after he played a suspected lady killer in *American Gigolo* (1980). **Lillian Gish** and her sister Dorothy were hired by D.W. Griffith in 1912, and first appeared in *An Unseen Enemy*. Three years later, Griffith and Lillian Gish achieved international fame with the release of *Birth of a Nation* (1915).

The Locked Door (1929) was Barbara Stanwyck's first Hollywood-made film, and is also notable as the film debut of **Paulette Goddard**. She later appeared opposite her long-time love Charlie Chaplin, in his classic comedy *Modern Times* (1936). In 1934, long before the "Sir" was added to his name, **Alec Guinness** made his film debut in *Evensong*. His journey toward knighthood began in earnest after he played no less than eight roles in the classic Ealing comedy *Kind Hearts and Coronets* (1949). **Daryl Hannah** was an extra in the Brian de Palma thriller *The Fury* (1978), but made a much bigger splash as a mermaid in *Splash* (1984). She had an I. Q. of 172, but **Judy Holliday** is still remembered as one of the movie's great dumb blondes. She debuted with a bit part in the long-lost film *Too Much Johnson* (1938), then won an Oscar as Billie Dawn in *Born Yesterday* (1950).

Star of stage, screen, radio and television, **Bob Hope** found his theme song, "Thanks for the Memories," while making his film debut in *Big Broadcast of 1938*. His movie career skyrocketed after Hope teamed with Bing Crosby for the first in a series of "Road" films, *Road to Singapore* (1940). **Leslie Howard** appeared in the short *The Heroine of Mons* (1914) before making his feature debut in *The Happy Warrior* (1917). In *Berkeley Square* (1933), his character was mystically transported back to the eighteenth century, and Howard was praised for playing the kind of steadfast but melancholy romantic hero on which he built a career. **William Hurt** needed only one movie to break through, but *Altered States* (1980) was a hard movie to forget; Hurt plays a scientist who is obsessed with discovering man's true place in the universe, and gets more of an answer than he wanted.

Jeremy Irons first captured the public's attention in the British TV miniseries *Brideshead Revisited*. *Nijinsky* (1980) was his first film; *The French Lieutenant's Woman* (1981) his first hit.

Legendary, stone-faced silent film comedian **Buster Keaton** began his career playing the foil to Roscoe "Fatty" Arbuckle in *The Butcher Boy* (1917). His ascent to stardom was gradual, but the film that left no doubt about his genius was *The General* (1926), a masterpiece that still turns up on top ten lists of the best movies ever made. **Veronica Lake** enjoyed a brief but colorful reign as the movies' "girl with the peek-a-boo bang." She made her debut under the name Constance Keane as an extra in *Sorority House* (1939). At the age of seventeen she played her first significant role, as a nightclub singer in *I Wanted Wings* (1941). Her hairstyle was emulated in beauty salons across the country.

Janet Leigh went through several ingenue roles, beginning with *The Romance of Rosy Bridge* (1947), before landing more significant parts. One of her best was opposite James Stewart in the superb Anthony Mann western, *The Naked Spur* (1953). Many film historians believe that **Peter Lorre** never topped the tour de force performance he delivered in his film debut, as a child-killer in Fritz Lang's *M* (1931). A bit part in the silent film *Girls Gone Wild* (1929) launched **Fred MacMurray**'s six-decade career. His seven films with Claudette Colbert, beginning with *The Gilded Lily* (1935), made him a star. Buxom platinum blonde **Jayne Mansfield** can be glimpsed as a cigarette girl in her film debut, *Pete Kelly's Blues* (1955). She became Hollywood's most marketable successor to Marilyn Monroe in *The Girl Can't Help It* (1956).

Critics thought the crime drama entitled *The Dummy* (1929) was aptly named, but **Frederic March** overcame this inauspicious debut and three films later he earned an Oscar for his amazing performance in *Dr. Jekyll and Mr. Hyde* (1932). After achieving superstardom on the stand-up comedy stage, **Steve Martin** made his film debut in the ill-fated BeeGees musical, *Sgt. Pepper's Lonely Heart's Club Band* (1978). In *The Jerk* (1979), Martin established his box-office credentials and his status as heir apparent to Jerry Lewis. **James Mason** debuted in *Late Extra* (1935); twelve years would pass before his first significant role, in Carol Reed's *Odd Man Out* (1947). In *The Housekeeper's Daughter* (1939), **Victor Mature** debuted as a gangster named Lefty. He exchanged a tommy gun for a six-shooter as Doc Holliday in John Ford's classic *My Darling Clementine* (1946). Diminutive **Dudley Moore** made his film debut with his then-partner Peter Cook in *The Wrong Box* (1966). He exchanged Cook for Bo Derek in *10* (1979), a good trade by any yardstick.

Roger Moore started his career with a walk-on part in *Vacation From Marriage* (1945), became a star on television in *The Saint*, and then became James Bond number three in *Live and Let Die* (1973). Television also launched the career of **Nick Nolte**; after debuting in the Grade-Z exploitation flick *Return to Macon County* (1975), his performance in the miniseries *Rich Man, Poor Man* led to better big-screen roles. The hilarious football satire *North Dallas Forty* (1979) was a breakthrough. **Chuck Norris** played (what else?) a karate expert in his film debut, *The Wrecking Crew* (1969). His ascent to the top echelon of action film stars began with *Good Guys Wear Black* (1979). **Anthony Perkins** will always be best-remembered as *Psycho*'s Norman Bates, but his first job was as a disturbed teenager in *The Actress* (1953), and he first achieved notoriety as baseball player Jimmy Piersall in *Fear Strikes Out* (1957).

The erudite **Vincent Price** played a country bumpkin in his film debut, *Service De Luxe* (1938), before finding fame and fortune as one of Hollywood's most bankable horror movie stars. *House of Wax* (1953) may be his best. **Richard Pryor** made his film debut among a talented group of comics, including Jan Murray, Bill Dana and George Jessel, in *The Busy Body* (1967), but in his greatest films, beginning with *Richard Pryor --Live in Concert* (1979), he always played himself. **Anthony Quinn** was Hollywood's foremost ethnic chameleon. He was an Indian in his film debut, 1937's *The Plainsman*, and received a career boost after playing a Mexican revolutionary in the classic *Viva Zapata!* (1952). **Basil Rathbone** made his first appearance in the British silent film *Innocent* (1923). After several high-profile villain roles in such films as *Anna Karenina* (1935) and *Captain Blood* (1935), he became Hollywood's best Sherlock Holmes in *The Hound of the Baskervilles* (1939).

Roy Rogers was one of the Sons of the Pioneers in his first film, *The Old Homestead* (1935), but three years later he was challenging Gene Autry for the title "King of the Cowboys" after starring in *Under Western Stars* (1938). In *It Happened At the World's Fair* (1963), Elvis Presley sings to Joan O'Brien, and **Kurt Russell**, who would later play Elvis in a TV movie, makes his debut. One of the few child stars to find work after puberty, Russell became an action hero in *Escape From New York* (1981). You'll see **Meg Ryan** first in *Rich and Famous* (1981), but you'll never forget her in the diner scene of *When Harry Met Sally* (1989). **George C. Scott** first appeared in the western *The Hanging Tree* (1959), then left the country for the city in *The Hustler* (1961).

Peter Sellers, who played numerous dual roles, began his film career doing double-duty in *Penny Points to Paradise* (1951). His performance as a pompous union shop steward in *I'm All Right, Jack* (1959) won him a British Academy Award. **Norma Shearer** was Queen of the MGM lot throughout the 1930s, but was already a star when movies began to talk. Shearer debuted in *The Flapper* (1920), and scored a hit in Ernst Lubitsch's *The Student Prince in Old Heidelberg* (1927). Fourteen-year-old **Jean Simmons** was picked from a group of dance students to appear in *Give Us the Moon* (1944). Four years later, as Ophelia in Laurence Olivier's *Hamlet*, Simmons proved she was more than a beautiful face. **Christian Slater**'s dead-on rendition of a teenage Jack Nicholson in *Heathers* (1989) made him famous overnight, but he first appeared on screen four years earlier in *The Legend of Billie Jean* (1985). **Donald Sutherland** played a male soldier and a female witch in his film debut, the Italian horror flick *Castle of the Living Dead* (1964). *MASH* (1970) was the film that got him noticed.

The Will Rogers comedy *Handy Andy* (1934) contains the first appearance of **Robert Taylor**, who became a star as a playboy turned surgeon in *Magnificent Obsession* (1935). When the death of **Rudolph Valentino** drove female fans to suicide, it was one of the first demonstrations of the power of a moving image on the big screen. Valentino's first movie was *My Official Wife* (1914), and he became the cinema's first great lover in *The Sheik* (1921). Movie audiences first heard the voice of **Orson Welles** in 1940, as the narrator on *Swiss Family Robinson* (1940). The following year, they saw the face that went with the voice in *Citizen Kane* (1941). At the age of five, **Natalie Wood** played a tiny role in *Happy Land* (1943). Her grown-up career began with *Rebel Without a Cause* (1955).